DYLAN THOMAS

A NEW LIFE

DYLAN THOMAS

A NEW LIFE

ANDREW LYCETT

THE OVERLOOK PRESS
Woodstock & New York

B
Thom

First published in the United States in 2004 by
The Overlook Press, Peter Mayer Publishers, Inc.
Woodstock & New York

WOODSTOCK:
One Overlook Drive
Woodstock, NY 12498
www.overlookpress.com
[for individual orders, bulk and special sales, contact our Woodstock office]

NEW YORK:
141 Wooster Street
New York, NY 10012

∞ The paper used in this book meets the requirements for paper
permanence as described in the ANSI Z39.48-1992 standard.

Cataloging-in-Publication Data is available from the Library of Congress

Manufactured in the United States of America
FIRST EDITION
ISBN 1-58567-541-5
1 3 5 7 9 8 6 4 2

CONTENTS

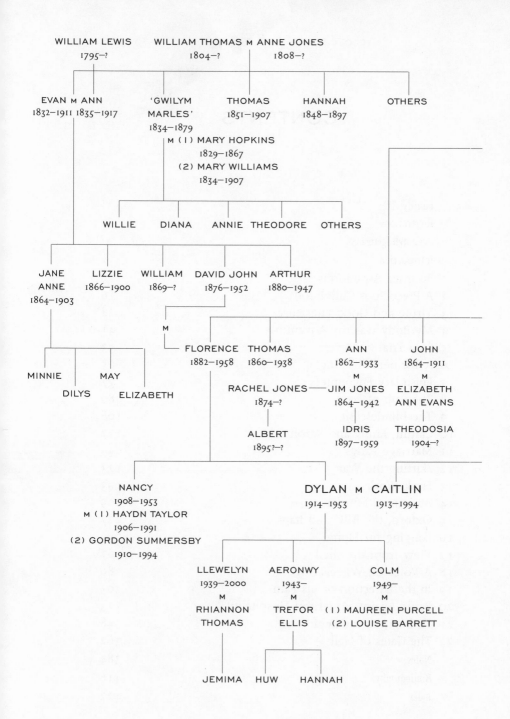

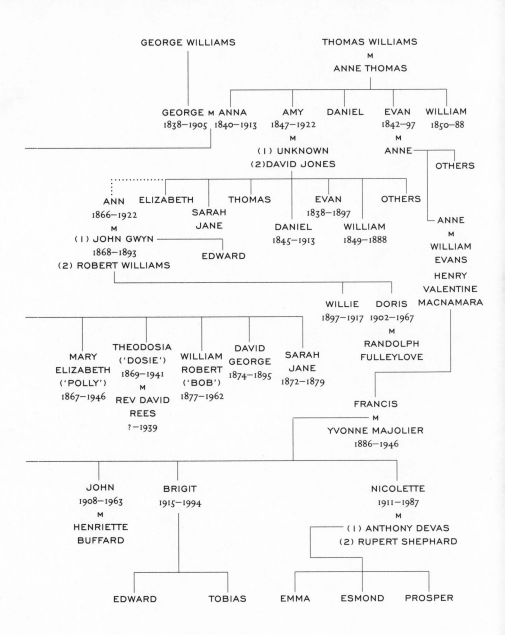

ILLUSTRATIONS

Between pages 178 and 179:

Dylan's father, David John, known as Jack or D.J., as a young schoolmaster[1]
Dylan's mother, Florence (née Williams), as a young woman[2]
Dylan as a child[3]
Dylan's mother's family (the Williamses)[2]
Dylan's father's family (the Thomases)[4]
Dylan's uncle Gwilym 'Marles' Thomas[3]
Dylan and sister Nancy on the beach at Swansea[4]
Dylan's cousin Idris (Jones)[2]
Dylan's Aunt Annie (Jones)[2]
In his school play, Strife, in spring 1931, with his friend Charles Fisher in the female lead[4]
The boily boy, in a Little Theatre production of Hay Fever, 1934[20]
Dylan – studio portrait taken at Arding & Hobbs, Clapham Junction, 1934[3]
Dylan and his mother[6]
Dylan and his first love, Pamela Hansford Johnson (three pictures)[5]
American in London: Emily Holmes Coleman[14]
Bert Trick[21]
Fooling around at Penard: Vernon Watkins and Dylan[4]
Runia Tharp (painting by Charles Tharp)[22]
Swansea society: Fred Janes, unknown, Vera Phillips and Charles Fisher[20]
Nautical girl: Dylan's sister Nancy[23]
Caitlin Macnamara – studio portrait, 1936[24]
Young Caitlin[25]
Caitlin – party scene[25]
Dylan and Caitlin – newly married at Blashford[25]
Dylan and Caitlin – on a beach in Dorset[25]
Dylan, Caitlin and their new-born son, Llewelyn[3]
Dylan at the Salisbury pub in Saint Martin's Lane, London, 1941[6]
Dylan and Caitlin, unfinished portrait by Ralph Banbury, c.1939[7]

Between pages 242 and 243:

Dylan discusses his role in the BBC radio play The Careerist with Louis MacNeice, author of the piece, and Pat Griffiths, who did the sound effects[8]
Dylan in London, 1941[9]
Family group at Blaencwm in 1942, with Dylan and Caitlin, Florrie, Llewelyn and family friend[10]
Dylan and John Davenport (photographed in 1952)[11]

Dylan with poetry producer Patric Dickinson at the BBC[12]
Dylan, Helen McAlpine and Caitlin in Ireland, 1946[26]
Helen McAlpine and Caitlin at the Boat House, Laugharne[13]
At Brown's: Bill McAlpine, Caitlin, Ebie Williams, Mary Ellidge, Dylan, Ivy Williams, Mabley Owen (with young Aeronwy in front)[13]
Domestic scene on the veranda at the Boat House: Caitlin, Aeronwy, Dolly Long, Shelagh Long[14]
Margaret Taylor[30]
Marged Howard Stepney[31]
Dylan in Persia, 1951[15]
Dylan with the actors Griffith Williams and Mario Cabre on the set of the film Pandora and the Flying Dutchman at Pendine Sands, July 1950[10]
Dylan at work in his hut above the Boat House in Laugharne, 1953[16]
Dylan's father, D.J., in typical pose – reading a newspaper at Pelican in Laugharne[10]
Dylan at a Foyle's literary luncheon in January 1953, receiving an award from Foyle's chairman William Foyle[8]
Oscar Williams's snaps of Dylan in the United States in 1950: with Williams himself, the quizzical tourist, with Stanley Moss[17]
Dylan and his American friend and promoter John Malcolm Brinnin[27]
Dylan and Caitlin in the United States, 1952[10]
Dylan and Pearl Kazin, London, September 1951[14]
Liz Reitell[18]
Dylan at a rehearsal of Under Milk Wood[19]
Dylan at the White Horse Tavern, Greenwich Village[28]
Dylan in Vancouver, April 1950[29]
Caitlin, Dan Jones and Fred Janes[4]
Dylan on television in August 1953[4]
Dylan, the family man, with Caitlin, Aeronwy, Colm and dog Mably[4]
Dylan at play at Vernon Watkins's house, the Garth, on the Gower in 1951[4]
Dylan the genial companion[10]
Dylan the consummate professional showman[4]

The author and the publishers offer their thanks to the following for their kind permission to reproduce images:

1 Swansea Grammar School Magazine/Swansea Library; 2 National Library of Wales; 3 Unknown; 4 Jeff Towns/Dylan's Book Store Collection; 5 Lady Avebury; 6 Bill Brandt Archive; 7 Peregrine Banbury; 8 Topham Picturepoint; 9 National Portrait Gallery; 10 Reg and Eileen Evans; 11 John Deakin/Vogue/Condé Nast; 12 Hulton Picture Library; 13 Mary Ellidge; 14 University of Delaware; 15 BP; 16 John Jones Publishing Ltd.; 17 Oscar Williams/University of Indiana; 18 Lois Gridley/Andrew Lycett; 19 Rollie McKenna; 20 Swansea Little Theatre; 21 Kerith Trick; 22 Silvia Tharp; 23 Joan Rubeck; 24 Edward Marnier; 25 Nora Summers/Jeff Towns/Dylan's Book Store Collection; 26 Harry Ransom Research Center/University of Texas; 27 G.D. Hackett/Jeff Towns/Dylan's Book Store Collection; 28 Bunny Adler/Jeff Towns/Dylan's Book Store Collection; 29 Geoffrey Madoc Jones; 30 Amelia Fell; 31 Molly Murray Threipland

ACKNOWLEDGEMENTS

Every book brings new friends, new acquaintances. In the former category I am privileged to count Swansea bookseller, Jeff Towns. He is an essential point of contact for anyone writing about Dylan Thomas. I'm sure that when he heard someone else was embarking on a biography, he inwardly groaned. But, from the very first occasion I met him, he was a fountain of information, encouragement and superior gossip. He also generously made available his vast collection of Dylan Thomas books, letters (some unpublished) and other material. I doubt I could have written this book without him. However I am also glad to say that I surprised him with some hitherto unknown Dylan-related material and characters I discovered.

Even before meeting Jeff, I had been to visit Aeronwy Thomas, Dylan's daughter, in Surrey. As everyone who meets her quickly recognises, she is a remarkable character – humorous, tenacious and very fair-minded. Dylan is lucky to have her flying the flag for him.

So thanks to her for her support, and also to the following people to whom I am particularly grateful:

Bruce Hunter (who represents the Dylan Thomas estate at David Higham Associates), Reg and Eileen Evans (who allowed me to see their Dylan Thomas collection and use photographs from it), Rob and Cathy Roberts (whose willingness to give me access to the papers of Daniel Jones, Cathy's father, was remarkable – the model of the sort of relationship a biographer likes to have), and Professor Ralph Maud (who allowed me to read in proof form Where Have the Old Words Got Me? his summation of his lifetime's thinking about the poems of Dylan Thomas).

Andrew Holmes's advice on computers was invaluable. I benefited from a grant from the Authors Foundation, a fund administered by the Society of Authors.

At my publisher I have again enjoyed the editorial expertise and backing of Ion Trewin. His very able assistant Victoria Webb has been a delight to work with. Margaret Body did two fine jobs – first on the copy-editing and then on the index.

At home I have been spoiled by the love and support of Sue Greenhill.

I am happy to acknowledge my use of the comprehensive tape interviews made by the journalist Colin Edwards in the 1960s. Intending to write a biography that was never completed, he was able to talk to many people who knew Dylan but are no longer alive. His tapes were deposited in the National Screen and Sound Archive at the National Library of Wales by his widow. I am grateful to her and to the Library for permission to quote from them. In the same context, I drew on the excellent work done by Kent Thompson in producing his Ph.D thesis Dylan Thomas in Swansea for Swansea University in 1965. His background research papers are lodged in the university archives.

I would like to thank David Higham Associates (on behalf of the Dylan Thomas estate) for permission to quote for the works of Dylan Thomas.

In addition I would like to thank the following people who have all given me relevant permissions to quote:

Michael Taylor and Felicity Skelton (Haydn Taylor)
Professor Christopher Todd (Ruthven Todd)
Jacqui Lyne (Tom Herbert)
Nicola Schaefer (Cordelia Sewell)
Richard Brooks-Keene (Bunny Keene)
Charles Fisher
Julia Davies (Mary Ellidge)
Lady Avebury (Pamela Hansford Johnson)
Judy Gascoyne (David Gascoyne)
Gwen Watkins (Vernon Watkins)
Hilly Janes (Fred Janes)
Emeritus Professor Meic Stephens (Glyn Jones)
Alice Kadel (Mary Keene)
Sebastian Yorke (Henry Yorke)
Rob and Cathy Roberts (Daniel Jones)
Julius White (Augustus John)
Ben Shephard (Rupert Shephard and Lorna Wilmot)
Susan and Jane Bullowa (George Reavey)
Amelia Fell (Margaret Taylor)
Strephon Williams (Oscar Williams)
Peggy Fox (James Laughlin and New Directions)
Authors League Fund (Djuna Barnes)
Joseph Geraci (Emily Holmes Coleman)
Jeff Walden (BBC Written Archives)
Judith Dunford (Alfred Kazin)
American Academy for Arts and Letters (John Malcolm Brinnin)
Kerith Trick (Bert Trick)
The Masters, Fellows and Scholars of St John's College Cambridge (Nashe Society)
Eva Rhys (Keidrych Rhys)
Francis Sitwell (Edith Sitwell)
Sir Reresby Sitwell, Bart, and Francis Sitwell (Sacheverell Sitwell)

Much of the work on a book of this kind is done in libraries. I would like to thank the following librarians for their help and their willingness to answer my questions:

Rebecca Johnson Melvin (University of Delaware)
Tara Wenger and John Fitzpatrick (Harry Ransom Humanities Research Center at the University of Texas at Austin)
Helen Cole (State Library of Queensland)
Marilyn Jones (Swansea City Library)
Robin Smith (National Library of Scotland)
Ceridwen Lloyd Morgan (Manuscripts/National Library of Wales)
Dafydd Pritchard (National Screen and Sound Archive/National Library of Wales)
Chris Penney (Birmingham University)
Bill Hetherington (Peace Pledge Union)
Adrian Glew (Tate Gallery)
Robert Bertholf (Lockwood Library, State University of New York at Buffalo)
Judith Priestman (Bodleian Library, Oxford University)

Vincent Giroud (Yale University)
Tom Ford (Harvard University)
Michael Bott (Reading University)
Katherine Salzmann (Southern Illinois University)
Francis Lapka and Saundra Taylor (University of Indiana at Bloomington)
Stephen Crook (Berg Collection New York Public Library)
Dean M Rogers (Vassar University)
Paula Brikci (BP Archive)
Ann Butler (New York University)
Susan Beckley (West Glamorgan Archives)
Terry Wells (Carmarthen Archives)
Elisabeth Bennet (Swansea University)
Nick Mays (News International)

In addition to the above, many other people have given me significant help, for
which I am very grateful:

David Wagoner	Ros Tharp	Lois Gridley
Stanley Moss	Joe Pearce	Lorraine Scourfield
Desmond Morris	Michael Rush	Jessica Treacy
Silvia Tharp	Warren Hope	Paul Redgrove
Deanna and the late	Roger Horrocks	Ann Meo
Zubel Kachadoorian		

Various people have generously allowed me to stay in their houses during the course
of my research. I am particularly grateful to
David and Philippa Owen, whose cottage provided a welcome refuge when I was in
the Laugharne, Carmarthen and Swansea areas. Denis and Sue Balsam kindly allowed
me to use their flat in Aberystwyth. Colin and Mary Ellen Davies were, as usual,
excellent hosts in Washington, as were Tim and Fredda Brennan as I criss-crossed
New England.

Other people have also provided invaluable help. I would like to thank:

Sue Fox	David N Thomas	Geoffrey Madoc-Jones
Ruth Herschberger	Paul Ferris	David Vaughan-Thomas
David Markson	Fiona Green	David Rosser-Owen
Alastair Reid	Edward Marnier	Margaret Hepburn
David Slivka	Paul Willetts	Stephen Fothergill
Rose Slivka	Paul Duncan	Haulwen Morris
Jo Ellen Hall	Robin Darwall-Smith	Mark and Molly Murray
Sarah Jane Checkland	Thelma Shoonmaker	Thriepland
David Wolkowsky	Powell	Paul Busby
Bonnie Luscombe	Nest Cleverdon	Joe Hone
Robert Williams	The late Gilbert Bennett	Tommy Watts
Barbara Holdridge	Leslie Mewis	Maurice Brace
Charles F. Wickwire	Peggy Rust	The late Ann Starke
Jeny Curnow	Richard Ramsbotham	Colin Webb
Harry Ricketts	Cesa Milton	David Bryan
David Cowell	Prof Mario Curreli	Sheila and Ivan Caley
Bob Kingdom	Frederick Morgan	Canon Fred Cogman
Claire Manson	Terence O'Brien	Jane Dunn

Mark Law
Virginia Law
Lady Bath
Michael Luke
Jonathan Moffat
John Veale
Martin Starkie
Joseph Rykwert
David Mason
Jane Ridley
Roger Davenport
James Schevill
Jonathan Clark
Dr Geraint James
Dr Roger Seale
Michael Snow
Rona Lucas
Paul Rubenstein
Louise Levy
Ceri Levy

Vicky Magnus
Sonia Birch-Jones
Brian Davis
Jane MacKelvie Jutsum
Rebekah Gilbertson
Jane Gibson
Barbara Parry
Rita Bronowski
Susan Gentleman
Barbara Wall
Cecily Mackworth
Gordon Bowker
Bob Kingdom
Laure Pengelly Drake
Pamela Wilson (Time
   magazine)
Lady Spender
Michael Holroyd
Jeremy Lewis
Anthony Thwaite

Conrad Goulden
George Tremlett
Philip Ziegler
Audrey Davies (and the
   Eastside Historical Society)
Edward Williams
John Bodley
Anthony Penrose
Ilse Barker
Joan Rubeck
John Goodby
Victor Golightly
Gabriel and Leonie
   Summers
Peter Conradi
David Woolley
Jo Furber
Victoria Walsh
Dr David Sutton

My publishers and I have done everything we can to seek out all copyright holders. If there are any we have inadvertently missed, we would like to be informed and we will note them in future editions of this book.

If any reader has comments on the book or further material to offer, please contact me at alycett@btinternet.com

INTRODUCTION

Type the title of Dylan Thomas's villanelle 'Do not go gentle into that good night' into the Google search engine on the world wide web; tell it you want those exact words, in that particular order, and it will provide 21,000 direct hits. A few of these responses are scholarly in tone, but most come from individuals stirred by the Welsh poet's passionate protest against his dying father's loss of faculties. Often the text of the poem is written out in full as a memorial to a loved one.

Half a century after his untimely death in New York in November 1953 Dylan Thomas still has the power to move. He always had a special ability to engage his readers and listeners directly, while still providing enough interest, through his intricate word play and rhythms, to excite the most severe of poetry critics. So you find him depicted on Peter Blake's cover of the 1967 Beatles album, *Sgt Pepper's Lonely Hearts Club Band*, and also represented in the austere pages of *The Criterion* magazine. Not many artists were favourites of both John Lennon and the determinedly high-brow T. S. Eliot.

Dylan's across-the-board appeal encouraged me to write his biography. As the Beatles recognised, he is an important figure in twentieth century culture, bridging the gap between modernism and pop, between the written and spoken word, between individual and performance art, between the academy and the forum.

His mediatory role has long been recognised, but it has usually been presented in terms of his position between England and Wales or, alternatively, on the cusp of empirical Anglo-Saxon and mythic Celtic traditions. In the past, this perception has done him few favours. He has often been scorned in his homeland for seeking acclaim and financial reward in the world of English letters, rather than accepting his responsibilities for forging a vibrant Welsh culture.

Recently, however, this nationalist line has softened. In today's devolved, Europeanised principality, the Welsh way of life is no longer under such threat. While English remains the dominant language, Welsh holds its own in areas where it has traditionally been spoken. The dragon's two tongues have become symbols of possibility, rather than division.

This has allowed new approaches to Dylan's work to flourish. His brand of Anglo-Welshness is now welcomed for bringing a fresh lyricism to the metropolitan poetical experimentation of the 1930s. Greater attention is paid to his interaction with radio and film. He is feted for invigorating English literature by introducing it to different sounds, intonations and ways of thinking. (Although he did not speak Welsh, he could not escape its influence. He heard it on a regular basis from his relations and in the surrounding community.) In this reading he is as much a precursor of English as a world language as Salman Rushdie and other Anglo-Indian authors. His English and Welsh sides are recip-rocal sources of inspiration and innovation.

From a biographer's point of view, this has made Dylan a more interesting figure – if, paradoxically, more difficult to pin down, as he darts between, and hides behind, different personalities, groups of people, and traditions. Often he could only manage the necessary moves by lying, or by losing himself in alcohol. His childhood friend Dan Jones talked of Dylan presenting a 'fetch' or double to the world.

My main task has been to explain how the public wild boy, 'the Rimbaud of Cwmdonkin Drive', could co-exist with the private poet of such sensitivity. The obvious point of entry is Dylan's own writing, particularly his verse and his vastly entertaining correspondence. It annoys me when detractors suggest he was only a verbal pyrotechnist or, an alternative version, he produced a handful of good poems, but otherwise was a Welsh windbag. Haven't these people read 'Ceremony after a fire raid', for example? Here is Dylan in an often forgotten role as one of our very best Second World War poets.

For Dylan had a clear mission. He recognised the conflicting sides to his personality and sought to reconcile them through poetry. That is how I read his lines: 'I hold a beast, an angel, and a madman in me, and my enquiry is as to their working, and my problem is their subjugation and victory, downthrow and upheaval, and my effort is their self-expression.' Perhaps they are over-dramatic, with their shades of Milton, though one of the delights of reading Dylan is the light touch of his learning: he can surprise with unexpected references, from Restoration comedies to 1930s musicals. As he explored internally and externally – first, his own mind and body and, then, the natural world and the wider universe – he let a 'host of images ... breed and conflict'. He toyed with the idea of God, acknowledged its value, but discarded it. His was a humanistic view of creation:

'Man be my metaphor', as he put it in his early poem 'If I were tickled by the rub of love'.

Coming from the land of bards, Dylan expected to be supported in this project. But bourgeois society is unsympathetic to artists, particularly those who flout its rules. Dylan retaliated as best he could. He became drunk, he borrowed money and did not return it, he stole his hosts' clothes and vandalised their houses, he propositioned women and went to bed with as many as he could. His struggle for poetry against propriety and convention ultimately cost him his life. He should have lived in an earlier age when medieval princes cared for their poets such as Dafydd ap Gwilym.

Dylan was sustained by his strong-willed wife Caitlin. She recognised his genius, but tired of living in his shadow, particularly when she felt threatened by other women. The story of their tempestuous marriage runs through this book. Inevitably its details are contested. Take one topic, alcohol, which played such a central and destructive role. There are tales of her in the pub, looking on angrily as Dylan wasted yet more money and work time, playing the fool for a band of well-wishers. Or was it as his friends allege? That without her fondness for whisky, he would have nursed a pint of beer through an evening and been saved from his furies.

I wonder how I would have got on with him. We had similar backgrounds in at least one respect: our fathers were school-masters and we both attended schools where they taught. I would certainly have enjoyed Dylan's company, but found his unreliability annoying. (He failed to turn up as best man for Vernon Watkins's marriage. His friend quickly forgave him, but Watkins's wife Gwen never quite got over it.)

At times during my research, the catalogue of Dylan's vices seemed to grow inexorably. Yet, even at his most exasperating, he retained an appealing innocence – the cherub-like image captured by Augustus John in his 1937 portrait. Dylan's mentor Bert Trick was by no means alone in regarding him as a secular saint – someone almost Christ-like in his awareness of suffering and in his sensitivity to others.

Was this another of Dylan's poses, like the 'conscious Woodbine' he adopted when he became a journalist? I don't think so. What was often described as his 'sweet' nature went hand in hand with a joie de vivre – one of the many Dylan paradoxes which, when given verbal form, make his poetry so rich and his life so interesting.

At root was his artistic integrity. When the alcohol created a haze around him and the internal masks began to slip, he may have joked about his phoniness. But he could do this because he knew it was not true. Throughout his life he maintained his intense vision as he stuck heroically to his poet's 'craft or sullen art'. These qualities, when reflected in his verse, ensure his continued, enthusiastic following.

Andrew Lycett

May 2003

ONE

SWANSEA ASPIRATIONS

Finding the right balance between Celtic sentiment, nationalist roots and the uncompromising demands of upward mobility has always been a feature of life in mainly Anglophone Swansea. By buying a new house in Cwmdonkin Drive, an unfinished terrace tilting alarmingly down a hill in one of the burgeoning suburbs to the west of the town, taciturn local Grammar School master D.J. or Jack Thomas and his lively wife Florrie were following a clearly defined path away from their family roots in rural Welsh-speaking Carmarthenshire.

The usual staging post was Swansea's industrial centre a couple of miles east, around the clanking docks which had sprouted at the mouth of the river Tawe to service the coal-mines and belching copper and tin-plate works a little inland. This was where most of the town's immigrants from the countryside had settled in the nineteenth century. But over the years the more respectable and ambitious among them had pushed westwards towards the salubrious Gower peninsula, colonising sea-facing ridges in haphazard fashion.

When Florrie became pregnant in early 1914, the Thomases staked their claim to bourgeois respectability. They had been living with their eight-year-old daughter Nancy in rented accommodation in Cromwell Street, close to the Grammar School, nearer the centre of town. But a residential construction boom had followed the innovative South Wales Cottage Exhibition in Swansea in 1910. When local builder W. H. Harding advertised a neat new row of houses to the north of Walter Road, the main thoroughfare leading out of Swansea towards Gower, the family raised £350 to buy a ninety-nine-year lease on a four-bedroom, semi-detached house, with bay windows, in Cwmdonkin Drive.

The purchase was financed with a 5 per cent mortgage, which was just about manageable on a teacher's salary of around £120 a year. The Thomases also paid a small ground rent, but this was reduced in the first year, probably because the house was unfinished. Although the surrounding area, known as Uplands, was well developed, only one other dwelling in their street had been completed in 1914, and that was occupied by Harding himself.

Unusually for a couple of modest means, the Thomases' house was owned by both husband and wife – a reflection, perhaps, of the greater financial resources in her immediate family, the Williamses. Florrie's mother Ann (or Anna) had died the previous year leaving her with, inter alia, an interest in a couple of leasehold shops in Pontypridd.

The youngest of eight children, Florrie herself had been born and brought up in St Thomas, a polluted dockside quarter on the lower reaches of Kilvey Hill on the other side of town. Both her parents hailed from farms in the Llanstephan peninsula to the south of Carmarthen. Following one of the few assured routes out of rural poverty, her father George had joined the railways in Swansea in the 1860s. Originally a porter, he worked his way up to shipping inspector on the docks for Great Western Railway – a responsible job which involved monitoring freight in and out of the busy port. (He was even mentioned, along with the local stationmaster, in the Swansea commercial directory for 1900.)

Not that his life was easy. He, his wife Ann and their family lived in a cramped house in Delhi Street, carved out of Lord Jersey's Briton Ferry estate. The date of the development is clear enough, as intersecting streets have the names Inkerman and Sebastopol. This part of St Thomas was built after the Crimean War and Indian Mutiny to accommodate people who flocked to Swansea from the countryside to find work in the rapidly expanding port, following the opening of the North Dock (in 1852) and South Dock (in 1859).

Until his death in November 1905, the 'quiet, retiring' George was a pillar of a poor but busy working-class community. Around him was strewn the human and physical evidence of an uncaring industrial society. Political consciousness was stirring: in 1898, a vociferous trade unionist from St Thomas called David Williams (no relation) became the first Labour candidate to win a seat on Swansea Council. George Williams's approach to improving society was different: an old-fashioned Nonconformist, he was a deacon of the English-speaking Canaan Congregational chapel and superintendent of the local Sunday School. One daughter, Florrie's sister Polly, played the organ there, while another Theodosia (Dosie) had married the former minister, the Reverend David Rees. Two sons, John and Bob, worked in the docks.

In his thrifty way, George salted away some money. He managed to buy number 30, the house next door to his own at 29 Delhi Street, as well as his two shops in Pontypridd. Willie Jenkins, son of his neighbour on the other side, also worked hard, founding a leading coal shipping agency, before becoming an MP and Mayor of Swansea in the 1940s, and being awarded a knighthood. He probably helped George's son, John, on the road to prosperity. John Williams was a stevedore, but people remembered him carrying out his own coal trading business down at the port. By the time of his death in 1911 he owned two of the plushier houses in the vicinity – one inhabited by the Reverend J. Llynfi Davies, a former minister at Canaan, to which John had demonstrated his largesse by donating a Bible and hymn-book for the pulpit.

With residents such as the Williamses, the Jenkinses and also the Leyshons, who were teachers, St Thomas was a lively old-fashioned neighbourhood, with a proud tradition of self-help. Not surprisingly, Florrie looked there, rather than to the spruce environs of Cwmdonkin Drive, for domestic assistance when she was pregnant. Her need for someone in the house had increased following the death of her mother in July 1913. Her sister Polly knew a St Thomas girl, Addie Drew, who was 'in service' with the Leyshons. For six shillings a week, plus board and lodging, Florrie was able to hire this eighteen-year-old as maid-cum-nurse.

On the morning of 27 October 1914, she sent down to St Thomas again for a trusted midwife, Gillian Jones, whose family ran the grocery shop opposite the Canaan chapel. With Dr Alban Evans, the stout Miss Jones had helped deliver the Thomases' daughter Nancy. She cheerfully made her way by tram across town to take her place once more beside the same doctor. Some time that evening (reports differ as to the hour, though by general consent it was a few days later than expected), Florrie gave birth to a seven-pound boy in the main front bedroom of her still uncompleted house.

Now it was her husband's turn to defer to his antecedents. This was unexpected since he, more than Florrie, seemed to have consciously kicked over all traces of his rural Welsh origins. He taught English in an established, some might say snooty, English-style Grammar School which prided itself on preparing its best boys for university. Parents at Swansea Grammar School made a decision that they wanted their sons educated in the language in which business was conducted, scientific progress debated, and continents governed. This pragmatism percolated down the social scale: to many, including both Thomases' families, English was the language of economic advancement. They might, like many of Florrie's relations, including her mother, continue to speak Welsh among themselves. But they were determined their children would benefit by learning English.

This was controversial, of course. Wales had an independent history, an expressive language, and a distinguished literature – older than English, in fact. But teaching in Welsh had been banned by the Blue Books in 1847, ostensibly to counter poor standards in Welsh-speaking schools. This blatant piece of cultural colonialism had been reversed a quarter of a century later. But the damage had been done. A majority of the one and a half million strong population still spoke Welsh, but they were predominantly country folk in dead-end agricultural jobs. The emerging middle-class spoke English, and the political challenge to this linguistic hegemony would not come for another two decades.

Nowhere was English more entrenched than in Swansea and its environs. The coastal strip beside the Bristol Channel had long offered invaders – whether Romans, Danes, Normans or Plantagenets – a foothold in the mysterious mountain fastness of Celtic Britain. By the early twentieth century a two-tier principality had developed, with North and West Wales maintaining their native culture, with its language and traditions, while the South and East had fallen, at least superficially, to the English from across the border. That is not to say there were not major discrepancies. For example, Swansea was a centre for dissenting Nonconformism (otherwise a rural phenomenon). In their chapels, the urban working classes, recently arrived from the countryside, clung to traditional values in the face of maritime cosmopolitanism. As a result Swansea was a town of twitching curtains (with all the attendant hypocrisy) as well as of intellectual energy and commercial drive.

Jack Thomas, the graduate of University College, Aberystwyth, embraced all this, and knew which way he was going. Slim (at this stage) and clearly vain, he wore his hair slicked like a younger member of the royal family. Later, the slick was trained to cover a bald patch and when that became too obvious, he wore a hat. He was always smartly dressed, adopting the style of an English country gentleman in suits, checks at weekends and brogues. The shelves in his new study groaned under the weight of standard English texts from the Dent and Everyman libraries. His greatest delight was Shakespeare. Walking the three-quarters of a mile from Cwmdonkin Drive to the Grammar School on Mount Pleasant (a journey he made twice most days, as he liked to come home for lunch), he even invented a new identity. To the outside world he was no longer known by the familiar 'Jack' but by the more remote initials 'D.J.' which he deemed more fitting for a serious-minded schoolmaster.

However, when he named his new suburban villa and his infant son, nature proved more powerful than nurture, and he drew directly from his Welsh background. The house later became widely known by its number, 5 Cwmdonkin Drive. However, for a dozen years after its construction, it also had a proud Welsh name, Glanrhyd. And, as for the baby, he was called, mellifluously and romantically, Dylan Marlais.

*

The house looked back to Glanrhyd y Gwinil, the smallholding where his grandfather had lived in the middle of the last century in the Cothi valley, thirteen miles north of Carmarthen. Ostensibly the families of both D.J. (as he will be styled) and Florrie came from the same county, west of Swansea. But the bleak, spectacular hills of its northern reaches provided a much tougher environment than the rolling plains around Llanstephan, where seafaring and the railways helped stimulate the mainly agricultural economy.

With his forty acres, nestling beneath the royal forest of Brechfa which covered the Llanybydder mountains in a green expanse of oak and ash, D.J.'s grandfather William Thomas should have made a decent living. But the 1830s were a decade of material hardship and political struggle, culminating in the Rebecca riots of 1843. His son, also William, born in 1834 and later known throughout Wales as the radical preacher and bard Gwilym Marles, was forced to leave his parents and live nearby with a devout uncle Simon Lewis, who was a cobbler. (The Marles – or Marlais – was a stream which joined the Cothi two miles up the valley.) As soon as they were able, he and his two brothers, Thomas and Evan (D.J.'s father), made a hasty exit from these economically depressed hills.

William's (or Gwilym Marles's) career was the most interesting, with parallels to his great-nephew Dylan's. He was brought up an Independent Congregationalist, one of several Nonconformist branches which had taken root in Wales. By dint of hard work, he gained a place at the influential Presbyterian College in Carmarthen. There he discovered Unitarianism, an intellectual strain of religious dissent which denied the Trinity and advocated social reform. Although known (and frowned upon) for his heavy drinking and love of theatre, he won a scholarship to Glasgow University (Oxford and Cambridge still being restricted to Anglicans). While there between 1856 and 1860, he wrote widely, including a novel, book of verse and several tracts. One long winter holiday he acted as tutor to another William Thomas – no relation, but a greater poet, under the bardic name Islwyn.

Quite when Gwilym Marles adopted his own bardic name is not clear. In 1860 he became minister of three Unitarian chapels in southern Cardiganshire, just over the mountains from his birthplace in Brechfa. At his house in Llandysul, he set up a small school which took in boarders from as far away as London. After studying the teachings of the fiery American Unitarian preacher Theodore Parker, his own views became increasingly radical as he battled for the rights of tenant farmers and landless labourers. Welsh country folk were supposed to vote according to the wishes of their landlords. But in the 1868 general election, they defied convention and, when the Liberals gained a famous victory, local Tory squires hit back by evicting tenants from their farms.

As District Secretary for the Liberals, Gwilym Marles became a prominent advocate of the secret ballot – a political battle won in 1871. But this laid him open to retaliation: since owners no longer knew how tenants voted, they targeted their ministers instead. In 1876 an absentee landlord refused to renew the lease at Gwilym Marles's main chapel at Llwynrhydowen without a clause which prevented the incumbent from preaching there. The congregation stood firm and was duly evicted with its minister – an abuse of the rights of free speech which led to widespread protest meetings and drew financial support from liberal-minded people throughout Britain. However the strain took its toll on Gwilym Marles who died three years later, aged only forty-five.

His life was characterised by an unstable mixture of emotional exuberance and deep depression. He enthusiastically supported the Union in the American Civil War ('there is a vein of unmitigated barbarism in the South,' he wrote) and his respect for the United States was evident in the names he gave two of his ten children – Mary Emerson (after the poet) and Theodore (in honour of his preaching mentor). He translated Tennyson, Browning and Pope into Welsh (one obituary commented on his 'fine' rendering of Tennyson's 'Oh, yet we trust that somehow good may be the perfect goal of ill'), and read Socrates, Spinoza and Heine. He loved cricket and theatre, and holidayed in Europe. Yet from college days he suffered from severe headaches, a complaint known locally as *dic talarw* (thought to be a corruption of the French *tic douleureux*). In June 1877, he told a friend, 'I have been pursued by neuralgia for rather more than a twelvemonth, with hardly any respite, and latterly it has got to be so acute and distracting that I have been obliged to think something must be done.' A couple of years later, in one of his last letters, he implored this friend to 'find for me a good brain doctor in London: I also inquire, but first of all I presume I have a brain.'

Of Gwilym Marles's brothers, Thomas made his way to London where he became manager of the National Provincial Bank, Aldersgate Street and where, in 1879, he was trying to get the minister's wayward son Willie a berth on a merchant vessel. (Willie had by then run through a number of careers, including pharmacy, ironmongery, 'business', the army and the navy.) Meanwhile Evan, D.J.'s father, joined the railways, probably in 1852 when he was twenty and the South Wales Railway first reached Carmarthen. In the 1860s, after he married, he lived in Swansea, where his first three children, Jane, Lizzie and Willie, were born. Jane attended the Queen Street British School there. But in 1872 the Evan Thomases moved back to Carmarthen, where they acquired a green-flecked cottage called The Poplars in Johnstown, a hamlet favoured by railway workers on the outskirts of the main town.

At the time Carmarthen was on the verge of a railway boom. Both the South Wales and the Carmarthen and Cardigan (C&C) Railways had just been converted to narrow gauge. The C&C, which employed Evan as a guard, had ambitions to link the industrial heartland of South Wales with a deep-water port in Cardigan and with Manchester and the English north-west. However its line north from Carmarthen never reached further than Gwilym Marles's home town of Llandysul: useful, no doubt, for transporting boarders to his school. The C&C might have succeeded, but for a troubled financial history. It closed temporarily in 1860 — a possible date for Evan the guard's initial move to Swansea. Four years later it called in the receivers, having run up liabilities of £1 million. Nevertheless, traffic was buoyant and, helped by conversion to narrow gauge in 1872, it soldiered on until 1888 when, like the South Wales before it, it was absorbed into the much more powerful Great Western Railway.

D.J. Thomas was born in Johnstown in 1876. Around that time his older brother Willie died suddenly and no further mention is made of him. Perhaps to compensate, the Thomases had another son, Arthur, in 1880. But whereas he followed his late brother and his sisters to the National School in Johnstown, D.J. did not. As a bright child, D.J. probably went to the school run by his aunt, Mary Marles Thomas (widow of Gwilym Marles) in Quay Street, Carmarthen. From there he moved not to the ancient Grammar School (his parents could not afford the fees), but to the National and Practising School in Catherine Street, a charity institution like the British School his sister Jane attended in Swansea. It was run by the Anglican church, marking an early step in the Thomases' transition from their Welsh Nonconformist origins. At this establishment (subsequently known as the Model School) from 1891 to 1895, D.J. enjoyed the status of pupil teacher, paying for the latter stages of his secondary education (and earning a small wage) by instructing the younger boys. Significantly, on 14 September 1892, he was absent, suffering from the family complaint of neuralgia.

Two years earlier, his father Evan was earning twenty-three shillings a week. (This is known because he asked for a rise to twenty-five shillings, the pay of a colleague.) As a guard he followed a two-week rota. One week he came to work at 4.30 in the morning, taking the early train up to Llandysul, where he arrived at 6.50, returning to Carmarthen at 10.20. After a similar journey in the afternoon, he finished at 6.15 p.m. The second week he started at 8.30 a.m., working through until 10.30 at night. Replying to a query from head office in Swansea, his local supervisor commented, 'You will see by the above the hours are not excessive.'

Evan doubtless thought differently and encouraged his elder son to adopt an alternative career and become a teacher. D.J. was initially reluctant until forced to step into the shoes of the National School headmaster who was ill. As a result, he stayed longer than expected and was awarded a Queen's Scholarship which took him to the new University College of Wales at Aberystwyth. His undergraduate career was steady but undistinguished. The only extra-curricular field in which he made a mark was music, acting as secretary of the Musical Society in 1897–8 and leading a male voice party which sang a glee at a soirée given by the Celtic Society in February 1898. Like his Uncle William, he wrote verse and contributed to student magazines. Otherwise he concentrated on a variety of arts subjects, which he combined with teacher training. His crowning achievement came in 1899 when he received the only first class degree in English to be awarded by any of the three University Colleges of Wales.

According to his future wife Florrie, he was then offered a fellowship at Aberystwyth. She said he was invited to 'go abroad, go here, to anywhere he could go. But he'd got tired, I think. He'd worked so hard for those four years [at the university] that he felt, "Get out of it." He was sorry afterwards of course.' There is no record of the university's offer, which may have been for a research post. But it established a sense of thwarted ambition, which became a pattern in D.J.'s life. Later a myth developed that he applied for a lectureship in English at the University College in Swansea, but was turned down. There is no evidence for this either; he never even applied.

He did however see himself as a gentlemanly man of letters, holding down an academic post which would have enabled him to write his own essays and poems. Instead he turned back to schoolmastering, an idea that had arisen more from his father than out of any great enthusiasm on his own part. At least he would be able to pursue his great love of English literature, particularly of Shakespeare. But he realised that, to teach it properly, he would have to adopt its whole cultural infrastructure, down to its English-orientated secondary education system, complete with the petty bureaucracy of the staff common-room. Any literary ambitions of his own would have to be set aside.

So it was an already disappointed man who became a teacher, first (briefly) in Swansea, then for a year or so at Pontypridd County School, before returning in 1901 to Swansea Grammar School where he remained for the rest of his working life. By early 1901, the year of Queen Victoria's death, he was committed to his new profession. For on 31

March, a week before Easter, he was staying at his father's house in Johnstown, Carmarthen, when the census was taken, and he described himself as a schoolmaster. Evan the guard and his wife Ann were in a hospitable, if not festive, mood. They had acted as guardian to their granddaughter Minnie when she attended the local National School in the previous decade. (She was the daughter of their daughter Jane who was twelve years older than Jack.) Staying with them in March 1901, along with D.J., was Minnie's younger sister Lizzie, as well as Evan's own unmarried sister Hannah who hailed, like him, from Brechfa.

D.J. may well have met his wife over this Easter holiday. It has become part of the accepted history of this opaque man that he first came across Florrie at a fair in Johnstown. Although her immediate family was ensconced in St Thomas, they regularly travelled down to visit their many relations dotted around the farms and cottages of lower Carmarthenshire. That Palm Sunday Florrie's older sister Polly was staying at Pentrewyn, a property owned by the Williams clan in Llanstephan, where another sister Annie was married to a farmer called Jim Jones. Eighteen-year-old Florrie – playful, round-faced and petite – was working as a seamstress in a Swansea drapery store and may well have come down to join her sisters for the long Easter weekend.

Details of her courtship with D.J. are tantalisingly scarce – perhaps because he was preoccupied with settling into his new job at Swansea Grammar School. The couple were married in Castle Street Congregational chapel in Swansea on 30 December 1903, nine days after Florrie's older (and richer) brother John had taken the same plunge at the ripe age of thirty-nine. D.J. was a witness at John's wedding at the Paraclete chapel in Newton, a neat village on the edge of the Gower peninsula, and charge of Florrie's brother-in-law David Rees since leaving the Canaan chapel in St Thomas five years earlier.

Why did D.J. and Florrie not follow suit at the same 'family' chapel? There is a persistent rumour that she was already pregnant. This was not unknown around Llanstephan, where her aunt Amy had an illegitimate daughter Ann, who was close to Florrie. In a world where people's Christian and family names tend to be confusingly similar, this bastard Ann was often mistaken for Florrie's much older sister Annie, whose sister-in-law Rachel Jones also had a child born out of wedlock, a son called Albert. But the Swansea hinterland had a more rigid code of values. Blessing the marriage of a woman in this parturient state would have been anathema to the prickly David Rees. So twenty-seven-year-old D.J. and Florrie, just twenty-one, had to make do with an anonymous chapel (later the site of the Kardomah café) in the centre of the town, where neither of them had obvious connections. This would have annoyed D.J. and hastened his passage to the scepticism he had adopted from favourite authors such as Carlyle and T. H. Huxley. As near to being an atheist as possible in such a strongly Nonconformist environment, he would have been confirmed in his distaste for the outward hypocrisies of organised religion.

At the time D.J. retained his love of singing. One of his surviving personal effects is a copy of an arrangement by Victor Novello of Handel's Oratorio. But Florrie's likely miscarriage started a process of withdrawal from social activity. He began to plough his energies into his job at the Grammar School, while his wife, with little else to do, perfected the art of keeping house for which she was later celebrated. Towards the end of 1905 it was clear her father was fatally ill (with tuberculosis, she later liked to say), so her presence was required around the family in Delhi Street. But she had her own preoccupations. Once again she had conceived and in September 1906, less than a year after George Williams died, she gave birth to a daughter called Nancy Marlees (sic).

Like many schoolmasters who mixed with other people's children during their working lives, D.J. had difficulty showing his affection for his own offspring, later reportedly declining even to acknowledge them if he met them in the street. Raising a baby daughter in a series of rented houses only accentuated the gap between this bookish man, growing stiffly middle-aged, and his much more vivacious wife, who liked to meet people and entertain, but who had no intellectual interests of any kind. Florrie had to wait eight more fretful years before she was pregnant again. When her second child was born, D.J. looked again to his bardic uncle for one of their new son's names, Marlais. For the other, more surprisingly, he ransacked a classic text of the Welsh literature he normally affected to disdain. 'Dylan' was a minor character in The Mabinogion, one of the great mythical prose dramas in the Welsh language. The work (a series of books) had been rediscovered during the romantic revival of the country's Celtic past a century or so earlier, and had enjoyed wider success when translated into English by Lady Charlotte Guest, the scholarly wife of a Welsh iron magnate, in 1849. In the drama, Dylan was a golden-haired baby who, as soon as he was born, made for the sea: 'he partook of its nature, and he swam as fast as the swiftest fish. And for that reason he was called Dylan Eil Ton, Sea Son of the Wave.' 'Dylan' in other words means 'sea' or 'ocean'.

By coincidence Dylan's story had been turned into an opera by Joseph Holbrook, from a libretto by the wealthy North Wales aristocrat Lord Howard de Walden, writing as T. E. Ellis (his birth name). Howard de Walden was obsessed with Welsh myths, to the point of owning a yacht called *Rhiannon* and a speedboat *Dylan II*. As recently as July 1914, the opera *Dylan* had been staged at the Theatre Royal, Drury Lane, under the baton of Thomas Beecham. A decade later, when unemployment hit the coal-mining valleys of South Wales, Howard de Walden would pay Beecham to bring his orchestra to give concerts there.

D.J.'s undergraduate love of music carried over at least this far into his married life. Not that Dylan had golden locks at birth: his nurse Addie Drew remembered dark hair, though this quickly changed to angelic yellow curls, like his sister's. The name was supposed to be evocative, a throw-back to the time when D.J. secretly nursed his own ambitions to be a storyteller – perhaps in poetry, like his uncle. Yet it all seemed rather incongruous, settled in genteel Cwmdonkin Drive looking out over the generous curve of Swansea Bay. The infant Dylan was confronted by mixed messages: on the one hand, the pressing reality of Anglo-orientated suburbia; on the other, the liberating potential of Welsh myth (and, to complicate matters, his name was pronounced 'Dillon', as an Englishman might say it, rather than 'Dullan', in the Welsh style). Yet, out of such contradictory circumstances, artists are fledged, and Dylan Thomas was to make the most of them.

TWO

A PRECOCIOUS CHILDHOOD

It was not medieval romance that captured Dylan's imagination at an early age but modern battle. The First World War with Germany was twelve weeks old when he was born. On 27 October, the local *South Wales Daily Post* sought to generate an upbeat mood with a front page report on a local battalion of the Welsh Regiment leaving Swansea to join the British Expeditionary Force. The sombre tone of the main headline 'A Desperate Advance' could not be denied, even if the underlying article looked for the good news of the 'British Hacking Their Way Through'. The reality was that Allied troops had already become bogged down on the Ypres salient in the first great bloody stalemate of the war.

This accident of birth left a life-long impression on the young Dylan. Florrie used to tell how, returning from shopping, she would sometimes inform D.J. in her artless manner: 'Do you know who's gone to the front now?' And Dylan, who was just four when the war ended, would show concern and go to the lobby at the front of the house, in a fruitless search for the person his mother had mentioned. 'I could not understand how so many people never returned from there,' he later recalled.

He was not even a teenager when he started publishing poems about the Great War in his Grammar School magazine. He felt the conflict personally. A bit later, when he began to find his own voice and subject matter, he could look back on the moment of his birth in his first published book, *18 Poems* (1934), and see it in military terms, with all the horror of the battlefield:

> I dreamed my genesis and died again, shrapnel
> Rammed in the marching heart, hole
> In the stitched wound and clotted wind, muzzled
> Death on the mouth that ate the gas.

Birth and death, particularly the inevitability of decay from the onset of life: these were to be among his most potent themes as a poet. But that was in the future. Back at Cwmdonkin Drive, Dylan entered the physical world in the bedroom at the front of the house. As customary in middle-class families, the Thomases maintained certain rooms for 'best'. One was this bedroom and the other the living room directly underneath which Florrie ensured was kept spotless for relations making the journey from Carmarthen. The main door was set slightly to the side of the front of the house. The focus of domestic activity was towards the back where parlour and kitchen looked out on a small garden, bordered by utility buildings such as the coal-hole and wash-room. This was Florrie's domain, where she would cook and entertain. In later years Dylan's friends enjoyed visiting his house: his mother would serve them cakes and sandwiches, with slices of bread cut so thin, she proudly and revealingly liked to say, that you could see London through them. His future wife, Caitlin, was not so impressed at this show of Welsh maternalism: she saw it as obsessive behaviour and noted dismissively that Florrie could not pass a sideboard without wanting to dust it.

In between this social centre and the pristine front room D.J. bagged a study, known as his 'den', which he lined with books from floor to ceiling. Its seedy atmosphere, which mixed classroom chalk with smoke and beer from the saloon bar, was redolent of the disappointments of schoolmastering. A half-finished copy of *The Times* crossword usually lay on a chair. Otherwise the most obvious concession to external taste was a pair of Greek statuettes. In those days a door led from the study to the garden. If someone unwelcome came to the house, D.J. could escape through here and a gate at the bottom of the garden.

Upstairs much the same plan was replicated. Initially, at least, the bedroom at the front was kept for special occasions (and a birth certainly counted). It looked out onto a reservoir and, slightly down the hill, onto an open field attached to a school where, if the pupils were not playing a lop-sided version of football, a flock of sheep grazed con-tentedly. Beyond the reservoir was Cwmdonkin Park, a municipally owned area of trees, ponds, and well-manicured lawns, made more aesthetically pleasing by the jaunty gradient on which it lay. Dylan's parents slept at the back overlooking the garden, while Nancy, washing facilities, boiler and live-in help were all squashed in rooms in between. When Addie left after eighteen months, Dylan took over her box-like room next to the boiler: 'very tiny,' he later noted; 'I really have to go out to turn around ... Hard chair. Smelly. Painful. Hot water pipes very near. Gurgle all the time. Nearly go mad.'

From the outset Dylan was a petulant child. He cried, would not sleep, and had difficulty keeping down food. D.J. was heard to want to 'chuck the little bugger out'. Addie would resort to anything to make the baby smile. He seemed to like a game where she pretended to throw a vinegar bottle at him. But this backfired when the cap came off and the sharp liquid spurted all over his face, nearly choking four-month-old Dylan.

The park had a calming effect when he was in a temper, Addie discovered. From the depths of his pram, he seemed to enjoy the trees and the birds – the earliest evidence of his response to nature. After she left, the Thomases employed other maids who took him there, such as the tall, broad-shouldered 'Patricia', who featured in his story 'Patricia, Edith, and Arnold'. She may well have existed, for much of the other detail in that story rings true. A family called Lewis did indeed live next door, and one can imagine the alert, precocious young Dylan climbing on top of the coal in the shed so as better to hear Patricia's cross-fence gossiping with Edith, the Lewises' maid. The coal-hole was a station on the line of his imaginary railway, the Cwmdonkin Special, 'its wheels, polished to dazzle, crunching on the small back garden scattered with breadcrumbs for the birds'. When he became filthy from the coal dust and Patricia took him inside to change, he exposed himself to her in a typically forthright, wholly innocent, startlingly exhibitionist manner. 'He took off his trousers and danced around her, crying: "Look at me, Patricia!" "You be decent," she said, "or I won't take you to the park."' 'A precocious child,' he described himself in 1933, having once been 'a sweet baby' and before becoming 'a rebellious boy, and a morbid youth'.

Before long the park – 'a world within the world of the sea-town' – offered more promising opportunities for play than the garden. While the spectre of war hung over the town, Dylan responded manfully by carrying a wooden rifle which he used to shoot down 'the invisible unknown enemy like a flock of wild birds'. Although the park was not large, there was always some new area to discover. One day he and his friends would range over it 'from the robbers' den to the pirates' cabin, the highwayman's inn to the cattle ranch, or the hidden room in the undergrowth where we held beetle races and lit the wooden fires and roasted potatoes and talked about Africa and the makes of motor-cars, yet still the next day it remained as unexplored as the Poles, a country just born and always changing.'

Dylan's energy found an outlet in boyish pranks. Accounts abound of him climbing trees and taunting the park-keeper John Smallcombe by walking on the forbidden grass. Addie Drew specifically remembered him throwing missiles at the swans in the reservoir. Such tales (given to biographers and researchers over the years) are doubtless true, though they often seem to draw detail at least from Dylan's own recollection of his youth, put in the mouth of the park-keeper in his 1947 radio broadcast 'Return Journey': 'He used to climb the reservoir railings and pelt the old swans. Run like a billygoat over the grass you should keep off of. Cut branches off the trees. Carve words on the benches. Pull up moss in the rockery, go snip, snip through the dahlias. Fight in the bandstand. Climb the elms and moon up the top like a owl. Light fire in the bushes. Play on the green bank. Oh yes, I knew him well. I think he was happy all the time.' Once such a colourful self-portrait is established by an author, it is often difficult for others to contradict.

Dylan had a mischievous though never nasty streak. But often self-promoted stories of his laddishness gloss over another side to his development. Throughout his childhood, he was considered delicate and sickly. (He later described how this made him suitable for a career as writer, because 'the majority of literature is the outcome of ill men'.) His main symptom was asthma, which was ascribed either to a wheezy chest or to weak lungs. If his mother made more of this than warranted, she was terrified by the spectre of tuberculosis, her father's apparent killer. So much was made of the disease in the Thomas household that Dylan later liked to pretend he had been afflicted with it, as part of his poet's rites of passage. Florrie had another reason for caution. For two terms in 1922–3, her lively daughter Nancy was unable to attend the Girls' High School after picking up a blood disorder which meant that any cut threatened to become septic.

At least this gave Florrie something to do. She wrapped Dylan in scarves in winter, kept him in bed at the slightest symptom, and pumped him full of comfort foods, such as his favourite bread and milk – a regimen tacitly approved of by D.J. who was a fearful hypochondriac himself. The result was that Dylan grew up coddled by his mother, a warm memory he retained throughout his life.

Looking after her children's health also compensated Florrie for her disappointing relationship with her husband. Apart from regular Friday night sorties down town to the Empire Theatre on Oxford Street, her contact with D.J. was minimal. When not at school, he was either reading or drinking at the pub. Haydn Taylor, who was to marry Nancy, was astounded at the intellectual gap. Florrie never read and, when not scurrying distractedly around the house, concerned herself exclusively with local gossip. 'Daddy', as she always called D.J., looked on her with a 'mixture of genuine affection and amused contempt'. He made fun of her mental limitations and, if he imitated or repeated one of her sillier remarks, no-one laughed more heartily than she. Communal activity was strictly limited: D.J. sometimes read from Shakespeare or Keats, two favourite authors, or accompanied songs on a harmonium, a throw-back to his musical past. But it was hardly convivial. 'There was no sense of any shared "homely" atmosphere,' noted Taylor. 'This was no family that went off to the seaside in the summer or played foolish games around the fire at Christmas.'

Another writer D.J. rated highly was Thomas Hardy, whose novel *Jude the Obscure* he used to read and re-read with what Taylor described as 'morbid satisfaction'. The parallels are obvious: Jude was a poor boy whose ambitions to study at Oxford were foiled after he was trapped into marriage by the blousy barmaid Arabella, who feigned pregnancy to win him. Perhaps, bearing in mind those stories that the Thomases were forced to wed, the 'popular' Florrie from St Thomas was better versed in the ways of the world than she let on, and did something similar to snare her Aber graduate. It is true she did not follow Arabella in immediately abandoning her man. And whether there was a free spirit such as Sue Bridehead who offered D.J. a vision of a better life is not known. However there was something of the grumpy D.J. in the unhappy, heavy-drinking Jude of the latter part of the book. Jude's dying words were: 'Wherefore is light given to him in misery, and life unto the bitter in soul?' 'Bitter' was a word frequently used to describe D.J.

Was it Dylan's ill-health or his father's pernicketiness that took the family to Llandrindod Wells in the summer or autumn of 1918? The Thomases stayed in a boarding house in this once fashionable spa town in mid-Wales. Resident in the same establishment was Trevor Hughes, a Swansea Grammar School boy with literary aspirations who, although ten years older, later became a friend of Dylan. He must have been alarmed to encounter his English teacher while on holiday – a sentiment clearly reciprocated, because he recalled D.J. keeping to his room and not mixing much. Florrie, on the other hand, was typically outgoing, and it was at her side that Hughes first saw the 'little face of a boy aged three peeping out from behind his mother's skirts'.

Dylan's attachment to Florrie is evident from a photograph taken around this time in a Swansea studio. It shows a serious, slightly girlish child, head garlanded in a halo of golden curls, sitting staring disdainfully at the camera, as if he is practising an angry arrogant poet pose for the future. His chubby legs are crossed laconically, and his left hand is uncomfortably extended into the lap of his mother, who herself is caught in an emotional no-man's-land between showing affection and restraining her son. The only person enjoying the exercise is Nancy who stands with another woman, perhaps a relation, behind this couple. She looks confident and pretty, her hair tied in an extravagant bow.

With D.J. as father, Dylan might have found himself forced educationally. At school D.J. was known as a fierce taskmaster, as suggested by his nickname *Le Soldat*, with its Napoleonic connotations. His iron self-control extended to alcohol: though he liked to drink, he monitored his input, perhaps trying to lay the ghost of some youthful excess. But, as if exhausted by his daytime exertions, D.J. at home was indulgent to the point of laxity. According to Florrie, Dylan taught himself to read from second-rate comics such as *Rainbow*. From time to time he would climb into his parents' bed where his father would declaim some Shakespeare. When Florrie asked if the child (aged just four) was not too young for this, D.J. said he hoped some passages would stick. 'It'll be just the same as if I were reading ordinary things.'

A similarly laissez-faire approach was taken to his spiritual development. D.J. had no time for religion, but it is impossible to grow up in a Welsh household with Nonconformist ministers in the family without taking on board the rudiments of a chapel approach to life. Most weekends Dylan would accompany his mother on visits to her sister Dosie at the manse of Paraclete chapel in Newton, close to the Mumbles. Often he attended his Uncle Dai Rees's Sunday School, winning a certificate for Bible studies that he hung with no great enthusiasm on his wall in Cwmdonkin Drive. One of his uncle's interests was natural history: Dylan picked up much of his basic knowledge of fauna and flora from rambles with his uncle through rustic byways on the edge of the Gower peninsula. (There is no evidence he showed any interest in, or aptitude for, his uncle's other passion – golf.) Sometimes the family ventured slightly further into Gower where another of Florrie's brothers, Thomas Williams, lived. A hunchback variously described as 'Bohemian' and 'a complete humbug' (by his niece Nancy), he too had been a minister until a good marriage had given him the money and freedom to retire to a series of grand mansions, including Brook Villa at the entrance to the Clyne valley, where he and his wife Emma alienated neighbours by closing a former public right of way.

Dylan's formal education did not begin until the age of seven, when he was sent down the hill to Mrs Hole's school in Mirador Crescent. In later years he liked to describe this grandly, in the English manner, as his 'preparatory' school, and in a way it was. Started a few years earlier by Isabel Hole, an English widow in her fifties, it provided the more prosperous young children of the locality with a grounding in Latin, French, Arithmetic, History, English and Geography, gently propelling them on their paths to the Grammar School and Girls' High School. Surprisingly for parents such as Dylan's, it was not only religiously based (every day began with Bible reading, hymns and a prayer) but avowedly Anglican, with regular visits from the vicar of Christ Church, Swansea, Canon J. H. Watkins Jones.

Wearing a red and blue blazer, Dylan took his place in an all-purpose ground-floor classroom, arranged in a series of long hard benches, with girls at the front and boys behind. Mrs Hole sat authoritatively at a high desk, assisted by her sickly daughter Dorothy, whose job was to cuddle the youngest pupils if they cried or otherwise could not keep up. In the background lurked a son, with a reputation for enjoying his drink. Upstairs, in the late afternoons, Mrs Hole's maid, Eliza Sadler, was allowed to teach music. Children who had misbehaved during the day were forced to stay on in the empty classroom during this period, allowing Dylan plenty of opportunity to hear what he called the 'distant, terrible, sad music of the late piano lessons'.

Afternoons were also a time for reading aloud, perhaps one of Richmal Crompton's *Just William* books which Dylan enjoyed or, a more direct literary influence, the German children's classic *Der Struwwelpeter* (or Shock-headed Peter). These cautionary tales of youthful misbehaviour appealed to Dylan's Gothic imagination, particularly the one about Conrad, whose habit of sucking his thumb led to his fingers being chopped off by the tailor or 'great long-legged scissor-man'. Similar images occur in his own later output, for example, the half-naked girl with nails 'not broken but sharpened sideways, ten black scissor-blades ready to snip off his tongue' in his story of emerging adolescent sexuality, 'A Prospect of the Sea'. These have given Freudian-inspired commentators scope for speculation about Dylan's supposed castration complex. Did this result from his mother's over-protectiveness? There were indeed childlike elements in the way he later related to women. And was it linked to another of the psychoanalysts' bugbears, his supposed oral fixation? As he grew older, Dylan liked to stuff himself, not with good, nutritious food, but with sweets of the most infantile variety, such as gob-stoppers. He also found comfort in the breast: after the matrimonial conflict described in his poem 'I make this in a warring absence', he was able to relax in his knowledge: 'Now in the cloud's big breast lie quiet countries.'

Reading aloud meant group recitation, which Dylan hated. Chanting a poem in unison one afternoon, he put his hands over his ears and burst out, 'I can't stand it, I can't stand it.' Subsequently he and his fellow pupils were allowed to recite poems of their choice. Standing alongside Mrs Hole, the seven-year-old Dylan announced he was going to do 'my grave poem', and started to intone:

> 'Let's talk of graves, of worms and epitaphs
> Make dust our paper and with rainy eyes
> Mark sorrow on the bosom of the earth...'

He ended in stunned silence. His class had no idea he had been quoting Shakespeare's *Richard II*. But they could not help being affected by the sadness of the words and their delivery.

Declaiming poetry introduced Dylan to one pleasure he never tired of – the sound of his own voice. Another stage in his journey of inculcation into English ways came around this time when he was sent for elocution lessons. Swansea's aspiring middle classes were not content with the broad musical vowels of the Welsh valleys. In their search for respectability they had to imitate the precise modulated tones of the English. D.J. had already lost the warm burr of his forefathers; Florrie retained it only slightly. But they made sure that Nancy learnt to speak 'properly', and Dylan followed her once a week to the small academy in Brynymor Crescent run by Miss Gwen James, a grocer's daughter who had studied at London's Central School of Speech and Drama. She recognised that Dylan had 'a big voice for a small boy' and set about polishing its rougher edges.

His command of diction and his delivery set him up for leading roles in school plays at Mrs Hole's. In one end of term entertainment he was cast as a colonel required to sit and read a newspaper. This proved too passive for Dylan. He contrived to poke a hole in the paper with a walking stick and to spit orange peel through the gap. He then jumped up and started twirling his stick, as if leading a group of minstrels. The audience (including his mother) loved this impromptu act. Mrs Hole was not so sure and promptly brought down the curtain. But Dylan had discovered a talent for performing and gaining attention which never deserted him.

At Mrs Hole's he met his lifelong friend, Mervyn Levy, whose cosmopolitan Jewish family offered a very different outlook on life than most inhabitants of the Uplands. Mervyn's father Louis was an idler who ran a tobacconist's shop in Castle Street in the centre of town. His mother Havie was one of the rich Rubensteins who supported Swansea's small Jewish community. However soon after giving birth to her younger son Alban in 1920, she was stricken with cancer and died the following year. As a result Mervyn's home life was strained and disrupted, a situation made worse when he quickly acquired a step-mother, Dolly, whom he could not stand.

Dylan was happy to find a fellow misfit who wanted to get out of his house. In the narrow lane behind their 'dame' school, the two boys developed their creative talents, as they learnt to fib and make up stories with their friends. 'My Dad's the richest man in Swansea,' one would say, and the rest would try to trump that: 'mine's the richest in Wales', chimed another, and someone would claim no-one in the world had more money than his father. Dylan and Mervyn also enjoyed more laddish japes – taking out their penises and writing 'God Save the King' with their urine on the wall, observing a buxom nursemaid employed by the Levys naked at her ablutions (there was a story, no doubt apocryphal, that she played strip poker with them), and, inevitably, starting to smoke or, as Dylan later called it, indulging in the 'Boy Scout's Enemy'.

Through his school and his parents, Dylan came to know the children of several local families. The heads of these households were not usually tradespeople. Nor were they from the polluted working-class communities on the other side of town. Dylan might visit relations in Gower and further afield in Carmarthenshire, but he seldom ventured to see his aunts and uncles in St Thomas. Instead the social circle encouraged by his parents included boys such as Jackie Bassett, whose father, the mayor in 1926–7, owned several of Swansea's leading hotels and lived in a large house, Rose Hill, abutting waste land on Town Hill, above Cwmdonkin Drive. On Richmond Road, the street immediately below the Thomases, lived Ivan and George Grant-Murray (the Murrays of 'Return Journey'), whose father William ran the municipal art gallery, and also Hugh, son of William Crwys Williams, a distinguished Baptist minister whose poetry was considerably more successful than D.J.'s. Crwys won the crown at the National Eisteddfodd in 1919. He went on to become Archdruid of Wales, but also found time to be secretary of the British and Foreign Bible Society in Wales and a Governor of the Grammar School.

Dylan showed no interest in the paintings and art books strewn around the Murrays' house. Nor, being monolingual, was he inspired by Crwys Williams's Welsh language verse. Dylan did, however, follow up the professional interests of another inhabitant of Richmond Road. A fellow pupil at Mrs Hole's was Joyce Daniel, daughter of a metal merchant. In his memoir 'Quite Early One Morning', Dylan recalled how he once filled the unfortunate girl's galoshes with snow. When he visited her parents' house, he was fascinated to learn that her mother Winifred had had stories published. When he said he wanted to be a writer, she lent him a copy of the *Writers' and Artists' Yearbook*. She even recalled that he used it to enter a competition which he won.

The Murrays were leaders in the youthful gang wars fought out on the exposed scrubland up the hill from Cwmdonkin Drive. Dylan joined them in fierce battles with the Mitchell brothers, otherwise known as the Sioux Indians. He had learnt about the Wild West from regular visits to the Uplands cinema. Every Saturday morning he and his friends went to the children's matinée. Part of his weekly ritual was that he first went to Mrs Ferguson's shop opposite the flea-pit picture house where he bought a three-penny bag of sweets, comprising gob-stoppers, liquorice allsorts and wine-gums. Apart from providing welcome, perhaps even needed, sugar input (some observers have described his abiding fondness for sweets as a physical addiction caused by a form of diabetes), these acted as ready missiles when the film started. Then he and his friends would stand up on their broken seats and would shout, jeer and throw anything they could lay their hands on at the screen.

Throughout his childhood Dylan showed a talent for getting into scrapes. His mother recalled how, when he was 'very small', he was playing in the upstairs nursery at the Crwys Williamses. 'Crwys's little boy Huey came down complaining of a pain in his tummy, Dylan stayed upstairs but leaned over the banister, mocking Huey and saying, "Oh I've got a pain in my tummy, Mummy." He leaned too far and fell down, flat on his nose. It was flat to his face.' He was rushed to hospital but, despite an operation, his features were never the same. Thenceforward, he was burdened with his flat boxer's nose. Another accident occurred when he and a friend played see-saw on a plank outside a new house being built on Cwmdonkin Drive. The inevitable happened: after jumping on one end without a counter-balancing weight at the other, Dylan tumbled over and was knocked unconscious.

Around the age of ten, he was given a new bicycle (probably a present for gaining a place at the Grammar School in September 1925). The following June he wanted to ride over and watch the annual regatta at Mumbles, but his father forbade him, saying the road to the seaside resort at the western edge of Swansea Bay was too busy. Dylan's good intentions were quickly challenged by some older boys, who persuaded him that his bicycle was too big and he should swap it with one of theirs. He was careering down the hill by West Cross when he found that the brakes on his replacement machine were non-existent. In order to avoid a stopped bus, he swerved into the road, and was hit by an oncoming delivery van owned by the big department store, Ben Evans, where his Great-Uncle Dan (his maternal grandmother's brother) had once worked. The result was a multiple fracture of both wrist and arm which kept him in hospital for three weeks – an early instance of the 'chicken bones' that regularly afflicted both him and his family.

Afterwards, unable to write, he had to stay at home to convalesce. In her maternal way, Florrie put a table in the garden so he could practise writing with his left hand. She was shocked to look out of the bedroom window and see her son not writing but casually smoking a cigarette. She said nothing at the time, but waited until her husband returned from school. D.J. was unconcerned: he suggested waiting until the weekend when Dylan was likely to have stocked up with cigarettes before visiting the cinema. Then he would swoop.

Apart from moving pictures, Dylan's imagination was stirred by words. Even before he could read, Dylan had shown signs of enjoying their sound as revealed in nursery rhymes. 'I did not care what the words said, overmuch, nor what happened to Jack & Jill and the Mother Goose rest of them; I cared for the shapes of sound that their names, and the words describing their actions made in my ears; I cared for the colours the words cast on my eyes ... I fell in love – that is the only expression I can think of – at once, and am still at the mercy of words.'

He later claimed he was six or seven when he began to understand how words could be strung together euphoniously in what was known as poetry or, as he once jokingly put it, 'the Spinster's Friend'. His mother dated this epiphany to a couple of years later when verse suddenly started pouring out of him. He wrote about literally anything. Sometimes he would ask his sister Nancy for a subject and, if she suggested the kitchen sink, he would turn neat rhymes on that. For paper he used whatever came to hand. A favourite medium was the cardboard that came back from the laundry as stiffener inside D.J.'s freshly ironed shirts. Visitors to Cwmdonkin Drive often found these pieces of card, duly filled with Dylan's neat, rounded script, hung on the walls of the back parlour, allowing them to follow the progress of a poem around the room from one storyboard to the next. Dylan liked his poems to be visual, engaging the eye as well as the ear. From an early age he also drew spikey little pictures – another addition to the parlour décor.

He later showed one of these laundry cards to his friend Tom Warner. Perhaps the earliest example of a Dylan Thomas poem, it read succinctly:

I Like
My Bike.

However, dating, or even laying hands on, his juvenile work is difficult. One reason is that most was destroyed. The Thomases used to keep Dylan's output in what has been described as a 'dinner wagon' with two cupboards. At some stage, so the family story goes, Florrie tidied the contents of this oversize trolley into two piles – one to keep (containing his juvenilia), the other to throw out – and she accidentally despatched the wrong material.

Some person did transcribe parts of Dylan's output, but that does not make chronology any easier. One can only point to some youthful talented work. The University of Texas owns a manuscript of a poem called 'My Party', with an identification (not in Dylan's hand), 'Dylan Marlais 5 Cwmdonkin Drive Swansea', but not dated. The subject-matter is clearly a child's:

> If I had a party at Christmas
> I'll tell you who I should invite
> I'd ask the wee mouse in the corner
> Who only comes out in the night...

Young Dylan runs through the other animals he would like to join his festivities, including a toad and a bat. But unfortunately his nurse is afraid of them, leaving him to conclude that he will have to wait until he is older and then have his party when nobody knows.

Even at this age, Dylan was able to knock off competent pastiches of known verse forms. In 'Decision' he recalled some rousing imperialistic boys' epic:

> As eager captains pent behind the wall
> Of some sieged city, yearn for clash of steel
> And thrust of sword; for battle close and real
> And fiery onset when fierce foemen fall...

Despite over-indulgence in alliteration, the lines show a keen appreciation of the poetic qualities of words. On the manuscript someone has pencilled in the sharp reminder: 're/al is two syllables & cannot rhyme with steel.' Probably it was his father, perhaps even his sister Nancy who had left school in April 1925 and was hosting a regular reading group for her friends at Cwmdonkin Drive. By that date Dylan's childhood freedom was coming to an end. In the autumn he was set to enter the Grammar School, where tiresome rules extended to everyday behaviour as well as to language and literature.

THREE

VIRTUE AND GOOD LITERATURE

Just before eight o'clock every morning, a mad scramble occurred on the hill outside the imposing Gothic Revival edifice of Swansea Grammar School. For several minutes beforehand, caretaker William Marley had tolled a bell summoning pupils from all quarters of the town. Then two or three minutes before the hour, he stopped, slowly walked across the courtyard, and then abruptly brought down a bar across the main front door. Anyone still outside was late and was duly punished.

On his first morning at his new school in September 1925 Dylan almost certainly made the journey there with his father. Florrie had dressed him in his uniform of bright red blazer, with matching cap, and had added a scarf to protect the sickly boy against Swansea's changeable elements. Then he and D.J. took the back route – a fifteen-minute stroll along Terrace Road to the school on Mount Pleasant.

Founded in 1682 by the Bishop of Waterford and Lismore, Hugh Gore, and set in a commanding position overlooking Swansea Bay, the Grammar School was, like its senior English master, D.J. Thomas, a curious mixture. A visitor might imagine he or she had strayed into a typical British public school, with its quaint traditions, daily religious observance and academic bias – a scholarship at Oxford or Cambridge university being the goal for the more ambitious pupils. Nevertheless, headmaster Trevor Owen, a stocky North Walian with a top degree in Mathematics from Cambridge, had little of the usual public school enthusiasm for games. Beatings did occur and masters were known to cuff pupils around the head. But generally the atmosphere was easy-going and discipline relaxed. Certain teachers had to endure endless ragging, among them W. S. 'Soapy' Davies, the senior classics master who was D.J.'s regular Wednesday lunch-time drinking companion at the nearby Mountain Dew. Classroom wags would torture Jimmy Gott, who taught art during Dylan's first year, by asking him distractedly, 'Sleep with your wife, sir?', and when asked for clarification, would say: 'Lend me a knife, sir?'

The school had moved up the hill from the town in the 1850s. A carved inscription above the main door read 'Hear instruction, be wise and refuse it not', a sentiment subtly echoed in the school motto, 'Virtue and Good Literature'. Arms of the founders and early trustees adorned the stained glass windows in the main assembly hall where the mitre was the most obvious decorative motif, though another surprising feature was the preponderance of pen nibs. A favourite pastime was to steal a fellow pupil's pen, add a dart-like paper tail and launch it at the ceiling where dozens of these lethal missiles were imbedded.

During the First World War the school had sprung dutifully to the defence of the Empire. A cadet corps was set up and drilled by the physical training master, Sergeant O. A. Bird, a former NCO known to Dylan and his friends as 'Oiseau'. But the conflict took a heavy toll: of around 900 old boys who volunteered, seventy-six were known to have died, including all but one member of the 1917 upper sixth form. Nearly a decade later the losses were still mourned. With so many former pupils among the casualties, D.J. felt some shame at having avoided the blood-bath. Commemorating the dead became a personal crusade. Daniel Jones (Dylan's best friend at the school) recalled how, beneath his outward calm, the senior English master seethed with a barely controllable rage. Once, when a pupil dared to giggle while a war poem by Wilfred Owen was being read, D.J. lost his temper and administered a savage beating. D.J. had had 'a hard time school-teaching' during the war, remarked Jones.

D.J.'s unease was not helped by a new breed of younger master, usually without a university degree, but with a maturity that came from wartime service at the front. Their casual manner was in marked contrast to older teachers in their stiff collars. One of the school's most distinguished old boys, Llewelyn Gwynne, Bishop of Egypt and the Sudan, and war-time Deputy Chaplain General to the British Army in France, came back to address the pupils. The general atmosphere of a nation still struggling to come to terms with the battlefield carnage could not fail to have made an impression on young Dylan. When the school commissioned a bronze memorial, unveiled by local grandee Lord Swansea in June 1924, Florrie noted that her nine-year-old son was 'very impressed'.

By then the school had long outgrown its Victorian shell. Seventy years earlier it had taken boarders, but now its dormitories were commandeered for use as chemistry laboratories, while the main classes were conducted in a filthy asbestos-ridden corrugated shed at the back of the main building.

A traditional feature of the establishment was the ritual chastisement meted out to new boys by their peers. During their first week, recent arrivals would be taken to the lower of the school's two playgrounds, beside the fives courts and cricket nets, and unceremoniously thrown into the brambles and bushes beneath. With a resilience that belied his delicate physique, Dylan survived this barbaric initiation and began making his mark on the school. For his first couple of years, he played the game as a member of Mansel House, called after an early patron of the school. In the fast-stream class 3A, he had a reputation for being bright but lazy. When, despairing of Dylan's repeated failures to complete any homework, his young Latin master, J. Morgan Williams, boxed him around the ears, he was surprised to hear a staff colleague advise against such punishment, as D.J. would disapprove. Dylan usually played on this perception, trying to get away with doing as little as possible, because he knew that most masters stood in awe of his stiff father.

Initially at least, Dylan's Latin improved under this regime and he may not have been as bad a student as his proud boast of being thirty-third in trigonometry would suggest. One of his physics exercise books survives, and it shows a conscientious second-year pupil who, despite a tendency to scribble random verses and sign his full name – Dylan Marlais Thomas – wrote up his experiments neatly and regularly received good marks. One doodle showed his interest in the physical properties of light. 'Light', he wrote. 'Light is invisible/Light travels in straight lines.' It could almost have been a draft of his early poem 'Light breaks where no sun shines'.

As other snatches of his back of the class verse suggest, however, his mind was never fully occupied in his studies, for he was already more interested in poetry. At the end of his first term, when he was just eleven, his 'The Song of the Mischievous Dog', an accomplished humorous ditty reminiscent of Hilaire Belloc, was published in the school magazine. This was followed a year later by 'His Repertoire', a delightful ballad in rhyming iambic hexameters, about a boy who only ever learnt one piece, called 'Alice', to play on his violin. When his friends, who were tired of this, demanded an encore at the school concert, he surprised them by launching into a wailing piece they had never heard, let alone expected. Questioned about this afterwards, he replied:

'Well you know of encore pieces I have always been bereft,
So I gave you Alice backwards; that was all,' he said, and left.

Some of Dylan's critics might be tempted to read this as an insight into his manner of poetic composition. It suggests that, as he searched for his own voice, he was wrestling with issues of creativity. These became more marked as he entered a phase of writing war-related poetry, which reflected his father's concerns, if not direct influence. 'The Second Best', published in the *Boy's Own Paper* in February 1927, focused on the poignant quality of the memory of ordinary unheroic people killed in battle. The following month Dylan returned to the school magazine as an outlet for 'The Watchers' which adopted the blustering heroic style of Sir Henry Newbolt to ask the 'mighty dead ... who rest by Ypres and Pozières by Vimy and Cambrai' if they heard the progress of the Allied armies overhead, marching victoriously towards the Rhine. 'Missing', just over a year later, called on the sun to seek out a dead soldier on the battlefield and 'bless/His upturned face with one divine caress'.

Such was Dylan's facility with this material that when fellow pupil Idwal Rees read one of these poems in the school magazine, he suspected the hand – or at least assistance – of D. J. Thomas. This was indeed possible because Dylan was not above discreet plagiarisation. In January 1927, he sent the *Western Mail* another war-related poem, 'His Requiem', which he had cribbed directly from the *Boy's Own Paper* four years earlier. When this appeared under his own name in the 'Wales Day by Day' column, he feigned such delight that, as he noted in his story 'The Fight', he plastered the cutting on the mirror in his bedroom, close to a treasured picture of Rupert Brooke, and scrawled on it, 'Homer Nods.' (His deceit was not noted until the verses were published in a posthumous edition of his poems.) A couple of years later he was caught out offering his school magazine a short sentimental poem called 'Sometimes' about a man who catches sight of his boyhood self and wonders what he might have been. Originally written by the American Thomas S. Jones Jr., this had appeared in Arthur Mee's *The Children's Encyclopaedia*. Ironically, as senior English master, D. J. Thomas supervised the school magazine. When alerted to his son's theft by the editor, E. F. McInerney, he could only make a suitable show of shock, and the poem was withdrawn.

Why did a bright boy, who clearly knew how to write verse, resort to such deceit? The answer is that this was his way of dealing with the various pressures on him. His introduction to poetry at Cwmdonkin Drive had been, not unexpectedly, didactic, with assimilation and imitation the main techniques of instruction. He himself recorded how, in the evenings, before settling down to homework that was seldom completed, he would sit in his father's dim book-lined 'den' and read indiscriminately, until his eyes hung out. D.J.'s shelves contained 'nearly everything that a respectable highbrow library should contain'. Inspired by the magic of words, Dylan began to experiment with the techniques of his favourite literary practitioners.

I wrote endless imitations – though I never thought of them as imitations, but, rather, colossally original, things unheard of, like eggs laid by tigers – I wrote imitations of whatever I happened, moon-and-print struck, to be goggling at and gorging at the time: Sir Thomas Browne, Robert W. Service, de Quincy, Henry Newbolt, Blake, Baroness Orczy, Marlowe, Chums, the Imagists, the Bible, the Magnet, Poe, Grimm, Keats, Lawrence, Austin Dobson and Dostoievski, Anon and Shakespeare. I tried my little trotter at every poetical form ... I had to imitate and parody, consciously and unconsciously: I had to try to learn what made words tick, beat, blaze, because I wanted to write what I wanted to write before I knew how to write or what I wanted to.

Copying the masters was one thing; passing the results off as his own another. It showed Dylan's need to demonstrate his poetic ability to his parents, partly to his indulgent mother, who made copies of his work, but rather more to his remote father whose laissez-faire attitude to learning in the home belied his firm ambition for his son. It was no coincidence that Dylan's main act of plagiarism involved a poem about the war – a topic of such emotional significance to D.J. – nor that it appeared in the Western Mail, the main outlet in Wales for traditional English literary values. Dylan's parents were so proud of his success that they kept the cheque for ten shillings he had won and did not allow him to cash it. No wonder he felt the need to display his prize poem in his room.

Having D.J. in the school put the boy under additional pressure. By his third year, Dylan was beginning to concentrate on writing poetry to the neglect of academic subjects. His father was heard to ask staff colleagues what he should do with his son. Since there was no simple answer, Dylan found one way of maintaining his father's good will was to keep up his own enthusiasm for English literature. The result was an extraordinary trade-off which was perhaps never mentioned, but which almost certainly existed. Recognising Dylan's talents and recalling his own thwarted poetic ambitions, D.J. learnt to turn a blind eye when his son ignored much of his school curriculum and concentrated his cerebral energies on poetry.

Something else was going on. With his commitment to a classical liberal education in the tradition of Matthew Arnold (who, though sympathetic to Celtic culture, denigrated the Welsh language) D.J. represented an uncompromising rationality that his son respected but found increasingly difficult to emulate. Dylan could sense that his own approach to life was likely to be more emotionally based, with fewer obvious intellectual certainties.

Dylan had read enough to understand that English verse was going through a period of profound change – a topic he wrote intelligently about in an article on modern poetry in the school magazine in December 1929. After an initially crude and emotional response to the war, he suggested, poets were finding themselves in 'a more contemplative confusion, a spiritual riot'. He may well have decided that, until he found his own voice in this mêlée, it was no bad strategy to continue to imitate. At least that way he could sometimes impress his father. 'No poet can find sure ground,' he added, reflecting his own lack of firm footing. 'Today is a transitional period.'

Away from the classroom and from literary endeavours, Dylan enjoyed a varied and even successful school career. At the end of his first year, in June 1926, when only eleven, he won the under-15 mile race at the school sports, though his victory reflected not just the school's poor standard of athletics, but also the substantial start he enjoyed under the handicap system because of his age. Nevertheless his supremacy in this race was repeated again in 1928 and 1929 when he also won the quarter mile. The following year he was second in the senior cross-country race. These performances belied his apparent frailty, reflecting his tenacity and sending a none-too-subtle message to his overweening mother that he was stronger than she would have the world believe. This was important to him and, until his premature death in 1953, he carried in his wallet a cutting (complete with his photograph) from the Cambrian Daily Leader reporting his 1926 triumph. Although he never made the school team, he also enjoyed playing cricket, frequently turning his arm as a medium-paced bowler. Throughout his life one of his favourite forms of relaxation was watching first class-cricket, starting at an early age with games involving Glamorgan at the St Helen's ground in Swansea.

As he rose through the school, he became a leading member of the debating, dramatic and reading societies. He was helped as a debater by his elocution lessons which enabled him to project his powerful voice. In one classroom colloquium, he was required to argue that modern poetry made a greater contribution to literature than anything from the past, while his more studious friend Daniel Jones presented the opposing case. Jones later recalled how he methodically researched his own thesis, with telling references to poets from Homer to Browning. But Dylan won convincingly by simply keeping his fellow pupils amused. Jones doubted whether his opponent even mentioned one contemporary poet or quoted a single line of verse. Dylan was not so lucky when he proposed the motion 'that the modern youth is decadent' in the full debating society. When he abandoned his proven crowd-pleasing technique and sought to impress with his knowledge of aestheticism, he was defeated. He put this down to his youthful audience's unwillingness to admit to the sin of decadence. However he relished the opportunity to be iconoclastic: 'I ran down everything, especially tender! subjects like religion, sanctity, sport and sex.'

His plummy voice proved an asset when he picked up the acting career he had started at Miss Hole's. If asked for an enduring image of Dylan, his contemporaries would almost certainly have pointed to one of his roles in the school plays. It might have been him as a fourteen-year-old impressing as Edwin Stanton in John Drinkwater's *Abraham Lincoln*, or the following year in the title role in the same author's *Oliver Cromwell*, when his character's distinctive wart lacked adhesive and kept slipping to other parts of his face. Most likely he would have been recalled as Roberts, the strike leader, in John Galsworthy's *Strife*, in the spring 1931 production. The school magazine praised his performance, though with reservations, for he 'seemed to lack the coarseness and toughness of fibre necessary for the interpretation of Roberts; his vowels were occasionally too genteel; and he was innocent of gesture, an essential part of the demagogue's equipment.'

Dylan was clearly too much of a respectable Uplands child to be entirely convincing. As the magazine had joked in an earlier feature on 'Things We Cannot Credit', 'That D.M.T. should mispronounce a word'. And there was indeed an irony in his well-endowed Grammar School mounting a play about class conflict during a period of growing industrial unrest. Part of the school's income came from an estate in the upper Ogmore valley in Glamorgan where a coal-mine had been sunk in the 1860s. South Wales had suffered crippling unemployment for the best part of a decade, though Swansea, with its new oil refinery at Skewen and its seams of 'modern' anthracite, had been spared the worst effects. In the late 1920s, however, the slump came to Dylan's 'ugly, lovely' home town. Dole queues lengthened, conditions in St Thomas became more difficult, and boys in the Grammar School's distinctive red cap were targets of abuse if they strayed outside their narrow suburban confines. Pupils had always been politically conservative and socially exclusive, an inevitable consequence of their type of education. But now these traits became more pronounced. One young master was surprised to find that no-one in the sixth form supported him in his opposition to capital punishment. When he remarked on this in the staff common-room, he found that everyone there was a hanger and flogger as well.

Dylan could not escape the effects of this social conditioning: as he would later tell his girlfriend Pamela Hansford Johnson, 'You don't know how True-Blue I really am, and what a collection of old school ties my vest conceals.' But a couple of months afterward, he was capable of making a complete volte-face: 'Don't you go about jeering at my Old School Tie. I hate Old School Ties.' Finding an appropriate attitude to his socially exclusive alma mater was always a problem, one made no easier by the fact that the school was so clearly identified in his mind with his father. So a solution was to bury and later find himself in poetry.

He was helped by his friendship with Daniel Jones, whom he met at the very start of his school career. Jones was older (by twenty months) and should not really have been in the same class. But he had attended a preparatory school run by his aunt in his family home and no-one at the Grammar School realised how well he had been taught.

Dylan gave a fictionalised account of his first meeting with Dan in his story 'The Fight'. He invested the incident with great significance, telling how he had been trying, with unusual bloody-mindedness, to goad a Mr Samuels who lived next to the school playground. He knew exactly what was needed to get an angry reaction from a man who simply wanted to read a newspaper in his garden. As soon as he was successful, he intended going home to lunch. His easy victory was interrupted when he was pushed down the bank by someone whom he had not heard approach. Dylan threw a stone at his assailant, leading to a bloody fracas, enthusiastically egged on by Samuels. But the adult's intervention quickly caused the two youths to stop their fighting and join forces in throwing sand in his direction.

Dan has dated this encounter to his first week at school in September 1925. This would explain Dylan's unfamiliarity with his classmate. But his story does not describe a new pupil's behaviour. Its detail comes from slightly later, around 1929. Not that this matters because 'The Fight' is about two artistic boys bonding against the adult world. With curly black hair and thick round glasses, Dan looked like a school swot, but his studious manner was offset by a twinkle in his eye and a naughty smile which played through his slightly pudgy features. In him Dylan found a kindred spirit, someone highly intelligent, who shared not only his interest in poetry but his impish sense of humour.

Dan was barely fifteen and living at Ballarat House in Eversley Road in Sketty when he wrote his first known letter to thirteen-year-old Dylan, dated 30 December 1927. Accompanying this precocious note was a mythological ballad Dan had composed called 'Persephone'. Indicative of the level of his discussion with Dylan, he mentioned that the poem had been difficult to write because of its 8.6 metre, with a rhyme at the end of every eight-syllabled line. He suggested he might have to resort to Chaucerian scansion to get the correct number of syllables. Even at this stage, Dan bowed to Dylan's poetic skills in signing off, 'Acknowledging your superiority in this Art, and hoping my poor attempts will arouse a little pleasure in your condescending breast'.

The following month the Jones family moved a short distance along the same road to a larger house called Warmley, the appealing backdrop to the domestic scenes in 'The Fight'. In this story Dylan disarmingly describes how he always wanted to invite a friend to his room at Cwmdonkin Drive, with its plagiarised poem from the *Western Mail* on the mirror. But no-one ever came. So he was always happy to take the ten-minute walk to Warmley where, as its onomatopoeic name implied, the atmosphere was welcoming, cultured and unconventional – a far cry from the pinched respectability with which he was familiar.

Dan's father, Jenkyn Jones, was a Welsh-speaker who earned his living as a bank manager. But that gave no clue to his alternative calling as a church organist and composer of choral music (which he regularly judged on the Eisteddfod circuit). He was a great raconteur with a fund of general knowledge, particularly about astronomy and entomology. Others in the family were equally accomplished. Dan's Scots-born mother had exhibited her intricate needlework, his older brother Jim was a competent musician with a fondness for jazz, and his Aunt Alice had her preparatory school. Dan himself played the piano to a very high standard and, following his father, composed reams of music. In 'The Fight', Dylan mentioned his friend's seven historical novels, but that only skimmed the surface of his output of poems and stories.

Dan's previously unknown diary for 1928 gives fascinating insight into his hitherto only dimly discernible relationship with Dylan. Written partly in easily penetrable code (useful practice for his Second World War job as a cryptanalyst at Bletchley Park), it captures the boys' mixture of intellectual curiosity and youthful fun. On 29 January, Dylan visited Warmley and listened to Dan playing the piano. A few days later he came and read his own poems. In between the two boys played cards and fooled around fencing in the basement. On 9 February, 'Dylan read a tuppenny horrible "One Punch Chris", Jim [Dan's brother] put on the gramophone, and I read *Ben Hur*. We made up poems, alternate lines.'

Dylan's fondness for trashy books was to endure throughout his life. But the collaborative poems characterised an important stage in his creative development. Temporarily forgetting the 'official' rules of great poetry, as drummed into him by his father, he relaxed and tested grandiloquent words and phrases in playful competition with Dan. Several such early efforts survive: seldom great poetry, often nonsensical, occasionally attaining an ingenious surrealism which suggests familiarity with contemporary Dadaism. When the two attempted short stories in a similar way, writing every second sentence, they were not so successful, Dan later recalled. The narrative line simply became too diffuse. But they did manage joint plays and other bits of prose. Dylan found all this experimentation extraordinarily liberating.

Dan's real talent was as a musician and in particular as a composer. Before long the boys were collaborating on songs and more elaborate operatic scores, with music by Dan and words by Dylan. The earliest which can be dated exactly is 'Vier Lieder' (Four Songs), composed on 27 April 1928. Another piece, 'Four horizontal Christmas carols', op. 181, had alternate lines by the prolific M. R. Tonenbach. It was written for chorus in four parts and dated 22 December 1929.

When Dylan was asked by Dan if could play the piano, he replied that he could do chords but not tunes. This proved no problem: the two youths, and anyone else around, learnt to render Dan's compositions on an assortment of instruments, including saucepan lids, whistles from Woolworth's and an old motor horn. Impervious to his neighbours' banging on the walls, Dan recalled the results were never trite, and at times interesting pieces of musique trouvé did occur.

M. R. (or more usually Max) Tonenbach was one of several exotic names they devised for their musical collaborations. Other alter egos included X. Q. Xumn and the estimable Reverend Alexander Percy, who came complete with cod biography, detailing his imagined exploits, such as being the first man to crawl from London to Brighton on all fours. Their poetry was often in the joint hand of Walter Bram, supposedly a homage to Bram Stoker, but with more than a hint of the Welsh word for 'fart' (which is bram). These names peppered the meticulous programmes they made for musical and literary evenings by Mr D. J. Seffrendi and Mr Dylan Marlais at Warmley.

Dan referred to the house having 'an artistic compulsion in the air'. But, even in this supportive environment, there was one art Dylan never mastered. When the Jones family went to the seaside, they brought back the grey-blueish clay of Swansea Bay for moulding. Dylan tried to learn this skill but, after a week of mucky effort, threw up his hands, crying, 'I'm fed up with sculpture'.

On 2 February 1928 Dan noted in his diary that he and Dylan were preparing to write a journal called The Era. An unpublished letter from Dylan to Dan also refers to this. Confirming his cavalier attitude to classroom attendance, he says he has not been in school since their last meeting and hopes not to go again for some days. He makes no suggestion that he is ill: 'This luxury has its inconveniences, though, because it prevents me from going out in the nights, at least temporarily.'

So he asks Dan to take the unusual step of calling at Cwmdonkin Drive where they can attend to the 'Small Review'. Dylan counsels: 'Bring your Rosetti essay & finish it here while I can go on with D H L[awrence]. You shall also get your facts about Mahler or any other composer you like. Come definitely. There's no need for embarrassment or whatever makes exterior company nauseous to you. We shall be QUITE ALONE. I shall expect you. Dylan.'

The first and only volume of *The Era* was a small hand-written publication of eight pages, dated 'January and February', and priced ambitiously at two shillings and sixpence. With D. J. Jones and D. Marlais Thomas as editors, the contributors were listed as these two, plus Dan's father and brother, and also Dylan's father and twenty-one-year-old sister Nancy. D.J. had agreed to be associated with the venture. But although his name was on the masthead, he did not write anything, unlike Jenkyn Jones who penned an amusing foreword which noted he had been commissioned to report from Mars, adding that the editor Dylan Marlais was 'already called (even by his rivals) "the second Milton" and "Byron re-hashed" '. Dan was in-house essayist and critic, while Dylan had a dual role, as a poet, trailed as 'one of the proverbial long-haired ilk, [who] will sing often in our columns in surging verse and delicate haunting refrains', and as a storyteller, he himself promising that 'Mr Marlais, our specially engaged poet, will write for our unflinching perusal deep, vivid, sensational and bizarre stories of the world as it is, black and wild, filled with the tortured spirits of souls worn out by the perpetual grind and tear of our pessimistic and miserable lives ... Not pleasant, but a wonderful change from simpering sentimentality.'

Dylan's draft for an introduction that did not appear in the review indicates his high regard for his own work: 'It is unfortunate that the younger an artist is the less he is credited with being an artist and that [a] young audience is put down as immaturity, because the splendour of youth should be recognised before possible disillusionment. If a child writes an astonishingly good poem, that poem should be regarded in the light of its own merits, not as the precocious and unnatural outpouring of an unhealthy little brat.'

Dylan's reference in his letter to 'exterior company' may have reflected a degree of friction between Dan and D.J. This was curious, since Dan, on the face of it, was one of the schoolmaster's best pupils. After leaving the Grammar School in 1931, he went on to gain a first class degree in English from Swansea University. Possibly D.J. was resentful that Dan was the attentive, academically inclined pupil Dylan never was. He probably balked at anyone getting too close to him or his family. Dan described D.J.'s relationship with his son as 'very strained', though he recognised Dylan's respect for his father. He also noted Dylan's attitude to Nancy, whom Dan found attractive, as she 'whirled away, leaving behind an exotic perfume of fur and scent'. In the blurb for *The Era* she was described as 'well known in society and acting circles'. But Dylan regularly put her down, leading his friend to speculate that either he hated her, or wanted Dan to hate her – an incestuous variation on the Thomases not wanting intruders.

Aged fifteen in early 1928, Dan took a great interest in the opposite sex. His diary is full of stories of his being attracted to various girls when he is out. At one stage neighbours accused him of molesting their daughter and threatened to call the police. Dylan was slower in his sexual development. But by the time he reached the same age he began to catch up. The broadcaster Wynford Vaughan-Thomas, who was at school with him, though slightly older, used to tell of taking a girl for a walk in Cwmdonkin Park and hearing Dylan's voice whispering from the bushes, 'Tell her you love her, boy. Tell her you love her.'

In the spring of 1930 Dylan accompanied another Swansea school-friend Cyril James on a short holiday to St Dogmaels near Cardigan. James's impoverished Welsh-speaking cousins ran a farm, Yr Hendre, in a beautiful spot looking out over Cardigan Bay. The two boys walked along the coast, took a trap into Cardigan, and frequented the local pubs. Dylan wrote a short poem in an autograph book which James's cousin Bonnie had recently been given. Though she was only ten and their friendship entirely innocent, Dylan managed to inject some sexual innuendo into a delicate ditty starting:

> He said, 'You seem so lovely, Chloe:
> Your pretty body and your hair ...

The visit had an unfortunate upshot. Dylan and his friend stayed a week longer than expected. Having come with only one pair of trousers, he borrowed another from Bonnie's father, who never got them back. In addition, Dylan's parents failed to pay for his visit, as arranged. Bonnie's Aunt Ethel wrote several times to Florrie Thomas without receiving an answer. Eventually, it seems, the debt was written off.

That summer Dylan joined some boys from the Uplands on a camping trip to the Gower peninsula. This was a local rite of passage when the sun beat down and tourists flocked to Swansea Bay. He and his friends took a bus down to Mewslade and pitched their rented Bell tents in a field at Pilton, a mile from the rolling Rhossili strand. So far as any of them could remember, Dylan played his part. He did some fishing and even helped with cooking, but showed no interest when, in return for ham and eggs, his colleagues helped a local farmer with haymaking.

The reason soon became clear. Staying in a cottage in nearby Llan-gennith were three attractive High School girls who were known to some in the party. One was Evelyn ('Titch') Phillips, daughter of an insurance salesman. She had convinced her mother that a spell in the country would aid her revision for forthcoming exams. She was told she had to wear dresses, not shorts. Before long she had linked up with these boys at a dance in Llangennith, and she and her friends were invited back to the camp. When she went over, she encountered someone she had not met previously. 'Suddenly I heard someone speaking in a voice such as I had never heard before, and I remember turning to see who owned this voice, and I could see nothing except a couple of boys I already knew and a little shrimp of a boy with light curly hair.' She asked Glyn Thomas, with whom she was acquainted, about this waif-like creature. She learnt it was Dylan, son of D. J. Thomas, with whom she was familiar because her family also lived in Uplands and her brother Billy had been at the Grammar School.

Although two years older than Dylan, she was immediately captivated by his sense of fun: 'he really brightened up their camp.' Since English was on her examination syllabus, he asked if she would like to read some poetry he had written. When she agreed, he gave her a small exercise book, full of jottings in pencil. It was clear that he had been filling this book while the others cut hay. 'We both lay on our stomachs in the grass and read the poetry,' Evelyn recalled. 'I didn't understand it all, I must confess.' She knew about sonnets and the sort of poetry she studied at school. But this was quite different – 'more poetic', she felt, leaving a sensation that was even more memorable than seeing it all on the page. Even at that age, Dylan impressed on her that he wanted to become a poet. And he had an added advantage: he was the only person around who could tell her the meaning of the word 'idiosyncrasy' which she found in one of her textbooks.

This was the first indication of the notebooks in which Dylan had begun his early personal experimental verse. Writing to Geoffrey Grigson in spring 1933, he referred to 'innumerable exercise books full of poems'. He later said there had been ten, of which four survive, incorporating just over two hundred poems which satisfied Dylan between 1930 and 1934. These show Dylan at his most prolific, beginning to take his creative powers seriously. Much of his published verse originated in one form or another during this short period.

FOUR

MY BODY WAS MY ADVENTURE

While Dylan's trips to West Wales and Gower developed his awakened interest in a natural world beyond the Uplands, his regular visits to his relations in Carmarthenshire introduced him to the starker realities of rural existence which had shaped both sides of his family. Here Dylan discovered a tight-knit Welsh-speaking world where, amid inevitable hypocrisies and compromises, the chapel still dominated the community, the Bible served as literature and inspiration, and the preacher engaged his congregation with emotional orations, known as hwyl (meaning literally 'full sail'). The sensitive bookish boy from Swansea's Uplands found it both repellent and fascinating. As much as he sometimes tried to escape its influence, he always returned to it.

The journey from Swansea was usually made by bus (occasionally by train) via the bustling county town of Carmarthen which, with its disputed reference to Merlin in its name, acted as a gateway to an older, darker world of Celtic myth. From there Dylan would take a bus run by the Thomas brothers from Llanstephan. After crossing the railway at Johnstown (close to The Poplars where old Guard Thomas had lived), he would wind up the escarpment to Llangain. Dylan described making the journey by pony and trap in his story 'A Visit to Grandpa's', though he himself never visited a grandfather in this area (Evan Thomas died in 1905). He probably heard the tale from his father who was referring to his own maternal grandfather, William Lewis, a local man (born in Llangunnock) who, in his eighties, lived at The Poplars when D.J. was a boy.

The straight road through Llangain passes Capel Smyrna, the Congregational chapel, where some of Florrie's family worshipped. Just before this thoroughfare dips towards Llanstephan, the main town of the peninsula with its ancient castle, a lane on the right leads down to a brook, rising, on the other side, past a small wood of poplar and fir trees which sheltered a ramshackle white farmhouse, Fernhill. This was where Florrie's sister Annie lived with her husband Jim Jones and son Idris. The interior was cold and dank, with stone floors and smiling china dogs. After the cleanliness of Cwmdonkin Drive, Dylan found it 'insanitary'. But the surrounding fields were full of natural excitements, later providing the backdrop (as Gorsehill) for Dylan's story 'The Peaches', before being immortalised as a romantic paradise in one of his most famous poems, 'Fern Hill'.

Dylan's 'ancient peasant Aunt' Annie was a bent creature with a 'cracked sing-song voice' and 'fist of a face'. She was generally kind, larding him with bread and broth when he arrived, and sending him money she could ill afford when he was away. But there was another side to her peasant character – the 'well of rumours and cold lies' Dylan noted in an early draft of his poem about her funeral in February 1933.

With his ruddy countenance, moustache and bowler worn at a rakish angle, her husband Jim was either a loveable rogue or an alcoholic layabout, depending on one's point of view. His family owned a local farm, Pentrewyman, but, as the post-war agricultural depression deepened, he was too lazy to apply himself to that, leaving the job of running it to his sister Rachel, Dylan's 'Auntie Rach'. In 'The Peaches' he sold pigs to support his drinking habit – a plausible enough caricature of a man whom one family member recalled selling his horse's shoes to the local blacksmith so he could have enough money for a pub crawl. He considered himself a cut above his fellows, living in a gentleman's house (bigger than the local norm) and preferring to worship in the Anglican parish church of St Cain in Llangain rather than in a Non-conformist chapel with the rest of his Welsh-speaking relations. (This latter point may have encouraged Dylan's English-orientated parents to entrust their sensitive and often unhealthy son to the Joneses.)

In 'The Peaches' the Joneses' son, Dylan's cousin Idris, comes across as an amiable boyo, with an energy that could be turned equally to either sexual conquest or silky preaching. In real life, he was a ruddy-faced wimp, who shared his father's aversion to any form of toil. Before the war, he had worked in Ben Evans's department store in Swansea (where his and Dylan's Great-Uncle Daniel Williams had also been a salesman). One result was an unctuous salesman's accent that even his friends found laughable. Unable to avoid being called up, he had served with the Royal Garrison Artillery. After being demobbed he could find no proper job. He liked acting in local amateur theatrical productions and, as in the story, may indeed have seen a future as a man of the cloth. But he failed to capitalise on this calling, and Dylan's image of him as a Lothario was probably the natural hero worship of a young boy for a relation seventeen years his senior. The reality was Idris masturbating in an outhouse with a book in his hand (a memorable image in 'The Peaches'), while sublimating his sexual drive in revivalist religion, full of Welsh hwyl, or emotional fervour. The pantheism of his sermon in the story initially seems attractive, until it becomes clear it is a humorous vehicle for Dylan's later sense of the oneness of nature: 'Oh God, Thou art everywhere all the time, in the dew of the morning, in the frost of the evening, in the field and the town ... Thou canst see everything we do ... Thou canst see all the time. O God, mun, you're like a bloody cat.'

Fernhill opened Dylan's eyes to a different way of life. He fished in the brook, spent time at the blacksmith's, and when a horse sank in a muddy field, he played his part in the rescue by lending his weight to others tugging on ropes. Rural values were certainly not those of the Uplands. Had he not seen his Uncle Jim, coming out of a pub and kissing two fat giggling women full on the lips? The countryside was also more raw, elemental and, so he discovered, strangely spiritual. To an adolescent boy, its rhythms were liberating: he could, as he put it in 'The Peaches', feel 'all my young body like an excited animal surrounding me ... I was aware of me myself in the exact middle of a living story, and my body was my adventure and my name.'

It was also a place of mystery and fascination. Until the beginning of the century Fernhill had been owned by Robert Evans, a former hangman who, in an effort to escape his notorious past, had in retirement changed his name to Anderson. Stories of Evans's temper and sexual appetite abounded: he was said to have constructed bars on the house's lower windows to prevent his daughter escaping to meet her lover. When he died in August 1901, the Carmarthen Journal noted that Wales had 'lost one of the most eccentric of her sons', around whose memory 'weird, creepy sensationalism' would always hang 'like a veil'. This sense of the macabre appealed to Dylan's imagination, contributing to the Poe-like feel of his early stories in the 1930s. The ghoulish detail could be used back in Cwmdonkin Drive, where literary fancies came to him 'in the warm, safe island of my bed, with sleepy midnight Swansea flowing and rolling outside the house'.

Not everyone could handle the profound change of culture. Once his friend Jack Bassett joined him as a paying guest of the Joneses. He arrived with his mother in a Daimler, suggesting the year was 1926–7, when his father was Mayor of Swansea and would have had access to a chauffeured limousine. But when Mrs Bassett refused to eat the peaches Aunt Annie served as a delicacy in her best room, an incident ensued. When young Jack overheard Jim Jones, probably drunk, complaining about this unintended slight, he too took umbrage and, despite his uncomplicated friendship with Dylan, demanded to return home.

Dotted around Fernhill were Florrie's other relations. Auntie Rach's farm, Pentrewymen, was a mile further on toward Llanstephan, beyond the weir and along the rushy mill-race (known as Fernhill Brook). As an attractive girl in her early twenties, she had become pregnant out of wedlock, and had never subsequently married. Thirty years on, her dozy son Albert was even more of a wastrel than his cousin Idris. Dylan would often wander over from Fernhill. If still there at sunset, he would eat his *cawl* (a Welsh stew of mutton and leeks) and sleep overnight – sometimes, as a child, sharing a bed with May Edwards, one of many foundlings employed as servants on local farms.

Opposite Pentrewymen, on the eastern bank of the stream, stood the grandiosely named Llangain Woollen Factory, a relic from the days when the natural combination of sheep, fresh water and access to the sea contributed to the economy. A smaller 'factory' operated a few hundred yards further on, beside a woody lane just off the main Carmarthen-Llanstephan road. At the top of the lane stood Waunfwlchan, where Florrie's mother had been brought up, as well as Llwyngwyn, another farm in the extended Williams family, and Mount Pleasant, a smaller property owned by Annie Jones and her home after she and her husband gave up the tenancy of Fernhill in 1929.

At the bottom, abutting the 'factory', were two small cottages, known as Blaencwm, which, over the years, accommodated different family members. This was where Dylan used to go after Fernhill was no longer available. One cottage became the home of his Aunt Polly and Uncle Bob, who had sold the old family house at 29 Delhi Street (though they retained number 30, which provided a rental income). Polly, one-time organ player at the Canaan chapel in St Thomas, was the pleasantest of Florrie's siblings, but Bob was difficult. He was mentally unstable, which made him hostile and anti-social. His problems may have been the result of family inbreeding or may have had a more tangible cause: Nancy used to suggest that he had been gassed in the First World War. If so, this would have helped explain D. J. Thomas's attitude to the conflict.

Another relation in the vicinity was Ann Williams, nominally Florrie's first cousin though consanguinity may have been closer. Ann's mother Amy was Florrie's aunt (her mother Anna's sister). Some time around 1860 young George Williams, Florrie's father, came to work as a labourer at the family farm at Waunfwlchan. The son of a local smith, he struck lucky and married his boss's daughter, Anna (who, since she shared his surname, may have been a cousin). He had the first three children by Anna (including – to confuse matters further – Ann, later Dylan's Aunt Annie Jones), before decamping with his wife and family to Swansea where he led his apparently blameless life on the railways.

In 1866, shortly after their move, Anna's sister Amy had a daughter, also called Ann. In the 1871 census this girl was described as a niece of Anna and Amy's parents, Thomas and Ann Williams, at Waunfwlchan; ten years later as a granddaughter. On her birth certificate Ann was reported to be the daughter of her grandfather Thomas Williams, but that was probably done for convenience. She may well have been the child of David Jones, a coxswain at Ferryside on the other side of the river Tywi. He was married at the time but, later, after his wife died, he wed Amy Williams, with whom he was having an affair, and had three more children by her. But another story persisted that, earlier, Amy had become pregnant by her sister Anna's husband, George. That might explain why five-year-old Ann Williams was described as a niece of the family in 1871. This was the version told to Florrie by her cousin Doris, who was Ann's daughter and Amy's granddaughter.

In her early twenties, this Ann Williams married an Anglican clergyman, the Reverend John Gwyn, but he died within three years. She then took another husband (Robert Williams, almost certainly also a cousin), and they had two children, Doris and William, living together in Llanstephan and later Ferryside. However in August 1917 William was drowned in a bathing accident (on the same day that his grandmother, Amy died). William's death came a year after that of his half-brother, Edward Gwyn. Ann Williams never recovered and herself died in May 1922.

Dylan would have known this background because afterwards Doris Williams became a frequent guest at Cwmdonkin Drive where she was close to Nancy Thomas, her junior by four years. She later met an Abergavenny dentist called Randolph Fulleylove who, on the evidence of an undated letter from Dylan to his sister, also befriended the Thomas family. Dylan looked up to him and plied him with wordly questions he could not ask his father. In this letter, Dylan wrote a verse titled 'Say Good Bye when your chum is married'. He asked Nancy to give it to 'Rudge', almost certainly a nickname for Randolph, who wed Doris in 1928, and this was Dylan's way of celebrating the betrothal.

The following year (1929) Dylan and D.J. visited the newly married couple in Abergavenny. Doris recalled how, on the journey home to Swansea, her husband lost control of his car on the steep road winding down from the Brecon Beacons. When Randolph brought the vehicle to a halt, he was sweating profusely. Dylan, who was sitting in the back seat with his father, was nonplussed: 'Lovely, Uncle,' he said. 'Can we go back and do it again?' As when hurtling down hills on a bicycle, Dylan enjoyed immediate sensations and had little sense of danger.

*

This Abergavenny trip probably took place during a period in 1929 when D.J. was sick and unable to attend school. Because of his ill-health, he declined the opportunity to become the Grammar School's second master when Trevor Owen and his deputy Hockgate Hockin both retired at the end of the academic year.

His presence at Cwmdonkin Drive led to unexpected tensions with his daughter Nancy who was twenty-two. By then she had been out of school for four years. But apart from working in a shop and helping the Missions to Seamen over Christmas, she had achieved little. Her feline sexiness was appreciated by Dan Jones. But being in the house brought out a neurotic class-conscious side to her personality. Her cousin Doris told how she and Nancy would go into the centre of town and treat themselves to tea at the bustling Kardomah café on Castle Street. There Nancy would say, 'For God's sake, Doris, don't eat more than one little sandwich and one little cake. It isn't correct.' But as soon as the girls were back in the Uplands, Nancy would tell her mother they were starving and demand something to eat.

With her training in elocution from Miss James's nearby academy, she still harboured an ambition to be an actress. An opportunity arose that summer (1929) when, in an effort to reach a wider audience, members of the established Swansea Stage Society set up an offshoot, the Swansea Little Theatre. Taking their cue from the popular Little Theatre movement in the United States, and boosted by the dynamic chairmanship of Councillor Willie Jenkins, the shipping magnate who had once lived opposite the Williams family in Delhi Street, they acquired a lease on a church hall in Southend, Mumbles.

At a promotional garden party given by Alan and Vesta Gill, two prime movers behind the project, Nancy met another theatre enthusiast, Haydn Taylor, an ambitious twenty-three-year-old building materials salesman from Bristol. He had arrived in Swansea three years earlier when offered the whole of Wales to carve out as his territory. He had ridden out some of the worst years of the slump, although his life in Swansea bedsitters had opened his eyes to the distress suffered by even the genteel middle classes of the Uplands – the 'lace curtains and no breakfast' crowd, as Dylan dubbed them. Haydn came from a family of work-orientated Nonconformists. When he first left home, he had abandoned a girlfriend called May after his mother suggested that the liaison might be a distraction from his career. However, with a father who played the organ for chapel services, and a brother called Handel who was a professional musician, Haydn was encouraged to sublimate his youthful energies in the arts.

At the Gills' party, he noticed Nancy, with her brown curly hair and large brown eyes, and ended up driving her home, rather than his original date. As a friendship grew in the weeks of intense preparation before the theatre's first production in November, he was invited back to Cwmdonkin Drive. On an early visit D.J.'s railwayman brother, Uncle Arthur, was also there from Port Talbot. At lunch, the talk turned to the new theatre, with an actor called Bennett singled out for particular praise. Haydn agreed, adding it was a shame about this player's facial twitch which not even his make-up could hide. For good measure, he gave an impression, and when his audience (the four Thomases and Arthur) did not react, he repeated it. It was only when he looked at Uncle Arthur, sitting on his side of the table, that he understood the reason for his cool reception: D.J.'s brother had a chronic tic, much worse than the man he was trying to portray.

Before long Nancy had a regular suitor. Haydn would court her in the parlour at Cwmdonkin Drive next to the kitchen. However their privacy was limited because the upper panel of the door was made of coloured glass and, at intervals, Florrie would peer in. Haydn had no doubt: 'Her interest was that of the Peeping Jane – she had a nasty mind – rather than the guardian of her daughter's virtue.'

Catching the theatre bug, Dylan penned 'Desert Idyll', a short sketch satirising the vogue for Rudolph Valentino-type matinée idols. This appeared in the December 1929 issue of the school magazine, which, along with the stage, was the main outlet for his energies during his last couple of years in education. He was no longer interested in any classroom subject, except English, and exam failures ruled out going on to university. If his fellow pupils remembered his acting, he himself gained most satisfaction from his journalism. Having been a sub-editor in the summer of 1929, he became joint editor that December. For the three issues in his last academic year (1930–1) he was sole editor.

He used the magazine to explore the more public aspects of the crucial debates going on in his head and in conversation with Dan Jones. His article on 'Modern Poetry' in December 1929 highlighted the unsettled ground on which poets were having to build after the ravages of the war. He traced the development of modernity which he argued was about freedom in content and form. He saw its origins in Gerard Manley Hopkins, a poet whose sprung rhythms were often later said to have influenced his own metrical experiments. This new approach began to flower in writers such as Robert Bridges, Walter de la Mare and Sacheverell Sitwell, all of whose styles are discernible in Dylan's early work. Licence extended to tackling new subject matter (he quoted Eliot's 'cigarettes in corridors, and cocktail smells in bars'), examining twilight states of consciousness (Yeats) and adopting exotic imagery, though he claimed to find the unsentimental hardness of the Imagists, associated with Richard Aldington, too flashy – 'the rush of coloured words producing a kaleidoscopic effect that cannot stimulate or satisfy the imagination'. (Ironically, he was soon criticised for such verbal pyrotechnics.) Dylan argued that such innovations could not take root in mainstream culture, however, without some major historical or intellectual justification. And this, he felt, had happened with the Great War, which had changed the course of English poetry, allowing practitioners such as D. H. Lawrence and Ezra Pound to build anew.

He was also thinking about other media, particularly film, where, as he wrote in the school magazine in July 1930, he recognised that the recent introduction of sound had created similar flux and opportunity. His favourite films were still the Westerns he watched in the Uplands flea-pit. From an artistic point of view, he noted that D. W. Griffith's silent movie The Birth of a Nation was 'easily superior' to anything else before the war. But the standard of 'talkies' had so far been poor. Directors did not seem to understand they were dealing with 'something new' (i.e. sound) 'which cannot be tackled by any old methods but which requires a special way of approach'. An innovative D. W. Griffith for the age of talking films was required.

A third approach to modern art came from the pen of Dan Jones who wrote for the magazine on 'Tendencies of Modern Music'. In this field, he argued, modernism had built on the attempt by composers such as Debussy to portray nature more precisely. However he had reservations about the dissonance of certain works and, while he referred jokingly to a futurist ballet involving six brass plates, sixteen mechanical pianos, six leaden plates and sixteen electric bells (shades of the Warmley repertoire), he expressed doubt whether 'any but musical instruments will take part in the real music of the future'.

The common theme to all three articles was Dylan's interest in a synthesis of the arts. This was the most fruitful period of musical collaborations between him and Dan, including the carols at Christmas 1929. In his own writing he would be recognised for exploring how the sound and even shape of words could contribute to a poem's effect, helping attain the quality Dryden described as 'articulate music'. Cinematic references abound in Dylan's verse, and he later enjoyed a subsidiary career penning film scripts. In his more cerebral way, Dan played an important supporting role, implicit in his university thesis on the relationship between Elizabethan poetry and contemporary music.

Dylan's contributions to the magazine in his last couple of years at school included 'Brember', a horror story with a musical sub-theme, and 'The Sincerest Form of Flattery', a witty concoction of parodies on topics from Osbert Sitwell to modern realistic drama. His poetry was limited to polished adolescent conceits, such as 'Armistice Day', which reprised his interest in the war, and 'In Borrowed Plumes', two further skits on the theme of Little Miss Muffett as written by Ella Wheeler Wilcox and W. B. Yeats. While amusing and technically proficient, this material was largely derivative, composed for a formal external audience.

His more personal and experimental efforts were confined to his notebooks. These showed a new resolve from the beginning of 1930. The previous year had been problematic, with D.J. absent from school, with important changes in his wider family living arrangements after Aunt Ann left Fernhill and Aunt Polly and Uncle Bob moved to Blaencwm, and with Nancy embarking on her first love affair. These events unsettled Dylan, contributing to his disaffection with his academic studies. They threw him back on himself, helping to heighten his poetic awareness, to the extent that in January 1930 he and Dan discussed forming a group of poetry lovers who would pay a fee of five shillings a year and be affiliated to the Poetry Society in London.

Material evidence of his poetic industry comes in his first notebook, sub-titled 'Mainly Free Verse Poems', covering the period 27 April to 9 December 1930. This shows he was still under the influence of the Imagists, but trying to extend his range with the more varied palette of modernists such as T. S. Eliot whose interest in other cultures is apparent in the first poem 'Osiris, Come to Isis'. Inspired by their range, Dylan begins to explore deeper realities of the universe in verses about light, time, nature and freedom. He hits on a personal theme, the relationship between his body and the external world.

He even attempts some tortured adolescent love poems. At one stage, as reflected in 'Osiris, Come to Isis', he worries that sex makes a mockery of true love. In May he cannot cope with an imaginary girlfriend's animal passion:

> I want something more of you,
> Something sexless and unmechanical:
> ... Let me dispense with the animal:
> The animal is not enough.

A week later he is more relaxed:

> And so the new love came at length
> Healing and giving strength ...

Tempting though it is to link these poems to 'Titch' Phillips, he seems
not to have met her until his holiday in Gower later in the summer. As
the year progresses, his concerns do not abate. He wants to be free but:

> When I allow myself to fly,
> There is no sense of being free...

By November, the time of his poem 'Written in a classroom', he
begins to understand the root of the problem. As his teacher drones on,
leaving 'no tail/Of reason', he realises that:

> Shaft of winter morning light
> Is realler than your faces, boys.

The problem with love is that reason intrudes. He is left to contemplate
his fantasies 'upon the island of my palm'. As the last poem in the
notebook, beginning 'How shall the animal' (later revised for his 1940
collection The Map of Love) makes clear, this is a burden. Whenever he
chases his flights of imagination, he is brought back to earth by the
forces of language and logic, his 'bantering Philistine'.

This sort of subject matter continued into his second notebook,
covering the years 1930 to 1932. He was going through a period of
typical teenage angst, as is evident from the letter he wrote from school
to Percy Smart, his former co-editor on the magazine, but by December
1930 working for Barclays Bank: 'Even that third-former, who is running
along the corridor now, has probably an inherent cancer, or a mind full
of lechery. The child grows from the cradle, soaked in a morbidity and
restlessness he cannot understand, does a little painful loving, fails to
make money, builds his life on sand, and is struck down before he can
accomplish anything. Is it worth me lifting up my pen to write? Is
anything worth anything?'

That did not stop him trying. The next time he wrote to Smart, the
end of his school career was fast approaching. With his father's curious
connivance, he had long since given up any pretence of regularly
attending classes. Dan Jones, who had become a prefect, noted a
transitional period when no-one was quite certain if Dylan was a pupil
or not. Those absences allowed Dylan to concentrate on more congenial
pastimes such as debating, acting and editing the magazine. Now, in
the midst of these, he proposed setting up a new quarterly literary
journal called Prose and Verse. It would be original, highbrow and funded
by subscription. He ran through some of the contributions already on
file, among them a poem by Dan, a short story ('v.g.') by 'Titch' Phillips,
and a mixture of his own poems, stories and essays, including a piece

on aesthetes which anticipated his arguments on decadence and youth, presented to the debating society in March.

Dylan asked Smart to place a notice about the venture in the local paper, the South Wales Daily Post. But by June he had only twelve out of the two hundred subscribers he needed to start the publication. He may have had ideas about contents and even promotion, but he lacked basic business nous: when his new headmaster John Grey Morgans gave him ten shillings towards the venture (significantly more than the standard subscription of two shillings) Dylan promptly went out and got drunk.

One reason for his resort to alcoholic release was continuing domestic pressure. His father was still regularly absent from school; Smart believed because of 'shingles', though more likely from a form of depression. The previous August Nancy had noted, 'I have realized how terribly worried Daddy is and how sad he is.' Dylan would have sympathised with her complaint to Haydn: 'I used to be always happy,' she informed Haydn. At Blaencwm the following June she repeated the same story: 'Daddy is not any better and has been home from school all week.'

Having produced the July or summer edition of the school magazine, Dylan was left feeling wistful. He admitted to Smart he would have liked to stay on and produce another issue which, he said with no false modesty, would be remarkable, because he was learning on the job all the time. He added that his father had impressed on him the importance of experience – an unusual acknowledgement of his father's guidance. Now, through regular practice and revision, Dylan was seeking to bring this quality of experience to his poetry.

A more immediate concern was how he was to earn his living after finishing school. Since there was no question of Dylan accompanying Dan Jones to university, D.J. asked a neighbour, Herbert Bassett, the brother of the former mayor, to enquire of Malcolm Smith, the managing editor of the Daily Post, if he could find his son employment on the paper. Jobs being at a premium in those economically depressed times, Dylan seems to have been offered some brief 'work experience' at the Post in July, perhaps even before the school term had formally ended. His friend Wynford Vaughan-Thomas told of accompanying Dylan on his first assignment, an interview with music hall star Nellie Wallace.

In the meantime Percy Smart had managed to place a brief notice in the paper about his friend's proposed new literary journal. In response Dylan received a letter from Trevor Hughes, a wiry Great Western Railway clerk with literary ambitions, whose accompanying story so impressed Dylan that he was invited to Cwmdonkin Drive. Hughes was greeted by 'a rather short, slightly built, almost girlish figure, with a fine head, light brown curls, and the eyes and ears of a poet'. Neither of them was aware at the time of a previous connection: Hughes was the former Grammar School pupil who had chanced upon the Thomas family in a Llandrindod Wells boarding house a dozen years earlier. Initially the focus of attention was on Nancy who had just bought a gramophone record of Paul Robeson singing a negro spiritual.

With this song in the background, the two youths settled on a sofa to discuss poetry, a topic, Hughes noted, that came as naturally to Dylan as football or films to another teenager. Reminded of Shelley, he had to make an effort to remember his host was so young: '[Dylan] showed the insight of a man in whom reading had become experience ... He had no small talk ... There was nothing spurious about him. He lived for poetry, which is the very act of loving. He loved, and marvelled at, every living thing. He loved words and the music of words.' When Dylan began reading his poems, he looked intently at Hughes, watching for any reaction. He was at a stage of rejecting his early, immature poems, and if Hughes showed any sign of distaste, Dylan made a mental note to bin what he had written. 'Sometimes, when he had read a poem, no word passed between us,' wrote Hughes. 'He would just look up at me, and, satisfied, start reading the next poem. And if, while he was reading, he found that a poem was unfinished, he would lie down, boylike, on the carpet, and finish it. Most of us must be moved by extraneous things, but it seemed, even at that time, that his apprehension was direct. His power was in and about him, and was always accessible to him. And to be with him was to be within the atmosphere of that power.' Here was a poet in direct communication with his muse. But before he could devote himself to his life's work he had to discover another aspect of the writer's craft – in a newspaper office.

FIVE

SORE TRIAL

Rising seventeen, Dylan looked faintly ridiculous when he arrived for work at the Castle Bailey Street offices of the South Wales Daily Post. Hoping to strike the attitude of a seasoned reporter, he wore a loud check overcoat, perched a green pork pie hat with a peacock feather on his head, and hung a 'conscious Woodbine' cigarette from his lip. As often, a tough-boy exterior hid an uncertain inner self.

The Post was a conventional evening newspaper, with cosy links to municipal movers and shakers (the reason he got a job), and with no propensity to rock the boat politically. It may not have been the house journal of the Conservative Anglo-Welsh gentry, like the Western Mail, published in Cardiff, but as part of Lord Rothermere's right-wing Northcliffe Press, it had no sympathy for Labour. Rothermere had bought the paper and its stable-mate the Cambria Daily Leader in 1928, merged them a couple of years later, and would change their name to the South Wales Evening Post in April 1932, shortly after Dylan joined.

The young recruit's first few weeks were spent in the copy department, learning to read incoming wires and check journalists' finished articles. After a while he moved to the newsroom where he was not popular, since he had a habit of arriving late and keeping to himself. Colleagues recalled him gazing vacantly out of the window and doodling. More likely, he was putting the finishing touches to a poem. Never having learnt shorthand, he found that, when allowed out of the office, he was assigned the dullest of routine jobs, such as the daily calls to the British Legion or the hospital. Occasionally he might accompany another newsman to the police court or a council meeting. Only if very lucky did he attend an evening dinner or cultural event. Even then, he hardly distinguished himself. Standing in for the elderly chief reporter Bill Hatcher at the annual dinner of the Licensed Victuallers Association, he found the hospitality so generous that he passed out before the President's speech.

At least getting out of the office gave him an opportunity to familiarise himself with his home town. His reporter's rounds took him on a wide circuit from Sketty and the Mumbles on one side of Swansea to Skewen (by the new oil terminal) on the other. His peregrinations took on greater significance when an older reporter Freddie 'Half-Hook' Farr befriended him and introduced him to the local low life. As detailed in Dylan's romanticised story 'Old Garbo', first published in 1939, Farr acted as a father figure initiating him in necessary rites of passage. Rotund, wise-cracking, and down at heel, he was the antithesis of the stiff pedagogic D.J. At one stage in 'Old Garbo', he makes an irreverent comment to Dylan about their puritanical news editor Edward Job (Old Solomon in the story). Dylan feels a pang of guilt in observing: 'I wished that I could have answered in such a way as to show for Mr Solomon the disrespect I did not feel. This was a great male moment.' The last sentence could have come from a twenty-first-century men's magazine: such bonding was important to Dylan's progress from immature lad to young adult.

Farr took Dylan under his wing and taught him the finer points of journalism. As Bill Hatcher's deputy, he was responsible, every Friday, for passing reporters' expenses claims. When Dylan failed to show the necessary creativity in massaging his accounts, Farr threw them back, with the cry, 'You can do better than that, Thomas.' After he had promised to take Dylan on a pub crawl, the young reporter hung around the office one Saturday, his half-day, pretending to work and hoping Farr would remember. Eventually Farr took pity and, after a ritual insult – 'Some people are too lazy to take their half-days off' – invited Dylan to join him at the Lamps at six o'clock.

Dylan briefly returned home to inform his mother he was taking a long walk and she should not keep his evening meal waiting. He spent the afternoon at the cinema, where he blagged himself a free seat by claiming press accreditation. Making his way through the late Saturday afternoon crowds, he reached the Three Lamps, on Temple Street, more or less opposite the *Post*'s offices, slightly earlier than Farr. In 'Old Garbo' he records how he sat between an alderman and a solicitor in the back bar, half wishing his father could see him there, chatting up a plump middle-aged barmaid. He liked the idea of D.J. being furious at the angle of his cigarette and at 'the threat of the clutched tankard' which reflected his growing taste for beer. At the same time he was rather glad D.J. was away visiting his Uncle Arthur.

At the appointed hour, he saw Farr approaching from the High Street, 'savagely' ignoring the laces and matches thrust at him by persistent, impoverished street vendors. According to Dylan, Farr 'knew that the poor and the sick and the ugly, unwanted people were so close around him that, with one look of recognition, one gesture of sympathy, he would be lost among them'. But this was more Dylan's own reaction than Half-Hook's. He was learning about Swansea's social and economic inequalities. And though he felt for those less fortunate than himself, he was still enough of a journalist to want to absorb the local colour.

The Three Lamps was in a commercialised (and therefore salubrious) 'down-town' area, close to the Ben Evans store. It was a regular reporters' pub, along with the Mackworth and the Bodega (part of the Bassett hotel empire). Sensing Dylan wanted something a bit different, Farr suggested they go to the Strand, the seedy area behind the Castle and the *Post*'s offices, on the other (eastern) side of the main thoroughfare, which ran down along High, Castle Bailey and Wind Streets. A throwback to the heyday of the North Dock in the mid-Victorian era, the Strand was the centre of a maze of alleyways and small courts where visiting sailors could find boarding houses, cafés, bars and brothels to suit all tastes. (By Dylan's time the new Prince of Wales Dock had begun to take pressure off this facility. Later, hastened by the decline in shipping that accompanied the 1930s slump, the North Dock was gradually filled in and cleaned up. Today it is no longer discernible as the foundation of a multi-storey car-park and a super-store.)

On this occasion Farr took Dylan to the Fishguard on the Strand. He told Dylan about 'sailors knitting there in the public bar'. But Dylan only came across the keeper of the mortuary underneath the nearby Arches. When he later visited this facility and saw a dead body for the first time, he fainted and had to be revived with three pints of beer. It was rough all right: on another trip to the Arches, he learnt of the brutal murder of a prostitute who had been attacked by a sailor with a broken bottle. At the Fishguard he witnessed the scam perpetrated by a Mrs Prothero, who raised money claiming that her daughter had died in childbirth, spent the proceeds on drink, and later drowned herself when it was discovered that her daughter was still alive. A rather different scene was to be found at the Lord Jersey on Market Street, where Dylan and Farr met an effeminate colleague who enthused about a young man dancing with a handkerchief round his head. Other colourful haunts Dylan visited around the Docks included the rowdy Cornish Mount and Spanish Joe's, a 'very rough' café in the Strand where the Hispanic proprietress had had the end of her nose bitten off. Further afield he frequented an Arab café in Port Tennant Road.

Although discovering an exciting Apaché world beyond the Uplands, he still had some growing up to do. On his first night out with Freddie Farr, he drank too much, was sick and did not even have the money for the tram fare home. 'The revolving hill to my father's house reached to the sky,' he wrote. 'Nobody was up. I crept to a wild bed, and the wallpaper lakes converged and sucked me down.' His bank of experience was expanding, however. The very next day, after the worst effects of his hangover had worn off, he sat down and wrote the first three lines of 'a poem without hope' – possibly the notebook poem which refers to 'head in the oven, no nearer heaven' and ends:

> Senselessly lifting food to mouth, and food to mouth,
> To keep the senseless being going.

The detail of 'Old Garbo' indicates that Dylan's pub crawl with Farr took place shortly before Christmas 1931, and this is the only poem in the 1930–2 notebook which fits that chronology.

Now that he received a weekly wage, Dylan could afford to drink, and that, as Haydn Taylor recorded in an unpublished memoir, brought problems. Haydn was sitting with Nancy at Cwmdonkin Drive one Saturday night, waiting for the prying Florrie to go to bed, when he suddenly heard a series of confused noises at the front door, followed by the sound of running feet. It was clear Dylan had returned home drunk and was being sick. His parents dealt with the problem and shuffled Dylan off to bed. Nothing further was said about the incident. The two young men remained outwardly friendly, occasionally joining forces to watch Glamorgan play cricket at St Helen's ground in Swansea, and Dylan even felt able to sting Nancy's 'steady' for a loan now and again. However Haydn was certain Dylan disliked him, particularly after the older Thomases began holding up the salesman's sobriety and hard work as an example to their increasingly wayward son.

Despite Farr's paternal influence, it was soon evident that Dylan was not cut out to be a professional journalist. One of his editors, J. D. Williams, described the boy's time on the paper as 'entertaining, but a sore trial to the chief reporter'. The feeling was mutual, as Dylan came to dread being woken from his reveries by the sound of the telephone or the sub-editors' door swinging open. Within six months of joining the *Post*, he had decided that, despite his efforts to take on the correct attitude, reporting was not for him. In February 1932, he told Trevor Hughes portentously, 'I am at the most transitional period now. Whatever talents I possess may suddenly diminish or may suddenly increase.' The journalistic lifestyle meant he was drinking excessively. 'It's odd,' he continued to Hughes, who had moved to the outskirts of London, 'but between all these' (his working schedule of 'concerts, deaths, meetings & dinners') 'I manage to become drunk at least four nights of the week. Muse or Mermaid? That's the transition I spoke about.' In other words, should he devote his energies to writing poetry or to dissipation at the Mermaid, a favourite pub in the Mumbles? The paper did not come into

the equation. And he posed his rhetorical question again, answering it
in a typical throwaway manner: 'M or M? I'd prefer M any day, so that
clears the air a lot.'

The Mermaid was where members of the Little Theatre liked to relax
after performances. In a snub to his editors, Dylan had joined them at
the start of the year, after hearing they needed male leads for a revival
of *Hay Fever*, Noel Coward's comedy about a quarrelsome theatrical
family. In February Dylan played the part of the artist Simon Bliss, whose
emotional outbursts were uncannily similar to his own (a point which
Nancy, who was also in the cast, with Haydn Taylor, no doubt impressed
on the producer.) His lively interpretation of the 'bright young things'
of the period contributed to what the *Post* described as 'two hours of
almost continual chuckling'.

A couple of months later, Dylan was back on stage, playing Count
Bellair in George Farquhar's eighteenth-century comedy, *The Beaux' Stratagem*. In the intervening period, Dylan added no poems to his notebook
(the young journalist was too occupied with acting, if not with
reporting), and then, as Professor Ralph Maud has remarked, came 'a
remarkable blossoming'. The first signs of this flowering are found in
the last few poems of his 1930–2 notebook, covering the period April
to July 1932 when he was still at the *Post*. A journalist's descriptive
power combines with a new technical and rhythmical assurance in
poems such as 'The hunchback in the park', written in May, an earlier,
slighter version of his later published poem of the same name. Its wistful
romanticism is reflected in 'Being but men', which weighs up the
relative merits of childhood and adulthood (opting, unsurprisingly, for
the innocence and sense of wonder of the former). There is another
journalistic touch in his reference to the new Cefn Coed asylum on the
hill in 'Upon your held-out hand', where he also feels that he cannot
yet articulate clearly his frustration at words' failure either to describe
the wonder of the universe or to stave off the inevitability of death.

Dylan's newspaper apprenticeship was saved from total disaster by the
astuteness of J. D. Williams, a stalwart supporter of the Little Theatre
whose other great passion was bounding up mountains in North Wales.
Williams edited the *Post*'s weekend paper, the *Herald of Wales*, which took
more features than its news-dominated evening sister. Williams had
noted Dylan's talent in his role as Cromwell in the school play in
Llewellyn Hall where 'he stood out shoulder high above the rest of the
cast: not alone because his part called for it, but because of a certain
distinction of voice and bearing.'

Offered the opportunity to write for the *Herald of Wales* (which meant
extra money), Dylan gave full vent to his opinions in a six-part series

on 'The Poets of Swansea' which ran between January and June 1932. He focused on writers who had made their names in Swansea from the widely known Walter Savage Landor (an adopted Englishman) to the more parochial S. C. Gamwell (which he managed to render as Camwell), a resolute high Victorian in the age of Oscar Wilde, and E. Howard Harris, whom he dubbed 'the first poet of Gower' for artistic vision, but cliché-ridden, derivative and bathetic in execution. This article drew an angry response from fifty-six-year-old Harris who did not take kindly to this treatment from a teenager. It was no coincidence that Harris was a schoolmaster. In accusing him of having 'great difficulty in expressing his thoughts in any but other people's words', Dylan was commenting partly on D.J. and partly on his own need to find a distinctive poetic voice.

In choosing poets who all wrote in English, Dylan showed his cultural limitations, for he ignored a host of local Welsh-language bards and hymnists, including his neighbour William Crwys Williams and the nationalist Saunders Lewis, a lecturer at the University College of Swansea. But this might have undermined his argument, that reflected his perhaps barely acknowledged self-interest, that Swansea poets needed to see more of the world. 'In calling Landor one town's poet,' he wrote, 'you call him a local poet. Landor is national, international; he should never be localised.' Even Howard Harris won praise for wanting to 'extend the Celtic message to the widespread English-speaking peoples'.

After a year in Lord Rothermere's employment, Dylan perked up when an old school-friend Charles Fisher joined the paper. The two had appeared together in school plays: with his good looks, Fisher often performing the female parts such as Dylan's (or his character Roberts's) wife in Strife. The son of the paper's head printer, Fisher wrote poetry and ostentatiously enjoyed country pursuits such as riding (sometimes appearing at work in britches) and fishing (he wrote an angling column under the name 'Blue Dun'). On Saturday nights he donned top hat and tails and attended society dances at the new Brangwyn (Town) Hall - one of middle-class Swansea's ways of keeping up its spirits during an economic depression.

Dylan often met Fisher at the Kardomah café, opposite the newspaper in Castle Street. Converted from the Congregational chapel where D.J. and Florrie had married in 1903, this establishment was conveniently split into a downstairs section, where middle-aged matrons came for morning coffee, and a more secluded upstairs area where the town's younger set disported themselves. Now at Swansea university, Dan Jones brought along some of his expanded Warmley circle, including Tom Warner, an Oxfordshire vicar's son who lived with two maiden aunts in the Uplands and studied the French horn, Mabley Owen, a teacher with a dry sense of humour and a fondness for drink, Thornley Jones, a composer and Fred Janes, a meticulous painter who had just won a scholarship to the Royal Academy Schools in London largely on the basis of his study of a fellow student at the Swansea School of Art, Dylan's old friend Mervyn Levy. Occasionally they were also joined by Titch Phillips and her lively younger sister Vera. At the weekends they ventured further afield to the Langland Bay Hotel on the edge of Gower.

These bright young things were witty, artistic and, like their *Brideshead* contemporaries, self-consciously affected. Charles Fisher admitted that one of their literary heroes, Sir Thomas Browne, epitomised English letters at their most mannered. He wondered why Dylan always ordered his beer with the words 'Beer, I may?', until he realised his friend was referring obliquely to James Joyce's character Leopold Bloom and his talismanic potato. One of the many word jokes which had them in stitches ran:

'Knock, knock?'
'Who's there?'
'Sir Sacheverell.'
'Sir Sacheverell who?'
'Sir Sacheverell people.'

This group was to become known as the 'Kardomah boys'. Together with others who joined later, such as the poets Vernon Watkins and John Pritchard, they have been portrayed as the vanguard of a 1930s Swansea cultural renaissance. This is to pitch their influence too high: Fred Janes doubted if they ever all sat in the same room. But, as individuals, they were highly talented and demonstrated Swansea's eagerness to absorb and contribute to the best of the wider world.

In 'Return Journey' Dylan records three lists of topics they discussed: 'Einstein and Epstein, Stravinsky and Greta Garbo, death and religion, Picasso and girls ...' Each time he finishes with 'and girls', a subject much on his mind. Although now close to the Phillips sisters, whose mother's house in Bryn-y-mor Crescent was as welcoming as Warmley, he had no regular woman in his life. He fantasised about a girl called Edith who worked at the *Post*. His friend Dilys Rowe, a contributor to the *Post*, recalled to Colin Edwards how Dylan took out a girl who worked at Woolworth's. She found this shocking for a Grammar School boy – an interesting insight into Swansea's rigid class distinctions.

She may have mixed this girl with Linda Slee whom Dylan mentioned to Kenneth Tynan in 1948. Dylan boasted of romps with Linda, giving the impression he lost his virginity to her. The daughter of the caretaker at the Rhyddings Congregational church, Linda lived at the back of the cricket ground on St Helen's Avenue, mid-way in the social pecking order between St Thomas and the Uplands. Exactly Dylan's age, she had been forced to work in a shoe shop (not Woolworth's) after finishing at Glanmor School for Girls when she was fifteen. Her daughter Jill Davies remembered her mother talking disparagingly about Dylan. She believed they had mixed as teenagers, but added, 'I shall never know what was behind her disapproving tone.' Dylan certainly knew Linda's artistic future sister-in-law Violet Dabbs, with whom he appeared on stage at the Little Theatre.

During the summer Haydn and Nancy decided to get married. Since this commitment brought new responsibilities, Haydn decided hastily to move to London in search of not only a better job but also a house in the English home counties where he and his future wife could live. Dylan greeted his sudden departure in early September with a back-handed farewell notice in the *Post* diary column. This celebrated Haydn's successes in the theatre (even noting his excellent 'facial contortionism' in *Hay Fever* – a private joke recalling their first encounter at Cwmdonkin Drive), while also revealing that he had left his thespian colleagues in the lurch. The Little Theatre had chosen Haydn to produce its forthcoming play, John Masefield's *Witch*. Now it was left with 'the problem of appointing a new producer at lamentably short notice'.

So long as Haydn was around, Nancy was reasonably content. But, with her fiancé in London, she felt trapped. D.J.'s health had deteriorated again in the summer and he was frequently bad-tempered. If Dylan had been closer to his father, he might have engaged with him. D.J. would have welcomed a discussion of, perhaps, the finer points of Shakespeare on which he put great store. But his adolescent son had other interests. Relegated to the diary rather than to regular reporting and going nowhere in his newspaper career, Dylan wanted to stay out late and get drunk. Florrie, in response to these pressures, became increasingly neurotic.

On 23 September, a Thursday, D.J. felt well enough to go out on the town, his first such excursion for some time. He returned home at 11.15 p.m., looking and smelling awful, noted Nancy. The following night Dylan, having been paid, followed suit, coming in 'very drunk', at fifteen minutes after midnight. 'Then there was much row,' remarked Nancy and she became involved. 'Nowadays, of course, I come in for Pop's nightly, nay hourly, grumbles ...' At the time she wrote Haydn a four-page account of 'all the horrible things that happened'. She later thought better of it, and tore up this letter.

The next morning she fled into town with her friend Gweveril Dawkins. After coffee at the Kardomah, she returned for lunch with her mother at 1.30. They were eating peacefully when, at around 2.45, her father lumbered in, probably from the pub where he usually repaired after Saturday lessons ended at noon. It was not a pleasant encounter: 'A very usual Saturday scene,' recorded Nancy balefully. 'Mother raving and in tears – I, tiniest bit frightened, rush upstairs, dress, & go out in the rain. It pours down & the wind howls.' Since she had no money – a not unusual occurrence, she made clear – she could only walk back into town. When she returned at teatime, her father was more composed. But she was unenthusiastic about the 'cheerful prospect' of having to remain at home all evening and then spend 'all a long Sunday sitting with the family – a family who are nervy & quarrelsome'.

Nancy supplied many other instances of the Thomases' dys-functionalism. In October, she was eating alone in the dining room, when her garrulous mother began to 'grumble at me', leading to a mild altercation. When the impetuous D.J. heard, he threw a book at his daughter. After swearing at her, 'using language that I couldn't repeat', he blustered, 'Who are you? Nobody cares what happens to you, it's a pity you're alive. All you & your beautiful brother do is to take my money from me.' Incensed at being classed with Dylan, Nancy kept increasingly to herself, telling Haydn, 'I honestly do wish I were dead.'

Money was a perpetual problem, particularly with D.J. who com-plained, when she made coffee for visiting friends: 'I will not have you making food for half Swansea. If they want to eat tell them to go home. Who pays for this food I'd like to know?' Florrie, who was anything but her usual 'sweet' self, did not help. When Nancy asked for money to buy materials for a coat, her mother maliciously suggested that she was preparing to get married. When Nancy denied this, Florrie claimed she was 'only teasing'. But she had probably picked up the idea from reading her daughter's correspondence. When she found that Haydn had put sealing wax on his letters, she was incensed. This was 'quite the rudest thing I ever heard of', she screamed. Nancy told her fiancé that she could 'manage to stick her, but Daddy I can't stick. Shortly I think he will go bankrupt; Dylan home, all helps to completely unnerve him. He now revenges for everything on me.'

An example occurred at the end of the autumn term, when she thought she would please her father by cooking him a special pie. But he would have none of it: 'he grumbled & grumbled & raved & swore'. When she remonstrated, he flew off the handle, asking her 'who the bloody hell' she thought she was, dictating to him in this way. He'd screw her 'bloody head off'. When she dashed upstairs for safety and emerged with a small bag, saying she was leaving, he taunted her: 'No such luck, you'll come cringing back, I know.'

Nancy sought refuge at Blaencwm in Carmarthenshire. But, although she enjoyed Aunt Polly's company, Uncle Bob was more trying than ever. 'Last night Uncle Bob was terrible,' she told Haydn. 'I do wish we could have him put away.' The next morning she arrived down to breakfast to find her aunt in a state because Bob had not lit a fire and refused to allow the oil stove to be used. 'Thank God you're not living in a mean, small in all senses, petty village & house. Where each lump of coal is looked at & thought about. Where you have bread and butter for breakfast, boiled ham for dinner (cake for tea when you are down or when any visitor arrives), otherwise bread and butter for tea & supper. This menu daily. How would you feel? A really potty man & a dear old aunt who has a dreadful cough & spits − & has some skin trouble. Can you let me live on like this? Not if you love me & want me sane. Or shall I return home? Where they are all potty...'

As the year drew to an end, Nancy became desperate to leave Cwmdonkin Drive. She implored Haydn to find her a job in London. Anything, even a post as a governess, would do. She thought of spending Christmas at her Aunt Polly's. Normally she could rely on festive cheques from her aunts and uncles. But these had not arrived, so, to post a letter to Haydn, she had to borrow three half-pennies from the maid.

When the couple announced their engagement at Christmas, they received short shrift from the Thomases. Florrie told her daughter not to expect any favours. 'Your wedding − remember Daddy won't have any money & any sort of fuss will kill him. If you expected any sort of special fuss or clothes you ought to be ashamed of yourself...'

By then the Thomases had additional reason to be concerned about money, for Dylan's short newspaper career had come to an end. One of his last pieces, in the Herald of Wales in early November, was partly a paean to his uncle the Reverend David Rees who was retiring as minister in charge of the Paraclete Congregational church in Newton. He had little time for his uncle, who epitomised the worst of organised religion for him. The feeling was mutual: the preacher once became so exasperated with his nephew that he suggested he should be sent to a mental asylum. So Dylan's apparently warm encomium was a lie, an example of his ability, which he deprecated, to spin out specious 'little (Oscar) Wilde words'. 'Give me pen & paper − the trick's done: a thousand conceits, couched in a hermit's language, spoiling the whiteness of the page.' He could turn it on when he wanted, but municipal politics and rugby reports did not inspire him even that far.

Around November he simply stopped working for the Post. There is no evidence to support his claim that he was offered a five-year contract and turned it down. Rather, his obvious lack of interest in his work, his increasingly drunken behaviour (probably linked to bouts of depression) and his own desire to concentrate on his poetry led to the only possible conclusion – that he should leave the paper. Although the parting was probably a mutual decision, he admitted he was 'already showing signs of a reporter's decadence' and feared 'the slow but sure stamping out of individuality, the gradual contentment with life as it was, so much per week, so much for this, for that, so much left over for drink and cigarettes. That be no loife for such as Oi!' Since he kept no notebooks as such from July 1932 to January 1933, it is difficult to match his verse to his mood.

However his Irishism (or was it Joyceism?) indicated his determination to put a brave face on his circumstances. In November he was back enjoying himself with Dan Jones at Warmley. With Tom Warner's technical help, the two friends set up the Warmley Broadcasting Corporation, an elaborate trail of wires and loudspeakers which allowed them to transmit from an upstairs drawing room to a small sitting room below. Their innovation was initially unknown to others in the house. After Dylan innocently asked Dan's father if he could listen to a foreign station on the radiogram, he seemed to tune in some Beethoven piano music. After a few bars, the notes began to sound increasingly discordant. Jenkyn Jones went through various stages of being quizzical, perplexed and annoyed. Only then was it revealed that the music was coming from Dan upstairs. (A note in the Henry Ransom Center in Austin attributes the WBC's founding to Daniel Hautboy Jones and Dylan Moreorless Thomas, with assistance from Tom (Tiptoes) Warner, advisory mechanician.)

Although not included in a notebook, his remarkable poem 'Especially when the November wind' expresses some of the exhilaration and at the same time trepidation he feels about his 'chosen task' of poetry 'that lies upon/My belly like a cold stone'. Experiencing his youth 'like fire', he speculates again about the restrictive nature of words, and finds comfort in being able this time 'to feel November air/And be no words' prisoner'.

With little else to occupy him, Dylan, on a whim, attended the funeral of his old French master R. M. 'Lulu' Lewis in Ystalyfera, an industrial village outside Swansea in early December. As he told Percy Smart, he had been trying to develop the Zen-like facility of dissociating himself from the emotions of others. He observed the obsequies 'as morbidly & as selfishly as a Russian dramatist', wondering if, when he died, his mother would 'turn on her ready tap of recollections and, cloaking misdeeds with tears, dwell tenderly upon such virtues as I may present at the gold gates.' (She was to do exactly that twenty-one years later.)

Once again Dylan was determined to tough it out. He counselled

Smart to heed the words of P. G. Wodehouse in his 1922 novel *The Clicking of Cuthbert* where the celebrated Russian novelist Vladimir Brusiloff tells a sedate literary gathering in England: 'No novelists any good except me. Sovietski – yah! Nastikoff – bah! I spit me of zem all. No novelists anywhere any good except me. P. G. Wodehouse and Tolstoi not bad. Not good but not bad. No novelists any good except me.' This was a sentiment Dylan clearly shared: after quoting this in haphazard fashion, he added, 'I cannot say better than that.' Despite his inability to hold down a job, his regard for his own writing skills remained healthily intact.

SIX

A TORMENTED THING

Only a few weeks into the new year of 1933, Dylan suffered a dramatic adverse reaction. With no job and no visible means of support, he stayed in bed most mornings, and then would rise in a fearful temper, 'rushing & raving like a tormented thing'. He tried to write in the afternoons, before going to Warmley in the evening. But Dan was immersed in his university studies, and Dylan often found himself at a loose end. If he had any money, he spent it in pubs. But it was never clear where he found his cash. On more than one occasion in January, Nancy thought that he had stolen sums from her or her friends. 'What will become of him Heaven knows,' she tut-tutted to her new fiancé. She was hardly mollified by the way her mother fussed over the teenage prodigy and on one occasion forced her to stop writing to Haydn because the ink was required by Dylan who had just risen from his bed. 'Dylan has to get up to work & now no ink, etc.' Nancy interpreted. 'Not fair for the child, etc.' As a cushion for his freelance writing career, Dylan had wrung a promise from J. D. Williams to take occasional articles. Whether his former editor felt so happy about this arrangement after the first offering is doubtful. In a piece for the Post in early January, the young would-be poet explored the thin line that artists trod between sanity, eccentricity and madness. He quoted the examples of several writers who interested him, including William Blake, Oscar Wilde, John Donne and John Keats. For some reason, he also threw in a modern case of 'eccentricity' – the painter Nina Hamnett, Welsh-born doyenne of the louche Bohemian set who congregated in London's Fitzrovia. Dylan stated that Hamnett's recent autobiography, Laughing Torso had been banned. Since this was untrue, she threatened legal action, forcing the paper to make a hasty climb-down.

His interest in such subject-matter was linked to his own fragile state of mind, as suggested in a poem in April:

> Within his head revolved a little world
> Where wheels, confusing music, confused doubts
> Rolled down all images into the pits

Where half dead vanities were sleeping curled
Like cats, and lusts lay half hot in the cold.

Women appeared to him as distant monsters with 'serpents' mouths and scolecophidian voids'. ('Scolecophidian' is not in the Shorter Oxford English Dictionary. It is a showy Dylanism meaning 'worm-like'.) For the first time, a questing spiritual dimension was to be found in his work. In common with adolescents through the ages, he could not help wondering: in a threatening world, where was God? where was love?

To absent friends such as Percy Smart and Trevor Hughes, he tried to paint a rosier picture. He talked of using his new-found leisure to write not just poems (which he described as his 'incurable disease'), but stories and even a short novel. Beginning to hanker after a wider audience, he claimed that Sir John Squire had accepted a story for the palely Georgian *London Mercury*. Luckily, perhaps, nothing further was heard of that initiative, while an approach to Geoffrey Grigson, icono-clastic editor of the recently founded journal *New Verse*, only resulted in the return of Dylan's poems.

The reality, he was forced to admit to Hughes, was more banal: 'I continue writing in the most futile manner, looking at the gas oven.' His disposition was not improved by the death of his Aunt Annie from cancer of the womb in February. Even as she lay dying in Carmarthen Infirmary, he was both concerned and also rather pleased that he could feel no emotion. 'She is dead. She is alive. It is all the same thing.' This was the same numbness to others' emotions he had felt at 'Lulu' Lewis's funeral a couple of months earlier. It reflected partly his own self-absorbed anger, and partly a feeling that this was the proper literary response – a Wildean defiance of conventional morality that would allow him to concentrate, as a poet, on his own emotional reality. After her funeral, he could only dash off a sour verse response. (Five years later, he had second thoughts and revised this notebook poem in a more upbeat fashion.)

In Rayners Lane, Hughes was, if anything, more doleful, looking after his arthritic mother, mourning a dead brother, and trying to write stories himself. Despite his own problems, Dylan had to counsel his friend not to be so morbid, but to look for that 'fountain of clearness' to be found in an extraordinary quintet comprising Bach, Mozart, D. H. Lawrence, W. B. Yeats and – a growing preoccupation – Jesus Christ. He chided Hughes for thinking that suffering helped the cause of art. 'The artistic consciousness is there or it isn't. Suffering is not going to touch it.' And he tried to explain his own idea of the artist's role. Everyone, he believed, had to live in the outer world, with its hardships and unhappiness.

'Where the true artist differs from his fellows is that that for him is not the only world.' He has an 'inner splendour', and it is his business to reconcile those external and internal experiences. Despite his efforts to articulate his aims, he admitted he seldom achieved them: most of his poems were 'outer poems' and therefore unsatisfactory.

Part of Dylan's confusion arose from his sense of impotence in the face of local developments. Swansea was no longer protected from economic realities by its anthracite fields or even the Anglo-Persian oil terminal. Unemployment had risen (28,000 people were jobless, or 20 per cent of the population, according to one estimate), and social conditions deteriorated. As in the good times, the town responded in its own peculiar way. The Labour party's control of local affairs had stimulated a right-wing reaction among the normally complacent petit bourgeoisie. Soon after its formation in 1931, Sir Oswald Mosley's British Union of Fascists opened an office in Walter Road – clear evidence that recession had reached the Uplands.

Swansea's religious and political conservatism created a moral backlash Dylan found distasteful. In February he pilloried the role of the Watch Committee as guardian of public morality. He must have known of the decision by the local Council's Library and Arts Committee to refuse a portrait of the writer Caradoc Evans who had made a career out of satirising the religious-based hypocrisy of his fellow Welshmen. Evans, a favourite of Dylan, thanked the Committee 'for proving the accuracy of some of my pen portraits of the Welsh people'.

This censoriousness reinforced the town's ban on Sunday drinking, but Dylan found a way round it. Although four miles from Cwmdonkin Drive, the Mermaid in the Mumbles was nominally a hotel, and the stout, hard-drinking landlady, Miss Spiers, showed scant regard for the letter of the law. Dylan passed many agreeable weekend hours at her bar, consuming, as he put it, 'too much out of too many bottles'. When once, in a drunken stupor, he slipped and fell, his ankle blew up like a balloon. He stayed overnight at the hotel, and found his parents none too happy when he arrived home for dinner next day.

Dylan was buoyed through these difficult early months of 1933 by two factors. One was his involvement in the Little Theatre. This not only enabled him to get out of the house, but gave him an excuse for drinking. If he stumbled home late at night (or even the next day), he could claim he had been in Mumbles rehearsing. He even had some status, if not exactly clout, in the company. For months he and Eric Hughes, his former colleague at the Post, had been clamouring to put on Peter and Paul by H. F. Rubinstein. Their wishes were finally granted and the play was staged in March. Reviewing it in the *Post*, J. D. Williams claimed he at last understood why the 'young Turks' at the theatre had lobbied for this piece. It was because of the 'fat parts' and 'acting chances it gave them'. The story revolved around two men who were shown from youth to old age – one (Dylan) who led a conventional life, working in his father's business, while always haunted by the knowledge that he wanted to write; the other (Hughes) who suffered great hardship because of his determination to follow his calling as an author. Williams probably did not realise that these two fictional characters reflected Dylan's own struggle while at the *Post*: should he stay unhappily at his job, or should he write and be poor?

In cast photographs of the time, Dylan appeared thin, languid, wide-eyed – the image of an affected thespian. The Little Theatre did at least allow him to lose himself. His colleagues might sniff at his unfashionably rhetorical style. 'Dylan liked a bit of old ham,' noted Eileen Davies, who appeared with him in *The Beaux' Stratagem*. But they loved his company. She recalled meeting Dylan at Oystermouth station one beautiful summer evening, when the rest of humanity was out enjoying the sun. 'Oh dear, we've got to go in and under-act again,' he complained. His energy perked up when, after rehearsals, the company decamped to one of two regular pubs, either Fulton's, popularly known as Cheese's after the landlord, or, a bit further away, the more plush Mermaid, where the thespian banter flowed with the drinks. As in most social situations, Dylan loved playing word games – partly to ward off boredom and introspection, partly to show off. One evening, complaining of feeling 'fed up', he suggested such an exercise. When asked what he had in mind, he said, 'Well, take any noun describing something on the table. Then let's find an adjective that is the most opposite. For example, see that jelly. There you are: "static jelly".'

Once, after a widely reported rabies epidemic, Dylan and his former school-friend Wynford Vaughan-Thomas, recently down from Oxford, used this as a cue for some spontaneous horseplay. They went down on all fours and crawled around the floor of the pub, pretending to be rabid dogs, biting people's ankles. When Dylan tried this on the actress Ruby Graham, she feigned anger and shooed him out of the door. She was astonished to see him continue across the pavement to a lamp-post. 'I thought he was going to pee on it,' she recalled. Instead, he bit on it, leaving him with a broken tooth for the rest of his life. (Afterwards, he used to tell her he remembered her every time he smiled.) As always, Dylan could always appear the life and soul of a party, even when his internal world was in turmoil.

The second stabilising influence for Dylan – and the more important –

was his friendship with Bert Trick, whom he described as 'a communist grocer with a passion for obscurity and the Powys family'. Trick was an unusual character, a self-taught radical with a quasi-religious view of the perfectability of man. The first part of Dylan's description has often been noted, without much attention being paid to the rest. Works such as *The Religion of a Sceptic* by John Cowper Powys played an important part in Trick's intellectual development. Born a bit later, he might have been a sandalled academic. His family, originally from Devon, controlled the meat trade in Neath, six miles east of Swansea. His prosperous middle-class existence was disrupted in 1914 when his depressive father (also called Albert, after Queen Victoria's Prince Consort) committed suicide. When the family butcher business began to falter in the slump, Bert joined the civil service, but found the salary insufficient to marry on. His solution was to buy a grocery store in Swansea in 1928. However he was never a convincing shopkeeper and his choice of location – Glanbrydan Avenue, a residential street in the Uplands, with little passing trade – was poor. When the economic downturn reached the suburbs, he started attending Labour party meetings and contributing to local papers. With the rise of the Mosleyites, he became increasingly left-wing and saw the world from a Marxist perspective.

One evening Trick was standing among the biscuit tins, when a slim young man entered his shop, wearing a trilby and an over-sized sports jacket. Dylan said he had written some poems and had been advised to show them to Trick by Thomas Taig, a Swansea University English lecturer who in his spare time produced plays for the Little Theatre. Since it was late in the day, the two men agreed to meet for further discussion on another occasion.

A few nights later Dylan called again at Glanbrydan Avenue. After some small talk he pulled out a notebook and started reciting his poems (or 'pomes' as he insisted on calling them). He refused to allow Trick to look at them on the page, saying that they needed to be heard: 'that is the only way to get the music out of the poetry.' Trick was so impressed that he called in his wife Nell, and they both sat spellbound. Appreciative of this positive response, Dylan invited Trick to Cwmdonkin Drive where he gathered some friends. Trick reciprocated, asking Dylan's Kardomah crowd to join a group of his own, which included John Jennings, a radical journalist who would become editor of the *Swansea and West Wales Guardian*, and Leslie Mewis, a would-be writer stuck in a dead-end job at the Fifty Shilling Tailors. For a while they all attended a series of evening discussion meetings covering politics, music and art, usually at the Thomases on Wednesdays and above the shop at the Tricks on Sundays.

The only regular participants at these soirées – the ones who met, even if no-one else turned up – were Dylan and Trick. Despite a sixteen-year age gap, they enjoyed each other's company. 'We'd start on modern poetry and end up discussing the dialectics of Karl Marx,' recalled Trick. 'It was all terribly exciting and stimulating.' They also shared a passion for words. In a memoir towards the end of his life, Trick wrote: 'Many were the times I skipped out of 5 Cwmdonkin Drive, my arms full of books, my head full of stars and feet of feathers. I didn't walk down the hill to my home, I was levitated. There was no need for strong drink, we were intoxicated with words – ideas and words. The magic of language was ours: the play of words to produce paradox, to twist the tail of a platitude to make an epigram, to change the juxtaposition of words in mundane prose to produce an explosion.'

At just the right time, when he was embarking on his own writing career, Dylan found someone with the patience and good humour to answer his probing youthful questions – Freddie Farr's more cerebral brother, who would introduce him to the literary and philosophical possibilities of the grown-up world. As an outsider, Leslie Mewis could observe: 'Dylan had no politics at all, but he appealed to Trick. I remember him saying to Bert, "For God's sake, Bert, explain that!" As a man Bert was very balanced. You felt in his company you would get down to sincerities rather than polemics.' With his understanding of Dylan's ambitions as a writer, Trick took the verbal gymnast of the Warmley era and strengthened his intellectual equipment.

He counselled his young protégé to temper his indiscriminate poet's passion with reasoning, in the manner of John Donne, a writer they both admired. If Dylan wanted to act like an angry young man, he should be angry about something worthwhile. 'So I began to interest him – I'm quite sure I did – in social justice,' claimed the grocer. 'There was no doubt that the whole of Dylan's life was coloured by his love for his fellow men – particularly if they were disabled or mentally handicapped or despisedly used.' Despite his special pleading, Trick did help Dylan channel his energies more sympathetically and creatively, giving him what Dylan's future wife Caitlin recognised as 'mettle'. Except that Trick saw it in a different, more personal way. He talked of Dylan having a 'deep compassion' that at times was 'Christ-like'. This, in his estimation, was at the heart of the 'unjudging innocence' of some of Dylan's best fictional characters. (He was referring in particular to Dylan's later work, Under Milk Wood.) That 'simple innocence' – found in William Blake and negro spirituals – was 'the very touchstone of Dylan'. And it came, Trick believed, from a basic spiritual consciousness that saw man as both 'the creature and creator of his own world'. Dylan understood this basic religious insight and determined to render it in his own modern way.

At one stage Dylan spent so much time at Glanbrydan Avenue that his mother, feeling rejected, asked Nell how she made her jellies and blancmanges, her son's favourite foods. Despite Dylan's sweet tooth, the secret was not in the food, but, as at Warmley, in the ambience. At the Tricks, no subject was off limits. When Nell recalled how, as a girl, she used lie down at night and feel her head getting bigger and turning to rubber, Dylan said he had experienced exactly the same sensation. 'Then we went on to talk about dreams. He said that whenever he had a dream he was always flying in the air – over a mountain, over the trees.' On another occasion Nell let slip that her young daughter Pamela had enquired out of the blue: 'What colour is glory?' Dylan was delighted with the phrase and incorporated it into his poem 'Why east wind chills', originally from July 1933, which addressed a topic occupying him at the time – the impossibility of reaching eternal truths about the world.

The conversation was by no means all high-minded. Having discovered a mutual love of the cinema, Dylan kept the Tricks amused with impersonations of stars such as Edward G. Robinson and Harpo Marx, his favourite Marx Brother. He was possessive about his idols: the only time Trick remembered Dylan losing his temper was when a female visitor had the temerity to suggest Greta Garbo could not act.

Exactly when Dylan first met Trick is not clear. In his authorised biography, Constantine FitzGibbon gave the date as 1933. However Trick said that Dylan was still a cub reporter, and elsewhere stated that his visitor was seventeen, at one stage placing this encounter specifically in spring 1932. This is possible: Taig was one of the producers of The Beaux' Stratagem in April 1932. Dylan would have known that Taig was the author of Rhythm and Metre, a manual on writing poetry, published in 1929, and sought his advice. As Maud noted, Dylan's poetical flowering in his notebooks commenced around this time.

What is certain is that Dylan's relationship with Trick took off in early 1933 after he had quit the Post. Some early poems in his third notebook, started on 1 February, still reflect his teething problems as he readjusted to a poet's life. Gradually, however, his subject-matter became clearer and more confident, as he moved from the passing of the seasons (dismissed in February as 'nothing more/Than hot and cold markings from one to four') to the fleetingness of existence – a concern brought home to him partly by his aunt's death, and partly by his almost wishful belief that, now he was a poet, he was doomed to die young and was indeed already wasting away with tuberculosis. Several recollections note this obsession at the time: 'He would tell Nell that he wouldn't live till 40,' said Trick, who charitably used this as an excuse for Dylan's reluctance to tackle political subjects. Dylan had his own poetical agenda which he needed to complete before he 'burnt out'.

In March there was a brief hiatus in his output as he concentrated on his theatrical role in *Peter and Paul*. Then he returned to his task. Seeking to make that connection between his outer and inner worlds, he contrasted the wonder of light in the universe with his own fear of the dark. There were precocious poems about man's megalomania ('men want the stars to hang on cherry trees') and his own continuing distaste for the mechanistic couplings of sexual love.

In April his interests came together in a powerful early version of 'And death shall have no dominion' which arose out of a friendly competition with Trick to write a poem on immortality. Dylan used rhyme, a form of versification he had recently eschewed, and pointed to texts ranging from John Donne to the Bible.

Trick was so impressed that he suggested Dylan try another London outlet, one that reflected the grocer's own interests. This was the *New English Weekly*, a recently established vehicle for the quirky mystical leftist views of A. R. Orage, former editor of *New Age*, which had published Shaw, Wells and Yeats a generation earlier. Dylan received an enthusiastic letter from Orage, accepting his poem and asking for more. But even though this was his first publication in a London periodical, Dylan was muted in celebration because he was not paid.

A feature of Dylan's work was its religious input, often presented from an unorthodox Christian perspective. Under Trick's influence, Dylan began to see Jesus Christ as an archetypal figure of compassion, who had tried, as he was doing, to reconcile the worlds of the flesh and the spirit. As he moved through his nineteenth year, Dylan had never been more spiritually curious. Traditional he was not: his quest arose from a literary fascination with death, inspired by the works of Donne and Thomas Lovell Beddoes, whose imagery suffused his poems. His heaven was a Buddhist-style nirvana – 'a state of being unbounded by traitor senses' – and his hell the church's personification of religion, 'the fallacy of fancies/That gave god whiskers to his navel/A tail and two horns to the devil'. His views were made clear in his vitriolic 'Matthias spat upon the lord' which closed this third notebook in August. This was an attack on conventional religion as peddled by 'The Reverend Crap, a pious fraud'. And to make sure no-one was unaware of his target, he wrote 'Rev David Rees' in the margin beside the poem. This – and not his recent fulsome notice in the *Post* – showed his real attitude to his uncle's Bible-thumping.

As he explored the universe, he was inspired by its infinite possibilities:

> A football has its moon and sun,
> A single syllable its many words

His main complaint, as is clear from his remarkable 'We have the fairy tales by heart', was that human beings had lost their capacity for mystery and wonder. But even in a world where

> We have by heart the children's stories
> Have blown sky high the nursery of fairies

there was no escaping the inevitability of death.

As his spiritual horizons expanded, so did his geographical, a yearning expressed in 'I have longed to move away' in March. By the time he wrote 'The first ten years in school and park' in late April he seemed confident he had overcome the worst of his personal demons and even went so far as to express satisfaction that he had found a balance between the opposing mechanistic and natural worlds. He drew on Dan's musical experimentation in his observations on harmony. But when he claimed, 'Now I've sterner stuff inside', he was referring to the intellectual ballast Bert Trick had given his life.

More tangibly, the atmosphere at Cwmdonkin Drive changed after Nancy's marriage in May. (The catalyst for this event seems to have been the death of Aunt Annie in February. Within days of her death the Thomases were able to increase their mortgage by £150, thus easing their immediate financial difficulties and allowing them to host their daughter's wedding.) She and Haydn moved to the English home counties, where they lived in the Betjemanesque Wisteria Cottage at Laleham, near Chertsey in Surrey, and where, because they were keen sailors, they also rented a houseboat called *Fairyland* which they kept nearby on the River Thames. With his parents' house strangely quiet, Dylan often went to the Tricks' weekend bungalow at Caswell Bay on Gower. As summer drew on, he would read them stories in the making. More than thirty years later Trick recalled how Dylan span an engaging fantasy about the inhabitants of a typical South Wales village called Llareggub. When Trick expressed surprise at the Welsh name, which was an unusual departure for Dylan, the young man gave a naughty smile and urged him to say it backwards.

Rather than anticipating *Under Milk Wood*, Trick may well have misremembered 'The Orchards', a typical short story from his young friend's pen at this time. Although there were exceptions, Dylan's tales weaved myth and dream with more tangible themes of paganism and religious fanaticism he had witnessed in Carmarthenshire (fictionalised as the Jarvis hills and valley). Paradoxically, even when dealing with madness – as, for example, in 'The Mouse and the Woman' – they are full of surprisingly domesticated detail, as if emphasising the tension in Dylan's mind between the worlds of suburbia and the imagination. 'The Orchards' was more autobiographical than most in its portrayal of 'Marlais, the poet' who leaves his 'top-storey room in the house on a slope over the black-housed town' for a dream-like flight over valleys and 'water-dipping hills', to a place of a hundred orchards where a fair girl makes him tea and, taking a phrase from Florrie Thomas, 'cut the bread so thin she could see London through the white pieces'. The academic James A. Davies is correct to see this as a statement of Dylan's general inability to escape his Uplands background: 'as always in Thomas's life, despite his journey and changed, disreputable appearance. In his end is his beginning.' In his narration, Dylan described 'The Orchards' as 'more terrible than the stories of the reverend madmen in the Black Book of Llareggub'. This was probably the reference Trick recalled, and it suggests that, even at this stage, Dylan was planning a series of such tales, perhaps leading to a novel.

This would explain the curious item in the *Evening Post*'s diary column in early July, almost certainly penned by Charles Fisher, who was as natural a reporter as Dylan was not. This noted that Dylan had tried his hand at journalism, but now 'his aspirations are for another branch of the craft of writing'. It added intriguingly that he had completed a novel which was under consideration by publishers and that the previous week one of his poems had been read over the wireless. The novel must have been the one he mentioned to Hughes at the start of the year. No other details are known, certainly no manuscript has been found, though Haydn Taylor did claim that, as a conciliatory gesture towards his feckless brother-in-law, he once sent some of Dylan's writings to the publisher Allen Lane, a friend from his Bristol days. Lane, who was to found Penguin Books three years later, was running the Bodley Head. He seems to have rejected what he read of Dylan, and nothing more was heard of it. Dylan returned to the drawing board with his 'novel'. The wireless broadcast – the first of many – did take place, however. On 28 June, Dylan's poem 'The Romantic Isle' was read out on the BBC National service, having been selected from entries to a BBC poetry competition. Unfortunately this too does not survive – either in the BBC archives or in Dylan's own papers.

One warm mid-July evening Dylan was sighted at a Little Theatre performance of Sophocles's *Electra*, given in the grounds of the Sketty mansion of Major and Mrs Bertie Perkins. He had gone to support Dan

Jones who had composed special music for harp and drums. When Eileen Davies in the lead role saw him lurking in the background, smoking a cigarette, she feared a snide review. However the piece he submitted to the Herald of Wales was a poem which used the circumstances of the Greek tragedy being played in an open air garden to explore a favourite theme of nature's indifference to suffering. 'A pigeon calls and women talk of death' ran the last line. But Dylan was going through the motions: his pondering on the pros and cons of going to London was apparent in his poem a few days later:

> Shall I run to the ships,
> With the wind in my hair,
> Or stay to the day I die,
> And welcome no sailor?

He was plagued by an old dilemma: unless he took a chance, he might be destined to a life of quiet sterility at home.

Within a couple of weeks he had taken the plunge and left for London, clutching a sheaf of typed poems. The capital's literary world was taking a collective breath after the perturbations of the post-war decade. Modernism was still in the air, but its excesses had been tamed. The pretensions of the Bloomsbury group had been pricked by Wyndham Lewis and the South African-born poet Roy Campbell. Surrealism remained a minority calling. The emerging movement was more concerned with social realities, but the verse of W. H. Auden and his fellow public-school Marxists had yet to find a wide audience. But there were still plenty of literary publications and, as always, they were keen to find new voices. A Welshman who mixed modernism and lyricism and had a musical way with words fitted the bill. But none of the existing schools particularly attracted Dylan who had his own subject-matter and his own style, and was unlikely to change them.

Eight years later Dylan wrote a colourful fictional account of his leaving home in January (the month was wrong) 1933. In Adventures in the Skin Trade his alter ego rose early to deface the school essays his father was marking and to smash his mother's crockery. In London he fell naturally into a world of cafés inhabited by tarts, bed-sitters and sleazy clubs. Dylan's sense of anger at the restrictions of Cwmdonkin Drive was realistic enough. But his progress in the capital was rather more conventional. In real life, he stayed first with Trevor Hughes in Rayners Lane, from where he and his host made at least one sortie to the Fitzroy Tavern, well-known drinking spot for Bohemians such as the litigious Nina Hamnett. He also visited Nancy and Haydn on their houseboat, where, so the story goes, he had to be pulled out of the Thames with a boat-hook one night after returning home drunk. During the daytime, he peddled his wares, but without much success. One literary figure he did meet was John Middleton Murry, former editor of *The Adelphi*. This was probably Trick's suggestion since Middleton Murry, friend and biographer of D. H. Lawrence, was a mystical Marxist of the type he favoured. He had visited Swansea in May when he lectured the Workers' Educational Association on 'Marxist Socialism and British Conditions'. His most recent work had been an article on William Blake, an author whom Trick encouraged Dylan to take seriously. As Dylan had told Hughes, Murry 'is interested in the symbols of the world, in the mystery and meaning of the world, in the fundamentals of the soul.'

Dylan and Murry met at the Chelsea flat of Sir Richard Rees, a flamboyant Eton and Cambridge-educated baronet and former diplomat, who had taken over editing the *Adelphi* in 1931. Dylan left some poems with Rees who was impressed and published 'No man who believes, when a star falls shot' in his next (September) issue.

A couple of other rendez-vous were more nebulous. Dylan may have met A. L. Orage, editor of the *New English Weekly*, which had published his first poem in London in May. There is a story that Orage asked him bluntly if he were a virgin. Dylan may also have encountered the bibulous Malcolm Lowry who was recently down from Cambridge and had published his first novel, *Ultramarine*. But none of these figures was likely to do much to further his career. Dylan returned to Wales little clearer about his ultimate literary direction. That is the inference from the wry epigram in his latest and final notebook, started on 23 August: 'To others caught/Between black and white.' And he might equally have written – between Muse and Mermaid, life and art (opposites he told Hughes he had difficulty reconciling), or even London and Swansea.

SEVEN

EPISTOLARY ENCOUNTERS

Dan Jones came to Dylan's rescue when he returned from a short summer holiday in Sussex, telling of his attendance at a literary tea party in Steyning hosted by Victor Neuburg, an eccentric middle-aged poet enjoying a new lease of life as editor of the Poets' Corner section of a maverick London newspaper, the *Sunday Referee*. An 1890s aesthete manqué, Neuburg had first published poems as a Cambridge under-graduate in the early years of the century. His career plummeted after he fell under the malign influence of the occultist Aleister Crowley who, in the guise of exploring mysteries, adopted him as his homosexual slave. After a girlfriend committed suicide (with Crowley heavily implicated), the mild-mannered Neuburg suffered a breakdown and retired to Steyning where he set up the unsuccessful Vine Press (named after his cottage) and played host to free-thinking leftist friends.

'Vicky' or 'Vickybird', as he was known, spoke in an affected manner, coining his own neologisms, such as 'ostrobogulous', meaning anything interesting with a slightly risqué connotation (the word is attributed to him in the Oxford English Dictionary). He had a habit of using abbreviations: TAP meant Take a Pew and when he raised a glass, MEGH, Most Extraordinary Good Health. He also inspired great affection. Ted Hayter-Preston, literary editor of the *Sunday Referee*, had been his sergeant during Vicky's ill-starred period of active service in France during the First World War. When he heard about Vicky's hand-to-mouth existence in Sussex, he prevailed on his editor Mark Goulden to find his old friend a job. So was born Poets' Corner in April 1933.

When Dan mentioned his tea-time meeting, and the literary company at Neuburg's, Dylan made a mental note of a potential outlet and sent the editor of Poets' Corner his pensive poem 'That Sanity be kept', which notes, behind the smiles of the people in the park, the 'grief' and 'vague bewilderment/At things not turning right'. Dylan was delighted when his lilting, quasi-romantic offering was published in the *Sunday Referee* on 3 September, and even more so when his success was followed by a fan letter from another poet who had featured in the same slot – a young woman called Pamela Hansford Johnson.

A couple of years older than Dylan (and half a foot shorter than his five foot six inches), she had sultry, dark-haired good looks. Brought up in the Gold Coast, she lived with her widowed mother in Clapham, travelled each day to an unsatisfactory job in a bank, and dreamed of being a writer. Dan had noticed her, looking bored, at Neuburg's, but they did not hit it off, and he later told Dylan that she had a nice body but poor brain. However she did not lack for male attention, given the number of references to 'osculatory adventures' she recorded gleefully in her diary. One admirer remembers her as being fascinated with sex. Not many girls of her age owned The Sexual Theories of the Marquis de Sade. But when another suitor became too amorous she was still primly self-conscious enough to write, 'What are our boys coming to?'

An engaging mixture of blue-stocking and flapper, Pamela was the sort of bright, well-read girlfriend Dylan might have scripted for himself in his fantasy life. Although her late father had been an austere colonial civil servant, her maternal grandfather had moved in racy theatrical circles as treasurer to Sir Henry Irving. Since her father's death, her mother had been forced to take in lodgers. But Pamela wanted to make more of her life than waste away in an office. The two young poets fell into an intense flirtatious correspondence, exchanging photographs and poems, as well as personal detail and criticism of each other's work. Dylan introduced himself as 'a thin, curly person, smoking too (many) cigarettes, with a crocked lung, and writing his vague verses in the back room of a provincial villa'. He explained how, 'for some mad reason', his name was derived from the Mabinogion and was pronounced to rhyme with 'Chillun'.

When he wrote a second time, he was down in Carmarthenshire, because the previous month his father had discovered, during a routine visit to the dentist, that a lesion at the base of his mouth was cancerous. D.J. had been quickly admitted to University College Hospital, London, where Haydn Taylor, the only relation with a car, drove him to start treatment with radium needles on 10 September. At such times, the extended Welsh family rallied round. To relieve his mother, Dylan reluctantly agreed to go to Blaencwm where his Uncle David Rees and Aunt Theodosia had retired to one of the cottages. He took his father's illness badly, as is clear from his observation 'Flesh is suffered, is laid low' in his poem 'Take the needles and the knives'. The cancer also reminded him of his concerns about his own body. He claimed in the autumn that his self-diagnosis of tuberculosis had been confirmed by a local doctor and that he had been given four years to live. The truth is more likely to have been that, given his history of asthma and lung trouble, he was advised to cut down on drinking and smoking. But tuberculosis remained a potent killer. Middleton Murry had lost two wives to it. With romantic connotations of 'consumption', the poet's disease, it was adopted by a lugubrious Dylan as a device to win sympathy and enhance his artist's mystique. If nothing else, the idea of having, as he put it to Pamela, 1340 days and nights to live was a spur to getting work done.

Dylan made a second trip to Carmarthenshire over his birthday in October. He no longer felt much affinity for the drab countryside, with its 'thin, purposeless rain, hiding the long miles of desolate fields and scattered farmhouses'. With the weather and snaring of rabbits the only topics of conversation, he too felt trapped. The bus from Swansea had taken him through some of the dingiest industrial towns in the area, where he had observed groups of coal-miners, 'diseased in mind and body as only the Welsh can be', standing outside the Welfare Hall. Their women were 'all breast and bottom', their houses 'jerry-built huts' for them to breed and eat in. With no Trick on hand to steel his political will, he could only rant to Pamela that all Wales was like this: 'It is impossible for me to tell you how much I want to get out of it all, out of narrowness and dirtiness, out of the eternal ugliness of the Welsh people, and all that belongs to them' and, significant additions to his list, 'out of the pettiness of a mother I don't care for and the giggling batch of relatives'. He finished this tirade with a cry, which even he admitted sounded melodramatic: 'I'm sick, and this bloody country's killing me.' No wonder he was excited by the prospect of London where professional adulation might be accompanied by touching scenes of domestic bliss, such as Pamela demonstrating to him 'the poetry of cooking'.

Despite low spirits, he remained both prolific and creative. In August he had composed a manifestly political poem as a homage to Bert Trick, to whom it was dedicated. 'The hand that signed the paper felled a city' showed Dylan had not completely ignored Hitler's accession to the Chancellorship of Germany in February and that country's quick descent into dictatorship. It was his personal protest against the arbitrariness of brute power. But he had no desire to emulate the social realism of the Audens and Spenders of his generation. His calling, poetry, was about higher things than politics, he maintained.

His reading matter at Blaencwm reflected his interests: an anthology of poetry from Jonson to Dryden provided a literary overview of a seventeenth century every bit as ideologically split as the twentieth; a volume of John Donne's prose took him to the heart of the fleshy, cadaverous English metaphysicals, while Bernard Hart's pre-war textbook, The Psychology of Insanity, introduced Dylan to the workings of the mind (as it had the Imagists a decade or so earlier when Ben Hecht called it a 'blueprint of modern thinking').

Such works provided stimulus for Dylan's output over the autumn. 'Light breaks where no sun shines' showed his determination to portray the development of human form and consciousness at all stages from conception to death – and to do so in as individual and as poetic a manner as possible. A couple of months earlier, he had written a similar, if more ambitious, poem which described in its opening lines the very first moments of a Christ figure's incarnation:

> Before I knocked and flesh let enter
> With liquid hands tapped on the womb

Delighted with the result, Dylan sent it to Pamela, though his ambivalence about his subject-matter is still clear from his mischievous lines scribbled opposite this poem in his notebook:

> If God is praised in poem one
> Show no surprise when in the next
> I worship wood or sun or none:
> I'm hundred-heavened   rainbow sexed
>   and countless

He looked again at the growing foetus in 'From love's first fever', adding a sequel which explored another Thomas theme, the formative power of language:

> I learnt man's tongue, to twist the shapes of thoughts
> Into the stony idiom of the brain...
> I learnt the verbs of will, and had my secret;
> The code of night tapped on my tongue;
> What had been one was many sounding minded.

This poem, with its lines:

> The nervous hand rehearsing on the thigh
> Acts with a woman

suggested (as did 'My hero bares his nerves along my wrist' the previous month) that Dylan used masturbation both as a physical release and as a means of getting to understand his body. His frustration at finding no other outlet for his sexual drive intensified his late teenager's sense of the physicality not only of life but also of looming death – as he was determined to show, in homage to his favourite metaphysical poets. 'Here lie the beasts of man', written in Llangain in October was one of several stabs at writing in the style of John Donne about a dead body lying in the earth: 'And silently I milk the buried flowers.' His best portrayal of that physicality was 'The force that through the green fuse drives the flower' with its dark lines, marrying Gothic and metaphysical, and ending:

> And I am dumb to tell the timeless sun
> How time has ticked a heaven round the stars.

> And I am dumb to tell the lover's tomb
> How at my sheet goes the same crookèd worm.

One of the work-sheets for this poem suggests that, despite his Anglophone upbringing, Dylan did know, and use, some Welsh. Under-neath the line 'How time has ticked a heaven round the stars', he has written 'am/sêr np 339 round stars'. This shows Dylan playing with puns in Welsh. 'Amser' is the Welsh word for 'time'. It comprises two other Welsh words, 'am' meaning 'round' and 'sêr' or 'stars'. The obscure 'np 339' refers to page 339 of the two-volume 1925 edition of Spurrell's Welsh–English Dictionary, which gives the definition 'sêr np stars', 'np' being an abbreviation for 'noun plural'.

Such poems provided the backdrop to Dylan's exchange of ideas with Pamela over the autumn. His love of words spilled out: whatever language they came from, they were the centrepiece of his trade. There was only ever one word to use in any given context, he told Pamela uncompromisingly. When he wanted to, he could work extremely hard: in his search for the mot juste, he made long lists of words and rhymes, from which he would choose for his poems, often re-writing his entire text several times to accommodate his changes. As a result he only completed two lines of verse an hour. A throwback to his schooldays, he seemed to understand things better if he saw them in front of him in black and white. Later, as a performer, not only would he copy out the text of poems he intended to read (so that he could fully understand the author's intentions), but he would make dozens of fair copies of his own work. (Harvard University has 166 worksheets showing the progress of his much later 'Prologue'.) At this stage, his favourite word was 'drome' (it 'nearly opens the doors of heaven for me'), while a range of homophones – bone, dome, doom, province, dwell, prove, dolomite – also excited him. 'God moves in a long "o",' he commented.

Attention to detail did not mean stinting on creativity, he argued. Part of a poet's job was to take well-worn words and give them new life. A political agenda prevented this because it called for a premeditated opinion. For Dylan, poetry only brooked one limitation – form. It was vital that 'form should never be superimposed; the structure should rise out of the words and the expression of them. I do not want to express only what other people have felt; I want to rip something away and show what they have never seen.' (He could have been quoting directly from the famous Imagist manifesto of 1915, written by Amy Lowell and Richard Aldington.) Rhythm was also one of his craftsman's tools - as essential to poetry as to music. However rhyme as such was not so important. It was an area where he liked to experiment, noting his use of consonantal and half-rhymes in his poem 'The force that through the green fuse drives the flower'.

In the face of Pamela's objections to the 'ugliness' in some of his poems, he defended his 'physical' imagery, arguing that the body was a fact of life, as much as death and disease. More fancifully, he claimed the body was like a tree, with roots in the same earth as a tree. In this he was only reiterating John Donne, from whose meditations on having typhus, *Devotions upon Emergent Occasions*, he freely paraphrased a passage, 'How little of the world is the earth! And yet that is all that man hath or is!' adding his own gloss: 'All thoughts and actions emanate from the body' and have a physical dimension. Thus, 'every idea, intuitive or intellectual can be imaged and translated in terms of the body, its flesh, skin, blood, sinews, veins, glands, organs, cells, or senses'.

Donne had first used the phrase 'No man is an island' in his *Devotions*. Appropriately, Dylan continued his lecture to Pamela: 'Through my small, bonebound island I have learnt all I know, experienced all, and sensed all. All I write is inseparable from the island. As much as possible, therefore, I employ the scenery of the island to describe the earthquakes of the heart.' However Dylan was never too immersed in theorising to see the humour of any situation: in this case, the image of himself – 'naked-nerved and blood-timid' – banging on about the brutality and horror of existence. He suggested that this was on a par with the weak Nietzsche praising life's strength or the complex-ridden D. H. Lawrence emphasising its wholesomeness.

When Pamela trumpeted the virtues of simplicity, he agreed that things should be said as simply as possible. But that did not mean that they had to be simple for the sake of it. Just because he liked Mozart did not mean he should abjure the 'bewildering obscurity' of later Scriabin, a favourite of Dan's. 'It is the simplicity of the human mind that believes the universal mind to be as simple.' Sometimes a degree of obscurity was necessary to convey the full extent of something's beauty which, according to one of his instant definitions, was the 'sense of unity in diversity'.

The sort of thing she liked was his 'dream' poem, 'The eye of sleep', written on 5 October, a conventional account of a nocturnal reverie, with wonderful lines, such as:

I fled the earth, and, naked, climbed the weather

But he told her that, only on the most superficial level, could this be described as visionary. He preferred 'Before I knocked', from the previous month, which had more of what he considered important in his poetry.

His comments on her poetry – sometimes gentle, sometimes waspish – were revealing about his own efforts. She had a 'tremendous passion for words', he granted, and a good grasp of form. Her poems generally tried to create rather than, as was the curse of most modern poets, to record 'none too clearly' the chaos of the contemporary world. But he was not afraid to criticise. ('A physical pacifist and a mental militarist, I can't resist having a knock,' he commented.) His main grouse was that she lacked ambition and 'soul'. Her phrases, such as 'Mother-of-pearl into pallid primrose', were 'too easily pretty'. In another poem her words 'unquiet mouse' were meaningless: the adjective (particularly as it was a negative one) failed to add to what was known about the mouse. A proper poetical adjective should either embrace all the associations of the noun it is qualifying (so in the case of a mouse it might incorporate fear, colour and texture) or else it should break down all associations, thus making the mouse something 'new'.

As for her finished product, he commented on her poem 'February' that she should look beyond the mere evidence of her eyes. 'Unless the spirit illuminates what the eyes have mirrored, then all the paraphernalia of the winter scene is as valueless as an Academy picture of Balmoral Castle.' Generally speaking, her output showed her to be like the little girl with the curl over her forehead: 'when you are good, you are very, very good, and when you are bad, you are horrid.' He urged her to look inside herself for subject matter: 'There is too much doing in life, and not enough being ... Man is preoccupied with action, never believing Blake's "Thought is Action." ' Her problem was misplaced romanticism when she should have been 'attempting a far higher thing – the creation of a personal poetry, born out of Battersea, Mrs Johnson, and wide and haphazard reading'.

Although he could be patronising, referring to one of her poems as 'sweet girlish drivel', his tone tended to be amusing, rather than didactic, as in the gentle fun he poked at Pamela for her fondness for traditional English expressions of the arts – from the music of the Promenade concerts to the poetry of Kipling, one of his bêtes noires, and Wordsworth ('a human nannygoat with a pantheistic obsession'). Dylan described Wordsworth as platitudinous and boring, without 'a spark of mysticism in him', and wanted him drowned along with Matthew Arnold, another Englishman he detested. Additional hate figures included Sir Edward Elgar, who had 'inflicted more pedantic wind & blather upon a supine public than any man who has ever lived', and, less predictably, Geoffrey Grigson, partly because Dylan recoiled from intellectuals who appeared to be smarter than himself (he feared the gaps in his learning), and partly because Grigson's New Verse promoted what Trick called the 'public school Pinks', poets such as Auden and Spender, whose political agenda Dylan was convinced ran counter to the stuff of great poetry.

Despite Dylan's epistolary lectures, there was no doubt which of the two correspondents was having the greater fun and success. That autumn Dylan thought he might revive the Prose and Verse magazine he had discussed a couple of years earlier with Percy Smart and Trevor Hughes. He intended it to fill a much-needed gap as a forum for Welsh writing in English. However Trick's support failed to materialise and Dylan went off the idea. He was left knocking on the doors of London editors who could not make up their minds about this unusual prodigy from west of the river Severn. Sir Richard Rees requested more work, though tempered his enthusiasm by saying Dylan's poems had an 'insubstantiality, a dreamlike quality' which disconcerted him and reminded him of automatic writing. He did at least agree to send them to Herbert Read who, in his role as a poet, straddled modernism and surrealism, and who in turn passed them on to his friend, T. S. Eliot. Since Dylan had a high regard for 'Pope' Eliot, this was at least encouraging.

Meanwhile Pamela had been making new friends at the 'creative arts circle' which Victor Neuburg held at the St John's Wood house he shared when in London with his exotic sounding mistress, Runia Tharp. This way Pamela met (and sat for) Reuben Mednikoff, an artist of Russian Jewish extraction, later better known for his 'automatic' paintings. Another acquaintance was David Gascoyne, a young poet (younger even than Dylan) who had recently burst onto the London scene with his excursions into literary surrealism.

Pamela kept Dylan amused (and a little jealous) with stories about these affected gatherings, presided over by the bird-like 'Vicky' in the company of the formidable Mrs Tharp. Born Winifred Simpson, the daughter of a senior police officer in India, she had studied at both Cambridge University, where as a woman had been unable to take a degree, and at the Slade School of Art. At the latter institution, she had left her first husband Leslie Bellin-Carter, art master at Eton and later

Wellington, and married Charles Tharp, a fellow student who became a prominent portrait painter. According to Arthur Calder Marshall, she spoke of Shaw, Wells, Havelock Ellis, Freud, Marx and D. H. Lawrence in the same breath. Marriage did not feature in her progressive view of the world, so, when she tired of Tharp, she left her family and turned to Vicky with whom, she told Calder Marshall, she was 'Trying the Modern Experiment'.

Dylan found Pamela's descriptions hilarious. He already had a low opinion of the quality of contributions to Poets' Comer, which he described as the sort of thing to be expected from 'agèd virgin(s)'. He claimed he had muttered the magic names 'Runia Tharp' so often that it was 'enough to Runia'. Resorting to satire, he warned Pamela of Mrs Murgatroyd Martin who would tell her of Pater and Pankhurst and the joys of morris dancing and poetry teas. As for Gascoyne, he was 'raving mad', with 'more maggots in his brain' than Dylan himself.

That did not stop Dylan sending Neuburg another poem, 'The force that through the green fuse drives the flower', which was published in the Sunday Referee's Poets' Corner on 29 October, a couple of days after his nineteenth birthday. The same issue brought even more exciting news for Pamela. Despite never having written more than thirty proper poems in her life (or so she told Dylan), she won an award for submitting the paper's best work over the past six months. Her prize was the opportunity to have a book of her poems published under the auspices of the Sunday Referee. Although the project dwindled in concept (a book designated for the Victor Gollancz imprint was later self-published), Pamela was plunged into a round of parties, including one given in her honour by Neuburg and Runia Tharp.

Back in Wales, he was having trouble sleeping. One night, he walked what he claimed were three miles (more like one mile) from Blaencwm into Llanstephan to buy some cigarettes. The combination of insomnia and the countryside had a strange effect. Looking up at the vast starry sky, he felt, 'It was as if the night were crying, crying out the terrible explanation of itself. On all sides of me, under my feet, above my head, the symbols moved, all waiting in vain to be translated. The trees that night were like prophets' fingers.' Although out of love with this part of Carmarthenshire, he still found it stimulating enough to want to convey its elemental qualities in a series of short stories, one of which, 'Uncommon Genesis' (later known as 'The Mouse and the Woman'), he was trying to finish in November.

Home in Cwmdonkin Drive, his wakefulness did at least allow him to turn over passages of poetry in his mind. Sometimes he would lie in a bath, smoking a Woodbine, and chanting aloud every poem that interested him. 'The neighbours must know your poems by heart,' he told Pamela; 'they certainly know my own, and bound to be acquainted with many passages of Macbeth, Death's Jester, and the Prophetic Books. I often think that baths were built for drowsy poets to lie in and there intone aloud amid the steam and boiling ripples.' (Death's Jester was actually Death's Jest-Book, the Elizabethan-style play written in the nineteenth century by Thomas Beddoes, whom Dylan referred to as 'my great Beddoes'.)

After a hot summer, the weather had turned very cold and, when he worked, he huddled round a stove in his back upstairs room, where the wall was hung with his occasional dabblings in paint. These showed pictorial evidence of his current obsessions – a large religio-surrealist pastel which he described as the 'Two Brothers of Death' – a syphilitic Christ and green-bearded Moses, both the colour of figs and both perched on a horizontal ladder of moons.

If he had nothing else to do, he would escape to the mists and heather of Gower, which he told Pamela, while promising to take her there one day, was 'as beautiful as anywhere'. Sometimes he walked beyond Newton to Caswell where the Tricks had their bungalow or he went on to Kittle where the beer and sandwiches in the Beaufort Arms were a draw. Near to this pub was an old limestone quarry whose deathly connotations loom in his poem 'See, says the lime, my wicked milks/I put round ribs that packed their heart' and in his famous 'The force that through the green fuse drives the flower' with it bleak lines

> And I am dumb to tell the hanging man
> How of my clay is made the hangman's lime.

At other times he took the bus to Rhossili, the furthest point on the peninsula. The four mile arc of the bay – the 'wildest, bleakest, barrennest' bay he knew – always appealed to him. In his lugubrious state he would make for the Worm, a desolate headland set a little off the shore. He liked the way the grass on the rock made a special sucking noise under his feet and gave off an odour like rabbits' fur after rain' – 'the most grisly smell in the world'. On this 'very promontory of depression', with seagulls swirling overhead and rats scurrying around him, he would read and write, imagining himself in a scene from Edgar Allen Poe. Once while reading, he fell asleep and the tide came in, trapping him from the shore. He was forced to stay on the Worm from dusk to midnight, with the rats increasingly menacing. After the water receded, he had an eighteen-mile walk home – an experience similar to that he recorded in 'Who Do You Wish Was With Us?' (In the story, his companion Raymond Price was based on Trevor Hughes, whose mourning for his dead brother provided the context for the question in the title.)

By contrast with Gower, Swansea was 'a dingy hell, and my mother a vulgar humbug', Dylan told Pamela. His father's illness did not help: D.J. was at home, apparently cured (though he did need further treatment), but 'exceedingly despondent'. Dylan's spirits were kept up by further commitment for the Little Theatre, a production of Rodney Ackland's *Strange Orchestra*, and rehearsals for William Congreve's *Way of the World*, which was being taken on a tour of nearby mining villages. Dylan complained about being cast in the effeminate role of Sir Wilfull Witwoud in the latter, an observation which led him to fulminate against the increasing openness of homosexuals. Having recently seen a girlish boy cavorting with a drunken black man, he claimed that this was the only vice that revolted him; even incest was preferable. His attitudes reflected a Welsh provincial upbringing, perhaps even alluding unconsciously to an incestuous dimension to his relationship with Nancy. When he left for London, he became more relaxed about homosexuals, who featured among his drinking companions, though he never entirely gave up his prejudice.

On 11 November he managed to sleep for the first time in a month. Since it was Armistice Day, he sounded off to Pamela about the Great War and the iniquity of the 'legion of old buffers' and of the armaments industry behind it. Using his favoured terminology of the moment, he ranted, 'What was Christ in us was stuck with a bayonet to the sky, and what was Judas we sheltered, rewarding, at the end, with thirty hanks of flesh. Civilisation is a murderer.' Donning a politicised hat he normally eschewed, he claimed that Revolution was the only solution to an outgrown and decaying system. 'The day will come when the old Dis-Order changeth,' he promised. Despite his attacks on capitalism, however, his rhetoric would not have gone down well in Marxist circles, for it was dominated by a fuzzy anarchistic individualism that maintained, 'Everything is wrong that forbids the freedom of the individual.' And included among his list of 'committees of prohibitors' were governments, newspapers, churches ('because they standardize our gods') and even poets when they look at the past rather than 'the huge, electric promise of the future'.

This harangue reflected part of his complex Trick-influenced view of the world. Dylan viscerally loathed any bullying force that snuffed out God-given sparks of goodness, light and individuality. But occasionally he indulged in Welsh hwyl. In this case, his real feelings were masked by the provincial boy waving evidence of his political virility before his London girlfriend.

By the year's end a meeting with Pamela was imminent. Dylan told her there was nothing – not even 'the personal delivery of Miss Garbo in a tin box' – he would have liked better than to spend the holiday season with her. But his father remained unwell, and was due back at the London hospital in early January. So Dylan was condemned to Christmas with his family, a group supplemented by Nancy, Haydn and Uncle Arthur. It was not a prospect that filled him with pleasure. 'Great fun will be had by all,' he told Pamela. 'Will it, hell! We'll eat too much, I suppose, read the newspapers, sleep, and crack nuts. There will be no Yuletide festivity about it.' It was very different from the warm, busy image summoned by his later, sentimentalised story 'A Child's Christmas in Wales'.

His bleak mood was reflected in a short poem, 'This bread I break' that he wrote on Christmas Eve. This was one of his verses about transformation – about man turning the oat and the grape into bread and wine. But a twist of perspective changed these staples into the flesh and blood of Christ, a reading that became clearer in a draft which had the last line as 'God's bread you break, you drain His cup', and in a title Dylan gave this draft, 'Breakfast before execution'.

Despite the cold gloomy weather, the festivities passed agreeably enough. After lunch, washed down with cheap port, Dylan settled down in mellow mood to read the book he had been given by one of his uncles, a complete volume of William Blake, including his letters. He received several other good presents, including a cigarette case from Haydn, a smart black hat from his mother (who had tired of his increasingly floppy trilby), and a number of additional books, including the Koran from Tom Warner and an anthology of *Recent Poetry* 1923–1933 (containing contributions from both Pamela and David Gascoyne) from Bert Trick.

Indicative of his personal inclinations at the time, Dylan gave himself a couple of pamphlets by James Joyce. Disappointingly, Pamela's present was fifty Player's cigarettes (which did not go far – he was a forty a day man), but this was her thoughtful response to his complaints about having to roll his own with Sailors' Plug Tobacco. His gift to her was a volume of poems by Robert Graves, one of the 'heroes' of his Grammar School magazine article on 'Modern Poetry' who had 'built towers of beauty upon the ashes of their lives'. At some stage (the date is unclear), he even wrote to Graves. Dylan's original letter is lost, but Graves, no great enthusiast for Thomas's subsequent output, recalled much later, 'I wrote back that they were irreproachable, but that he would eventually learn to dislike them ... Even experts would have been deceived by the virtuosity of Dylan Thomas's conventional, and wholly artificial, early poems.'

EIGHT
THE RUB OF LOVE

'No, I don't really spit in the piano,' Dylan assured Pamela about his impending visit to London. 'So there'll be no need to nail the top down.' He often indulged in ironic self-mockery about his humble Welsh origins, though usually interwove it with more than a hint of braggadocio. So he made no such pledges about not singing lewd roundelays. This was a party piece and he promised that, unless he turned shy and locked himself in the lavatory, he would indulge it. His only domestic vice, he confessed, again with evasive humour, was sprinkling cigarette ash.

His new year resolutions for 1934 repeated the sort of expansive views about poetry and the universe he had been developing over previous months. 'I want to imagine a new colour, so much whiter than white that white is black.' And he had a novel prescription for achieving this goal. He felt man's lack of vision derived from his rigid upright stance. He would be much wiser if he adopted a different perspective, lying on his back to view the sky and on his stomach to see the earth.

Dylan was preparing himself for the most important year of his career. Despite this waffle, he was still determined to break new ground, both as a poet and as a man. But he was plagued by a dilemma. On the one hand he could never quite shrug off his sense of his own ridiculousness; for all his fine words, he remained 'a short, ambiguous person in a runcible hat, feeling very lost in a big and magic universe'. (This was both his weakness and his strength, certainly a large part of his charm.) On the other hand he struggled manfully to understand and portray the world in his own terms. His best poetry brought an openness to technical innovation together with a personal, if unpredictable, quest for universal truth.

Since Nancy was able to come home and look after D.J., Dylan was finally free to go to London to meet Pamela in late February. He telephoned her three days in advance to say he was coming. She was immediately impressed by his 'rich fruity old port wine of '06 voice'. When he first arrived at her mother's house in Battersea Rise one dull evening, he showed his nerves by asking, 'Have you seen the Gauguins?'

His obligations to metropolitan culture discharged (he had been practising the remark, which referred to a current London exhibition, all the
way from Swansea), he relaxed and she found him 'charming, very
young-looking' and – a feature often noted – with a 'most enchanting
voice'.

Although staying with Haydn in Laleham, he managed to spend a
long weekend with Pamela, her mother and aunt in Clapham. On that
occasion, he quickly polished off the quarter bottle of brandy he had
brought, before repairing to the off licence for a more favoured tipple,
beer. While they both chatted and played records (he particularly liked
a syncopated old 78 'The Beat of my Heart', by the American bandleader
Ben Pollack), Pamela gained the correct impresssion that, although well
informed about poetry, he knew rather less about novels, music or art.
Despite being tied up with rehearsals for a revue she had written, she
introduced him to friends, including Victor Neuburg and Runia Tharp,
whom he bewitched with his 'glorious hokum', and took him to Sean
O'Casey's lacklustre new play *Within the Gates*. The only moment of
concern came before breakfast one cold foggy morning when Dylan
wanted to go out for cigarettes. He was still in his pyjamas, over which
he had draped a vast blue and violet dressing gown once owned by
Pamela's uncle, and on top of his head was his new black felt hat, his
mother's gift at Christmas.

In between times Dylan made the rounds of publishers' and editors'
offices where, as he had no regular source of income, he was as
interested in finding a regular job as in selling his recent work. No
employment ensued, though his poems and stories created interest and,
within a short time, had been printed in the *Adelphi*, *The Listener* and *New
English Weekly*. He left Pamela happily typing up 'The Tree', one of his
mystical stories about the Welsh countryside, for the *Adelphi*. Within a
couple of days of returning to Swansea, he wrote to say he loved her,
which threw her into happy confusion.

The publication of his haunting 'Light breaks where no sun shines'
in *The Listener* on 14 March proved a turning point. It brought welcome
letters of encouragement from Stephen Spender, Geoffrey Grigson and
T. S. Eliot. The magazine had to fend off correspondents who objected
to the supposed obscenity in lines such as:

> Nor fenced, nor staked, the gushers of the sky
> Spout to the rod
> Divining in a smile the oil of tears.

Dylan claimed disingenuously that this was a metaphysical image of rain and grief. But he was smart enough to realise that a degree of controversy would not hurt his cause. And he thought it worthwhile to visit London again at the end of March.

He made another circuit of editors, among them Janet Adam Smith, young assistant editor responsible for the poetry pages of The Listener. A product of Cheltenham Ladies' College and Somerville College, Oxford, she invited him to tea in her flat, where he met her fiancé Michael Roberts, a robust poet and Auden propagandist earning a living as a mathematics teacher, and Desmond Hawkins, another young man making his way on the London literary scene. Hawkins got the mood of the occasion right: 'The tea-party, for all its friendliness, was inevitably intimidating as a kind of initiation ceremony.' But the cucumber sandwiches brought the expected results: over the next couple of years both Adam Smith and Roberts were to include Dylan's work in influential poetry anthologies. They probably sparked in him the idea (never realised) of compiling an anthology of English-language poems and stories by modern Welsh writers.

Dylan now found himself actively wooed by Victor Neuburg who, after printing three more of his poems, made him the second winner (after Pamela) of the Poets' Corner prize, again with the promise of publication of a poetry collection. Pamela recognised the shrewd 'Vicky' had found a new star to succeed her.

In Clapham, Dylan played the dutiful suitor, inviting both Pamela and her mother to the Cock pub on the Common. Although abstemious by his own standards, he shocked Pamela by drinking too much. She noted how he knocked back his alcohol in a manner he thought expected of a poet. But she did not care; she was now infatuated, her diary full of references to 'darling Dylan'. 'I find I have to keep his name on every page' she wrote on 20 April. She was even happy to meet his father who was up in town for a medical check-up.

After his extraordinary output the previous year, Dylan was less prolific in the first few months of 1934. Nevertheless he produced a handful of fine poems. Among them were 'A process in the weather of the heart', whose oblique viewpoint successfully pulled it back from parody of his usual 'death implicit in life' subject-matter, and 'Where once the waters of your face', which explored the experience of the womb through increasingly favoured images of the sea, which had the same eternally nurturing and destructive powers as the weather in the other, slightly earlier poem (both of which were published in the Sunday Referee).

Then in April, after returning to Swansea from his second visit to Pamela, he wrote two of his greatest poems. 'I see the boys of summer' arose from looking out from Cwmdonkin Drive in what must have been a fairly depressed mood. 'I wish I could see these passing men and women in the sun as the motes of virtues,' he explained to his girlfriend in London; 'this little fellow as a sunny Fidelity, this corsetted hank as Mother-Love, this abusing lout as the Spirit of Youth, and this eminently beatable child in what was once a party frock as the walking embodiment of Innocence. But I can't. The passers are dreadful. I see all their little horrors.' Looking on as one of the 'dark deniers' who, in his verses 'summon/Death from a summer woman', his tripping poem captures the fateful sense of tragedy and decay discernible in even the happiest of youths (whose careless state is suggested in simple metaphors of 'gold', 'apples' and 'honey'). Dylan's genius is to overlay his central concept of life's inevitable progression with a sense that this leads to the necessary overhaul or even overthrow of one generation by the next – a throw-back to his heart-felt if unsophisticated political rantings the previous year.

> But seasons must be challenged or they totter
> Into a chiming quarter
> Where, punctual as death we ring the stars.

This was Dylan showing that his poetry did not have to be overtly political (in an Auden sense). He had his own way of invoking change, whether it was seasonal, personal, cultural or political.

At the end of the month he concluded his fourth notebook with 'If I was tickled by the rub of love', which, reflecting his unconsummated affair with Pamela, manages to be both physically suggestive and puritanical, railing against sex for failing to overcome death ('The words of death are dryer than his stiff'). Despite a sense of the futility of life (indicated in 'And what's the rub?' with its *Hamlet* associations) and an underlying imagery of masturbation (the 'rub of love'), set within a familiar geography of the womb, Dylan finds solace in the mere act of being human. And so his positive last line, 'Man be my metaphor' which encapsulates his concept of his body being the centre of his universe. Dylan told Pamela that, despite its faults, this was the best poem he had written. He implied it would take its place in the *Sunday Referee*'s promised book of his poems. Indeed he had already determined that 'I see the boys of summer in their ruin' should be the first poem in that volume.

Despite the patronage of the *Sunday Referee*, he refused to be typecast. When Neuburg described him as an experimentalist in a blurb accompanying the announcement of Dylan's prize, Dylan claimed not to recognise himself. He protested too much, but indicated his cussedness, when he asked Pamela to tell the editor, 'I am not modest, not experimental, do not write of the Present, and have very little command of rhythm ... I don't know anything about life-rhythm. Tell him I write of worms & corruption. Tell him I believe in the fundamental wickedness and worthlessness of man, & in the rot in life. Tell him I am all for cancers. And tell him, too, that I loathe poetry. I'd prefer to be an anatomist or the keeper of a morgue any day ... And I don't like words either.'

The publication of 'The Woman Speaks', a Donne-like poetic fragment from a play, in *Adelphi* in March brought a letter of appreciation from Glyn Jones, a Cardiff schoolmaster with roots in the mining valleys. No matter that – strangely for a Welshman – Jones had been bamboozled by the poet's first name and imagined he might be addressing a woman (even stranger when the verses were more gory than Dylan's usual cerebral evocations of death). The two men immediately hit it off. Dylan was delighted to find someone with similar professional interests, aspirations and sometimes style. Jones had family links in the Llanstephan peninsula and a keen sense of the London literary market. (He too had appeared in *Adelphi*.) In general he was a more reliable sounding board for discussions on writing than the lacklustre Trevor Hughes.

Dylan tried to explain to Jones what he was trying to do. Although he claimed to be a Socialist (and presumed Jones was the same), he dismissed the recent poems of Auden or Day-Lewis because they were neither good propaganda nor good poetry. ('The emotional appeal in Auden wouldn't raise a corresponding emotion in a tick,' he said damningly.) His own ambitions were set higher. He was not worried about being obscure, taking his cue from Eliot's dictum that meaning could be subordinate to overall effect: it was a trick to 'satisfy one habit of the reader, to keep his mind diverted and quiet, while the poem does its work upon him'. Most modern writers evolved their own types of obscurity, from Gertrude Stein and the French-Americans around the Paris magazine *transition* who had tried, mathematically, to strip words of their associations and bring them back to their literal sound, to the heavily culturally laden outpourings of Eliot which required, he joked, an intimate knowledge of Sanskrit weather reports. His own obscurity he described succinctly as based on the cosmic significance of the human anatomy.

Since he was again wrestling with his stories-cum-novel about Carmarthenshire (or Jarvis valley) life, and they both had local ties, Dylan and Jones agreed to meet over Whitsun on their ancestral Carmarthenshire turf in Llanstephan at the mouth of the river Tywi. From there, they would walk over the great headland called Parc yr

Arglwydd (the Lord's Park) and take the ferry across the Taf estuary to Laugharne. Dylan immediately fell in love with what he called the 'strangest town in Wales' – an enclave of Norman England, with an ancient charter, unique borough privileges and a castle, where Richard Hughes, author of the 1929 bestselling novel *A High Wind in Jamaica*, lived. He found Jones rather prim and disapproving of his habit of drinking pints of Guinness at lunch. But Laugharne itself was remarkable, with its cockle-pickers, cormorants, sea-carved rocks and lowering skies. 'I wish I could describe what I am looking on,' he told Pamela. 'But no words could tell you what a *hopeless* fallen angel of a day it is ... I can never do justice ... to the miles and miles and miles of mud and grey sand, to the un-nerving silence of the fisherwomen, & the mean-souled cries of the gulls and the herons ...' Just over four years later he would be married and living there, and would indeed do justice to the unique qualities of the place. Brown's, the pub he enjoyed, would become his regular, and later he would live at the Boat House, next door to the ferryhouse, home of Jack Roberts who had rowed him across the Taf. While lying in a field of buttercups on this first visit, examining an army of scarlet ants playing over his hand, he had picked up a sheep's jawbone and written of death. It was all so 'incorrigibly romantic', he trilled, as if putting into action his new year resolution about seeing things from different perspectives.

At Laugharne he sounded relaxed. But this was illusory. Pamela had been urging him to see a doctor about his health, but he could not bring himself to make an appointment. He was still drinking heavily and sleeping badly. On his way back to Swansea, he stopped in Gower where he stayed with an old reporter friend called Cliff. The first night he was there, Cliff's fiancée joined them. She was 'tall & thin and dark with a loose red mouth & a harsh sort of laugh'. Dylan claimed that, after a heavy session at the pub, she started making passes at him. When they went to bed, she refused to sleep with Cliff and came to join Dylan. He later told Pamela apologetically that he had slept with this girl over the next three nights. He added that he did not know why, because he loved her, Pamela. He implied it must have something to do with his drinking, for he was 'on the borders of DTs' (delirium tremens). And he begged her forgiveness. Doubts have been raised about whether this incident took place as he said, or even happened at all. Was he trying to put Pamela off? Or did he want to suggest his worldliness and sophistication? Clearly he was in a depressed state made worse by alcoholic poisoning. Pamela was devastated to receive his letter telling her about this incident, and resolved, reluctantly, to have no more to do with him.

A fortnight later, in mid-June, she had given him another chance and Dylan was back in London, asking her to marry him. She decided to keep him waiting. So Dylan shuffled between her house and Trevor Hughes's in Rayners Lane, visiting editors such as Richard Rees and finding himself an agent – David Higham at the established firm, Curtis Brown – who had only limited confidence in the marketability of Dylan's poetry, suggesting that his ongoing novel about the Jarvis valley would be a better proposal to try to sell.

Dylan himself was hardly bullish about the putative book, which he described – not inaccurately – as the 'hotch-potch of a strayed poet, or the linking together of several short story sequences', and he feared he might soon have to scrap it. A week later the book had progressed slightly: it had a name – *A Doom on the Sun* – and had become 'a kind of warped fable in which Lust, Greed, Cruelty, Spite etc., appear all the time as old gentlemen in the background of the story'. He described a scene in which Mr Stipe, Mr Edger, Mr Stull, Mr Thade and Mr Strich watch a dog dying of poison. By the end of the month, progress remained slow, but the project was 'as ambitious as the *Divine Comedy*, with a chorus of deadly sins, anagrammatised as old gentlemen' and a host of other characters including 'a bald-headed girl, a celestial tramp, a mock Christ, & the Holy Ghost'. These old gentlemen appeared, with the letters of their names rearranged, in Dylan's story 'The Holy Six', which also referred to Llareggub, leading back to 'The Orchards' which was originally known as 'Anagram'. It was clear now that Dylan's stories were parts of a novel in which word-play featured. But these alphabetical constructions had no role but to amuse their author as symbols of the world's topsy-turvy nature.

There was at least a new mercenariness to Dylan's approach. Only recently he had told Pamela that novels were the best way for a writer to earn a living. By comparison, short stories did not pay and 'poetry would not keep a goldfinch alive'. One reason for such thinking was, so he claimed, that his father was retiring from Swansea Grammar School at the end of the summer term, and 'after that I face the bitter world alone', inferring that, even now, he received some form of parental allowance. (In fact D.J. did not leave his job for another three years.) Dylan had considered working in the docks or a provincial repertory company. He had thought seriously about asking Lady Rhondda, daughter of the former D. A. Thomas, one of the richest colliery-owners and industrialists in South Wales, for a job on her right-wing journal *Time and Tide*. But, determined to make his way with his pen, he had forced himself to turn down trips to the Mediterranean and, bizarrely, to the Soviet Union with a Welsh Communist organisation. 'It's all useless', he said, rather sensibly, 'for, when I came back, I'd be just where I was before I went away – a little less pale perhaps, but as green as ever as to what I must do in this dull, grey country.'

Back in Swansea, John Jennings, a member of Trick's evening discussion group, had been hired to edit the *Swansea and West Wales Guardian*, a new weekly Swansea edition of an established Pembrokeshire newspaper with a radical agenda. During the summer he had been campaigning strongly against the entrenchment of the right wing in Swansea politics, where an influential councillor, a coal merchant called W. T. Mainwaring Hughes had switched from Tory imperialism to Mosley's British Union of Fascists. When Hughes arranged for Mosley to hold a rally in the town, a group of anti-fascists, including Trick, friends in the Socialist League (a Marxist splinter group from the unenterprising, bureaucratic local Labour party), and members of Swansea's small Jewish community, tried to stop him. Dylan weighed in with a letter to the local *Guardian* which clearly had Mainwaring Hughes in mind as it fulminated against 'Christ-denying Christians, irrational Rationalists, and the white-spatted representatives of a social system that has, for too many years, used its bowler hat for the one purpose of keeping its ears apart'. (The paper gave it a large two-deck headline TELLING THE TRUTH TO THE PUBLIC / EXPOSE HUMBUG AND SMUG RESPECTABILITY.) Mainwaring Hughes retaliated that he could make 'neither head nor tail' of the letter: 'It is indeed too bad that Mr Dylan Thomas should have to stay in such a town, or for that matter, in such a country. What's the matter with Russia as the spiritual home of one who wants to "teach to hate and then to believe in the antithesis of what is hated", or Cefn Coed?' (This was the psychiatric hospital above Cwmdonkin Drive, which Dylan had referred to in his 1932 notebook poem 'Upon your held-out hand'. He told Hughes, 'It leers down the valley like a fool, or like a snail with the two turrets of its water towers two snails' horns' – an image he later appropriated for St Martin's Church in Laugharne in his 'Poem in October'.)

Trick and his colleagues failed in their efforts to ban the rally from going ahead in the Plaza cinema, the largest in Wales with 3,500 seats. Surrounded by Blackshirts and swastika regalia, Mosley unleashed a tirade against the Jews and their influence in society. When he said he would take written questions, the first out of the hat came from the Reverend Leon Atkin, who said he had worked for a Jew for a long time and wondered if he should change his employer. Mosley answered affirmatively, adding that he would be certain to find a more reliable Gentile. When Atkin rose to his feet in clerical garb, pandemonium broke out and the meeting had to be abandoned. Dylan claimed to

Pamela that he was thrown down the stairs, though there is no corroborating evidence. He added that he had left the Socialist party and joined the Communists, but again this seems to have been in his head. He did however follow up his earlier letter to the *Swansea and West Wales Guardian* with another which inveighed, even more forthrightly, against 'the obscene hypocrisy of those war-mongers and slave-drivers who venerate [Christ's] name and void their contagious rheum upon the first principle of His gospel'.

He tried to explain his political views to Pamela, but they were incoherent. In the same paragraph he could call for an intellectual, rather than a bloody, revolution, and also say that if constitutional government were unable to achieve this, property should be taken by force. What he really wanted was what he called 'Functional Anarchy', but this was an adolescent fantasy of freedom – of playing truant from his school-master father and avoiding any orders. Typically, at the same time as he was indulging this political pipe-dream he was preparing to visit Swansea's St Helen's ground to watch Glamorgan play a county cricket match. Throughout his life he loved to sit on the boundary of a cricket ground, drinking and chatting, with the sound of willow against leather in the distance. He even played the odd game himself, bowling thirty-four overs in one game in late July, conceding only sixty runs, and taking three wickets.

The first thing he did on his return to London in mid-August was accompany Pamela to a Promenade concert – either a very loving gesture or hugely hypocritical, given his roasting of her only a few months earlier for enjoying this musical institution. The focus of their social activity now shifted from the Cock in Clapham to the Six Bells across the river Thames in Chelsea where Dylan could be closer to his new literary friends. Despite his still very limited output, he had been approached by John Lehmann for some contribution for *The Year's Poetry*, another anthology, and by Geoffrey Grigson, who asked him (and several other poets) to answer a questionnaire about his writing.

His replies provided the latest update on his ideas about his craft. He stressed the hard work, both physical and mental: 'Poetry is the rhythmic, inevitably narrative, movement from an overclothed blindness to a naked vision that depends, in its intensity, on the labour put into the creation of the poetry.' His own output was the record of his 'individual struggle from darkness towards some measure of light'. He reiterated Eliot's observation about narrative, in the sense of meaning, satisfying one habit of the reader, adding his own gloss: 'Let the narrative take that one logical habit of the reader along with its movement, and the essence of the poem will do its work on him.' Asked if he had been influenced by Freud, he answered unconvincingly in the affirmative, for reasons roughly in keeping with his general thesis. Like Freud, he argued, his job as a poet was to expose what was hidden and to make clean. To another question about his politics, he waffled, 'I take my stand with any revolutionary body that asserts it to be the right of all men to share, equally and impartially, every production of man and from the sources of production at man's disposal, for only through such an essentially revolutionary body can there be the possibility of a communal art.'

On the last Sunday of the month, Dylan spent half the day with Pamela before departing on his own to have tea, which seems to have meant a long drinking session, with Grigson at his open house in Hampstead. He did not return until after one o'clock the next morning, which annoyed her. Grigson had a full-time job as literary editor of the *Morning Post*, the sale of review copies from which helped subsidise his own venture, *New Verse*. As a result, he had a wide circle of friends and acquaintances whom Dylan enjoyed meeting. Among them were Norman Cameron, who had been at Oxford with Grigson, and T. S. Eliot, though, initially at least, Eliot and Dylan did not hit it off. Dylan complained that Eliot treated him as 'as if I were "from pit-boy to poet"!'

Slight cracks in his relationship with Pamela were appearing. Despite having been introduced to Hughes (with whom she established a watch committee to prevent their mutual friend from drinking too much), she felt Dylan kept his friends apart. She found it 'wounding' if, when they were both strolling down the King's Road, he saw someone he knew, usually a poet, and, without asking her to join him, crossed the road for a chat. She was probably not fully aware of his worries about money. In Grigson, he thought he had found someone he could tap for occasional loans. This was the gist of a letter he penned to the *New Verse* editor the day after his 'tea' party – the first of many such plaintive requests for money he was to send to various potential patrons over the next two decades.

This did not mean he had given up on Pamela. Determined that she should meet his family, he invited her, a couple of weekends later, to Laleham, but she found his sister and brother-in-law obsessively conventional. She was happier when, at the end of the following week (Dylan's fifth in London), he went home to Wales and, since she was due some holiday, she accompanied him, taking her mother as chaperone.

The Hansford Johnsons stayed at the Mermaid hotel in the Mumbles, from where Pamela and Dylan made sorties into Gower (there are photographs of the young lovers cavorting in Caswell Bay) and to Cwmdonkin Drive for meals with the Thomases. Pamela thought D.J. charming, but, like her mother, found Florrie's interminable chatter wearying. (On this matter she had been warned by Dylan, but he did add that his mother was at least kind.) Any free moment Pamela worked on a novel, originally called Nursery Rhyme, but at Dylan's suggestion, renamed, more suggestively, This Bed Thy Centre (from John Donne's 'The Sun Rising'). She would probably have been better at home, because it rained a lot and there was nothing relaxing about the combination of her work and Dylan's moody behaviour. At one stage she collapsed from nervous exhaustion and had to consult a doctor in the Uplands.

Dylan was now thinking of moving permanently to London. Before leaving, he agreed to accompany Glyn Jones on a pilgrimage to Aberystwyth where they both wanted to see one of their favourite authors, Caradoc Evans, the 'best hated man in Wales'. Originally from near Llandysul, home of Dylan's great-uncle, Gwilym Marles, the Welsh-speaking Evans had grown up in Cardiganshire, where he had enraged the locals with his savage satires on chapel and peasant life. His recollections of making his way as a journalist in London, where his literary friends included fellow Welshman Arthur Machen, were particularly useful to Dylan at this stage.

Evans's wife, the prolific novelist Oliver Sandys (also known as Countess Barcynska from her first marriage) left a conventional account of Dylan's visit. Her maid announced the two young men: 'One of them is a poet, or says he is – hopes he is.' Dylan unravelled some typewritten notes and began reading his poems in his usual mellifluous voice. But both Dylan and Jones were more interested in talking to Evans about short stories than poetry. They made a tour of local pubs with their idol, 'drinking to the eternal damnation of the Almighty & the soon-to-be-hoped-for destruction of the tin Bethels'. Back at their hotel Jones told Dylan about Dr William Price, the eccentric Chartist who liked to stand naked on a South Wales hilltop, chanting Druidical rites. In 1883, when in his eighties, Price fathered an illegitimate son called Jesus Christ who died in infancy. Price burnt the infant's body, leading him to be charged with manslaughter. However he was acquitted, thus legitimising the rite and practice of cremation. Dylan was so fascinated that his cigarette burnt several holes in his sheet. However the details stuck, appearing as a central motif in his scandalous story 'The Burning Baby' which strayed deep into Caradoc Evans territory in its depiction of a preacher indulging in incest with his daughter. Dylan also drew on his Carmarthenshire experience in his detail of the girl's brother bringing a dead rabbit into his house. Showing how Dylan's ideas shuffled round his imagination, the story also included a sow-faced woman called Llareggub (again) who sexually initiated the girl's brother – the first published instance of the name of the town in Under Milk Wood.

Dylan's journey to Aberystwyth in October was the furthest he had ventured into rural Wales. Having enjoyed the experience, he wanted to repeat it, and the following year accepted a commission (which he did not fulfil) to write a travel book about his country. Contrary to popular misconception, Wales remained a focus for his literary endeavours. Still toying with his novel about the Jarvis valley, Dylan was influenced, so Glyn Jones recalled, by Caradoc Evans, T. F. Powys and Thomas Hardy and wanted to make South Wales like Hardy's Wessex.

Dylan's Celtic heritage is less obvious in his poetry. In May he had told a prospective editor that his poem 'I dreamed my genesis' was based on Welsh rhythms. But critics who argue Dylan's familiarity with Welsh prosodic devices such as the *cynghanedd*, with its strict syllable count and internal rhythms, are often disappointed. Dylan was promiscuous in his borrowings, and his use of Welsh metres were often mediated through English writers such as Gerard Manley Hopkins and Wilfred Owen. His attitude to Welsh (and Irish) verse is better described in one of the reviewing jobs he was beginning to pick up in London. He argued in *Adelphi* in September that 'the true future of English poetry, poetry that can be pronounced and read aloud, that comes to life out of the red heart through the brain, lies in the Celtic countries', with their tradition of ballads and folk-songs, and their intellectual and artistic traditions unburdened by the dictates of a numb university-educated elite. In other words, English verse needed an injection of Celtic energy.

However Dylan needed to earn a living and, as an English-speaker, that meant working in London, even if he intended to draw on his Celtic background. He was ambitious, as Glyn Jones realised on an early visit to Cwmdonkin Drive. Dylan had just returned from London and was telling his mother about eminent literary figures he had met – Eliot and so on. When she reminded him he had also encountered the humorist and later MP, A. P. Herbert, he spat out dismissively, 'Oh, he's nobody' – a curious comment, since Dylan enjoyed most people's company, but it was indicative of his desire to ingratiate himself with certain sections of the establishment.

That did not mean he had to be fawning. Reviewing in *New Verse* in December, he tore into Stephen Spender's extended epic 'Vienna', repeating his nostrums about poetry having to come before politics or any such other consideration, and suggesting that his fellow poet, who had encouraged him personally, had failed to make either good verse or good propaganda. Dylan called 'Vienna' 'a bad poem; the images are unoriginal singly, and ambiguous, often meaningless, collectively,' though he never made it clear if he understood much about the event

Spender was writing about – the bloody Dolfuss putsch in Vienna which left hundreds of workers dead. Bert Trick claimed that, in the same issue of *New Verse*, Dylan's 'My world is pyramid' contained his real attitude to events in Austria, particularly the stanza:

> My world is cypress, and an English valley.
> I piece my flesh that rattled on the yards
> Red in an Austrian volley.
> I hear, through dead men's drums, the riddled lads,
> Strewing their bowels from a hill of bones,
> Cry Eloi to the guns.

(This was the final version of the poem containing Trick's daughter's comment: 'What colour is glory?') The grocer may well have been right, and Dylan was giving an object lesson in the reality he had tried to convey to Glyn Jones earlier in the year: 'And as for the Workers! People have been trying to write to them for years. And they still don't give a damn. The trouble is that in attempting to write for the workers one generally writes down. The thing to do is to bring the workers up to what one is writing.'

Before leaving Swansea, he agreed to address a genteel literary club, known as the John O'London's Society, after the weekly magazine of that name. The society was run by a Mrs Bates from a room over her husband's ironmongery shop near Singleton Park. When a member, Leslie Mewis, told Mrs Bates he had met Dylan Thomas at Trick's, she insisted that the young poet, who was beginning to make a name for himself, should address the members. Against the advice of Trick, who sensed disaster, an invitation was despatched, and Dylan offered to talk on 'Obscenity in English Literature'. According to Mewis, Dylan initially kept to his thesis, arguing that the most obscene aspect of English literature was its triviality. But he got carried away by the prospect of shocking his mainly female audience (Dylan described them as middle-aged virgins), and launched into a tirade of filth and bad taste. In Dylan's account, having been introduced as a 'Young Revolutionary' he preached the Communist gospel of free love, ending his talk with the rallying cry, 'Let Copulation Thrive.' Mewis recalled that, as a bemused audience drifted away, Dylan could be heard swearing profusely.

Dylan enjoyed shocking in the manner of his new friend Caradoc Evans. 'The more I see of Wales,' he told Pamela, 'the more I think it's a land entirely peopled by perverts. I don't exclude myself, who obtain a high & soulful pleasure from telling women, old enough to be my mother, why they dream of two-headed warthogs in a field of semen.'

Poet, revolutionary or buffoon: there was no doubt what was the most important to Dylan. The final spur to his moving to London was his dissatisfaction with the way Neuburg was dealing with his collection of poems. As with Pamela's book, trade publishers had been mooted but failed to materialise. Dylan managed to retrieve his selection of twenty poems and send them to Eliot at Faber & Faber. Eliot's secretary sent an express letter to Cwmdonkin Drive, asking Dylan to do nothing until the great man had made up his mind. But Eliot delayed just long enough to allow Neuburg to find the resources and a publisher to bring out the book, as originally intended, under the auspices of the *Sunday Referee*.

Dylan had found someone to live with in London — Fred Janes, a mercurial occasional member of the Kardomah crowd who, having discovered abstract art in Cork Street galleries, had dropped out of his old-fashioned course at the Royal Academy Schools and was hoping to launch his professional career. Another Swansea painter, Dylan's child-hood friend Mervyn Levy, was at the more adventurous Royal College of Art. He lived at the top of a student hostel in 5 Redcliffe Street, where the lower reaches of Chelsea merge into Fulham. Dylan and Janes managed to rent one room, with a bathroom, on the floor beneath him.

In early November Janes's greengrocer father drove the two young men to the capital. Weighed down with an oversize suitcase, Dylan wore his trademark pork-pie hat and a vast check overcoat that blew like a marquee over his slight frame. From somewhere he and Janes acquired a couple of camp-beds, a table and a gas oven. By chance, only the previous week, the Hansford Johnsons had moved across the river from Clapham to a new flat in Chelsea. Since some of their furniture was in storage, Dylan asked Pamela if there was anything he could borrow. Still enraptured by 'darling Dylan', she provided an iron bedstead (which saw service as a wardrobe — tipped up, with a curtain covering its outward-facing castors), a few chairs (one of which became Janes's easel) and a dozen yellow dusters. Having helped the two Welshmen settle into this seedy room on 13 November, she was upset not to hear from Dylan for four days. He then sent 'an entirely fogged note' which convinced her he was no longer interested in their relationship. Janes and Trevor Hughes tried to reassure her that this was not so and that Dylan was ill. She went round to Redcliffe Street again, and found Dylan indeed in bed, and very bad-tempered. He had been drinking heavily (though this might not have been immediately obvious to Pamela): he admitted to Glyn Jones the following month that alcohol had become 'a little too close and heavy a friend for some time now' and, as a result, he had not been eating much.

He made life difficult for Pamela over the following month. The day after her visit, he had recovered enough to tell her that the reason for his lack of communication was that he wanted to marry her and was arranging to do so in three weeks. She was completing the final stages of her novel (fast work: she had only started in September). He offered to take it away to read, but did not return it, so she had to send her mother round to retrieve her text, which he despatched the following day, without a note. Only after she had handed her book in to her agent did he write – to say that drink had won, which, as she confided to her diary 'upset me plenty but surprised me little'.

The background to this shadow play was the forthcoming publication of Dylan's book, and his shrewd notion that, in order to promote it, he needed to be seen and recognised as a writer of verse. That meant continuing to seek out, drink with, and develop his poet's persona in the company of his literary peers. Having been spurred by Eliot's interest, Neuburg arranged for Dylan's poems to be published by the Parton Press which operated out of the back of a bookshop in Holborn.

Situated on the outer edges of the main publishing area of Bloomsbury, this was a centre for fringe literary activity. Close to where Harold and Hilda Monro's Poetry Bookshop had once been, two other local book-shops now operated as occasional publishers. One was the Blue Moon Bookshop, in Red Lion Street, between Holborn and Theobald's Road. It was owned by Charles Lahr, a resolute bearded anarchist of German Jewish origin, whose dabblings in publishing had brought him the friendship of D. H. Lawrence, as well as T. F. Powys and Rhys Davies. Dylan later became firm friends with several Blue Moon writers including Keidrych Rhys, Oswell Blakeston, Ruthven Todd and John Gawsworth.

The other was the Parton Bookshop, run by David Archer, the effete left-leaning scion of a Wiltshire landowner. Situated on the ground floor of number 2 Parton Street, a run-down Georgian alley (since built over by the Jeanetta Cochrane Theatre) between Southampton Row and Red Lion Square, this provided a refuge and often a bed for aspiring young writers, such as George Barker, David Gascoyne and Maurice Carpenter. In 1934 it also gave space to *Out of Bounds*, the revolutionary anti-public school movement headed by Winston Churchill's shabbily dressed nephew, Esmond Romilly.

Upstairs was the headquarters of the Promethean Society, founded four years earlier following an appeal, headed 'The Revolt of Youth', in the magazine *Everyman*, calling for opponents of 'the humbug and hypocrisy, the muddle and inertia that everywhere surrounds us today'.

Taking their cue from D. H. Lawrence, the Prometheans emphasised sexual as much as political revolution. They published another leftist literary magazine, *Twentieth Century*, where one of the assistants was Desmond Hawkins, the aspiring poet whom Dylan had met earlier in the year at Janet Adam Smith's.

The atmosphere in the Parton Bookshop was leisurely, idealistic and camp. The stock was interesting enough to attract regular customers such as Colonel T. E. Lawrence. However the shelves and even the pavement were strewn with copies of the *Daily Worker* and other left-wing journals. Archer (described by Barker as a cross between Proust's Robert de Saint-Loup and P. G. Wodehouse's Bertie Wooster) was totally unbusinesslike. He frequently shut up shop and walked across the road to Meg's Café, the social centre for aspiring artists and revolutionaries in the vicinity. His business partner was nominally his friend David Abercrombie, son of the Georgian poet Lascelles Abercrombie. (They had been to Russia together in 1931.) But in 1934 David Abercrombie started lecturing at the London School of Economics. His interest in the shop devolved on his brother Ralph who lived above Meg's Café with Roger Roughton, a languid teenage writer who later committed suicide in Dublin.

In discussing how Dylan came to be published by this uncommercial outfit, Runia Tharp told a Gothic tale about walking home with Neuburg one foggy evening and seeing an arc of light which drew them to the Parton Bookshop. Asked if Dylan Thomas had ever ventured there, Archer replied, distractedly, 'It is known to all *poets.*' However, ever generous in his literary patronage, he agreed to put up £20 to publish Dylan's collection, while Mark Goulden, editor of the *Sunday Referee*, promised a further £30.

Over the summer Dylan had been quietly casting through his four notebooks before deciding on what were now to be eighteen poems for his collection. From this material, mainly from the fourth notebook, he chose (and where necessary improved) twelve poems, plus one earlier one, and he wrote a further five between 'I dreamed my genesis' in May and 'When, like a running grave' in October. The resulting package remains exciting – a concentrated young man's attempt to refashion the lyrical, hierophantic traditions of his craft in the contemporary idiom of modern poetry. His Welshness played its part, providing not only a vitality but also an alternative vantage point from which to spy out his assault on the metropolitan cultural redoubt.

Personal contact was a natural part of his game plan. His circle of London literary friends, which had started with the old-fashioned Middleton Murry, Rees and Orage, and had grown with Neuburg's idiosyncratic Creative Circle and Grigson's wide company of contributors to *New Verse*, now expanded to include a more unorthodox group of working writers. Acquaintances from these often overlapping groups regularly filtered into the West End where they drank with Dylan in the Fitzroy and other public houses around Charlotte Street.

Dylan's drinking habits in London have become mythologised, though the broad outlines are simple enough. At this stage one would most likely find him in either the rowdy Fitzroy or the quieter, better upholstered Wheatsheaf, two pubs in Fitzrovia, a working-class area, full of European immigrants, on the other (west) side of the Tottenham Court Road from literary Bloomsbury. Closing time in these two establishments was (according to the licensing laws of the borough of Holborn) 10.30 p.m. So when the clocks approached this hour, drinkers often made a dash south to the rougher Marquess of Granby in Rathbone Place or the Highlander in Dean Street which, being under different jurisdictions, were allowed to stay open until eleven.

Not liking the run-down drinking spots around where he lived, Dylan gravitated naturally to the Fitzroy and Wheatsheaf. These two pubs still attracted some older artists, such as Augustus John and Percy Wyndham Lewis, both of whom had once had studios in the area. They also provided starting points for sorties to eating places ranging from Mrs Buhler's café at the top of Rathbone Place to exotic foreign-owned restaurants such as Schmidt's and Bertorelli's, or, if someone else was paying, Rudolf Stulik's Eiffel Tower, with its first-floor room decorated by Wyndham Lewis.

Two regulars were the ageing good-time girls, the artist Nina Hamnett and 'artist's model' Betty May. Both had written autobiographies detailing their scandal-ridden lives. Hamnett's was *Laughing Torso*, the book which had brought Dylan a libel threat at the *Evening Post* three years earlier. The title came from her nude bust sculpted by her one-time lover Henri Gaudier-Brzeska, about which she told the writer Ruthven Todd, 'You know me, m'dear – I'm the one in the V&A with me left tit knocked off.' Like Augustus John, she had been born in Tenby, another English-orientated town on the South Wales coast, and had studied at the Slade. A fine draughtswoman, she now hung around the Fitzroy cadging drinks, often from immature provincial youths told to look her up by fathers who had known her in better days. Her preference was for rougher trade, particularly sailors, 'because they leave in the morning'. Richard Aldington referred to 'poor Nina' as 'a curious mixture of slut and whore, but a very decent chap'.

The petite Betty May brought to Fitzrovia the panache of Paris where she had danced in a café chansant and lived with the leader of an Apache gang. (*Tiger Woman*, the title of her autobiography, came from the nickname she gained after fighting off a knife attack from a woman who thought she was this French thug's rightful girlfriend.) After turning her back on prostitution, she married Raoul Loveday, an Oxford under-graduate who was an acolyte of Aleister Crowley. When they were both visiting Crowley's abbey in Sicily, Loveday died in mysterious circumstances – she thought because he had been forced to drink the blood of a sacrificed cat. (The story recalls Victor Neuburg who, as part of an occult initiation ritual, had suffered the indignity of being turned into a camel by his homosexual lover, Crowley.) Hamnett had told Loveday's story in *Laughing Torso*, which resulted in Crowley unsuccessfully suing her for libel.

Although many years Betty May's junior, Dylan had hopes of bedding this still attractive woman, boasting to Trick in December that he was going to ghost an article on her behalf for the *News of the World*, and his payment would not be monetary. Apart from obvious fellow poets of his own age, he also claimed to have met the sculptor Henry Moore (possibly through Vera Phillips who was studying interior design under him at Chelsea Polytechnic), as well as the anti-fascist poet Edwin Muir and his wife Willa, and Wyndham Lewis, who were all part of Grigson's circle.

Finding his level in this world, while waiting expectantly for his book, proved distracting for Dylan. He was forced to adapt his pose slightly: no longer was he the leading light in a small group of provincial aesthetes; posing as Keats or Wilde was hardly original in London. Dylan found that one way of keeping his new friends amused was playing the professional Welshman. He joked to Grigson how in Carmarthenshire he had lived on carrots, and then adding that this was not quite true: he had had onions as well. But he found Londoners generally had little interest in Wales. To them it was an industrial wasteland, or else, as he once said to Pamela, 'I, to you, move in a fabulous, Celtic land, surrounded by castles, tall black hats, the ghosts of accents, and eternal Eisteddfodau.' So he learnt to grab his audiences' attention with different ruses. His powers of mimicry allowed him to conduct elaborate con-versations in the guise of characters such as an Indian intellectual or an Austrian professor. His regional accents were so true that he once convinced a visitor from Yorkshire that they had lived in the same road in Bradford. But these thespian tricks complemented his greatest social asset which was his ability to spin out a tale. He did not go in for side-splitting punch-lines, but his skill in adopting the tones and sending up the attitudes of the motley characters in his elaborate shaggy-dog stories kept everyone riveted. His warm, often inspired, generally theatrical delivery was the most obvious aspect of his Welshness.

Gradually Grigson noticed Dylan becoming more confident as his persona evolved from literary fop to Toughish Boy or the Boy with a Load of Beer. In those first few weeks in his new digs, he appeared to do little writing, telling Trick that it was impossible to concentrate or even find anywhere to work in his cramped living space, where any piece of paper was immediately liable to be covered in egg and mashed potato. One solution, he admitted, might be for someone to do the washing up. At least he earned a small amount of money from reviewing for *Bookmen* and *New Verse*. And that small income enabled him to buy the necessary rounds and keep up his job of self-promotion in the Fitzroy.

It was a lifestyle he enjoyed. On 20 December he went round to Pamela's, presumably to give her a copy of his book which had been published two days earlier in an edition of 500, though only half that number were bound and finished (the remainder had to wait until 1936). But he did not make himself welcome. His behaviour was so obnoxiously self-centred that her diary mentioned nothing of his triumph, only: 'Shopping in morning. Dylan came round in afternoon and boasted of all his rather revolting Bloomsbury fun and games.'

A couple of days later Dylan returned home for Christmas, without saying goodbye to her. In Swansea he parked with Tom Warner fifty copies of 18 *Poems*, which, from time to time, he would ask him to send out to designated recipients. On new year's eve Pamela thought he was being romantic when the telephone rang and she heard some Dylan-like noises, before being cut off. She later learnt that this had not been Dylan, but someone else playing a cruel joke. Nevertheless she had begun to rumble Dylan's way of promoting himself. At the end of her diary she scribbled a 'Song for DT', which included the damning verses:

> Princess, as you can see, my aim
> Has been to lift myself to fame
> No more I'll need to toil and moil
> For I've been thrown out of the Café Royal . . .
>
> I never trouble now to write,
> For I have set the town alight.
> And who would waste the midnight oil
> When they've been thrown out of the Café Royal.

NINE

THE BLINDEST BIT

One of Dylan's last acts of self-advertisement before leaving for Swansea was to send an inscribed copy of 18 *Poems* to the well connected but as yet unfulfilled critic and editor, Cyril Connolly. The gesture was an instant success: as soon as he read the first line of the book – 'I see the boys of summer in their ruin' – Connolly was 'completely ensnared . . .: it was so utterly unlike the hearty hopeful group therapy to which I had grown accustomed & I made haste to meet its engaging author.' On his return to London, this new young literary sensation from Wales was invited to visit Connolly and his American wife Jean, who together took him for drinks with their friends, the novelist Anthony Powell and his wife Lady Violet at their flat in Great Ormond Street. These two Old Etonian writers were not Dylan's usual Fitzrovia cronies; they belonged to a more moneyed literary-cum-social set. The Welshman made enough of an impression to be asked back to a formal dinner with the Connollys.

On this next occasion, things turned out differently for Dylan. He must have had wind of who was coming and taken fright. The other guests were the Powells, up-and-coming Roman Catholic novelist Evelyn Waugh, travel writer Robert Byron, Bloomsbury acoloyte and *Sunday Times* columnist Desmond MacCarthy and several 'ladies representing fashion rather than literature'. Dylan was never averse to advancing his interests but he did not like the sense of being paraded. As when he failed to turn up to meet the municipal worthy at Trick's house, he proved markedly reluctant to make his way to the Connollys' flat above a shop in the King's Road at the accepted time. He spent the early part of the evening in a nearby bar. By the time his friend Norman Cameron had plucked him from there and parked him at the Connollys' door, Dylan was not only drunk but late.

He immediately made his mark, but not as expected. There was a hush in the noisy room when Dylan drawled in answer to his host's enquiry as to what he wanted to drink, 'Anything that goes down my throat.' He joined conversation with the elderly Desmond MacCarthy about Swinburne, but did not seem to know that the latter's novel *Lesbia Brandon* dealt with flagellation. Connolly recalled MacCarthy 'revert[ing] to the schoolboy language which cuts through age and class' and saying, ' "Yes, he likes swishing." After a long silence, a wide-eyed Dylan replied, "Did you say swishing? Jesus Christ." '

Geoffrey Grigson gave a second-hand version of this encounter suggesting MacCarthy felt affronted. But this reflected his own later antipathy towards Dylan. Waugh was not aware of any rudeness; only that MacCarthy had been slightly embarrassed as he 'did not like talking smut to a man of a different age & class'. According to Connolly, it was Waugh who was discomfited, the novelist having to leave early because he saw so much of his own youthful behaviour and appearance in the Welshman. (And it is true that Dylan, when he filled out some fifteen years later, was to look very similar to both Waugh and Connolly.) Dylan must have felt uncomfortable too, because he did not mention this dinner, even dismissively, in any letter. He seems to have accepted it as part of the learning process of making one's way in the capital. He never liked formal grand gatherings, but this one alerted him to the wide, perhaps irreconcilable gulf between Swansea suburbia and London society. From then on his relations with Connolly and company tended to be restricted to professional matters, though he did join Connolly and David Gascoyne on a day trip to Selsey where they had some sport pelting pebbles at bottles placed in the sand to represent such respected literary figures as John Lehmann, Michael Roberts, Edith Sitwell and Virginia Woolf.

The year 1935 had started promisingly for Dylan in Swansea with his old editor J. D. Williams using his regular diary column in the *South Wales Evening Post* to puff his first book. Unable to resist an avuncular swipe against modernist poets, Williams admitted his recent faux pas in describing Dylan (apparently to his face) as one of the T. S. Eliot, Ezra Pound and Auden school. Confident of his own status, Dylan had retorted, 'Eliot! Pound! Auden! They are back numbers in the poetical world.' This was a robust comment to set beside his riposte in an interview, obviously given when still in London and published in the *Sunday Referee* under the headline 'Our Literary "Gangsters": Young Poet Attacks Modern Writers': 'Most writers today move about in gangs. They haven't the strength to stand and fight as individuals. But even as "gangsters" their machine guns are full, not of bullets, but of dried peas.' By being himself, Dylan was positioning himself as the angry young man avant le mot of English letters.

Publication of 18 *Poems* stimulated a modest debate in the *Swansea Guardian*, albeit one conducted largely by his friends. Bert Trick downplayed the importance of his young protégé's politics: 'one knows instinctively his politics are correct, but they hover like a faint perfume above the lines of his poetry.' John Jennings praised Dylan's use of words and their ability to touch the subconscious: Dylan's method was 'to get hold of one of the violin strings of a man's inward being and twang it till it hurts.' However Trevor Hughes, writing from Harrow, felt it was too early to make extravagant comparisons with the great poets. His carping attitude – the result, it soon became clear, of professional and sexual jealousy – sparked a quick rebuttal from Trick who claimed it was perfectly reasonable to talk about Dylan's descent from Webster, Beddoes and Blake. Dylan, he said extravagantly, had 'snatched today from the procession of time, and made it eternal'.

Meanwhile J. D. Williams chipped in with another diary column item in his paper, this time about the admiration for Dylan felt by the sea-loving novelist Richard Hughes, who had recently moved to Laugharne. On 12 January the Post's more literary stable-mate, the Herald of Wales, printed one of the first reviews of 18 Poems – an encomium by Spencer Vaughan-Thomas, whose brother Wynford had acted with Dylan at the Little Theatre.

By then, Dylan had returned to London. He made at once for Pamela's flat where he pitched up at 11.30 on the evening of 2 January. It was not a happy reconciliation. He was very drunk and she was entertaining another boyfriend. Three nights later, a Saturday, he was back, staying until midnight. Once again, the story was depressingly similar. 'Very trying time,' recorded Pamela. 'Still says he loves me but can't resist Comrade Bottle. Am just watching and praying. What else can I do?'

Others close to him were in a similar quandary. His mother and father had become so concerned about his physical and mental well-being in Swansea over Christmas that, within a fortnight of his return to London, they made the 185-mile journey to see him. Dylan spent some time frantically cleaning his dingy room in Redcliffe Street. When he invited D.J. to sit on his camp-bed, the structure collapsed. His parents had to wait for Fred Janes and a friend to finish their tea before having a cup themselves. Florence looked on disapprovingly: 'If there was one empty, dirty milk bottle, there were twenty,' she later recalled.

The Thomases tried to reassure themselves with the knowledge that their son was sharing a flat with the reliable Fred Janes to whom, it seems, they sometimes wrote about their son's well-being. They also felt they had an ally in Pamela. But when they decided to visit the Hansford Johnsons on this trip, they unwittingly blurted out the – to Pamela – unexpected and unwelcome information that Dylan was to have his twenty-first birthday in October. He had led her to believe that they were exactly the same age.

Dylan took up where he left off. He still frequented the Parton

Bookshop, meeting prominent Communists such as A. L. Morton and Claud Cockburn, editor and foreign editor of the *Daily Worker* (though the latter was already better known for publishing his own radical newsletter *The Week*). He made a note of telling Bert Trick he had come across the anti-public school activist Esmond Romilly. And he also mentioned a couple of leftist writers, John Lehmann and John Pudney, whom he described as pseudo-revolutionaries. But they all only helped to convince him of the incompatibility of poetry and politics. The Welsh puritan in him took strongly against their generally privileged backgrounds and their advocacy of 'what they priggishly call "the class struggle" . . . They are bogus from skull to navel.'

During February, further reviews of 18 *Poems* tumbled out, confirming the value of Dylan's amateur public relations. These appeared anonymously in *New Verse* (Grigson's vehicle), *European Quarterly* (where the volume was described, probably by Edwin Muir, one of the editors, as 'one of the most remarkable books of poetry which have appeared for several years') and *The Listener* (where assistant literary editor Janet Adam Smith had printed one of his first verses), and under the bylines of Rayner Heppenstall in *Adelphi* and of Desmond Hawkins in *Time and Tide*, the latter of whom spoke Dylan's own language: 'The Audenesque convention is nearly ended; and I credit Dylan Thomas with being the first considerable poet to break through fashionable limitation and speak an unborrowed language, without excluding anything that has preceded him.' These last two reviewers, Heppenstall and Hawkins, were the sort of unpretentious literary friends Dylan liked. He had met Heppenstall, a slim young Yorkshireman with a passion for French culture, just before Christmas, when, at Richard Rees's suggestion, he had knocked at his door in Chelsea and given him a signed copy of 18 *Poems*. Before long the two men were, in Heppenstall's words, 'very thick'. They both enjoyed drinking, though neither had a particularly strong head. Heppenstall's memoir, *Four Absentees*, contains several stories of their bibulous exploits – on one occasion, being thrown out of a nightclub called the Blue Mask; on another, getting into a fight somewhere around Parton Street, with the result that Heppenstall, later, like many of Dylan's friends, a stalwart of the BBC, spent the night in detention at Clerkenwell police station. At Bertorelli's in Charlotte Street, the two men dined with Richard Rees and a young Etonian with pale blue eyes called Eric Blair, who had written two books under the pseudonym 'George Orwell'. That evening ended in a basement bar in the King's Road frequented by young Blackshirts, another with Heppenstall giving Dylan a black eye.

Hawkins was a daytime drinking companion. Dylan would meet him in the mornings at the Wheatsheaf or one of the pubs around Charlotte

Street. At closing time in mid-afternoon, the two men would move on to a more accommodating drinking club. Hawkins was now associated with the quarterly *Purpose*, of which he became literary editor the following year. Dylan offered to write for it on 'Poetry, Jacobean and Metaphysical, and music, minus the more intricate technicalities, mysticism (honest), and psychology (abnormal for preference)'. Looking back, Hawkins felt this list represented Dylan's interests. 'He had a fund of stories about madness, lunatic asylums and strange symbolic possessions – usually funny stories, not solemn ones. He had a quick, volatile, chuckling relishing sense of humour. He certainly loved the "Gothic".'

Dylan's interest in music had been stimulated by Dan Jones over the years and revived more recently by Pamela Hansford Johnson taking him to the proms. In a letter to Pamela he described listening to Monteverdi's *Ballet of the Ungrateful Ladies* as 'very happy music'. He also loved Alban Berg's then little-known opera *Wozzeck*, which put a suitably avant-garde gloss on his respect for the common man. Although often teasing Dylan about his precious 'Kensington' manner of speaking (the direct result, he realised, of his friend's upwardly mobile Swansea background with its elocution lessons), Hawkins loved the Welshman's uninhibited use of words and the theatricality of their delivery. ('Words to him were like flags and banners, to be seized and waved in tumultuous signallings.') The two men agreed to collaborate on a satirical thriller about the murder of a fictional Poet Laureate, whom they dubbed 'the King's Canary'. As summer drew on, he and Hawkins enjoyed devising spoof names for a cast of thinly disguised literary figures whom they both knew.

Thrillers became a regular topic of discussion after Dylan began reviewing them for the *Morning Post* where Geoffrey Grigson, keen to help, realised the young man could at least earn extra money by selling any books he had finished to a dealer in the Strand. Grigson also saw that Dylan lacked either the confidence or the will to storm what he called modernism's 'Inner Command', meaning Eliot and Wyndham Lewis. This was indeed a problem for Dylan. He did not lack ambition but, afraid of being shown up intellectually, he tended to steer clear of the elder statesmen of his profession. He genuinely preferred to operate independently of all 'Commands'.

This was clear in his choice of another friend. Through Grigson he had met Norman Cameron, a tall, shambling Oxford graduate of Scottish origin who also ploughed his own furrow. Cameron had been one of the few poets able to work with Robert Graves and his tempestuous mistress Laura Riding. Supported by private means, he lived with them in Majorca, where they encouraged him to marry one of their 'tribe', a German girl called Elfrieda Faust. In 1933 he returned with her to London but, rather than join the gaggle of hollow-cheeked young men trying to survive through occasional poems and reviews, he found work (and a comfortable existence) as a copywriter with the advertising agency J. Walter Thompson.

In many ways Cameron was very different from Dylan. His verse, which had been published by Auden and Day Lewis in their edition of *Oxford Poetry* in 1927, was lean, sometimes witty, but often surprisingly emotional. It owed something to Graves but was individual enough to be seriously compared to the Movement of the 1950s, which emphatically turned its back on the supposed romanticism of Dylan and his fellows over the previous decade. With his tailored suits, Cameron's personal style was also a long way from Dylan, who still sported the fancy dress of a Bohemian poet.

Dylan was unconcerned by these differences. He was happy to find someone unstuffy, whose professional opinion he respected. The poet John Pudney (who married A. P. Herbert's daughter Crystal and probably introduced an ungrateful Dylan to his humorist father-in-law) recognised what was going on: 'Dylan suddenly appeared chez Norman, playing the enfant terrible to Norman's nanny.' These unlikely confrères struck up a bantering relationship. Dylan called Cameron 'Norman the Nagger', a comment on their personal dynamics, or, simply, 'Normal' which, as Grigson noted, was like calling the largest man in an RAF unit 'Tiny'. (The nickname came after Elfrieda revealed that, the first time they made love, her husband had turned over and said, 'Thank you.') To Cameron, Dylan was 'Ditch', as if it described the place he had crawled out from.

The Camerons lived in a large loft-like flat in British Grove, Hammersmith, where there was always room for Dylan to spend the night after he and Norman had started an evening's drinking at Hennekey's, close to the latter's workplace in the Aldwych. Cameron's biographer Warren Hope records that Cameron initially thought that Dylan had been influenced stylistically by the American Hart Crane, another heavy drinker who had committed suicide in 1932. But Dylan said he had never heard of the poet.

Nominally Dylan was still living in Redcliffe Street, but he was seldom there. Janes recalled him as 'tremendously restless, coming and going at all times, now a furious burst of work, often sitting up in bed with his hat and coat on to keep warm'. Levy also remembered Dylan sitting in bed in the mornings, eating apples, drinking beer and reading thrillers. Since the place was teeming with mice, he and Dylan would indulge in elaborate fantasies such as speculating how many of these rodents would be required to pull the London to Glasgow express. Janes found time to paint a fine portrait of Dylan, capturing his wide-eyed charm, crinkly golden hair and boyish good looks. (This was exhibited at the Everyman Theatre in Hampstead in August.) But Dylan never considered Redcliffe Street as his base and more often was to be found at the Camerons.

There his general health began to cause concern, particularly as Dylan was never reticent about his professed tuberculosis or how his doctor had given him only so long to live. In April Cameron suggested that Dylan might like to get out of London and visit his friend, Alan (A. J. P.) Taylor, a history lecturer at Manchester University. Taylor, scion of a Lancashire cotton merchant, had known Cameron as an undergraduate at Oriel College, Oxford. In Vienna in 1930, he met Margaret Adams, the artistic convent-educated daughter of a chief inspector of mines in India, and married her the following year. The young couple set up home in Didsbury, on the edge of the Pennines, five miles south of Manchester, where their social circle included an assortment of academics and writers, some, like Malcolm Muggeridge, associated with the local newspaper, the *Manchester Guardian*.

Cameron convinced the sceptical, often curmudgeonly Taylor that Dylan would be an entertaining guest. Initially the two men took to each other, staying up late, laughing and reading Rabelais aloud. Then Dylan's drinking habits became excessive, even for Taylor, who kept a beer barrel in his house. Dylan consumed between fifteen and twenty pints each day, and Taylor was forced to ration this intake. The historian probably sensed another problem: his attractive and emotional wife Margaret had developed a tendresse for the young poet. As a result of her attention, which probably reminded him of his mother, Dylan stayed much longer than expected. Despite his lack of enthusiasm for aspects of the Taylors' life, such as long walks in the Derbyshire peaks, he remained with them for nearly a month until mid-May. When he eventually left, he found he had lost the return half of his railway ticket and asked Alan Taylor if he could borrow £2 to buy another. His host told him bluntly, 'I lend once and, unless repaid, once only.' By then he would have done anything to speed the departure of the sponging Welshman. He never expected to see his money again, and he never did. Not that he cared, for he hoped he had experienced the last of Dylan.

The young poet was in not much better shape when he returned to London. The tenancy at Redcliffe Street had ended, and Janes and Levy moved round the corner to share a flat in Coleherne Road with another artist, William Scott, later well known for his abstract paintings. They witnessed Dylan's social life becoming ever more bizarre. After periods of absence, he would often return to the house with a new friend, such as a down-and-out he had met on the Embankment. Mosley's Fascist party was at its height, which made life difficult for Levy, who not only looked very Jewish but tended to dress as a prototype punk, with trousers slashed to the knee and with one side of his face shaven, the other not. On more than one occasion, Levy was confronted by right-wing thugs in his neighbourhood. But this brought out the best in Dylan who, despite his personal excess, showed the innate compassion that Trick admired and often muddled with political commitment. After a huge Moseleyite rally at Olympia on 7 June led to violent running battles, Dylan found a battered Communist hiding from Fascist gangs. He turned out to be an American boxer down on his luck. Dylan invited him back to stay with the 'gang'.

Still in peripatetic mood, on 20 June Dylan went to visit Dan Jones and his family, now living in Harrow, north-west of London. Dan was pursuing his music studies in London, while still nominally enrolled at Swansea University College completing his MA thesis on the links between the Elizabethan lyric and contemporary music. As a result the two friends often seemed to miss each other, one being in Swansea, while the other was in London, or vice versa. Dan saw more of Fred Janes who kept him apprised of Dylan's relationship with Pamela. In Swansea a few months earlier Dan had stayed briefly with the Thomases while simultaneously conducting steamy affairs with two women. On that trip he had also met Thomas Taig, the English lecturer connected to the Little Theatre, who remarked on Dylan's poor understanding of rhythm – at least, as an actor. He linked this to Dylan's lack of control over his muscles.

So Dylan's visit to the Joneses was a return match. However he did not endear himself to his old friend by failing to turn up at a rendezvous. He had got drunk, picked up a girl – 'a Jewess with thighs like boiled string' – and woke up with a fearful hangover. It was, he was forced to admit, 'the same old story'.

His other companions did what they could to help re-write the script. Grigson, who had moved into a new flat in Keats Grove, Hampstead, found Dylan examining himself in an agitated manner after developing a rash all over his body. Dylan was packed off to an Irish doctor in Bloomsbury who told him he had nothing to worry about; all he needed was to take more rest and drink less alcohol. In order to facilitate this, Grigson – at Cameron's urging – agreed to take Dylan with him on holiday to a remote spot near Adara in County Donegal in the Irish Republic, where they stayed in a small cottage, once a donkey-shed, made habitable a few years earlier by Rockwell Kent, the American artist who loved wilderness. Although mid-summer, it rained continuously and they had to build turf fires. Drinking less frenetically, eating nutritious local food (including fish which Grigson taught him to catch) and keeping regular hours, Dylan began to relax. He grew a beard and took long walks on the cliffs overlooking the Atlantic Ocean, where he and Grigson sang 'The Ram of Derbyshire' to the gannets, puffins and black seals on the rocks below. They frightened themselves when they shouted 'We are the Dead' to the surrounding mountains, and the words echoed back to them, three-fold.

Grigson was never sure if Dylan fully appreciated their rural setting. He felt Dylan enjoyed it, and was even encouraged to write, but somehow failed to engage on a deeper level. Dylan confirmed as much in a letter to Trick: 'I find I can't see a landscape; scenery is just scenery to me.' With a sneer at the locals' religiosity, he referred passionlessly to this 'wild, unlettered and unfrenchlettered country, too far from Andara, a village you can't be too far from'. But encouraged by an offer from Richard Church at J. M. Dent to publish his next book of verse, he did complete some work, ranging from a vampire tale which managed to spook him out further on dark, rainy nights, through his picaresque novel (which developed into 'Prologue to an Adventure'), to approximately six poems, the most ambitious of which was 'I, in my intricate image'. These he sent to John Lehmann, editor of the anthology The Year's Poetry, asking ominously if he might have payment in advance to cover his local debts and enable him to return to England. Lehmann generously advanced a sum from his personal pocket.

However even this failed to meet Dylan's requirements. Grigson had only been able to spend a fortnight in Ireland, so he had left Dylan on his own in the cottage, supplied with money to cover the rent and other necessities. The nearest porter bar was at Glendrumatie, ten miles away. Poteen, the local illicit brew which had become his tipple, was cheap. So what Dylan found to spend his money on is unclear. Nevertheless by the time he came to leave at the end of August, he was penniless, and was forced to depart without notifying or paying Dan Ward, the farmer who owned the place.

Details of the next two weeks in London are sketchy. Grigson was furious, and temporarily put an end to his helpful practice of giving Dylan thrillers to review for the Morning Post – though Dylan's failure to deliver copy may also have contributed. Having paid off the debt to the Irish farmer, Cameron joined Grigson in reading Dylan the riot act: 'we had a blistery scene with Dylan, who on such occasions always sucked and pouted and acted the injured Suckling,' recalled Grigson. Temporarily denied admittance to Cameron's flat, Dylan responded by going on 'the blindest blind in the world'. He did not know the day, the week 'or anything', he told Desmond Hawkins. One consequence of his bender was that he managed to lose his few possessions, including his papers, amongst which were notes for his fictional collaboration with Hawkins.

At one stage he visited Pamela who noticed he was shaking, probably from the effects of alcoholic poisoning. This did not stop him taking her on a crawl of Chelsea pubs including the Cadogan where they happened to see what she described as his 'prossy Miriam (or Shirley)', possibly the Jewish girl he picked up earlier in the summer. His sexual profligacy during this period of drunken confusion led him, almost inevitably, to pick up a dose of gonorrhoea. (Whether the woman responsible was Miriam, Shirley or the one he blamed, an improbable sounding 'chorus girl with glasses' called Fluffy, is unclear.) This time there was no friendly Irish doctor to placate him. Antibiotics were not yet available, and the only cure was regular washing out of the urethra. Dylan was forced to retire to Swansea to recuperate, both mentally and physically. From there he sent a desperate note to Grigson, who had backtracked slightly, begging him to continue sending thrillers to review and, 'for the love of the great grey cunt of the world', not to reveal any details of his state, except to Norman Cameron, because otherwise his own 'lecherous chances' might be ruined. Later Dylan liked to tell how, when in Swansea, he heard his mother talking to a neighbour, who asked, 'And how is your boy, Mrs Thomas?'

The conversation continued: 'Oh, we don't know what is wrong with him.'

'What is the matter?'

'Every time he goes to the lavatory, he screams.'

Although he could joke about this, Dylan had been through a traumatic period which had taken him to the edge of a nervous breakdown. The strain of making his way in London had been more than he had imagined. He had kept going partly because his mother selflessly sent him an allowance of £1 a week, which she could afford only because she was sharing the rental income from 30 Delhi Street. Even she recognised her son had been 'ill' and acknowledged Cameron's role in looking after him. But she was partly to blame. Her homeliness, making sure that meals were always on the table, had given Dylan little preparation for fending for himself. One reason he had overstayed his welcome at the Taylors was that the woman of the house had been prepared to cook for and look after him like his mother. However he realised he could not live happily again in Swansea. In a letter to Trick from Ireland, he reminisced about the Uplands and the Mumbles, and concluded reasonably enough that he could never feel at home, even when at home. 'Everywhere I find myself seems to be nothing but a resting place between places that become resting places themselves.'

In his state of feverish activity, he found some solace in recalling the fantasy world he had once created with Dan Jones. 'I'm surer of nothing than that that world, Percy's in Warmley, was, and still is, the only one that has any claims to permanence; I mean that this long out-of-doored world isn't much good really, that it's only the setting, is only supposed to be the setting, for a world of our own.' They had both been happier, he wrote to Jones from Ireland, happier even in their unhappiness, when WARMDANDYLANLEY-MAN inhabited this WARM-DANDYLANLEY-WORLD. (He hermetically enclosed their two names within the friendly embrace of Dan's old house in Swansea.) This imaginative construct also included individuals such as Fred Janes and Tom Warner, together with all the Swansea haunts where they had once gathered. It was a sad exercise in nostalgia, with its longing for a cosy past rather than addressing the problems of the present. Dan Jones called it 'nothing but a protracted dirge' but charitably attributed the cause to 'the uninspiring atmosphere, or rather lack of atmosphere in London: the three of us who have tried or who are trying to live here, Dylan, Fred and I, have decided that the country is the best place for our work ... Next year I shall probably be in Vienna, and Fred and Dylan in Swansea writing and painting as hard as they can; they have both given up the idea of living in London.' (Dan had recently won a coveted Mendelssohn scholarship to study music in the Austrian capital.)

Dylan was to stay for a while in Swansea, albeit involuntarily, but it would be some time before he would forgo living in London which seemed to offer economic, social and sexual liberation. And he would always retain the fond idea of a happier past which would bear artistic fruit in his poetic renderings of a bucolic Welsh countryside and in his invention of the complete universe in the town of Llareggub.

While in Swansea in September Dylan made a valuable new friendship. Despite his Cambridge education, Vernon Watkins had a humble job in the St Helens Road branch of Lloyds Bank. Like other poets, he managed to combine working in an office with a passionate commitment to verse. Although eight years older than Dylan, no-one in Swansea was better equipped, both emotionally and intellectually, to relate to him. The gentle Watkins had been despatched by his well-off, once Welsh-speaking parents to English public school at Repton where he had been a contemporary of Christopher Isherwood. He abruptly left Cambridge after a row with A. C. Benson, Master of Magdalene College. After his father insisted that he adopt banking as a career, Watkins had a nervous breakdown, which led him to destroy around two thousand of his poems. He also returned to Repton and attempted to kill the headmaster Dr Geoffrey Fisher (later Archbishop of Canterbury). Subsequently he became a Christian, adopting a quietistic version of the religion which enabled him to proceed calmly, almost ethereally, through life. Even so, enough of his psychopathic nature remained to establish a strong bond with the equally headstrong Dylan.

Shortly after 18 *Poems* appeared in the window of Morgan & Higgs' bookshop in Swansea, Watkins bought a copy and was impressed. A little later, he ran into Dylan's uncle, the Reverend David Rees, former pastor of Paraclete Congregational church, where his own parents had worshipped, before moving to Pennard in Gower. Rees suggested Watkins might like to talk with Dylan and gave him the address of Cwmdonkin Drive. Dylan was in London when Watkins visited, but Florrie promised her son would get in touch when he returned.

Dylan duly telephoned and the two men arranged to meet at Watkins's parents' house where, after a walk along Dylan's beloved Gower cliffs, Watkins read his new acquaintance some recent poems. The following week Watkins went to Cwmdonkin Drive where Dylan returned the compliment, declaiming 'Ears in the turrets hear', earlier rejected from 18 *Poems* as 'terribly weak' but now sounding crisper, and 'Should lanterns shine', a mature meditation on the confusing nature of time, interwoven with insights into the powerful, even destructive, properties of light, thus giving the poem a contemporary feel, playing on the idea of relativity.

The sequel to 18 *Poems* had been on Dylan's mind for the best part of a year. Even when mired in London pub life, he had still found time to write verse. And, remarkably, his bluff seventeenth-century metaphysics had given way to a more compassionate view of nature which attained its highest manifestation, a state of grace akin to the innocence of childhood, in Christ's sacrifice on the Cross. Quite how a non-practising Christian of his temperament arrived at this theological position is difficult to fathom. It owed much to his conversations with Bert Trick and his view of Jesus Christ as a 'social revolutionary'.

This was the theme behind something else he read to Watkins – seven out of the ten sonnets in his 'Altarwise by owl-light' sequence. Although Dylan later dismissed them as 'the writings of a boily boy in love with shapes and shadows on his pillow', these verses punningly detailed his own spiritual odyssey in idioms both Christian and pagan that reminded commentators of James Joyce's *Ulysses*. The sacred nature of the exercise was evident in the words 'altarwise' and 'tree' that begin and end the sonnets. Dylan was expressing his autochthonous sense of religion, an elemental force summoned more in the bardic utterances of his Celtic forefathers than in the Calvinistic prescriptions of his uncle's church.

He also had his poet's reasons for arriving at his position. He recognised his poetry sometimes teetered on the edge of self-parody. As he later admitted, he had made a conscious attempt to 'get away from those rhythmic and thematic dead ends, that physical blank wall, those wombs, and full-stop worms'. Now, in the middle of reading to Watkins in his parents' house in Cwmdonkin Drive, he stopped for a moment, on reaching the last line of the seventh sonnet, 'On rose and icicle the ringing handprint', and looked up. The lamp behind his head made a halo of his golden hair. With Dylan's words hanging in the air, it was a moment Watkins never forgot. 'I was aware that I was in the presence of a poet of extraordinary genius,' he later recalled.

After finishing, Dylan asked if his visitor used a dictionary. When Watkins conceded that he occasionally did, Dylan looked unimpressed and said he meant a real dictionary. He pulled from his shelf a brown paper folder – a rhyming dictionary which he had compiled himself and called his Doomsday Book. Around him were strewn pieces of cardboard box covered in his tiny, backward-slanting, childlike hand. These were his stories, from which he read Watkins 'The Orchards' (with its reference to Llareggub) and two others. He explained how he liked to see a story take shape and how a friendly draper gave his mother boxes which he cut up, wrote on and hung around his room – another example of his visual approach to his craft.

Settling down to a prolonged stay in Swansea, Dylan introduced Watkins to his friends. With Dan out of town, his Warmley group at last began to take on a new lease of life as the more eclectic Kardomah crowd. Dan looked on paternally from afar, indulging his own form of nostalgia. When, following his show at the Everyman in Hampstead, Fred Janes sold two paintings to the Glynn Vivian Art Gallery and his study of Dylan was shown in Cardiff, Dan could not help remarking, 'As Kneller was to the Kit-Kat Club, so Fred may be to the W.S. [Warmley School]!' Even he admitted he missed 'the artistic stimulation of the "united" school very greatly'. Without Dan, Dylan saw more of Tom Warner who had suffered a nervous breakdown the previous year. On Mondays, they regularly visited the cinema, after which Tom took Dylan back for supper with his aunt. When she served a boiled egg, Tom was astounded to see Dylan had no idea what to do and she had to cut off its top.

Slowly Dylan's psychological and physical health improved. In October Tom wrote to Dan, 'Dylan is still here, and never a day passes without some little plan; maybe a coffie [sic] in the Kardomah, or again a visit to some picture-palace, anon the evening meeting, which beggars description, but always the gay laughter, the merry quip, the Warmley pun, the mutually seen cameos of the streets, that woman's nose, or the wooden leg of this man; the smile of the girl in the cash desk, the uncertain gate when approached by that certain gait, all those things called life.'

Dylan's twenty-first birthday passed uneventfully, if agreeably, after a generous gift of money from his sister and brother-in-law allowed him to kit himself out in a new suit, grey hat and sundry other items of clothing appropriate for an aspiring literary gentleman. With Watkins's help, Dylan foraged through his notebooks again, revised some poems, and prepared them for Richard Church, the poetry editor at the established firm J. M. Dent, which he hoped would take on his next book. But Church, who had been alerted to Dylan's talent by the sons of his friend Lascelles Abercrombie, was conservative in taste and his initial response was cool. He felt Dylan's verse was unnecessarily obscure and, worse, infected with surrealism – a charge Dylan countered robustly, if slightly misleadingly, saying that, until recently, he had never heard of surrealism, he had not read any French poetry since failing to translate Victor Hugo at school, and his knowledge of modern verse in general was regrettably poor.

Watkins felt Church had a point. He encouraged Dylan to leave out two of his intended poems, the sparse 'Now say nay', and showy 'How Soon the Servant Sun', arguing that reviewers would latch onto them to damn the entire collection. But Dylan was unconcerned: 'Oh, give them a bone.' He himself was more worried about 'And Death Shall Have No Dominion', the poem he had written in competition with Bert Trick in 1933. But after reading it aloud many times, a diagnostic technique he favoured, he relented, and the poem was to become one of the general public's favourites.

By the end of the year, Dylan was passably fit and ready to contemplate his next move. A vague plan to share a flat with Rayner Heppenstall having fallen through, he idly contemplated following Roy Campbell and, more recently, Laurie Lee, another graduate of the Sunday Referee, and going to Spain. But he realised he would be lost without either money or command of the language. So he returned to London where, making no attempt to find permanent lodgings, he centred himself on Norman Cameron's flat in Hammersmith. There he renewed his association with Ruthven Todd, a pasty-faced young Scottish writer in glasses, with a remote family connection to Cameron.

Todd had first met Dylan at the end of 1934, when Geoffrey Grigson had entertained them both in a café in Mitre Court, close to his office in Fleet Street. He had returned to his home town of Edinburgh where, for a short while, he was assistant editor on *Scottish Bookman*. In this capacity he sought a contribution from Dylan, who stipulated a fee of £2 for his poem 'Do you not father me'.

Back again in London and temporarily supporting himself with a job in an art gallery, Todd witnessed Dylan resume his bare-faced, if good-natured practice of sponging off Cameron – something noted also by Pamela Hansford Johnson who used Cameron as a model for Clement Maclaren in her 1968 novel *The Survival of the Fittest*. In the garden of the Six Bells, a Dylan-like character suggests a trip to the Fitzroy, saying that Clement is rich and will pay.

But Dylan was such good fun, it did not usually matter. His aura of charm, openness and vulnerability tended to work to his advantage. Sitting in a pub, he often started quietly. When the alcohol took effect, he sprang to life and could be side-splittingly funny. He was seldom malicious: for all his self-centredness, perhaps because of it, he retained a fund of sympathy for less fortunate individuals. He saw himself in them: he was the common man. Even the surly Grigson could, in charitable mood, write of him, 'When he disappeared, it was a relief; when he reappeared, a pleasure.' And this was the basic sentiment of Cameron's subsequent, slightly sour poem 'The Dirty Little Accuser' which started:

> Who invited him in? What was he doing here?
> That insolent little ruffian, that crapulous lout?
> When he quitted a sofa, he left behind him a smear.
> My wife says he even tried to paw her about.

Late at night, Cameron's guests amused themselves with games of verbal wit. Even when flooded with alcohol, Dylan's brain could toss off bits of verse, often parodies or obscene limericks such as:

> Now Jove was a kind of a bloke
> Who looked for his bit of a poke
> And when he found Mary
> Had been fucked by a fairy
> He didn't think much of the joke.

Cameron had been working on a campaign for Horlicks, which suggested that a regular glass of malted milk could ward off the pangs of 'Night Starvation'. Dylan seized on this slogan, devising an alternative panacea called Night Custard. The assembled party hooted as they imagined ever more fanciful ingredients, such as fluff from under beds, and uses for the product, from hair cream to vaginal jelly.

As an advertising man, Cameron had several visually creative friends. Len Lye, another former associate of Robert Graves, lived round the corner from British Grove with his wife Jane. He was a jazz-loving artist-cum-film-maker whose experimental abstract work had brought him into contact with similarly ambitious, multi-media British painters, including Ben Nicholson, Julian Trevelyan and Humphrey Jennings. His animations for John Grierson at the GPO Film Unit led him, for all his New Zealand nationality, to be dubbed the 'English Disney'. As a result of his innovative techniques of painting directly onto film, he was hired to do special effects on Alfred Hitchcock's 1936 movie *Secret Agent*.

Oswell Blakeston was a witty homosexual painter who lived with Max Chapman in a run-down house in St John's Wood. Born Henry Hasslacher into an Austrian wine-importing family, his first name was derived from the dandyish, discreetly gay Osbert Sitwell, while his surname was based on his mother's. Dylan struck up an immediate rapport, indulging in long-running fantasies in which Blakeston took on the role of Dearest Mouse or Darling Slime. Sitwell could not have done them a better favour when he wrote his satirical ballad 'National Rat Week', attacking the hangers-on who ditched King Edward VIII after his abdication in December 1936. Dylan enjoyed peppering his letters to Blakeston with references to rats: 'it'll be Rat Week always,' he pronounced. Both Blakeston and Chapman later claimed to have had affairs with him. Given Dylan's puritanical Welsh aversion to what he called 'the only vice that revolts me', this seems unlikely. However, Dylan was never dogmatic about his masculine sexual identity. 'Sex – male, I think,' he described himself to Pamela, and he often indulged in hermaphrodite imaginings. It is possible that, after a drunken evening, he and Blakeston did find themselves in bed, and he only took evasive action when, as Ruthven Todd has noted, his companion brought out the Vaseline.

He could now rely on his friends and contacts to publish most of his output. At Cameron's suggestion, he ventured further afield and sent his poem 'Hold hard these ancient minutes' to *Caravel*, a publication in Majorca. A story, 'The Phosphorescent Nephew' was despatched to an unspecified publication in America, since when it has never been heard of. Negotiations continued with Church at Dent about the composition of his next book. Various titles were discussed and rejected – *Twenty-Three Poems*, *Poems in Sequence* and *Poems in Progress*. Dylan preferred a simple numerical indicator, but admitted at one stage he could no longer remember how many pieces he had submitted.

As *18 Poems* went into a second issue in February, he found a new patron in the quaint reactionary modernist, Edith Sitwell. She had taken against his first published work in 1934, telling the academic and poet John Sparrow that Dylan 'ought to be dashed off to a psycho-analyst immediately before worse befalls'. But she had changed her mind and printed a fulsome, if belated, review of *18 Poems* in the *London Mercury*. She subsequently invited him to a party, telling a friend Robert Herring, editor of *Life and Letters Today*, 'I want to ask him some questions and give him some advice.' Such occasions usually scared Dylan, but he also knew Herring who had recently published a fragment of his 'Altarwise by owl-light' sequence – a compromise after a typical Dylan cock-up in which the editor found that the poem Dylan had sent him for publication, 'A grief ago', had already been printed elsewhere. 'She isn't very frightening, is she?' Dylan asked Herring about their bird-like hostess. 'I saw a photograph of her once, in medieval costume.' Even when Dylan inexplicably failed to keep a subsequent date, Sitwell was undaunted: he 'stands a chance of becoming a great poet, if only he gets rid of his complexes', she told her friend Christabel, Lady Aberconway. Another welcome supporter was T. S. Eliot whom Dylan hoped to interest in a book of his short stories. Over lunch Eliot expressed concern for Dylan's professed 'rheumatism'; he spent the meal describing his own symptoms and recommending cures. Although no contract with Faber was forthcoming, Dylan described Eliot as 'charming, a *great* man, I think, utterly unaffected'.

Dylan's condition was as much self-inflicted as anything. His return to London had taken its toll, and once again he was suffering from chronic alcohol poisoning. In early April his thriller reviews for the *Morning Post* (which had kept him solvent in Swansea) suddenly came to a halt. He had hoped to supplement this work by editing a regular book column for the *Swansea and West Wales Guardian*. In the paper's pages, he had delivered one of his best summaries of his literary beliefs when he announced grandiloquently that he and his fellow reviewers would share:

a horror of bunkum, of pretence, of pretentiousness, and a knowledge of the havoc that has been wrought by modern ethics of common-sense on the great Blarneys of the past; ... a tolerance far from divine for nearly all social and moral behaviours; ... [and] the will to call the long-standing bluff of the English gentleman of letters, those arm-chaired adventurers with their arch humour, their quaint apologetic egoism, their eminence socially and academically, each in his own right a gentleman and a gas-bag, who, in the words of Cyril Connolly, have gone down before the modern spirit and divided their mantle between the professor of literature and the Sunday journal buffoon.

But, as tended to happen when he was in an editorial role, this project had failed to develop, despite his writing to publishers to ask for books, using the names of friends as potential contributors. Among these was Rayner Heppenstall, a recent convert to Roman Catholicism, who remembered him, at the end of a drunken evening, not having made arrangements where he was going to stay the night. Dylan went to a telephone box somewhere near the Euston Road, emerging to declare wearily, 'Oh God, I'm so tired of sleeping with women I don't even like.' Dylan was reduced to asking for loans from his new friend Vernon Watkins. Again Cameron came to his rescue and packed him off for a rest cure with his (and Blakeston's) friend, Wyn Henderson, a large red-headed woman with appetites and energy to match.

Having been declared bankrupt, she had recently decamped to the village of Polgigga close to Land's End in Cornwall where she hoped to bring stability to her own roller-coaster life by running a bed and breakfast establishment. Born Winifred Lester to unmarried parents in South Africa, where her mother used to sing out of the back of a truck, she was a gifted musician who had once opened for the actress Ellen Terry. Wartime marriage to Kenneth Henderson, a rich English Guards officer, soon ended in divorce, after he decamped to Argentina to look after business interests set up by his uncle, Lord Faringdon. Having trained as a typographer, she was employed by various small publishers, including Nancy Cunard's Hours Press in Paris, from where she returned to London to work in a similar business with Desmond Harmsworth. She lived next door to Virginia Woolf's brother Adrian Stephen and his wife Karen in Gordon Square where she also ran a well-attended musical salon. But when Harmsworth merged his business with Francis Meynell of the Nonesuch Press, she found herself out of a job and was soon being sought by her creditors.

A 'new woman' of a type Dylan had seldom encountered (her son Nigel talked of her 'shattering procession of lovers'), she liked to talk about her liberated sex life and prided herself on having been psychoanalysed. Over Easter she took him to hear a performance of Bach's St Matthew Passion which, throwing some light on his interest in the symbol of Christ, he interpreted as a powerful homosexual love story. Dylan tired of her anecdotes of friendship with the pioneering sexologist Havelock Ellis (who usefully had taught her how to pee standing up). But he found her good company when drunk and, although eighteen years her junior, at some stage (the exact dates are uncertain) enjoyed a fleeting affair.

However his heart was never in it, for shortly before departing for Cornwall, he had met Caitlin Macnamara, the girl he was to marry the following year.

TEN

CAITLIN, EMILY AND VERONICA

Caitlin had been brought up by her mother Yvonne to think she would marry a duke. In contrast to Dylan, she did indeed have something aristocratic in her background and attitudes. Her quixotic father Francis Macnamara was a fine leonine specimen of a man but, in socio-political terms, a sad relic of the Protestant Anglo-Irish ascendancy. His own father Henry Valentine Macnamara had been High Sheriff of the beautiful desolate Irish county of Clare, much of which he owned, including the entire village around his mansion, Ennistymon House. After Magdalen College, Oxford, Francis had trained as a barrister in London. In 1907, he married Yvonne, after she had eloped from her disapproving family which mixed similar Anglo-Irish landed stock with a more dominant haut-bourgeois French Quaker strain. His letters were unusual for the time in their forthright avowal of his desire to 'fuck' her – a consequence, perhaps, of his friendship with the randy Welsh-born artist Augustus John who enthusiastically welcomed the publication of his book of poems, Marionettes, in 1909. As a result, in the balmy, high Edwardian days before the First World War, he decided to 'drop out' and pursue his interests in poetry, philosophy and sailing.

The young Macnamaras had four children – John, Nicolette, Brigit and, in December 1913, Caitlin, generally considered the prettiest of the girls. Before long, however, the would-be Bohemian Francis turned his back on marriage and children, leaving Caitlin in particular feeling resentful. He had long professed his Irish nationalist sympathies, provoking a split with his father, known as Henry Vee, who was a British loyalist. Feeling unable to support the Great War against Germany, Francis returned to Ireland where, in the wake of Synge, he conducted quasi-ethnographic research into the Celtic customs of the Aran Islanders, off the coast of County Clare, close to his own seat of Doolin House on the Atlantic Ocean. He avoided the fate of his father who was wounded in the arm and face while gamely resisting an Irish Republican ambush in 1919. Within three years Henry Vee was forcibly asked to leave his land. He finished his days in London on a dwindling income, his tenants having long asserted their rights to his property.

In his role as literary Bohemian, Francis translated Balzac's pioneering sex treatise, *Physiology of Marriage*, put out by the Casanova Press in 1924. While occupying himself in a series of affairs, he encouraged his wife and children to live near and in effect become an appendage of his friend Augustus John's extensive, gypsy-like family in Alderney Manor in Dorset. For a while he stayed in the vicinity trying to earn a living as a guru-like teacher (of John's son Romilly, among others) and editor of the respectable *Wessex Review*. But his philandering took him elsewhere, encouraging Yvonne to turn her back on heterosexual relationships and engage in an affair with a neighbour, Nora Summers, a brooding painter and later photographer who had known John's circle while studying at the Slade School of Art with her husband Gerald, who came from a rich family of steel manufacturers in North Wales. Caitlin and her sisters came to resent the woman who distracted their mother from caring for them. By the mid-1920s they were living in genteel poverty in a rambling former pub, New Inn House, at Blashford, near Ringwood, in Hampshire, roughly halfway between the Summerses (in Ferndown) and the Johns who in 1927 moved to Fryern Court, near Fordingbridge.

With few obvious parental constraints, the Macnamara children enjoyed a carefree upbringing. With the younger Johns, they romped around the countryside on the edge of the New Forest. When money became tight, they were sent briefly to stay with their Majolier grandmother in Provence, where the fiery Caitlin railed against French middle-class restrictions. Encouraged by Nora Summers, one of their 'two mummies', Brigit and, in particular, Nicolette were encouraged to paint. Caitlin threw her energies into riding and dancing, for which she shared a passion with Vivien John, Augustus's youngest daughter. (They were effectively cousins because in 1927 Francis Macnamara had married Edie McNeill, the small dark sister of Dorelia ('Dodo') McNeill, Augustus's long-term mistress, and mother of his four later children.)

With her bright blue eyes and tangle of golden hair, Caitlin was an attractive uninhibited creature. In her memoir *Two Flamboyant Fathers*, her sister Nicolette portrayed her, with a touch of jealousy, as someone who from the age of twelve was a 'honey pot for men', thoroughly enjoying the power this gave her. According to this version, Caitlin 'unfairly romped through adolescence with a perfect nubile figure, a joy to men and a pleasure to herself. She always seemed to get away with murder.' But it was not quite that easy. The other side of Caitlin was the stroppy country girl, with a propensity to puppy fat. Her first boyfriend, in her mid-teens, was Caspar, one of the good-looking John sons, who had embarked on a naval career. But when, staying at Fryern, Caitlin dolled herself in a frilly nightgown and crept into the future Admiral of the

Fleet's bed, he did not want to know, thus adding to her feeling of rejection.

She spent two predictably miserable years at a second-rate boarding school in Bournemouth where the headmistress called her 'my little New Forest pony'. While still there, she and her friend Vivien John ran away to become dancers in London. Vivien had arranged an audition with her father's friend, the theatrical impresario C. B. Cochran, known for his troupe of high-kicking girls. Despite an impressive display of tap dancing and girlish gymnastics, Caitlin was apprehended and sent back to school. But she had made enough of a statement for her mother to allow her to return to the capital the following year to attend the Dillon School of Dancing, off Shaftesbury Avenue.

Despite several boyfriends, her sexual confidence was not improved when a Colombian painter she met through her sister Nicolette, now a student at the Slade, committed suicide after, but not necessarily because of, expressing his undying love for her. Her virginity was disposed of by Augustus John. She later claimed that the 'old goat' had pounced when she was posing for him in his studio in Mallord Street, Chelsea. That did not stop her going back the next day, and the same thing happening again. In her version, this rape by her father's friend put her off sex. But others suggest she was coquettish and perfectly capable of seducing the priapic artist. That was the background to the recollection of another young artist bowled over by her striking looks. Rupert Shephard painted her several times, but 'all too often, a large car, driven at some danger to others, would scream into the back yard [at Blashford] and Augustus would step out ... All activities stopped – the old stag had arrived to round up and take away his young doe.'

Around 1933 Caitlin temporarily set aside her stage ambitions and went to stay with her father in Ireland. If Francis Macnamara hoped for rapprochement, he was to be disappointed. In his grand town house in Dublin, she found his egotistical bluster and intellectual posturings more off-putting than ever. He accused her of being 'surly' and was not content, or so she said, until she burst into tears and tore from the room. With little money to hand, she much preferred the life in County Clare where, now that the 'Troubles' had abated, her father was thinking of turning the family's Ennistymon House into a hotel. With the daughter of one of her father's friends, she explored the dark smoky recesses of Irish peasant cottages, drank whiskey and danced with great exuberance at ceilidhs.

In Dublin she met an Austrian woman, Vera Gribben, who claimed to have studied with Isadora Duncan, California-born pioneer of free-flowing modern dance. Under her tutelage, Caitlin took to Duncan's sinuous movement and philosophy of self-expression. On her return to England, she was photographed by Nora Summers in various tripping poses, occasionally wearing an ill-shapen diaphanous garment, at other times – her mother's lover's speciality over the years – next to nothing.

She and Vera Gribben began to perform their fashionable mode of dance at select gatherings in London. A couple of years earlier Caitlin had wanted to go to Paris to join the Folies Bergères, but had been forbidden until she was twenty-one. Having attained her majority, she flew at Mrs Gribben's suggestion that they might both spend some time there on the first stage of a terpsichorean tour of Europe. Once in the French capital, not a great deal was heard of her dancing, though she did attend a school run by Isadora Duncan's brother. She had a relationship with an older Polish Jewish artist called Segal. She had only recently returned to London and was drinking in the Wheatsheaf with Augustus John (clearly more a sugar daddy with whom she slept than the rapist she later portrayed) when she bumped into Dylan.

Dating this encounter exactly is difficult. Caitlin has put it specifically at 12 April but there is no evidence for this. By then Dylan was down in Cornwall. He is likely to have met Caitlin during his few days in London prior to this trip. He described them to Vernon Watkins as living up to the conventions of his 'Life No 13: promiscuity, booze, coloured shirts, too much talk, too little work'. But this period appears to have been a boozy, masculine affair, with Dylan catching up with his literary friends. He would have had no time for the other part of the myth of this first meeting: that within minutes, they were in bed together at the Eiffel Tower where they took pleasure in charging the room to Augustus John – something she would have been able to get away with because the proprietor Rudolf Stulik had often seen her there with the painter.

More likely, Dylan met Caitlin briefly at the Wheatsheaf prior to going to Cornwall. He was pleasurably struck, but made no known reference to her during his month away. His wooing and bedding of her probably took place when he returned from the west country in mid-May. While staying with Wyn, he had polished up some poems for his next book, including the final sonnets of 'Altarwise by owl-light', which first saw print in July in Roger Roughton's small circulation *Contemporary Prose and Poetry* (the outlet too for several stories including his long gestated 'The Burning Baby').

The enigmatic Roughton was one of the group behind the International Surrealist Exhibition in June. The main instigator was the artist Roland Penrose, together with the young surrealist poet David Gascoyne. Penrose had been introduced to Gascoyne in Paris the previous year by their mutual friend, one of the fathers of French surrealism, the poet Paul

Eluard, whose first wife, a Russian woman nicknamed Gala, had left him for the Spanish painter Salvador Dali. Gascoyne, who as a boy of seventeen had enthusiastically reviewed modernist exhibitions at the Mayor Gallery for Orage's *New English Weekly*, was in the French capital to write his *Short History of Surrealism*. He and Penrose conceived a plan to bring an exhibition of European surrealist artists to London where the local inhabitants, in Penrose's words, needed to be freed 'from the constipation of logic which conventional public school mentality had brought upon them'. Having enlisted the help of Herbert Read, the all-purpose art critic and historian, they appointed Eluard and his fellow surrealist André Breton to select what works should be brought to London.

A girl in a mask of red roses stood outside when Breton opened the show at the New Burlington Galleries on 11 June. He and others had chosen nearly four hundred paintings, sculptures and art objects to represent the surrealist spirit, including works by Picasso, Miró, Max Ernst, Man Ray, Marcel Duchamp and Henry Moore. Dali, another exhibitor, wore a diving suit as he gave a graphic talk on his love life with Gala. Dylan's contribution is unclear: the critic John Davenport remembered him shepherding Augustus John round the exhibition (a surrealistic touch in itself); according to Gascoyne, he 'came in and tied a mouse to an exhibit'; while another story had him approaching participants with a cup of boiled string and asking in a loud voice if they wanted it weak or strong (although this last sighting sounds similar to an item on show, Meret Oppenheim's fetishistic 'Object' – a cup, saucer and spoon covered in gazelle fur). If not a surrealist in practice (he was too much of a traditional lyricist), Dylan supported Gascoyne's premise that 'man's imagination should be free, but everywhere is in chains', and he enjoyed the controversy surrounding the event, which was denounced by the *Daily Mail* as responsible for 'decadence and unhealthiness of mind and body, the unleashing of low and abnormal instincts, a total lack of reason and balance, a distasteful revelation of subconscious thoughts and desires'.

The organisers included not only Roughton and Gascoyne but a couple of new friends, the engraver Bill (S. W.) Hayter and, in particular, George Reavey, Hayter's some-time flatmate and collaborator in Paris and now a fellow author with Dylan at Dent. Small and entrepreneurial, Reavey had been brought up in Russia, the son of an Armagh linen manufacturer who made his fortune by building mills. He was part of the Cambridge University generation of the late 1920s which produced challenging poets and artists of the calibre of Malcolm Lowry, Kathleen Raine, Charles Madge, Humphrey Jennings, Julian Trevelyan, John

Davenport, James Reeves, William Empson, Michael Redgrave and Jacob Bronowski (later better known as a scientific populariser). After graduating, Reavey decamped to Paris where he immersed himself in the avant-garde culture of the early 1930s, writing his own poetry, translating Russian literature, and setting up his own Europa Press, which published the first book of poems by the Irish writer Samuel Beckett. In 1936 he returned to London to set up an offshoot of the Europa Press in Red Lion Square, where one of his first projects was a translation (by Beckett and others) of Paul Eluard's poem under the title 'Thorns of Thunder'. His contacts made him the ideal choice to arrange an adjunct to the main surrealism exhibition, a poetry evening in the New Burlington Galleries on 26 June where Dylan proudly followed the main speaker Eluard in reading some of his own poems.

A week later Dylan was back in Cwmdonkin Drive, regaling his local friends with tales of Dali's lobster telephone and his own plans to write a play for Rupert Doone's fashionably leftist Group Theatre, where his new girlfriend Caitlin had once danced. He caught up with her again in mid-July in Laugharne, the Carmarthenshire seaside town which he had enjoyed visiting with Glyn Jones a couple of years earlier. Fred Janes was back in Swansea, teaching part-time at the art school, developing his meticulous style of still life painting. Fred had entered a painting in an exhibition (to be judged by the Pembrokeshire born Augustus John) at the National Eisteddfod in Fishguard. Since Fred intended to borrow his father's car, Dylan offered to accompany him. As Laugharne was roughly halfway between Swansea and Fishguard, Dylan took the opportunity to invite himself to call on Richard Hughes, the local author whom he had missed on his earlier visit.

Despite his enthusiasm for Dylan's early work eighteen months earlier, the bearded seafaring Hughes was not the sort of person Dylan would normally have sought out. He was a rarefied mixture of English elite (having been educated at Charterhouse and Oxford) and deep Welsh roots, with a family tree that stretched back to Beli the Great, a quasi-mythical King of the Britons in the days of Julius Caesar. Dylan had no real desire to see him, but he knew that Augustus John and Caitlin would be staying there en route to Fishguard. Hughes and his wife Frances lived in Castle House, a pink-washed Georgian house adjacent to the ruins of the Norman castle, which they had rented together from a locally established family, the Starkes. They and their two guests were sitting down for lunch when Dylan and Janes arrived and were asked to join them. Caitlin recalled that John was immediately put on edge – not surprisingly, since he must have known Dylan was his young mistress's lover.

Frances Hughes saw things differently: 'I remember Dylan coming into the dining room at Laugharne and thinking this was one of the most vivid and alive young men I'd seen in years.' With his smallish stature and unkempt appearance, he was hardly attractive, but his latent energy, his 'brilliant eyes and curly hair' and his 'somewhat ethereal' quality impressed women in Wales as much as in London. Her approval helped smooth over a potentially difficult situation, and in the afternoon everyone, bar the Hugheses, drove westwards to Fishguard. On the way the party stopped at several pubs, John did his judging (he did not like what Janes had to offer), and they returned, repeating their pub crawl along the way. After one stop, Dylan left Janes's car and climbed with Caitlin into the back seat of John's black six-cylinder Wolsey, 'the Bumblebee'.

In his mirror, John had to endure the sight of his passengers 'osculating assiduously'. When he reached St Clears, he resolutely failed to turn off the main road for Laugharne but continued another eight miles into Carmarthen. There the drinking continued at the Boar's Head. John said very little, but Caitlin knew he was furious. When they prepared to leave, she heard a scuffle and, as John jumped into the car and drove off at high speed, she saw Dylan lying on the ground, having emerged the worse from a fight. John had simply refused to transport Dylan back to Laugharne. He wanted Caitlin, and was not prepared to brook any rivals. She finished the night unsatisfactorily, staring at the ceiling, wondering when he would be finished having his way with her.

The following morning Dylan turned up again and the Hugheses witnessed an entertaining French-style farce as he and John scurried around the battlements, the one emerging for a rhetorical scene with Caitlin as the other exited through a door stage left. Dylan returned by bus and train to Swansea where next morning he wrote a passionate letter to Caitlin in Blashford, reminding her that she had not demurred when he had mentioned marriage. His promising London flirtation had become a full-blown affair. But even he realised nothing would happen for some time, because he lacked money. There was a note of desperation in his confession to Desmond Hawkins that he thought continuously of 'possessing it in great milky wads to spend on flashy clothes and cunt and gramophone records and white wine and doctors and white wine again and a very vague young Irish woman whom I love in a grand, real way but have to lose because of money money money money.'

He travelled to London to spend the August bank holiday weekend with Caitlin. John had calmed down enough to agree to draw the frontispiece for a travel book about Wales that Dylan was hoping to tout around London publishers. Dylan had been toying with the idea following the success of J. B. Priestley's *English Journey* in 1934 and Edwin Muir's similar *Scottish Journey* in 1935. He had no doubt heard about W. H. Auden and Louis MacNeice's on-going expedition to Iceland. He hoped John's involvement would help him secure a contract.

In the context of Wales, the project was topical. A phenomenon of the past decade had been the emergence of the Welsh Nationalist party, Plaid Cymru, which, although as yet small and electorally insignificant, threatened to fill the political gap left vacant, particularly in rural Welsh-speaking areas, by the decline of the Liberal party. (The former Liberal leader David Lloyd George had denounced it at the Eisteddfod attended by Dylan and his well-tanked party in Fishguard.) Led by Saunders Lewis, a powerful writer who lectured at University College, Swansea, Plaid Cymru had grown, alongside other Welsh cultural organisations, as Welsh intellectuals contemplated the long-term consequences of the emigration and economic devastation which accompanied the continuing slump. In 1936 a fund to help the unemployed was launched by Lewis in Dowlais, in the Rhondda valley, where in November that year the beleaguered King Edward VIII visited the derelict iron and steel works and declared 'something must be done'. Partly to distance itself from Anglo-Saxon cultural hegemony and partly reflecting the views of Lewis, a Roman Catholic convert, and other similarly inclined leaders, the party adopted an Idealist form of nationalism which, drawing on the ideas of French Catholics, such as Maurice Barrés and Charles Maurras, saw Wales as part of a greater Christian Europe.

Plaid's right-wing tendencies, which were reflected in its close alliance with the quasi-Fascist Action Française, helped explain its lack of electoral success. However in May 1935 it was handed a propaganda opportunity when the Baldwin government announced it intended to build an RAF bombing school at Penyberth, near Pwllheli, in the Lleyn peninsula in Caernarfonshire. Plaid attacked this on the ground that it was an assault on Welsh rural values. Its opposition became more virulent in September 1936 when Lewis and two other Plaid leaders, the Reverend Lewis Valentine and D. J. Williams, participated in an arson attack on the partially built school. They were arrested and, when the case was transferred to the Old Bailey in London where the 'Penyberth three' refused to give evidence in English and were sentenced to nine months imprisonment, the party gained its first martyrs and was rewarded with an upsurge in support.

As this political confrontation was brewing, Keidrych Rhys, a young Welsh journalist in London, hatched plans to launch a new leftist review which, while sympathetic to nationalist aspirations, would showcase the extraordinary range of Welsh writing in English. Born William Ronald

Rees Jones in 1915, Rhys was, like Dylan, a product of a Welsh Grammar School (Llandovery) who spoke with a fruity cut-glass accent. (Unlike Dylan, he wore the immaculate tweed suits of a country gentleman.) His initial approach to Dylan was a suggestion that they should collaborate on an anthology of Anglo-Welsh writing – something Dylan had long wanted to do himself.

Although this idea fell through, Dylan realised that there was copy to be written about his country. The main event of the summer had been the outbreak of the Spanish Civil War in July, which introduced some hard reality into the wacky world of the surrealists. In keeping with his claim that surrealism was not a retreat from but a principled assault on reality, David Gascoyne travelled to Spain where he was joined in the struggle against Franco by others among Dylan's acquaintances, such as Roland Penrose and Stephen Spender. On a different front, Gascoyne was discussing another unlikely offshoot from surrealism with two brilliant Cambridge graduates, Charles Madge, a poet working on the Daily Mirror, and Humphrey Jennings, who had made documentary films with Len Lye. Together they were developing the idea of Mass Observation, a meticulous record of the everyday experience of ordinary Britons, though they came to it not as sociologists but as avant-garde poets, who regarded their documentation as a collage which would provide a snap-shot of the national unconscious. In the autumn the Jarrow march served to emphasise another more political aspect of social reality, and again the importance of looking to one's community.

Dylan received encouragement in writing about Wales from the poet and critic William Empson, who in between teaching posts in the Far East and having just published his Poems, was often in the Fitzroy where he recalled meeting Dylan, scrounging for money and talking about going to work as a checker-in at a Welsh mine or as a grocer. Often the strength of Dylan's views about his home country have been ignored. But Empson noted revealingly:

> What with the Welsh nationalism, the vague and balanced but strong political interests of this man, the taste for violence in his writing, and the way he was already obviously exhausting his vein of poetry about events which involved the universe but happened under his skin, it seemed to me that being a checker-in was just what he wanted; and I shouted at him for some time, against two talkers I should otherwise have been eager to hear, to tell him that he was wasting his opportunities as a Welshman and ought to make full use of a country in which he could nip across the classes.

Typically Dylan dismissed Empson's suggestion, but kept to his own idea of a travel book about Wales, though he took his time to get round to writing it. In September he claimed Dent had taken him by surprise when it published his *Twenty-Five Poems*. The critical response was generally more equivocal than for *18 Poems*. Even his friend Desmond Hawkins said in the *Spectator* that he had been less successful than before in 'subduing his material to a communicable form'. However, despite his having missed a rendezvous with her, Edith Sitwell's enthusiasm was undimmed. She arranged to review the book for the *Sunday Times* and pestered the literary editor Cyril Lakin when her notice did not appear at the expected time. Lakin had somehow failed to take up her imperious request to review *18 Poems* a year earlier. But this time the *Sunday Times* did deliver, and her notice on 15 November was followed by an avalanche of letters. Twenty of them were printed over the following two months, providing a forum on the pros and cons of modern poetry and a high-brow alternative to the gloom of Jarrow and Edward VIII's abdication in December. This level of interest was reflected in the sales of *Twenty-Five Poems* which raced through its first impression of 750 copies and had three more impressions, making it one of the more successful poetry books of the 1930s.

Convinced she was responsible for the popularity of her protégé, Sitwell sought to promote him further. She asked Richard Jennings, a compliant acolyte at the *Daily Mirror*, to find him a job. But even Jennings could see the drawbacks. He was already working in the office with Charles Madge who had been recommended by T. S. Eliot, and he feared Dylan would fight not only with Madge but the rest of the staff. 'I would do, or attempt, anything for you,' he told Sitwell, 'so must, I suppose, try again. But is there nobody else? Won't T. S. E[liot] help him on the *Criterion* or wherever?' So the intrepid lady turned to Kenneth Clark: 'Have you seen young Dylan Thomas' *Twenty-Five Poems*? He is the boy I told you about when I sat next to you at dinner at Sybil Colefax's. The poems are very obscure, and very strange, but singularly beautiful, and I think it is certain that he is going to be a great poet.'

By the start of 1937 Dylan was beginning to find a wider audience. As the *Sunday Times* debate suggested, the public was bored with modernist experimentation and happy to make acquaintance with, as Grigson sourly put it, 'a Young Poet untainted with Eliot or with Auden etc. (or with the Left), whose poems, though a bit unintelligible, sounded at least familiar in an old grandiloquent way'.

Professional recognition was no help in his blossoming relationship with Caitlin. That was undergoing an unexpected hiatus after she contacted gonorrhoea from another man and retired to Ireland to recuperate. As her confidant, she turned to Rupert Shephard, her sister Nicolette's friend from the Slade who had been so smitten with Caitlin's looks at Blashford four years earlier that he insisted on painting her. They had kept in touch, usually when she wanted something, such as a person to store her French lover Segal's paintings which she had hoped to sell in London. He was quite happy to act as an amiable lapdog, even if it meant receiving Caitlin's confidences about her future with Dylan. She told him that she was smitten, though 'for internal doctoral reasons', she needed to cool the relationship and go to Ireland.

Over the next four months there was little holding back Dylan, buoyed as he was with his taste of success. In the Six Bells shortly after Christmas Oswell Blakeston introduced him to Emily Holmes Coleman, an eccentric, impulsive American writer whose one auto-biographical novel, *The Shutter of Snow*, published in 1930, had dealt with her breakdown and incarceration in an asylum following the birth of her son six years earlier. For much of the previous decade she had lived in Paris where, in between writing for *transition*, she had been secretary to both the international anarchist Emma Goldman and the flighty heiress (and later art collector) Peggy Guggenheim. Through the latter she had met Djuna Barnes, for whose experimental novel *Nightwood* she had originally come to London to find a publisher. The book was good enough to interest T. S. Eliot who had put it out under the Faber imprint earlier in 1936 — albeit with an ambiguous introduction, distancing himself from the lesbian content, and saying it would 'appeal primarily to readers of poetry' (amongst whom Dylan was a great enthusiast of the work).

Coleman, whose stream of consciousness style was one of Barnes's influences, had stayed on in London, living in Oakley Street, off the King's Road in Chelsea, where she was trying to make sense of her complicated love life. Dubbed 'Little Annie Oakley' by Eliot, she had conducted a long unsatisfactory affair with a brilliant civil servant called Peter Hoare. When she weaned herself off that, she conceived a grand passion for the young poet George Barker, but that was complicated by his bisexuality, a problem which also prevented her proceeding with her friendship with David Gascoyne. In her search for sexual satisfaction she had alighted on Humphrey Jennings, the handsome young poet and film-maker who flitted between Cambridge literary cronies, Cameron's advertising world and surrealism. But he was too caught up in a Byronic vision of himself, driving her to the verge of suicide.

So the fresh-faced full-lipped Coleman was immediately 'delighted' to meet Dylan — 'a round-eyed animal, with a chuckling guttural laugh, and a rosy personality'. He looked at her and pronounced, approvingly,

'Not a hard line in her face!' On the ensuing pub crawl, a Welshman called Richard Hughes tried to bed her (not the author in Laugharne but a sculptor who later changed his name to Huws). But she was more interested in Dylan who 'opened [her] heart' by 'raving' about the work of another friend, the troubled author Antonia White, whose own novel, Frost in May, an intensely personal account of convent life, had been published in 1933. Dylan said he wanted to meet her, which surprised White when she learnt this the following day.

Although Norman Cameron warned Coleman about Dylan's history of sexual disease (there was a suggestion he had picked up another dose of gonorrhoea from a prostitute around the time of the surrealist exhibition), she and the young poet (sixteen years her junior) were soon conducting a passionate affair 'in pubs and clubs and cinemas and beds'. Through Peggy Guggenheim, the news quickly reached Paris from where Djuna Barnes took Coleman to task on 10 January 1937 for failing to write: 'Your new love affair must be "hurried" to account for it! I asked Peggy about you and she said it was someone called Dillon Thomas, or Thomas Dillon. She could not remember which – I wonder can it be the one who was Edna Millay's sweetie, and who helped her with what are said to be the worst translations of Baudelaire in existence? I suppose not.'

Having once been hospitalised for apparent mental illness, Coleman was fascinated by William Blake – a point of contact with Dylan who had some astute comments on her friends who teetered on the edge of insanity. After meeting Antonia White, he felt that, having once been mad, she could never quite recover the peace of mind she craved. 'She wants to be tame again, but she's been let loose once.' As for Gascoyne, he had knocked on the doors of madness, but had held back and never allowed himself to enter. 'A poetical surrealist in a looney-bin is a literary freak, but a surrealist who hangs around outside, pimping through the bars at the looney-logical activities of the inmates, can always be a man-of-letters and an acknowledged authority on the dark bits of the brain.' Despite occasional aberrations resulting from drink, Dylan's own adolescent psychoses had abated. Apart from some virulent spots, he was in better shape physically and mentally than for a long time.

Although sleeping with Coleman and saying he loved her, Dylan readily discussed his engrossing relationship with Caitlin. He spoke of marrying his 'Ireland', but wondered if she had the psychological resilience for the emotional ups and downs of living with a poet, though he was cheered to an extent by the knowledge that she was not squeamish about physical pain. He recalled Caitlin's imperviousness when she boiled a live lobster, driving others, including Dylan, from the kitchen because they could not bear to hear its screams.

For a while Coleman genuinely thought he was divided between her and Caitlin. 'He said he was. But no doubt he did not find me as congenial as she; though I followed him from pub to pub, I simply detested the life. And those "clubs"! ... They were (some of them) the saddest places I have ever been in. I wasn't bored with Dylan but I hated his kind of life. I enjoyed him alone, but he could not stand not drinking ... I just wasn't crazy-bohemian enough for him. Caitlin was.' She recalled how Dylan used to say admiringly of Caitlin, 'She's really crackers!' – though Coleman shrewdly suspected that being resolutely Bohemian required a rigid frame of reference that is ultimately conventional. (Coleman could be equally unconventional: once, in Hennekey's with Dylan and Cameron, she refused to allow the barman to close because, she said, two of Britain's greatest living poets were there and wanted to continue drinking.)

To contemplate these matters Dylan returned in late January to Swansea, where he also had another task. His father had finally retired in December and Dylan had to help his parents rent out Cwmdonkin Drive (it was not sold until 1943) and move into a smaller house close to the sea in Bishopston, one of the first villages leading out of Swansea into Gower. However this process was delayed by his mother's neuralgia, which confined her to bed unable to move the muscles in her face.

In between the two stages of this moving operation, Dylan dashed to Cambridge to fulfil a commitment to Wyn Lewis, a young undergraduate friend of Vernon Watkins, to give two talks to the Nashe Society in St John's College. He had not intended to take Coleman, but for some reason she accompanied him, perhaps as a result of some deal after he had written a review of her friend Djuna Barnes's *Nightwood* for *Light and Dark*, a short-lived Oxford periodical, where he described it as 'one of the three great prose books ever written by a woman'. (One of the others was almost certainly *Wuthering Heights*, whose author, Emily Brontë, he described as 'the only woman I've ever loved'.)

On Saturday 13 February he attended a formal Cambridge cocktail party, where he drank sherry and then whisky to steel himself, before falling asleep and then rousing himself to read a long (nearly two hours) paper on 'Modern Poetry et cetera'. Amidst 'brilliant, bitter, and sometimes bawdy invective' he elaborated on his distaste for the school of Auden and Spender and the 'inevitable compromises and vulgarisation attending works of propaganda'. He refused to answer questions, but ended by reading not only an Auden ballad but one of his favourite poems at the time, 'Captain Carpenter' by John Crowe Ransom. He may well have been alerted to its simple religious symbolism by Ransom's fellow American Coleman who was to follow her friend Antonia White into the Catholic church in 1942.

The following night he gave a more informal though animated reading of three short stories and part of his 'Altarwise by owl-light' sonnet sequence. During his visit he attended a lively party in his honour at the house of Gordon Fraser, a hospitable Cambridge bookseller. Fraser's wife Katherine had befriended a forlorn fellow Illinois graduate student, John Berryman. Dylan took to the hard-living Yeats-loving Berryman, a depressed version of himself, who was to become one of America's leading poets before committing suicide in 1972.

On the train to Cambridge Coleman taxed Dylan on the meaning of one of his sonnets. Despite his explanation, she felt it did not convey what he wanted it to say. 'It was clear to me then that he was sincere, and that some block in him (evident enough what it was) prevented his communicating in a way to be comprehended.' This block which she identified as his inability to handle reality was apparent in one incident at Cambridge. Professor E. M. W. Tillyard, a world authority on Shakespeare, came to meet Dylan (probably at the Saturday night party) but found him in one of his drunken poses – down on the floor, playing bears. In some embarrassment, Coleman tried to engage the eminent scholar in a discussion on Milton but found him 'naturally upset'. The following day Dylan knocked out a sad note to an unidentified correspondent. He was eating prairie oysters in Fraser's bookshop, waiting for the pubs to open, with the 'filthiest feeling in the world'. As a consequence, he apologised for not calling 'to do a Richards with you', suggesting he was going to participate in a repeat of an exercise pioneered by the former Cambridge (now Harvard) don I. A. Richards, who had given his students unidentified poems by famous writers and asked for comments.

Dylan's warm reception in Cambridge confirmed that, with the publication of his second book and following the controversy in the pages of the Sunday Times, he was – for a poet, at least – famous. At Edith Sitwell's suggestion, he followed her lead in appointing David Higham as his literary agent. Higham, a courteous, effective, old-school operator of Jewish origin and military background, had recently left Curtis Brown to set up his own company with two colleagues, Nancy Pearn and Laurence Pollinger. He was to become skilled in bailing Dylan out of difficult situations. Almost immediately he had to deal with his old agency which he discovered was touting around Dylan's book of short stories. Dylan apologised, saying he was a business dunce and explaining, unconvincingly, that he had been approached personally by the eponymous head, Spencer Curtis Brown. So Higham initially had to ensure he had exclusive representation.

Dylan had already begun to ask Higham about American publishers when he revealed his idea for a book about Wales, which he said was not intended to be a nationalist tirade or a naturalist's ramble but 'an intimate chronicle' of a personal journey by foot, bus and train. He intended to visit writers and painters he knew such as Richard Hughes and Caradoc Evans, and he still hoped having a frontispiece portrait by Augustus John would make it an attractive package for a publisher.

In London, en route from Cambridge back to Wales, Dylan and Coleman decided, rather than go to her flat, they would spend a night in a dank hotel, where he upset her with his bluff exclamation, at the mention of Caitlin, 'Oh, I've never told you anything about that. That is between us.' In Gower, he helped install his parents in their new house, with its garage and lawn much more of a suburban villa than Cwmdonkin Drive. From there on a balmy Easter Monday he wrote blithely to Coleman, making no reference to any misunderstanding. Instead he enthused about a sweater Caitlin had knitted him, while telling Coleman, 'I miss you deeply, and want to come back to London soon; I remember everything, and it's all good to remember. You are very, very near to me.'

Describing the Welsh bank holiday (in a way which foreshadowed his later story 'Holiday Memory'), he told Coleman he particularly liked such crowded days because – confirming something Trick liked to say – that was when he could observe humanity in all its tragic, comic, democratic variety, adding revealingly, if hardly correctly, 'It is only among poor failures that I find the people I like best.' He clearly liked this line for he elaborated on it to George Barker a few days later. For some reason the two young poets had never been introduced (though they had attended a party at David Archer's). Tentatively, Barker had made contact via Coleman with the idea of starting a poetic dialogue. Dylan readily agreed, claiming: 'All my friends are failures, I think the glories of the world are mingy, and the people I know and like best – hack Fleet streeters, assistant assistant film-producers, professional drunks, strays and outlaws, who are always, & always will be, just about to write their autobiographies – are too big to want them or get them.' Barker wrote 'Epistle to D. T.' which was printed in the May issue of *New Verse*, but from Dylan nothing more was heard.

One reason was that it was time for his long-discussed journey through Wales. On 6 April, his first day out, he made slow progress, travelling by meandering, stopping train, as far as Machynlleth, one of the centres of Welsh language activism in Montgomeryshire, though, so far as Dylan was concerned in a telegram to Coleman, it was 'Gods knows where'. En route, he had spent part of the afternoon in a wet and windy Aberystwyth where, chastened by the force and unpredictability of the sea, which had fascinated him since his Swansea youth, he proceeded to Machynlleth, from where he set out walking late that same evening. It was madness, something quickly brought home to him by his hostile environment.

'I was not the only one abroad that foal of a night,' he wrote in an unpublished fragment based on his journal. 'An hour after closing time, a white queen rat, big as a Persian cat, ran by the hedgeside; she was not followed by her common rats, as the queen rat is in all stories; there was no need to climb a tree, or throw my safe stone. She ran on into the darkness, There were vampires in all the hedges, pale girls & clergymen's wives – small respectable women, with set red smiles & long eye-teeth; the fiend who follows a lonely man should catch him up. It was a bad beginning.'

Within a very short time he had had enough. He may, as he had said in his bank holiday letter, have wanted to get back to Coleman. Or he may have got wind that Caitlin was due from Ireland. Either was good enough reason to hang up his hiking boots. Since Caitlin was not in London, he immediately sought the comforts of his American girlfriend, planting himself in Coleman's flat and declaring with the conviction of a small boy returned from a perilous adventure, 'Safe, at last.' They were together in the crowded Fitzroy when, as Coleman recorded, 'all of a sudden a blonde childish head with a pretty pink face appeared through the mass, put out a hand & took Dylan's; & he with a smile of delight went right out with this girl.' From this woman's hair and general demeanour, Coleman thought she must be a pub whore, and sat back, waiting for him to return. But Dylan never came back. Coleman was so upset when Dylan did not contact her over the next three days that she went looking for him with a friend, Phyllis Jones. Jones found Dylan and his blonde girl in a pub near Charing Cross. He introduced his companion as Caitlin, back from Ireland, and stated he was going to marry her.

On 13 April David Gascoyne ran into Dylan and his fiancée in Piccadilly, where they were on their way to a cinema to see the horror film The Golem. He accompanied them part of the way, but, en route, Dylan got some dust in his eye and had to divert to a chemist for an eye-bath – an ungainly sight, Gascoyne noted, along with his impressions of a muted Caitlin, whom he described astutely as having 'a hard innocence, obtuse, hermetic, and a concealed but very precise knowledge of how to deal with anyone she might want to deal with'.

Three days later, Dylan had recovered enough to meet Berryman, the young American from Cambridge, who was in London to meet his hero, W. B. Yeats, at the Athenæum. According to Berryman, Dylan heaped scorn on Yeats, as well as his usual bêtes noires such as Auden, and tried to get him drunk at lunch-time prior to his important engagement. Around this time Coleman saw Dylan again for the first time since the Fitzroy. Caitlin was temporarily back in Blashford, and he was looking doleful. Coleman asked him to choose between her and Caitlin, but he would not. Back at her flat, she made him sleep alone, which infuriated him. Next day she told him never to come back. With Nigel Henderson, his friend Wyn's artist son in the room, Dylan sat slumped in the sofa, not saying a word.

It is not difficult to guess what happened afterwards. The following week he was due to make his first important broadcast, reading his and other people's poems, in 'Life and the Modern Poet', a fifteen-minute programme for the BBC for which he was being paid an inclusive fee of four guineas. On the day of the broadcast Bert Trick met D. J. Thomas on a bus in Swansea. The recently retired schoolmaster proudly told him to listen to the wireless that evening, though he also added, 'Do not be disappointed if the announcer says that Dylan Thomas has been indisposed and he has to play Debussy.' And so it almost came to pass. Having received a second £25 tranche of his advance for his account of his Welsh journey, Dylan completely forgot he was supposed to record his contribution for the newly established Welsh region in Swansea. A couple of hours before he was on air, he was dragged from a London pub by John Pudney and taken to Broadcasting House, where a land-link with Swansea was hastily rigged. No-one who listened was any the wiser as to the background. However Dylan's behaviour and, even worse, his failure to provide a script afterwards, caused over the next couple of months a flurry of unanswered letters to him and of related bureaucratic memos within the BBC, including one to the Welsh Programme Director: 'A nice mess-up all round.' He was not invited back for eighteen months.

Clearly his no-show was the result of an extended period of over-indulgence following his dumping by Coleman and subsequent reunion with Caitlin. He ended in a nursing home with bronchitis and laryngitis, while Caitlin returned again to Blashford where he wrote longingly, telling her that being away from her was 'absolutely a physical removal ... If I lost a hand when you weren't with me, when you came back it would grow again, stronger & longer than ever. That's my cock words again, though all it means is true as heaven.'

He could not, to put it crudely, keep his cock away. Needing somewhere to stay, he was taken in by Veronica Sibthorp, a rich partially crippled artist whom he had met in Cornwall the previous year. While he continued to tell everyone about Caitlin, he seems to have been happy (possibly as a quid pro quo for somewhere to stay) to sleep with Veronica, though the exact timing of their sexual affair is uncertain. She lived in Great Ormond Street, opposite the nurses' home where Ruthven Todd used to say that the spectacle of the girls dressing and undressing was better than anything he later saw in Jersey City. Estranged from Jake Sibthorp, a rich printer who drove a Bentley, she was an excellent cook, who possessed an unusual luxury, a refrigerator. Her flat provided a civilised alternative venue to Norman Cameron's for raucous parties and inventive word games. She would park her disabled leg, dubbed 'Gilbert', on a stool and, if she needed to move around her kitchen, she would hop. Calling Dylan 'the Angelic Pig' (a friendlier alternative to Cameron's 'the Ugly Suckling'), she used to bathe him daily (perhaps to alleviate his spots).

They used to meet Todd in the Swan pub, where others in their circle included William Empson and Bob Pocock, a former policeman beginning a broadcasting career. On one occasion Dylan managed to stab himself in the eye, eating a plate of meat-balls. Another time he and Todd talked their way into the Café Royal where a man bought them a Pimms No. 1 and extolled the financial rewards of writing pornography. Dylan thought he could do the same and knocked out a ten-page story overnight. But when he re-read it, he thought it was so bad that he tore it up. He reserved his licentiousness for rhymes made up for his friends, along the lines of:

> The last time I slept with the Queen,
> I repeatedly muttered 'Ich Dien',
> She called me a shite
> And said,'Put out the light.
> A Queen should be served but not seen.'

Veronica kept an album of Dylan's occasional verses and drawings from this period which is now in the National Library of Wales. Apart from two more serious items – Dylan's short introduction to his Welsh trip and the draft of an interesting though later abandoned poem, based on hunting images, starting 'For as long as forever is', which he read to Vernon Watkins around this time – this portfolio describes a relationship that was childish and bawdy. The influence of the recent surrealist exhibition is evident in several cartoons in Dylan's hand, including one captioned 'Egocentric, egocock', and another with Veronica's caption 'Child surprised by size of cock'. A self-portrait by Dylan carries his legend: 'I'm young but I can learn', while his caricature of Caitlin has the words: 'Augustus' model (she hopes)'. There are three delightful sketches titled 'Lazy', including 'Welsh lazy' with an annotation by Dylan:

> Oh oh there's lazy I
> am
> Damn
> It all I am, aye

Hermaphroditism is a theme in several drawings, but the essentially sexual nature of Dylan's liaison with Veronica was evident from a doodle depicting a bee and someone in bed. With the rubric 'Bear in bed', it carries Dylan's two-line 'Poem to Veronica':

> Wherever there's honey there's bees & bears there
> And I'm a bad bee & you're a good bear.

And if that was not clear enough, he also wrote:

> I love my love with an A because she Answers
> Both my hands, while both her Breasts are dancers.
> I love my love with a B because she beats
> All others at Lighthousing up her teats.

In 'Shouldn't', one of several crisp short stanzas, Dylan took a more humorous attitude to death than usually found in his poetry:

> All I know about death
> Can be said in one breath:
> It's tall and it's short
> And it shouldn't ought.

His salacious schoolboy humour is most apparent in another poem:

> Up in the belfry sexton stands
> Pulling pud with grimy hands.
> Parson in vestry upward yells
> 'Stop pulling pud, pull fucking bells.'
> Groaning at the thought of working

Sexton goes on pulling gherkin.
Pausing not to say his prayers
Parson stamps up belfry stairs,
Just when reaches peak so high
Stops a packet in the eye;
Sexton, having shot his spray,
Buttons up and puts away,
Turning round to parson yells
'Now perhaps I'll pull fucking bells.'

Moral
The moral of this story's plain
And should be taught in schools again
Never mix up work with play
Pull pud by night & bells by day.

Dylan was in London for the Coronation of King George VI on 12
May. Elizabeth Fusco, a Scottish dancer turned actress, watched the
procession with him from the Trafalgar Square offices of the *Courier*, a
literary magazine written almost entirely by Gerald Kersh, an author of
novels and short stories much valued by Dylan. Except that Dylan refused
to look at the ceremony and sat with his back to the window. 'He didn't
like the pomp,' recalled Fusco, while expressing surprise because he
normally enjoyed 'colour and gaiety and brass bands'. Fusco had recently
arrived in London from Glasgow and was working in films as Elizabeth
Ruby. Dylan rescued her from a sophisticated movie set she disliked.
She was impressed by his hands and particularly by his voice: not so
much his accent – 'he could have been Hungarian' – but his 'wonderful
tones'. What she described as a 'romance' rather than affair ensued as
they explored London on foot, visiting pubs and restaurants, talking a
lot, perhaps ending in an all-night café by the Thames, where she
retained an image of him, lonely and sad, reflected in the river. The
Coronation hardly featured as a topic of conversation among their
Bohemian acquaintances. More important was the war in Spain and the
rise of Nazism in Germany. But though Dylan was aware of developments,
he did not want to think about them – probably, Fusco thought, because
it hurt too much.

His empathy with fellow human beings was obvious, even if
sometimes sentimental. 'He used to be horribly upset by any sort of
suffering,' such as the sight of a waiter limping or news of an
unmarried girl who was pregnant. Fusco did also witness another,
more hurtful, side to his character. When she showed affection

towards a baby with a scar, he laughed and said, 'Serves it right.' He made great play of accosting women in bars and trying to seduce them. To the amusement of male hangers-on, he would offer his stud services in a flurry of four-letter words. He took particular pleasure in abusing English women.

Inevitably this behaviour incited physical reaction from husbands and boyfriends, and Fusco found it curious that this peaceful man could sometimes provoke such violence. She ascribed it to a quality of saintliness in Dylan. This may sound a paradox, but she was by no means the only person to remark on his fall-guy innocence – a trait noted by Bert Trick as the secret of not only his character but his creative output. At the same time, Fusco noted 'he was obsessed by death and creation' – the subjects of most of his jokes. Indeed the first joke he told her was about coprophilia, a word he had to explain to her. But she found him extraordinarily vivid and learnt more with him about life, people and art than with anyone. 'He educated me into the Bohemian idiom.'

Meanwhile, at Veronica's, Dylan had been trying to write up his account of his Welsh journey, but had made little progress, Despite his colourful social life and romps with his landlady-cum-lover, he thought incessantly about Caitlin, building her up as a symbol of youth and innocence. (He still was not aware that she was slightly older than he.) He fantasised about the two of them operating a close conspiracy, 'a sort of mad bewilderment and astonishment oblivious to the Nasties and Meanies', and based on a shared innocence that 'goes awfully deep, and our discreditable secret is that we don't know anything at all, and our inner secret is that we don't care that we don't.'

She also had been thinking and, having reacquainted herself with Celtic culture, could imagine many less satisfying roles than playing the wild Irish muse to a penniless poet. She agreed to accompany Dylan to a cottage owned by Veronica's husband, Jake, in Lamorna Cove, Cornwall, close to where he had stayed the previous year. On 9 June Caitlin's father, Francis, married for the third time to Iris O'Callaghan, a tempestuous young Irishwoman who had been at finishing school with another of his daughters, Nicolette, in Paris. It cannot have been entirely coincidence that on the following day Dylan in Cornwall composed a careful letter to his own parents. He apologised for not being in touch for two months; his behaviour was 'careless, callous and quite unreasonable'. The reason, he explained, along with a routine request for clean clothes, was that he was finalising plans to marry Caitlin the following week in Penzance registry office. He said he intended to come to Swansea when the ceremony was over. He was going to continue his perambulation of Wales, while Caitlin returned to Blashford until they had enough money to live together.

Events moved more slowly than he wished. His parents became alarmed and put their son-in-law Haydn Taylor to tracking Dylan down. Taylor telephoned Yvonne Macnamara, advising her not to let her daughter marry this man. At some stage Dylan and Caitlin were in London, where they bumped into Emily Holmes Coleman drinking with Mervyn Peake in the Wheatsheaf. Coleman noted how, even though the wedding had yet to take place, Caitlin showed off her ring with childish glee. The American claimed she took Dylan outside and told him not to dare to let his fiancée down.

This visit probably allowed Augustus John to complete his portrait of a radiant, strong-featured Caitlin and to work on his study of Dylan which was to be the frontispiece to the Wales book. The painter had written to her in Cornwall: 'I spent some time combing the London pubs in hopes of finding you & getting you back for a bit to finish that pink picture which I rather bank on. If I came down soon would you come back with me do you think? I could do Dylan's drawing at the same time ... I hope you haven't caught any more diseases from Dylan, or others. Keep the fun clean also your [word undistinguishable] my little seraph ... P.S. I take it you are not spliced yet.'

The journey to London (as well as drinking both there and in Cornwall) ate into what little money Dylan and Caitlin had. They spent the £3 they had carefully hidden to pay for their wedding licence. But eventually, after two postponements, love triumphed. D.J. resigned himself to the fact that 'the young irresponsibles are bent on their supreme act of folly' and sent them a welcome gift of £5. Even so, Wyn Henderson, who had opened a guest-house with the painter Max Chapman in Mousehole, a few miles round the coast from Lamorna, had to take in the couple and then arrange and finally pay for their low-key wedding in Penzance registry office on 11 July. With Dylan in his regular garb of corduroy trousers, tweed jacket, check shirt and no tie, and Caitlin wearing a simple blue cotton dress, the couple exchanged two cheap Cornish silver rings which he had bought in Penzance without telling her – a romantic touch she liked. The ceremony had taken place, Dylan delightedly told Vernon Watkins, 'with no money, no prospect of money, no attendant friends or relatives, and in complete happiness'.

ELEVEN

MARRIAGE PANGS

At some stage in their marriage Dylan and Caitlin played the truth game, filling out a form titled 'Qualities: The New Confessions Book' which appeared in The Weekend Book, a popular annual for the more literate of the pre-television age, comprising humour, poetry and short stories. It is impossible to say when they did this, though it was probably earlier rather than later in their liaison. Since the book was published by the Nonesuch Press which Wyn Henderson had worked for, the Thomases may well have found it on her shelves and submitted themselves to its silent self-analysis while down in Cornwall.

The book requires its readers to assess themselves and others on fourteen personality traits, giving marks out of twenty. Caitlin thought Dylan was strong on sensibility (a maximum 20), moral sense (19) and sincerity (18); less so on will power (7), discretion (3) and humility (0). He was appreciative of her sincerity (18), sensibility (18) beauty, taste and sensuousness (all 17), but not of her humility (4), tact (4) and discretion (2). Turning their gazes on themselves, Caitlin felt she had sincerity (20), sensibility (19) will power and humility (both 18), but little sense of humour (6), moral sense (5), tolerance (3), discretion (1) or tact (0). Dylan was proud of his sincerity, sensuousness and sensibility (all 18), but admitted he had ground to make up on taste and tact (both 8), discretion (5) and humility (2).

In sum they both saw themselves as full of sincerity and sensibility, while low on tact and discretion. Ironically, these latter qualities were quickly required when the newly married couple had to withstand Wyn Henderson's excited pleas to join them in a threesome while they were making love. (Caitlin was apparently agreeable, but Dylan would not have it.) They soon vacated her guest-house, the Lobster Pot, and moved into Max Chapman's small studio overlooking the harbour in the seaside village of Newlyn, halfway between Mousehole and Penzance. The view was pleasant enough, the air invigorating and gulls flew in for breakfast, even if the overall quality of the environment left something to be desired, with the smell from the fish-market directly in front, the dust from the coal-yard below, and the ubiquitous fleas and other insects from the municipal dump behind. Furnishings included an ancient primus stove, but neither of them could cook. As if Dylan did not already know it, his new wife was quite capable of drinking, however. He joked that they ate in the morning, as they were both too unsteady in the evening to open the tins they had bought.

As the Spanish Civil War entered a more bloody phase, Dylan and Caitlin were surrounded by second-rate artists and writers, some left over from an Edwardian high age, others simply trying to escape if not blot out the grim realities of the late 1930s. They met Dod Procter, the celebrated expressionist painter who was the grande dame of the Newlyn art scene. In her mid-forties, she fancied Dylan – or so he thought – which may explain why when, on preparing for an excursion, she asked for time to 'powder her nose', Caitlin piped up brusquely, 'Why don't you put it in a bag?' One evening Mulk Raj Anand, an Indian novelist feted by the Bloomsbury group, made them a fiery curry. As Dylan told the story, another guest looked at her plate where she saw a curious rubbery thing like a discarded French letter. Out of curiosity, she picked it up and found it was the entire skin from her tongue. In the vicinity was Dylan's friend, Rayner Heppenstall, also newly married and in a religious phase. He recalled Dylan walking in a bright sunny field above Newlyn, drinking from a bottle of lethal 'champagne tonic wine', and talking animatedly. Suddenly he stopped and said, 'Somebody's boring me. I think it's me.'

With several friends risking their lives in Spain, Dylan felt pangs of acute existential anxiety that he should be doing something. Acting out of character, he took daily trips out to sea with the Newlyn fishermen. He probably thought his young wife would enjoy seeing him in this masculine role, that it would remind her of her father's love of the sea. He even talked of sailing round Land's End to Swansea, but this was a pipe-dream.

Certainly Swansea and its environs promised to be more lively when he and Caitlin went there to stay with his parents in late August 1937. After a false start the previous year Keidrych Rhys had managed to get his review, called simply *Wales*, off the ground. The first issue had appeared in June, billed as 'an independent pamphlet of creative work by the younger progressive Welsh writers'. It came with a bald manifesto which emphasised the feeling among English-speaking writers and artists in Wales that they had something special to offer both their own nation and a wider Britain. That feeling might be presented in an over-rhetorical, even paranoid way, but it reflected an idea that became clearer with the emergence of English literature in the Indian sub-continent, Africa and the Caribbean – that minority Anglophone status in a larger culture allows unique insights and (in the vocabulary of academic theorists) a 'liminal' voice that can enhance both the art and experience of people on both sides of the equation.

Taking its tone from ideas on culture elaborated by Scottish nationalists such as Hugh MacDiarmid, the *Wales* manifesto derided England's contribution to British culture, claiming there was 'no such thing as "English" culture; a few individuals may be highly cultured, but the people as a whole are crass.' Welsh literature, on the other hand, was 'carried on, not by a clique of moneyed dilletantes [sic], but by the small shopkeepers, the blacksmiths, the non-conformist ministers, by the miners, quarrymen, and the railwaymen. The Kelt's heritage is clear as sunlight, yet the burden of English literature had also fallen upon him. The greatest of present-day poets are Kelts.'

After their earlier failure to collaborate even on an anthology, Rhys felt notably cool towards Dylan. A dispute over a girl had further fuelled his antipathy: in an incident in a London pub, Dylan had displayed a feudal droit du seigneur towards the womenfolk of the small Anglo-Welsh literary community. Relating this to Glyn Jones, whom he was also trying to recruit, Rhys likened Dylan to Dafydd ap Gwilym, the great skirt-chasing anti-clerical Welsh poet of the fourteenth century, who 'mustn't miss his ten beauties a day, not even if it means taking my girl friend, a little slut who I was happy to lose, though Dylan didn't go up in my estimation, there [being] some old puritan spirit left. Dylan's only affinity with the Gogynfeirdd [medieval court poets] is his vanity and use of I – I, Dylan, the poet and fucker ... He could never become a truly representative Welsh poet. Can a poetic person with his sensitiveness ignore the industrial mess where he lives? Or am I being unduly cynical and catty?' And just to make sure his attitude to Dylan was not misunderstood, he added, damningly, '[He] reminds me of these fake nostalgic bourgeois reincarnations of boyhood of some compatriots, who've never really lived intensely or felt. A teashop gossip – a beauty at remove.'

Jones admitted that Dylan could be very annoying, though he had great affection for him. 'I've told him how absurd all this drinking and so on is, suicidal for a man like him, but it makes no difference of course. It's a tremendous pity he kids himself so much. His work suffers I think – his "Life and Letters" story is piffling. You see, he hasn't the energy or determination to acquire any background, so he is reduced to spinning fantasies out of his navel. And soon his navel won't have another fantasy left.' (The story, 'A Prospect of the Sea', was about a boy's sexual initiation in an idyllic West Wales where, though 'he did not believe in God ... God had made this summer full of blue winds and heat and pigeons in the house wood.' Still in Dylan's mythopoeic style, it anticipated the rural romanticism and religious agnosticism of his later poems.)

Despite such caveats about his political commitment, his lifestyle and his imaginative range (specifically in his stories), Dylan was the leading (in the sense of the most widely recognised) young Anglo-Welsh writer of the mid-1930s. He was a catch who had to be included in any review of the type Rhys envisaged. When Rhys raised this subject again in early 1937, Dylan still wanted the magazine to be 'very experimental and not left'. But then he relented and, taking an opportunity to cadge some money off the slightly wealthier Rhys, offered to act as literary advisor to the venture. He provided one particularly good contact in Vernon Watkins, whom Rhys visited in Swansea in April.

Rhys had moved to a farm in Carmarthen and was taking seriously his role as god-father of modern Anglo-Welsh letters. He sought a middle way between authoritarian nationalism and the cultural colonialism favoured by institutions such as the BBC and, in particular, the *Western Mail*, the Cardiff based paper which looked down on Welsh literary aspirations with all the enthusiasm of a suburban English drawing room. He could call on a large and varied pool of talent from the established Caradoc Evans to Goronwy Rees, the brilliant young assistant editor of the *Spectator*, who promised a short story. And, as always, there was 'verse by gently nurtured County Sandhurst gentlemen, sadly reminiscent of Evan Morgan's youthful outpourings'.

In Swansea Rhys also met Charles Fisher, Fred Janes and Tom Warner, who accompanied him in a party of 'ten of Dylan's boys and girls' to a protest meeting against the detention of Saunders Lewis. According to Rhys, they all clapped at his command, and then repaired to the Grand Hotel where the main topic of discussion was their worries about Dylan. Their eager response to *Wales* indicated the extent to which this small group of educated, not very political, friends was looking for direction on how to express their Welshness without disowning their English-style upbringing – an issue which was always rather more difficult to resolve in Swansea's hybrid culture. But the problem with this crowd was that they looked to Dylan for intellectual leadership and were lost without him, a point recognised by Rhys: 'they all try and write like Dylan and talk about him every minute. Imitate his slobbery slop. They too have a particular form of oblique humour, which I wasn't used to.'

Dylan's story 'Prologue to an Adventure' graced the front cover of the first issue, published in June. 'Confident, ear-catching and barely comprehensible', this was a curious relic from a couple of years earlier when he had been trying to marry his prose and verse styles. He had worked on it while in Ireland, from where he had explained it to Bert Trick as a reverse *Pilgrim's Progress* – the tale of Anti-Christian's (or Daniel Dom's) travels from the City of Zion to the City of Destruction. One reader wrote in appreciatively that it was 'a marvellous blend of Dali and St John the Divine'.

But such an esoteric mix was never going to win Dylan a large readership. As with his travel book on Wales, he seemed to be marching alone into a weird and inhospitable landscape without getting anywhere. This was the gist of Nigel Heseltine's review of *Twenty-Five Poems* in the second issue of *Wales* in August. While applauding the book's ambition, Heseltine, the prickly Eton-educated son of the Edwardian musician Philip Heseltine (better known by his schizoid alter ego Peter Warlock), felt the material was 'often raw and unshaped', and couched in 'typically Sitwellian image-confusion'. As he told Rhys in accepting the commission: 'The main obstacle to [Dylan's] fulfilment is the man himself. I have a feeling that at present he is a vehicle not a creator. I have seldom had the impression of anything so spineless as Dylan half-tight. He should never get tight, it shows him up too much.'

Rhys bumped into Dylan back in Swansea on 6 September and found him unchanged. 'I'm afraid he'll always remain an emotional brainless creature, nice, of course.' The next day Dylan sent a short encomium on Auden to Grigson for inclusion in a special double issue of *New Verse*. This could be read as either an endorsement of Rhys's view or a subtle presentation of Dylan's differences with Auden – that he 'admire[d] intensely the mature, religious, and logical fighter, but deprecate[d] the boy bushranger'. This phrase has been much debated: it suggests Dylan approved of Auden's propensity for radical cultural change (along the lines he himself had noted in his poem 'I see the boys of summer'), while disapproving of the way his political tub-thumping got in the way of his poetry. But Rhys was more of a follower of Auden. 'The only thing a young Welsh writer should do is revolutionary writing, without heeding criticism,' he wrote to Glyn Jones, in a curious manner for an editor of an intellectual review. 'It's the only thing – delivering a message in this wobbly world before it's sunk. "Good writing" seems so silly in war fascism unemployment.'

More than ever, Dylan's cultural role was to act as a gadfly – a point negatively noted in a poem Nigel Heseltine sent Rhys a few days later:

> A young fellow of Swansea called Tummas
> creates a disturbance among us
> with a purgative pill

> he produces at will
> effects that are published by some ass.

Not that Dylan was particularly concerned with this anguished debate. He was contentedly introducing Caitlin to his parents and friends. Bert Trick recalled meeting the newly married couple in a party with Caitlin's sister Nicolette and other members of her family who were returning from a holiday in Pembrokeshire. Swansea had a long history of ties with the Basque country and, after the bombing of Guernica in April 1937, had taken in a group of eighty Basque children and installed them in Sketty Hall where Trick was part of the reception committee. Dylan brought his new bride and her relations to see him there. Dylan amused the refugee children by climbing into a tunnel and getting stuck.

When the young Thomases went to dinner with the Tricks, Bert's wife Nell pronounced that Caitlin had the most beautiful complexion she had ever seen. Vernon Watkins also was entranced by the woman he dubbed 'Caitlin ni Houlihan' after the heroine of W. B. Yeats's eponymous play. He noted, 'When she smokes a cigarette she looks very much like Dylan and her remarks are like his but softer, and in a lower key.' He found Dylan on good form socially, but not looking very well physically, the result, he thought, of having been depressed in Cornwall. Watkins quickly forgot the annoyance he had felt when he opened the first *Wales* and saw that his poem 'Grief of the Sea', which he had given to Dylan as the magazine's literary advisor, had been inexplicably altered. He went round Swansea bookshops changing it, wherever possible, back to his original. Dylan apologised for his 'Thowdlerized' version, explaining it was a private doodle and he had not meant it to reach Rhys, let alone be printed.

Having grown to know and love a witty drinking man, Caitlin was surprised by her husband's meekness in the company of his parents. Dylan cut out his usual swear words and addressed D.J. and Florrie conventionally, even reverentially. His mother continued to fuss over him, drawing him a bath every evening. It did not take him long to get annoyed and to go out drinking with his friends. But when he turned up the following morning with a hangover he had regained his placidness. Florrie would say he was ill with the 'flu and give him bowls of hot milk filled with chunks of bread, his preferred cure-all throughout his life.

Nicolette was also fairly recently married, to a society painter Anthony Devas, by whom she had a year-old daughter Emma. On her visit, she noted, 'Mr Thomas owned a lot of books and Mrs Thomas was a great chatter-box. It was a cramped menage with Caitlin and Dylan added.'

For this reason her sister and brother-in-law soon moved to the more ample (thirteen-roomed) Macnamara family house in Blashford where they spent much of the next six months. There the newly-weds quickly fell into a routine. The Macnamaras had fashioned a large back room out of the wood shed. Francis Macnamara had supplied a carpet to make it slightly more comfortable, but the general décor and standard of cleanliness were rudimentary. Dylan remarked how nice it was not to be followed around by somebody with a dustpan and brush. (His wide-eyed sister Nancy gushed that it was the most artistic house she had ever seen.)

He would work for two or three hours each morning before the grandfather clock told him it was 12 o'clock and time for him and Caitlin to take the bus into Ringwood for a drink before lunch at the Old Oak. They returned an hour later, armed with fizzy drinks and bags of sweets about which Nicolette noted Dylan had views as marked as any wine connoisseur. The couple then retired upstairs to bed where, as they munched their way through their sweets, they read to each other, perhaps from one of Dylan's hoard of comics or one of the many thrillers he found in the library. In the evening they went back to the pub, often accompanied by Caitlin's sister Brigit or her brother John, if he was home on leave from the navy.

During their brief honeymoon in Wales, the Thomases had played croquet and table-tennis (a sport which Caitlin enjoyed so much that Dylan contemplated buying her a table). In Hampshire, they were more sluggish (even though these had hardly been strenuous activities), tending to relax with games of shove-halfpenny and skittles in the Old Oak. Caitlin burnt off excess energy in bouts of dancing and occasionally managed to drag Dylan out for a walk or even a bicycle ride in the country. They also visited nearby beauty spots, such as Durdle Door in Dorset, where he and Caitlin were photographed by Nora Summers, who also captured him in studied, tough-boy pose – hair tousled, lighting a cigarette, wearing cravat and thick woolly cardigan probably knitted by his wife; a poetic, sensual James Dean before his time. Dylan sent a copy of this snap to Vernon Watkins, telling him he could use it to advertise Kensitas cigarettes in his front window. Watkins responded with 'Portrait of a Friend', almost a love poem, delicately celebrating the marvel that this vulnerable, impenetrable figure could have such poetic range, covering the holy, the deathly and the earthy.

Poetry was poorly represented at Blashford, either on the library shelves or in general conversation. For an exchange of ideas about his work, he relied on postal communication with Watkins, whose sensitive judgement he trusted and with whom he swapped suggestions about metre and, in particular, apposite words. One poem he revised many times was 'I make this in a warring absence'. First mentioned the previous September, it coincided with the occasion Augustus John turned up in Cornwall and revived jealous memories of his affair with Caitlin. This suggests Dylan was more troubled by his wife's infidelities than seemed apparent. Caitlin certainly saw it this way, out of a sense of self-confidence or even arrogance (as she later put it) which meant she never questioned that Dylan was hers 'for keeps'.

The poem tells of his limp and jealous state when his lover's sexual passion is withdrawn. Only after a process of purgation is he able to forgive and welcome her when she sweetly returns. As he explained to Desmond Hawkins, he sought conflicting images and let them fight until they reached a resolution. He repeated this line to Henry Treece, a poet and critic who approached him in February 1938 hoping to write a book about his verse. Treece advocated the virtues of romantic poetry in an age of high politics and aimed to appropriate the Welshman to his cause. While making his usual self-deprecatory noises, Dylan was happy to find such interest in his work and took the trouble to explain, 'I make one image – though "make" is not the word: I let, perhaps, an image be "made" emotionally in me and then apply to it what intellectual & critical forces I possess: let it breed another; let that image contradict the first, make, of the third image bred out the other two together, a fourth contradictory image, and let them all, within my imposed formal limits, conflict.' Out of his host of warring images, he hoped he achieved 'that momentary peace which is a poem'.

Claiming he had no access to a typewriter, Dylan asked Watkins to type up 'I make this in a warring absence' (also known as 'Poem [for Caitlin]') so he could send it to T. S. Eliot at The Criterion. Watkins was so inspired (Caitlin thought besotted) that he happily complied, not only with copies of Dylan's own verse but also of poems by himself and others, particularly Yeats, which his young friend wanted to use in his increasingly regular public readings (for example, to students at Goldsmiths' College, London in January.) With nothing much to distract him, Dylan found writing (and particularly rhymes) surprisingly easy, though most of what he sent to Watkins were revisions of earlier work – pieces such as 'After the Funeral' (based on the notebook poem he had composed following the death of his Aunt Annie in 1933), 'How shall my animal', and (though the dating is more problematic) 'When all my five and country senses' whose title and general sentiment suggests his general contentment and provides a foretaste of rural themes to come.

'I make this in a warring absence' appeared not in The Criterion but in Twentieth Century Verse, a new small poetry magazine edited by Julian

Symons, which aimed to be a more accessible alternative to Grigson's *New Verse*. Its appearance reflected subtle changes in the London intellectual climate. In the art world, for example, the down-to-earth Euston Road school of painting was emerging after the excesses of surrealism.

With his poetry flowing, Dylan's main concern was his stories and, in particular, the collection he had put together with a view to publication. This had been retrieved by Higham from Faber (where it had been sent by Curtis Brown) and returned to Dylan, minus 'The Orchards' which was used not only in *The Criterion* but also in two Faber anthologies of short stories. At the time Dylan was still supposed to be working on his book on Wales, but made no further progress – one of several incidents that led to an early, if short-lived souring of his relations with Higham. With minimal income coming to Blashford, he became increasingly desperate for money and in December, without consulting Higham, made a deal directly with George Reavey's new Europa Press to publish his collection of short stories under the title *The Burning Baby*. The book was supposed to come out in both popular and limited editions. For the latter Dylan supplied a list of around thirty potential subscribers, including his richer friends such as Vernon Watkins, Emily Coleman and Augustus John, as well as less obvious figures including the travel writer Robert Byron, the academic Lord David Cecil, Alan and Margaret Taylor with whom he had stayed outside Manchester in 1935, and Constantine FitzGibbon, an Irish-American undergraduate at Exeter College, Oxford.

Before Christmas he and Caitlin went to London to pick up the first £15 tranche of his much needed advance. Reports filtered back to Carmarthen that Dylan was seen in the Café Royal after the pubs closed, causing Keidrych Rhys to observe: 'He should do some real work before Bloomsbury drop him.' The Thomases stayed with Reavey's friend Anna Wickham, a rugged Australian-born poet whose house in Hampstead was a haven for impoverished writers and artists. A notice in her hall invited: 'Saddle your Pegasus here. Creative Minds Respected. Meals at all Times.' With no mind to conventional domesticity, she wore football stockings and slept with a stinking chamber pot under her bed. She also had a fierce temper, so it was no surprise when the Thomases soon fell out with her and were expelled into a cold snowy evening. While still persona grata, Dylan met one of her visitors, Lawrence Durrell, who caught his ear by talking about Henry Miller, author of the banned novel *The Tropic of Cancer* which he much admired. Durrell and Miller were trying to turn *The Booster*, the ponderous official publication of the American Country Club in Paris, into a lively literary magazine. Dylan offered them his Caitlin poem, 'I make this in a warring absence', which appeared in the magazine in April 1938, along with three poems by Antonia White, two of which dealt with her damaging affairs with both Nigel and Ian Henderson, Wyn's sons who were hardly out of their teens. (Wyn would push them on her friends, but Nigel, in particular, was sexually ambivalent and liked to reminisce about being groped by Dylan.) Soon afterwards the magazine antagonised the club grandees by printing an obscene story about an eskimo and moved, under the name *Delta*, to the more liberal atmosphere of London.

In January the Thomases were back in London, having hitched a lift to town from Augustus John. One pressing reason was to pick up the remaining £5 of the advance for *The Burning Baby*. Reavey was reluctant to pay, but recognised his friend's need. The cheque was cashed on 25 January by Nigel Henderson, an indication that Dylan had attended the opening the previous day of Guggenheim Jeune, the London branch of Peggy Guggenheim's avant-garde Paris gallery, which was run by her 'Leporello', Nigel's mother Wyn. The opening show quickly gave way to exhibitions of Kandinsky and of contemporary sculpture. The latter caused a sensation when, on the advice of James Bolivar Manson, director of the Tate Gallery, British customs refused to allow sculptures by Brancusi, Arp, Alexander Calder and others into the country. In March, Wyn Henderson organised a petition signed by a number of artists including Henry Moore and Graham Sutherland.

A month later another gallery opened next door to the Guggenheim Jeune in Cork Street. It was the London Gallery, financed by Roland Penrose and dedicated to surrealism. Penrose asked Dylan for a contribution for his related magazine the *London Bulletin*, edited by the Belgian surrealist Edouard Mesens and Humphrey Jennings (both, together with Samuel Beckett at this time, lovers of Peggy Guggenheim). Dylan replied enthusiastically, though his sotto voce request for payment may have put Penrose off since nothing of his appeared in the *Bulletin*. Clearly, however, through his connections with Reavey, the Hendersons and others, Dylan was now considered a fixture on the avant-garde London art scene, which received a further boost with the exhibition of modern German art, held at the New Burlington Galleries in the summer in direct defiance of the Nazis' growing attacks on 'degenerate art'.

While Durrell introduced him to expatriate circles in Paris, Dylan's name was also beginning to be known in the United States. The previous year he had received an enquiry from the State University of New York at Buffalo which wanted to acquire manuscripts and other papers for a new poetry library. In February 1938 he was contacted by James (known as Jay) Laughlin IV, wealthy Harvard-educated heir to a Pittsburgh steel dynasty, who had turned his back on industry and ploughed his money into New Directions, a publishing company specialising in avant-garde literature, mainly poetry. Starting with anthologies before turning to books, he had quickly attracted some of the most exciting modern writers. Dylan quoted approvingly a list which included works by Jean Cocteau, Henry Miller, Gertrude Stein and William Soroyan. (He could have added to it, among others, Ezra Pound, William Carlos Williams and Laughlin's old Harvard tutor Delmore Schwarz.) Alerted originally by Edith Sitwell and more recently by the American poet Charles Henri Ford (an interesting pair since Sitwell was livid with Ford for replacing her in the affections of the emigré Russian artist Pavel Tchelitchew,) Laughlin told Higham's New York associates, the Ann Watkins agency: 'I have been watching [Dylan's] work for three years now and it seems to me that he is full of beans.'

Since Dylan's relations with Higham had broken down, he was approached directly by Laughlin. He replied enthusiastically, suggesting that New Directions might like to publish an American edition of *The Burning Baby*, which was in production with Reavey's Europa Press. Laughlin agreed to take 500 sheets, though Reavey grumbled that the figure was too low. However in February the Europa Press ran into difficulties when its printer, William Brendon in Plymouth, refused to set Dylan's stories on the grounds that they were obscene.

Probably at Durrell's suggestion, Dylan was offered an alternative outlet for this book by the Obelisk Press, a Paris publisher specialising in pornography. But, as he told Bob Rees, an old schoolfriend who was teaching in London, he refused, not for moral reasons but because the money was so paltry. Rees had approached him, on behalf of a fellow schoolmaster, for some background information on Dylan's poetry. As often happened in such cases, Dylan replied courteously, saying that he had never read Gerard Manley Hopkins with any thoroughness, though his influence might have intruded 'when my "work" was fluid enough (perhaps I mean watery enough) to find room for any number of foreign bodies, some of which still unfortunately remain, occupying too much space'. He confirmed that he did not know 'any Welsh poetry at all' and added, in a significant unpublished statement of his poetic ends:

I think I am always attracted to the idea of extremely concentrated poetry; I never could like the poetry that allowed itself great breathing spaces, tediums and flatnesses, between essential passages; I want, and wanted, every line to be the essence of the poem, even the flourishes, the exxagerations [sic]. This, naturally, I never could achieve, but it still remains an ideal for me. (I believe that, despite his own verse which is all a marking-time, Poe wanted the same.) I never could reconcile myself to reading six weak lines, lines of mechanical verse or, worse still, of poetical mechanics, in order to get to the strong (qualified) poetry of the seventh. My determination to avoid this had led to the mixed monotony of many of my own poems.'

Although he occasionally managed to get up to London, Dylan was not happy about his situation. Living with the Macnamaras was a stop-gap: he did not mind their generally matriarchal society (that was familiar from Wales). But he found that even their unconventional menage had its rules, often related to gradations of class, in ways unknown to a boy from the curtain-twitching Swansea suburbs. Nicolette told a story about how, when Dylan invited a friend to Blashford, he sought to reassure her mother, 'He's all right. He goes to cocktail parties.' For all her broad-mindedness and an affection for Dylan which had her mothering him with bowls of his bread and milk when he was feeling 'seedy', Yvonne could never banish her prejudice that he was not quite good enough for her daughter.

His state of mind was not improved by lack of finance. Although Yvonne helped him out with small gifts of money, he was already complaining to Durrell in January, 'We are stages beyond poverty.' The following month he was seriously homesick: 'Swansea is still the best place,' he wrote to Charles Fisher. 'Tell Fred [Janes] he's right,' referring to his painter friend's decision to return and make his base in his home town. Dylan even looked forward to living in neat domesticity in a Dan Jones-inspired Percy Villa in Swansea. By March he had almost had enough. 'I'm leaving here next week for nowhere,' he indicated to Keidrych Rhys. 'I want to be in Wales, but it offers me nothing at all; I'm facing starvation, which is a pity.' He hung on a little longer, enough time to plead with Laughlin for funds. 'We are completely penniless. I do not mean that we just live poorly; I mean that we go without food, without proper clothes, have shelter on charity, and very very soon will not have even that shelter. I have now less than a shilling; there is no more to come; we have nothing to sell, nothing to fall back on.'

It was a measure of Dylan's perilous position that he concluded this request with a rash promise to give Laughlin the American rights to 'all my books, past, present and future'. In addition, he offered to dispense with future royalties, in return for immediate money up front. Laughlin sent him $20, with the promise of a further $20 to come. Dylan said this would be enough to get him and Caitlin to Wales, where he hoped to be able to live more cheaply. En route through London Reavey showed them paintings by his friend the Dutch surrealist Geer van Velde who was shortly to exhibit at the Guggenheim Jeune. But the Thomases were too poor to stay and attend Reavey's party for van Velde and Samuel Beckett. At the end of April they continued to Swansea. After a short period with Dylan's parents, they found themselves, with Richard Hughes's help, a small cottage in Laugharne, the village whose natural beauty and charm Dylan had found instantly attractive when he visited with Glyn Jones in 1934.

Dylan's return to live in Wales was a turning point. Throughout his life, he was never good at venturing far from the beaten track. This was the emotional price he paid for pushing at the boundaries of imagination and language. He always needed to return to familiar, ordered territory, whether Cwmdonkin Drive after the wild spaces of Gower or Emily Coleman's flat following the ravages of West Wales. Now he had a gut understanding of his need for the security of his Welsh roots at a time when, professionally, he was starting to venture overseas and, domestically, he was about to embark on having a family. Not that he knew about the latter at the time. But shortly after he and Caitlin had set up in Eros, their appropriately named fisherman's dwelling in Laugharne, she learnt she was pregnant. Dylan claimed this was a mistake, a line echoed by Caitlin who said it was 'totally unexpected'.

They particularly wanted to live somewhere close to water, for Dylan an ever-present symbol of the unrelenting power of nature; for Caitlin, a source of more immediate pleasure for swimming and outdoor frolicking. Eros was a damp dingy two bed-roomed house with no bathroom and an outside lavatory. Its redeeming feature was its long narrow back garden which gave onto the pellucid Taf estuary where local women gathered cockles when the tide was out and the men went out in smacks to fish at night.

Dylan felt immediately at home, describing Laugharne as 'a good place' and 'a sociable place too, and I like that, with good pubs and little law and no respect'. Nevertheless the Thomases were happier when, after three months, they moved up the hill towards the centre of the town and settled in a larger, still ramshackle house called Sea View (a misnomer, since the water could only be seen from one top-floor window). This was owned by Tudor Williams, a member of the extended family who ran the town in parallel with the established Corporation. On the official level, Laugharne operated through an ancient charter, granted by Edward I to the marcher lord Sir Gwydo de Brione. One of only two in Britain (the other is Malmesbury's), this charter gave the town a measure of fiercely guarded independence, with its portreeve (or mayor) and medieval panoply of governance that continues into the twenty-first century. On a day to day basis the Williamses ensured the place worked, owning not only the electricity generating station but the main bus company, as well as around fifty houses, many of them acquired from the Corporation on preferential terms.

One family enterprise was Brown's Hotel, the most appealing of several pubs in Laugharne. It was acquired for 625 gold sovereigns by Tudor's mother Esther in 1934, partly because the attached stables provided garaging for the family's buses. Another son, Ebie Williams, ran the pub with his wife, Ivy, a bright, homely woman not unlike Dylan's mother. Although there was a Victoria Cross in her husband's family (won by Esther's nephew Lance Corporal William Fuller while serving at the battle of Aisne in 1914), Ivy considered herself a cut above the Williamses. During the First World War, her hard-drinking Scottish father Lieutenant Commander Douglas McDermott had travelled every day to Milford Haven where he was officer in charge of the harbour's boom defences. Seeing Dylan as an educated gentleman, she was happy to trade gossip about the town for snippets of information about literary life. He was delighted to find a bolt-hole at Brown's. He would go there in the morning, return home for lunch, work in the afternoon and again walk to the pub in the evening, a routine Caitlin was happy to let develop and to participate in when she could.

Ivy Williams quickly became Dylan's best friend in town. She cashed his cheques and allowed his credit to pile up when he could not pay. Though dismissive of 'jive-man' Richard Hughes's work as whimsical, Dylan nevertheless relied on the author of High Wind in Jamaica for intellectual stimulation, particularly in his first months in Laugharne. Not for the last time, he and Caitlin took advantage of someone trying to help. During the summer, as she began to swell with her child, they often relaxed in the grounds of Hughes's uninhabited Castle, where Dylan found he could work in a gazebo high in the battlements overlooking the estuary. One day they saw the nautical-looking owner disappear into the bowels of the Castle and emerge with a bottle of wine. Having established this was where he kept his wine cellar, they regularly raided it (a practice they justified to themselves because they felt Hughes, though rich, was unnecessarily mean: he would produce his wine at meals but not offer it to them). Their thieving practices had to be curtailed after Dylan was surprised in the gazebo by Hughes. He was reading and sipping a glass from some carefully laid down vintage. He hurriedly hid the bottle under his bottom from where, to his horror, it began to drip.

In the gazebo, with its view of the sea and the sounds of the town in the background, he began to experiment with a new type of writing. He had become bogged down with surreal mythical stories of the sort

George Reavey was still trying to publish in *The Burning Baby*. While at Blashford he had produced a more realistic story, 'A Visit to Grandpa's', which, while not based directly on his personal experience, recreated the sights, sounds and way of life of the rural Carmarthenshire he had known since boyhood. He had sent this to *New English Weekly* where his friend Desmond Hawkins, now literary editor, published it in March 1938. Writing to Hawkins at that time, in a letter illustrated by pornographic sketches from a larger 'utterly filthy' work, he claimed to have more or less discounted his 'Europa mistake' and, although he did not think the new style any better, he was hoping to write many more stories 'like that one you liked about Grandpa, stories of Swansea and me'. Over the summer he followed this up with two more stories in the same genre, 'One Warm Saturday' and 'The Peaches' – the basis of the collection to be known as *Portrait of the Artist as a Young Dog*.

Although he wrote another piece in the earlier style, 'An Adventure from a Work in Progress', he was making a break with what he termed 'free fantasy'. Caitlin had her phrase for it: 'surrealism and pornography', a genre she found muddled and did not like, any more than his 'complicated' poems. Ironically a similarly revisionist attitude was being bandied around by some of his fellow contributors to *Wales* where, despite evidence of Dylan's fecklessness, Keidrych Rhys was still struggling to produce a magazine. Rhys had printed Dylan's mythopoeic story 'The Map of Love' in his third (October 1937) issue, along with his simple, effective poem 'We lying by Seasand'. The story, however, was not so successful: 'very Lawrence in style', Rhys told Glyn Jones, ' "strange continents" etc ... Dylan's self-criticism is going to pot I feel.' In March, having received Dylan's 'In the Direction of the Beginning', described as a 'fragment of a work in progress', he added 'Dylan's aren't so much stories as exotic rhapsodies – music inspired by Tom Warner – shallow spirituality perhaps, and rather ruthless.'

Nigel Heseltine, never a fan, took much the same line, describing this piece as 'not up to standard. I have enjoyed his stories in the past. This fragment which he is confident enough to put in as if we hung on his every word no matter how scribbled, proves that he is not yet a great enough artist to throw off fragments even if Joyce does.' Heseltine, just back from a visit to the Balkans which had turned him against nationalism, thought David Jones's recently published poetry and prose epic *In Parenthesis* superior – the 'first truly Welsh Anglo-Welsh product' to set alongside Joyce's quintessentially Anglo-Irish *Ulysses*.

Based on the experiences of its author, an Englishman of Welsh origin, *In Parenthesis* was a heavily annotated paean to the timeless qualities of the British fighting man, drawing on British literature stretching back through Shakespeare and Malory to The Mabinogion and Y Gododdin. Only through its highlighting of Welsh epic poems much earlier than anything in English can it be described in Heseltine's terms. But the great debate on what comprised Anglo-Welsh writing had been joined. The nationalist leader Saunders Lewis made his position clear in an address titled 'Is there an Anglo-Welsh Literature?' to the Urdd Graddedigion Prifysgol Cymru Cangen Caerdydd the following December. Referring to the opening sentence of Dylan's 'Prologue to an Adventure' which had appeared in Wales, he said this (like most of the author's work) stood in the mainstream of the English literary tradition with its deliberate echo of Bunyan. 'Mr Dylan Thomas is obviously an equipped writer, but there is nothing hyphenated about him. He belongs to the English.'

Dylan recognised this criticism and, although he claimed he did not understand 'this racial talk', he was concerned, if not embarrassed. Having set aside his travel book about his homeland, he adopted a different approach. Spurred by his London friends' experience with Mass Observation, which had produced an 'Oxford Collective Poem', he suggested that Wales devote an issue to a mass-poem comprising verse reports by the magazine's contributors on their areas.

Although nothing came of this, the combined effects of hostility from his countrymen and more personal criticism from Caitlin were encouraging Dylan to reassess his approach to his craft. From around this time, he began to write more simply and realistically, particularly about Wales, and his change of tack was also apparent in his poetry. There were sound financial reasons for this: his old high literary style was not making him any money (and this must have affected his wife's attitude as well). His bank balance was not helped by problems related to Reavey's editions of The Burning Baby and to his own budding relationship with the American publisher, Jay Laughlin.

Through the summer he continued to chivvy Reavey about his book of stories which failed to appear, as had been announced, in May. When, for want of other information, he tentatively suggested 'Prologue to an Adventure' might be causing the printer offence (which would have been odd since it had already been published in Wales), he offered one of his 'new' realistic tales, 'A Visit to Grandpa's', as an alternative. He also hinted that Durrell and Miller, his friends in Paris, might be prepared to publish the book. To complicate matters, Augustus John had completed his portrait for the frontispiece but was not satisfied with it. In addition, David Archer's Parton Bookshop, or rather the Fortune Press which had taken on its publishing interests, was offering Reavey its remaining stock of Dylan's 18 Poems, together with the copyright (which it did not possess).

At least Dylan had been encouraged by his correspondence with Laughlin, who mixed flattery, commercial sense and informed literary gossip. 'How much younger are you than Auden?' the preppie publisher wrote from Rapallo where he was visiting Ezra Pound, another of his authors. 'It will help if I can bill you as "the most important English poet of the generation following Auden" or some such crap. America, having decided that Auden is a poet, which I doubt, now *has* English poetry ... and will with reluctance realize that there is anybody else.' However, he cleverly tried to tie Dylan to his publishing house, noting that Ann Watkins, Higham's associates in New York, had been reminding him that the Welsh author was their property. Dylan himself was adamant that he had only signed up with Higham for *Twenty-Five Poems*, that his royalties through them were 'minimal', and he did not need an agent. Laughlin did nothing to disabuse him of this view: 'What they (i.e. Ann Watkins) want is to collect commissions on what I pay you. Naturally I am not anxious to do this.' He hoped he would be able to 'politely tell them to go to hell'. However he was not amused to find that, contrary to Dylan's desperate promise in March, Reavey, rather than he, held the rights to the American publication of *The Burning Baby*.

Tackled on this last point by Laughlin, who thought the wool was being pulled over his eyes, Dylan claimed ignorance, adding that Reavey had simply taken advantage of his vagueness and stupidity. When Laughlin sought to clarify his position with regard to the rights of *Twenty-Five Poems*, Dylan admitted that David Higham probably had those, though he stressed the agent had only acted for him over that one book and the royalties had been minimal, around ten shillings a quarter. 'I don't require any more the services of an agent,' proclaimed Dylan, just as Laughlin was drawing up a contract giving him a 15 per cent commission for his exclusive right to place Dylan's stories and poems in America.

When Laughlin informed Ann Watkins of this, making clear that he also considered any payments he had already made to Dylan as advances on future royalties, the agency came back with 'queries galore'. Apparently winning his covert battle to usurp Higham's influence, Laughlin kept at his publisher's business of raising Dylan's profile in the United States. He had plans to print three poems and two stories in his 1938 anthology *New Directions in Poetry and Prose*. Provided Dylan worked through him, Laughlin intended to push his work in American magazines such as *Poetry* (Chicago) and *Partisan Review* where Dylan already had contacts. He was also approaching the radio networks. 'The propaganda is underway,' he assured Dylan in June. 'Squibs have appeared in the newspapers to the effect that the best young English poet is soon to be published in America etc.' As he explained to Ann Watkins, amid claims that Higham had been abandoned because he 'virtually stole' from Dylan, 'My plan for Thomas is to spend about six months placing his poems in American magazines and spreading publicity for him. Then when he is "ripe" I'll bring out a book of about forty poems, followed by the stories the following year.'

Laughlin even arranged for Emma Swan, one of the richer American poets he published, to send Dylan a regular financial subvention. He had been hoping to travel to Laugharne to stay with the Thomases at the end of his European trip in the early summer, but never managed it. There was no shortage of visitors to Sea View, however. Blustering through in August, Augustus John took a liking to the 'stage house, with a certain air of mystery about it', and used it as a base from which to settle affairs relating to his father's death in Tenby four months earlier. He disrupted Dylan's routine for four days, reporting back to his consort Dorelia, '[The Thomases] live in frightful squalor and hideousness.' From London came Norman Cameron, and Mervyn Levy, hitch-hiking on his way to Ireland; from Blashford Yvonne Macnamara and her 'neuter' friend Nora Summers who photographed the young marrieds drinking in Brown's Hotel; and, from Swansea, Vernon Watkins and Charles Fisher, who had taken over from Hawkins as Dylan's collaborator on the literary thriller *Death of the King's Canary*. Fisher happened to be there during Augustus John's visit when he found Dylan already drunk in the afternoon. After a hard session at Brown's in the early evening, Dylan returned to the house for supper and then had to retire, saying he was unable to speak. John and Fisher sent out for a bottle of whisky, and continued to talk 'about Paris, about art, about everything in the world'.

While Fisher had a car, Watkins used to travel the forty-four miles from Pennard by bus or by bicycle (his chosen method of transport on his return from a visit to Yeats in Ireland). He often brought provisions such as ham and tinned fruit from the market in Carmarthen. At one stage he noted that Dylan had given up smoking in the house and taken to a pipe which he shared with his wife. In September he arrived in his friend Wyn Lewis's car which everyone, including Dylan, took turns to drive on the nearby Pendine flats, where fourteen years earlier Malcolm Campbell had clocked 146 miles per hour in breaking the world land speed record. With the throttle fully extended, Dylan managed 10 mph before grinding to a halt in the sand. When Dylan called on his parents a few days later, Watkins was there, clutching a volume of Lorca, which the two men read avidly.

Dylan savoured these meetings with Watkins. Unlike his often strained performances for noisome London poets, he could act naturally with his Swansea friend, who instinctively understood the subtle balance he was trying to strike in his work between Welsh cultural and English literary influences, and between the outside world and own personal development. He sent Watkins his beautiful poem of welcome to his unborn child, initially called 'In September' because, he said enigmatically, 'it was a terrible war month'. He was referring with disgust to the Munich pact signed on 29 September and the attendant mobilisation of the British fleet, issuing of gas-masks and stepping up of air-raid precautions.

Not that his position on the treaty which led to the dismemberment of Czechoslovakia was particularly sophisticated. As a pacifist he had no wish to fight against Germany, yet his gut reaction was to oppose this cowardly capitulation. Despite this fearful background (reflected in phrases such as 'agony has another mouth to feed'); he described it as an optimistic poem, with rhythmical effects that excited him. He gladly accepted Watkins's alternative title 'Poem in the Ninth Month', which gave a connotation of near-culmination of pregnancy. However it became known by its first line, 'A Saint about to fall' – a simple expression of its central image of an angelic child leaving an apocalyptic Miltonic heaven.

This poem provides an early evocation of the Laugharne landscape with its 'squawking shores'. Similarly his 'Twenty-four years' was the first of three main poems reflecting on the state of his life around the time of his October birthday. Significantly, birthdays meant little to him on a day to day basis, but anniversaries more generally acted as inherent reminders of the immutable workings of the cosmos. As 'A Saint about to fall' reflects the potency of an innocent child in a crazy world, so this short poem reprises a favoured theme of the absurdity of life in the midst of mortality. In it, Dylan is 'Dressed to die, the sensual strut begun'. Resurrecting a line from a discarded poem penned at Veronica Sibthorp's two years earlier, he intoned, 'I advance for as long as forever is.'

Another visitor was Henry Treece, who was hard at work on his critical study. In response to letters and to ongoing chapters he was sent, Dylan took pains to avoid being typecast. Distancing himself from Louis MacNeice, Stephen Spender, W. H. Auden and Cecil Day-Lewis was not too difficult. He scornfully referred to this quartet of politically engaged poets (dubbed 'Macspaunday' by his later friend Roy Campbell) as the 'Brotherhood of Man – love thy neighbour and, if possible, covet his arse'. They were 'a disappointing school-society, and I cannot accept Auden as head prefect'. However he denied Treece's assertion that he lacked social awareness, pointing to images he had drawn from the cinema and other mass media, though admitting he thought a squirrel stumbling was of at least equal importance as Hitler's invasions, the Ashes and a host of contemporary goings-on.

Asked about Hopkins's influence on his poetry, Dylan again claimed to have read him only lackadaisically and never to have studied him. He argued that, rhythmically at least, Swinburne had been a greater influence and noted that 'the people to be found in those early poems were the Elizabethans and George Peele, Webster and, later, Beddoes, some Clare (his hard, country sonnets), Lawrence (animal poems, and the verse extracts from The Plumed Serpent), a bit of Tennyson, some very bad Flecker and, of course, a lot of bits from whatever fashionable poetry – Imagists, Sitwells – I'd been reading lately.' The surrealists might have featured in this list of fleeting influences, but Dylan dismissed them as 'a highbrow parlour game'. He said he could not read French, so had only encountered the original surrealists in weak translations by David Gascoyne. He denied any knowledge of the middle ages, pleaded his education had been poor, and asserted he never read anything but in Modern English.

Nevertheless he was keen to refute any suggestion, as made in a review by Spender, that 'Thomas's poetry is turned on like a tap; it is just poetic stuff with no beginning or end, shape, or intelligent and intelligible control'. The exact opposite was true, he said: 'Much of the obscurity is due to rigorous compression; the last thing they do is to flow; they are much rather hewn.' And he came up with a classic statement of his professional purpose: 'I hold a beast, an angel, and a madman in me, and my enquiry is as to their working, and my problem is their subjugation and victory, downthrow & upheaval, and my effort is their self-expression.'

Despite Dylan's tendency to contradict Treece's views, the two men maintained a healthy mutual respect, which survived his dogged inter-preter's coming to Laugharne in August. However they fell out towards the end of the year when Dylan refused to sign a manifesto promoting the Apocalypse Movement. This was an attempt by Treece and others to establish a group of mainly Celtic poets on a wildly romantic, neo-surrealist platform designed to take the place of the tired politicised values of metropolitan Macspaunday. The group's theoretical output was not unattractive (and in keeping with the sense of doom felt as a result of political developments at the time), but its practice was often a parody of Dylan at his most bombastic. Not opposed to being cast as a romantic, and even willing to contribute to Seven, the main magazine of the new faction, he reserved his right to stay clear of any such labelling.

Dylan hardly left Laugharne during the summer and autumn. He made only occasional sorties to Swansea, once to see a Noel Coward play (at the invitation of Watkins's mother) and again to catch up with Bert Trick whose sense of community service had led him to join the Civil Defence. (This was in August and no doubt influenced Dylan's outrage at the time of writing 'A Saint about to fall'.) In October the BBC sent Dylan his third-class rail fare to travel to Manchester to take part in a discussion on 'The Modern Muse' with various poets, including all the members of the dread Macspaunday. 'What a mincing lot we were!' Dylan gleefully told John Davenport, a robust, well-connected critic from the gifted Cambridge generation of the late 1920s, who had recently returned from a spell as a Hollywood screenwriter. Back in the BBC fold, he fired off a letter to the Corporation's Welsh regional director T. Rowland Hughes in Cardiff suggesting a programme of his readings of Welsh poets in English. Hughes was more interested in knowing if Dylan would compose a long dramatic programme in verse. Dylan demurred, saying he wrote too slowly and 'the result, dramatically, is too often like a man shouting under the sea'. But another seed of his later work, Under Milk Wood, had been sown.

The main thing holding Dylan back from going anywhere was lack of money. In August he approached the Royal Literary Fund for a grant. Despite the formidable backing of T. S. Eliot, Edith Sitwell, Charles Williams and Walter de la Mare among others, and despite quoted earnings of less than £30 over the previous year, he was turned down, leading him to enquire if he was too young: 'Must you be a Georgian writer of belle-lettres, suffering in Surrey? ... Thirty pounds would settle everything.'

The combination of his poverty and the chaotic state of his business affairs led him to swallow his pride and seek to return to the David Higham fold. He made little apology for not having answered the agency's letters over the previous months. Higham welcomed him back as if nothing had happened and immediately set about regularising his dealings with Reavey and Laughlin. The former he brusquely informed that his client was withdrawing his book, The Burning Baby, because the Europa Press had failed to publish it within the time stipulated in the contract. Since Reavey had made no progress, he had little option but to return the manuscript, with a plea that he might be repaid some of the £20 advance if the stories were printed elsewhere. Laughlin put up more resistance to Higham, claiming he had now advanced Dylan $60 (a figure initially denied by the recipient, but later accepted) and demanding that Dylan commit all his future books to him in America. 'I will not spend a lot of time and money developing a young fellow, only to have him swiped by somebody,' he told Higham's New York associates Ann Watkins. 'Thomas has promised me the books and has taken money in return for the promise. Accordingly he must keep his word. There is no question of that.' On this Higham had to give way.

The London agent then reacquainted Dylan with Richard Church at the publisher, J. M. Dent. There was little love lost there: Dylan considered Church 'a cliché-ridden humbug and pie-fingering hack', particularly for telling him that a genuine artist spurned financial gain. It did not help that Dylan had unilaterally abandoned the Welsh travel book he was doing for Dent. But Church was astute enough to see that Dylan was a rising star who would bring kudos to a stuffy company. He sent thirty shillings to bring Dylan to London to see him shortly before Christmas. Despite his disdain for Auden, Dylan was not averse to telling Higham that he had met the poet in Manchester and that Auden had suggested that the Hogarth Press (with which he was associated) might be interested in his new book and would pay an advance of £50. Now Higham was able to use this as a bargaining ploy with Church who agreed to abandon the travel volume and publish a new book, comprising fifteen poems and five stories, provisionally titled In the Direction of the Beginning.

By then Dylan and Caitlin had moved to Blashford to await the birth of their child in the bosom of the Macnamara family. In London he ran into Wyn Henderson and also met James Meary Tambimuttu, a wild English-speaking Tamil who was talking of starting a poetry magazine, one of several ventures looking to take on New Verse's mantle as arbiter of poetry's development. But behind the tinkling of glasses in the Fitzroy, he could hear another more disturbing sound – the crescendo of chatter about the forthcoming war. In December a national register of war volunteers had been started. As Auden and Isherwood prepared to travel to a new life in the United States, Dylan realised he would need to decide what action he would take in the event of hostilities.

Drawn one way back to his past and another towards his future, Dylan returned to his pregnant wife in a poor way, partly because he had indulged too much, and partly because, as he explained to Watkins, he had had something of an epiphany: 'It really is an insane city, & filled me with terror. Every pavement drills through your soles to your scalp, and out pops a lamp-post covered with hair. I'm not going to London again for years; its intelligentsia is so hurried in the head that nothing stays there; its glamour smells of goat; there's no difference between good & bad.'

Despite the bitter cold, Christmas in the English countryside was tolerable. He might jokingly complain that all he did was 'sit and hate my mother-in-law'. But he was able to sit back and listen to Arthur

Askey on the wireless, read a copy of the banned *Black Book* given him by its author Durrell, and play charades and seasonal games from a Compendium, a present from Watkins. There was promising news on the book and other negotiations from David Higham, and Dylan had learnt he had been awarded the Blumenthal Prize for Poetry (worth $100 or £20) in America, He was even treated to a Christmas stocking, stuffed with sweets, cigars, a mouth-organ and some cherry brandy.

His aversion to London did not prevent him returning over the new year to see Lawrence Durrell who was now publishing *Delta* (the new name for *Booster*) there rather than in Paris. He tried to invite Durrell to Hampshire, telling him, 'I've got the willies of London & it makes me ill as hell.' But this could not be arranged, and Dylan cadged a lift to the capital, probably with Augustus John. Durrell was staying with Henry Miller in a flat lent them by Hugo Guyler, Anais Nin's rich husband. Miller had expressly said he wanted to meet Dylan. But on the evening they arranged, Dylan did not appear. They had given him up, when he telephoned from a nearby pub. He was not drunk but, upon questioning, admitted he was afraid at the prospect of meeting Miller, one of his literary heroes. Durrell went to the pub, had a drink with him, and brought him back to the flat where Dylan was immediately at ease, joking and declaiming. He described Miller to Watkins as 'a dear, mad, mild man, bald and fifty, with great enthusiasms for commonplaces'. But London remained a 'nightmare' and again he returned a 'wreck'.

Caitlin meanwhile had been getting mellower and more rounded. At the end of January, she was taken into the Cornelia Hospital in Poole where, after protracted and painful labour, she gave birth to a son, Llewelyn Edouard, on the 30th. Dylan did not witness the arrival of the 'Mongolian monkey', his term for the bad-tempered blue-eyed baby, who weighed just over six pounds. Caitlin thought he was cavorting with a girlfriend, a leggy black dancer from the Dollin school whom she called Joey the Ravisher. More likely he was in the back room at Blashford polishing his poem 'Because the pleasure bird whistles'. The mellifluous title sounded up-beat, but the content was full of dark and perhaps drug-induced imaginings about the co-existence of pleasure and pain. Drawing on his painful experiences in London, it also conveyed, with heavy shift of editorial emphasis, his anxiety about his failure to confront problems encountered in the past.

This poem, with its mixture of Bunyanesque and Biblical allusions, was used as a grace, or brief prayer, at the start of *The Map of Love*, the revised name of the book under discussion with Church at Dent's. It complements the shorter 'Once it was the colour of saying', written slightly earlier, over Christmas. There, in lines redolent of Cwmdonkin Drive, Dylan made a more explicit statement that his artistic direction was changing, in line with his overall life: The gist was that his recollections of his childhood had once come in bright higgledy-piggledy confusion. But:

> Now my saying shall be my undoing,
> And every stone I wind off like a reel.

Or, being interpreted, he intended taking a more methodical approach to deciphering his past, and he was worried that this would not only be personally challenging, but also possibly too mechanical, like the unwinding of a reel, with its dual sense of both fishing and films.

Just before Christmas he told Watkins, 'Last year at this time Caitlin and I were doing an act in a garret. This time we're just as poor, or poorer, but the ravens – soft, white, silly ravens – will feed us.' With his mock imprecation to the providential birds of the Old Testament, this oddly religious man who lived outside any formal creed was abandoning himself to his fates, as he faced the last few months of peace before the Second World War, carrying for the first time the responsibilities of fatherhood.

TWELVE

SKIRTING THE WAR

Dylan was, by his own admission, drunk for two weeks after the birth of his son. In true country gentry style, Yvonne Macnamara had re-engaged her trusted family nanny to look after her first grandson. New Inn House was dominated by women at the best of times; now it was also regimented. Dylan showed no particular interest in the mewling baby; Caitlin claimed he never wanted to hold or even look at Llewelyn. She on the other hand was besotted, and Dylan found himself taking second place in his wife's affections. A more mature man could handle this, but Dylan resented the rivalry. Caitlin feigned lack of concern: she had come to recognise Dylan's needy infantile behaviour, and later bitterly recalled how he had always been like a child to her, even in bed, an exceptionally gifted child.

Drink was one way of signalling and at the same time coping with his dependency. It had its side effects: with the additional intake of regular meals at Blashford, he put on over two stone during the first few months of 1939, as his weight barrelled up to twelve and a half stone. He thought he looked like a 'small square giant'. No longer was he the stick insect of the Little Theatre stage or even the narrow-faced Renaissance courtier of Augustus John's portrait in the autumn (the artist's second and well-known attempt to capture his likeness, having been dissatisfied with the first). Now his looks fell the wrong side of a thin line between l'homme moyen sensuel of Nora Summers's photographs the previous year and chubby libertine.

He was not totally idle. He managed a sonorous poem about his son's birth 'If my head hurt a hair's foot', ostensibly a dialogue between the 'bunched monkey' embryo and his mother. He hoped it would fit into his forthcoming book for Dent, for which he was sorting out a running order and, in particular, trying to find the right balance between verse and prose. The fastidious Church was not happy with his story 'A Prospect of the Sea', which he felt had 'moments of sensuality without purpose', a curious description, Dylan felt, for his references to fish. But both sides were keen to finalise a deal. Dent played their part by writing off any money given him for his abandoned Wales book, and offering an unprecedented £70 in advance for this new one (to be called *The Map of Love*), even if not all was immediately available and £20 needed to be returned to George Reavey to ensure he would never have claim to any rights in *The Burning Baby*.

Dylan welcomed whatever sum he received because he had been afraid that he would not be able to return to Laugharne where he still owed rent on Sea View. Having sorted this matter out, he thoughtfully wrote to Frances Hughes asking her to ensure that the house was properly aired for his family's return in late March. Stopping in Bishopston for a day to show off his son to his parents, he took time out to see Bert Trick who later recalled Dylan's outrage at hearing the news of the fall of Madrid to Franco's forces (on 28 March) and also confirmed the young man's deep concerns about how to respond to the coming war.

First engagement in Laugharne was Llewelyn's christening in the parish church, St Martin's, a High Gothic Anglican establishment which had attracted Samuel Taylor Coleridge at the start of the nineteenth century. The ceremony was surprising since the baby's parents had shown little enthusiasm for formal worship. It was enlivened by the presence of Augustus John as godfather. Unable to follow the service, he chimed in with the words 'I desire it' when he saw fit. He also provided additional furniture (unwanted after his father's death) for the house, adding to items that had already come from Blashford. The other godfather, Vernon Watkins, was unable to attend (bank clerks do not enjoy the leisure time of artists). However he sent a wireless set to enliven the Sea View atmosphere, a present particularly welcomed by Caitlin who used to tune in to the commercial station, Radio Luxembourg, and dance round the house to its music.

Within an alarmingly short period (before the end of April), Dylan was again without money and forced to pawn one of Llewelyn's christening gifts, almost certainly the silver spoon and fork from Vernon Watkins. By mid-May he was worrying that debts to local tradesmen would land him in court. Off his own bat, he rifled through his bottom drawer and discovered two old tales, 'The True Story' and 'The Vest', written in his abandoned mystical-poetical style. Such was his need that he sent them to his rich Irish-American friend, Constantine FitzGibbon, who had graduated from Oxford and started a new avant-garde literary magazine *Yellowjacket*. Even Dylan admitted they were 'very paltry', but he needed the guinea each one earned. Higham meanwhile did his best to obtain any money owed Dylan, ranging from anthologies to an HMV recording of 'And death shall have no dominion'. He finalised details of Dylan's contract with his American publisher New Directions, which had abandoned plans for a book of poems in favour of a mixture of prose and verse, similar to Dent's, but more comprehensive, incorporating forty poems and eleven stories from earlier books and articles. Entitled *The World I Breathe*, it was scheduled for publication by the end of the year.

Higham was cheered by Dylan's promise that his exertions in the Castle gazebo were progressing and his new style of more realistic stories about his childhood and immediate Welsh environment were developing into his 'sort of provincial autobiography' for Dent. Surprisingly it was Church who had first suggested three years beforehand that his young protégé might write a story about his 'earlier world'. This was Church's way of weaning Dylan off his often unreadable essays in literary surrealism.

Dylan also kept up his regular exchange of ideas and poems with Vernon Watkins. His bitter lines beginning 'Friend by enemy I call you out' harped on his unhappy experiences in London:

> My friends were enemies on stilts
> With their heads in a cunning cloud.

Happier in mood was another poem for Caitlin, 'Unluckily for a death', which described his wife in mystical, life-enhancing terms, referring positively to his willingness to subjugate his ego to hers. Soon Dylan was promising Higham a further selection of poetry and verse similar to *The Map of Love*. But work in progress did not pay his bills. Encouraged by John Davenport, he adopted an idea of Henry Miller to ask a dozen friends, ranging from the inevitable Norman Cameron to Peggy Guggenheim, to contribute five shillings a week to his Thomas Flotation Ltd. 'As I can't make money by what I write, I think I should concentrate ... on getting my living-money from *people* and not from poems.' When this notion came to nothing, Dylan was reduced to pleading with Higham to negotiate advances on his two proposed books from Dent. His publisher proved surprisingly accommodating, offering an immediate £30 to cover his debts, as well as a retainer of £8 per month.

Meanwhile the spectre of war was concentrating minds on the fringes of Britain where, consciously or unconsciously, nationalists saw coming hostilities as an opportunity to advance their cause. On the literary front, the magazine *Wales* had, after an initial salvo, faltered and Keidrych Rhys had temporarily given up day-to-day editorship to Nigel Heseltine, a move that did not inspire Dylan who had already accused Rhys of printing lightweight reactionary material. 'Why not an article on Firbank, too?' he asked cattily after one effort, going on to lecture Rhys for letting 'the possibility of a possibly great magazine almost slip away'.

Dylan's passion about this venture was genuine; in correspondence with Watkins, he even entertained ideas of taking over the editorship. Unrealistic at the best of times, these became more so after a new Anglo-Welsh journal appeared in February 1939. Edited by Gwyn Jones, a lecturer at Aberystwyth University, The Welsh Review had none of its rival's avant-garde aspirations, but covered a wider literary and political canvas.

While Wales staggered on, Rhys and Dylan retreated to their fall-back position of editing an anthology of Anglo-Welsh writing. As a taster, they (or rather, Rhys, on their behalf) pitched a series on Anglo-Welsh poets to the BBC in Cardiff. Simultaneously Dylan liaised with the Swansea Little Theatre producer, Thomas Taig to compile a programme of Anglo-Welsh verse to run alongside Vernon Watkins's masque The Influences at the Mercury Theatre in London. Once again, both projects indicated Dylan's commitment to the idea of Anglo-Welsh writing, if not to the practical task of propagating it in a regular journal. (His journalistic abilities had peaked at school.)

Recalling his poor track record in these matters, someone at the BBC demanded, 'We must have this man's script before he appears in the studios.' However neither broadcast nor masque took place owing to events beyond Dylan's control. His book The Map of Love (now comprising sixteen poems and seven stories) was published by Dent on 24 August, but the timing could not have been worse. Immediate reaction was mixed: James Agate's devastating attack on his wordiness in the Daily Express was matched by positive reviews by Desmond Hawkins in the Spectator and, particularly, Herbert Read who wrote in Seven: 'It is mainly a poetry of the elemental physical experience: birth, copulation, death ... A unique book ... It contains the most absolute poetry that has been written in our time, and one can only pray that this poet will not be forced in any way to surrender the subtle course of his genius.'

Not that it mattered what anyone said: the book's reception was completely overwhelmed by the hubbub leading to the Second World War. The previous day had seen the signing of the Nazi-Soviet pact, with attendant shattering of illusions among Dylan's leftist friends. This paved the way for Germany's threatened take-over of the Polish city of Gdansk (or Danzig), and, given Britain's treaty obligations, the inevitability of conflict. On the 25th, a Friday, Dylan admitted to Watkins he was having difficulty thinking about the masque programme because, even from Laugharne, the prospect of war filled him with 'such horror & terror & lassitude'. However he could still comment cheekily on Laugharne's position as an English enclave within Wales, describing it as 'a little Danzig'.

At the weekend his father travelled across from Llanstephan with

Dylan's Aunt Polly. With his experience of the Great War, D.J. was keen to ensure that the young Thomases were well provisioned. While Polly Williams searched the Laugharne sands for snails, D.J. helped his son construct bookshelves in Sea View, contributing a large dictionary as the physical and intellectual basis of his son's library. By Tuesday, Britain had mobilised and prospects were considerably more dangerous. Thanking his father for the dictionary, Dylan wrote: 'If I could pray, I'd pray for peace. I'm not a man of action; & the brutal activities of war appal me – as they do every decent-thinking person.' Locally, the war atmosphere had become 'thick and smelling': while children danced in the streets, mobilised soldiers sang 1914–18 marching songs in the pubs, and wives and mothers wept around Laugharne's dilapidated war memorial. At least the Thomases were yet to be affected personally and Dylan did his best to allay his parents' concerns: 'Our own position is, *so far*, quite comfortable.'

The town was gearing up as a military transit centre. Before long any spare room, at Brown's Hotel or elsewhere, was commandeered by soldiers on their way to serve abroad. The small army firing range at Pendine became a large weapons research establishment, after absorbing a similar facility from Essex. New people came to South Wales; new relationships were formed. On the way from Swansea to see Dylan on Sunday 3 September, Vernon Watkins and Thomas Taig heard Prime Minister Neville Chamberlain announce Britain's official declaration of war. Laugharne was in total confusion, and Brown's bar bedlam. Watkins noted that two military policemen who had come in pursuit of deserters ended up drinking with those they were supposed to arrest.

As evidence of intent to stay, the Thomases acquired a cat, unimaginatively called Pussy. Dylan found Dent's monthly allowance covered their basic expenses, and even paid for his Players' Weights. Caitlin coped as best she could as a novice mother without help, though there were alarming stories of her dropping Llewelyn on the stone floor. One visitor recalled her shaking a frying pan over the brick oven in the living room while tending her young son on his chamber-pot. Her most striking dish was a large stew (described by the charitable as pot au feu), consisting of whatever she had to hand, usually cockles, but, on one occasion, an entire rabbit, including the skin. Her domestic forte was needlework, a matter of pride to Dylan who liked showing off to friends a shirt or sweater made by his resourceful wife. Even so, in October he had to borrow a suit from the ever-supportive Watkins so he could fulfil his duties as best man at Keidrych Rhys's wedding in Llanstephan to Lynette Roberts, a highly strung poet of Welsh-Argentine extraction.

Dylan's personal contribution to the smooth running of Sea View was minimal. When Watkins offered to clear the table, he was told (by Dylan) that this was women's work and that the two of them had business with their poems. Watkins recalled his host requesting, in a soft, wheedling voice, 'Ca-at. Can I have a plum?' When met with silence, Dylan asked again, 'Ca-at. Can I have a plum – a very little one?' Whereupon she picked up a bag and threw at him every piece of fruit it contained. Dylan waited with eyes closed until the hail of plums had finished. 'Right,' he then said. 'Now we can get on with our poems.'

Once, when Caitlin was incapacitated with a poisoned finger, he offered to bring her a cup of tea. He came back with a curious greasy concoction, explaining he could not find a top for the pot, so had covered it with half a pound of cheese. Asked to get his wife some water, he rushed to attend to the task, but came back empty-handed. When admonished, he said, 'Well, I did hurry to get it, you can't expect everything.'

Dylan soon gained a local reputation for drinking, brawling and not paying his bills. However he was protected by Ivy Williams (to whom he had surreptitiously lent a copy of Henry Miller's banned *Tropic of Cancer*, one of his favoured genre of 'good fucking books') and, more generally, by the often superstitious townspeople's recognition that he had some God-given role in their community as a poet. When, having imbibed too much, he knocked someone down outside the pub, the policeman agreed that the victim had had it coming to him.

With its history and traditions, Laugharne was also broad-minded enough to recognise Dylan's sweeter, more innocent side. His politeness to old people was noted. It did not matter if they were illiterate cockle-pickers or genteel, often Anglicised middle classes – the type who attended St Martin's church: Dylan always had a cheerful word for them: Among the latter category was the Starke family, long established in Laugharne but originally from Devon. Mrs Janet Starke, a widow, owned the Castle and leased it to Richard Hughes. When the Thomases were invited to dinner with her mother, a Mrs David, at Minerva, a large Georgian house in the High Street, they were joined by a raw young curate. After the meal, Dylan was asked to read and unfurled some crumpled pages of a story remembered as 'to do with Daniel in the lion's den' – probably the suggestive 'Prologue to an Adventure'. As he launched into it, the curate began to fidget and finally could take it no longer. 'I'm sorry, Mrs David,' he announced. 'I've got to go.'

For regular moral support, Caitlin looked to Richard Hughes's eccentric, aristocratic wife, Frances, who had studied at the Chelsea School of Art. Since Hughes was away much of the autumn, writing at his house

Dylan's mother, Florence (née Williams), as a young woman

Dylan's father, David John, known as Jack or D.J., as a young schoolmaster

Dylan as a child

Dylan's mother's family (the Williamses): (from left) (standing) John Williams, the Reverend David Rees, the Reverend Thomas Williams, Bob Williams; (seated) Florrie, Dosie Williams, Polly Williams

Dylan's father's family (the Thomases) outside the Poplars in Johnstown, Carmarthen, c. 1909: (from left) (standing) Tom Thomas; his wife; Arthur Thomas; Florrie Thomas; D.J. Thomas; (seated) Eva Thomas, young Nancy Thomas, Ann Thomas

Dylan's uncle Gwilym 'Marles' Thomas

Dylan and sister Nancy on the beach at Swansea

Dylan's cousin Idris (Jones)

Dylan's Aunt Annie (Jones)

In his school play, *Strife*, in spring 1931, with his friend Charles Fisher (fourth from right) in the female lead

(Seated centre) The boily boy, in a Little Theatre production of *Hay Fever*, 1934

Dylan – studio portrait taken at Arding
& Hobbs, Clapham Junction 1934

Dylan and his mother

Dylan and his first love, Pamela
Hansford Johnson

American in London:
Emily Holmes
Coleman

Runia Tharp (painting
by Charles Tharp)

...rt Trick

Fooling around at Pennard:
Vernon Watkins and Dylan

A youthful Dan Jones

Swansea society: (from left) Fred Janes, unknown,
Vera Phillips and Charles Fisher

...autical girl: Dylan's sister Nancy

Caitlin Macnamara –
studio portrait, 1936

Young Caitlin

Dylan and Caitlin – newly married at Blashford

...itlin – party scene

Dylan and Caitlin –
on a beach in Dorset

Dylan, Caitlin and their
new-born son Llewelyn

Dylan at the Salisbury pub in Saint Martin's Lane, London, 1941

Caitlin and Dylan, unfinished portrait by Ralph Banbury, c.1939

in North Wales, Frances, pregnant with her third child, often invited the Thomases to meals at Castle House, where they drank good whisky and gorged themselves on rich, extravagant fare such as goose. As local chatelaine, she felt duty bound to sponsor a Christmas entertainment in aid of the Red Cross. Drawing on his Little Theatre background, Dylan offered to put on a short play as part of an overall programme of music, acting and dancing (including a lively rendition of tap by Caitlin). In early December, he was still seeking his former mentor Thomas Taig's advice on possible plays. The upshot was that, just before Christmas, he appeared as the poor tanner in his own production of an amateur dramatic society staple, Ernest Goodwin's one-act farce *The Devil Among the Skins*. As post-production celebrations stretched into the night, Dylan started talking about a play about Laugharne, with the local people playing themselves. While Hughes was sceptical they would do this, Dylan was more confident: 'They're so convinced that they're absolutely sane normal people. I think they'd be delighted to prove this on stage.' *Under Milk Wood* was coming more firmly into focus.

Dylan's suggestion was stimulated by his efforts over the autumn to complete his stories recalling his earlier years in Swansea and Carmarthenshire. He cavalierly described tales such as 'Extraordinary Little Cough' (published in *Life and Letters* in September) and 'Just Like Little Dogs' (in *Wales* in October) as 'vulgar' and as 'pot-boilers'. Life in the Llanstephan peninsula was that much easier to recall because it was so close. Often he would ask Jack Roberts, whose family ran the ferry, to take him to visit relations on the other side of the estuary where, he told Richard Hughes, so many people were mentally unbalanced that a bus made weekly trips to the asylum. When Hughes asked if they were 'wild mad or just melancholy', Dylan replied, 'Just more or less sad; everything anyone said of them they think is true' – another pointer to the play he was germinating.

His autobiographical stories were delivered to Dent before Christmas under the 'flippant' mock-Joycean title *Portrait of the Artist as a Young Dog* (devised by Hughes, or so he claimed, and favoured by Dent for its commercial potential). At much the same time New Directions put out *The World I Breathe* in a handsome edition Dylan much admired.

Apart from finishing his book, his main concern over the latter part of 1939 had been what to do during the war. For the time being, conscription applied only to men younger than himself. But he realised that sooner or later he would be called up. Claiming 'all I want is time to write poems', and adamant he did not want to fight, he pulled what limited strings he could to secure an agreeable pen-pushing job, perhaps in a government department. He wrote to Sir Edward Marsh, the

Georgian poet turned civil servant who was a friend of Richard Hughes, asking for preferment in the Ministry of Information. He tried the same approach with Humbert Wolfe, another bumbling poet in Whitehall, and was amused to receive back a wrongly directed letter indicating Desmond Hawkins had done exactly the same. He also began to look for openings in the film business.

When these approaches drew a blank, he enquired about becoming a conscientious objector. After contacting the Welsh branch of the Peace Pledge Union, he attended an objectors' tribunal in Carmarthen, but was discouraged by the proceedings. The only way to ensure exemption from military service, he surmised, was to plead religious conviction, but he felt unable to take this hypocritical approach. Seeking advice from Bert Trick, 'as one Daddy to another', he painted a rosy picture of his baby son, bursting with energy, with 'the familiar Thomas puffed innocence about him'. But Dylan himself admitted to being confused: there was nothing he could contribute to the war with a bayonet, and even the government's incessant propaganda about the evils of Hitlerism only encouraged 'the rebellious pacifism of anti-social softies like myself'. Perhaps a nobler course now was 'for some life to go on, strenuously & patiently, outside the dictated hates & pettinesses of War'.

As usual, Trick proved a sympathetic listener, accepting that Dylan was 'completely outraged' by the prospect of war. 'The very thought that millions would lose their lives, that homes would be shattered, and all the ugliness and horrors and hatreds that war meant, was abhorrent to Dylan.' Trick was later at pains to disabuse an interviewer of any notion of cowardice. Dylan would have been 'prepared to die for something in which he profoundly believed. But war to him was a senseless brutal return to the savagery of the jungle.'

Increasingly conscious of his weight (he described himself to Trick as 'like a walrus' and wondered to Desmond Hawkins if he should declare himself a neutral state or join up as a tank), Dylan circulated some fellow writers, including Rayner Heppenstall, with the idea of compiling a joint article entitled 'Objection to War'. Heppenstall mimicked an earlier stance of Dylan and was dismissive of such communal efforts. Naughtily, he wondered if a writer eager for experience should not join up for that very reason – a suggestion scornfully dismissed by Dylan who said no-one could write if he was killed. As for Heppenstall's objection to working in the civil service, Dylan replied: 'Is it any worse to receive a good salary for muddling information, censoring news, licking official stamps, etc. than it is to kill or be killed for a shilling, or less, a day?'

When no satisfactory answers were forthcoming, no anti-war article was written, and no job offers appeared in the post, Dylan took these reverses badly. Asked by Watkins what he might like for Christmas, he replied morosely, 'I want a war-escaper – a sort of ladder, I think, attached to a balloon – or a portable ivory tower or a new plush womb to escape back into.' Although he settled for a copy of The New Yorker annual, his reaction to the war had become something of a personal crusade, as if battling to find a position which would atone for his father's disappointments a quarter of a century earlier.

Forced again to seek temporary refuge from creditors, he transported his family to Blashford where, as the 1940s were ushered in, his own black mood was not assuaged by news that only 280 copies of The Map of Love had been sold. While publicly adopting a philosophical stance and attributing this poor performance to the war, he must have felt it as another assault on his peace of mind by the forces of darkness. He could only urge Higham to capitalise on his United States publication and sell his latest stories to high-paying magazines in New York.

Passing through London at the end of December, he met Heppenstall who noted his friend's unaccustomed gloom, the physical manifestations of which were all too clear in his growing weight and the cast in his eyes. Dylan 'seemed a prey to some large resentment'. On the one hand, his stand against the war had come to nothing; on the other, he was experiencing the loss not merely of innocence but also of the comforting sense that anything was possible if he approached it with his usual swagger – the unusually personal subject of his fine poem, 'Once below a time', written at Blashford.

This was complemented that spring by a satirical poem, 'The Countryman's Return', in which Dylan poked fun at himself as a suburban 'singing Walt', adrift in 'low-falutin' London', before making his way back uncertainly to a more regular rural existence. Uncertain what to make of it, he sent it to Watkins for perusal. By the time he had touched on its protagonist's 'delusions of all embracing humanitarianism', he rather liked it. With obvious references to cinematic technique, the poem attempted to portray elements of London low life such as:

> girls from good homes
> Studying the testicle
> In communal crab flats
> With the Sunflowers laid on.

In documentary style, it highlights:

All the hypnotised city's
Insidious procession
Hawking for money and pity

and tells how 'that sin-embracing dripper of fun' (or Dylan himself) has to sweep away this false glamour 'like a cream cloud'. With nods to Eliot's Prufrock, it offers documentary detail about Dylan's periods adrift in the capital's underworld. It seems to relate back to his few nerve-shattering days in London a year or so earlier. It also points forward to the sequel to *Portrait of the Artist as a Young Dog*. He described what was to be called *Adventures in the Skin Trade* to Laughlin in April as 'a proper city book, and far free-er in style than the slight, "artful" other stories.'

The Thomases stayed in Blashford for the first three months of 1940. This was longer than expected, partly for financial reasons, partly out of fear of the perishing cold at Sea View and partly because, at Augustus John's suggestion, Dylan had written for a job to Sir Kenneth Clark, Director of the Film Division at the Ministry of Information. He wanted to be reasonably close to London (or at least closer than Laugharne) if he were called for an interview. Time was pressing, since men of his age were scheduled for military call-up in April.

Clark, who had heard about Dylan from Edith Sitwell three years earlier in 1937, had nothing to offer. So Dylan asked the well-connected Herbert Read to remind Clark. He had already thanked Read effusively for his review of *The Map of Love*. Now he claimed that conscription would hinder his writing. 'I refuse to fight, but I'm willing to do some kind of work, any kind of work of which I'm capable.' After he contacted Clark again, emphasising his pressing need and his wish at least to find a non-combatant job in the army – 'my great horror's killing' – Clark's wife Jane recommended him for a position in her friend Captain Victor Cazalet's battery. Cazalet was a music-loving former MP and friend of Winston Churchill who had managed to set up his own unit of anti-aircraft gunners, largely as a bolt-hole for writers and artists who he knew would not be able to stomach military life.

At the end of March Dylan and his family returned disconsolately to Laugharne where they were joined by Caitlin's artist friend Rupert Shephard, accompanied by his South African wife Lorna Wilmot who, pointedly unlike Dylan, had found a niche in the film industry. Although they stayed in Brown's, the Shephards spent much of their free time at Sea View. It was not always a relaxing experience. Wilmot frequently clashed with Caitlin, whom she found 'as wild and unscrupulous' as Dylan. The Thomases took their visitors to Llanstephan to meet the Rhyses – both Ernest Rhys, a veteran Dent editor who regaled them with stories of Whitman and Swinburne, and Keidrych Rhys and his new wife whom Wilmot identified as 'Welsh mystic patriots'. Shephard was struck by Caitlin's enduring beauty, though Dylan's Falstaffian girth was not so appealing. He painted them both, his study of Dylan stressing a different side to his sitter's personality than the wide-eyed visionary of Augustus John's recent portrait. Shephard showed an unusually subdued Dylan, sitting and working amid the domesticity of Sea View.

Dylan's moderation reflected his worries about his military status. As legally required, he registered for military service on 6 April, still hoping to join Cazalet's anti-aircraft battery. His friends were receiving their marching orders: Watkins to the Royal Air Force, Dan Jones to the government cipher centre at Bletchley Park, and Charles Fisher to the army. Dylan at least enjoyed the way Fisher communicated this news – in a clerihew:

> The poet Charles Fisher
> Will be compelled to join the militia
> With a lot of other pricks
> On June sixth.

But that did not ease his own problems, among which money was again pressing. Publication of *Portrait of an Artist as a Young Dog* in early April gave him an excuse to travel to London to make further enquiries about his candidacy for Cazalet's battery. But his main reason was to ask his richer friends and admirers for financial help. Wilmot, who was remaining in Wales, offered him the use of her flat in Crawford Street, on the Portman estate north of Oxford Street. From there, he telephoned Henry Moore who, with Stephen Spender, Henry Read and Peter Watson, wealthy proprietor of the newly established literary journal *Horizon*, agreed to put their names to a letter which went to a dozen or so potential subscribers asking for at least £70 which would enable Dylan to pay his immediate debts. While Cecil Day Lewis, Bryan Guinness, Lord Esher and others responded with cash, raising a total of £126. 12s. 0d, H. G. Wells meanly declined, claiming that he had many dependents and had never read Dylan.

Having unfettered exclusive access to a handsome mansion block property went to Dylan's head. Unhinged by drink and depression, he invited two low-life friends to join him. The upshot was that several of Wilmot's prized possessions, including silver, furs, a gramophone and a typewriter, went missing. When she returned home, she was incensed to find not only had these items disappeared, but also her flat was strewn with half-eaten meals, and with love letters belonging to one of

Dylan's friends, a Fitzroy denizen known as Mab Farrogate, and the clothing and make-up of another, the cross-dressing Brian Dean Paul.

Over the previous three years there had been strong indications that Dylan had been taking drugs. His paranoia following his trip to London in December 1938 strongly suggests a reaction to a bad drug experience. His association with 'Napper' Dean Paul confirms his close involvement with London's prevalent drug sub-culture. 'Napper', the generally disliked son of an ineffective Irish baronet and grandson of the famous nineteenth-century Polish violinist Henryk Wieniawski, openly took cocaine and, rather more furtively, heroin. His promiscuous sister Brenda, another junkie, was more popular, having made a career as mistress to a variety of men about town, from David Tennant, the owner of the Gargoyle Club, to Peter Quennell, the author. The onset of the war had only accentuated the (to Dylan) alluring social fluidity of an amoral world where aristocrats and influential men of letters mixed with drug addicts and bums.

At 3.30 on the morning following Wilmot's return, Dylan turned up drunk at the flat but, unable to handle any confrontation, promptly bolted. An hour later Dean Paul arrived and did the same. After recovering some of her goods from a pawnbroker, Wilmot found a woman in the Fitzroy wearing her University of Cape Town scarf. She wrote angrily to Dylan in Wales, threatening police intervention. He cabled immediately, begging her to 'call off the hounds' and promising to restore all. On his return to London, he said his friends had let him down. 'You do believe me, don't you?' he pleaded implausibly. 'My honour is about the only thing we have got left now, Lorna. It's pretty valuable to me.'

He had only gone back to Wales because his army medical was scheduled in Llandeilo, east of Carmarthen, at the end of April. With his secondment to Victor Cazalet's battery still unconfirmed, he decided the best condition in which to approach this examination was very drunk. When he entered the clinic, he could hardly stand. His lungs, not to mention his liver, were in such a damaged state that the doctor had little hesitation in giving him C3 status. This meant that, while he was technically capable of serving in the army, his health was so poor that he would be one of the very last people to be called up.

Still creditors pressed for payment. Until funds arrived from his benefactors, he and his family were forced to 'sneak away' from Laugharne and spend most of May with his parents in Bishopston. There he saw a lot of Watkins, his companion for renewed exploration of Gower. One day he was again nearly caught by the tide on the Worm, off Rhossili. Watkins remained his usual supportive self, conscientiously sending Dylan a pound he had earned for some short poems he had written for his godson Llewelyn. Dylan used the money to make payments on a bed he had bought on hire purchase from a Swansea store.

Watkins liked a poem his friend had written at Blashford earlier in the year. 'There was a saviour' captured Dylan's unease at the start of the war, contrasting the sense of false comfort experienced under a Fascist dictatorship with the satisfaction of the complexity of Christ's universe. With Miltonic cadences and exciting rhythms, it is on one level the first of his sonorous war poems, on another a paean to God's creation. Over the early summer Dylan worked on 'Into her lying down head', the latest in his series about his relationship with Caitlin. Dealing with jealousy, innocence and reconciliation, it recalls 'I make this in a warring absence' but in a more amusingly detached manner.

At the beginning of June Dylan received the proceeds of his London friends' appeal and for a few weeks returned to Laugharne where he was able to lash out on a new coat of distemper for his house. But once again his financial security did not last. In late July, with the phoney war ended, the Battle of Britain lighting up the skies over southern England, and bombs starting to fall in Swansea, he closed up Sea View and took Caitlin and Llewelyn to stay in the Malting House, John Davenport's eighteenth-century mansion on the High Street in Marshfield, on the edge of the Cotswolds between Chippenham and Bath.

Portly, bucolic yet lithe, like a light-heavyweight past his prime, Davenport was a complex character, whose loud actress mother, Muriel George, was the antithesis of his own gentlemanly ideal. Destined never to write anything substantial on his own account, he was however successful as a critic, and his theatrical connections had done him well: after making his mark as a poet (and boxing blue) at Cambridge, he had married Clement, a beautiful painter from New England who was great-niece of the actor Sir Johnston Forbes-Robertson. His mother had then found him lucrative employment as a scriptwriter for MGM in Hollywood. The combination of his transatlantic earnings and an inheritance of his wife's enabled him to acquire his elegant house and furnish it with modern paintings by artists such as Picasso and Tanguy. A grand piano took pride of place in a long upstairs drawing room. This became a refuge for artists still unclear about their roles in the war.

Others in this cultured, often neurotic menage included the composers Lennox Berkeley and Arnold Cooke, the music critic William Glock and the writer Antonia White who was on the verge of returning to the Roman Catholic church. When not amusing himself playing piano duets with Glock, Davenport became the latest person to work on Dylan's long-gestated spoof thriller about the murder of the poet laureate. Now that Fisher had been called up, the talented Davenport proved an ideal partner for *The Death of the King's Canary*. The two writers had fun devising thinly disguised portraits of prominent literary figures and composing pastiche poems to go with them. Among those caricatured were Vicky Neuburg (as the murdered poet laureate Hilary Byrd), T. S. Eliot (J. L. Atkins), W. H. Auden (Wyndham Nils Snowden), Cyril Connolly (Basil Minto), George Barker (Albert Ponting), Augustus John (Hercules Jones), the Sitwells (the Laceys) and Dylan and Davenport themselves (Owen Tudor and Tom Agard). Owen Tudor promises, when rich, to give up writing and 'just be absolutely disgusting'. Suggestive of Dylan's narcotic dabblings, he smokes marijuana and asks, 'Do they make you ... full of fun? I mean, do they make you want to do things? ... Larks.'

The two friends shared composition of the main prose storyline, though, contrary to expectation, Davenport wrote most of the verse parodies. Two definite exceptions were 'Parachutist' and 'Request to Leda', based on Spender and Empson, which Dylan later sent to *Horizon*. Strangely, his mildly homo-erotic Spender spoof was set up for printing and then pulled – Cyril Connolly, the editor, claimed through lack of space. Instead the inferior Empson villanelle was retained and, on the page opposite, surely as a joke, Connolly published 'The Dirty Little Accuser', Norman Cameron's exasperated recollection of Dylan.

In August Dylan went to London hoping to find a job somewhere in the BBC's expanded wartime service. The blitz had yet to reach London, but already Dylan was alarmed by the evidence of the air battle being fought over southern England for the future of Britain. When he met Pamela Hansford Johnson, now married to an Australian journalist Gordon Stewart, he paranoidly inscribed a photo from six years earlier: 'August 12 1940. Dylan-shooting begins.'

Back in Marshfield, his collaboration with Davenport helped take his mind off the war. But too often for his liking, he heard German bombers droning overhead at night, en route to drop their loads on Bristol. Then, as Caitlin recalled, he would hide his head under the sheets in their exposed top-floor bedroom and he would whimper. To Watkins he confessed he was having 'burning birdman' dreams, including one in which airmen were fried in a huge pan. Another fearful fantasy was 'greyclothed, grey-faced, blackarmletted troops marching, one morning, without a sound up a village street ... That's what Goebbels has done for me.' News of intensified bombing raids on Swansea only added to his unease. The Germans had identified the town's port and nearby oil installations as crucial targets. Their attacks crept closer to home in early August when Titch and Vera's family, the Phillipses, were forced to vacate their house in Bryn-y-Mor Crescent after the Girls' High School was also destroyed. On 1 September came the biggest raid yet, when thirty-three people were killed and over a hundred injured.

There were additional unsettling forces at work. Caitlin had loyally supported Dylan in his feud with Lorna Wilmot, firing off a telegram inveighing against the South African's bourgeois attitude to her London flat. But, after three years of marriage, Dylan's wife was tiring of her subsidiary role as poet's muse and nappy-washer. At Marshfield she practised her dancing in a local Roman Catholic chapel, but lacked creative outlet for her talents both as a stage performer and as an occasional versifier in her own right. She resented being left often penniless on her own with Llewelyn while Dylan made regular restorative trips to London, particularly as she was convinced, correctly, that he used these occasions for dalliances with other women.

To preserve her amour propre, she developed a tendresse for another Marshfield inhabitant, the fair-haired Glock (who was also romantically involved with Clement Davenport whom he was later to marry). Caitlin arranged to consummate what she described as her first serious affair since marrying Dylan in a hotel in Cardiff. As an alibi she told Dylan she was visiting his parents in Bishopston. But the canny Florrie Thomas worked out that her daughter-in-law had spent one unaccounted night en route, and the story emerged. Caitlin's hotel rendezvous with Glock turned out to be a limp farce, but Dylan was furious, especially when the liaison carried on for a while. His fights with his wife grew more bitter; on one occasion he threw a knife at her, and for a long time refused to come near her. Llewelyn picked up on the bad blood and, according to the testimony of Antonia White's younger daughter, Lyndall, he wet his bed continuously. Extraordinarily White herself saw the Thomases as pillars of sanity in this frenetic war-traumatised community: 'when I tell you I clung to them,' she told Emily Coleman, '... you will get an idea of what it was like!'

Dylan failed to convince anyone at the BBC to give him a full-time job. He told Vernon Watkins that a putative opening, though well paid, would have meant writing tedious news summaries for the Empire Service, thus more or less admitting he did not want to be tied down in this way. Yet he realised he needed the money, and his desultory requests for indentured employment at the BBC were to become a regular theme over the next dozen years as if, in addition, someone, possibly D.J. or Florrie, though more likely his own atavistic idea of what might please them, pricked his conscience from time to time and reminded him of his obligation to provide for his family.

His parents were clearly keen for him to be seen to be doing useful war service. A few months earlier Florrie had optimistically told her daughter Nancy that Dylan had joined up. But this was wishful thinking, and in the meantime Mrs Thomas had had to come to terms with the break-up of Nancy's marriage. Unlike Dylan, Nancy had done the patriotic thing, signing up to the ATS as a driver. (Caitlin's sister Brigit also joined the same service in France, later becoming a member of a vital barge transportation crew.) Nancy's duties took her from home and introduced her to officers' messes, while her husband Haydn wrestled with a new job as manager of a brick factory near Redhill and with the ongoing problem of his wayward brother Handel, a Fascist sympathiser under regular police surveillance. The sexual temptations proved too much for Nancy who in 1940 decided to leave Haydn and join an officer with the Indian Army in Poona. Although the Thomas family had weathered extra-marital relationships, this was its first divorce – a shocking departure for the Uplands.

On another foray in early September, Dylan was terrified to find himself in London on the weekend the blitz started. He had gone to see Donald Taylor, boss of Strand Films, leader in the thriving market making documentaries for the government. Either Davenport or Cyril Connolly had given him the address of Peter Rose Pulham, a painter turned fashion photographer, as a possible place to stay. When Dylan turned up at Pulham's flat in Chelsea and asked in his plummy Welsh voice, 'Is this Mr Pulham's residence?', Pulham's girl friend, an aspiring actress called Theodora Rosling, thought he must be a debt collector. Having established his bona fides, Dylan joined a small party which included the young diplomat, Donald Maclean. In the early evening they all repaired to a local pub, but were prevented from returning home because of the ferocity of the first major German bombing raid on London which left much of the East End in flames.

Assigned to Pulham's sitting room sofa, Dylan hardly slept either that or the following (Sunday) night, when the bombing was repeated. On the Monday he met Taylor in a pub in St Martin's Lane (probably the Salisbury which was favoured by artists and film-makers). The interview seems to have gone well, but Dylan loathed the destruction around him (and feared more to come). He beat a hasty retreat to the Davenports' in Gloucestershire where he worked on his 'poem about invasion'. He had mentioned this to Watkins earlier in the summer, but his London experience inspired him to complete 'Deaths and Entrances', into which he poured all his concerns about the threat around him. Taking up well exercised themes of birth and death, it was the first of several deeply felt poems in which he engaged with war.

The blitz put a temporary halt to discussion about employment in the film industry. Dylan had to be content with resuming his freelance activity at the BBC, which did at least allow him occasional trips to London, as much to escape from Caitlin and the fouled atmosphere at Marshfield as to keep up with his drinking companions. John Royston Morley, a producer and former literary crony, hired him to write a feature on the nineteenth-century Brazilian army commander, the Duque de Caixas, even lending him books which he later had to request back. This was followed by programmes on Christopher Columbus and on the Czech legion in Russia in the 1914–18 war. The Christopher Columbus script was a confused mish-mash and was not used, though someone in the copyright department took the trouble to plead with the Corporation's accountants to pay Dylan: 'He came in to see me today (12 December), in an exceedingly nervous state, having been bombed.' As for the Czech legion commission, Dylan used it to hone his skills at writing for different voices, boasting to John Davenport that it called for five different announcers. At least he was getting practice for employment as a film scriptwriter.

In December the various tensions at the Davenports' caused Dylan to beat a retreat from the Malting House and to park himself and his family temporarily with his parents. His personal pain was startlingly evident in 'On a Wedding Anniversary' published in January 1941 in Poetry London, the journal edited by Tambimuttu, a rising star of the literary scene. This short poem minced no words about the breakdown of a relationship which had 'moved for three years in tune' but 'Now their love lies a loss.' Similar suffering was the engine of his 'Ballad of the Long-Legged Bait', which describes in dramatic Freudian dream sequence a fisherman at sea in an ocean of desire. After a period of wild sexual activity, the sailor becomes sated and agrees meekly to marriage, an inevitable sacrifice in 'the furious ox-killing house of love'. When a child is born, he recognises this as another trick played by cruel Time, an unstoppable force whose role is simply to advance one rapidly to death. Recalling his inability to cope with metropolitian stresses a couple of years earlier, he rails against 'O Rome and Sodom To-morrow and London'.

At the end he is left standing disconsolately at the door of his house, with the organ of his love onanistically in his hand. Vernon Watkins, who had helped the ballad through many versions, noted that it was 'so much a visual poem that [Dylan] made a coloured picture for it which he pinned on the wall of his room [at Bishopston], a picture of a woman lying at the bottom of the sea.'

Having finished The Death of the King's Canary, his collaboration with Davenport, Dylan was also working on Adventures in the Skin Trade which he now described as a semi-autobiographical novel – 'a mixture of Oliver

Twist, Little Dorrit, Kafka, Beachcomber, and good old 3-adjectives-a-penny belly churning Thomas, the Rimbaud of Cwmdonkin Drive'. But his heart was not in it and he admitted it was badly written, a view readily endorsed by Dent which, amid stern comments about Dylan's 'literary irresponsibility', declined to publish the book.

By January 1941 Dylan's situation was again unbearable. He and his wife were living in cramped conditions at his parents' house. (When the pipes burst, Caitlin spent the whole day mopping up.) They had no money, and Llewelyn had been sent to his Macnamara grandmother. Desperate for funds which might allow them to rent a small cottage somewhere in Wales or in Cornwall, Dylan wrote to the wealthy Lord Howard de Walden, an Augustus John contact (and, in a roundabout way, the source of his name), who had helped him in the past. He also applied to the Royal Literary Fund which granted him £50, though not before Alec Waugh, a half-hearted supporter of his request, had commented to Davenport that Dylan should write more stories and fewer letters. ('When I want advice from Alec Waugh, I'll go to his brother,' commented Dylan, testily.) One writer Dylan approached about his application was Walter de la Mare who generously sent £5 to tide him over. Dylan promised to repay this as soon as the Fund delivered. But by the time this money arrived in February, it was all otherwise accounted for, and Dylan had to write a letter of grovelling apology to de la Mare.

In the midst of grave problems on both domestic and war fronts, there were still moments of defiant pleasure. Over the festive season he and Caitlin attended a loud party given by students from the Swansea College of Art over a laundry opposite the Slip looking out across Swansea Bay. The Thomases went with the Phillips sisters who, after their house had been bombed, were preparing to decamp to Cardiganshire, their mother's original home. While guests drank a mixture of rum and milk brewed in the kitchen, Dylan and Vera Phillips sang a strange personal opera in which they made up both the words and the tune. Vera's sister Evelyn (Titch) recalled how everyone stopped dancing to watch Dylan and Caitlin perform a 'particularly brilliant' ballet burlesque in the middle of the room. Caitlin was even more hopelessly drunk than Dylan. In order to sober her up before returning to his parents' house in Bishopston, Dylan tried to make her vomit by putting a finger down her throat. She bit him hard, causing him to remark, 'She bites the hand that makes her sick.'

But the war was relentless. In late February Swansea suffered its worst air raids ever. Two hundred and thirty people were killed during a three-night blitz in which the area around the High Street was devastated. The following morning Bert Trick went to the offices of the air-raid service (of which he was a warden) on the corner of Union and Oxford Streets. The building had been destroyed and, as he contemplated a surreal scene of smouldering masonry and serpentine fire hoses, Dylan and Caitlin walked round the corner. 'There had been a pub on the corner,' recalled Trick. 'It was a blackened mound. Dylan said, "Our Swansea has died," and by God he was right. The pubs and familiar places we knew had gone for all time.'

With Swansea seemingly as dangerous as London, Dylan wrote again to Edith Sitwell's friend Sir Kenneth Clark about the possibility of a job in the film industry. He suggested he would be more useful writing films than working in a munitions factory, adding for emphasis, 'I'm not, by the way, thinking of film-work because I imagine it to be easier than other jobs.' A few days later he rather back-tracked when, echoing his alter ego Owen Tudor in a letter to Clement Davenport, he indulged a fantasy about employment in a munitions factory: clocking in, socialising in the canteen, turning and hammering all day – all 'to help to kill another stranger; deary me, I'd rather be a poet anyday and live on guile and beer.'

His still basically iconoclastic attitude to the world was clear in a telegram he wrote to his old friend Len Lye. With the vision of an experimental artist, Lye had composed a political-cultural manifesto for the post-war world. Anticipating the hippy movement by a quarter of a century, this was based around the slogan Individual Happiness Now (IHN). Dylan could only signal his enthusiastic approval, sending (with the painter and designer John Tunnard) a cable which read: 'Hurrah for IHN'. Although aware that this might have been written after a session in a pub, Lye was delighted at such an unsolicited testimonial, describing it to Robert Graves as 'the right kind of lift'.

Despite his immediate woes, Dylan maintained his regular poetic output. Horizon had taken 'Deaths and Entrances' in January. 'Love in the Asylum', published in Tambimuttu's Poetry (London) in May–June was a light, ironic yet passionate appreciation of Caitlin's role as a turbulent muse who stimulates his imagination – the woman he could not live with, nor live without. A more sceptical view of sexual relations came in 'On the marriage of a virgin', originally written around the time of his sister Nancy's wedding in 1933, and one of two poems (the other was 'The hunchback in the park') which he now radically revised from his notebook versions eight and nine years earlier. Both were printed in Life and Letters Today, as was his latest angry report from the battlefront, the sonnet 'Among those Killed in the Dawn Raid was a Man Aged a Hundred'.

The Swansea of Dylan's adolescence may have died, and now he moved to draw a line under another relic from times gone by. For over three years he had fielded requests from the State University of New York at Buffalo for manuscripts to form the basis of a poetry collection at its new Lockwood Memorial Library. In June Dylan agreed to sell the university five of the notebooks in which he had methodically written his poems during his teenage years (four containing poetry, one short stories). The London bookseller Bertram Rota was paid just over $140 (or £35) as agent on the deal. Dylan clearly received significantly less. He had sold the cream of his creative work for the equivalent of around £1,200 in 2003. Dylan was twenty-six at that time. Although his biographer Constantine FitzGibbon drew over-fanciful parallels with John Keats, who died in his twenty-sixth year, Dylan was indeed sloughing off a youthful skin. A period of intense poetic activity had drawn to an end. Dylan had already written more than eighty per cent of his published verse. Now, signalling a different sort of creative potential, he was free to join the commercial world of film.

THIRTEEN

HACK WORK

Two additional factors speeded Dylan's return to London in the summer of 1941. One was the death of his Aunt Dosie in Carmarthenshire in April. Unlike with Aunt Annie eight years earlier, this did not lead directly to Dylan writing a poem. More prosaically, it allowed his parents to cut their Swansea ties and move permanently to Blaencwm. Since Dosie's husband, the pious Reverend Crap, David Rees, had died two years earlier, Florrie had often been in Llanstephan looking after her older sister. Dosie now left her share in the two cottages which made up Blaencwm to Florrie. Dylan's parents were able to give up living in Bishopston, sell Cwmdonkin Drive (a transaction completed in April 1943) and move permanently to Llanstephan where they had the upper of the two cottages and Aunt Polly and Uncle Bob the lower.

The other development was that the worst of German bombing of London appeared to be over. (The blitz is officially said to have ended in May.) Although demonstrably a city still at war, with sandbags shoring up vital buildings, and egg powder and Spam the staples in every kitchen cupboard, the capital began to return to some semblance of normality – one sign of which was the reopening of the Gargoyle Club in Meard Street, Soho, in June. Originally founded in 1925 with a dual role as a nightclub and a meeting place for avant-garde artists, the Gargoyle had, by the start of the war, become an after-hours watering hole for the rich. In December 1940 its well-heeled owner David Tennant, son of Lord Glenconner, closed it down, partly because of the bombs and partly because, with internment, it was impossible to find experienced Italian waiters. When, six months later, he opened its doors again, he was determined to return to the club's original raison d'être and to admit a wider clientele, from writers and artists, to officers of the various émigré forces such as the Free French who had brought a degree of sophistication to the beleaguered capital.

Tennant was only reflecting a general spirit of camaraderie. For two years social divisions and sexual inhibitions had broken down as the pubs of central London had drawn in the itinerant bands of war, whether East European refugees, Commonwealth soldiers en route to some distant battlefront, vital workers from the Celtic fringes, or East Enders simply seeking a break from the domestic front line. A gallows intensity inevitably hung over proceedings, and this was found also in literature and the arts, which were both flourishing. Paper might be rationed and the number of books printed down, but sales were up, as any printed work was immediately devoured by an eager public. (Another wartime paradox was that, despite the flourishing of pub culture, people spent more time than usual quietly at home.) Reading was a way of passing the hours, obtaining information and also, particularly in the charged atmosphere of the moment, exploring eternal verities. This was good for poetry, where the political concerns of the 1930s had given way to the neo-romanticism of the apocalyptical school that had tried to claim Dylan. Edith Sitwell did her bit, springing into verse for the first time in a decade to give the horrors of war a Christianised context in her poem 'Still falls the rain'. Magazines of the Auden decade such as *New Verse* and *Twentieth Century Verse* folded and were replaced by Tambimuttu's *Poetry (London)* and Charles Wrey Gardiner's *Poetry Quarterly*. A wartime phenomenon was the anthology: from May 1940 the government banned the publication of new magazines, but could not prevent entrepreneurial publishers who used their often hoarded supplies of poor paper to put out collections of verse and short stories that they called books. Where magazines flourished, they were pocket-sized and comprehensive, in the style of John Lehmann's *New Writing*, Cyril Connolly's *Horizon* and periodicals for the fighting man such as *Lilliput* which printed pictures of semi-naked girls.

All of this was good news for Dylan. During the summer he, Caitlin and baby Llewelyn had been staying with Frances Hughes in the house attached to Laugharne Castle. (Frances enjoyed the company as her husband was away, working for the Admiralty in Bath.) Confident at last that the bombing in the capital had really abated, Dylan decided to return there in August. Caitlin opted to accompany him, fearing that if she did not make the effort, he would be drawn inextricably back to pubs and their easy women. Reluctantly, or so she claimed, she was forced to leave two-and-a-half-year-old Llewelyn with her mother in Blashford, where he remained for much of the rest of the war. (En route, as she recounted in harrowing detail to Frances Hughes, she managed to lose the unfortunate child on the train between Cardiff and Bristol.)

This time Dylan was ready and willing to take up Donald Taylor's offer of a job with Strand Films. The spectacled, dark-haired Taylor was a leading light in Britain's documentary film movement which had grown up over the previous decade and been further boosted by government propaganda commissions during the war. Taylor had started making films in the 1930s in partnership with Ralph 'Bunny' Keene, a sharp-featured jack of all trades who was originally an art dealer. Together they worked closely with Paul Rotha, a director who was also a leading theoretician of their trade. Taylor's wife Marion (herself a film-maker) was the sister of John Grierson, the acknowledged pioneer of British documentaries, with his work for the Empire Marketing Board, the General Post Office film unit and, before the war, the oil industry. By 1941 the market had grown so substantially that Keene opted to leave Strand and set up his own company, Greenpark. Through friendship with documentary-makers such as Len Lye and Humphrey Jennings, as well as his own love of the screen, Dylan was well acquainted with this branch of film. His own poetry used cinematic references, and he almost certainly knew W. H. Auden's clattering verse commentary on the Night Train for the GPO film unit.

Taylor must have wondered where Dylan had been over the past year, for he did not hire him immediately. When Dylan wrote to Vernon Watkins from Horizon's offices on 28 August, four weeks after arriving in London, he was still looking for a film job, though he claimed to have been offered work on several scripts. Taylor later said that Dylan was recommended to him by Ivan Moffat, another of his scriptwriters. Moffat was the witty talented son of sybaritic American artist Curtis Moffat and of socialite Iris Tree, whose father was the actor-producer Sir Herbert Beerbohm Tree. With these credentials, he was an ideal front-man for the Gargoyle Club, whose owner David Tennant charged him with bringing in new, livelier members after the establishment reopened in June. One person he commandeered was Dylan who took readily to the louche atmosphere of the club. Dylan had probably met Moffat through his one-time benefactor Peter Watson, Horizon's financial backer and Gargoyle habitué, or through Augustus John, a friend of Ivan's father Curtis, who, the painter pointedly noted in his autobiography, had introduced him to hashish. Either of them might have seen Dylan mooching about and urged Moffat to find him a job.

Indisputably, before long, Dylan was perched at a desk in Strand's 'ringing, clinging' offices, initially in Upper St Martin's Lane and then, as the workload increased, in Golden Square, in the film-making heart of Soho. He was paid £10 a week, or around £350 a week at 2003 prices, for contributing his share of ideas, scripts and voice-overs to the output of Britain's leading documentary production company which, under contract mainly to the Ministry of Information, put out seventy-five films, ranging from five-minute shorts to substantial features, in 1942 alone. As little more than a propaganda arm of the government,

Strand's role was to pump out basic information, raise morale and, increasingly, prepare Britain's war-weary population for a brighter future. Two of Dylan's early efforts in the summer of 1942 show how easily he took to wielding his pen in this manner: *Balloon Site 568* is an eight-minute recruitment vehicle for the Women's Auxiliary Air Force (WAAF), while *New Towns for Old* uses dialogue in similar fashion to treat of plans for post-war reconstruction, with 'new schools, new hospitals, new roads, new life', adding a populist note with the rallying cry: 'You're the only folk that can make these plans come true.'

Dylan might have known how to paint a bright future in the movies but, closer to home, in the summer of 1941, he still had as much difficulty as ever supporting himself and his family. Occasionally he and Caitlin were able to stay with her sister Nicolette in Markham Square, Chelsea. But the differences in way of life between the Devases and the Thomases were vast – a point brought home to Nicolette during air-raids when, while most others tried to disguise their fear, Dylan covered himself in an eiderdown and lay, moaning and cursing in a corner of the room, in a manner that made everyone else more frightened. Since Nicolette was pregnant with her second child – a son called Esmond, who was born in November – Dylan and Caitlin soon moved to the seedy Mars Hotel, above a restaurant in Frith Street, near his place of work in Soho. From there he complained to Watkins of sitting in his room, thinking darkly about those who could afford to go out to eat.

The alternative, as always, was the pub, but here the ambience and even the venue was changing. Dylan still made his way north of Oxford Street to the shambling, old-fashioned Fitzroy and Wheatsheaf. Increasingly, however, he was drawn to the more functional film-makers' hostelry, the Highlander in Dean Street, or to the actors' haunt, the Salisbury in St Martin's Lane. He also frequented two drinking spots which epitomised London's shifting population – the York Minster at the southern end of Dean Street, known as the French pub since becoming the bar of choice for all who had crossed the Channel with General de Gaulle after the fall of France, and the unambiguously named Swiss pub on Old Compton Street. If he needed food, there was always the Café An' in St Giles Passage off the Tottenham Court Road, the second part of whose name alluded to its additional attractions, such as girls. But wherever Dylan went, however much he earned, he never had money to spare.

One encouraging sign was that the younger generation of consciously post-Auden poets regarded him as a mentor. In the autumn of 1941 Routledge published *Eight Oxford Poets*, an anthology of undergraduate verse. One of the editors was Sidney Keyes, soon to be killed in action.

At the age of twenty-one, he affirmed, 'We have on the whole little sympathy with the Audenian school of poets.' Since Dylan was clearly in the same camp, he was invited to Oxford in November to address the English Club. Looking smarter than usual in a borrowed dinner jacket, Dylan attracted an eclectic audience, amongst whom was the young Philip Larkin, up at St John's, who noted appreciatively: 'Hell of a fine man: little, snubby, hopelessly pissed bloke who made hundreds of cracks and read parodies of everybody in appropriate voices. He remarked, "I'd like to have talked about a book of poems I've been given to review, a young poet called Rupert Brooke — it's surprising how he has been influenced by Stephen Spender ..." There was a moment of delighted surprise, then a roar of laughter. Then he read a parody of Spender entitled "The Parachutist" which had people rolling on the floor. He kept this up all night — parodies of everyone bar Lawrence — and finally read two of his own poems, which were very good.' (Dylan was winning over his student audience with excerpts from *The Death of the King's Canary*.) Afterwards he was invited to a party in Christ Church given by Michael Hamburger, a pale dark-haired member of the club who translated Rilke and Hölderlin. He was unaware he had offended some student hearties with obscene comments at the end of his talk until they broke into Hamburger's rooms, dragged out Dylan, and tried to throw him into the pond in the main college quadrangle.

Hamburger, later a distinguished poet and translator, struck up a friendship with Dylan, imitating his verse, and seeking out his company in Soho pubs during vacations. Often he was accompanied by his undergraduate friend John Mortimer who had recently lost his virginity to Susan Henderson, daughter of Wyn, who lived in the same Oxfordshire village of Turville Heath. One drunken lunch Dylan, adopting what Mortimer called his 'breathy, Charles Laughton voice', announced he was looking for a girl with an aperture as small as a mouse's earhole and took the two undergraduates to the usually welcoming offices of *Horizon*. By then Mortimer was too drunk to recall if Dylan was successful in his quest.

For much of the rest of 1941, the Thomases led an unseemly peripatetic existence. Theodora Rosling compared Dylan to the Master of Hounds in R. S. Surtees's 'Handley Cross':

> He will bring his nightcap with him,
> For where the MFH dines he sleeps,
> And where the MFH sleeps he breakfasts.

Theodora herself was posing naked for her boyfriend Peter Rose Pulham for a series of tasteful photographs which appeared in the new magazine Lilliput, where the Polish-born Mechtild Nawaisky, a Chelsea drinking friend, was art editor. Through this connection, Dylan was commissioned to write verse captions to accompany a series of photographs, titled 'A Dream of Winter', by the celebrated photographer Bill Brandt, which appeared in the magazine in January 1942. A few months earlier Brandt had captured him on camera for a series 'Poets of Democracy' in the same magazine. Laurie Lee, part of this group, called it 'a gallery of hideous morons & gargoyles', with Dylan looking 'sick in a pub'.

With Theodora and Pulham, Dylan went round for dinner at Donald and Melinda Maclean's flat near Regent's Park. On the menu were some dried onion flakes which, because of rationing, a friend had thoughtfully sent from the United States. Dylan put his fellow guests off their meal by remarking sweetly that this delicacy looked like old men's toe-nails.

When at a loose end, he often accompanied Theodora to the cinema. Although they usually enjoyed horror movies, they both found Fritz Lang's M stomach-turning, particularly Theodora, who could not help remarking that Peter Lorre, in the lead role of a child murderer, looked uncannily like Dylan. When they went to the French pub for a restorative drink, they were accosted by an oldish man whom Dylan knew and clearly disliked. Wielding a pad of paper, this fellow asked them to make a drawing. When they finished he sent over a piece of paper on which he had sketched exactly the same thing. Already discomfited by the film, Dylan went white and insisted on moving immediately. When Theodora asked why, he said they had just met Aleister Crowley and they needed to get as far away from him as possible.

Some respite came in early 1942 when John Pudney (never Dylan's favourite poet, though always a loyal supporter) prevailed on his father-in-law Alan (A. P.) Herbert (another about whom Dylan had been unduly scornful) to allow the needy Thomases to live in one of his two adjacent houses in Hammersmith Terrace, Chiswick. Staying nearby was Cecily Mackworth, a well-born Welsh woman who had befriended Henry Miller while living in France. Forced to flee Paris in 1940, she was working with the Free French in London. Once when she was ill, a friend brought Dylan along to help cheer her up. Dylan sat on the end of her bed and talked seriously about the pain of being in love. Eyeing her sympathetically, he said he hoped she did not have tuberculosis, as he did. They next met at a party at Durham Wharf, the Chiswick house of their mutual friend the painter Julian Trevelyan. This time Dylan was accompanied by Caitlin who took offence when he and Mackworth struck up a quiet but intense conversation. No doubt imagining wrongly that her husband was flirting with a mistress, she came up behind her supposed rival and, without saying a word, stubbed her cigarette down hard on the back of Mackworth's hand. Then she said, 'Hullo' and walked calmly away to talk to someone else. 'Dylan looked only a little embarrassed and not at all surprised,' recalled Mackworth.

Without the distraction of Llewelyn, Caitlin was bearing the brunt of her husband's errant ways. As she explained to her sister Brigit, Dylan veered between a life of impeccable domesticity and irresponsible abandon. Sometimes he disappeared and she did not see him for several nights. Then he would return home without explanation and everything appeared fine – even if she found his behaviour all very curious.

One of the perks of Dylan's job was that he was occasionally able to get out of town. In June he went to the north of England to research a film about the arts. The idea was to show music and theatre continuing to thrive in grimy industrial towns and idyllic country villages. Dylan had a miserable time until, in Bradford, he met Ruth Wynn Owen, a young actress with a touring company, who epitomised the innocence he had once seen and loved in Caitlin. Deeply struck by her, he arranged to meet her again, even trying to reschedule a talk in Cambridge so he could be there when, a short while later, her company played the university town. But he had forgotten that, by then, the undergraduate term had ended. When her production of The Merry Wives of Windsor came to London in August, he was drunk and outrageous on the only occasion they met, and then failed to link up with her a second time. Nevertheless he managed to conduct a discreet and probably chaste romance. Part of her charm was her fey North Welsh mysticism which in later years became more marked as she became one of Britain's leading 'white' witches, heading the Plant y Bran branch of the Wicca, or ancient British religion. Although she had many followers, particularly in the acting profession, she was denounced as a fraud and died in obscurity in 1998.

In early July Caitlin accompanied her husband on a recce for a film in Scotland. The couple visited David Archer, the gentle rich ingenue who had published Dylan's first book. He had set up the short-lived but influential South Street Art Centre in Glasgow, which, coincidentally, had attracted several excellent refugee artists, such as the Polish painters Jankel Adler and Josef Herman. With his European touch (he had been a friend of both Klee and Picasso), Adler helped inspire a school of Scottish neo-romantic artists, including Robert MacBryde and his partner Robert Colquhoun (together known as 'the two Roberts') who became friends of Dylan after moving to London.

As Adler was to young Scottish artists, so Dylan became to a rising generation of Scottish poets – an example of a 'foreign' (in his case Celtic) writer with a distinct style that steered clear of Anglo-Saxon public-school orthodoxies. Already Dylan had been courted by Scottish poets such as J. F. Hendry and William Montgomerie linked to the apocalyptic group. Not that he had done much to reciprocate their interest: as he had told another Scots poet, Hamish Henderson, a couple of years earlier, he had little enthusiasm for Scottish or Welsh nationalism and, as for the New Apocalypse, they were 'beneath contempt'. But he was prepared to help individual poets. Four years younger than Dylan, the tall, energetic Sydney (W. S.) Graham was working in a weapons factory in Greenock while turning out powerful verses which were compared to the Welshman's. With the South Street Centre already falling apart, Dylan encouraged Graham to pursue his ambition of producing a Scottish number of Life and Letters and promised assistance if he came to London. Even Hugh MacDiarmid, the uncompromising old man of Scottish culture, welcomed Dylan's visit, falling heavily for Caitlin's looks (he remembered reading her father's poetry before the First World War) and arranging a programme for them at the house of the composer, F. G. Scott, who played and sang his settings of MacDiarmid's lyrics for the Thomases 'so that they could get the right idea of the sound of the Scots language'.

But this interlude only confused Caitlin further. As she told Brigit, she felt she was wasting away in London and dreamt of a healthy, outdoor life in Scotland. Somewhere she had heard that the left-wing writer Naomi Mitchison had gathered a group of artists and writers on her family farm near Campbeltown on the Mull of Kintyre, and Caitlin wondered if she might join them.

In the middle of this mayhem, Caitlin discovered she was pregnant. Instead of returning to Scotland, her temporary solution was to escape to the west coast of Wales and join Dylan's old friends, the Phillips family who, after leaving Swansea, had taken a large house called Gelli at Talsarn in the Aeron valley, not far from the busy fishing port of New Quay. Caitlin probably decided this while she and Dylan were staying at Vera Phillips's flat in Old Church Street, Chelsea. Vera had lived a semi-Bohemian existence in London since the mid-1930s, initially studying interior design, occasionally working in the theatre, sometimes supporting herself as a waitress at the Chelsea Pensioner, a café partly owned by a friend, Elizabeth Taylor, whose husband was an artist. Since 1940 she had been romantically involved with William Killick, an Old Harrovian officer in the Royal Engineers, whom she had met at the bar of the Antelope near Sloane Square. But since he had been called up, she was free to join her family in Wales, and Caitlin went with her.

Staying on at Old Church Street, Dylan realised his recent behaviour had been appalling and went through what was to be a frequent ritual of apology, as he begged to be allowed to join his pregnant wife. He convinced Donald Taylor that he could do some useful research on the Welsh strand of the 'Pattern of Britain'. Although he was only at Gelli for just over a week, he again enjoyed being away from the capital. With access to fresh milk, cheese and eggs, he felt his health improving. And as he plaintively wrote to Tommy Earp, a much older crony of Augustus John, with whom he used to drink in the afternoons at the Horseshoe Club in Wardour Street, he did not feel the pressures of London: he was under no obligation to admire the trees and 'the country's the one place you haven't got to go out in, thank Pan'.

In early September he was back in the capital, again looking for somewhere to live. Remembering that Dan Jones had once inhabited the grandly named Wentworth Studios (in fact, a row of run-down shacks) off Manresa Road, round the comer from Peter Rose Pulham and Theodora Rosling, he checked out the place and found it empty. With Theodora's help, he secured the tenancy on a dilapidated square room, which stank of cat's pee. It had an ancient bathroom and a skylight that leaked when it rained. Visitors marvelled how, when Caitlin came back, she managed to turn this tip into a liveable space, initially using Dan's books as tables, and adorning the walls with Dylan's passe-partouted drawings and any other reproductions she could find.

Although Dylan and Caitlin both continued to move around, Wentworth Studios provided a base for the next couple of years. (There is a Bill Brandt photograph of them there the following year, looking almost proprietorial – having secured the use of a handsome circular Victorian table – but also ineffably sad.) When Dylan had money, he would take his wife to the Pheasantry, a nightclub in the King's Road, where Caitlin's high spirits bubbled out. Wearing a pink skirt, she once tried to teach Dylan (in her mother's cast-off sweater) the basics of dancing. Realising she was wasting her time, she twirled around the room, lifting her skirt to enthusiastic shouts of 'Olé' from Augustus John – 'a free floor show'.

Various tensions of the period boiled up one evening after Dylan met Caitlin's brother John Macnamara in the Markham Arms and was invited back to dinner at the Devases. When John began talking about his wartime experiences with the Commandos (he had participated in the Dieppe raid in August 1942), Dylan took him to task for boasting of murdering Germans. An angry John countered that his brother-in-law was quite happy to have his dirty work done for him, whereupon the two men squared up for a fight. For a while tempers abated, but then Dylan started up again in his wheedling way, accusing John of being a Nazi and enjoying the war. This was too much for everyone, particularly

Henriette, John's French wife, who demanded that Dylan leave the house.

To an extent Dylan was fooling around: this was an infantile annoying version of his drunken banter. But there was a more serious side to his behaviour. Because of his non-combatant status, and his history of troubled attitudes to war, stretching back to childhood, he had problems relating to soldiers. He 'would walk up to the tallest man in uniform in the pub and insult him, his country and the war so grossly that almost inevitably a fight developed'. By any standards, his comments were insensitive during a war.

In early March 1943 Caitlin went into St Mary Abbot's Hospital to give birth to a baby girl, who bawled like her brother at that age and looked a prettier version of her father, with curly golden hair and brown eyes. As with Llewelyn's birth, Dylan was nowhere to be found. Nicolette had to haul him out of the Anglesea pub, but Caitlin was again convinced he had been with another woman. This was clear, she claimed, when she returned to Wentworth Studios and found it in greater disarray than usual: their matrimonial bed showed signs of recent love-making and there was no cot for the infant. Shortly afterwards Theodora Rosling was standing outside the Sunlight Laundry in the King's Road when Dylan approached. He told her about the baby, who was called Aeronwy (regularly abbreviated to Aeron, after the river beside which she was supposed to have been conceived, though this was nonsense as Caitlin was already pregnant before going to Wales the previous summer). When he added plaintively that his daughter had nowhere to sleep, Theodora emptied her laundry basket and gave it to him.

Before the end of the month Dylan had escaped to Tickerage Mill, the Sussex house of Dick Wyndham, a hard-drinking artist and adventurer who had recently been invalided out of the army after a nervous breakdown. Wyndham was unwittingly at the centre of various of Dylan's circles. A witty, aristocratic habitué of the Gargoyle, his pre-war travels and painting in the Sudan have been seen as a model for Charles Ryder in Evelyn Waugh's novel, Brideshead Revisited. He had connections in films, being a close friend of Donald Taylor's former partner 'Bunny' Keene who, in his previous incarnation as director of Tooth's Gallery, had promoted Wyndham's early artistic career. He was also a cousin of David Tennant, who encouraged Dylan to follow in the tradition of poets such as Dafydd ap Gwilym at the Welsh courts in the middle ages and to become a sort of licensed troubadour to the well-heeled Gargoyle crowd. Usually his drink bills were tactfully forgotten, though once or twice he (and his wife) overdid it, as Sacheverell Sitwell told his sister Edith. Having had his card marked by Ivan Moffat, Sitwell found Dylan 'an utterly impossible but quite fascinating person'. Caitlin was simply formidable: 'dressed like the trainer in a boxing ring with about seven jerseys one over the other, and ... trained to knock [Dylan] out when he comes home'. Sitwell told how Caitlin had gone berserk in a nightclub and broken the arm of the recently married Virginia Gilliatt, a cousin of the Sitwells.

Seeking to go one better than his wife, Dylan had raced into the Gargoyle one night, spinning down the stairs so fast that Moffat had likened his figure to a series of circles, as in a comic drawing.

> Once on the dancing floor (he was poetically dressed in tweeds, with curls of hair like Bacchus, shoes, but no socks), he ripped off both shoes and danced barefoot, for a while, in a sinister but distracted fashion. Then his purpose became evident. He moved up to the table where David Tennant was sitting, drinking a valuable bottle of claret, poured it into his own shoe and drank it, finished the bottle, and then with an extraordinary gliding movement, like a sea serpent, traversed the entire floor to the far end of the room, and landed on the divan nestling his head against the thighs of Harold Nicolson, whom he hates. After that there was general furore, and a sort of pêle mêle struggle, of which the results were long in doubt, owing to the extraordinary bravery and resources of Mrs Dylan T. Eventually, much to the regret of many persons, they were ejected.
>
> It shows infallible taste and instinct, doesn't it?

For a while the couple were banned from the establishment. But two months later, Tennant and his wife Virginia invited them both down to East Knoyle, their house in Wiltshire, where Dylan and his host sat up late into the night declaiming Milton and Shakespeare.

In July Dick Wyndham's fun-loving twenty-one-year-old daughter Joan came to London, looking for respite from the tedium of institutional life in the Women's Auxiliary Air Force. She had recently met Julian Maclaren-Ross, a tall, loquacious man with crinkly dark hair and literary aspirations, who was in the process of being invalided out of the army on psychiatric grounds. He had invited her and her friend Zoe Hicks, a fellow WAAF officer and daughter of Augustus John, to join him on a trip to the capital. They quickly ditched him and went to the Wheatsheaf where Dylan, apparently unaware of any connection, eased himself beside her and introduced himself: 'I'm Dylan Thomas and I'm fucking skint. Be nice to me, Waafie, and buy me another Special Ale.' His friend Ruthven Todd soon informed them that the drink was running out (a common wartime occurrence) and they had better go elsewhere. On a subsequent pub crawl, Joan quickly twigged that Dylan's acquaintances were split broadly into two camps – those who lionised him, and those who regarded him as a drunken bore and took steps to avoid him. In a taxi back to Todd's flat behind the British Museum, she was alarmed to be smothered in wet, beery kisses by Dylan. Since by then, the bombs had begun to fall, they both had to stay at Todd's. Given the spare room, Joan was just dozing off when she heard someone fumbling with the lock and chanting, 'I want to fuck you! I want to fuck you!' She managed to bolt the door and prevent Dylan's entry.

Next morning, they both went out for breakfast. Dylan told Joan about his baby daughter and she politely tried to engage him in conversation about poetry, saying that, although she liked his work, there were a lot of lines she did not understand. Dylan told her not to worry: his verse was 'like a walled city with many gates, it doesn't really matter which door you go in by – in fact it doesn't matter a tinker's toss if you don't go in at all.' He added disingenuously that poetry was not the most important thing in life: 'Frankly, I'd much rather lie in a hot bath sucking boiled sweets and reading Agatha Christie.' She concluded that Dylan was much nicer in the mornings than in the evenings.

The following month Dylan found himself sharing the lift at Strand's offices with Joan's dandyish friend Maclaren-Ross who, it turned out, had been hired as the third member of the company's scriptwriting team with Dylan and Philip Lindsay, the youngest, sleepy-looking member of a formidable Australian literary family. In camel-coloured overcoat, cream silk shirt and peach-coloured tie, sporting dark glasses and carrying a silver-topped cane, Maclaren-Ross became enough of a Soho personality to be immortalised in print as X. Trapnel in Anthony Powell's *A Dance to the Music of Time*. Joan said he looked 'a real toff if a little frayed at the edges'. To Anthony Burgess, he was 'an Oscar Wilde with less talent but no homosexuality'. An alternative view was that he was a tedious solipsist.

Maclaren-Ross's *Memoirs of the Forties* provide a snap-shot of Dylan in the office – with his bow tie and collar pinched too tight, looking like a provincial young farmer up in town for the day. Taylor put them both to work on a *Dad's Army*-type film about the Home Guard which was never finished. Smoking incessantly, Dylan wrote in a soft 2B pencil, which he also used to make funny, frequently obscene, drawings on his blotter. The two men quickly adopted a routine which involved generous periods of recuperation in the Wheatsheaf and Highlander. However Maclaren-Ross's monologues could be overbearing, and Dylan was often happy to escape from his company into the Horseshoe. As their mutual friend the New Zealander Dan Davin noted, they were wary of one another, since they both needed audiences: to see them holding court was like watching rival condottieri.

Apart from drinking, they shared a passion for art-house cinema classics. They dreamt of producing a film called The Whispering Gallery or The Distorting Mirror in the style of The Cabinet of Dr Caligari. Dylan suggested a plot vaguely reminiscent of The Death of the King's Canary, involving fairgrounds and stately homes. When they were unable to decide whether the villain should be male or female, Dylan suggested the character should be both – or should have a sex change halfway through. (His fascination with hermaphroditism may have come from his father-in-law Francis Macnamara who had retired to his sick bed, convinced he was both male and female.)

Dylan and Maclaren-Ross also wanted to write a complete screenplay, including such details as instructions to cameramen, instead of the prosaic treatments they usually did. Taylor who was also tiring of documentaries and harboured an ambition to make feature films, encouraged them, even suggesting a version of Dylan's semi-autobiographical Adventures in the Skin Trade which had been turned down by Dent early in the war. For a while Dylan carried a copy of this work which he lent to Tambimuttu who claimed he might be able to get him a publisher's advance on it. When Tambimuttu temporarily lost it, Dylan was furious, the only time Maclaren-Ross ever saw him angry.

An unpublished script survives for what appears to be a radio play about the dangers of talking too much during the war. In his own hand, Dylan contrasts the great conversationalists of the past, neatly parodying the witty circumlocutions of Wilde and Beardsley and the epigrammatic style of Samuel Johnson speaking to Mrs Thrale, with the vapid effusions of modern novelists, bright young things, blimpish military men and ordinary people, whose speculations about the progress of the war might, it is suggested, prove useful to the enemy.

Although his more creative ideas had to be put in abeyance, Dylan, in mid-1943, was enjoying his most prolific period as a scriptwriter. His short stay in Cardiganshire the previous summer contributed to Wales – Green Mountain, Black Mountain, the documentary in the 'Pattern of Britain' series, on which he is credited as both producer and scriptwriter. Appealing to different ideas of Welshness – the industry of the coal-mines, the agricultural richness of the hillsides and the timeless community of the chapel – the film summons a sense of nationhood that supersedes any distant Anglo-Welsh squabbling and joins in 'terrible near war ... against the men who would murder man'. Until recently, Dylan would have cringed at his portrayal of the beneficent influence of the chapel, whose slate roofs are linked cinematically to mines lying under grey mountains, and thus to the essence of Welshness. But this was wartime, this was propaganda, and the underlying message was that there had been enough suffering in the valleys.

> Remember the procession of the old-young men
> From dole queue to corner and back again . . .
> Remember the procession of the old-young men.
> It shall never happen again.

At first even this rousing script was deemed too controversial: the British Council argued that its hint of unemployment would prevent its being shown abroad, while the Ministry of Information's Welsh Office in Cardiff wondered if Dylan was the right person to write it because, as an inhabitant of London, he was not even a 'real' Welshman. Such was the knee-jerk censorship of a nation at arms. But there was ample scope for extra work in the wartime propaganda machine. Now he was based in London, Dylan was more easily accessible to read poems and write literary-related talks for the BBC on a freelance basis. In January 1943 he recorded a programme for the Corporation's Welsh service on 'Reminiscences of Childhood', looking back at his early days in the 'ugly, lovely town' of Swansea. He also began doing work for George Orwell in the Indian section.

Even so, political sensitivities intruded, as when the BBC cancelled at short notice a broadcast, in which Dylan had a role, of In Parenthesis, the epic prose-poem about the First World War written by another great Anglo-Welsh writer David Jones. The poem wrapped up Welsh nationalism in the greater good of Britain in a more telling than Dylan's efforts for the screen. However, in drawing on the sixth-century Welsh poet Aneirin's Y Gododdin, which told how a Welsh raid into Saxon Britain left all but one person dead, it raised not only thorny issues of nationalism, but also quasi-pacifist notions of the brutality of war.

The regulators also got at Is your Ernie really necessary?, a short satirical feature film Dylan made under Strand's aegis with Oswald Mitchell, a well-known director and half-brother of his old Swansea artist friend, Denis Mitchell (himself soon to forge a new career as assistant to the sculptor Barbara Hepworth in Cornwall). Poking fun at the government's slogan 'Is your journey really necessary?', the film starred Hay Petrie in several roles, including a full chorus line, who was edited and reproduced twelve times to look like a chorus line. But this inventive touch was too much for documentary veteran Arthur Elton, film supervisor at the Ministry of Information, who banned it.

All the while Dylan continued to contribute to Strand's stock films on subjects ranging from the global reach of war (*Battle for Freedom*) to the development of antibiotic drugs (*Conquest of a Germ*). Later he wrote about the rebuilding of the bombed city of Coventry (*A City Re-born*) sprinkling his commentary with post-Beveridge promises of new hospitals, schools, suburbs and roads. He even incorporated progressive thinking about future transport needs, adding that the roads would be built 'round the city of course; you can't have great big lorries roaring through the centre'. Unsuitably, perhaps, he also tackled the psychological readjustments which families would need to make when their loved ones returned from fighting abroad (*A Soldier Comes Home*).

Understanding that Dylan's creative juices were hardly stimulated by this fare, Donald Taylor gave him licence to come up with innovative scripts for two much praised documentaries. In *These are the Men*, released in March 1943, Hitler and various German leaders bear witness to their evil fascistic pasts in extravagant rants dubbed over clips from Leni Riefenstahl's record of the 1934 Nazi party congress at Nuremberg. Edgar Anstey, another veteran of early documentaries, adjudged in the *Spectator* that the film 'combines political passion and technical ingenuity in the most pitiless condemnation of individual Nazi leaders that has yet appeared in the cinema'.

More ambitious, *Our Country*, in April 1944, provides lyrical filmic accompaniment to the poems Dylan was then starting to write about the war. Framed by the device of a journey by a merchant seaman home on leave, it ranges urgently over Britain, using poetic imagery and metres to evoke a sense of *rus in urbe*, with the fauna and flora of the countryside starting to regenerate a nation long at war. It anticipates themes in Dylan's later output, such as the restorative powers of nature, and more general techniques, including his celluloid-inspired facility to create simple verbal pictures and tell an unfolding story. *Our Country's* opening phrase – 'To begin with the city' – is close to *Under Milk Wood's* 'To begin at the beginning.'

Denied a screenplay, Dylan was seeking a creative meeting between poetry and cinema. He did not want this script to appear verbatim in the programme for the premiere (particularly after it had been cut) because 'the words were written to be spoken & heard, & not to be read'. He had insisted, from an early age, on the importance of the sound of his verse, and there was no reason to stop now. Dylan's experimental approach did not please all the critics, but Taylor thought it worth promoting and booked the Empire Theatre, Leicester Square, for the premiere. The *Spectator* reviewer was again complimentary, describing *Our Country* as 'the most exciting and provocative film ... for many a long day'.

Dylan himself needed convincing because, all too often, he disliked what he was doing, describing it as 'hack work'. 'I hate films,' he told his wife. 'There is nothing but glibly naïve insincerity.' The fact that she tended to agree – indeed that she felt he was prostituting his talents – did not help matters. His sense of frustration only fuelled his anger, which he sought to assuage by increasing his input of alcohol during the latter two years of the war.

FOURTEEN

ATTEMPTED MURDER

From late 1943 Caitlin began to spend less time in the unhealthy environment of Wentworth Studios. While she was there, Aeronwy had to sleep with an open umbrella over her pram to prevent rain falling on her from the skylight, and even then the baby caught pneumonia. For a while, when heavy bombing resumed in early 1944, the family found refuge in a house in Bosham, on the Sussex coast, where they acquired a poodle puppy called Dombey but found themselves, unwittingly, in the middle of noisy preparations for D-Day. With V-1 and then V-2 pilotless bombs falling in London from the summer, the Thomases also stayed in Buckinghamshire with Donald Taylor who had set up a new company, Gryphon, to make feature films.

In between Caitlin escaped with Aeronwy to Wales (where she could take her pick between staying in Laugharne, Blaen Cwm and Talsarn) or to her mother's in Hampshire. Stuck in London, ostensibly for reasons of work, Dylan was on his own at Wentworth Studios with the freedom and funds to indulge his tendency to dissipation. He could now roam freely in an arc between the pubs and clubs of Chelsea and those of Soho and Fitzrovia. His after-hours companions included artists such as the stroppy flamboyant gays, 'the two Roberts' Colquhoun and MacBryde, who led the Scottish migration to London after the closure of David Archer's South Street Art Centre. They drank in Soho, but shared a tenement in Bedford Gardens off Kensington Church Street with Jankel Adler who, between draughts of his favourite tipple, Armagnac, found Dylan strangely sympathetic to his Hassidic-inspired stories of Jewish suffering. Other tenants in the same building included another neo-Romantic painter, the 'horse-faced and Byronic' John Minton, who was a member of the china manufacturing family, and the assistant editor of Lilliput, Kaye Webb, who had recently commissioned the first St Trinian's cartoon from artist Ronald Searle who would become her husband.

At work Dylan's preferred drinking companion was not the verbose Maclaren-Ross but the more congenial Philip Lindsay who was also an historical novelist. Gerald Kersh recalled these two on 'a bender': 'An

account of this alone would make The Lost Weekend sound like Southey's
Life of Nelson. Dylan got his penis stuck in a two ounce honey pot. Why
he put it there I don't know. On the same occasion he pushed a shirt
button up his nose and couldn't get it out either.' Kersh also remembered
being out with Dylan and Augustus John. Dylan 'made up a poem about
the smell of his wife's drawers, and Augustus let loose a reminiscence
. . . about how he wore, for months on end, the bloomers of a girl he
loved, which were caulked at every seam.'

Drink often rendered Dylan oblivious to his surroundings, even to
the bombs that usually scared him. Elizabeth Fusco, who had re-
emerged on the Soho scene after a broken marriage, recalled him
'skipping' down Tottenham Court Road, ignoring the doodle bugs.
John Banting, an artist attached to Donald Taylor's production
company, recalled 'one Hogarthian night when Oxford Street was a
sheet of ice. Dylan, a stray sailor and myself all bravely (and beerily)
crossed it. Both of them performed a sort of "cake-walk" or "knees-
up" before they fell. I laughed so much that surprisingly I did not.
In a side street we stood in a solemn row spouting vomit and piss.
And went on to yet another pub.'

Alcohol also brought out Dylan's emotional side. Fusco witnessed him
breaking down and saying a prayer, after a mutual friend, following
close behind them, was killed by a bomb on the short walk from the
French to the Swiss pub. Fusco was struck by the decline in Dylan's
health since first meeting him half a dozen years earlier. Once when he
visited her flat in Charlotte Street, he kept her awake all night with his
vomiting. She was afraid that the mucous he coughed up indicated
something worse than the effects of drink – perhaps an ulcer. 'It was
dreadful. He really suffered all night long. And he was resigned.' To
Philip Lindsay's leftist brother Jack, Dylan acknowledged, with some of
the misplaced romanticism he used to speak of his tuberculosis, that he
had cirrhosis of the liver. His condition was not helped by the fact that
often, the more he drank, the soberer he seemed. Jack Lindsay recalled
Dylan's first visit to hospital for treatment around this time. Dylan had
also been to a psychiatric unit, seeking a cure for alcoholism, but had
not met a sympathetic response.

Dylan's resignation about his physical condition, linked to the wartime
prevalence of death, seemed to heighten his libido. Lindsay himself
witnessed its consequences, according to his brother Philip, who recalled
that Dylan 'fucked Jack's previous girl, then used her to look after the
baby while he and his wife went to the pub or the pictures'. Jack saw
a direct correlation between Dylan's fear of death – the theme of his
adolescent poems – and his need for physical release. (He also noted

Dylan's fascination with pornography, particularly a periodical dealing with rubber fetishism.)

One night Dylan would be seen with Pamela Glendower, whose Welsh connections stimulated fond memories; the next with Netta Macnab, former wife of Richard Aldington, one of his Imagist heroes; yet another with Joan Graham Murray, who dabbled in the occult and boasted she slept with Dylan when she had jaundice. Her unpopular artist husband, James 'the Shit' Graham Murray, introduced Ann Meo to Dylan in the Gateway Club in Bramerton Street, Chelsea. Meo, a painter's daughter who later worked at the BBC, had noticed the poet in the Eight Bells, quarrelling with Caitlin. She admits she succumbed to Dylan's sexual pestering, but found him a disappointing lover. Not that she had any illusions: 'He was completely promiscuous. I don't know why he did it. It was simply something he had to do.'

His priapism extended to his place of work. For a brief period he was entrusted with watching for fires on the roof above Strand's offices. Accused of taking a girl up there, wrapped in a sleeping bag, he replied, blandly, 'Then she must have been a very little girl.' Dylan did not allow his wife to behave in a similar way, of course. He was fiercely protective and jealous about her. When Philip Lindsay briefly came to live with the Thomases in Wentworth Studios, Dylan refused to allow him to sleep there on the nights he went out fire watching. Their colleague Maclaren-Ross recalled Dylan talking bawdily about sex in general, but never about a woman in particular. The reason became clear when he asked a girl who had slept with Dylan what it was like. She said it was not bad: the problem was his guilt the following morning.

That guilt was linked to the repressed emotion that often emerged in inappropriate situations and left him in tears. Fusco recalled Dylan picking up a young provincial girl near a railway station. He was weeping when he later told Fusco, 'Do you know what she said to me when I went to bed with her? She said, in a very north country voice, "I hope you don't stuff me."' Fusco, always prepared to argue Dylan's essential innocence, noted he was moved by the girl's uncertain use of idiom. 'People who were not articulate hurt him terribly. He suffered for their lack of expression.' A more down to earth view came from Augustus John who said Dylan 'robs his £3-in-Post-Office mistresses of their honest earnings, drinks the cash, and leaves the c − t'.

The tale of his personal deterioration can be told through three London-based weddings. In August 1943 he was happy to act as best man when his friend Vera Phillips married her officer beau, William Killick, at Chelsea registry office. At the same venue the following March he was expected as a witness to Theodora Rosling's marriage not to

Peter Rose Pulham, whom she had dumped because he could not support her, but to Constantine FitzGibbon, the Irish-American literary adventurer who had first met Dylan while at Oxford. FitzGibbon wore the uniform of an American army officer – a new group bringing jollity and liquidity to the London social scene. Dylan missed the ceremony, but this was accepted because his train journey from the south coast had taken him through 'Bomb Alley', where most of the destruction of the V-1 and V-2 flying bombs was concentrated. At a reception at the Ritz Hotel, FitzGibbon was approached by a footman who said, 'There's a personage in the bar, sir, who *says* he's a member of your party.' FitzGibbon found Dylan, curiously festooned with several scarves. When, on a subsequent pub crawl, the party picked up an old tramp who played the guitar, Dylan complimented the newly married couple on their good fortune, complaining that he had never had troubadors at his wedding.

In October 1944 he simply failed to turn up as best man when Vernon Watkins was married at the church of St Bartholomew the Great (appropriately on the Smithfield site of a priory founded by Rahere, Henry I's court jester). Like Dan Jones, Watkins had been seconded to work with the code-breakers at Bletchley where he had fallen in love with an Oxford graduate called Gwen Davies. At the Charing Cross Hotel for a pre-wedding lunch, he received a call from Gryphon Films that Dylan was on his way. When his friend did not appear, Vernon, ever ready to make excuses, told his bride-to-be that Dylan had probably gone straight to the church. But when he was not there either, the normally placid Vernon exploded, saying, 'That's the end of Dylan as far as I'm concerned.' Extraordinarily he heard nothing from Dylan for another four weeks. Then he received an envelope from Dylan containing two fawning letters, one apologising for having failed to post the other; and the other claiming that, in a confusion of missed trains, Dylan had forgotten the name of the church where the Watkinses were getting married. Vernon was immediately mollified; his new wife, who had never met Dylan, rather less so.

By then Dylan had given up Wentworth Studios and moved back to Wales. With Caitlin and his children seldom in London, and his work for Donald Taylor geared increasingly to feature films which did not require him in the office, he decided to make a decisive move from the capital. For a few weeks in July and August he and his family stayed with his parents in Blaencwm. The change suited him well. Before the end of August he was sending Vernon Watkins the texts of three recent poems. He had written the first, 'Ceremony After a Fire Raid', earlier in the summer after visiting the bombed city of Coventry while working on the film *A City Re-born*. It shows his remarkable ability to compose great verse out of and in the middle of the direst situations. Starting from a modernist's diverse perspective ('Myselves/the grievers') and building to an expressionist vision of the apocalypse, he powerfully conveys the sense of a ceremony to the dead, moving, with the help of various liturgical references, from prayer, through sacrament, to thunderous musical acclamation. He had already sent it for publication in the ephemeral magazine *Our Time*. But Watkins had yet to see it.

There were two other poems he was still tinkering with at Blaencwm. According to Watkins, he had been talking about 'Poem in October' for three years, and possibly longer, for Dylan referred to it as 'a Laugharne poem: the first place poem I've ever written', though the latter bit was hardly correct. In the same way that he had sat upon some of his early notebook poems, Dylan had put this aside and gone back to it later. He may have thought its easy lyricism did not accord with the harsh realities of the world around the start of the war. But he had sloughed off the more jagged elements of his earlier poetical style, and his return to Wales had enabled him to pick up his neat, personalised description of the changing Carmarthenshire weather patterns and weave it into one of his most memorable verses.

The third poem 'Vision and Prayer' is an extraordinary one-off statement of Dylan's religious belief. Presented in twelve pictographic stanzas – six shaped like diamonds, six like chalices – this describes how Dylan is unable to ignore the presence of Christ who seems to live so close to him, as if next door. As in Francis Thompson's 'The Hound of Heaven' (one of the few influences Dylan was ever happy to acknowledge), this Christ figure is undeniable. (Dylan also admitted that the image of 'you/Who is born/In the next room' came to him after reading an English translation of Rilke, almost certainly the poem 'Du Nachbar Gott' from the *Stundenbuch*. Dylan has to die, or shed his ego (at the end of the first six verses) and then finds his true personality by losing himself in Christ. There seems to have been no particular incident that sparked this powerful sentiment. Dylan did not have a conversion. He did however retain an indomitable religious passion, that manifested itself from time to time in magical, even holy, statements of belief. Dylan was not one to define such glimpses of ecstatic truth into a prosaic creed: this was a personal, poetic vision. Yet it was an enduring part of his nature, an indefinable spark of divinity that some people, such as Elizabeth Fusco, recognised in the most unlikely areas of his life.

In early September he moved with his family to New Quay on the west coast of Wales, where Vera Killick (as she now was) was living in Ffynonnfeddyg, a bungalow overlooking Cardigan Bay, not far from her mother. New Quay was a popular destination for people seeking to escape the war. Many 'Cardis' who had opened dairies in London at the turn of the century flocked back. They were joined by a motley assortment of crachach (Welsh gentry), artists and simply holiday-makers in a lively seafaring town where many of the menfolk were merchant seamen, working in tankers, bringing precious fuel across the Atlantic to Britain. The damage wrought by the latest generation of V-2 flying bombs in London made it easy for Dylan to decide to rent a spartan bungalow, made of wood, with thin asbestos walls, next door to Vera. It was called Majoda, after the Christian names (Marjorie, John and David) of the three children of the owner. Amenities were basic: no running water, lighting by liquid gas and a paraffin stove. However there was a fine view not only of the terraced town a mile or so to the south, but also of the wide expanse of the Irish Sea, a prospect that had inspired and slightly overwhelmed Dylan on his abortive Welsh trip seven years earlier.

Dylan quickly settled into the easy pace of Cardiganshire life. Before the end of September he had the measure of the town, where he told Tommy Earp in good-natured verse, 'no-good is abroad'. On the 'wild, umbrella'd and french lettered/Beach' he could hear 'rise slimy from the Welsh lechered/Caves the cries of the parchs and their flocks.' And already he was observing the rich cast of characters:

> There slinks a snook in black. I'm thinking it
> Is Mr Jones the Cake, that winking-bit,
> That hymning gooseberry, that Bethel-worm
> At whose ball-prying even death'll squirm
> And button up.

The following week Augustus John came to New Quay and helped introduce the Thomases to local notables. Ostensibly he had a commission to paint a neighbour who had been headmistress of a girls' grammar school in Wrexham. Staying at the Black Lion pub in town, he visited his friend Lord Howard de Walden who had a comfortable summer house, Plas Llanina, in the woods above. Having already provided Dylan with financial support, Howard de Walden offered him use of the Apple House in his grounds, as a place to work, away from the pressures of family life at his 'shack at the edge of the cliff where my children hop like fleas in a box'. John also met Alastair Graham, a former lover of Evelyn Waugh, who had settled in New Quay before the war and was trying to lead a respectable life, giving no indication of his scandalous past when he was run out of society following his affair with another aristocratic Welsh patron of the arts, Lord Tredegar (otherwise the poet Evan Morgan). Here Graham was an officer in the Observer Corps, played the oboe, did embroidery, published *Twenty Different Ways of Cooking New Quay Mackerel*, and used his influence to prevent the closure of the lifeboat station. Although he entertained discreetly, few people in town would realise in 1945 that he was a model for Sebastian Flyte in Waugh's *Brideshead Revisited*.

Tom Herbert, an ambitious Welsh-speaking vet, left an unpublished account of a party at Graham's house, Plas y Wern. He had come to know Dylan through treating the Thomas dog, no longer the poodle of Bosham, but a black labrador. He was having an affair with Tessa Dean, a bright, hunt-loving member of the fading aristocracy who congregated in Cardigan seeking anonymity. She was the daughter of the theatrical producer and director Basil Dean and grand-daughter of Daisy Warwick, the famous Countess of Warwick who was mistress of King Edward VII when Prince of Wales. Graham's uncle, Willie Low, had also been part of the Prince's Marlborough House set. (He had first employed Rosa Lewis, later chatelaine of the Prince's favourite hotel, the Cavendish. Waugh said Graham was one of two people who taught him all he knew about the Cavendish, which he portrayed as Shepheard's Hotel in *Vile Bodies*.) Graham and Evan Morgan had once shocked the guests at one of Tessa Dean's London parties by coming dressed as women.

Although his memoir appears to be an amalgamation of recollections at different times and perhaps in different places, Herbert tells of Dylan arriving drunk at Graham's party, also attended by Augustus John. Dylan attracted an audience with his account of the story of Daniel in the lion's den. John called to him, 'All you are is a pot-bellied purveyor of pornographic poetry.' Dylan replied, 'And you, Gus, you are a bearded begetter of bastards.' As the guests later peeled away, Dylan was left helping himself to drinks, and Graham complaining that the poet had never been invited and was always asking for money. When someone suggested he could at least comfort himself with the thought that he was helping genius, Graham replied, 'Bugger genius. I am the only genius I want to support.' John certainly attended a party at Plas y Wern, his account of which may explain some of Graham's antipathy. Complimenting Graham's hospitality, John said of him, 'Caitlin wasn't exactly polite to him as his guest when he gave us a slap-up dinner. She kept calling him a bugger which he disputed.'

More often the Thomases were down in the town, where they gained a reputation as agreeable eccentrics. Some people did not like their 'Bohemian' habits, epitomised by the way Caitlin would leave her two children unattended in the Black Lion while she went boozing elsewhere.

But New Quay's history of ocean sailing had contributed to a legacy of cosmopolitanism and sexual freedom. (Women left at home while their master-mariner husbands were at sea had a habit of taking lovers.)

Caitlin found her life on the West Wales coast isolated and dull. But, with Vera Killick for company, she was not totally discontented, and Dylan, when not in the Black Lion, was left free to pursue his various professional interests. Still employed by Donald Taylor's company Gryphon, he had finally got a chance to write a screenplay based on the lives of the nineteenth-century Edinburgh body-snatchers, Burke and Hare. In New Quay he started afresh on an adaptation of *Twenty Years A-Growing*, Maurice O'Sullivan's lyrical memoir of childhood on the west coast of Ireland. John Ackerman, who collected and edited Dylan's filmscripts, describes this as 'seminal in the evolution of his later narrative, visionary, sea-and bird-haunted pastoralism'.

Dylan also had plans to work with Philip Lindsay on a film life of Charles Dickens, but the terms were poor and the two men did not see eye to eye. Dylan wanted to use Dickens's own words, an approach his collaborator thought 'too intellectual'. Lindsay clearly hoped Dylan would bring some of his populist style to the job, for elsewhere he remarked on Dylan's penchant for detective fiction. 'Only once did I catch Dylan reading a good book, and that was *Dombey and Son*, for he had a natural love for Dickens, one of whose characters he might well have been.'

Elsewhere Dylan continued to work for the BBC. He had found an enthusiastic supporter in Aneirin Talfan Davies, a producer in the Welsh service, who lobbied his superiors in London to allow Dylan to broadcast his impressions of New Quay. After G. R. Barnes, the Corporation's head of talks, grudgingly gave his consent, Dylan recorded 'Quite Early One Morning' in December. This was another dry run for *Under Milk Wood*, from its repetition of the phrase 'The town was not yet awake', through its evocation of the dreams of tidy Miss Hughes or seafaring Captain Evans, and its introduction of Mrs Ogmore-Pritchard, who demands 'And before you let the sun in, mind he wipes his shoes', to its coy reference to Phoebe – in real life, Phoebe Evans, a New Quay cleaner who, like the memorable sweet-singing Polly Garter she became in *Under Milk Wood*, could not stop having babies with different partners. Even so, Barnes was unimpressed, complaining Dylan failed to do 'justice to his script until he came to the excellent character speech of the last page'. He felt Dylan 'was wrong to use that breathless poetic voice for the words don't seem to us to carry it' and the wit would have been 'better appreciated if it had been read caustically, or, at least, drily'. The talk had to wait until the following August before it was broadcast. But

Dylan's style of delivery was being seen as a feature, as he began to be recognised as a performer as much as a poet.

His ability to knock off brisk poetic travelogues gained him a commission to write captions to another Bill Brandt photo-essay in *Lilliput*, this time about Chelsea. David Gottlieb at the publisher Peter Lunn was impressed enough to ask him to pen a similar short text to an illustrated book about London entitled *Twelve Hours on the Streets*. Dylan drew up a grandiloquent proposal, incorporating elements of Dickens – 'not the great thoroughfares, described, written, painted a thousand times, but the side streets, the back streets, the smaller worlds of life and death' – with homages to Edgar Allen Poe and German expressionist film, not forgetting the documentaries he had been working on. (Dylan's proposal ended fawningly: 'The streets one would like to see in the future. This section which is really a discussion of town planning schemes as they exist now in this country would make the book have, I think, a positive and creative end.') Dylan turned to his office colleague John Banting to do the drawings. When Banting demurred, saying this was not his sort of thing, Dylan 'at once reassured me that I would be free to use my own kind of Surrealism. "Fitzroy Street could be paved with tits and the houses built of bottoms." I was on.'

Although paid a £50 advance (part of which he may have picked up in London on the day of Vernon Watkins's wedding, causing him to embark on a pub crawl and forget his other commitments), Dylan failed to make any progress on this commission in New Quay. Dylan made a series of excuses about illness and family problems, but, despite Banting giving way to John Piper as the designated artist, nothing emerged. Eventually, two years later, Gottlieb was forced to sue for the return of the advance.

This abortive project was the latest example of Dylan funding his drinking habit by deceitfully doing a deal behind his agent's back. At the start of the war, he had caused confusion by selling the rights to his first book 18 *Poems* to Reginald Caton, a miser whose hoarding of paper allowed his Fortune Press to bring out books when few other publishers were able. Caton, whose more lucrative sideline was sado-masochist homosexual erotica, put out a series of 'first editions' which confuse the unwary collector. Since a range of projects was put at risk, J. M. Dent paid Caton £150 in 1948 to retrieve the 18 *Poems* copyright.

By the time Dylan got to New Quay, his publisher was preparing a further collection of his work called *Deaths and Entrances*. Dylan was thankful for the prospect of another £50 advance. He did not want exactly the same book (essentially all his poems since *The Map of Love*) published in the United States, as some of the contents had already been printed there in a thin 1943 volume, *New Poems.* New Directions had put this out in response to the interest in *The World I Breathe*, his comprehensive collection of poems and prose in 1939. Although only 700 copies were printed, *The World I Breathe* was generally positively reviewed by poets such as Robert Lowell, Conrad Aiken, John Berryman and Dunstan Thompson. Several of Dylan's poems had subsequently found United States markets, 'Into Her Lying Down Head' being published in *Vice Versa*, a short-lived journal edited by the religious-minded Thompson who, to Dylan's delight, had turned up in London as part of the American military invasion. Oscar Williams, a New York poet and literary entrepreneur, had begun to collect Dylan in his regular anthologies (which became better known than his own verse) and to correspond with him, making a pitch to place his poems in US magazines – a role Dylan was happy to encourage because it brought much needed extra cash, even if again it cut across the responsibilities of his accredited New York agent, Ann Watkins.

As a result of this activity, the consensus emerged that New Directions should put out a cheaper selection of Dylan's poetry and prose, with an introduction by John L. Sweeney, a Harvard academic who had been associated with *transition*, the house magazine of experimental writers in Paris a generation earlier. (This was to be *Selected Writings of Dylan Thomas*, published in 1946.)

In early 1945 Caitlin invited Mary Keene, a friend from London to join her in New Quay. Tall, enigmatic and wiltingly pretty, Mary had overcome an impoverished, abusive East End childhood to sit for artists including the young Lucien Freud, Augustus John and Matthew Smith. Although Ruthven Todd described her as 'the most beautiful English girl I ever saw', she had one notable defect: as a girl she had lost her lower leg in a traffic accident and wore a tin prosthetic. By dint of personality, she had moved effortlessly from artist's model to muse. Still in her early twenties and nominally married to Donald Taylor's former business partner, Ralph 'Bunny' Keene, who gave her financial security, she had been the mistress of (probably) Louis MacNeice and (definitely) Matthew Smith and Henry Yorke, the Etonian businessman who wrote novels as Henry Green. Although a cooler character, she had Caitlin's untutored intelligence and careless ability to make her presence felt. Having met in artistic circles, the two young women became firm friends, particularly after Mary had a daughter, Alice, in May 1944, just over a year after Aeronwy's birth.

The worst of the latest wave of bombing was over by early 1945 when Mary Keene decided to take her baby daughter to join her friend in Wales. She asked advice on travel and accommodation in New Quay from Augustus John, who also informed her that when he had last met Dylan he had found him 'very dignified, articulate, and charming. I could readily have embraced him.'

The next time he wrote in early March, he had changed his tune: 'Dylan has a split personality of course. He can be unbearable and then something else comes out which one loves' – an observation which she soon played back to Henry Yorke: 'Dylan is an extraordinarily abnormal person, is the most uncivilised I've known, he never has a hot drink always beer, has the most terrifying speech when annoyed, not terrifying now because one knows it means nothing. I have mingled emotions of hating and liking him.'

Mary must have described to Augustus John an incident in New Quay, probably during a visit to Plas Llanina, because he told her that Lord Howard de Walden was 'a gentle soul', adding that Dylan's 'class consciousness' was a 'perfect disease': 'it takes the form of sponging on his "social or financial superiors" and then abusing them – thus is his amour propre preserved whole.' When she related the same story to Henry Yorke, he was more damning: 'I'm delighted that Thomas' cloven hoof is beginning to show and am impatient for you to get impatient over it. It is inverted snobbery at its most odious. Exactly like the Tatler, only the other way round.'

It was not Dylan's class warfare or even basic insecurity which caused Mary to alter her generally favourable opinion about New Quay, but Vera's husband, William Killick. After the events of 6 March, Mary described the place as an 'open air loony bin'. On that day Dylan was playing host to two employees of Gryphon Films, the director John Eldridge and an assistant Fanya Fisher who had come to help him finish a script, probably an abortive project, Suffer Little Children. Around 8.30 p.m. the three of them went for a drink in the Commercial pub. Already in the bar was Killick, an impulsive twenty-eight-year-old Captain in the Royal Engineers, just home after a strenuous period of secondment with the Special Operations Executive in Greece. As with many servicemen who had recently witnessed colleagues being killed, he had difficulty adjusting to the apparent normality of life in Britain. Consequently he objected when his wife's friend, the best man at his wedding, failed to acknowledge him. Dylan may have been indulging his well-known aversion to soldiers, but more likely he needed to talk to his colleagues. Killick took offence and went to Dylan's table to make his presence felt. A heated exchange about the war ensued. When Killick remarked on the role of the Jews, Dylan and his friends objected. Fisher, who was Jewish, is reported to have said, 'You cad.'

Discomfited, Dylan took his party down the road to the Black Lion where Killick followed. This time they had a more amicable conversation, though Killick laboured the point that they did not know what it was like fighting 'out there'. The mood changed again when, at closing time, Fisher had to squeeze past Killick, and angry words were exchanged. He slapped her, she struck back, and Dylan also traded blows. Only the intervention of Alastair Graham prevented a bloodier brawl. After Eldridge and Fisher went to their rooms upstairs, Graham drove Dylan back to Majoda where they found Caitlin and Mary Keene, in liberated style, entertaining a couple of male friends.

Around forty minutes later, they were all enjoying a late nightcap when, suddenly, without warning, they heard bullets being fired close at hand. Killick had returned from the Black Lion, with the incident playing on his mind. At Ffynonnfeddyg, he had pulled out one of his two machine guns, walked to Majoda next door, and started firing into the air above the bungalow. As all the adults inside ducked (the two baby girls were asleep in the bedroom), he dispatched a further four to eight shots into the building. When he finally stopped, he was found to be holding a grenade. The fact that this had no detonator went some way to supporting his subsequent plea that he had wanted to give Dylan a taste of front-line action. He may also have suspected, or simply heard, a local rumour that his wife was having an affair with Dylan. (Vera Killick never really denied this, telling her family shortly before her death that she retained one great secret. But if she did have an affair with Dylan, it is more likely to have been in Swansea or in London before her marriage.) He was definitely incensed that Vera had been using part of his soldier's pay to support the Thomases' Bohemian lifestyle. The appearance of two additional film-makers from the flesh-pots of London unhinged him.

Mary was furious that the subsequent police investigation forced her to stay on in what had become a nightmare town. She objected when the local constabulary refused to take down what she said verbatim and insisted – 'as if one were visited by the Gestapo' – on writing 'I came in accompanied by Mrs Thomas' when she said 'I came in with Mrs Thomas'. Despite such delays, the case came quickly to court on 21 June 1945, after the Special Operations Executive claimed Killick was needed back on duty. An SOE officer, Lt Col. David Talbot-Rice, travelled to Lampeter Assizes to appear in Killick's defence. By then tempers had abated, and even Dylan and Caitlin were unwilling to say much against him. Following Killick's acquittal, Henry Yorke commented to Mary: 'I'm sorry Dylan was no good and that you weren't allowed your say.

Well done for speaking up though ... My God, Killick has got away with something, hasn't he?'

Extraordinarily, only a week before the shooting, Dylan had written in a glum letter to Vernon Watkins: 'The ordinary moments of walking up village streets, opening doors or letters, speaking good-days to friends or strangers, looking out of windows, making telephone calls, are so inexplicably (to me) dangerous that I am trembling all over before I get out of bed in the mornings to meet them.' In his next letter at the end of March, Dylan detailed the incident, adding his friend must have thought he was exaggerating about his 'daily terrors'. Now he was as 'frightened as though I had used the Sten gun myself'.

Dylan's problems were as usual exacerbated by worries about money and about his parents. His mother came to New Quay to look after the children during the preliminary trial hearings, leaving his father at Blaen Cwm, 'awfully ill' with suspected heart disease, and even more glum than usual. Even so, Dylan was able to send Watkins four poems in the wake of the shooting. He had been working on them at Majoda, chipping away, Watkins observed, like an old carpenter. Writing was indeed more laboured, Dylan admitted, but at least it was more meaningful. 'Less passes Uncle Head's blue-haired pencil,' he told Watkins, 'that George Q. Heart doesn't care about', and the result 'if only to you and me, is worth all the discarded shocks, the reluctantly-shelved grand moony images, cut-&-come-again cardpack of references.'

'A Winter's Tale' is a measured version of 'The Ballad of the Long-Legged Bait': using the seasons as a metaphor for the power of sexual love, without the frantic thrashings of the earlier poem. Dylan's distance from London had encouraged a more relaxed way of observing his environment. His recent experience in film also helped: this poem includes several imprecations to listen and to look, as if screenplay notes to cameramen and directors. Even Dylan's references to death have a mellowness removed from the harsh realities of the Metaphysical poets he once valued. One line, anticipating the inescapable life and death process in 'Fern Hill' and the authorial tone of Under Milk Wood, runs: 'Time sings through the intricately dead snow drop. Listen.'

In 'This Side of Truth', this quietism took on a different, Calvinistic form, an acceptance that life was both uncaring and predestined:

> And all your deeds and words,
> Each truth, each lie,
> Die in unjudging love.

He had written these verses 'for Llewelyn', after his son had fallen and split his tongue in February. (They came with a companion poem 'The Conversation of Prayers'.) As during most of the war, Llewelyn stayed with his grandmother in Ringwood where, it was hoped, the regular routine would suit his sensitive nature. According to Caitlin, expressing a guilt they both must have felt, Dylan was disappointed their son was not a more natural lad, a kicker of balls. Llewelyn was just six and, as 'This Side of Truth' suggests, too young to understand the relativism of a world where good and bad are 'two ways/Of moving about your death'. Dylan was not the first poet to see the indifferent universe in this way – Shakespeare anticipated him by over four centuries. But the critic Ralph Maud is right to suggest that Dylan gave this philosophy a modern existentialist perspective.

Dylan was pushed in this philosophical direction by his reaction to the horrors of war. 'A Refusal to Mourn the Death, by Fire, of a Child in London', the other poem he sent Watkins at this stage, was the latest of his magnificent war verses. He conveyed his disgust at the manner of this young girl's death (in an air-raid) by affirming, in a hymnic voice that took off from the swirling organ sound of 'Ceremony After a Fire Raid', that he would not trivialise her passing with the usual sort of personalised elegy. But after the Christian sentiment of some of his poetry, such as 'Vision and Prayer', this was avowedly unreligious. Following up on his existentialism, he refused to accept the possibility of a second life or death (as suggested in the Book of Revelation). Simply: 'After the first death, there is no other.'

The Christ figure beckoning from the other room in 'Vision and Prayer' had dissolved. Or possibly the earlier poem was Dylan's last desperate attempt to give representation (both verbally and graphically) to his religious feelings. But the atrocities of the final year of the war had undermined this. It was not just the bombing raids on Britain. It was also knowledge of the conditions in Nazi concentration camps, which featured in a gruesome waxwork exhibition in London from 1944. Then in April 1945 came film from the newly liberated Belsen and Buchenwald camps. 'Crowds queued for hours,' wrote Philip Ziegler in London at War, 'watched in shocked silence, left without applauding or even passing casual remarks.' Finally in August came news of the first atomic bomb – an appalling event for someone with Dylan's sensibilities. Throughout the year, his letters are peppered with barbed references to Belsen, bombs and atoms which mask his terror at what these meant. 'Behind me, two months when there was nothing in my head but a little Nagasaki, all low and hot,' he wrote to Oscar Williams.

It is impossible to say how much the Majoda shooting acted, as has been suggested, as a catalyst to such feelings. It did put an abrupt end to his and Caitlin's affair with New Quay. During his trips to London in the summer, she felt isolated and depressed. As she chronicled in letters to Mary Keene, who was back in the capital enduring her own private hell of a divorce from Bunny Keene, she fell off her bicycle, grazing her hands, knee and face. She blamed her accident on a mixture of alcohol, the sun and steep country roads. Although Mary tried to help by sending small sums of money and a wheelbarrow as a present for Aeronwy, Caitlin missed her friend's company (and that of her small daughter Alice). She felt herself trapped among people with whom she had little in common, while her own children were all too demanding – a complaint that was to become familiar. She feared her sensations of weakness and dizziness might indicate another pregnancy and, when that did not seem to happen, she worried that she had lost her Dutch cap.

From Mervyn Peake's flat, off the King's Road in London, Dylan made noises about his efforts to find a new flat, even enthusing about the possibility of a house in the unlikely venue of Bovingdon in Hertfordshire. Dylan removed some pressure from Peake, who was putting the finishing touches to his novel *Titus Groan*, by taking his young son Sebastian to see the Disney cartoon *Dumbo*. Sebastian was surprised because Dylan had previously refused to take him to the cinema. He did not know that this was exactly their guest's type of comfort movie. In this infantile state, Dylan simultaneously wooed and tried to placate his wife with expansive statements of his love.

My dear my dear my dear Caitlin my love I love; even writing, from a universe and a star and ten thousand miles away, the name, your name, CAITLIN, just makes me love you, not more, because that is impossible, darling, I have always loved you since I first saw you looking silly and golden and much too good forever for me, in that nasty place in worse-than-Belsen London, no, not more, but deeper, oh my sweetheart I love you and love me dear Cat because we are the same, we are the same, we are the one thing, the constant thing, oh dear, dear Cat ... You are the most beautiful girl that has ever lived, and it is worth dying to have kissed you.

But Caitlin was beginning seriously to resent her situation. The best Dylan could offer was a further stay with his parents in Blaencwm in late July. While he was in London on VJ (Victory in Japan) Day in September, making enquiries, inter alia, about accommodation, she was stuck in Carmarthenshire, without even a drink. With Aeronwy suffering from acute indigestion and looking pale and withdrawn, Caitlin could stand it no longer. Fed up with her domestic chores, she wrote pleading to Mary Keene, saying she needed a break or she would go mad. Dylan was exploring some promising developments, but in the meantime she wondered if she and Aeronwy could stay with Mary in London.

Dylan's position was not much better. He was sick of his work for Donald Taylor. Even in Cardiganshire he complained about having to turn out socialist propaganda or, as he put it, 'filmscripts on Rehabilitation, Better Housing, Post War Full Employment, etc. for the socialist film department of the Ministry of Information'. He had a row with Taylor about this Labour bias, and was forced to recant. The producer tried to maintain Dylan's interest by involving him in more congenial feature projects about the murderer Dr Crippen and Scots poet Robert Burns, but nothing came of them.

Sensing a way out, Dylan wrote to Oscar Williams from Blaencwm, asking his help in finding a job in the United States, where he thought naively that Time magazine might like to employ him and Harvard University give him a lectureship. Showing he could still turn it on, he played up for his American correspondent the eccentricities of rural Wales, 'where the Bible opens itself at Revelations' and where a farm labourer was convinced that the stream by his cottage was Jordan water – 'and who can deny him'. He also emphasised the ravages of socialism, where, in the Orwellian Ministry of Information, ideas are shuffled by 'dead young men in briar pipes that are never lit in the office but which they always have protruding from their mouths like the cocks of swallowed bodies'.

His cynicism was jolted when he began to read an edition of D. H. Lawrence's poems which he had been sent by the BBC so he could make a selection for a reading in September. Dylan was particularly impressed by Lawrence's laconic 'Ballad for Another Ophelia' with its 'green glimmer of apples in the orchard'. This inspired him to one of his greatest poems, 'Fern Hill', which summons up the delights of his childhood in that part of Carmarthenshire, before subverting them in the realisation that they are all passing, indeed past. As three of his most memorable lines describe:

> Oh as I was young and easy in the mercy of his means,
> Time held me green and dying
> Though I sang in my chains like the sea.

With the war over, Dylan finally found a place to live in London, a flat in Markham Square across from the Devases. Having moved his family there at the end of September, he was able to increase his output for the BBC which was now prepared to let him do talks on, as well as readings of, a range of literary subjects. He also worked on the proofs of his new book of verse, *Deaths and Entrances*, which he insisted to Dent should include 'Fern Hill', even though the poem was not on his original list of contents. 'It is an *essential* part of the feeling & meaning of the book as a whole.'

Part of 'Fern Hill's appeal is that even its author could not decide if it was 'for evenings and tears', as he told David Tennant in August, or if it was 'joyful', his description to Edith Sitwell six months later. This reflects its shifting nature for, as James A. Davies has noted, it is the epitome of the modern Welsh poem in English – using the forms of English literature to summon the Carmarthenshire countryside. Davies evokes the critic Homi K. Bhabha, who writes on the changing patterns of English in an age of global multi-culturalism. In the terms of this debate, 'Fern Hill' mixes the best of Welsh and English traditions in a manner that is all the more original because not specifically oppositional.

'Fern Hill' was first published (with 'A Refusal to Mourn the Death, by Fire, of a Child in London') in the October issue of *Horizon*. The magazine had kept faith with Dylan through the war and published most of his major poetry. Its editor Cyril Connolly described the furtive routine he used to go through when Dylan appeared with a batch of new poems. He offered cash and the transaction would be concluded 'as if they were packets of cocaine'. Out of love with most contemporary verse, Connolly recognised Dylan's achievement in the award of *Horizon's* prize for 1945 worth £50.

With *Deaths and Entrances*, which appeared in February 1946, Dylan accomplished a popular breakthrough. A decade earlier, *Twenty-Five Poems* had made his name, but only among a small literary circle, while any response to *The Map of Love* in 1939 had been lost in the drift to war. With the end of hostilities, the British public was looking for a new voice, one to help them reflect on their experiences of the previous six years (which Dylan did supremely well in his four main war poems 'A Refusal to Mourn the Death, by Fire, of a Child in London', 'Deaths and Entrances', 'Ceremony After a Fire Raid' and 'Among those Killed in the Dawn Raid was a Man Aged a Hundred'), while at the same time looking forward to a future where, even with the atomic bomb, the poetic truths of love, nature and God were still addressed. Dylan's title *Deaths and Entrances* incorporated this balancing act: it echoed not only John Donne but Rudyard Kipling, a poet Dylan affected to despise, in the way it signposted the contents of the book, while describing the deeper level of the subject-matter – about the process of life in death, and vice versa. As early as May 1940 Dylan had alighted upon this as the title of his next book 'because that is all I ever write about or want to write about'.

In addition, he had begun to rein in the excesses of his poetical style, making his verse more accessible. (Wartime paper rationing may well have had an effect here.) He astutely requested another late addition to the book, 'In my craft or sullen art', with its simple, near perfect description of the poet's job – to write 'not for the proud man apart/... But for the lovers ... /who pay no praise or wages/Nor heed my craft or art.' Dent printed a first edition of 3,000 copies, and four further impressions. At last Dylan was being widely and enthusiastically read.

FIFTEEN

OXFORD, THE BBC AND ITALY

A chance encounter during the war set up the pattern of Dylan's life for the next three years. He had left Alan and Margaret Taylor under a cloud, after overstaying his welcome at their house in the spring of 1935. The Taylors had subsequently moved to Oxford, where he taught history at Magdalen College, while his wife busied herself as a hostess cum impresario, 'a sort of middle-class Lady Ottoline Morrell', putting on lunch-time concerts. A regular performer at her musical events was the pianist Natasha Litvin, who had married Stephen Spender in 1941. The Spenders escaped the worst of the bombing in London as paying guests at Holywell Ford, the Taylors' nineteenth-century house in the grounds of Magdalen next to the Cherwell river. One evening the gregarious Margaret Taylor, who had a mission to bring the arts to Oxford's cold intellectual world, asked the Spenders to bring back some guests for the weekend. 'Anybody will do,' she said, doubtless expecting a *Horizon* regular. The newly marrieds duly obliged, turning up with Dylan and Caitlin Thomas.

Dylan fell into advising Margaret Taylor on her poetry. He gave her the sort of general advice he had doled out to Pamela Hansford Johnson a decade or so earlier, stressing how she should strive to bring a new interpretation to any words she used. He did it in a clever, encouraging, somewhat sycophantic way which led, in March 1946, to Dylan and his family being invited to live in a summerhouse on the banks of the Cherwell at the bottom of the Holywell Ford garden. Dylan had just spent four days in St Stephen's Hospital, London, with 'alcoholic gastritis' and wanted somewhere to continue his recovery. His new quarters in Oxford were damp, with no running water (nothing unusual for the Thomases), though there was gas and electricity. The kindly Margaret said the children could sleep (and have baths) in the main house, one hundred yards away.

Dylan's living arrangements suited him well. He was within easy reach of Oxford railway station, starting point for day trips to London where the expanding BBC was happy to find room for the author of *Deaths and Entrances*. His participation in a poetry reading, attended by Queen

Elizabeth and her daughters Princess Elizabeth and Margaret, at the Wigmore Hall in May only improved his marketability, one advantage of which was that no-one queried his travel expense claims.

Indicative of his new status, he played a small part in arranging the royal event – one of the only occasions he was entrusted with an organisational role. In overall charge was the Society of Authors, whose Secretary, Denis Kilham Roberts, was a poet he had known since his early days in London. Dylan was co-opted onto a committee to choose the programme and performers, who included the poets John Masefield, Edith Sitwell, Walter de la Mare, Louis MacNeice and, for added professionalism, the actors Edith Evans and John Gielgud. On the day, there were warning signs that everything was not right with Dylan. Though everyone was asked to arrive early, he turned up two minutes before due on stage, looking particularly unkempt in a pair of blue and white check trousers. He acquitted himself well, with renditions of three poems – D. H. Lawrence's 'Snake', his own 'Fern Hill' and William Blake's 'Tyger! Tyger! Burning Bright', which he read at such a stately pace that one actor remarked on it. 'Well, I took it as fast as I could,' returned Dylan, slightly aggrieved.

The fireworks came afterwards. Caitlin was reported to have approached the Queen and said, 'I say, do you like this? I don't. I think I shall ask for my money back.' According to Edith Sitwell, Caitlin then flicked some ash on the Queen's dress. That part of the story might have been embellished after what happened when the participants and their spouses were invited to join Sitwell for dinner at her club, the Sesame in Grosvenor Street. After Sitwell's sister-in-law Georgia announced, 'There is a woman in the cloakroom more roaringly drunk than anyone I have ever seen in my life', Dylan intoned grimly, 'That will be my wife.' And so it turned out. Caitlin was sitting next to John Hayward, the crippled bibliophile and close friend of T. S. Eliot. When she spilt some ice-cream on her arm, she asked him to lick it off. When Hayward refused, she let fly, 'Mother of God! The insults of Men. You great pansy.' Improbably, Sitwell thought that Caitlin had taken a fancy to Hayward, whom she insisted on calling 'Old Ugly'.

Dylan joined in the act, attacking the encroaching Leavisite academic consensus, which had not wanted Milton read earlier in the evening, and even taking Eliot to task for publishing 'such awful poetry'. Sitwell claimed Dylan had been as 'good as gold' with her. But she said the date of the evening would, after her death, be found inscribed on her heart, like the word 'Calais' on Queen Mary's. 'I am worried to think how his friends will be driven away if she goes on like that. He is such a wonderful poet – a really great one, and has very endearing qualities as a person.' Regarding him indulgently as the son she never had, she was even prepared to overlook the fact that he failed to turn up to lunch with her the following day – 'I suppose because he would have had to apologise for her'.

His more regular fare on the wireless involved him declaiming and pontificating on a wide range of poets, from his beloved Milton to Walter de la Mare in series such as 'Book of Verse' (produced for the Overseas Service by his friend John Arlott), 'Time for Verse' (edited by Patric Dickinson) and 'Living Writers' (the last two for the new arts-orientated Third Programme, which started broadcasting in September 1946, further adding to his range of outlets).

Building on his 'Reminiscences of Childhood' and his New Quay portrait 'Quite Early One Morning', he developed a line in sharply observed talks, often incorporating a version of his own experiences, such as his 'Memories of Christmas', a warm evocation of Swansea yule tides he might have liked, but seldom had. This originally went out on the BBC Wales 'Children's Hour' in December 1945, but was recorded in London where Derek McCulloch, director of 'Children's Hour', was a trifle over-anxious: 'There is a tremendous risk in taking Dylon [sic] "live" in the programme for reasons I do not think I need enlarge upon. He is notoriously tricky.' Dylan later amalgamated this talk with a piece for Picture Post in a Christmas article for the American magazine Harper's Bazaar. This provided the text for one of his most enduring pieces, 'A Child's Christmas in Wales', recorded by the commercial firm Caedmon in New York in February 1952.

In July 1946 he expanded his repertoire with a short radio drama, The Londoner, described as 'a day in the life of Mr and Mrs Jackson, Ted and Lily, of number forty-nine Montrose Street, Shepherds Bush, London, W12', Part documentary about the post-war capital (picking up from his stalled book on the streets of London), part prototype radio soap opera, this production anticipated Under Milk Wood, to the extent of using an omniscient narrator and starting (and ending) with dreams. It even included allusions to the atom bomb and to television. Laurence Gilliam, the BBC's director of features, described it to Dylan as 'a most sensitive and successful piece of radio'. No-one was surprised that, when Dylan recorded another colourful talk 'Holiday Memory' in October, Edward Sackville-West should ask in the New Statesman 'why this remarkable poet had never attempted a poetic drama for broadcasting'.

Dylan's trips to London allowed him to meet friends who had also found berths in radio, a medium which reflected the educational and egalitarian ideals of the new Labour government. Many were poets whose special status at the BBC was recognised in an illustrated feature for *Picture Post*, titled 'A Nest of Singing Birds'. Among them was John Arlott, who had only recently graduated from being a poetry-and cricket-loving policeman to a BBC producer. He valued Dylan as a reader of verse, describing him standing at the microphone, 'feet apart and head thrown back, a dead cigarette frequently adhering wispily to his lower lip, curls a little tousled and eyes half-closed, barely reading the poetry by eye, but rather understanding his way through it, one arm beating out a sympathetic double rhythm as he read.' As a narrator, Arlott thought Dylan 'a trifle too explosive, but stimulating if used only occasionally'.

A day at the BBC involved protracted lunch-time drinking at a nearby pub, usually the Stag's Head in New Cavendish Street or (Dylan's preference) the George (christened the 'Gluepot' for obvious reasons) in Great Portland Street. When he was producing, Roy Campbell, the tall, iconoclastic South African poet, was careful to make sure that Dylan stayed off whisky, at least until after he had recorded. Once he failed to do this, and heard Dylan slur his introduction to 'Ode on Shaint Sheshilia's Day'. Nevertheless Dylan was the 'best all-round reader of verse' Campbell ever produced. His blind spot was 'correct' poets, such as Pope and Dryden. But he made up for this with his superlative performances of 'wild and woolly' poets such as Blake and Manley Hopkins. Then he 'became almost Superman'.

Dylan's BBC friends included Louis MacNeice, who had recently acquired Tilty Hill House, a part-fifteenth-century mansion near Dunmow in Essex, from Dylan's one-time girlfriend Veronica Sibthorp and her latest paramour, the painter John Armstrong. Ruthven Todd lived down the hill at Tilty Mill. When he invited Dylan to stay, he was initially fearful of the impression his friend would make. However Dylan charmed the locals, showing intelligent interest in country life. When Todd moved to the United States in 1947, Tilty Mill was taken over by George Barker's former lover, Elizabeth Smart, who shared it with the painters Robert MacBryce and Robert Colquhoun (the two Roberts) who either 'caused havoc' or, according to one's taste, proved excellent nannies for her children. In London, MacNeice and Todd introduced Dylan to two of his favourite BBC cronies – Bob Pocock, another poetry-loving policeman who had been on the fringes of Soho pubs and broadcasting for some time, and R. D. (Reggie) Smith, an amiable, thick-set former student of MacNeice at Birmingham, whose novelist wife Olivia Manning chronicled his days as a British Council lecturer in her Balkan and Levant trilogies.

Radio also attracted musicians, such as the composer Elizabeth Lutyens, who had rebelled against the values of both her father, Sir Edwin

Lutyens, the imperial architect, and her mother Lady Emily, who devoted her life to the Indian guru, Krishnamurti. Instead Lizzie (as she was called) concentrated on writing twelve-tone serial music, which gave some order to a dishevelled life, though she had recently turned to more conventional film scores. A natural Soho-ite, she befriended the Thomases around 1942. For a short while they were tenants of her and her second husband, Edward Clark, also a composer, off Tottenham Court Road. Her status as Aeronwy's godmother indicated she was persona grata with both Dylan and Caitlin. She had few illusions about Dylan's trickiness, remarking he was 'as difficult to pin down as quicksilver with his ever-changing moods from solemnity to giggles'. At one stage he annoyed her by failing (despite, she claimed, having been paid £50) to provide the words he had promised for The Pit, a politically committed composition about coal-miners that she had written for William Walton.

By her account, Dylan, although in demand, still had some basic learning to do in radio. In September 1946 she accompanied him and Reggie Smith to Kent to record some 'actuality' for a programme about the seaside resort of Margate, part of an exchange with the American station WOR which was supplying a similar feature on Coney Island. In the spirit of his wartime propaganda exercises, where detail was not so important as overall effect, Dylan had already roughed out a breezy script, full of bathing beauties, girls in 'Kiss me Quick' hats, and his stock-in-trade, a documentary-style 'Voice of Information'. He then celebrated with Smith, leaving them both with massive hangovers. Dylan had forgotten that Margate was entering the off-season. When he and his colleagues went to reconnoitre the sea-front, they found only one middle-aged matron with bunions, while Dreamland, the amusement arcade, was deserted. When Dylan spied a pretty girl selling scent and made a bee-line for her, he was fended off by her boyfriend who squirted one of her cheapest products at him. As a result Liz had to keep leeward of him for several hours. Back at the hotel, he made a statutory 'alcoholically-polite' pass at her, before crashing out.

This story makes sense of an anecdote told by Wynford Vaughan-Thomas. Dylan returned to London to have lunch with Edith Sitwell, with whom he had resuscitated his friendship of the 1930s, after she had written an enthusiastic review of Deaths and Entrances. For some reason, he was unusually apologetic. 'I'm sorry to smell so awful, Edith, it's Margate.' She could only placate him: 'Yes, of course, my dear boy, naturally it's Margate. Of course, I quite understand that.'

After a day's work at Broadcasting House, Dylan would have a few pints at the Stag or George, before catching an early evening train back to Oxford, where he was often in time for a dinner party or more drinks, preferably at the Turf, or sometimes, when the beer there had run out the Gloucester Arms, or even White's, a club until recently popular with American servicemen, where Dylan liked to order gin fizzes. One of his drinking partners was John Veale, a young composer whose first symphonic study was being produced locally. Although grateful to Dylan for introductions to MacNeice, Lutyens and Roy Campbell, Veale was disapproving of the older man's lifestyle. When they first met, Veale had not yet been demobbed. Despite having little money, he lent Dylan three shillings and sixpence for a taxi, but was taken aback two weeks later when he asked for the money back and was greeted with 'a look as if I'd delivered an unforgivable insult'. Margaret Taylor adopted Veale as one of the creative talents with whom she liked to surround herself. He recalled 'ghoulish' dinners attended by MacNeice, Lutyens, Joyce Cary and Graham Greene, whose estranged wife lived in Oxford. They were all so carefully orchestrated as to lack any warmth or spontaneity.

As for Margaret's favourite, there was no doubt. Veale said she lionised Dylan, though this downplays the strong emotional attachment she felt towards him. She had a history of throwing herself at younger men, such as Robert Kee, a handsome student of her husband. After joining the RAF as a bomber pilot, Kee was shot down over Europe and imprisoned in Stalag Luft III. In bland letters to the Taylors, he sent odd messages to non-existent aunts, which were in fact coded references to his fellow inmates. After Kee escaped, Margaret rented and decorated a flat for him in London's Percy Street, but was put out to find that, while working on his prison memoir (published by Greene at Eyre & Spottiswoode as a novel *A Crowd is not Company* in 1947), he used it to entertain Janetta Woolley, a pretty girlfriend, who was part of Cyril Connolly's *Horizon* set.

Initially Alan Taylor had indulged his wife over Dylan, thinking, against his better judgement, that their new tenant would help take her mind off Kee. He even agreed to take him in to dinner at Magdalen's High Table where Dylan and the College President, the distinguished scientist, Sir Henry Tizard, sought, in Taylor's words, 'to impress one another, a very curious conversation'. The historian was distraught when Caitlin told him bluntly that his wife had simply transferred her affections from Kee to Dylan. Part of Margaret genuinely believed in the poet's talent, and was prepared to indulge him out of a private income, but another wilder part relished the spirit of dionysiac mayhem he brought to staid Oxford gatherings. She took him to literary societies, accompanied him to pubs, and invited him to her distinguished dinner parties where, more often than not, his behaviour was appalling. Once Dylan returned drunk from London to find that she had cooked a dish of jugged hare. When he said he was not hungry, she insisted. 'All right then', he grudgingly agreed. 'I'll eat the hare of the bitch that dogs me.' On another occasion, he was in an even worse state at a gathering for Lord David Cecil and Hugh Trevor-Roper, who recalled, 'He promptly overturned a full decanter of claret – good claret too – drenching the fastidious Lord David. That dinner party was not a success.'

Veale was not impressed: 'Dylan was accustomed to being trailed around by people in whose eyes he could do no wrong. He was allowed to get away with anything. I didn't approve of it. I had a sneaking sympathy with Alan Taylor who thought Dylan was a fraud.' Certainly there was no love lost between Dylan and Taylor who recorded succinctly in his memoir, *A Personal History*, 'I disliked Dylan Thomas intensely. He was cruel. He was a sponger even when he had money of his own. He went out of his way to hurt those who helped him.'

Margaret Taylor's generosity allowed the Thomases to pick up the threads of normal life. Over the summer of 1946 several friends visited them, including Dan Jones, Norman Cameron and Roy Campbell. John Arlott, who was beginning a parallel career as a cricket commentator, stayed when in town to cover a match between Oxford University and the Indian tourists. Dylan accompanied him, MacNeice and Cecil Day-Lewis on a welcome day out in the Parks. When Edith Sitwell came to Oxford, she gave a party, where another guest was the hostess Lady Sibyl Colefax, who had been impressed enough by Dylan's reading in front of royalty at the Wigmore Hall to invite him to tea, a measure of his growing social success. Surprisingly, given their different poetic styles, Dylan also struck up a liaison with John Betjeman, who was beginning a stint as secretary of the Oxford Preservation Trust. The two men lunched at Blenheim Palace where Betjeman, until recently, had worked for the Books Division of the British Council. A regular broadcaster himself, he recognised Dylan's more positive side, recalling how beautifully the Welshman read Thomas Hardy's 'To Lizbie Brown' when they both dined with the Taylors at Holywell Ford.

Over the year Dylan contributed to over fifty radio programmes, earning about £700, or £19,000 in 2003 figures. Showing some application, he noted details of his finances in a small diary. Although he was not writing poetry and his film work had dried up (without assured government contracts, Taylor had been forced to put his companies into liquidation), Dylan could call on his BBC income, fees from talks, and royalties from books, with the result that, on paper at least, he was not destitute. At the end of May he was owed £85 (around £2,400 in 2003), and by the end of July this had risen to £89. 18s. 4d., including £2. 15s. for a one-hour afternoon talk to sailors at Morley College.

By then Dylan and Caitlin were preparing to go to Ireland with their new friends, the McAlpines. They intended visiting the Puck Fair at Killorglin in County Kerry, an area that had intrigued Dylan since working on a film script of Maurice O'Sullivan's memoir *Twenty Years A-Growing* a couple of years earlier. The trip had taken on an added urgency after Caitlin's father died in Dublin in March, his last dispirited words being, 'Tried in the scales and found wanting.' Bill McAlpine and his wife Helen were obvious travelling companions. He was a bibulous engineer from Ulster, with an acute intelligence and a deep knowledge of literature, in particular of James Joyce. He was able to indulge this hobby, because Helen, a free spirit who struck an immediate rapport with Caitlin, had been married to a millionaire. When he died she was left no money but a substantial house overlooking the river Thames at Richmond.

Dylan and Bill had reputedly met as fire-watchers but, more likely, they shared pints in the Wheatsheaf or French. On 5 August they and their wives flew to Dublin, where they spent four days, before proceeding to Kerry. Dylan had managed to inveigle a £50 advance out of *Picture Post* for a story on the fair, a three-day pagan festival turned drinking extravaganza, based loosely round the totem figure of King Puck, a crowned billy-goat. But the commission was never completed for Dylan drank so much he had no idea what was happening. Caitlin and Helen simply left their menfolk and danced with handsome Irish boys.

Dylan did not mind. He had a wonderful time, even managing to squeeze in a day on O'Sullivan's Blasket Islands. Back in the United Kingdom, he descended on his parents in Carmarthenshire, where his mother was unwell. From there, he described his Irish trip to Vernon Watkins 'We ate ourselves daft: lobsters, steaks, cream, hills of butter, homemade bread, chicken and chocolates: we drank Seithenyns of porter and Guinness: we walked, climbed, rode on donkeys, bathed, sailed, rowed, danced, sang.' Seithenyn was a legendary Welsh prince whose love of drink caused him to neglect his duties attending the dykes which protected a low-lying kingdom in Cardigan Bay. As a result the sea overwhelmed this community, whose remains, it is said, could be seen at low tide. Dylan's reference indicates how details of Welsh mythology swirled around his mind, possibly, in this case, contributing to his description of the drowned souls in *Under Milk Wood*.

Another letter (of thanks) went to Osbert Sitwell who was enjoying success with his autobiography. Having recently been left some money, he had joined his sister Edith in supporting Dylan, in his case, with funds which helped allay the costs of the Irish trip. But once he had assessed his financial situation, Dylan realised he needed to return quickly to work. So he also wrote to his BBC contacts and to Donald Taylor to whom he admitted 'in this tremendous quietness, feel[ing] lost, worried about the future, uncertain even of now. In London, it doesn't seem to matter, one lives from day to day. But here, the future's endless and my position in it unpleasant and precarious ... I've reached a dead spell in my hack freelancing, am broke, and depressed.'

After a few months of relative ease, Dylan was again under pressure. One way out – apparently encouraged by Caitlin – was to revive his plan to work in America. With typical professional naivety, he had tried to advance this idea earlier in the year by entering unilateral negotiations with at least three American publishers keen to get him on their books – William Morrow, Reynal & Hitchcock and Henry Holt. Oscar Williams played a role in leading these firms to believe that Dylan had no commitment to New Directions beyond his forthcoming book of *Selected Writings*. At one stage it was suggested that Laughlin's firm might share Dylan's publishing with Reynal & Hitchcock and Henry Holt, which played its trump card by offering to pay Dylan's passage to the United States. Holt's new editor of belles-lettres, the respected Southern writer, Allen Tate, was so keen to sign Dylan that he suggested an advance of $750. Another Holt director went to the trouble of inviting Dylan to lunch when he was in London, even paying the Welshman's expenses for the journey from Oxford.

Predictably James Laughlin was not amused when he learnt of these initiatives. New Directions' edition of Dylan's *Selected Writings* was due out in December with an expanded print-run of 4,000. On an autumn visit to Europe, he forced Dylan to sign a stringent new contract. Dylan promised not to enter discussions with any other American publisher and gave New Directions carte blanche to handle the placing of his articles in US periodicals. While in Italy, Laughlin made a typically canny response and asked the noted typographer Hans Mardersteig of the Officina Bodoni to produce an expensive limited (200 copies) edition of Dylan's poems.

For his part, Dylan felt that his unequivocal commitment to New Directions allowed him to pester Laughlin again about visiting the United States, a country which, in the atomic age, seemed more congenial than dank Britain. He had enjoyed his wartime encounters with various people attached to the US military. And the feeling was reciprocated: after meeting him in May, the poet Conrad Aiken described him as 'a delightful fellow, full of good humour and gusto, and a fine drinker. He thinks of going to the U.S., which I'm not sure is a good idea, but who knows? He might emerge unscathed.' From friends, Dylan probably heard of Gerald Kersh who, after an extraordinary few years in which he deserted from the British army and emerged as an American war correspondent, had prospered on the other side of the Atlantic, both as an author and a journalist.

So, in November, Dylan was emboldened to ask his publisher's help in finding him a house in the countryside, near New York (perhaps in the Adirondacks). He suggested that he could use this as a base for writing, broadcasting and lecturing in the United States, where he promised everything he wrote was 'yours without any condition to print, publish, in the United States'. He claimed that Edith Sitwell had offered support in setting him up with lectures and readings. Generally, however, she feared the combination of drink and spiralling expenses, telling John Lehmann she was 'aghast' when she heard of Dylan's plans and quoting Margaret Taylor that his mania for crossing the Atlantic was like measles – 'you have to have it and get over it.'

A year or so earlier Laughlin had counselled Dylan against rushing to America. He had said that it was too soon: the young academics and critics who would appreciate him were yet to return from the war. This time there is no evidence he was any more enthusiastic. So Dylan was forced to remain at Holywell Ford, doing much the same as before. He talked with Higham about a new book for Dent, a compendium of the personal reminiscences he had been doing for the BBC, together with some unwritten stories, which he listed as 'Bob's My Uncle', 'Poor Will', 'Opera Story' and 'Welsh Script', all packaged under the unlikely working title of *Top Hat & Gasworks* or, alternatively, *Bob's My Uncle*. (At least that last bit was true.)

He could always find work at the BBC, which had latched on to the potential of his 'organ' voice. MacNeice realised this could be used, in tandem with Dylan's character, 'for all sorts of strange purposes'. He cast his friend as Aristophanes in his 'panorama of Aristophanic comedy' *Enemies of Cant* and then as 'a funereal but benevolent raven' in his dramatised fairy story *The Heartless Giant*. In November Dylan appeared as Private Dai Jones in Douglas Cleverdon's held-over production of David Jones's *In Parenthesis*, causing him to complain to his agent that he should be getting an actor's fee rather than the rather lesser payment for a talk. 'He took his radio acting very seriously,' noted MacNeice, 'and between rehearsals would always keep asking if he were giving satisfaction. He was a joy to have around the studio, causing a certain amount of anxiety to the studio managers, who could never be quite sure that he would speak into the right microphone, and a great deal of delight to the rest of the cast who particularly admired the queer little dance steps that he always performed (it seems quite unconsciously) while broadcasting.'

Dylan still hoped his war-time script for The Doctor and the Devils (based on the Edinburgh body-snatchers Burke and Hare) might prove financially rewarding. Donald Taylor talked vaguely of bringing this to the screen, but Dylan wanted to speed up the process. Bypassing Higham again, he sent the manuscript to Graham Greene, one of whose hats was as a director of the publisher Eyre & Spottiswoode. Dylan made typically self-effacing noises about the work, but had a canny notion of Greene's influence in the worlds of both books and films, something which Margaret Taylor followed up on his behalf. After Dylan mentioned that Michael Redgrave had expressed an interest in playing Dr William Salter, the dour Edinburgh anatomist (based on the real life Dr Robert Knox) at the centre of the story, Greene took the trouble of confirming this with the actor. When Greene suggested that the Rank Organisation, the dominant force in post-war British cinema production, might be interested, Dylan became excited and wondered if he might write something specially for Redgrave. The combination of Dylan's unilateral approach and Greene's intervention spurred all concerned, including Taylor, Higham and Dent. After Gainsborough Films bought an option on The Doctor and the Devils (in a deal which would net Dylan around £400), Dent offered to publish the text, though it would be a long time before either film or book came to fruition. (His script for Redgrave appeared the following year as The Shadowless Man, a story steeped in German Romanticism, about a man who sells his shadow. The film industry showed no interest in a nebulous treatment, which Margaret Taylor is said to have played a part in writing.)

Christmas passed pleasantly enough in the circumstances. Osbert Sitwell sent a cheque which Dylan acknowledged fulsomely: 'It was all Christmases and birthdays the morning of getting it ... it was new shoes and sweaters for the voley river cold, and school bills paid with a flourish, and some Algerian [wine], and books I've wanted for months, and a heater for our hutch, and such happiness to think that you were thinking of us and could spare, in the taxed dark, such a very marvellous gift.' Florrie sent two fat chickens from Carmarthenshire, one of which Dylan and Caitlin cooked for themselves and Aeronwy for lunch on Christmas Day. In the evening they had a big dinner at the Taylors, with turkey and Christmas pudding, and on Boxing Day they took the other chicken to the Veales, where they were joined by Ernest Stahl, a German don at Christ Church, and his wife Kathleen, who both later became good friends. But Dylan was worried about Llewelyn, who spent the holiday season with his grandmother in Ringwood. The boy was suffering badly from asthma; he also seemed very nervous and Dylan noticed he walked in a peculiar manner. After a doctor recommended a change of climate, Margaret Taylor had offered to pay for him to go to a holiday-school on the Isle of Wight. Dylan still had to meet the ongoing medical bills for Llewelyn, and now an unfortunate relic of his past had come back to haunt him: after dodging solicitors' letters for some time, he had finally been served with a writ for the return of his advance for the unwritten book *Twelve Hours on the Streets* (of London).

Dylan shrugged off these problems (which must have made America seem all the more enticing) and took Caitlin to the Chelsea Arts Ball, a fancy dress event to see in the new year of 1947 at the Albert Hall in London. Showing an uncanny ability to find money when required, he went as a chinaman and she as a flouncy Spanish lady. They accompanied several friends from the BBC, including Michael Ayrton, a young neo-Romantic artist with a fondness for the occult. Ayrton had a flat in All Soul's Place, round the corner from the BBC, where his friend, the composer Constant Lambert, lived in the ground floor flat with his mistress, the ballerina Margot Fonteyn. He had met Lambert through another composer, Cecil Gray, who had admired Caitlin's father Francis Macnamara enough to make him godfather to his daughter Pauline.

Soon after this new year encounter, Dylan was convinced that he and Ayrton had agreed to work on a full-length opera for William Walton who, having made his name with the music for Edith Sitwell's *Façade*, had recently composed the score for Laurence Olivier's gung-ho end of war film version of *Henry V*. Dylan even told his parents he was going to do the libretto and Ayrton the 'décor', but, before they were 'definitely commissioned', they needed to reconnoitre the Thames estuary, 'as I want to set the opera in a near-docks area. A very modern tragic opera, in the bombed slums of wharfland. If this ever comes to anything, it will be the biggest English operatic event of the century.' He looked forward to taking off six months to write the piece which Covent Garden had promised to stage in 1949. (Possibly this was the 'Opera Story' he was offering to Dent.)

How this project took on these fanciful proportions is unclear. The only suggestion that the putative composer knew anything about it came from John Veale who heard from Dylan that Walton considered it too avant-garde. The momentum came from Ayrton who had been working on the sets for Covent Garden's first big post-war production, a version of Purcell's opera *The Fairy Queen*, conducted by Lambert. He was eager to follow this up with something similar and swapped ideas with Dylan who was keen to break into a new medium. The two men did make their voyage down the Thames in mid-January, but by then their objective had changed: Ayrton was talking of doing an illustrated version of Hogarth's *Peregrinations* and wanted Dylan to write an introduction. They took a boat as far as Gravesend but, on the way back, Dylan, who had been drinking, showed the pressures on him, when he began to scream, 'The birds, the birds are getting at me.' After falling into the cold river (a perilous occupation at that time of year), he was taken to a nearby hostelry where he was revived.

Dylan was again at a low ebb, as was clear when he cancelled two BBC engagements in February. One was run of the mill – a recording of *How Green Was My Valley*, but the other was a commitment to accompany Louis MacNeice to Belfast to narrate 'The Hare' by the latter's friend W. R. Rodgers. Ferry tickets from Heysham to Belfast had been bought, but at the last moment Dylan cried off, claiming food poisoning. He did manage to participate in the Third Programme's daunting series 'The Poet and his Critic', in which Tommy Earp addressed his work, and Dylan replied in what he himself described as a 'warm-hearted and dull' manner.

On his sickbed in his 'converted ark' at Holywell Ford, Dylan had been thinking about what might have been. In an uncollected poem, with references to William Johnson Cory and Eliot, he mused about how his life might have turned out if he had buckled down at Swansea Grammar School and proceeded to Oxford University.

> Oxford I sing, though in untutored tones, alack!
> I heard, long years ago, her call, but blew it back;
> ... Ah, not for me the windblown scarf,
> The bicycle to the Trout, the arm-in-arm sweatered swing,
> Marx in a punt, Firbank aloud round the gas-ring;
> Never in flannelled and umbrella'd youth did I
> Tire the sun with talking and drive him down the High.
> But is it now too late? I'll wear my bottom rolled
> And never dare to smile to show time's fag-stained mould,
> Comb, over the blitzed bits, my gravely tumbled hair,
> And walk about the place as though there's no-one there
> But I, single, aloof and eager, cynic, wit,
> With hands that never shake, aged twenty and a bit;
> And after climbing up one flight of stairs I must
> Remember not to faint,

Here he has crossed out 'nor chase with squeals of lust/Botany lecturers from women's colleges' and has added:

nor must I pour my gin
Into my whisky 'just to make it taste', nor pin
My first born's school report above my little bed
Nor dare let on I knew old poets since snuffed.

(The last word was originally 'dead'.)

His tone was reflective, touching, a bit solemn, underlined in the way he steered away from 'squeals of lust' to the pressing matter of his son's school report. At the same time, in a notebook dated 1947, he collected anecdotes about Oxford University, including bits of its history, excerpts from its statutes, details of its eccentric figures, such as Dr William Buckland, the Geology Professor who ate his way through the animal kingdom, and a page of local quotations by authors such as Wordsworth, Swinburne and Pepys. He even wrote a line to remind himself to find the 'exact modern duties' of the university policemen, the proctors and bulldogs.

This could have been background research for another talk, but was more likely a labour of love. Looking back, Dylan felt he might have enjoyed being an undergraduate, with a licence to be supercilious. But his own career path had been different, so, by way of compensation, he invested considerable time and emotional capital in researching his real background for a BBC programme about Swansea. He spent two days visiting the town and talking to friends such as Fred Janes, Vernon Watkins and Walter Flower. Concerned to have the correct details of its wartime destruction, he wrote to a municipal official to obtain the names of all the shops in the High Street destroyed by German bombing. Looking for further information about his school, he wrote to his old classics master John Morys Williams and was surprised to learn of the extent of the damage it had suffered. In his script for 'Return Journey', he passed through Swansea, conducting quasi-fictitious interviews in bars, school, newspaper office and finally Cwmdonkin Park, as he searched for memories of his youthful self. Neatly turned vignettes summoned up his childhood, such as when a young girl he was trying to pick up on the Promenade said to her friend, mocking his Grammar School accent, 'No thank you, Mr Cheeky, with your cut-glass accent and your father's trilby! I don't want no walk on no sands. What d'you say? Ooh, listen to him, Het. He's swallowed a dictionary.' The result was good radio both technically and emotionally, because it created a paradox: with his charm, sense of character and felicitous phrases, Dylan evoked the spirit of his youth, but, he also made clear that the past was dead. Much as he might want to go back, he could not.

While he was indulging in this exercise in nostalgia, Edith Sitwell had been working behind the scenes on his behalf. If she did not think he was ready for America, she realised he needed a break. So she prevailed on the Society of Authors, where her brother Osbert was deputy chairman and she was responsible for a committee which awarded travelling scholarships, to give Dylan £150 so he could take himself and his family to Italy. By the time 'Return Journey' was broadcast in June, the Thomases were ensconced in a villa in Florence.

At the age of thirty-two Dylan ventured outside the British Isles for the first time. The railway journey to his interim destination – a small pensione at San Michele di Pagana, a mile outside Rapallo, on the Mediterranean coast – might have put him off the experience. He went in an unruly family party, including not only his wife, son and daughter, but also his sister-in-law Brigit Marnier, who was there as a glorified nanny, and her son Tobias, a companion for his cousin Llewelyn with whom he had been brought up at Blashford. The trip, via Switzerland, took three days, largely because the party's baggage was lost at the Italian border. Dylan and Caitlin had to spend their first morning in Italy in the Kafkaesque bowels of Milan station, trying, through judicious bribery of officials with English cigarettes, to find out what had happened.

Italy was lively and chaotic, where Britain was dour and accepting of continuing austerity. Both countries were coping in their different ways with the aftermath of war which, in political terms, meant getting used to a continent of Europe divided into capitalist and Soviet camps, both protected by atomic weapons. But whereas Britain had come through the hostilities battered but victorious, with its institutions intact, Italy had not only been defeated, but had experienced the trauma of Fascism. With Marxism on its borders, threatening its political core, its response was to dissolve its compromised monarchy, formally ban the Communists from government (in May 1947, the month after Dylan arrived), and stitch together an uneasy American-brokered coalition, fronted by the Christian Democrats with links to the Mafia.

En route, Dylan had been horrified by the blown-up bridges and other signs of war. In San Michele, he was taken aback by the hordes of dirty children who followed him wherever he went, and fascinated by the intricate workings of the black market which, once he had mastered the system, allowed him to double the spending power of his English pounds. He quickly adapted to his bright sunny environment. His pensione on the sea-front was delightful – like 'a clean pink ship in the sea', he told his benefactress Edith Sitwell. It served generous meals starting with spaghetti, followed by meat (with artichoke, spinach and potatoes), then cheese (including his favourite gorgonzola), all sorts of fruit, and coffee, washed down with delicious red wine. Red, pink and white villas glistened kaleidoscopically among the fir trees in the surrounding hills. As Dylan knew, Rapallo had a reputation as a retreat for artists and writers. Yeats had visited and commented appreciatively, while Max Beerbohm still entertained at his house on the edge of town. Only the previous year Dylan had signed a letter of support for former resident Ezra Pound who had been accused of treason, found unfit to plead, and incarcerated in a psychiatric hospital.

But Dylan had no intention of staying. For all its good points, the town of Rapallo was a Riviera hotspot and the area was likely to become expensive later in the summer. Dylan told Edith Sitwell that he wanted not a holiday, but a place to live where he intended to work 'like a fiend, a good fiend'. Before settling down, however, he wanted to go to Rome where he knew Ronald Bottrall, head of the British Council and a published poet. He had fond notions that Bottrall might set him up with lucrative lectures and even find him a job in the burgeoning Italian film industry. Friends such as Stephen Spender seemed to be earning a decent living on the international lecture circuit. But Bottrall was a Leavisite with little sympathy for Dylan's poetry. The best he could do was give a party for the visiting British poet and his wife, who had travelled to Rome by bumpy overnight bus. Dylan met some local authors, including Mario Praz, an Anglophile historian of art and literature, who had made an international name for himself with The Romantic Agony, his study of the romantic imagination.

Unable to stomach the idea of a sixteen-hour return bus ride, the Thomases caught a bucketing army plane to Genoa, within easy reach of Rapallo. Five days later, they were off again to Florence, where they hoped to find a house for a long-term stay. There they bumped into Stephen and Natasha Spender, with whom they enjoyed a couple of good meals. Through the British Council they had an introduction to Eugenio Montale, a left-wing man of letters who was to win the Nobel Prize for literature in 1975. He invited them to meet some 'intellectuals' over dinner. Dylan had never shown much enthusiasm for such gatherings and, when Montale, in the formal spirit of the occasion, came to pick up his guest at his hotel, he found that Dylan, after drinking, had locked himself in a cupboard and refused to come out. Eventually prised from his hiding place, Dylan did not prove a scintillating dinner companion. When Montale arrived to collect the Spenders for a similar event the following day, he informed them severely, 'Monsieur Thomas est un homme tres étrange.' As a result, he cancelled his planned ceremonial dinner, and took them out for a more relaxed and agreeable tête-à-tête.

Dylan (centre) discusses his role in the BBC radio play *The Careerist* with Louis MacNeice (right), author of the piece, and Pat Griffiths (left), who did the sound effects

Dylan in London, 1941

Family group at Blaencwm 1942, with Dylan and Caitlin (standing), Florrie, Llewelyn and family friend

Dylan and John Davenport
(photographed in 1952)

Dylan's surrealist-influenced painting for John
Davenport's children, late 1940s

Dylan with poetry produ
Patric Dickinson at the B

Dylan, Helen McAlpine a
Caitlin in Ireland, 1946

Helen McAlpine and Caitlin at the Boat House, Laugharne

At Brown's: (from left) Bill McAlpine, Caitlin, Ebie Williams, Mary Ellidge, Dylan, Ivy Williams, Mabley Owen (with young Aeronwy in front)

Domestic scene on the veranda at the Boat House: (from left) Caitlin, Aeronwy, Dolly Long, Shelagh Long

Margaret Taylor

Marged Howard Stepney

Dylan in Persia, 1951

Dylan with the actors Griffith Williams and Mario Cabre (right) on the set of the film *Pandora and the Flying Dutchman* at Pendine Sands, July 1950

Dylan at work in his hut above the Boat House in Laugharne, 1953

Dylan's father, D.J., in typical pose – reading a newspaper at Pelican in Laugharne

Dylan at a Foyle's literary luncheon in January 1953, receiving an award for the best volume of poetry in 1952 (his *Collected Poems 1934–1952*) from Foyle's chairman William Foyle

Oscar Williams's snaps of Dylan in the United States, 1950 – with Williams himself (above left), the quizzical tourist (above), with Stanley Moss (left)

ylan and his American friend and promoter John Malcolm Brinnin at a book signing with Frances Steloff at the Gotham Book Mart, New York, 1952

Dylan and Caitlin in the United States, 1952

Liz Reitell

Dylan and Pearl Kazin, London,
September 1951

Dylan at a rehearsal of *Under Milk Wood*

Dylan at the White
Horse Tavern,
Greenwich Village

Dylan in Vancouver, April 1950

...aitlin, Dan Jones and Fred Janes

...ylan on television: in August 1953, ...ylan recorded *The Outing* for tele-...sion as *A Story*. (Unfortunately no ...cording survives; nor indeed is ...ere any moving image of Dylan)

...lan, the family man, with Caitlin, Aeronwy, ...lm and dog Mably

Dylan at play at Vernon Watkins's house, the Garth, in Gower in 1951: (from left, adults) Dylan, Caitlin, Fred Janes, Gwen Watkins (seated), Ethel Ross

Dylan the genial
companion

Dylan the consummate
professional showman

Dylan's Florentine contacts did come up with a suitable house, however. Belonging to a local lawyer, the Villa del Beccaro was a substantial mansion, complete with colonnaded swimming-pool, set among pine-trees and terraced vineyards, in the hills five miles south-west of the city. Possibly because the place had served as the German army headquarters during the war, the rent was a manageable £25 for two and a half months until the end of July. Although Dylan liked the setting, he did not find it conducive to work. The children made such a din round the pool all day that he was forced to take a room in a peasant's cottage on the estate. He claimed he was writing a long poem, 'In Country Sleep', but in letters to friends he indicated his tortuously slow progress. He also told David Higham he hoped to finish a radio play, possibly Under Milk Wood, though nothing more was heard about it on this trip.

Much as Dylan talked up Tuscany and its food in letters to his parents and to Margaret Taylor, it was clear, as the summer became hotter, that he was not enjoying himself. His creative spark was missing. Often he took a horse and trap to nearby Scandicci and then caught a tram into Florence, where he sat disconsolately in the well-known Café Giubbe Rosse, sheltering behind what local poet Mario Luzi called a 'small forest of bottles'.

Florentine writers and artists tended to speak French, so they found conversation with him difficult. If they invited him to dinner, he fell asleep during the meal. When he reciprocated and asked them to the Villa del Beccaro, he felt an obligation to amuse them: 'I have to stand on my head, fall in the pool, crack nuts with my teeth, and Tarzan in the cypresses.' By then he was fed up with Italian 'intellectuals', describing them as 'rarefied and damp: they do not write much but oh how they edit! They live with their mothers, ride motor-scooters and translate Apollinaire.' Dylan had little of Spender's aptitude for the fierce if finely tuned cultural diplomacy of the period. Having been stifled under Mussolini, these literati were keen for outside contacts, but equally they realised their biddable position in the ideological struggle between Communism and liberalism. With his British Council contacts, Dylan seemed to offer a possible entrée into a world of artistic slush funds or, at the very least, invitations to prestigious conferences abroad. But he refused to play that game.

He did notice his wife was learning Italian, but did not understand the significance there either. Not only was she thoroughly at ease in a sexually charged Latin culture which valued buxom golden-haired women – having her bottom regularly pinched was the least of her worries – but she relished the tables being turned. For once she did not have to play the retiring wife while Dylan basked in the limelight. Rather the opposite: she was the centre of attention, while he was a Welsh nobody, all the more isolated by his inability to speak the language.

Despite Brigit's presence, there were rows. On one occasion, he wrote Caitlin a rambling, maudlin letter from the Giubbe Rosse. It suggests he may have physically assaulted her, perhaps burning her arm with a cigarette. He admitted he felt so guilty that he had expunged the details from his account. 'There is shame, and disgrace, and grief, and despair, but there is only love about which I know nothing except that what I feel for you must be love because, to me, it is religion, and faith, and the world. I love you, Caitlin. I think you are holy. Perhaps that is why I am bad to you.'

His homesickness tended to abate when the postwoman appeared at the door with letters from England, particularly those from Margaret Taylor. She had been with her husband in Yugoslavia, making his life a misery by constantly saying how much she would have preferred being in Italy with the Thomases. Now back in Oxford, she sent Dylan welcome reminders of the life he was missing – light novels, magazines, and British newspapers which he relished for their crosswords and cricket scores. Margaret's books were invariably published by her friend Graham Greene at Eyre & Spottiswoode, among them a seedy sub-Greene thriller, *Deadlier than the Male* by 'Ambrose Grant', otherwise known as James Handley Chase. Dylan pronounced it 'very good' but not as good as Patrick Hamilton. To buoy his spirits more, he twiddled the knobs on a wireless set and picked up his friend John Arlott commentating on a test match at Trent Bridge.

He was relieved when Margaret picked up on his none-too-subtle requests for assistance in finding a place where his family could live on their return to England. 'I am domestic as a slipper,' he claimed. 'I want somewhere of my own, I'm old enough now, I want a house to shout, sleep and work in. Please help, though I deserve nothing.' She reported back that she had discovered the grandly named Manor House at South Leigh, a village in the countryside near Witney, some twenty minutes by train from Oxford. Having come into some money following her mother's death, she proposed to buy and rent it to Dylan for a pound a week. (Her husband Alan claimed he paid for it as a way of getting Dylan off his back. It is clear, however, that she was the purchaser.) With his mind anywhere but on his immediate work, Dylan wondered how he could furnish it, and where he could send his children to school. Once again, Margaret came to his aid, offering to use her patronage to obtain Llewelyn a place at Magdalen College School, founded in 1480 and alma mater of William Tyndale, Richard Hooker and Thomas

Hobbes. As so often, Dylan had ambivalent reasons for wanting to send his son to a fee-paying boarding establishment he could ill afford. As the son of a schoolmaster, he knew the value of giving Llewelyn the best possible education. At the same time, not wanting an extra child under his feet, he convinced himself that a further period away from home would be good for Llewelyn's and everyone's well-being.

By mid-June it had become so hot that Dylan, sweating profusely, could only work for two hours a day. When he went into Florence, the heat was 'like a live animal you fight against in the streets'. Even the children wilted, becoming restless and bad-tempered. He had been hoping for the distraction of visits from the McAlpines and from John Davenport. When for various reasons none of them could make it, he was disappointed.

In July he began to think of his journey home to England. But a new problem arose when he realised he had not booked his train tickets and was down to his last £10. Having tried unsuccessfully to borrow £100 off the British Council, he begged Margaret Taylor to send him £5 (in single pound notes – nothing else was negotiable) and, of course, she did. He subsequently found he could pay for his tickets from England. But no railway passage was available until mid-August. So, having acquired extra funds through an illegal exchange with an Italian who was coming to London, he decided to take his family to Elba for the fortnight between the end of the lease on his villa and his trip home. (Three years later the Italian was still politely enquiring if he could bank the two undated English cheques Dylan had given him for £175, and his debtor was skilfully eluding him.)

Best known as the place of Napoleon's exile in 1814–15, Elba was a starkly beautiful island in the Mediterranean, south of Livorno. Yet to be discovered by tourists, it was recommended by Luigi Berti, one of the Florence-based intellectuals who originally came from there. Berti, who made his living as an editor and translator, was taking his summer holiday with his family at Rio Marina on Elba's east coast, and suggested the Thomases might like it too. Professionally Dylan had little time for Berti: he was scornful that a man who had rendered Henry James and Virginia Woolf into Italian could say, 'In Elba oo veel lak der skool di fishdog', apparently a reference to schools of dogfish. But he was happy to have someone he knew close at hand.

To his surprise, Dylan loved Rio Marina, a small unostentatious town where the only occupations were fishing and working in the iron mines. The latter had been exploited since Etruscan times, leaving a mottled grey-blue landscape, and adding to the general air of pagan antiquity. During the day, when cold beer was like 'bottled God', Dylan even ventured into the sea, where he would lie in the shallows, smoking a cigarette, and reading the *New Statesman*. In the evenings he drank cheap potent brandy with the Marxist mayor. The combination of pre-Christian culture and Communism appealed to him: 'Communism in Italy is natural, national, indigenous, independent.' It reminded him of the best aspects of Wales. In his enthusiasm he failed to notice that his wife was flirting (and she later claimed sleeping) with their hotel-keeper.

By the time Dylan began his journey home, he had been away for four months. In his luggage he carried just one work to show for his labours – the first draft of his long unsatisfactory poem 'In Country Sleep'. Reflecting his difficulties not just in writing but in communicating with Italians, this work retreated from his recent moves towards simplicity of vocabulary, prosody and meaning. It assembled a mass of religious, fairy tale and rural images, permitting a number of interpretations, of which two predominate – that he was writing about either his relationship with Aeronwy or, perhaps, the destructive power of jealousy in his marriage with Caitlin. The poem allows for both these, and is also about Dylan's own sense of well-being or, in religious terms, his faith which, in order for him to feel alive, needs to be under assault from some malevolent force – call it the devil, the 'thief' (as in the poem), or, as Dylan put in a late interview, perhaps drink. 'Alcohol is the thief today. But tomorrow he could be fame or success or exaggerated introspection or self-analysis. The thief is anything that robs you of your faith, of your reason for being.' One would be hard pressed to gather that Dylan had worked on these verses in a foreign country. The only hint comes in the suggestion of atomic catastrophe threatening the country idyll. Then, as the last line promises, you shall find 'your faith as deathless as the outcry of the ruled sun'. This last image, implying man's baleful harnessing of the sun's energies, lies in contrast to the benevolent 'lawless sun awaking' five lines earlier. When the clowning in the Villa del Beccaro stopped, the shadow of Hiroshima was one of the few subjects Dylan and his Italian literary acquaintances could agree on.

SIXTEEN

LONGING FOR HOME

The symbolism is inescapable: no sooner had Dylan returned to England than he broke his right arm – the one he used to write. He had arranged to stay with the McAlpines in London before going on to Oxfordshire. But they were away and, in his attempt to gain access through a window, he slipped and injured himself. This was not the first or last time he fractured a limb, a tendency which ran in his family. Ironically, he told Philip Lindsay in outraged tones that he had been sober at the time. If so, noted his old scriptwriting colleague, it was a malicious act of the gods, since Dylan had 'probably fallen down more times unhurt than any man in London'. Nevertheless alcohol consumption was bound to have affected his spatial sense and, because of related poor diet, weakened his bones.

Belying its grand name, the Manor House at South Leigh was a damp, ungainly Edwardian edifice, set in a low-lying area, next to a farm. It had neither electricity nor bathroom, and made do with an outside lavatory. Most of the mains water was drawn off by a cattle drinking trough, halfway up the drive. The inside was soon dominated by Caitlin's distinctive decorative style, which relied on pictures and photographs randomly torn from magazines. The kitchen tended to be tidier, with the children's clothes hanging in front of the stove. By the light of the oil lamp, it could look quite homely.

Unspoiled and independent in spirit, the village was part of the estate of Michael Mason, a local landowner who, as an author, had befriended Rudyard Kipling and, as an explorer and spy, had served as a model for his one-time colleague Ian Fleming's fictional James Bond. Mason took little interest in this part of his property. Perhaps for this reason, South Leigh had a reputation in the wider county for the cantankerousness of its inhabitants. Somehow it enjoyed a quaint sort of local democracy, presided over by Albert Hopkins, owner of the pub, the Mason's Arms, and by Bill Mitchell, the station master who was always happy to keep the Oxford train waiting for a minute or two if he saw Dylan puffing up the road hoping to catch it.

In a cottage at the opposite end of the village from the Thomases lived Cordelia Sewell, a sprightly woman in her late thirties with a liking for the outdoor life. She was vaguely aware of the new residents, but did not meet them until around Christmas when Mrs Hopkins at the pub suggested she might find them congenial. When, one evening, she plucked up the courage to knock on their door and introduce herself, she found a party going on. A flushed Caitlin was dancing round the kitchen table, with a flower in her hair and another at the bosom of her velvet dress. People were making sandwiches and discussing a tea party, for which they eventually departed at around ten o'clock in the evening.

Caitlin showed no interest in learning that Cordelia had been to the Slade School of Art, knew her sister Nicolette and had even stayed at Blashford. But she did recognise a fellow soul whom she adopted as the latest in a line of 'best friends' – the qualifications being that they should drink, smoke, care little for anyone else's opinion and, above all, be good company. Granddaughter of the formidable Roman Catholic literary couple Alice and Wilfred Meynell, Cordelia and her two daughters had been parked in South Leigh during the war, after the breakdown of her second marriage. Within a week, she was looking after the Thomases' black cat, Satan, and, soon after, Dylan and Caitlin came round, complaining that they itched and asking if they could have a bath. Although they spent a long time, they never again availed themselves of this facility. Caitlin said she did not like Cordelia's bath-mat and thereafter performed her ablutions in the Mason's Arms.

Apart from drinking, their main point of contact was children. Llewelyn, who had been parked for so long at his grandmother's that he scarcely knew what it meant to live at home, struck up a friendship with Cordelia's younger daughter Nicola, who was the same age. The Thomases would drop him off at the Sewell house before going to the pub at night. 'Bring him back when you're sick of him,' shouted Caitlin, while Dylan matched her for insouciance: 'They're in bed already wearing each other's vests.'

In an unpublished memoir, Cordelia recorded how, when her new friends took to rolling their own cigarettes, Dylan admitted this was another of his Bohemian poses, in the way he coughed, produced a little machine, and chuckled, 'I use this and pretend . . .' The rest of his statement was lost, a regular occurrence with Dylan who seemed to mumble. Cordelia so often had to ask, 'What?' that she mentioned this to Caitlin, adding that she was surprised because his broadcasts were so clear. Dylan's wife answered, with a note of triumph, 'Not heard a bloody word for years.'

Cordelia's tales of Dylan's domestic ineptitude and Caitlin's heroic perseverance are often overlaid with a touch of macabre surrealism. In one, Dylan was failing to make a pot of tea in the kitchen and shouting for his wife, who was in the garden cutting grass with a long gleaming scythe. 'Cait's just had it sharpened,' observed Dylan. 'She cycled across Magdalen Bridge with it over her shoulder.'

Initially, at least, he warmed to South Leigh's rural anarchy. He honed his skills at shove-halfpenny at the Mason's Arms. If he needed to be ferried somewhere urgently, he could call on Bill Green, a bus driver (and son of the owner of the post office), who owned the only car in the village. For more social events, there was the van owned by Cordelia's friends the Colgroves who lived in Stanton Harcourt. Cordelia remembered an outing in this van with some other local people and Dylan laughing: 'Oh what a treat for Hitler! We'd be the first lot for the gas-pipe. Peasants, Communists, gypsies and intellectuals. Not much room for us in Russia either. A lot of layabouts living on other people.'

One of South Leigh's attractions was its proximity to Oxford, a twenty-minute journey on an old-fashioned two-carriage steam train. Dylan soon resumed his place at the bar of one of the city pubs – usually the Turf or the George but, occasionally, now he lived in that direction, the Perch or the Trout on the river to the north-west. New friends included Enid Starkie, a vivid Irishwoman who taught French literature at Somerville, and Dan Davin, a New Zealander working for the Oxford University Press. Dylan became excited when Starkie, a Rimbaud expert who had known Francis Macnamara in Dublin, told him she had discovered that the French poet had plucked some of his imagery from an eighteenth-century hermetic dictionary. Adamant that this was not cheating, Dylan said he wished he could lay his hands on something similar. However Starkie could never work out how much he had read of Rimbaud. He simply seemed to like the idea of 'this dissolute character who went into every sort of experience'. Starkie felt that Dylan himself was not 'a man of great education', knowing nothing of life outside Britain, nothing of history and nothing of art. But she loved his conversation and his voice. 'I wouldn't have minded if Dylan Thomas had read the telephone directory.'

After a good war on General Freyberg's staff, Davin had found himself full-time employment in publishing. Early in their friendship, he invited Dylan home to meet his wife and daughter. As a result, Dylan promised to bring Caitlin to tea the next day. But she rang shortly before the agreed hour to say that Dylan had passed out and they could not come. Davin was left with a suspicion 'that she might not be willing to meet any more of Dylan's pub friends'. He may have been closer to the truth in his observations of Caitlin when he got to know her. He noted how, when they were out drinking, she used to look on with an anger amounting to hate as Dylan regaled his Oxford friends with his stories. Her antipathy was directed at her husband as much as at the rest of the company. Davin was well aware of her artistic aspirations and could see that, once again, she resented having to play second fiddle. He also could sense her disdain for bourgeois literati with indentured posts at the university, as they bought Dylan's drinks and encouraged him to make a fool of himself, 'spend[ing] on us the strength and energy he should have reserved for himself, his poetry and her'.

In the background hovered Margaret Taylor. She had promised her husband that she would pull back once she had established Dylan in South Leigh. But, for various reasons, she found this impossible. Dylan, after all, was an artist who needed succouring. When she discovered that his financial affairs were in chaos, she saw to it, with the help of Higham, that he consulted an accountant, Leslie Andrews, in Sussex. The upshot was not as bad as feared: Dylan's total tax liability to the Inland Revenue up to April 1948 worked out at just £85, or slightly under £2,000 in 2003 prices.

But, as Cordelia Sewell could see, Margaret was also 'besotted, ill, daft, sick with love' for Dylan. This made matters difficult for Caitlin who, on a personal level, liked the don's wife, as she too was a mother with young children. She was even prepared to humour her for the sake of her husband's career and financial security. However, a letter from Margaret to Dylan which trilled, 'To sleep with you would be like sleeping with a god', went too far, even if Caitlin realised that, between the lines, this meant they had not been to bed together. When, by way of apology, Margaret sent her a pink taffeta petticoat, Caitlin cut it up and returned it.

Another time, Margaret suggested to Dylan that they should elope and arranged to meet him at Paddington station. Dylan did not go, and showed his cruel streak in his wry amusement at the thought of 'maudlin Magdalen Maggie' waiting there, suitcase in hand. 'She's desperate for me to poke her,' he told Francis King, an undergraduate at Balliol, 'but who wants to poke a bowl of cold porridge?' There was an added frisson in the idea of an Oxford don's wife fawning over him. By denying her, he gave himself a certain power in the relationship. The underlying psychology was complex: on the one hand, with his high opinion of his creative talents, he believed such adulation was due him as a poet; on the other, his shaky sense of personal esteem meant he thought that anyone who made a fuss of him was a fool and to be treated with disdain. In the background were the residual effects of his relationship with his mother whose indulgence had only brought his contempt.

In February 1948 Margaret was on hand to drive the Thomases to

Aldbourne, near Marlborough in Wiltshire. This was the domain of James Bomford, an art-loving millionaire who, during the war had served with Mervyn Levy in the Royal Army Educational Corps. Levy was living and teaching nearby, while Jankel Alder, another painter friend of Dylan, had a cottage in the grounds of Bomford's large estate. On Saturday nights the hedonistic Bomford used to hold lavish parties, to which he invited artists, writers and plenty of girls, such as Diana Fluck, a buxom blonde from the county's most industrialised town of Swindon, soon to become a famous Rank starlet under her screen name Diana Dors.

Also resident in Aldbourne was the writer Gerald Brenan, one of Dylan's drinking companions when he first arrived in London in the mid-1930s. On this trip, it emerged that Brenan had also known Caitlin around this period. When, during a pub crawl, he drunkenly tried to kiss her, she bit his lip. According to his biographer, Jonathan Gathorne-Hardy, Brenan had last met her in Churriana in Southern Spain in 1935. If true, this indicates Caitlin travelled well beyond Paris on her continental trip that year. It also suggests that Brenan had had a sexual relationship with her, which he expected to revive. In his inebriated state, Dylan seemed not to worry: leaving Brenan's house one night after the pubs had closed, he passed four large metal dustbins glistening in the moonlight. Throwing up his hands in mock terror, he cried, 'Ali Baba! Ali Baba!'

On his return to South Leigh, Dylan penned an introduction to the catalogue for a forthcoming exhibition of Levy's paintings in Swindon. His clichéd references to his old friend – 'Red chalk glows in his drawings because his passion for the human figure is glowing. His line is a line of love.' – suggest that, unusually for his published output, he had been drinking, or at least was not taking the task very seriously.

Dylan's mind may simply have been elsewhere. For, in time-honoured family fashion, his mother had slipped in wintry Carmarthenshire and broken her thigh. On at least two occasions, he dashed to visit her in Carmarthen Hospital. Luckily, his sister Nancy was back in England after spending most of the war in India. She had married an army officer, Gordon Summersby, whose first wife Kay had been American General Dwight D. Eisenhower's driver and mistress. As an army driver herself, Nancy was one of six women who accompanied British forces into stricken Singapore following the Japanese surrender in 1945. Her husband had briefly stayed on in India, working for IBM. But, well before independence in August 1947, he and Nancy returned to England, where he bought a trawler and established an up-market fishing business in the north Devon port of Brixham. From there she came to Blaencwm to look after her father, who was more glum than usual, partly because his brother Arthur had died the previous autumn and partly because he was suffering from a painful attack of angina. As a result of a family conference, Nancy agreed to have D.J. live with her in Brixham, while Dylan took home his parents' boisterous mongrel dog, Mably, who would otherwise have been destroyed.

Having been away, he managed to make his mother's misfortune the excuse for, first, not producing an article on London for British *Vogue* and, then, not keeping a long-standing engagement at a teachers' training college in Wrexham. The former was understandable: he had little stomach for recycling material from his unpublished book on London's streets. The latter was unforgivable, as it was brokered by Bert Trick, who was working in Wrexham for the Inland Revenue. Even the indulgent Trick was annoyed with his old friend.

When his mother was well enough, he arranged to rent Cordelia Sewell's cottage in South Leigh as a summer convalescent home for his parents. Florrie arrived in late April and was soon complaining about Dylan's friends. D.J. joined her a few days later, coming in an ambulance because his heart was still playing up. As usual when his parents were around, Dylan put on his most respectable Cwmdonkin Drive behaviour, while Caitlin dutifully scurried round with her home help Mary, trying to look after two households at different ends of the village.

The Saturday after his mother arrived, Dylan managed to escape to Oxford for a rendezvous with Margaret Taylor at the George. He had arranged to meet Bob Pocock and 'an actor friend of his', have a few pints, and saunter over to the Parks to watch some cricket in the afternoon. After three hours in the pub, someone remembered the game. When Dylan suggested taking some additional drink, Margaret – 'stupid bitch', commented Pocock – interpreted this to mean a bottle of rum. They saw ten minutes of the game, before opting to bowl at some undergraduates in the nets who were frightened away by their oafish drunken antics. Dylan then suggested opening the bottle of rum. Pocock, who had been going through a divorce, got paralytically drunk and had to be driven back to the Fleece Hotel in Witney where three months earlier Dylan, in his role as a celebrity, had introduced a roving BBC programme, 'Country Magazine', which featured the nearby Windrush valley. The planned Saturday evening's entertainment – a pub crawl with Cordelia and her friends the Colgroves in their van – had to be postponed.

The actor was almost certainly Harry Locke, whom Dylan had met at a party at the McAlpines'. Bill and his wife Helen enjoyed being surrounded by artistic, particularly theatrical, people. During the summer, when Dylan was up in town, he attended a reception at the House of Commons for the American boxer Joe Louis. The McAlpines turned up with the all-black cast of *Anna Lucasta*, an American play which was running in the West End. Earlier Dylan had 'declared drunken devotion' to Louis's former girlfriend, the singer Lena Horne. On another occasion he cherished the image of Helen singing Irish ballads to a group of West Indians. Locke was an Acton-born actor with regular slots on radio series such as the 'Will Hay Show' and 'Workers' Playtime'. He specialised in telling shaggy dog stories of the kind Dylan loved. At their first meeting, Locke liked to say, Dylan laughed so much he was sick. Locke came to South Leigh, where he recalled Dylan sitting at the end of the ailing D.J.'s bed feeding him bottles of beer. He also met Cordelia and they started an unlikely romance which was to result in her getting pregnant and marrying Locke. (The early blossoming of this relationship had been the spur to Cordelia vacating her house.)

Having her parents-in-law so close, Caitlin was soon at her wits' end, complaining to her sister Brigit not only about their surliness but also about the drudgery of her own work on behalf of five people – two very young, two very old and, always, 'Useless Eustace Dylan' (the thought of their dependency terrified her). Philip Lindsay heard from a friend: 'There is hell in the place, poor Caith [sic] with two kids being such a slave to the tyranny of the aged couple that she was unable to slip out even for one drink. Under such circumstances, having to support a wife, two aged parents and two children, the poor bastard will have no time for poetry. He was luckier when he was poor, for then at least he was free.'

Matters were not improved when the Thomas family was stricken with measles in June. Dylan claimed he had 'to cook and char', but the reality was conveyed in Caitlin's complaint to Mary Keene about the ailing older Thomases on her doorstep, together with hordes of screaming children and Dylan, being unusually anti-social and swearing at everyone in sight. Caitlin was left feeling not just very weak, but self-conscious about her measles spots. Cordelia saw her in the village wearing a typically striking hat, but with her face covered with a half-veil. Another time she witnessed what must have been the nadir in the Thomases' relationship – Caitlin with a bloody, swollen ear, and with her rings missing. But when Cordelia exclaimed involuntarily at this evidence of domestic violence, Caitlin did not want to talk about it.

Partly to convalesce and partly because she could stand it no longer, Caitlin upped with her children to her mother's, whereupon Margaret Taylor insisted on moving in on the pretext of looking after Dylan's parents. The experiment was not a success. Margaret drove D.J. mad with her patronising lectures on art and music. Feeling compromised, Dylan kept out of the way: on the one hand, he could not afford to alienate his generous admirer; on the other, he also bristled at her presence – or so he made out to the absent Caitlin, to whom he duplicitously described his benefactress as 'the bitch'. He had to bite his tongue when Margaret asked if he wanted her to go. Alan Taylor bicycled out to remonstrate with his wife whom he felt was making a fool of herself over Dylan. After angry scenes in the road, she was reduced to tears. In the circumstances, Dylan begged Caitlin to come back quickly because 'SHE will go then'. No doubt he did desire this, but he was torn by conflicting emotions.

These events provided the backdrop to Dylan's efforts to make a living. He wrote little poetry at South Leigh but, as his correspondence shows, he was in demand to give readings, even if he was not always the most enchanting guest. Invited to the Poetry Society in Richmond run by an attractive minor literary hostess, Wrenne Jarman, he arrived an hour late. He apologised profusely, but was clearly drunk. However the audience's annoyance was soon forgotten when he began to read. As they broke into applause at the end, Dylan turned his back and vomited into the fireplace. After another encounter – a dinner throughout which Dylan smoked – Miss Jarman was moved to ask, unrealistically, 'Don't you think the writing of poetry should be limited to gentlemen?'

Such considerations were not so important at the BBC, where he could always find some work. He had survived the critical mauling of his rendition of Satan in Milton's *Paradise Lost*. According to the Corporation's own magazine *The Listener*, Dylan's booming voice had 'swamped Milton, it swamped *Paradise Lost*, it occasionally swamped even the sense, for the louder Dylan Thomas shouts the more his articulation deteriorates, until one fails to hear the words for the noise.' Producer friends stood by him: Roy Campbell, for example, using him to read one of his favourite books *The Autobiography of a Super-Tramp*. In the field of talks, they knew Dylan could be relied on to spout entertainingly on anything from boxing to comic writing – a topic on which he bowed to the Americans, preferring Thurber and Perelman's contemporary social observation over Wodehouse's period charm.

However Dylan's creative energies were still directed less to radio than to films. This was another phenomenon of the times. In the years of post-war austerity, the public looked to the cinema for escape. Particularly in demand was light patriotic entertainment in the vein of the first Ealing comedy, *Hue and Cry*, produced in 1946. Gainsborough's interest in the script of *The Doctor and the Devils* encouraged Dylan to think that, with his documentary scriptwriting background, he could find a well-paid niche in the domestic feature film industry. This ambition received a significant boost in August 1947 when, seeking to save much needed foreign exchange, the Labour government imposed a 75 per cent import duty on foreign (mainly American) films. For a while British studios searched frantically for 'product' – anything that would fill the country's empty screens.

Dylan flirted with two of the leading studios, Ealing and Gainsborough. For Michael Balcon's Ealing, he re-wrote the dialogue for two scripts, *No Room at the Inn*, completed in April 1948, and *Three Weird Sisters*, which he worked on during the summer. These films are often glossed over, but they were interesting developments in Dylan's career. Contrary to prevailing trends, *No Room at the Inn* was a well crafted piece of social realism, about a sluttish woman who runs a home for evacuee children in the village of Market Norton, which could pass for South Leigh or at least Witney. Adapted from a 1945 stage play by Joan Temple, the script shows Dylan developing ideas that interested him, such as the sounds of children playing, the effects of rationing (with the butcher saying, 'Got a nice bit of tripe – under the counter for you, Agg'), and the sunny vicar with his head in the clouds. Dylan wrote the part of a spiv for Harry Locke, the actor's first role in a distinguished screen career.

Three Weird Sisters was another adaptation (from a book by an American mystery writer Charlotte Armstrong). It is the story of three sisters from the Welsh valleys who ask their mean London-based brother to give them part of the family fortune so that they can make good a promise to rebuild their village after it has suffered a pit collapse. When he declines, they attempt, in B-movie thriller style, to kill him and his stuck-up English secretary (and heir) Claire Prentiss. Dylan has fun with names, trying out new ones such as Daddy Waldo and Mrs Probert (later used in *Under Milk Wood*), and introducing those of friends in Mabli Hughes, Sergeant Flower and Beattie (a woman from South Leigh). A minister makes a chapel speech which refers to 'my people' (a nod to Caradoc Evans's book of satirical short stories). According to the script directions, this should be 'funereal, sanctimonious and plangent, and not without the emotional chanting hwyl'. One can see Dylan acting out his personal dilemmas about Wales, as he contrasts the brother Owen Morgan-Vaughan's visceral antipathy to his homeland with the steady human values of the miners in their distress.

Morgan-Vaughan is given a speech with a line often attributed directly to Dylan: 'Land of my Fathers! As far as I'm concerned, my fathers can keep it.' Summoning all the venom of the Welshman in England, this film character adds, 'You can tell he's a Welshman by the lilt in his voice. Huh, little back-biting hypocrites, all gab and whine! Black beetles with tenor voices and a sense of sin like a crippled hump. Cwmglas!

Full of senile morons and vicious dwarfs, old poles of women clacking at you like blowsy hens, self-righteous little humbugs with the hwyl, old men with beards in their noses cackling at you, blue gums and clackers. Oh the mystical Welsh – huh! About as mystical as slugs!'

This obscure speech has been taken to represent the sum of Dylan's attitudes to his country. In fact it was just one of his many ways of looking at Wales. On balance, the coldness and self-interest of London-based Morgan-Vaughan are presented as being much more unattractive than the solid virtues of the indigenous Welsh.

Dylan was not finished with Welsh themes or with Ealing. In July 1948 he was toying with writing a script based on an outline by a Welsh actor friend. Clifford Evans had asked his help in developing a comedy about two Welsh miners on a London spree after winning a productivity competition. Dylan attended several conferences about this project – originally called *A Nightingale is Singing*, later released as *A Run for Your Money*. But Ealing could not match the £1,000 per script which Gainsborough was then prepared to offer him. An added incentive for switching to Gainsborough was that Donald Taylor's old partner, Bunny Keene, had recently moved there as a producer-director, after a couple of lean years making documentaries, including one on Cyprus scripted by Laurie Lee and another on Assam with music by Lizzie Lutyens.

Dylan's work for Gainsborough had started earlier in the spring with an adaptation of Robert Louis Stevenson's *The Bridge of Falesa*, a story about a trader arriving at a copra-producing island in the South Seas, and an incumbent competitor trying to scare him off by playing up the forces of evil in the locality. In some ways, it suggested Carmarthenshire, with its depictions of a closed community, misdirected religion and, not least, the local missionary, a Welsh minister with hwyl. But Dylan's script was not much more than a conventional cinematic rendering of a classic text, albeit one he respected.

With the break-down of negotiations with Ealing over Clifford Evans's outline in July and with another project, *The Forgotten Story*, quietly sidelined, Dylan was able to turn to *Me and My Bike*, an idea he much preferred, touting it to Sydney Box at Gainsborough as 'the first original film operetta'. The story line was slight – about a man who measures his life through the bicycles he has owned and loved – penny-farthings, tandems, tricycles and racing bikes. When he dies, he is greeted by a heavenly chorus of bicycle bells. With the demand for British films, Box was so pleased to have Dylan on board that he put him on contract and gave him his head. 'For me, as a supposedly imaginative writer, it's got wonderful possibilities,' Dylan enthused to Keene about *Me and My Bike*. 'Sydney's carte blanche as to freedom of fancy, non-naturalistic dialogue, song, music, etc is enormously encouraging.' Now he had scope to make the kind of arty film he wanted, Dylan also intended to introduce elements of popular culture and song.

All other work at South Leigh was put on hold, poetry did not get written, as Dylan turned his hands to this remunerative script. Margaret Taylor gave him a gypsy caravan so he could work in the field next to the house, untroubled by his family's demands. Doubtless she felt she was being helpful; completion of the contract would go a long way towards righting Dylan's still precarious finances. But Caitlin was so infuriated that she knocked over her husband's bolt-hole. The single-minded Margaret simply moved it further away.

During the latter half of the year Dylan's Gainsborough film projects tended to crowd in on one another. He was still working on Me and My Bike while completing a revised script of The Bridge of Falesa in October. The following month, having done most of the 'first chunk' of Me and My Bike, he embarked on yet another script for the studio, Rebecca's Daughters. A return to more conventional narrative, this was the dramatic story of the Welshmen who dressed as women to protest against the crippling burden of tolls in the second quarter of the nineteenth century.

In the new year, Dylan moved on to yet another script, a version of Thackeray's Vanity Fair. But none of these projects for Gainsborough was ever put into production. In May 1948 the film import duty had been lifted and, within twelve months, Box's company had folded.

For a short time, while working for Gainsborough, Dylan's bank balance did look more secure. During the 1948 financial year he earned £2,482, against which he claimed business expenses of £612, leaving him with a profit of £1,872, or roughly £43,000 in 2003 prices. Unfairly to Caitlin and his family, who usually suffered in penury, Dylan managed to fritter away large proportions of his earnings on 'treats' while in London. Staying with Louis MacNeice in Canonbury in late July, when he was working for both Ealing and Gainsborough, he seemed almost opulent. One morning the two poets indulged themselves by going to Lords, but failed to ascertain that the cricket match they hoped to see had already finished. So they made their way across London to the Oval, stopping en route for lunch at a bar where they drank champagne. When they finally reached the Surrey cricket ground, Dylan 'poured out much curious lore about cricketers' private lives, all of it funny and most of it, I fancy, true'. In the evening they ate Portuguese oysters and, so it appears from a letter from MacNeice to his absent wife Hedli, went to a revue at the London Casino.

Dylan's love of cricket fascinated Philip Lindsay. Noting that his friend 'worships' the game, he wondered if this went with being a poet. He did not know any artists who liked cricket, but felt that 'something in the grace, the poise, the rhythm of the batsman probably appeals to the poet'. With the Australians touring in 1948, Lindsay hoped to see them at Lords with Dylan. When this did not happen, he told Dylan he put himself to sleep by imagining himself as the great Australian batsman Donald Bradman. Dylan replied that he often saw himself as a top English bowler. Lindsay thought of writing a piece about an imaginary encounter between their dream selves.

In truth, despite moments of extravagance, Dylan was still leading a perilously hand-to-mouth existence, though his liquidity had improved. In August he was forced to turn down a request for a loan from his friend John Davenport, who himself had fallen on hard times. He quoted a mountain of calls on his finances, from the Italian who still had not been paid for his trip to Elba, through a looming repayment he needed to make to Margaret Taylor, to Caitlin's desire for a new pressure cooker and a nightgown. Yet at the same time he was applying to join an expensive London club, the Savage, which catered for writers and artists. He was already an unlikely member of the National Liberal Club, a traditional, rather stuffy watering hole for politically minded London Welshmen following in the tradition of Lloyd George. But Dylan soon realised this was the wrong place for him. He called it the National Lavatory Club, after Lord Birkenhead, who used to call there regularly for a pee. When the hall porter challenged the Conservative politician, reminding him that this was a gentleman's club, Birkenhead replied, 'Oh is it that as well?' Dylan felt much the same and now, after just over a year at the National Liberal, he was applying to the Savage.

In early September Dylan travelled alone to Edinburgh where, as part of the newly established Festival, he gave a short talk on Hugh MacDiarmid to Scottish PEN. While there, he bumped into Kenneth Tynan, who was just starting a career as a theatre critic after leaving Oxford in the summer. Short of money and with a girl friend in tow, the flamboyant Tynan asked for a loan, and Dylan, unusually, was able to oblige. Dylan had many young friends such as Tynan at Oxford. Over the years he had become a familiar figure to undergraduates such as Alan Brien, at Jesus College, who remembered him in the Cornmarket on Saturday afternoons, 'staggering along loaded down with string bags, behind his striding, empty-handed Viking Irish wife – the very seaside postcard of a booze-flushed, snub-nosed, ox-eyed, hen-pecked slave husband, aching to slide off into a pub and lose wife, shopping and consciousness'.

Those students who knew Dylan better often found him friendly and supportive, imparting his knowledge in the pubs like a worldly tutor they might have liked. In the George, he discussed the Mistletoe Bough legend with Paul Redgrave, from St Catherine's College. Recently featured in an Alfred Hitchcock film *Rope*, this was the story of a bride who became trapped in a wooden chest while playing a game of hide and seek and was only found as a skeleton ten years later. Dylan said that it could be located at only three places in Britain, one of which was Minster Lovell, five miles from South Leigh. When Redgrave mentioned another Gothic tale about the village, which was also close to where he lived, Dylan proposed a visit by bicycle. When Redgrave arrived at the Manor House at ten o'clock the following morning, he found Caitlin peeling potatoes and Dylan still in bed. She offered him a drink from a murky bottle which looked like cough mixture but which she said was rum and cider. She knew nothing of Dylan's arrangement and, when told, remarked in a knowing tone that it was Thursday, market day in Witney, when the pubs were open all day.

Dylan emerged in an oversized fisherman's jumper which accentuated the whiteness of his legs. His breakfast consisted of two bottles of beer which were despatched to a four-foot mountain of empties at the door. After a perilous cycle ride, he and Redgrave were in Witney by eleven. Having drunk in every pub, they continued to Minster Lovell, where Dylan refused to eat lunch in another hostelry, exclaiming, 'Eating is the death of good drinking.' He would not allow the student to pay, saying he was a 'film mogul' earning £60 a week. At closing time, he leered at the barmaid and said slowly, 'How would you like to fornicate with an oval Welshman.'

After an unsuccessful attempt to locate the Mistletoe Bough, they ended back at Redgrave's cottage at Church Hanborough, where Dylan was intrigued to learn of a poltergeist in the local church. They agreed to go there later that evening and read from John Donne's sermons. Clutching a candle, Dylan mounted the pulpit and began to read 'Doth not man die even in his birth?' Realising this was a Dylanesque theme, Redgrave took a copy of *Deaths and Entrances* from his pocket and asked Dylan to read 'Fern Hill'. Having laid the poltergeist to rest, they proceeded to another pub in Eynsham. When closing time was called at ten p.m., Dylan said he was 'buggered' if he was going to ride home. He said there was a train due at half past the hour and he would take it. Dylan turned out to be the only passenger: as he was leaving, he lowered the window and shouted, 'Missed the Mistletoe Bough but caught the bloody Ghost Train! See you in the George.'

Such exuberance appealed to most Oxford undergraduates. Michael Hamburger, who had returned to Christ Church after war service and was feeling out of place, recalled seeing Dylan with Margaret Taylor in White's, off St Aldate's. For him, Dylan's presence brought the club to life. Although he had a sense of someone drinking himself to death, he felt he was at least experiencing something real: an authentic Soho Bohemian in the boring world of student poseurs.

But poetic fashions were changing. The neo-romanticism of the war years, which Dylan had tried to avoid, was giving way to a simpler conservatism, which would later be identified with the Movement. Some undergraduates now regarded Dylan more as an entertainer than a great poet. 'Our taste ran to austerity,' noted Alan Brien retrospectively, 'to spare, taut, tight-lipped verse slimmed of fat, slimmed of ornament, music and magic terms of abuse. What we wanted was the sound of a mind at work, a mind in battledress. Dylan's mind wore a ceremonial uniform of his own design, self-indulgent, and self-displaying, he was the Boy's Own Poet.'

Away from the university Dylan still had legions of admirers and imitators, including the unlikely figure of Harold Pinter, whose poetry was steeped in his imagery. Another fan was Muriel Spark, editor of the *Poetry Review* (the journal of the Poetry Society), who convinced the poet Derek Stanford of Dylan's greatness by reading him 'Fern Hill'.

But Philip Larkin, who had recently started his first job as Assistant Librarian at the University College of Leicester, was one poet who had changed his mind. Encouraged by his friend Kingsley Amis who could not stand 'that crazy Welch fellow Thomas', Larkin observed, 'I think a man ought to use good words to make what he means *impressive*: Dylan Thos. just makes you wonder what he means, *very hard*.' He noted Dylan's use of the words 'immortal hospital' in 'Holy Spring' in *Deaths and Entrances*. 'Now that is a phrase that makes me feel suddenly a sort of *reverent apprehension*, only I don't know what it means. Can't the FOOL see that if I could see what it means, I should admire it 2*ce* as much.'

Unconcerned with academic niceties, Tynan appreciated Dylan for his swagger and celebrity status. Once seeing Dylan swaying drunkenly down Oxford High Street, he asked if he could help. 'Get me some more bloody crème-de-menthe, you fucking idiot,' Dylan screamed. Recognising a fellow romantic soul, Tynan took him back to his rooms in St John Street. He was astute enough to remark at the time that Dylan was 'a surly little pug, but a master of pastiche and invective. Thinks himself the biggest and best phoney of all time, and may be right.'

For over a dozen years, Dylan had brilliantly carried off the role of a drunken Welshman adrift in the competitive world of Anglo-Saxon letters. But now he was tired; he could recognise he was out of sympathy with trends in poetry; and he was thinking of going home.

His parents' ailments provided a spur, but there were other reasons for his wanting to be back in Wales. At South Leigh he had been working on a play about a Welsh village, which had been gestating in his imagination since he first mentioned it to Bert Trick in 1933. His stay in Elba had stimulated him. Rio Marina reminded him of Wales, and some of the phrases he used in letters from there – such as 'fishers', 'webfooted waterboys' and 'sunblack' – were echoed on the first page of his manuscript of what came to be known as Under Milk Wood.

During 1947 he discussed the idea with Philip Burton, the BBC producer of 'Return Journey'. In March 1948 he referred to it in a letter to John Ormond at Picture Post: 'A radio play I am writing has Laugharne, though not by name, as its setting.' Ormond, a younger poet from Swansea, had been responsible for the magazine's earlier feature about poets at the BBC. On this occasion Dylan was seeking a commission from Picture Post about Laugharne. He promised not only details of the town's quaint history, but also no repetition of his 'disastrous' Puck Fair visit, when the magazine had stumped up expenses and he had failed to deliver. Mindful of that precedent, Picture Post decided not to throw good money after bad.

Dylan went to Laugharne nevertheless, and once more fell in love with the town. He was 'tired of living among strangers in a dark and savage country whose customs and tribal rites I shall never understand, breathing in alien air, hearing, everywhere, the snobcalls, the prigchants, the mating cries, the tom-toms of a curious, and maybe cannibal, race'. Over the summer, as he became disenchanted with Oxfordshire, the idea of moving back to Wales took hold. Caitlin could recognise the element of fantasy: Dylan thought he only needed to return to Laugharne and all would be right, exactly as it had been before the war. She also understood that he was filled with hiraeth, a Welshman's deep longing for home. This accounted for the many references to Wales in his work, not just in his radio play about Laugharne, but also in his filmscripts. He used them to air the arguments for and against living in Wales, once so oppressive to him but now increasingly beguiling.

Sometimes he veered one way, sometimes the other. His visit to Edinburgh to address Scottish PEN about Hugh MacDiarmid in September freed him to speak more candidly than usual: 'I am a Welshman who does not live in his own country, mainly because he still wants to eat and drink, be rigged and roofed, and no Welsh writer can hunt his bread and butter in Wales unless he pulls his forelock to the Western Mail, Bethesda on Sunday, and enters public houses by the back door, and reads Caradoc Evans only when alone, and by candlelight.' Perhaps the

Scotch whisky had begun to talk as he continued, 'Regarded in England as a Welshman (and a waterer of England's milk), and in Wales as an Englishman, I am too unnational to be here at all. I should be living in a small private leper house in Hereford or Shropshire, one foot in Wales and my vowels in England.' Although he did not mention returning to Wales, the sub-text was that he coveted MacDiarmid's ability to make a living and be respected in his home country of Scotland.

Having identified Gosport House, on the hill near where he had first lived at Eros Cottage, as a possible future home in Laugharne, he encouraged the ever-willing Margaret Taylor to negotiate with the owner on his behalf. When no deal could be struck, he tried a different tack. Knowing that Richard Hughes no longer wanted to live at Castle House, he wrote to him at the end of September, asking if he might take over the lease. (Coincidentally Hughes had just taken over from him as a scriptwriter on *A Run for your Money*.) Dylan's letter was followed a week later by another from Margaret Taylor who suggested that Castle House had become, for Dylan, a symbol of personal salvation. Since Hughes was tied up with films, his wife Frances replied to both Dylan and Margaret saying that the house was totally impracticable. Undeterred Dylan sent Margaret to Laugharne again to see if she could salvage something. Apologising to Frances that he too had been prevented from coming by film work, he said that in Laugharne he could 'work well. Here I am too near London.' But Mrs Starke, the ultimate owner of Castle House, knew Dylan well enough to be wary, and the move to Wales stalled.

When his former Strand colleague John Banting wrote from Dublin in November proposing a film about Ireland, Dylan replied he would love nothing better than to 'dawdle and doodle' through the countryside. However he feared his contract with Sydney Box and Gainsborough did not allow him to be hired by any other film company but 'that Rank growth'. He explained that at Gainsborough he worked under Bunny Keene and occasionally made appearances at 'inarticulate conferences'. But there was no mention of Wales, and otherwise only sadness in his catalogue of mutual friends in the film business whom he no longer saw. Donald Taylor had produced a 'big, bad' feature, 'Perrin & Trail' and had returned to the Crown Film Unit. Fanya Fisher was ill in hospital and he was annoyed with himself for failing to see her when in London. 'The 2 feature films I've so far written have had viperish notices. The Gargoyle is drabber, and empty of all except touts in well-fed suitings. The old pubs are fuller but empty of all friends.' If he ever did manage to come to Dublin, he asked Banting plaintively, 'can you put me up on bed, couch, or blonde?'

The same deflated mood was apparent in Dylan's letter to Vernon Watkins the following week. 'Nothing happens to me. I go to London and bluster, come back and sigh, do a little scriptwriting, look at an unfinished poem, go out on my bicycle in the fog, go to London & bluster.' After six months in South Leigh, his mother was no better and, although his father had improved, the old man was 'naggier' than ever. Since Cordelia was back in the village, his parents had had to move into the Manor House, leaving Caitlin to apologise to Mary Keene that, with three generations of Thomases under her roof, there was no further room in the house and her friend could sadly not come to visit. What was more, Caitlin's unmarried sister Brigit was pregnant with her second child. Having no money, she and her mother in Ringwood appealed unavailingly to Dylan, the supposed film mogul, for assistance.

As an act of solidarity, as much as anything else, Bill and Helen McAlpine took a cottage in South Leigh at the end of November. Bill had been searching, without success, for a job in newspapers, but his wife still had funds and he wanted to be closer to his friend Harry Locke who was now living with Cordelia. It must have been very soon afterwards that Caitlin discovered that she too was pregnant. This at least gave Dylan one more reason for going to Wales. He celebrated by again breaking his arm, the upshot of a pre-Christmas shopping trip with Bill to Witney. They went by bicycle and it was not so coincidentally 'market day'. On their return journey Dylan was knocked over by a lorry and his main purchase of assorted nuts spilled onto the road, leading to a variety of cracks about him losing or breaking his nuts. When Cordelia went to the Manor House to inform Caitlin her husband had been taken to hospital, she found her sitting happily, reading a Penguin and listening to Radio Luxembourg. 'Showing off as usual,' Caitlin spat out dismissively. 'Always has to be the centre of the stage. Dylan. Dylan. Dylan ... And what have I got? Another bloody baby to feed and change and prop up.' On her way home, Cordelia passed the Mason's Arms, where she found Dylan already ensconced, his presence advertised by the ambulance outside.

Dylan's injury gave him an excuse to delay various projects. But for all his skiving, he was still in demand professionally. The new year brought a couple of attractive offers from the BBC – an adaptation of William Wycherley's bawdy Restoration comedy The Plain-Dealer, and a new version of Ibsen's verse drama Peer Gynt for BBC television. Both ideas interested Dylan, even though the lead time for the Ibsen was just eight weeks and he had to admit ruefully that he had never seen a television drama and wanted to visit a studio to watch one being made.

Before he could do so, Margaret Taylor came up with welcome news.

After weeks of toing and froing, she had found him a place in Laugharne. Determined that he should have what he wanted, she had paid £3,000 for a lease on the Boat House, a six-roomed white cottage perched as if on stilts at the very edge of the river Taf. Dylan was thrilled: this was a place he and Caitlin had once identified as their dream house in Laugharne. What was more Margaret had arranged with Ebie Williams to rent a house on King Street, the main thoroughfare, for D.J. and Florrie. By February 1949 all the paperwork had been completed and Dylan was saying confidently, 'In the Spring, we go to Wales to live in a house on an estuary.'

Before that, he had one more place to go. In March, to his pregnant wife's disgust, he took up an unexpected invitation to visit Czechoslovakia, and so blundered unconvincingly into the international political arena. Over the previous two years Europe's bitter post-1945 divisions had hardened into outright Cold War, with the threat of atomic war ever present. Dylan was not the only person to feel frightened: at the other end of the social spectrum, Nancy Mitford had written to Evelyn Waugh about world events: 'I wake up in the night sometimes in a cold sweat. Thank goodness for having no children, I can take a pill and say goodbye.' Since then, the situation worsened. Hopes of pluralism in Eastern Europe were dashed with the Communist coup which overthrew the democratically elected liberal government in Czechoslovakia in February 1948. Although Marshal Tito's show of anti-Moscow independence in Yugoslavia bucked this trend, the opposing battle lines were drawn more firmly when Washington sped to implement its Marshall Plan for the economic regeneration of Western Europe, establishing the framework which led to the setting up of the North Atlantic Treaty Organisation in 1949, and the Soviet Union responded by preventing road and rail access to Berlin.

With the political tub-thumping came cultural diplomacy. Vast official gatherings of writers and artists (sometimes described as peace conferences) were held, encouraged by the West (with the United States's Central Intelligence Agency increasingly to the fore) in so far as they allowed intellectuals in Communist countries to maintain links with the outside world. Dylan had had a taste of the politicisation of culture in Italy. He also knew plenty of people who had attended such conferences. In August 1948 Alan Taylor had participated in the grandiose Congress of Intellectuals for World Peace in Wroclaw (formerly the German city of Breslau) in Poland. Although sympathetic to Soviet aspirations in Eastern Europe (anything was better than the Germans, he felt), the historian nevertheless angered his hosts by demanding that their attacks on imperialism should be directed towards Russia as much as to America.

Dylan knew many other Communist fellow-travellers. The combination of his political naivety, innate anti-authoritarianism and horror of war made him naturally sympathetic to talk of peace among his left-wing friends. Inevitably, mixing in interlocking circles of broadcasters, artists, film-makers, drunkards and academics, he came across many 1930s-style Communists, such as John Sommerfield, who had fought in Spain, and Jack Lindsay, brother of his former fellow scriptwriter. Dylan told Lindsay around this time, 'If all the party members were like you and John Sommerfield, I'd join up on the spot.'

Linked with these two, trying to ensure Marxism's continuing intellectual respectability, was the Wykehamist poet and journalist Randall Swingler who, inter alia, edited Our Time, a Communist party-sanctioned magazine which had first published Dylan's poem 'Ceremony After a Fire Raid' in May 1944. Having worked in various capacities at the Left Book Club and Daily Worker, Swingler had had high hopes of a Labour culture that drew on the working man's experiences of war. However, after fighting in North Africa and Italy, he was bitter that his brand of English radicalism and poetry in the tradition of Blake had been marginalised, and that Britain's new cultural commissars were bourgeois figures such as Orwell and Spender who, he wrongly suggested, had never been near a battle-front.

When the new Communist regime in Prague wanted British participants at the inauguration of a writers' union, Lindsay recommended Dylan to Aloys Skoumal, the sophisticated cultural attaché at the Czech embassy, who had translated classic English authors such as Swift and Stern. Dylan knew something of Czech poetry from a wartime acquaintance with Jiri Mucha, son of the art nouveau painter Alphonse Mucha. Mucha had worked with John Lehmann on Daylight, a cultural magazine for Czechs that operated as an offshoot to Penguin New Writing, and had also helped Norman Cameron translate the Czech poet, Vitezslav Nezval. In an earlier incarnation, Nezval had been a writer on Hedy Lamarr's sultry film Ecstasy in the 1930s; by a curious trick of history, he was head of the Czech Ministry of Information in 1949. After spending an evening at Skoumal's house in Willesden, north London, Dylan was happy to accept his invitation to go to Prague.

Louis MacNeice, the only other invitee, smelt a Stalinist propaganda ploy, and declined to reply. So Dylan was on his own when he flew to the Czech capital in March 1949. Caitlin would have liked to accompany him, but he preferred to escape family commitments, leaving her wondering if once again he was having an affair. She could only fulminate at the restrictions enforced by her pregnancy, while Dylan to her chagrin was enjoying himself in Prague.

The weather there was bitterly cold and the food poor, but he enjoyed playing the cultural tourist, which seemed to involve little more than talking, drinking and visiting the opera. He also liked the city, which John Davenport astutely remarked appealed to his Gothic imagination. (By the same token, Dylan's lack of sympathy with classicism had contributed to his unease in Italy.) An early call was lunch with Jiri Mucha, and he also met other writers, including the poets Nezval and Vladimir Holan and the novelist Jan Drda. He spent an evening with Edwin Muir, an acquaintance from his early days in London, and now Director of the British Institute in Prague. Because of the cold, Dylan bought a fur hat to wear with his yellow duffel coat. Apart from being coveted as a fashion item – a symbol of capitalist individualism, like jeans in later years – the coat marked him out as a foreigner when he walked around town. On such occasions, he liked to give his official minders the slip and disappear into a bar. He became so annoyed with the unwanted presence of one translator that he mounted the Charles Bridge, embraced a statue and threatened to jump into the river.

In his official capacity Dylan was more conciliatory, particularly when he attended the inevitable conference celebrating the writers' union. Unlike the combative Alan Taylor in Wrocaw, he gave a cringing speech about his respect for the Czech revolution. But at the end of six days in Prague his enthusiasm for the union had waned. He had initially liked the idea of an organisation that catered for creative people and paid them a wage even if they were not working. But local authors alerted him to their fears of creeping totalitarianism. On his last night in Prague he went to a small private party to meet Holan, an unusual event, since the poet hardly ever left his own flat. For one of the guests Dylan scribbled a poem which compared the union to a cage. Then he crumpled it up, saying he did not want it misused by the capitalist press. Holan left after an hour, but Dylan stayed all night, treating his hosts and their guests to some dialogue from his ongoing play about a Welsh village. On leaving he wrote in a visitors' book that he had been taught that there were only two kinds of people in Prague – slaves and bosses – but in this flat he had met people who were neither slaves nor bosses 'but my friends'.

SEVENTEEN

VIEW FROM THE SHED

Dylan was returning not just to a place he loved but to a way of life. With his mother and father also settling in the same Welsh village, he was rediscovering the world of his childhood. Why Caitlin, who had complained vigorously about D.J. and Florence in South Leigh, went along with this is curious. She probably believed what Dylan had told Frances Hughes – that at Laugharne he would be able to work.

The main change since he had lived there at the start of the decade was the war-related growth of the weapons research establishment at Pendine, which had become the major employer of former fisherfolk. Otherwise the ancient Corporation, with the portreeve at its head, still administered the town, while the ubiquitous Williams family provided for its more mundane daily requirements. As always, Laugharne's singular history and constitution attracted a broad range of unusual inhabitants, with the anarchic high spirits of South Leigh.

As its name implied, the Boat House gave Dylan a different perspective from his previous dwellings in the town. Originally two fishermen's cottages, it had been knocked into one in the early years of the century to serve as a holiday home for a Worcestershire doctor. There were six cramped rooms and a kitchen with a coal-fired Rayburn stove. Otherwise conditions were predictably basic. At the time Dylan moved in there was no electricity or running water, though Margaret Taylor soon helped install both. The house's position, set tight against a red sandstone cliff, made for dampness which was not helped by the sea lapping against its lower walls at high tide. It was a haven for rats.

On the other hand, not many buildings have their own private harbour at the back or an outside wooden verandah offering magnificent views over the Taf estuary. In her throwaway style, Caitlin transformed the inside, which had to cater for two children and another on the way. Her *pièce de résistance* was the lavish dressing table in the main bedroom, which she adorned with white net and ribbons and covered with her own exotic potions and scents. Since there was no handrail on the internal staircase, the rope banister became a feature, adding to a nautical feel, though Llewelyn, now aged ten and a boarder at Magdalen College

267

School, had different ideas, insisting on his own room which he decorated with photographs of African tribesmen.

Forty-one steps led above the roof level to a path, which ran along the side of the cliff and into the town. Some hundred yards in that direction stood a smallish wooden building, once the garage for the doctor's Wolsey, when it was the only motor car in Laugharne. This shed was commandeered by Dylan as his place of work. He plastered its walls with pictures of art plucked from magazines, including an Italian primitive and a Rouault, and with photographs of writers he admired such as Walt Whitman and a youthful Edith Sitwell. And then he began to write.

As his children soon learnt, Dylan had a routine. In the mornings he would read, before venturing along the cliff path for his daily visit to his parents at their new house, called Pelican, opposite Brown's Hotel, on King Street. He liked to stay there to complete *The Times* crossword with his father. Around mid-day he went across the road for a drink or two, and for an update on the local gossip from Ivy Williams. Florrie sometimes made noises about his pub visits – 'Now, don't think I'm interfering, dear, I just happened to be looking out of the window as you fell down Brown's steps' – but, according to Caitlin, she did 'that Welsh trick' of pretending her son did not drink. At two Dylan made his way back to his shed (now warmed, in the winter months, by the anthracite stove Caitlin had lit in the morning) and he wrote until the early evening. Then he would descend to the Boat House where, if he was lucky, Caitlin had boiled some water for a bath. He would sit in the tub, reading, eating sweets or pickled onions, and sipping a fizzy drink, until it was time for supper, followed by another visit to the pub. Llewelyn and Aeronwy were not allowed to disturb him during those crucial afternoon working hours. Even when they could hear him murmuring to himself, trying out lines of his endless drafts of verse, they knew they had to creep past.

From his 'water and tree room on the cliff', Dylan looked out over the estuary, where at low tide the sandbanks teamed with cormorants and the odd stately heron which reminded him of Edith Sitwell. To his right, he could see Sir John's Hill standing sentinel over the town. The hill epitomised the quirky history of Laugharne, taking its name from Sir John Perrot, one time occupant of the Castle and supposedly a bastard son of King Henry VIII. Lord Deputy of Ireland, Perrot died in the Tower of London after being sentenced to death for treason under Queen Elizabeth I.

The McAlpines accompanied the Thomases to Laugharne and helped them settle in at the beginning of May. By the middle of the month an increasingly pregnant Caitlin was beginning to feel at home. She too fell into a pattern – swimming in the river, sunbathing on the verandah (often, as quickly became known, in the nude), painting and sometimes, though she tended to hide her efforts from Dylan, writing poems. She sacked her first daily help, an 'old ugly dumbie', and took on her 'treasure', the dependable Dolly Long who, not unusually for Laugharne, came unmarried but with a child, five-year-old Desmond, a potential playmate at least for the Thomas children. She also saw off Lynette Roberts, who had left her husband Keidrych Rhys and seemed to think that the Thomases should accommodate her.

In mid-May Dylan felt relaxed enough to write a belated thank-you letter from his shed to Margaret Taylor: 'Here I am happy and writing.' Soon his first poem appeared – a meditation on the view towards Sir John's Hill which, like a judge with a wig of elm trees, looks out retributively on the unthinking, murderous ways of nature, as the 'hawk on fire' swoops on the feeding birds in the bay below. In 'Over Sir John's hill' with its assonantal rhymes in each stanza, Dylan creates a glittering verbal snap-shot of the Laugharne seashore, capturing both its diurnal langour and its fleeting moments of action, in a manner reminiscent of both the movement of a nineteenth-century Japanese print and the tooth-and-claw passion of a Ted Hughes poem. Since Dylan had written so little over the previous couple of years, Caitlin regarded this as a favourable sign and tried to encourage him by starting a notebook for him on 1 June – one where, as in the old days, he could assemble his preferred verses.

Dylan's sense of well-being was boosted when, around the third week of May, he received an invitation which would change his life. For years he had been yearning for some way of getting to the United States. In April 1949 John Malcolm Brinnin, an ambitious poet and critic in his early thirties, was appointed director of the Poetry Center at the Young Men's and Young Women's Hebrew Association (YM-YWHA) in New York. The Center had a regular programme of talks and cultural events. Wanting to make an immediate mark, Brinnin wrote, within ten days of starting his job, asking if, for a fee of $500, Dylan would like to read there. He also offered to act on Dylan's behalf in arranging additional lectures.

Because of Dylan's recent move to Wales, the letter took some time reaching him. Once he had digested it, he wrote a remarkably clear-headed and businesslike response (particularly as he claimed to be suffering from 'flu). He said he would be delighted to take up the offer, preferably in early 1950. But he insisted that, after having had his fares and expenses paid, he would have to return to England with some money in his pocket.

Laugharne was so attractive in early summer that the McAlpines came again in early June, intending to stay until Caitlin had her baby. Without the Thomases' company they had tired of South Leigh and particularly of Cordelia: 'We escaped London and ran smack into Charlotte Street of the 20s', they wrote jointly to a friend. They felt sorry for their actor friend Harry Locke who had just returned from filming in Austria. 'How he picks them – lesbians, blood-letters, spiders; and now a spiritual vampire. The little Acton boy rides on his love boat with a cargo of snakes.' With their extrovert manner and obvious wealth, the McAlpines were popular in Laugharne. But when Dylan took time off to entertain them, his work was quickly neglected. Though the BBC still required its commissioned scripts for Peer Gynt and The Plain-Dealer, he did not produce them. Instead he sent excuses, claiming so many varieties of illness that certain apparatchiks became cynical. After he had written to one producer, saying he had gastritis and was 'about to be X-rayed for many an ulcerous fear', someone in the office, clearly not a friend, noted, 'He looked pretty lively in Great Portland Street today.' At other times he complained of gout and difficulty peeing (perhaps a recurrence of his old gonorrhoea).

More seriously, now that his film work had dried up (only Vanity Fair remained to be finished) he was again in dire financial straits. Within three months of returning to Laugharne, his supplies of coal (vital for keeping the house warm) had been cut off, the milk was about to be stopped, and he was having difficulty paying his rates, as well as the butcher and the builder. On his trip to London, he had bounced several cheques at the Savage Club. Once again Margaret Taylor helped out, and Dylan was forced to acknowledge the national debt he owed her.

He and Caitlin did manage to travel to Wiltshire to stay with Mervyn Levy who had taken over the cottage he shared with Jankel Adler, following the latter's death in April. Levy took them up to the big house where James Bomford was holding one of his celebrated parties. Offered some punch by her host, Caitlin took hold of the jug and swigged directly from it. Dylan got so drunk that, although he somehow made his way back to the cottage, he was unable to rouse himself to go to the lavatory. Levy was disconcerted to discover the next morning that his old friend had wet his mattress.

That day Levy was joined by a former army friend, Desmond Morris, who was embarking on the career as a zoologist that would make him famous but who was at the time better known as an artist. Just before lunch Dylan emerged groggily, complaining of the poet's lot. One of Morris's paintings happened to be standing at the corner of the dining room. 'Now look at that,' said Dylan. 'You can sell that, can't you? The painter makes an object that can be sold. But not the poet.' He took from his pocket a piece of paper which may or may not have contained a poem. 'Now I can't sell that, can I? No one would buy that bit of paper, would they?' Morris was not particularly impressed by the juvenile animal jokes with which Dylan tried to amuse him. (Example: There were two rhinos and one said to the other, 'I wonder why I keep thinking it's Thursday.') But, after settling down to lunch, Morris came to understand the poet's qualities. Obsessed with the small size of one man the previous evening, Dylan skewered a potato with his fork and began to boom into it, as if a microphone, 'Our midget which art in heaven, miniature be thy name'. By the time he reached the end of his spoof Lord's Prayer with the words, 'For ever and ever, Tom Thumb', Morris was amazed at his facility with words. (Morris only met one other person with this gift – John Lennon, whose debt to Dylan was acknowledged by Paul McCartney: 'We all used to like Dylan Thomas. I read him a lot. I think that John started writing because of him.')

Soon afterwards Caitlin's travels came to a temporary halt. On 24 July, she had been swimming energetically near Pendine. On returning home, she experienced pains that she knew meant she was in labour. Since Dylan was nowhere to be found, she contacted Ebie Williams at Brown's Hotel who drove her into Carmarthen Hospital, where her second son Colm Garan (an Irish name followed by the Welsh word for heron) was born. Dylan greeted this event much as the births of his other children: he abandoned his wife and family, and went off on a binge. The details are sketchy, but he was down in London the following week to record a talk on Edward Thomas whose careful observation of nature had influenced 'Over Sir John's hill'.

In London Dylan stayed with Bob Pocock and with John Davenport (both of whom were newly married). Pocock sent an ambiguous note to Dan and Irene Jones hinting that their mutual friend had not only been drunk but had spent time in a seedy dockside brothel. Dylan did little to indicate otherwise in a letter to Davenport the following week, in which he mentioned feeling 'rather bruised' after his 'tearful jags' in London. He explained himself by reference to his financial problems, adding that he had had a minor breakdown.

Back in Laugharne he stirred himself to put the finishing touches to 'Over Sir John's hill' and send it to *Botteghe Oscure*, a Rome-based literary magazine which had solicited something of his work. It was run by the enterprising Marguerite Caetani, Princess di Bassiano. Born in Connecticut, she had joined the pre-First World War exodus of American women to Europe where she had married an Italian prince who shared her devotion to the arts. While living in Paris between the wars, she ran a journal called *Commerce* which published Paul Valéry and, in translation, Joyce and T. S. Eliot. After moving to Italy, she started *Botteghe Oscure*, meaning literally 'dark shops', after a district in Rome where the Caetani family had started in business, though it also housed the headquarters of both the Communists and the Jesuits, which gave the phrase a Machiavellian connotation in Italian. The multi-lingual magazine quickly developed a reputation for paying well for first-rate work by authors ranging from Truman Capote to Giuseppe di Lampedusa. The Princess seemed to know her man for her initial request to Dylan for a poem in June had come with payment in advance.

He was soon labouring over another more complicated offering for *Botteghe Oscure*. He told Vernon Watkins he spent three weeks on the first line of 'In the White Giant's Thigh' – 'Through throats where many river meet, the curlews cry'. The view from his shed is there, but the poem itself is the first part of a wider-ranging state of the universe message, as recorded around the time of his thirty-fifth birthday. As his more accessible 'Poem on his Birthday' showed, this was an important milestone: he felt he had reached the middle of his three score years and ten, and was on the slippery, depressing downward path. This required him to look out not just on the estuary below him but on the wider world, which was not a pretty sight. 'In the White Giant's Thigh' is ostensibly about Dylan's visit to an ancient fertility symbol – probably the Cerne Abbas giant in Dorset, not far from Blashford – and his empathy with the women who, after a life of active but barren sexuality, resorted to visiting this phallic centre in search of some sympathetic magic which would help them conceive. It is also an anguished reflection on his own failure to produce verse. As the introduction to a longer poem, it pointed to Dylan's despair at a godless world where the atomic bomb can reduce all to barrenness.

As usual, there were distracting trips, mainly to London where, unrealistically, he hoped for Louis MacNeice's BBC job after his friend joined the British Council in Athens, and to Swansea for a programme on the town and its recent artistic flowering, made with his old friends Vernon Watkins, Fred Janes, Dan Jones and John Pritchard. As compere, Dylan reprised his recent ideas about the difficulties of being a creative Welshman. With his uncanny knack, he struck the right note by remarking that Swansea was the most romantic town he knew.

He was supposed to attend the annual dinner of the Swansea branch of the British Medical Association as guest of honour in October, but, as he explained in an unnecessarily facetious letter of apology three months later, he had set off from London with good intentions. But before reaching Paddington station, he had met a rich friend with a sports car who offered him a lift as far as Bristol. En route the car had been involved in an accident. What he admitted sounded like 'a thin tall story' was, in fact, partly true: the friend was Tony Hubbard, the spoilt son of a Woolworth heiress and an old army colleague of Mervyn Levy, whom they were hoping to visit in Bristol. Hubbard dispensed his money liberally in projects which ranged from collecting early Francis Bacon paintings to subsidising Dylan Thomas. In late 1949 he was being courted by Dylan and various cronies to finance a new magazine which would offer a radical religious perspective on a world made more dangerous by the Soviet Union's recent explosion of its own atomic bomb. The people behind the project were John Davenport, a right-wing Europhile Catholic, and Randall Swingler, a Marxist who had tired of the British Communist party's kow-towing to Moscow and had let his Marxist magazine *Our Time* fold. Making their own literary Molotov-Ribbentrop pact, the two men had set up *Arena*, a 'literary magazine interested in values', with the slogan, 'European, with no Iron Curtain'. But, despite Edith Sitwell's support and Dylan's unfulfilled promises of contributions, that was already floundering. So plans were afoot to steer Hubbard's wealth towards a more marketable journal called *Circus*.

On the occasion Dylan was to address the Welsh doctors, he doubtless did think he would reach Bristol and take a train on to Swansea. But he, Hubbard and another passenger, the poet turned advertising man Bernard Gutteridge, stopped off in Oxford to see Dan Davin. Before long Hubbard had produced some chicken and a bottle of champagne from the back of his car, and Dylan used the opportunity to try out some verse he intended to read in America. When he reached the last of several poems by Hardy, he burst into tears. Davin remarked astutely in his diary the following day: 'Dylan is very emotional but like a good Welshman also very suspicious. Thus when he has expressed himself very warmly, in fact exposed himself, he will suddenly react violently towards a self-sneering cynicism. It imparts a curious rhythm to his talk.' There was also much talk of books and magazines, and the New Zealander gained the impression he was being paraded in his professional capacity as a publisher to impress Hubbard.

The upshot was that Dylan and his friends stayed the night. After a liquid lunch they then proceeded to Bristol. En route Hubbard's car did indeed have a collision, which led to Dylan spending the next night at Levy's and missing his appointment with the Swansea doctors.

He was prevented from giving one of his great unwritten speeches. He might have put some flesh on his amorphous left-wing views and articulated his true attitude to the new National Health Service, the pearl of the new Labour government, but he balked, perhaps alarmed, as often in the past, at having to make a public statement. His politics in this period did creep out, however. A couple of years earlier he had earned three guineas for his apothegm printed in the I-n-s-u-l-t-s column of *Strand* magazine: 'One should tolerate the Labour government because running down Labour eventually brings you alongside the Conservatives, which is the last place you want to be.' His Socialism was apparent in a later talk about America, in which he satirised 'the brassy-bossy men-women, with corrugated-iron perms, and hippo hides, who come, self-announced, as "ordinary British housewives", to talk to rich minked chunks of American matronhood about the iniquity of the Health Services, the criminal sloth of the miners, the *visible* tail and horns of Mr Aneurin Bevan, and the fear of everyone in England to go out alone at night because of the organized legions of cosh boys against whom the police are powerless.' In Laugharne, which was old-fashioned Welsh Liberal in its politics, this was dangerously left-wing stuff. When he voiced an opinion there about living in a slave state, he claimed he was almost struck down.

His most passionate political stance continued to be his opposition to war in the era of the atomic bomb. He battled to find ways of representing the threat of an impending holocaust in his poetry. But when it came to specific issues, he remained adamant that, as in the 1930s, politics had little place in the arts, excusing himself for failing to make yet another meeting with Davenport by poking fun at *Arena's* political commitment: 'I got caught up with rewording a petition against decadent tendencies in the cultural field.' On a practical level, however, he signed the Stockholm Peace Appeal in 1950 and the Authors' World Peace Appeal the following year. The former was a Soviet-inspired attempt to hijack the cold war pacifist movement, and the latter was a follow-up designed to attract writers and other opinion-formers. As with his trip to Prague, Dylan acted more with his heart than his mind. In matters of realpolitik, he remained an ingénue. However that is not to underestimate the strength of his feelings. When Julius and Ethel Rosenberg were executed for spying for the Soviet Union against the United States in June 1953, he described it as 'murder' which 'should make all men sick and mad'.

By the autumn, news of Dylan's impending visit to the United States was beginning to percolate through American literary circles. The prospect of hearing him speak was creating excitement. Lloyd Frankenberg was a New York-based poet and critic who had recently written *Pleasure Dome*, a well-documented book stressing the importance of a poet's voice in communicating the meaning of verse. Dylan, at his request, sent him a tape of 'Poem in October' and 'In my craft or sullen art' for re-mixing onto a long-playing record of poets reading their work. Frankenberg asked him to contribute to a series of poetry readings he ran at the Museum of Modern Art, where the work of his artist wife Loren MacIver was on display. In October the modest, inventive Elizabeth Bishop, Poetry Consultant (now known as Poet Laureate) at the Library of Congress, wrote to Brinnin saying she had seen advertisements for Dylan's forthcoming visit to the YM-YWHA and wondered how he might be contacted to give a similar talk at the Library in Washington.

Interest was further stimulated by New Directions' publication of an anthology, The New British Poets, edited by Kenneth Rexroth, a fiery San Francisco poet who inspired the pre-Beat generation of West Coast versifiers. Describing Dylan's impact as 'a cultural coup d'état', Rexroth enthused, 'If Auden dominated the recent past, Dylan Thomas dominates the present. There can be no question but that he is the most influential young poet writing in England today ... He takes you by the neck and rubs your nose in it. He hits you across the face with a reeking, bloody heart, a heart full of worms and needles and black blood and thorns, a werewolf heart...'

Once he learnt of the visit, James Laughlin, hoping to cash in, asked Dylan if he had any spare poems which might be collected in a book. But Dylan had nothing to hand except the few chapters of his book Adventures in the Skin Trade. Laughlin was not prepared to offer an advance on this 'because I have gotten the impression from your delay in finishing it that you are really not terribly keen about it'. The publisher had to be content with the forthcoming limited Mardersteig edition of Dylan's poems, which had been delayed as a result of illness and currency devaluations.

Oddly Dylan did not mention his American visit to Laughlin until mid-October when he casually asked, 'Have you heard that I'm supposed to be coming to the States in February 1950?' Laughlin almost certainly had, and it was probably he who encouraged Bishop to approach Brinnin. But Dylan was wary of his New York publisher who had not been keen on his travelling to North America three years earlier. So both men were happy to allow Brinnin to continue to take the lead in arranging this lecture tour. The Poetry Center director played his hand well. He offered Dylan a New York apartment, as well as what he described as a 'country retreat' in the upstate artists' community at Yaddo. He did not press himself too strongly, proposing, in return for arranging a country-wide programme of readings and lectures, to take just 15 per cent commission, rather than the usual agency fees which could amount to twice as much. One selling point he did put forward was his closeness to the college poetry market. But when, by the end of

November, requests for Dylan's presence began to mount up, he expressed genuine concern about the poet's ability to fulfil a gruelling tour. 'I don't want to turn your American visit into a kind of drudgery, and yet I hate to pass up opportunities which might enhance the financial aspect of your tour.'

One unresolved issue for Dylan was what to do with his wife. Colm's birth had left her physically weaker than with her previous two children. She admitted she was so worried she could not eat and she was more resentful than usual about being left on her own in Wales. When Glyn Jones went to Laugharne in mid-October to discuss with Dylan a BBC programme about being a writer, he found Caitlin by turns indifferent and hostile to her husband, to whom she snapped, 'I thought you were not going to broadcast any more. And this, giving away your secrets.' Jones was surprised at the deterioration in Dylan's appearance. His friend looked fat and comical in baggy trousers, his teeth were brown and crooked, his nose had grown vast and bulbous, and his once golden hair was dark and matted.

Another visitor to Laugharne was Allen Curnow, a young New Zealand poet whom Dylan had met in London at the start of the year and who, sharing his love of cricket, had accompanied him and Louis MacNeice to Lords. Down in Wales, Dylan was still working on his film script of *Vanity Fair*, though he fulminated that Margaret Lockwood, who had been cast as Becky Sharp, was 'a rotten actress'. He tried to drag Curnow to the Rhondda where he had been talking about setting a big new poem, 'a kind of colloquial Lycidas'. His other versifying seemed stalled, however, and he said despondently, 'The craze for me is over. They won't like what I'm doing now.' He was more interested in testing out his proposed readings for America – W. H. Davies, Yeats, MacNeice, Auden and Hardy, including a poignant version of 'To Lizbie Brown'. He wanted to make an immediate impact on his audience with modern British poems which he copied carefully into a large anthology. When he took Curnow to Brown's, he wept unashamedly when a Welsh girl with a crystal voice stood up and sang an unaccompanied Victorian ballad called 'Daddy', with the lines: 'They were given to me by your mother dear/The night before she died.'

In mid-November John Deakin, a louche young Soho photographer, came to shoot some pictures for *Flair*, a glossy new American magazine published by Condé Nast. Dylan took pleasure in taking Deakin to St Martin's church and having himself pictured in a grave, his unusually long hair blowing in the wind. Depending on the printing, the image can look remarkably ghostly.

Even now Dylan was still thinking Caitlin might accompany him to

America. He hoped Brigit would take Colm for three months, while Nancy and her husband Gordon moved to the Boat House to look after Aeronwy and his parents. But by the end of the month he had changed his mind: 'It would be difficult, expensive, and, I think, bad for her,' he told Margaret Taylor, apropos his wife. 'She wants a long and utter rest.'

This did little to appease Caitlin, who stormed off to Ringwood with her children for Christmas. Restless there, she joined Dylan in Oxford where they asked Dan Davin if they could stay a couple of days which became a week. They were not easy guests: Davin found a little of the Thomases went 'a long way – not that I tire of Dylan's company but I tire of its consequences. And also his mode of arguments – emotional and assertive – gets on my nerves a bit.' From an academic's perspective, which summed up Dylan's worst fears, he added, 'For he hasn't a first class brain, or at least a trained one, and a great deal of noise is spent on perceptions which are either obvious or absurd.' On this occasion Davin sensed that Caitlin was apprehensive about Dylan's imminent departure. 'She tended, when in the pub, to become distant, remote, hostile even. An uneasiness would spread out from her and it was difficult to know which of us was provoking it.' To Mary Keene she tried unconvincingly to remain upbeat, telling her of Dylan's plans, though she wondered what would happen to her while he was away.

His wife's anger did little to calm Dylan's own nerves. To add to his worries, he had fallen and cracked his ribs, his father had contracted pneumonia in the new year, and there were the usual financial concerns, which were hardly addressed by a generous if inadequate Christmas box from Marguerite Caetani. Having met her in London, he was now promising her a story which failed to materialise. When she expressed concern about his drinking, he assured her it was not a problem: 'it is only frightening when I am whirlingly perplexed, when my ordinary troubles are magnified into monsters.' Otherwise he was 'a dull, happy fellow only wanting to put into words, never into useless, haphazard, ugly & unhappy action, the ordered turbulence, the ubiquitous and rinsing grief, the unreasonable glory, of the world I know and don't know.' Quickly falling into her prescribed role as another rich patroness, the Princess further tried to ease his way in America by offering to put him in touch with the poet Archibald MacLeish, one of her contributors, and with her sisters in New York and Washington. But even at the end of January 1950, three weeks before his departure, his visa had not yet come through and he asked John Davenport if he knew any US consular official who might expedite matters. When he visited the American embassy in London, he found he had left his passport and cheque book in Laugharne, and Caitlin had to send them on. He did not help himself by showing annoyance when asked about his visit to Prague and its financing.

At this stage Brinnin was beginning to feel concern. A cultivated homosexual who lived with his mother in Connecticut, he kept hearing alarming stories (from W. H. Auden and e. e. cummings among others) about Dylan's tantrums and unreliability. 'Thomas's silence is a worry,' he confided to his more sexually adventurous lover Bill Read, 'and in another day or two I'll be ready to cable, to learn probably only the true extent of his defection.' This was all the more troubling as the invitations were piling up. The British ambassador Sir Oliver Franks had offered to hold a reception when Dylan came to Washington. Ruthven Todd, who was pursuing his idiosyncratic literary-cum-artistic career on the fringes of the abstract expressionist movement in Greenwich Village, had offered a bed in his study. And Brinnin was intrigued that the out-of-the-way Roman Catholic university Notre Dame in South Bend, Illinois, was getting in on the act and requesting a reading by Dylan.

Eventually, on 13 February, Dylan had to borrow money from his mother to travel to the American consulate in Cardiff to pick up his visa. He continued from there to London to visit a dentist and to finalise arrangements for Caitlin's finances while he was away. He turned to his rich friend Tony Hubbard who agreed to send Caitlin a regular stipend in return for Dylan penning a quick article on 'How to be a Poet' for his proposed magazine *Circus*. Though hardly qualified to address the sub-theme, 'Can poetry be made good business?' Dylan playfully charted the literary career of an unworldly civil servant turned poet. He sprinkled his text with unpromising in-jokes that he infused with his own brand of humour, such as his comment that if his hero Cedric Cribbe had written verse in the 1920s, it would have been 'a cunningly evocative pudding full of plums pulled from the Sitwells and Sacheverell other people, a mildly cacophonous hothouse of exotic horticultural and comic-erotic bric-à-brac, from which I extract these typical lines:

> A cornucopia of phalluses
> Cascade on the vermillion palaces
> In arabesques and syrup rigadoons...'

Incorporating a gag from his Kardomah days, this parody poked fun at Edith Sitwell in a way no-one else who knew her would have attempted, let alone got away with.

Dylan remained in London to fulfil an undertaking to appear in a reading of Picasso's surrealist play *Desire Caught by the Tail*, which was being presented at the Rudolf Steiner Hall to celebrate the second anniversary of the Institute of Contemporary Arts. He had lent his support to the Institute, the brain-child of his old friend Roland Penrose (whose wife Lee Miller had photographed him three years earlier, for American *Vogue* when it printed *Holiday Memory*). However there were still aspects of London sophistication which alarmed his Welsh Non-conformist conscience. Knowing that Penrose was a sado-masochist, with a penchant for whipping, he became alarmed when he learnt that *Vogue* journalist Rosamond Bernier was living at Penrose's house in Hampstead. 'I won't have you tied up,' Dylan told her earnestly. According to Bernier, 'Some girlfriend of his had been tied up in Roland's house. It was funny that Dylan, who was very hard drinking and living, had quite a conventional attitude to that. I told him, "thanks, but I can look after myself." '

But when it came to artistic expression Dylan had no inhibitions. Refreshing his avant-garde credentials in advance of his American visit, Dylan had, in his role as Stage Manager, to inform the audience of imaginary stage props and directions such as the 'immense bath-tub full of soap suds' from which The Tart 'gets out stark naked, except for her stockings'.

With his departure only four days off, he might have stayed in London. Instead he took his regular third-class sleeper back to Carmarthen in order to say goodbye to his parents. At the weekend a small party travelled from Laugharne back up to London. Probably driven by Billy Williams, it included Ivy Williams and Caitlin, as well as Dylan. Their immediate destination was Margaret Taylor's new house in Park Village East, just off Regent's Park, where she was living while her husband was taking a year's leave of absence from Magdalen. He had since tired of her obsession with Dylan and moved to a nearby flat. In her desire to give Dylan a rousing send-off, poor, scorned, infuriatingly ardent Margaret was free to gather the McAlpines and other friends for a bibulous party, followed by lunch of oysters and Guinness at Wheeler's the following day.

EIGHTEEN

A VOICE ON WHEELS

Dylan loved the United States for its cowboys and its cartoons. He had been attracted by them as a young boy and, to the surprise of many people who regarded him as a poet preoccupied with weighty issues of life and death, he had no reason to change his mind. Such examples of American culture epitomised for him the best of the country – its capacity for innovation, humour and surprise. That New World energy created the humorists he liked. It fuelled not just the films of the Marx Brothers but also the thrillers of Dashiell Hammett and the novels of Nelson Algren. It had been apparent in the cast of *Anna Lucasta*. It also threw up critics who were open to Dylan's subject-matter and technique. As John Sweeney, a Harvard academic with one-time links to *transition* in Paris, had written in his introduction to *Selected Writings*, Dylan's 'poetry springs directly from primitive and traditional sources, but it is peculiarly the poetry of his own time. It is the record of a struggle towards spiritual rebirth.' Such notes were encouraging, and helped maintain interest in Dylan's work.

Not that Dylan really knew much about the United States. It might be a place of great vitality and also a place where he could earn a decent living. But he had little idea of the profound changes that had taken place over the previous decade. By 1950 the influx of mainly Jewish refugees from Hitler's Europe was beginning to make its presence felt in America's intellectual and cultural life, and nowhere more so than in New York. Radical thinkers such as Erich Fromm at the New School for Social Research were introducing new psychoanalytical techniques to American criticism. Artists such as Max Ernst, often associated with the Guggenheim Gallery, were stimulating painters and sculptors and creating a new American genre known as abstract expressionism. Such influences – and others more locally generated, such as the prevalence of black music, particularly jazz – were entering the wider culture, where they were seized on by a generation of ex-soldiers eagerly seeking education under the provisions of the post-war GI Bill.

Within New York's avant garde, two tendencies were apparent, based, roughly speaking on the opposite sides of Greenwich Village. The West

Village tended to be more sympathetic to tradition (even if trying to go beyond it), slightly more affluent and more in tune with uptown media such as the New Yorker and Harper's Bazaar. The East side was less accommodating towards the establishment. It provided the crucible for the early work of Beat writers, such as Allen Ginsberg and Jack Kerouac, for radical film makers such as the youthful Kenneth Anger, and for Frank O'Hara and the New York school of poets who were determined to make something of the language of the American street in the way Wilhelm de Kooning and his colleagues had pioneered an indigenous school of painting in abstract expressionism.

For some Americans, these developments were proving hard to stomach. In Washington a patriotic strain of conservatism was emerging. In January 1950 the former State Department official Alger Hiss had been convicted of lying to Congress's powerful House Un-American Activities Committee about having once been a Russian agent. And on 9 February, less than a fortnight before Dylan's arrival, Senator Joseph McCarthy of Wisconsin announced he had a list of Communists working in the State Department. His great anti-Communist witch-hunt had begun.

Such thoughts were a long way from Dylan's mind when he first stepped out on American soil at Idlewild airport, New York, on 21 February. It was a bright, freezing morning, and he was glad of the warmth of his old duffel coat. Clutching a copy of Max Beerbohm's *Seven Men*, a parting gift from John Davenport, he shook hands cagily with the dapper, balding John Malcolm Brinnin, who had risen early to meet him. Then, complaining of a terrible flight caused partly by a massive hangover and partly by sitting next to a man in a dark suit whose opening conversational gambit was 'You know, Hitler was a much misunderstood man', he proceeded directly to the bar to order a breakfast of double Scotch and soda. Once refreshed, he could see the world in a better light. He was most impressed by the sight of his host's black Studebaker in the parking lot. Looking out over the unprepossessing suburb of Queens, as they sped towards Manhattan, he trilled, 'I knew America would be just like this.' As they entered an underpass on the throughway, Brinnin idly compared the experience to the womb. 'Ee-ee-EE,' roared Dylan, appreciatively. 'It does remind me of Mummy.' But when they came to the point where Manhattan's glittering skyscrapers appeared on the skyline ahead, the first-time visitor was stunned into silence by the magnificent sight.

He had another stunning panoramic view of the city from his thirtieth-floor room in the mid-town Beekman Tower Hotel. By this time the excitement was beginning to pall. Peering through a plate glass window at the teeming city below, he had vertigo and became apprehensive: 'it is all an enormous façade of speed and efficiency and power behind which millions of little individuals are wrestling, in vain, with their own anxieties.' After a bloody encounter shaving, he was happy to be brought down to earth, both literally and metaphorically, in Costello's, an Irish bar with a familiar feel, round the corner from the hotel.

On a whistle-stop sight-seeing tour, Brinnin claims to have been so alarmed at Dylan's coughing fits that he mentioned them to him. According to Brinnin's intriguing, not wholly accurate and occasionally self-serving memoir *Dylan Thomas in America*, Dylan said he had a liver condition, adding, as if it was nothing, 'I think it's called cirrhosis of the liver.' This was an unlikely comment but, for Brinnin, who was later accused of failing to prevent Dylan drinking himself to death, it helped establish that the Welshman was in poor physical shape when he first arrived in the United Estates.

After the RCA building, Dylan tired of tourism. Since Brinnin had business to attend to in the afternoon, Dylan telephoned his friends Ruthven Todd and Allen Curnow, the New Zealander who had recently visited him in Laugharne, and they came to join him. By the time Brinnin returned for dinner at an Italian restaurant in the Village, Dylan had been drinking all day (though he seems also to have enjoyed American food, particularly T-bone steaks, every one of which, he told his parents, was the equivalent of a month's ration for an English family). Afterwards they all went to the San Remo, a local cafe-bar on the corner of Bleecker and MacDougal streets frequented by writers. Even when an exhausted Brinnin was forced to call it a day, Dylan continued with Curnow and the young American poet Patrick Boland.

Extraordinarily, when Brinnin called at the Beekman Tower the following morning, Dylan was not only up but out, having left a note 'Dear John, Gone to 3rd Avenue. See you at Costello's. Come at once. (I like this peremptory tone.) Ever, Dylan.' Dylan turned out to be ensconced not exactly where he said but in a similar Third Avenue hostelry called Murphy's, together with Todd and Len Lye, another pal from London.

Basically a jazz-loving artist and experimental film-maker, Lye stood at an intriguing intersection between the worlds of culture and espionage. Through the intervention of Tom Matthews, an American who, like him, had known Robert Graves and Laura Riding in London and Majorca, and who had become an editor (later the editor) of *Time* magazine, Lye had worked on *March of Time*, the main newsreels shown in the United States during the war. In 1944 he went to New York, leaving his wife and children out of the reach of German bombs, staying at Todd's house in Tilty in Essex.

Immediately attracted to the liberating potential of abstract expressionism and to the general artistic flowering in Manhattan, he decided to stay. He picked up his friendship with Bill (S. W.) Hayter, an organiser of the 1936 surrealist exhibition in London, who was running the influential Atelier 17 design studio on East 8th Street. Hayter's studio was close to the Artists' Club where the post-war school of painters such as Barnett Newman and Mark Rothko hung out (shortly to be joined by Jackson Pollock). While his wife Jane was deciding whether to join him, Lye took up with Ann, the fun-loving American-born wife of 'Tommy' Hindle, a British journalist and secret agent. After working for The Times (of London), Hindle had represented the British Secret Intelligence Service (or MI6) in Budapest and Prague, and acted as assistant to the Anglo-Iranian oil company boss in the United States, before joining the United Nations. By the time Jane Lye did come to America, her marriage was all but over. Having gone to Reno, Nevada, for the quickest possible divorce, Lye married Ann Hindle there the very same day. The newly wed couple moved into an apartment in Washington Street in the West Village.

By then Ruthven Todd had also joined the exodus to New York. There he put the finishing touches to his 1949 book on William Blake and dabbled in print-making with his friend Joán Miró at Atelier 17, collaborating with him on a poem published by Tambimuttu's Poetry (London) in an issue which also included his tributes to Bill Hayter and Yves Tanguy (both similarly illustrated by the dedicatee). So it was natural that Dylan should want to see his old friends Todd and Lye and through them discover what was happening in the city.

They were joined for lunch by Harvey Breit, editor of the New York Times Book Review, who wanted to interview Dylan. But the discussion proved so bibulous and Dylan so elusive that Breit sat on his piece for the best part of three months and then made up most of his quotes. The Times would not have printed Dylan's answer to a question about his reasons for coming to New York: 'To continue my life-long search for naked women in wet mackintoshes.' But it did throw light on Dylan's estimation of the progress of his career, and on his dissatisfaction with it. When asked about success, he said it was bad for him: 'I should be what I was.' Breit pressed if he meant like thirty-five years ago. 'No, twenty years ago,' said Dylan, referring back to his first dabblings with mature verse. 'Then I was arrogant and lost. Now I am humble and found. I prefer that other.' As if to emphasise the point, at some stage they were joined by Lye's ex-wife Jane who remained friendly with

Todd. She is reputed to have said, 'Oh, Dylan – the last time I saw you you were an angel.'

Getting steadily more drunk, Dylan counselled Breit to make his story imaginary, 'a bard's eye view of New York by a dollar-made nightingale', declaring, 'How can I know what I like until I find out what I want?' When Jane Lye agreed he had never known what he wanted, he said, 'Until right now. I do know what I want.' Asked to expand, he poked his finger into Brinnin and announced, 'I want him'. After the sudden silence had given way to laughter, he added to the Poetry Center director, 'You couldn't manage to change your sex a bit, could you?' At least that was the way Brinnin told the story in an unpublished fragment of his memoirs. Whether this was a piece of gay wishful thinking is difficult to tell. Certainly Caitlin came to think that there was an element of homosexual love in Brinnin's developing relationship with her husband.

On this occasion Brinnin dragged Dylan back to his hotel and watched over him as he slept. After only two hours' fitful slumber, Dylan was ready for a full evening's entertainment. He and Brinnin first went to a dinner party at the 12th Street apartment of Marshall Stearns, a professor of English at Hunter College, with a particular interest in the history of jazz. Stearns had written an important introductory essay to Dylan's poetry in the *Sewanee Review* in 1944. As Dylan carefully informed his parents, the party's atmosphere was respectable and academic. One professor's wife even carried a notebook to take down the great poet's bons mots. That only encouraged Dylan to heights of outrageousness: he told scatalogical stories, propositioned women, and when asked to explain his 'Ballad of the Long-legged Bait', he stopped the conversation with his bawled reply, 'A gigantic fuck!'

The austere Brinnin, whose worst fears were being confirmed, had to transport him from there, through the sleet, to Harvey Breit's apartment in the mid-fifties where a star-studded party was being thrown in his honour. In the taxi, Dylan nodded off and was only jolted awake when his cigarette burnt down to his fingers. After a few more drinks at Breit's, he became even more embarrassing. Brinnin sensed W. H. Auden signalling to him, 'I told you so' and other guests imploring him to take the addled poet home. Having lunged at Charles Henri Ford's sister, the actress Ruth Ford, who neatly side-stepped, Dylan made a play for the elegant Southern writer Katherine Anne Porter who looked not unlike Caitlin. As she prepared to leave, he grabbed her, lifted her to the ceiling, and held her there, as if acting out a scene in some private ballet. The incident quickly became the talk of the town. It later provided a dramatic scene for Sidney Michaels' Broadway play *Dylan*, which portrayed it positively, with Dylan telling her that he wanted to raise her to the stars where she belonged, head and shoulders above any other writer. But her own recollection was different: 'He was most objectionable, trying to get his hands under my dress, and picking me up, until finally I just had to get out.'

Despite his reservations, Brinnin was enjoying himself, as he giddily admitted to his friend Jack Thompson: 'He's here, but I'm not sure I am. Two mornings ago his plane put down at Idlewild. Since then, I've had more to drink, less to eat, more to 'take in' and more to worry about, than in any other forty-eight hours of my existence. First of all (last of all), he's a wonder and a delight – simply because each of his long assumed virtues is subsumed by a quality of being – a human dimension, a human ampleur, a human quidditas (how the hell can I get it right?) of such unclouded sweetness as to signal the correction of heresies.'

The following day Dylan felt awful and vomited periodically, hardly a good augury for his first reading at the Poetry Center that evening. In the taxi up to the YM-YWHA at 92nd Street on Lexington Avenue, he veered maniacally between joyfulness and depression. Back stage in the Kaufmann Auditorium he demanded a cold beer. Five minutes before he was due to appear, he was seized with a coughing fit and retched convulsively. Unable to see how Dylan could carry on, Brinnin had to help him to his feet. But as the curtains parted, Dylan braced himself, puffed his chest, and walked out in front of a capacity house of over one thousand people. He launched into his repertoire of twentieth-century poets, finishing with a selection from his own verse. His audience, which included e. e. cummings and other often reclusive members of New York's literary aristocracy, was held spellbound, not just by the virtuosity of his delivery, but also by the nuances of his language. At the end, they demanded 'Fern Hill', and would not let him go until he obliged. After thunderous applause, a hundred people mobbed him in the vestibule, causing Brinnin to worry for his charge's safety.

Dylan had been invited to a post-performance party by Frederick Morgan, editor of the influential *Hudson Review*. But en route he was again sick and had to be taken back to his hotel. The next morning, the management of the Beekman Tower had had enough. It had tired of his endless calls for room service and demanded he vacate his room. A chastened Dylan telephoned Curnow and arranged to move into his more relaxed Midston House Hotel, on 39th Street at Madison Avenue. Luckily, he was not reading that night, but the following one. He was able to sleep (with the help of a doctor's prescription), to visit other parts of the city including Harlem where he insisted on buying some black magazines, and to see people, including Bill Hayter, the anthologist Oscar Williams, who was full of plans for selling his work to periodicals, and, at Dylan's special request, e. e. cummings, whose wife, the photographer Marion Morehouse told Brinnin over tea that her husband had been so moved by Dylan's performance that he had walked the streets alone for hours. After a second, equally successful, reading at the 'Y' that Saturday evening, his fifth night in New York, Dylan went to a party at the Greenwich Village apartment of Lloyd Frankenberg, the poetry impresario who had written to Dylan in Wales, and his wife Loren MacIver, another painter, whose recent portrait of cummings showed words from his poems billowing onto the canvas, as if from his head.

Over the weekend Dylan wrote to Caitlin – more informatively than his usual gushing protestations of undying love, this time telling her of his schedule, promising to buy her some nylons and even sending her a couple of cheques; and also to his parents – typically a more guarded letter, stressing his sobriety amid the unfamiliarity of America.

That was not how it looked on the ground. During his first few days in the United States, Dylan had exhibited the excesses and experienced the adulation which would later be associated with rock stars. He had even been thrown out of his hotel. As in the 1960s, it was a matter of being in the right place at the right time. Until Dylan's appearance, American poetry had been a modest, staid and introverted affair, caught in a strait jacket of academic textual criticism. There was not much new about his subject-matter – the age-old American concerns of nature and spiritual development. But he put them in a different, more challenging context, with his concertina of words and ideas, and he brought them to a wider audience, taking verse out of the printed page and into the auditorium just as culture was being democratised. He managed the former without the usual condescension of British poets and, as for the latter, he anticipated the beat poets with his sense of theatre and 'happening'. As a result, this small overweight Welshman was feted as a Promethean god – the reaction he had always longed for, though when described as the greatest reader since Yeats, he had still had enough of his self-deflating humour to be able to say, 'I'm afraid it's second-rate Charles Laughton.'

On Sunday 26 February Dylan ventured out of New York City for the first time. His initial destination was Brinnin's house in Westport, Connecticut, where he stayed a couple of nights before embarking on a short tour of New England universities. Brinnin had to apologise to his boyfriend Bill Read that he was neglecting him, 'but this weekend must be given over to Dylan'. He was buoyant at the success of the two

Poetry Center events and looked forward to them helping him to pay off his own debts. He took his Welsh guest to meet two sets of his neighbours – the novelist Peter DeVries, and his wife Katinka, and the critic Stanley Edgar Hyman and his wife, Shirley Jackson, a well-known short story writer. Drinks with the DeVrieses went smoothly enough, even if the host was later to use Dylan as the model for the poet, Gowan Glamorgan McGland in his novel, *Reuben Reuben*. Supper with the Hymans the next evening was a more problematic affair. Dylan and Shirley Jackson tried to outdo each other in constructing gory plots for murder mysteries. In *Dylan Thomas in America* Brinnin described the evening as ending 'gracelessly' – a tame description of a pathetic, drunken scene where Dylan, having propositioned the overweight Jackson, chased her round the house while Hyman fell asleep, watching baseball on television. In an unpublished memoir, Brinnin was more explicit, describing Dylan and his hostess emerging – 'she décolleté, her hair unstrung, he unbuttoned and unzipped.'

Dylan alarmed Brinnin with his depressed behaviour, as he lolled around at home, reading and guzzling chocolate bars. When he received a letter from Caitlin, he was reluctant to open it – probably, Brinnin sensed, because it contained news he did not want to read, though he was later keen to explain how wonderful his wife was.

Dylan continued his way north-eastwards, first to Yale which he found 'formal and donnish and altogether impossible', and then, having held a 'moist little waitress all the way', to Boston where Allen Curnow was at the railway station to greet and convey him to F. O. Matthiessen, the distinguished critic and academic who was his host at Harvard. Curnow was a last-minute replacement for Bill Read whom Brinnin earlier told: 'You'll be able to recognise him easily ... he's short, bumbly and a little wild-looking. He'll probably want to stop for a beer immediately, and you'll have to give in ... but it might be just as well if you'd say you had a definite time in which to deliver him. The best approach to him in all ways is the most casual; overt recognitions of who he is and what he's done, or any sort of "respectfulness" tend to put him off. Take him as he comes and he'll return the gesture.'

Curnow felt that, at Harvard, Dylan was subjected to 'what no poet should have to endure – least of all one so exciting and excitable as Dylan Thomas', performance at five, the *Advocate* newspaper's cocktail party at 6.30, dinner at Matthiessen's (attended by distinguished poets including Archibald MacLeish, Richard Eberhart and Richard Wilbur), party at the Wilburs' campus apartment from midnight to four in the morning, bed around five in a university hall. Matthiessen, who was to commit suicide exactly a month later, informed Brinnin the evening had been a success, though he could not help adding that he only wished 'for his own endurance that [Dylan] would stick to beer after as well as before his performances'.

After a short night's rest Dylan was ready to drive to a reading at Mount Holyoke and from there, next day, to Amherst (both in Massachusetts). By now the pressure (and the drink) were getting to him: before mounting the stage, he suddenly plunged his head in his hands and exclaimed, 'I can't go on. I miss my wife, I miss my children. I'm sure they're all dead.' Back home, if he had been working on a poem, he would have given up. But the actor in him realised the performance had to go ahead. He steeled himself and regaled his audience with his usual gusto.

Reuben Brown, a member of staff at Amherst, was alarmed at the overall spectacle. When he sent Brinnin the $100 fee for the evening (rather less than the average of around $150 Dylan was receiving for most engagements), he observed that the poet was 'a very sick man. He suffered terribly from the whole business, and it was hard to know whether to encourage or discourage him ... Isn't there a possibility of getting some grant for him that will give him a rest?'

Dylan was on the lecture treadmill, and there was no jumping off. He returned to New York where Brinnin found him 'in a heavy hung-overish desuetude', looking back on his brief New England tour (he had liked Harvard best) and proudly maintaining he had not missed an engagement all week. Dylan had a Saturday night dinner date at the Austrian restaurant, Stahl's, with Frederick Morgan, the Hudson Review editor whose party he had flunked. Brinnin was miffed that Oscar Williams, a friend of Morgan, also attended – an early instance of the rivalries that were to develop over Dylan between different factions. Williams was in his most fawning mode, eager to effect a sale to the magazine. But the dinner was marred by a row over religion, with a drunken Dylan making disparaging remarks about Roman Catholicism, the faith of both Morgan and his co-editor, Joseph Bennett, who was also present. Perhaps fearing he had talked himself out of a commission, Dylan was later – unusually for him – worried about having been indiscreet. Having found his guest obnoxious in the restaurant, Morgan warmed to him back at his hotel, where Dylan curled up on his bed and showed interest at the plight of Ezra Pound. Like many people, Morgan recognised Dylan's basic sweetness and, ignoring his indiscretions, happily paid over the odds for 'Over Sir John's hill'. (Curiously, another New Yorker, the Columbia professor William York Tindall, recorded Dylan attacking the Roman Catholic church – an indication, perhaps, that, feeling far from home, Dylan reverted to the anti-Papism of his forefathers. Generally, he was sympathetic to the faith of friends such as John Davenport, and drew on it for the theological underpinnings of his poetry.)

After a long weekend in New York, he ventured south again to Bryn Mawr, the Pennsylvania women's college (and alma mater to Ella Wheeler Wilcox whom he had parodied as a schoolboy), before proceeding, without ever feeling totally well, to Washington for his appearance at the Institute of Contemporary Arts. Unbeknownst to him, wheels had turned, and he was staying at the elegant Georgetown mansion of Marguerite Caetani's sister, Katherine, and her husband Francis Biddle, who had been President Roosevelt's attorney general during the war. The Biddles did their bit for Dylan, holding a reception, attended by Beltway cultural luminaries, such as Luther Evans, later the Director General of UNESCO, and Kimball Flaccus, author of an unfinished biography of the Kansas-born humorist Edgar Lee Masters, who had died earlier that month and was much admired by Dylan. Having been on his best behaviour all evening, Dylan went to the Library of Congress the following day and recorded his poems for its archive. Over lunch with Elizabeth Bishop and her friend Joe Frank, he plied her with questions about how American poets made a living. She could not help feeling frightened for his future: when she said something trite to her companion about him appearing to be bent on self-destruction, Frank said he felt Dylan did not want to live and gave him two or three more years.

With the Biddles away for a long weekend in Bermuda and Brinnin also out of town at an arts festival in Virginia, Dylan was left to his own devices for the next couple of days in Washington. On the whole he enjoyed himself, though Caitlin would not have known it from the way he went on about missing her, or about America – 'this vast, mad horror, that doesn't know its size, or its strength, or its weakness, or its barbaric speed, stupidity, din, selfrighteousness, this cancerous Babylon'.

She meanwhile was getting on with her own life. She had had one letter from him and, as she told Mary Keene, did not expect more until his return. The children were trying, and her eye had begun to wander to local men, but she was coping. Not so Dylan, who plied her from various hotel rooms with many more whining loving letters than she expected. Philip Larkin described this correspondence as 'all snivelling and grovelling and adoring and so very impersonal' which was unfair. It did express something of Dylan's torment – his remorse at leaving his family; not knowing if they had enough money or if perhaps Caitlin would seek sexual comfort elsewhere. This epistolary outpouring of emotion also sought to cover his failures in small things: having neglected to remember Aeronwy's seventh birthday, he tried to assuage his guilt by sending her a large box of chocolates from Washington.

On Brinnin's return, Dylan was waiting at the Biddles', smoking one of his host's cigars. Stung by a comment from a Yugoslav maid who had playfully said she knew he could not be rich because she had washed his underwear, Dylan also purloined a couple of Francis Biddle's shirts. 'Look!' he told Brinnin, pulling out a drawer from a Hepplewhite highboy. 'You could dress a regiment.' He made no secret of what he was doing, and Biddle did not seem to mind. But his pilfering was another example of his self-destructive biting the hand that fed him. Driving back to New York in Brinnin's new green convertible, Dylan was on good form, swapping stories with the composer John Cage, who was a passenger with the dancer Merce Cunningham. He was rested and felt no need to drink more than a couple of beers all day. In this relaxed state, Brinnin noted, Dylan showed an ebullience that most people needed several drinks to attain. Alcohol, he felt, was a device Dylan used to put a barrier between himself and emotions and situations he could not control.

This might have been the reason for his behaviour when he visited e. e. cummings's wife, Marion Morehouse, to have his photograph taken. Despite his respect for her husband, he arrived inebriated from lunch and quickly launched into an inappropriate seduction routine. He had hardly sat down, she recalled, before he started 'about the swan-like shape of my neck and how he'd like to snuggle up between the pillows of my breasts and sleep forever. He sounded like a Groucho Marx on a bad day.' For a while she listened to his childish sexual fantasies, continuing her job with a fixed professional smile. Eventually she had had enough: she dropped her camera and looked him in the eye. ' "You want to feel my tits? You want to snuggle up and nibble, or do you want to fuck?" The poor soul was so shocked the blood ran out of him ... Once he didn't have to play Priapus he turned into himself and God knows that's enough.'

After a reading at Columbia on the evening of Monday, 13 March, Dylan embarked the following day on the next stage of his journey to the mid-west and on to the Pacific coast. He first flew to Ithaca in upstate New York for a fleeting visit to Cornell university. David Daiches, a Scottish-born lecturer in English who was at the airport to meet him, was surprised when no-one of his description came off the plane. When he boarded the aircraft, he found Dylan still in his seat, the groggy victim of unaccustomed sleeping tablets which he had acquired to counter bouts of insomnia in New York. Dylan fell asleep again over an early dinner but, as usual, roused himself for his performance, telling

Daiches, 'I'm just an old ham. I always respond to an audience.'
Afterwards Daiches drove him to Syracuse to catch the train which
would take him to Ohio and through to Chicago, Illinois. Settling into
his seat, he looked frightened. 'Westward into the night,' he intoned,
adding he did not think he would come back: 'Perhaps I shall die in
Utah.'

His first stop in the mid-west was Kenyon College in Gambier, Ohio.
Once there, he complained to Caitlin that he never seemed to sleep in
a bed, but only in trains and planes. 'I'm hardly living; I'm just a voice
on wheels.' He added pathetically that he could find no paper or pencil
in his campus room, and was too scared to go out and ask. He continued
to Chicago to read at the university, which paid $250, his highest fee –
apart from the Poetry Center – so far, and on to South Bend, Indiana
(Notre Dame University), Champaign, Illinois (University of Illinois)
and Iowa City (the State University of Iowa).

He had developed a routine where he charmed his audience with a
Welsh version of blarney, delivered his quota of favoured poets (taking
care never to offer the same selection at more than one place), and
ended with a poem or two of his own (usually his later ones, and even
then they sometimes had to be dragged out of him). Afterwards he would
attend a party with faculty members (occasionally, with predictable
consequences, this came before the reading), and later there would
usually be some story of his making a pass at a professor's wife or
ogling a nubile young student. However tales of his sexual prowess have
been exaggerated. At Kenyon College, he was ill at ease with the students
who looked like 'bad actors out of an American co-ed film'. Earlier, at
Mount Holyoke, he said how beautiful girls would ask him to their
rooms, saying they were not really poets, but they wanted him to look
at verses they had written. 'And that's all they want you to do, look at
their beastly poems!'

He stayed longer than expected in Iowa because Brinnin had requested
for him to have much needed dental treatment there. A dentist took one
look at his mouth ('m'fuckin' curse', Dylan told Ray B. West Jr., his
English faculty host) and said remedial work would take up to six weeks,
which was not possible. Dylan was forced to kill time, sitting around
idly, drinking beer and feeling resentful. Each day, on his way to work,
West deposited him at a bar from where he was picked up for lunch by
the brilliant, troubled poet Robert Lowell, a visiting fellow, who prevailed
on him to address his writers' workshop. Dylan told West he loved his
daughter, but 'detested' his new-born son Colm because he felt jealous
of 'the little bugger, suckin' away there at his mummy's tits'. At the
house of Baldwin Maxwell, chairman of the English faculty, Dylan got

into an argument with a doctor's wife about Britain's new National Health Service. She described it as a Marxist front, which annoyed him intensely. He exploded with rage, reducing her to tears with his description of her as a 'bloody fucking bitch'. Such outbursts were more likely than any romantic interludes.

Unable to stand it any longer, he flew to the west coast on 26 March for what was to be the most enjoyable part of his trip. In San Francisco, his first port of call, he had been booked by Brinnin into the Palace Hotel where Oscar Wilde and Rudyard Kipling had once stayed. Without bothering to unpack, he went out looking for a bar, walking north until he found a suitably nondescript place off Columbus Avenue. After a few drinks, he asked some locals for directions to an address he had written on a crumpled piece of paper. It was the home of Ruth Witt-Diamant, professor of English at San Francisco State College. Dylan had a note – probably, she thought, written by Stephen Spender, who was the only English poet she knew – asking her to look after him in San Francisco. When he telephoned, she immediately offered to put him up in her house in Parnassus Heights. It was only three in the afternoon, but since Dylan had passed out, she drove over to collect him.

He struck lucky. Witt-Diamant was a kindly middle-aged Jewish woman from Philadelphia who was bored with academia and had good contacts in San Francisco's burgeoning artistic community. The city acted as a magnet for poets escaping WASP-dominated literary circles in the east. The headstrong, bewhiskered Kenneth Rexroth had acted as mentor to the so-called first San Francisco Renaissance of post-war poets such as William Everson and Robert Duncan, and was now paving the way for the beat poets of the 1950s, including Lawrence Ferlinghetti and Allen Ginsberg. Parallel to this, Witt-Diamant parlayed the growing interest in poetry, as both written and performance art, to cajole her faculty into establishing the Poetry Center at her college in 1954. Dylan's visit to San Francisco acted as a useful catalyst in this process.

With time on his hands before his reading on 4 April, he hung around the bars of North Beach playing pin-ball and drinking with Knute Stiles (later known as an 'underground' artist) at the Two A.M. Club in Mill Valley. Many of Stiles's friends were gay, such as the poet Tram Combs. Dylan told how a 'party of queens' befriended and took him around the bars. Although he appreciated their kindness and did his best to enjoy himself, he longed for a woman. In one bar, he saw an attractive girl on her own but, when he approached her he found it was a boy in drag. His sense of sexual frustration hardly abated when he met the Greek-born collage artist Jean Varda who worked in a decommissioned ferryboat in Sausalito and recalled meeting Caitlin when she was fifteen (almost certainly through Augustus John). Dylan could only longingly tell his wife how much he wished he had known her then.

He also spent time with Rexroth who, as early as 29 March, wrote to Laughlin 'Dylan Thomas is here. What a problem. It is sure hard to try to keep him from continuously drinking & throwing his money around ... I like him very much & he seems to like me. He is sure genuine. A vast relief after these nasty English poets. He is Welsh & proletarian to the core.' The sentiment was mutual: Dylan felt a natural affinity for the laid-back west coast. After the unreality of New York, it was like returning to Wales, only with sunshine, good wine and excellent food. In addition, Californian poets such as Rexroth wrote about their environment with the same modernist intensity he aimed for in his own writings on the natural world.

While Dylan was staying, Witt-Diamant had a lunch appointment with Noel Sullivan, a staunchly Roman Catholic millionaire who supported the local arts and lived on a rambling estate on the Pacific Ocean at Carmel near Monterey, south of the city. She asked if she could bring her house guest and enlisted as chauffeur Gavin Arthur, who was the epitome of the nascent counter-culture – a homosexual astrologer of advancing years, father-in-law of philosopher Alan Watts, teacher at St Quentin prison, and grandson of Chester Alan Arthur, the twenty-first President of the United States. Lunch with Sullivan went so well that he invited them all back for supper, saying he would also ask some local people who would like to meet Dylan. In the meantime, Witt-Diamant took Dylan and Arthur to the hot springs at Big Sur. (Now commercialised as Esalen, Dylan called them the 'pansied Pacific baths'.) On the way they passed Henry Miller's house. Since Dylan said he knew Miller, Witt-Diamant suggested that they knock on his door. This was answered by 'a pretty young Polish girl' (as Dylan recalled) who turned out to be Miller's wife, Lepska. She said her husband was resting and could not be disturbed. However Miller had been roused and duly appeared. He scolded his wife for being inhospitable and chatted happily with Dylan who found him 'gentle and mellow and gay'.

After leaving Miller and visiting the hot springs, it was time to prepare for supper with Sullivan and his guests in Carmel which was known for being stuffy and snobbish. When Witt-Diamant suggested they should stop in the town to buy ties, Dylan reached in his pocket for a crumpled neckpiece which he tore in two, saying that would make two bow-ties. One guest at Sullivan's ranch was Robinson Jeffers, a local poet with a wide reputation for writing about the surrounding sea and mountains though, unlike his colleagues up the coast in San Francisco, he had become reclusive and misanthropic and, not unusually, was drunk. After five minutes' social chit-chat, the two poets went into the garden and did not reappear until dinner when Jeffers went (or was taken) home. When Witt-Diamant asked Dylan about his encounter with Jeffers, he said they had hit it off perfectly. 'And what did you talk about?' she asked. 'We didn't say a thing,' answered Dylan.

Earlier Witt-Diamant remembered she had to telephone James Caldwell, a poet in the English department at Berkeley, who had arranged a party later that evening for Dylan. Dylan was having such a good time that he asked her to say he was sick. Caldwell was unimpressed. 'Is he drunk?' he asked. When she said no, he blustered, 'If Mr Thomas can't make his engagements, we'll have to make other arrangements.' Dylan stayed through the meal with the cream of Carmel society. They would have loved him to burst into poetry, but he never liked performing to order in that way. Inevitably he and his party arrived back in San Francisco too late to go to Caldwell who subsequently cabled Brinnin: 'Contact with Thomas reestablished after lapse. Will do all I can but cannot assume responsibility since he is indisposed to keep appointments. Trust he will meet engagement Tuesday.' In his archives, Brinnin has written an accompanying note, 'How many such communications I had to deal with!'

By the time Dylan gave his scheduled reading at Berkeley on 4 April he had certainly made his mark among the local chattering classes. He was scheduled to appear in a 300-seat hall, while a local zoology professor, Paul Needham, talked in the 1,000-seat Wheeler Auditorium. Shortly before these simultaneous events, it was clear that the numbers turning up for Dylan were larger than expected and would need the more spacious venue. A switch was tactfully arranged. From the moment Dylan started with a joke about not offering 'Henry Miller with demonstrations', he had a captive audience. Normally indifferent students suddenly found themselves appreciating what poetry was about. As Dylan excitedly relayed back to his wife, the university's Speech Department initiated discussions about inviting him back to teach on a six months' contract. But the dean of the faculty was less enthusiastic: he had heard of Dylan's reputation for drinking, and decided the Welshman would not be a suitable influence.

After San Francisco Dylan flew north to Vancouver for a couple of readings at the University of British Columbia and the Vancouver Hotel. Unexpectedly his old friend Malcolm Lowry came to listen to him at the second venue. The visionary alcoholic Lowry was living in nearby Dollarton with his second wife Margerie, an ex-Hollywood starlet. Struggling to pick up his career after the successful publication of his novel *Under the Volcano* three years earlier, he was trying his hand at screenwriting and had just completed an over-long treatment of Scott Fitzgerald's *Tender is the Night* for Frank Taylor. As a publisher in New York with Reynal & Hitchcock, the talented Taylor had been responsible for *Under the Volcano*. Bi-sexual, he had turned bi-coastal, and switched jobs to work for MGM as a producer.

Dylan found Vancouver 'a quite handsome hellhole' but, compared with San Francisco, too British. After two notably successful readings, he was happy to chat with Lowry about mutual friends such as John Davenport and Anna Wickham who had committed suicide in 1947, ostensibly in protest against an increase in the price of cigarettes. As they caroused into the night, 'the only noticeable drunks,' noted influential local poet Earle Binney, 'were the inevitable Malcolm Lowry and a certain undergraduate lion huntress who got herself blotto trying to seduce Dylan without success.' When the Lowrys called on Dylan the next morning to say goodbye, they found the girl 'hanging over him', as Margerie put it, and Dylan asking blearily, 'Won't somebody do something with this pest?'

Back in the United States, for a reading at the University of Washington in Seattle, Dylan was approached at a party by another old literary friend, John Berryman, who was teaching there. The two men greeted each other warmly but, after a short conversation, their hostess tried to prise them apart, accusing them of indulging in literary gossip. Berryman recalled that Dylan, who showed little sign of having drunk excessively, replied with slow deliberation, 'We were just discussing Hitler's methods of dealing with the Jews, and we have decided that he was quite right.'

From Seattle, Dylan flew directly to Los Angeles for one of the more bizarre episodes on his tour. Somewhere in his luggage he had found another crumpled piece of paper with a telephone number and the name of Christopher Isherwood, who had been living in California since 1939. On the morning of 10 April Dylan phoned Isherwood from the Biltmore Hotel, where he stayed overnight. The two men did not know each other, although they had several mutual friends. Dylan sounded particularly lost, as he recounted how he was due to give a reading at UCLA that afternoon, but the English department had declined to provide any transport, only telling him how to reach the campus by bus. Taking pity, Isherwood went to pick him up at the hotel. Dylan was touched and rewarded him with a tacky but treasured present – a small crab set in plastic, with a key-ring attached. Isherwood accompanied him to lunch with members of the UCLA English faculty who did not know what to make of this crumpled poet. 'They had conjured up this dangerous little creature,' wrote Isherwood, 'excited by the dangerousness of his poems, and now that they had him there in the flesh, he terrified and shocked them by those very qualities which are so admirable as long as they remain merely in the library.' By the time Dylan gave his reading he had been drinking steadily, but gave no indication of this. As had become customary, he was able to push himself out on the stage and deliver a commanding performance, though Isherwood noticed that the students clapped loudest while the academic staff looked on sour-faced.

Afterwards Dylan wanted only to relax and have a good time. Two other people he knew in the city were Ivan Moffat, his old sparring partner from the Gargoyle, Strand films and wartime London, who was working as a screenwriter, and Frank Taylor, the publisher-cum-producer. When they enquired what he wanted to do, he said he would like to meet Charlie Chaplin and 'the most beautiful blonde in Hollywood'. Both Moffat and Isherwood had worked with the buxom blonde Shelley Winters on a series of inferior films, so, having arranged to go on to Chaplin's house, they invited her to dinner at a popular movie business eaterie, the Players Restaurant (owned by director Preston Sturges) on Sunset Boulevard. During the evening, Dylan, by now well-oiled, became fascinated with Winters's cleavage. He asked if her breasts were real and, when she said they were, he asked if he could feel them. He was so excited at her assent that, according to Isherwood, he reached across and grappled her, and they both fell off their chairs.

The party proceeded to Chaplin's house on Summit Ridge Drive. Winters reported an unlikely-sounding interlude with Marilyn Monroe at her apartment, followed by a hair-raising drunken drive which ended with Moffat's Green Hornet car on Chaplin's tennis court. Dylan was certainly drunk, but Chaplin seemed not to notice. According to one version, he performed a routine where he opened his front-door as the butler. Dylan may have urinated on a flower-bed on the way out. But Chaplin remained good-humoured and even carried out his promise to cable Caitlin in Laugharne, after Dylan had said that his wife would never believe him. The evening ended in a bar where, when someone amicably told Isherwood that he did not think his latest book was as good as his previous ones, Dylan took offence on behalf of his new friend and attacked this very much larger man.

After further readings at Pomona College, in Claremont, east of Los Angeles, and at the University of California at Santa Barbara, Dylan returned to San Francisco for two more events. The bay area lifestyle proved so enticing that Dylan decided to stay longer than scheduled. Feigning illness, he postponed his next appearance on the other side of the continent in Florida. Instead he abandoned himself to a rich, eighteen-year-old girl called Bambi who drove him around in her yellow convertible and asked if he would mind waiting three years until she came of age, inherited her millions, and they could marry. 'My God what a swathe you have cut into the even quilt that covered the muddle I called my life,' wrote Witt-Diamant on his departure. 'Darling – everyone who heard you loves you – feels – really feels – communication with you – well deep – and everyone is better – healthier – because you were here – pray god you will be soon again.' Such gushing enthusiasm was impossible for Dylan to resist.

Passing briefly through New York, he flew to give his delayed talk in Gainesville, Florida on 27 April. However he was still not finished, returning to New England for engagements at Wellesley College and Brandeis University, and to the mid-west to the universities of Michigan, Wayne State and Indiana – all in a punishing schedule the following week.

At the University of Indiana in Bloomington, one of his duties was to address a group of film students after a screening of his own work for the cinema. He was given an official speech of welcome by the Tennessee-born John Crowe Ransom, a poet for whom he had great respect, who was teaching there for a year. Asked at a subsequent question and answer session if, 'as a poet', he felt something-or-other, he answered, 'I'm only a poet when I'm writing poetry. The rest of the time, I'm ... well, Christ, look at me.' David Wagoner, a young poet who had taken time off from teaching duties at DePauw University, some fifty miles away, noted the cigarette ash caught in the folds of Dylan's shirt and his seersucker suit. Wagoner and some others befriended the visiting Welshman and took him to a party where Dylan amused his hosts with his impressions and revealed that John Brinnin had bought him the suit as a good travelling outfit because it would never need pressing. 'But it's a misnomer,' he added. 'I'm neither a seer nor a sucker.' Dylan told Wagoner he wished he had known more about Ransom's origins. He would then have made a habit of reading his poems, such as 'Captain Carpenter', in a rich Southern drawl, rather than in his own 'usual evangelistic trombone'.

Back in New York for his final local appearances, he wrote to Caitlin on 7 May, saying that he was exhausted but was thinking of her, with too little money, alone in their little bedroom in Laugharne. ('Please Christ, my love, it is always alone.') He said his speaking schedule would be completely finished in just over a week. But he warned her that, since he was determined to travel back by sea rather than by plane, transatlantic passages were difficult to obtain at this time of year, and he might not be able to make it until early June.

He was not worried when it turned out thus. He based himself at the Hotel Earle on Washington Square, which allowed easy access to the San Remo and other Greeenwich Village bars. After his final appearance at the Poetry Center on 15 May (when he read prose rather than poetry), he received a call from Anita Loos, author of *Gentlemen Prefer Blondes*, who wanted to sound him out about appearing in a play she was interested in, Garson Kanin's *The Rat Race*. The idea of appearing on Broadway appealed to Dylan, but it came to nothing.

Instead he spent what he happily described as 'one liquid libidinous fortnight in New York' which ended with him being 'wheelbarrowed on to the *Queen Elizabeth*'. He went to parties at the Frankenbergs and at the Oscar Williamses, who epitomised New York artistic style with their penthouse at the top of a modest-sized office block in Lower Manhattan. Despite magnificent views over the water-front, such a place was considered beyond the pale by some New Yorkers, though it anticipated by thirty years the coveted yuppie lofts of the 1980s. In her long cape and beret, and with her raspy voice, Williams's poet-artist wife Gene Derwood chose one of their parties to paint Dylan. Asked to read from his poems by a fawning female fan, he at first tried to put his head under her dress and then launched into a ten-minute gobbledygook parody of his reading style, complete with bodily mannerisms, which created just the right element of frenzy for Derwood's portrait. Alcohol flowed, but when dinner was served by Williams, it consisted entirely of mashed potatoes.

The fastidious Harvard-educated Brinnin had no time for such antics. Stung by recriminations from Bill Read and other friends who said he was ignoring them for this 'monster', he left Dylan to himself. By chance the two men ran into each other at an artist's party on 8th Street. Dylan was in the centre of a crowd with Delmore Schwartz. Seeing Brinnin, he assumed a pouting wounded attitude and rushed towards the nearest window, as if to throw himself out. When asked the matter, he moaned, 'You've deserted me.' Brinnin claimed he was haunted by Dylan's rueful unforgiving look: he could not make out if it was acting or for real. On another occasion Brinnin drew up precise accounts of Dylan's trip and felt hurt when the poet showed no interest. Dylan had said something about not wanting businessmen involved in his affairs (they would certainly have charged him more than Brinnin's ungrasping 15 per cent). But Brinnin hoped to be recognised for the commercial good sense he had brought to Dylan's affairs. A complicated relationship, full of fondness, resentment, guilt and dependency, was developing.

By mid-May the word about Dylan had been buzzing in artists' circles for nearly three months. During his travels over that period, he had met an extraordinary range of American poets. At times he must have thought that half his audiences were composed of 'poets'. And still they wanted to meet him. At Brinnin's suggestion, Theodore Roethke came down from his retreat at Yaddo to talk, drink and go to Marx Brothers movies with him. Once he was taken by Dylan to a sing-song organised by an official group of Welshmen in North America. Roethke noted how 'to those hard-boiled business men Thomas was the first citizen of Wales, and nothing else.' When Stanley Moss, a young poet working temporarily at New Directions, recognised him and started chatting in the San Remo bar in Greenwich Village, he was struck by Dylan's courtesy. 'You know why I drink?' Dylan said to him. 'Because I don't do anything really useful.' One early morning, after the bars had closed, they found themselves at a funeral home in Bleecker Street where it was possible to buy some beer and drink it over a coffin. 'That appealed to Dylan's sense of sin,' recalled Moss, who also relished the memory of the Welsh poet, in a taxi, imitating God receiving T. S. Eliot in heaven.

After Eugene Walter, a camp import from Alabama, met Dylan through Ruthven Todd, he prevailed on a fellow poet, the gamine Jean Garrigue to throw a party for Dylan in his summer apartment on West 9th Street. Seeking to create what he thought was a British environment, Walter decorated the place with roses made from wet Kleenex, green wax paper and wire, and painted the tables and chairs dark green. Then, a more personal touch, he strewed the flagstones with sequins and diamond flitters. Guests included the proto-feminist poet Ruth Herschberger, as well as, from the artistic community, the young Andy Warhol and Curtis Harrington, an experimental film-maker later known for his suspense movies. At 3 a.m. Dylan had the stragglers in stitches with his impressions of Queen Mary's magpie tendencies. Regarded as lesbian, Garrigue nevertheless conceived a tendresse for Dylan and, for a brief while, was often with him. The affair petered out, though Dylan spoke nostalgically of it to Brinnin. Her tender poem 'A poet kissed me' suggests what it meant to her.

The problem was that Dylan was overwhelmed by the attentions of other New York women, and of two in particular. One was Jeanne Gordon, the chirpy ex-model wife of a Yale-educated up-town psychiatrist. According to Brinnin, she knew more about poetry than she let on. She took on a maternal role, worrying about Dylan's drinking and if his poetry was beginning to repeat itself.

Dylan liked to boast of his sexual exploits with her. In an unpublished memoir Brinnin recalled waiting in his car while she and Dylan enjoyed a prolonged tryst. It was cold and he had the heater turned up. When Dylan emerged, he made a crude remark about what he had done to make her bleed, adding, 'Christ, it's hot in here. Can we turn that thing down a bit?' In his book *Dylan Thomas in America*, Brinnin referred to Jeanne under the pseudonym 'Doris'. After its publication, he received a call from her husband threatening to sue and passing him on to Jeanne herself who remonstrated, 'Jesus, John, have you got it wrong. In the matter of taste alone, couldn't you give me a little credit? I tried to be nice to Dylan, that's all. Where did you get any other idea? And for God's sake, tell me this: who on earth in their right mind would want to go to bed with that fat slug of veal, with his matted hair and bad teeth?' She may have been protecting her reputation, particularly if she had enjoyed a passionate or out-of-character fling with the visiting poet. She may indeed have simply wanted to look after him, and he may have flattered her with his attentions and strung her along for the many presents she liked to give him. But another mutual friend has referred to her relationship with Dylan as a 'very intense affair', and it would not have been the first time for him.

The other woman, more important to Dylan, was Pearl Kazin, a striking dark-haired junior editor on *Harper's Bazaar*. The daughter of an immigrant house painter in Brooklyn, she had a traditional Jewish respect for education and a personal love of English literature, which she had studied at graduate level at Radcliffe, the female college of Harvard University. Sociable and intelligent, she had moved in similar circles to Brinnin since the war. Only the previous summer she had spent time with him and their mutual friend Elizabeth Bishop at Yaddo, the artists' colony, near Saratoga Springs in upstate New York. Her brother Alfred was a well-known literary critic and historian, whose friends included Norman Mailer and Saul Bellow. Having recently embarked on a career in literary journalism, she was delighted not only to meet Dylan but to sign him up to write a story for her magazine (a piece of information formally if grudgingly conveyed by agent Ann Watkins to David Higham on 24 May). To Dylan Pearl was the epitome of the sophisticated, open, young American woman of a type he had not encountered since Emily Holmes Coleman.

For the last week or so of his American trip, Dylan conducted simultaneous liaisons with both these women. Brinnin often unwittingly found himself at the centre of a French-style farce. On 28 May he picked up Dylan and Pearl at the Earle where, as he coyly put it, they were 'merry over Grand Marnier'. They proceeded, via the Frankenbergs', to a farewell party for Dylan given by a woman, who was described by a fellow guest, the novelist Dawn Powell, as 'one of those dumb-intellectual Jewish girls of the twenties'. Also there were Leo Lerman, an editor at *Vogue*, and the unfortunate Jean Garrigue. The hostess took pride in a large photograph of young Dylan on her wall, with an earring on it. 'Dylan at twenty,' she told Powell, probably referring to a picture taken by Nora Summers around the time of Dylan's marriage. 'Wasn't he gorgeous? And that's the earring I lost when I lost my honour.' Proceedings became farcical when she refused to allow a rival for Dylan's affections into her apartment, but this woman later returned and was rushed into a bedroom by him. According to Brinnin, this woman's husband had forbidden her to attend the party and locked her in a closet, but she had escaped. As Powell left, she noticed Dylan discard the two women on his lap ('a hand here, a hand there'), lift his shirt tail and perform a 'perfectly dandy dance'. She told Edmund Wilson, 'It is rare indeed for us to see an English [sic] poet have such a wonderful time – probably the Welsh coal-miner's Saturday night. Other reports are that he loves America madly (what kind of Britisher is this?) and at the Pleasure Club (Surrealists' party place near here) he started to take a swan dive out of the window in a peak of exaltation. Everybody loves him and perhaps this is partly due to his being the personification of the now-glamorized spontaneity of the twenties.'

The next morning Dylan's breakfast with Brinnin at the Earle comprised two raw eggs and a sherry. He departed for a dental check-up, before rejoining Brinnin at the offices of the Internal Revenue Service, whose permission was required if he was to travel two days later. Brinnin enjoyed quiet satisfaction at the importance his methodical accounting now assumed. Then Dylan went through his romantic opera bouffe: tea-time drinks with Jeanne Gordon at the Champs Elysées, followed by an evening with Pearl and one or two others.

On 31 May, Dylan's last day in New York, the partying started in his room at the Earle around 4 p.m. The place was strewn with clothes, manuscripts, empty beer bottles, chocolate bar wrappers, sleazy thrillers and faded flowers. As Brinnin offered to pack (someone had to), Dylan's New York friends, such as Oscar Williams and Gene Derwood, began to drop by. One visitor was James Laughlin who had been curiously inconspicuous throughout Dylan's visit. He told Rexroth that he had seen Dylan a few times but had not been able to 'get much sense out of him as he always seemed to be half cooked. It's just a shame.' He said Dylan's most recent reading at the Museum had been excellent, however. 'He cranks up that big voice and lets it moan.'

Brinnin was still packing when Jeanne arrived, loaded with expensive presents, including a new tweed jacket, some ties and a box of cigars for Dylan, and a space suit, cowboy outfit and archery set for his children. As she and Dylan broke into a medley of songs from musicals, she sprayed the room and his belongings with a scented air purifier.

Shortly afterwards the telephone rang with the news that Pearl was waiting downstairs. Taking the line of least resistance, Dylan invited her up. There were awkward moments, as Pearl remarked, 'What is that frightful odour?' and Jeanne, still squirting, countered, 'I like this odour. Don't you like it, Dylan?'

After a few drinks the atmosphere improved. A lively party proceeded to an Italian restaurant in the Village where Jeanne broke down in tears and rushed out. When someone went outside to try and bring her back, Pearl wondered coolly what her rival was doing there anyway. Three cars were needed to convey Dylan, his friends and his luggage to Pier 90 from where the Queen Elizabeth was due to sail at midnight. They all tried to stay on board with him until the last possible moment. When they had left the ship and were waving from the dockside, Jeanne teetered triumphantly down the gang-plank in her high heels. Brinnin noticed Pearl quietly weeping. They embraced silently as the liner pulled away from the pier.

NINETEEN

IN THE DIRECTION OF HIS PAIN

Dylan's progress through America had developed into a gripping soap opera. To people in the know, the delightful, bumbling, brilliant Dylan came across as a character in his own cartoon or, perhaps, morality play. Conrad Aiken, Elizabeth Bishop's successor as Poetry Consultant at the Library of Congress, suggested as much, with his barbed observation on how the 'kind friends who helped [Dylan] pack at his hotel, when of course he was blind to the world, thoughtfully packed about five hundred passionate love letters from all over the country, which naturally in due course his wife would unpack. Good clean fun.'

The numbers were exaggerated, it was never much fun, and there was an awful inevitability about the outcome. Despite prickly comments to her friends while Dylan had been away, Caitlin went to London to welcome her husband. There was immediate friction because she wanted to enjoy herself (having been cooped up in Laugharne for three months) and he wanted to go straight home (having had his fill of parties in New York). But they overcame these differences and, before long, she was again pregnant. The children were delighted with their presents from America and Dylan himself felt he had at last made a breakthrough in his career. He was enthusiastic about returning to the United States to teach and insisted that Caitlin would accompany him. Not that Ivy Williams and the inhabitants of Laugharne were interested in such matters: they only wanted to know about the stars he had met in Hollywood.

The main problem for the Thomases remained the perennial one of money. Dylan's American trip was supposed to put him on a firm financial footing. Yet he returned with very little to show for his time abroad. Caitlin was beginning to worry when she opened a present from Brinnin – a leather handbag, in which he had managed to secrete $800. He had noticed the speed at which Dylan was running through his earnings while in the United States and had astutely put something aside for the family, who he knew were living in difficult circumstances.

When the accounts were tallied, Dylan had earned a gross sum of $7,860 in America. Roughly two thirds of this had been generated by

Brinnin, who took his 15 per cent commission. In addition Dylan had incurred expenses of $2,860, as well as a US tax liability of $212. As a result, Dylan netted just under $4,000 or £1,425, the equivalent of around £29,000 in 2003. This was a reasonable return for three months' work for anyone. But Dylan had managed to dissipate much of it through drinking and other incidental pleasures, and the British taxman was waiting for his share of an already dwindling amount. The returns might have been better but for his need to pay for his travel and accommodation. If he were to get an indentured position at, say, the University of California, such outgoings would not arise.

Having been inconspicuous in the United States, James Laughlin thought it an appropriate moment to send Dylan a word of encouragement. 'New York, and, in fact, I am informed, the entire United States, seems very quiet after your departure. We all miss you a lot. You made yourself thousands of friends over here, and that is always a good thing.' However, as a publisher, he was also keen for Dylan to capitalise on his fame. 'As an author who almost never writes anything himself, I am always embarrassed about prodding others, but I do hope you will be writing again soon. Send along anything which you can turn out, as I shall be eager to see it.'

Dylan's more immediate concern was finding work in Britain. He resurrected his BBC contacts, but it was not easy to force a way back into their schedules. With MacNeice's position as a producer no longer vacant, Dylan suggested to Harman Grisewood, Controller of the Third Programme, that the Corporation might still find him some regular employment – possibly an attachment for a year or two. Margaret Taylor's controlling hand was discernible behind this. Living in London, she missed regular communication with Dylan. So, seizing on the possibility of Dylan working at the BBC, 'Maggs' took the initiative in trying to find the Thomases accommodation with the McAlpines. In July 1950 Bill McAlpine had finally found a job as scientific officer at the British Council. He and his wife celebrated by acquiring a large house in St James's Terrace in St John's Wood. As a closeish neighbour, Margaret Taylor hurried round to inspect the place. Caitlin was furious at this intrusion in her private life, without even her say-so.

Skilfully timing his trip to avoid a visit to Laugharne by Margaret, Dylan went to London in mid-August to discuss his prospects with Grisewood. Although the Controller himself was positive, and suggested Dylan might play some role in the BBC's coverage of the Festival of Britain the following year, others in the BBC were less enthusiastic and no job offer materialised.

Within a short time, Dylan's attentions were diverted, as his romantic entanglement with Pearl resurfaced. In June she had received an invitation from her friend Truman Capote to visit him in Taormina, Sicily, where he was renting D. H. Lawrence's old villa, La Fontana Vecchia, with a spectacular view of the sea and smoking Mount Etna. This raised the possibility that she might also see Dylan in London. She had had one letter from him – a mere two pages which she fondly described to Brinnin as long. This had stressed that she should write to him at 'my reactionary red-nosed club', the Savage. Apart from that, she had only heard rumours that he might be returning to the United States to teach. Still pining for him, she asked Stanley Moss, the poet who had befriended him in New York, if Dylan was serious about her. When he said he thought so, she decided to take leave of absence from *Harper's Bazaar* and devote several months to a European grand tour. Coincidentally, Capote invited another good friend, John Malcolm Brinnin, who was therefore also planning a rather shorter transatlantic trip in the late summer. Apart from his social commitments the Poetry Center director wanted to interview Alice B. Toklas in Paris for his ongoing biography of Gertrude Stein.

By early August Pearl had communicated her plans to Dylan. He was concerned the imminent intervention of the United States in the Korean War might delay her trip. 'Do you still arrive in England on the fourth of September, or will the war stop you, or some other madness?' he wrote to her as if from the Savage Club. 'If the dark leagues say No to you, I will declare war on America.' Although Dylan had taken the elementary precaution of asking Pearl to write to him at the Savage, he was careless what he did with the letters he received there. One day when he was at Brown's, Caitlin saw some pieces of paper in an unknown hand sticking out of his jacket. She read them and found they were love letters from Pearl. On Dylan's return from the pub, she confronted him. Typically, he tried to pass the matter off as inconsequential. This was the sort of thing he was always having to dodge from American women, he said. Caitlin wrote a blistering retort to Pearl, but remained wary. As usual when marital relations were tense, Dylan upped his alcohol intake. His wife complained that he had been drinking heavily since his return from America and had done no work, which was hardly the recipe for great advancement.

Dylan was back in London at the end of August. He claimed it was his duty to look after the visiting Brinnin who had not been there since before the war. Meeting Brinnin's boat train at Paddington station, Dylan looked not only well, but surprisingly smart (with his shoes polished for a change) and, as if to make a point, he was sporting a fat cigar. Over the next twenty-four hours or so, Dylan introduced his American tour agent to his London haunts – the Savage Club, where he seemed at home among the faded sepia photographs; the Salisbury, the pub in St Martin's Lane favoured by his acting friends; the Academy cinema in Oxford Street, where he smoked and then snored his way through the Marx Brothers' Duck Soup (which he must have seen countless times before); El Vino, the journalists' bar in Fleet Street, and the Mandrake, a Soho chess club which served – under its dishevelled patron, Boris Watson of the old Café An' – as an afternoon drinking dive.

At the last venue they were joined by Margaret Taylor, who knew about Brinnin from both Dylan and, more ominously, Caitlin, who had conveyed her suspicions of her husband's gadding about in the United States. With Maggs in her headmistress role, dinner at Wheeler's, a fashionable fish restaurant, was a frosty affair. Brinnin remarked how a drunken Dylan 'rather quickly sobered' over tasteless oysters and lobster. To prevent discussion straying onto the subject of, say, Pearl, Dylan suggested going to a revue at the London Casino where he insisted on paying for the best seats and then fell asleep. Afterwards the pubs were shut and even the Savage Club would not allow them a drink. While negotiating these matters with the hall porter, Dylan was called to the telephone. He was invited to a late night party which, according to Brinnin, was being given by the black actress Hilda Simms at her house near Regent's Park. She had played the lead in Anna Lucasta when Dylan had met the cast a couple of years earlier. On this occasion he spent most of his time talking to the singer Lena Horne. From their bantering manner, Brinnin correctly concluded that they had met before.

Over the course of a grey London weekend, Dylan treated Brinnin to more of his blowsy London hospitality. Then the reason for his glad rags and general sheen became clear. On the morning of Monday 4 September, Pearl arrived in town, after crossing the Atlantic in a bucketing English freighter turned passenger ship. As a surprise gift for Dylan she brought his watch which he thought he had seen the last of in New York after a friend dropped it in some beer. But the Frankenbergs had taken it to a repair shop, from where Pearl reclaimed it. Unfortunately within days he had lost it again – this time in Brighton. Brinnin arranged to meet them both for lunch at Wheeler's, but they did not turn up. Instead Dylan telephoned Brinnin's hotel and invited him to join them later at the Café Royal. Dylan was in ebullient mood, but clearly wanted to be alone with Pearl, so Brinnin discreetly left after one drink. The three of them met again at the Salisbury the following lunchtime. At Dylan's prompting, they strolled down to the Thames and took a river bus down the river to a point beyond Greenwich. As a series of photographs show, they were in good spirits. However Brinnin noticed that Dylan, for all his laughter, seemed perturbed. When Pearl went to refill their drinks at the bar, Dylan turned to him with a look of desperation and said, 'John, what am I going to do? I'm in love with Pearl and I'm in love with my wife. I don't know what to do.' (This was the version in Brinnin's *Dylan Thomas in America*. In a letter to Bill Read, he said, 'Dylan seems to be deeply taken with Pearl, to the point where he's wondering what might be done about it.'

With Brinnin leaving for France the next day, Dylan and Pearl escaped for a couple of nights à deux to the south coast, to Brighton. If there was an air of caution about this, it had disappeared by the time they returned to London, where, over lunch-time on a Saturday, Dylan squired Pearl around the Stag's Head without concern for the consequences. Rayner Heppenstall, who happened to be working at the BBC, described her as 'arty in clothes and manner, intelligent and full of suspicion'. Later in the afternoon the couple went to a party to celebrate George Reavey's wedding to the American artist Irene Rice Peirera. The wise old bird Wyn Henderson, who was present in her latest incarnation as housekeeper to BBC producer Bertie Rodgers, noted, 'He was with the Kazan [sic] girl and I thought they seemed much in love and that she was an exceptionally nice girl. I felt uneasy for Caitlin.'

Henderson was right to be wary. News of Dylan's activities reached Margaret Taylor who went to the Savage Club (where Dylan was nominally staying) and prevailed upon the hall porter to hand her Dylan's messages. Her suspicions confirmed, Margaret decided to punish her kept poet. Since the Thomases had recently installed a telephone, Margaret was able to dial Caitlin on their new number, Laugharne 68. She said she needed to see her immediately and, without further ado, announced she was catching the next train to Carmarthen. At the Boat House, she flung her arms around Caitlin, kissed her and followed her into the kitchen. Then she told her about Pearl.

What Dylan's benefactress thought would be gained by telling tales is hard to say. It was a personal, emotional reaction. She herself was jealous of the slim young American with the Juliette Greco fringe. She feared her own controlling influence in Dylan's life might end if, perhaps, he were to leave his family and go to the United States. No doubt, she also felt genuine concern for Caitlin and her children.

The immediate reaction was predictable. Caitlin was furious and thirsted for revenge. Only her pride held her back from abandoning her children and chasing after her husband in London. She waited until he returned later that week, and confronted him. Once again, Dylan tried to lie his way out of the situation and tell her she had got the wrong end of the stick. She remained unconvinced, sensing that this affair meant more to him than the others. More hurtful than anything was the thought of Dylan parading his girlfriend in the pubs they both used to frequent. It was this public humiliation that embittered her.

Dylan thought he had pacified her but, realising he was still in deep trouble, he wrote to Helen McAlpine begging her, if asked by Caitlin, to say that everything the 'grey scum', as he referred to Margaret, had said was LIES (and he capitalised the word for effect). 'All was LIES,' he reiterated. 'And, incidentally, it was. And, incidentally, the girl has gone to France, not to return.' In his alcoholic haze, he half-believed what he said: he could certainly argue that Pearl had known Reavey's new wife in New York. And it was true that Pearl had left for France. She had been escorted to the air terminal by Margaret Taylor, who continued to write to her telling her how lucky she was to be out of England.

As the autumn nights drew in, rows at the Boat House often turned into physical fights. On occasions Dylan would pass out and Caitlin would worry that she had killed him; other times she had to concoct elaborate stories about her own black eyes. Dylan was terrified that he had destroyed his marriage. And it is a moot point whether or not this was true. Caitlin admitted she never forgave him for this infidelity and she began to punish him with a series of her own affairs. At the same time, she was surprised at the degree of tenderness that still remained in her marriage. But Dylan could not see this. Within four months, he was writing to her, 'I'm in darkness because I do not know if you will ever love me again. And I'll die if you do not. I mean that. I shall not kill myself: I shall die.' And, without really trying, he did his best to speed the process.

He knew it was important to return to writing poetry, but found it difficult. He had promised Mike Watkins of the Ann Watkins agency in New York that his 'first task' on returning to England would be to write a poem for the agency to submit to either The New Yorker, Atlantic or the Hudson Review. But he made no progress on that score. The best he could do was polish up 'In the White Giant's Thigh' with a view to sending it to Botteghe Oscure. After one argument, Caitlin found a fair copy of the poem and somehow, being pregnant, took umbrage at its sexual connotations. She became so angry that she tore it up and threw it out over the verandah. Then, with the reverence for the creative act that was so important to her relationship with Dylan, she felt remorse and, while he was still asleep the next morning, tried to gather the pieces. He sent the sixty-line poem to Marguerite Caetani, complete with a note which placed it, as intended, in the context of a more ambitious work.

This way 'In the White Giant's Thigh' metamorphosed from a gloomy text into part of a more substantial celebratory poem, 'In Country Heaven'. This as yet unwritten longer work, which may have been gestating for over three years, was to start in the vein of 'In the White Giant's Thigh', with God weeping over the earth's self-destruction. (In Dylan's dizzying theology, God was 'the godhead, the author, the first cause, architect, lamplighter, the beginning word, the anthropomorphic bawler-out and black-baller, the quintessence, scapegoat, martyr, maker'.) But then the 'heavenly hedgerow men' who once inhabited earth begin to recall the contrasting pleasures and pains of life on that planet. 'And the poem becomes, at last, an affirmation of the beautiful and terrible worth of the earth. It grows into a praise of what is and what could be on this lump in the skies. It is a poem about happiness.'

In September Dylan recorded a version of this explicatory note for the BBC. It provided a framework for him to give a promised broadcast of his recent poems. Somewhat unconvincingly, Dylan claimed that two more poems – 'In Country Sleep' and 'Over Sir John's hill' – also formed part of the foreword to 'In Country Heaven'. With the addition of 'In the White Giant's Thigh', they at least gave Dylan something to read on the wireless and earn his twenty guineas. The programme's producer was Douglas Cleverdon, a former Bristol bookseller, who had featured Dylan's voice in a number of broadcasts, including In Parenthesis, Milton's Comus and the maligned Paradise Lost. Now Cleverdon wondered if something might be made of Dylan's long-held interest in writing the intimate history of a Welsh town, sometimes called Llareggub. Over the years this idea had evolved and even had dry runs, growing from discussions with Bert Trick and Richard Hughes before the war, through 'Quite Early One Morning' his evocative sketch of New Quay (or somewhere very similar) in 1944, to miniature radio dramas such as 'The Londoner' in 1946 and Dylan's later filmscripts.

The recent death of Edgar Lee Masters has concentrated Dylan's mind on the American author's Spoon River Anthology, about a mythical town in Illinois as seen through the eyes of the characters in the local graveyard, all keen to settle old scores. Cleverdon astutely set Dylan to editing the Anthology for a BBC programme, with the idea that the related subject-matter might also encourage him to finish his own radio play about an imaginary town. This latter project became known as The Town That Was Mad. As conceived in the autumn of 1950, this had a discernible plot about a town which, under obscure post-war legislation, was certified mad. In order to disprove this allegation, its inhabitants (with names familiar to Under Milk Wood) had to go to court where they were cross-examined by the blind Captain Cat. When the legal process was completed and the town's madness was confirmed, Captain Cat welcomed this verdict as a triumph for individuality.

Dylan took his family to London in September to work on these projects and to allow Caitlin to have an abortion (a topic on which there was never much debate). Initially they stayed in the Drayton Gardens flat of Mary Keene who had spent some time in Laugharne while Dylan was away and had liked the place. When Dylan became ill with something like pleurisy, Mary's doctor advised him to stop drinking. He replied predictably that he preferred the sickness to the cure. With Dylan in bed, Mary felt she had to move out with her daughter Alice and stay with friends. The Thomases seemed to have no sense that they were putting her out. When she returned, Caitlin said to her, 'I suppose you've come to throw us out.' Mary could only reply, 'Can't you see it's the other way round.'

Dylan then moved his family into a rented flat in South Kensington. With Cleverdon eager for a script that could be scheduled for the first quarter of 1951, Dylan at one stage escaped these cramped domestic quarters and moved into the Cadogan Hotel, once favoured by Oscar Wilde. When he and Caitlin visited Cleverdon and his wife Nest to read the work in progress, Philip Burton and his ward Richard were present. Nest Cleverdon was appalled that Caitlin could leave her three children, including one-year-old Colm, alone in a strange flat. But the reading was appreciated by all – all, that is, except Caitlin, who piped up at the end, 'Bloody pot-boiler'.

She might have been happier if it had been so and certainly if her husband had managed to finish it. But although Dylan sent Cleverdon a script of thirty-nine pages, he himself did not like it. The BBC offered him additional work to tide him along. In November he chaired a discussion on bad verse with several other poets including George Barker – somewhat ironically, since only the previous month he had stood at the bar of the Stag's Head and, hooting with laughter, had read out various sentences from Barker's new novel The Dead Seagull to Rayner Heppenstall, who also now worked for the BBC. The recording of the programme, 'Poetic Licence', was preceded by a 'lunch' for which, as the BBC archives dutifully record, Dylan had to borrow £5 from the producer. The lunch was clearly liquid, which led the reviewer in The Listener to note the 'cheerful animal noise from which only one or two human phrases emerged'. But the indulgent Corporation did not want to divert Dylan too much as its main objective was to secure delivery of its promised radio play.

With bills again piling up alarmingly, Dylan was forced to look elsewhere for money. Through the McAlpines he maintained good contacts in the film industry, where he claimed to be discussing a project with the young producer Ben Arbeid. (In an effort to curry favour with his patroness, he also asked Arbeid to look at *The Shadowless Man*, the filmscript he had written with Margaret Taylor. Arbeid indicated the project's lack of commerciality by tactfully suggesting it should be sent to Jean Cocteau.)

Another promising idea was that Dylan should write a radio series called 'Quid's Inn' with Ted Kavanagh, an Irish New Zealander whom he described as the 'best gagman in England'. Kavanagh, father of the poet P. J. Kavanagh, was at a loose end after ITMA, the comedy series which made his name, collapsed with the death of its principal actor Tommy Handley in January 1949. Dylan envisaged an ongoing story line based on the characters in a rural pub – a cross between ITMA, *Crossroads* and *The Archers*. Kavanagh drew up an outline and, although again nothing came of it, Dylan's involvement with a professional writer familiar with the comic possibilities of radio rubbed off and contributed to his handling of *Under Milk Wood*.

Despite subventions from the usual sources such as Margaret Taylor, Tony Hubbard and Marguerite Caetani, Dylan was forced in December to make a further plea for money to the Royal Literary Fund. Harold Nicolson backed the application, despite his caveats that Dylan was a 'very heavy drinker' and his wife 'almost equally unreliable'. Dylan was thankful for a prompt grant of £300 which was immediately swallowed up by school fees and local tradesmen's bills.

In December he began talking of a new most unlikely enterprise. Bunny Keene was again running his own film company, Greenpark, after an interlude at Gainsborough where he liked to claim he discovered James Bomford's Swindon friend Diana Dors (née Fluck) by casting her in his film *A Boy, a Girl and a Bike* in 1949. Returning to documentaries, he had been asked to make a film about Iran, following on his earlier successful feature about Cyprus with Laurie Lee. Greenpark's client was the Anglo-Iranian Oil Company (AIOC), which had the largest concession in the Middle-Eastern country. However it found itself in the centre of political upheaval, as nationalists made common cause with Islamic fundamentalists against the Shah's pro-western government, targeting the oil industry as the main area of the economy for fruitful agitation. Self-conscious about its image, Anglo-Iranian needed a good public relations job. A bibulous poet was hardly the most obvious candidate for such a task. However a literary man's overview had worked in the case of Cyprus. Anyway Dylan needed the money, and it seemed politic to get out of the marital home (though only after making sure that, while he was away, Greenpark paid Caitlin £10 a week out of his

£250 flat fee). On 8 January 1951, he and Bunny flew to Tehran, via Amsterdam and Lydda.

Their initial task was to set up the project and write a draft script. Filming, in glorious, expensive Technicolor, would follow. However, Bunny turned out to be an appalling hypochondriac, forever retiring to bed with pills and hot water bottles. Because of the growing political unrest, the bureaucracy was more obtuse and unyielding than usual. So Dylan spent his first few days in Tehran mooching around his oil company guest house, drinking with Scottish engineers, and waiting for Bunny – an unsatisfactory regime since it allowed him to think too much about Caitlin and if she still felt anything for him. At least he could call on Bunny for potions to send him to sleep.

His initial impressions were that the city was 'depressing and half-made'. He disliked oil men and their habit of 'running down the Persian wops'. The effects of poverty were painfully obvious, particularly when he visited a hospital and came across 'rows and rows of tiny little Persian children suffering from starvation: their eyes were enormous, seeing everything & nothing, their bellies bloated, their matchstick arms hung around with blue, wrinkled flesh.' On 17 January he and Bunny journeyed south by train to Ahwaz on the Persian Gulf, and on to Abadan, the centre of the oil industry, full of hissing state of the art refineries. In much hotter conditions, Dylan again despised the British oil workers, though he summoned some respect for the local people. One image struck him: four Iranians sitting on a small mudbank in the middle of a river. Their fatalistic ability to make the most of their situation inspired him to tell Caitlin that they too could both be happy in 'any dusty sunfried place'.

His timing was atrocious, for at almost exactly the same time his wife was telling Helen McAlpine that she had mentally cast Dylan out of her asylum. After a fortnight of silence, she had received his usual 'slop bucket douche' of a letter, leaving her wondering who was the fool. She felt he had her both ways. If he left her, she was still there, and if he came back it was the same. As a result she admitted that she had become exceedingly bitter.

Dylan was devastated when Caitlin wrote to him along these lines, saying she did not want to see him again. Lonely and unhappy as he already was in southern Iran, he had to wrestle from a distance with the awful possibility that his lifetime's relationship had broken down. Well might he answer in reply, 'Your letter, as it was meant to, made me want to die.' However he did not underestimate his wife's anger. He said that he would not return to Laugharne unless she wanted him – 'not as an inefficient mispayer of bills, but as myself and for you'. He asked her to leave a message for him at the McAlpines': if she did not, he would know 'everything is over'.

He tried opium as a palliative, but was not impressed, settling for vodka made from beetroot, which tasted like 'stimulating sockjuice', and a local beer full of glycerine. He can hardly have been great company when, with Bunny crying off sick with tonsillitis and opting to stay in Abadan, he took off to spend a couple of days camping with geologists in the hills. On his return, he and Bunny flew to Shiraz, the delightful tree-lined city of the poets Hafiz and Sadi, from where, suffering from gout, Dylan chose to write not to Caitlin but to Pearl, giving her a rather more jaundiced impression of 'lonely ... stricken' Iran and the sexually frustrated expatriates trying to run its oil industry.

The two colleagues returned from Isfahan to a snowbound Tehran for a week of scripting. On his last night, 13 February, Dylan gave a reading of his poems to the Anglo-Iranian Society at the British Council. At an accompanying party, he consumed so much vodka (the only available drink) that Olive Suratgar, widow of a head of English at the university, became seriously worried. Emotionally racked though he was, the trouper could still work his old magic: 'when he read so beautifully', Mrs Suratgar found herself 'shivering with delight'.

The following day Dylan flew to London where he found Caitlin had failed to carry out her threat and was again waiting for him at the McAlpines. It was a complicated, unhappy home-coming. Finding that his bored wife had been in town for several days, he suspected her of having an affair with the younger amusing South African-born poet David Wright. She admitted a romantic fling, but it does not seem to have been consummated. However Dylan had an excuse to flounce off and feel doubly hurt. His behaviour may have been linked to the fact that Pearl was passing through London, on her way back to America from Sicily.

Within a week he returned to Laugharne where a fraught situation became alarmingly worse when Caitlin found another batch of letters from Pearl, one replying to a cable from Iran reiterating his love and continued desire for her. Having been careless enough to let the letters be found, Dylan compounded his stupidity by still trying to assert that there was nothing to his affair with Pearl who, he said, was another Margaret Taylor. Caitlin was adamant that even someone as hare-brained as herself could not accept that.

It was a miserable start to a miserable year. Dylan was forced to find a temporary berth at the McAlpines, from where he pursued various unlikely possibilities of work, such as the Quid's Inn project. With no doors opening, the outcome was predictable. 'Dylan is here,' wrote his hosts to the newly married Reaveys. 'He came back last night like a prize fighter's sparring partner! An enormous black eye, shirt torn to ribbons. He said he tried to hit a fellow smaller than himself, but when he looked up at him from the floor, he was over six foot. (Overheard: Dylan's description of the weather in Wales: grey, wet, windy and cold like an old man's bum.)'

There was little respite at the BBC. Although sympathetic, Cleverdon at the Third Programme was reluctant to let him start on any new scripts 'until he has finished the two or three which have already been commissioned for some time'. Looking for a way round the problem, either Cleverdon or perhaps Margaret Taylor may have asked their friend John Betjeman if he could prevail on George Barnes, the former head of the Third Programme and now head of BBC Television, to find Dylan a job. Betjeman did his best: 'I like [Dylan Thomas] all right myself, and I like some of his poetry, and I know that he really understands poetry, and reads it and interprets it beautifully.' Noting that Maggs was coming to see Barnes about this, Betjeman stressed that Dylan was 'more important than I am. He can't provide for his family. I at least can do that.'

Although nothing came of this initiative, the Home Service was happy to take a piece from Dylan on Iran which, despite lifting a long paragraph directly from a letter to Caitlin, skilfully conveyed the country's delicate balance between progress and tradition. At the Welsh service in Cardiff Aneirin Talfan Davies expressed interest in Dylan reporting on the ongoing Festival of Britain, and giving it a Welsh twist. After the usual delays, Dylan prevailed on an Oxford friend, Mary Ellidge, to accompany him, telling her how he hated exhibitions. They went by way of a Bloomsbury pub, where they met Richard Huws, a Welsh sculptor whom Dylan had known before the war. Huws had designed several features for the Festival site, including a celebrated water mobile, and seemed an appropriate guide since Dylan was writing for a Welsh audience. He proved his worth by declaring that the most stimulating places in the twenty-two pavilions were the bars – all decorated with murals by different artists. When Dylan reached Huws's modernist steel and platinum water mobile, Ellidge remarked on the use of Handel's Water Music as accompaniment. 'Is that what it is?' said Dylan, noting this information on a cigarette packet. The detail duly appeared in his talk, together with colourful journalistic observations on places such as the Dome of Discovery and the Transport Pavilion. His comment on the British character – 'that stubborn, stupid, seabound, lyrical, paradoxical dark farrago of uppishness, derring-do, and midsummer moonshine all fluting, snug and copper-bottomed' – bears repeating, but his florid verbal picture of the night-time Thames was from the public relations side of his documentary film-making days.

Dylan kept up his occasional speaking engagements. But when he addressed a meeting of the English Society at Swansea University in April, he ran up against Kingsley Amis, to whom he was the epitome of a bombastic, old-fashioned style of poetry. Amis, an English lecturer there, treated his friend Philip Larkin to a venomous description. Dylan's 'conversation consisted of one or two written-out solos and a string of very dirty and not very funny limericks ... His talk was horrible: shagged epigrams topped up with some impressionistic stuff about America that I imagine he had inserted from another talk and with a backlash of dutiful impropriety.' Amis expanded on this in the *Spectator*, where he described Dylan as looking like 'a dissolute but very amiable frog'. He enjoyed an exchange where, when Dylan mentioned he had been in Persia, 'pouring water on troubled oil', Amis asked if he could write that down and Dylan replied he already had. Although he sensed signs of charlatanry, even Amis could not deny Dylan's voice was magnificent and his delivery 'infectious'.

During the first few months of the year, two out-of-town friends had acquired small houses in Laugharne. One was Mary Keene who prevailed on Matthew Smith to buy her a two-room cottage in the Lakes, a lane towards the bottom end of the town. Mary's daughter Alice fitted in well as a playmate for the Thomas children. Having been raised in London, she was astonished at the material poverty of the local people. She also recognised Caitlin's extraordinary spirit: 'I didn't like her, but she was terrific', bundling the children off for picnics and even taking Mary swimming with no regard for any embarrassment her friend might feel about her metal leg. Alice observed the rest of the Thomas family – D.J. pale and thin, a very different specimen from his son; Florrie laughing, with, as was common practice in the Welsh countryside, a village girl to share her bed and keep her warm; Llewelyn protective of his ground-floor room at the Boat House, which he perceived to be under threat from the girls; Aeronwy seeking to assert her independence in the face of her domineering mother. (She wanted to learn to cook, for example, when Caitlin would have her dancing.)

The other was Margaret Taylor who purchased a place on the Grist, from where she was able to monitor Dylan's progress. It soon became clear that the Laugharne experiment was not working. Dylan admitted he found it difficult to write when feeling guilty that the local traders had not been paid. A note of frustration with the Welsh town had begun to creep into his communications, whether to John Davenport, to whom he moaned about 'my horribly cosy little nest, surrounded by my detestable books, wearing my odious warm slippers, observing the gay, reptilian play of my abominable brood, basking in the vituperation of my golden, loathing wife', or to Lloyd Frankenberg and Loren MacIver, for whom he took to cummings-inspired verse:

> In this pretty as a stricture town by the eel
> y, oily, licking sea full of fish that taste like feet...
> under a bathwater sky...
> Nine hundred gabies, two chapels soprano with rat
> s; five catafalque pubs licensed to sell enbalming gin
> And aconite tobacc
> o: such is my home

To Brinnin, he simply said, 'I'm sick of Laugharne. It has rained here since last June.' Margaret Taylor understood the message and began talking about finding him a flat or house in London, possibly in Cheyne Walk, where he could once again be close to more lucrative sources of income, such as the film industry.

Perhaps it was her influence that led to Dylan completing some excellent poems during the spring and early summer. 'Lament' is a swaggering, punning account of a one-time sexual athlete's rise and fall back into the enveloping folds of family and religion. To an extent he is poking fun at himself, though the colliery imagery (emphasised in the title 'The Miner's Lament' used in one worksheet in Texas), gives the poem a more universal, and added metaphorical, appeal. 'Do not go gentle into that good night' is an anguished protest against his father's declining powers, particularly his loss of sight. But as often in Dylan's poetry it was more complicated than that. When he sent both these poems to Marguerite Caetani in quick succession in May, he said of the latter, 'The only person I can't show the enclosed poem to is, of course, my father, who doesn't know he's dying.' The reason was that, in its careful villanelle form, it was also about men discovering their lives had been failures – a category that included his father, if not Dylan himself. At the same time it is a plea to seventy-five-year-old D.J. not to lapse into sentimental religion of the kind satirised in 'Lament', but to retain his quality of fierce scepticism that had been such an important influence in Dylan's development. (In a talk the following year, Dylan would tell how his father was so firmly opposed to the notion of a personal God that he would stand at the window and growl, 'It's raining, blast Him!')

By July Dylan was promising the Princess another piece, a longish poem on a birthday theme which he said he liked better than anything he had written for a long time, 'which does not say a great deal'. This was 'Poem on his Birthday' which, from its internal reference to his thirty-fifth birthday, originated nearly two years earlier. Again on one level it is a personal record of Dylan's heightened sensitivities as he reaches the half point in his allotted Bible span and begins to 'sail out to die'. At first he approaches this subject-matter through a familiar gentle Laugharne landscape of cormorants and curlews. Typically of Dylan, he both 'celebrates and spurns' the anniversary. But, as he looks at nature, he realises not just the prevalence of death but how creatures seem unthinkingly to seek it out. Similarly, as he told Bill Read when he came to Laugharne with Brinnin that summer, a poet 'sings in the direction of his pain', or, put differently, toils 'towards his own wounds which are waiting to ambush him'. In a complicated exposition of his theology, Dylan recognises the attraction and mystery of religion. But it is not for him: his blessings are more tangible and earthly – the four elements and five senses. As he stated to Brinnin during this visit, his aim was to produce 'poems in praise of God's world by a man who doesn't believe in God'. 'Poem on his Birthday' is his statement of this position – a cosmically aware, religiously minded humanist's anthem, a personalised version of 'Do not go gentle into that good night'.

Despite his respect for a spiritual viewpoint, his own atheism had recently become more pronounced, perhaps the result of renewed proximity to his father. One night he stayed in Notting Hill with the Roman Catholic writer Bernard Wall, a friend of John Davenport. According to Wall, Dylan proposed translating with him the poems of Umberto Saba, a Jewish poet from Trieste. When, the following morning, Wall's wife Barbara made Dylan a cup of tea, they started talking about religion. At her mention of her faith, Dylan stated categorically, 'The after life is one of the most terrible things you Christians have thought up. When I'm dead I want to be buried and to feel the violets growing over me.'

As the crossings out on his worksheets attest, 'Poem on his Birthday' did not come easily. But it was a stunning work, fully justifying his personal note of satisfaction. Devastatingly, on its completion in August, he took it on one of his job-searching trips to London where, finding himself unable to afford the fare back to Wales, he sold the manuscript to the short-lived *World Review* which paid him a miserable £10, considerably less than his potential fee from *Botteghe Oscure*.

Dylan was still working on the poem when Brinnin and Read came to stay in late July. Having rediscovered London the previous year, Brinnin wanted to come back and develop his contacts in the English literary world. But, however much he might protest the contrary, he was also quietly determined to get Dylan back for another American tour. After meeting John Davenport, Edith Sitwell, David Gascoyne and others, he and his boyfriend travelled to Cardiff, where he was broadcasting on Dylan, and to Carmarthen where they were met at the station by the poet himself. Over the next three days the pleasures of their introduction to Laugharne and West Wales were dampened by their hosts' fighting among themselves and, in particular, by Caitlin's hostility towards the Americans personally. This surfaced when Dylan hired Billy Williams and his ancient Buick to take them all round Pembrokeshire. After stops at various pubs, Dylan was chatting garrulously to Billy in the front, when Caitlin began questioning Brinnin at her side in the back about Pearl, wanting to know what sort of a person she was, where she was now, and if she intended coming back to England. Brinnin squirmed with embarrassment, partly because of the topic and partly because Dylan was so close. He realised he had not satisfied her curiosity and, by the time the group reached St David's Head, at the far western tip of Wales, a distinct tension had arisen. A photograph taken in the ruins of the bishop's palace next to St David's cathedral shows an apparently contented group, though, according to Brinnin, 'the camera had never lied more gracefully'. Caitlin, who had insisted on taking a swim in the nude, refused to speak when they stopped for tea. Then, with the atmosphere darkening and everybody longing to return home, Dylan insisted on leading them to a place in Fishguard for 'a magnificent lobster dinner', which turned out to be nothing of the sort. On the return journey Caitlin sat in the front while Dylan slept on Brinnin's shoulder. Occasional snatches of her conversation would reach the back, such as her comment that she was looking forward to a visit from some 'real friends, not Americans'. Back at the Boat House, after Dylan went directly and silently to bed, Brinnin prepared to sleep on a sofa in the sitting room, while Read took Llewelyn's bedroom. As she swept upstairs, Caitlin turned and spat out the words, 'Now you can see what I mean. America is out.'

The two visitors sat up late in the night wondering what they could have done to offend her. They toyed with leaving but next morning she and Dylan were so charming and seemingly oblivious of any irregularity, that they decided to stay. But after a pleasant day meeting Dylan's parents and friends, reading his latest work and discussing an American tour, they were subjected to another alarming display. Dylan began sounding off over dinner on topics such as the need for compulsory execution of all sex offenders. Anything he said, Caitlin contradicted. Before long husband and wife were throwing things and assaulting each other. When Dylan finally broke away, she snarled at her dumbfounded guests, 'Thank you for helping a lady.' She then calmed down and poured out her woes which, for all the practical problems of money, boiled down to her feeling trapped with her family in Laugharne while Dylan lorded it in the United States. Reiterating a line she had already communicated to Brinnin by post, she accused him of flattering Dylan's ego. She said her husband was not going to America again without her and, as she was not budging, the decision was irrevocable.

Clearly this was an emotionally charged subject in the Thomas household. Earlier that month, it had seemed to be resolved, as Dylan had given Oscar Williams and Marguerite Caetani definite hints that he was going to America. Brinnin's presence had stirred in Caitlin memories of her unhappiness at the outcome of the previous trip. However Dylan's parlous finances had their own inexorable logic. Before long details of a new itinerary were being bandied across the Atlantic. By mid-August Laughlin was congratulating Brinnin on the 'good news' of Dylan's return to the United States in the new year. 'However, I hope you will beat him sternly and constantly on the head, so that he will write more poems, and not just spend all his time in bars. It is really tragic that he indulges himself so continually, and I don't see how he can survive long at the present pace.' In London later that month, Laughlin saw Dylan briefly and impressed on him the usefulness of having a new book to coincide with his visit. Dylan's output since *Deaths and Entrances* (or *Selected Writings* in the United States) amounted to six poems. But Laughlin seemed satisfied and asked Dylan if he wanted the book to take the title of one of the poems, with the addition & *Other Poems*, or if it might be called by one of the many fine phrases in the verse, such as 'The Hawk on Fire' or 'Under a Serpent Cloud'.

While these details were being worked out over the autumn, Dylan's relationship with Caitlin went from bad to worse. She remained implacably opposed to his returning to America. As a form of revenge, she started casually picking up men, even local youths in Brown's. Hearing about these one night stands from Ivy Williams, Dylan questioned Caitlin about them and, although she lied, he was relieved to hear her denial.

But the tantrums and the fisticuffs, as well as the bills and the summonses, continued. When Lizzie Lutyens came to stay at the Boat House, she found that her friend had a scar on her forehead and Dylan had fled the nest, threatening suicide. Caitlin was concerned that Dylan had telephoned from Swansea the previous night and announced dramatically, 'This is the last time you will hear my voice.' When, after two days, nothing further was heard, Lutyens, on Caitlin's behalf, telephoned Dan Jones who knew where Dylan was staying. Dan said that, although Dylan did not want to come home, he might be encouraged to meet Caitlin in a local pub. A stormy reconciliation ensued, which resulted in the Thomases missing their last train home and Lutyens (whom Caitlin had begged to accompany her) having to fork out for a taxi. The return journey was farcical, with Dylan demanding to stop for a pee at regular intervals, each time pretending to run away and having to be caught. Lutyens, who was living in the McAlpines' house, was one of several emotionally scarred women who did their best to give Caitlin emotional support. She was shocked at the way Dylan in Laugharne had taken on Welsh patriarchal attitudes. He even resented the two women going out for walks together. Lizzie encouraged Caitlin to keep up her dancing and felt privileged to be offered her poems to read.

This was a sideline that Caitlin had been quietly developing. Earlier in the year she had been in correspondence with Oscar Williams, thanking him and his wife for sending her some nylon stockings. When he replied, expressing interest in her own writing, she told him she had been trying to write him some verse, but found it difficult because whenever she asked Dylan the rudiments of his trade, he seemed unable to explain. So, if she felt under pressure, she resorted to writing down her thoughts as concisely as she could and she hoped that the results could be described as poetry.

One of her efforts recorded in some detail her contempt for Margaret Taylor, whom she portrayed as prim, emotionally repressed and rapacious. While her style might be faulted, her rhythm rattled along.

Unfortunately for Caitlin, this was the woman who was looking for a house for her and her family in London. Although unhappy at this prospect, Dylan realised he had little option. 'I hate to leave this sea but I must earn a living and will be writing filmscripts, class very B.' While still in Laugharne, he occupied himself with The Town That Was Mad project for the BBC. However in his desperation for money (he had been threatened with prosecution for not paying his National Insurance stamps), he was forced to offer a version of this to Marguerite Caetani. In October he sent her the first half of something he called Llareggub. A Play for Radio Perhaps, and promised to complete it soon. In anticipation of this, he begged her to send him £100 now, for the whole work. With this in mind, he took the trouble to explain some of the characters and say it was based on the town where he lived.

By November Margaret Taylor had found the Thomases somewhere to live in London. Unsurprisingly, it was not in Cheyne Walk, but a basement flat at 54 Delancey Street in Camden Town, within a quarter of a mile (across a railway line) of where she herself lived. Maggs convinced herself that if Dylan had a 'London dump', he could do his 'bread and butter work' in the capital and not have to go to America.

Dylan and Caitlin brought their Laugharne help Dolly Long (and her son Desmond) with them to look after the children. Maggs somehow managed to wheel up the old caravan from South Leigh and park it in the garden, allowing Dylan at least temporary respite from the din.

It did not prove a happy experiment. Again potential work projects kept collapsing underneath him: he had had hopes of writing scripts for Donald Taylor who was now a director of Regent Film Productions, with grand-sounding offices in London, New York, Hollywood, Hamburg, Cairo and Singapore. But nothing materialised, and Dylan was reduced to appearing on a BBC light entertainment show 'Say the Word'. Otherwise he explored the pubs around Delancey Street – particularly the Black Cat, where the Irish immigrants were always good company, and Old Mother Red Cap, where an undertaker kept him amused with tall stories about his trade, such as the time a coffin lid would not close because the corpse had an enormous erection.

At least Oscar Williams continued to work on Dylan's behalf. In June he bludgeoned Edward Weeks, editor of *Atlantic*, into accepting 'In the white giant's thigh' and paying $150. Weeks described the poem as 'a lovely thing, a sort of paean to the life force, musical, highly emotional, compact, full of beautiful pictures, & as one of my assistants says, "unhampered by any consensus to common place logic". We think it is Grade-A Thomas.' Williams begged Dylan to send more poems to him, in preference to *Botteghe Oscure* or other such publications. 'You are too good, & too well known, & too poor, for any magazine to lay down conditions. The Italian magazine will take months, literally months, before they publish. I can arrange American publication in the meantime, if I had copies of your poems ...' When in October Dylan sent 'Poem on his Birthday', along with a dire account of his financial and physical well-being, Oscar considered it 'a beauty; the strict vowel rhymes throughout add a freshness & simplicity unparalleled in modern poetry; it's lucid as moonlight on the Hudson on a clear night'. At *Atlantic*, Weeks agreed, in view of Dylan's hardship, to pay $200, though he felt $300 – the sum Oscar requested – would have been unfair to earlier contributors including Frost, Eliot and Auden. In return the magazine asked for a prose note to accompany the poem, as had been the case with 'In the white giant's thigh'. Oscar replied wistfully, 'I have never had much success in getting Mr Thomas to write anything special, within six months of the request.'

By now, for all Maggs's efforts, America could not be avoided. Surprisingly, however, Caitlin relented and made plans to accompany her husband to New York on the *Queen Mary* on 15 January. Maggs too changed her position: when the American embassy again queried Dylan about his trip to Prague in 1947, she asked Nicholas Henderson, a young friend in the Foreign Office, to see what he could do to speed matters along. As an added boost, the London publisher Allen Wingate contracted to take a 60,000-word journal of Dylan's American trip. The responsible editor was Charles Fry, an amiable alcoholic whom Dylan had known on the pub circuit for many years. He agreed to pay a £400 fee (£100 of which was up front), though the specified delivery date was tight.

The reason for Caitlin's change of heart is unclear. Perhaps she simply wanted to get away and have a good time. She may have been convinced by Maggs that she was better off beside her husband than away from him. She may also have heard that, in an effort to put Dylan behind her, Pearl had married Vincent Kraft, a photographer and former lover of Aaron Copland, and had moved with him to Brazil. As an augury of her new life, making a living by her own pen, Pearl had even sold a story to *Botteghe Oscure*. It was called 'The Jester', which could have been a wry comment on her relationship with Dylan. Although ostensibly about an energetic New York literary figure called Kuney, the piece was full of intimations of Dylan — not least, its second sentence: 'When his memory absorbs me now, I turn with strange formality to the extremes of the Earth's turning.'

TWENTY

BATTLE AGAINST AMERICAN HOSPITALITY

Brinnin had promised to roll out the red carpet if the Thomases managed to catch the *Queen Mary* on time. Halfway through their voyage they cabled him: 'See you Pier 90 Sunday Bring Carpet Love Dylan Caitlin.' He was there at the quayside, clutching a small square of red carpet and a box of gardenias, when they docked around mid-day on Sunday 20 January 1952 He and a small welcoming party waited for two hours until Dylan finally emerged from the customs shed, looking like a koala bear in a vast brown parka, followed by his wife, a character from *Anna Karenina* in a black fur ensemble.

Brinnin had arranged for them both to stay for a couple of days at the Millbrook, New York house of his photographer friend, Rollie McKenna, who specialised in writers' portraits. En route he was cheered to see how eagerly Dylan pointed out interesting sights and features of American popular culture to Caitlin. He thought this heralded an improvement in their relationship. He did not at first appreciate the significance of her sullen silence. She endured a photographic shoot on a bitingly cold morning, when McKenna took a well-known portrait of Dylan looking uneasy, climbing among, and as if hemmed in by, the matted vine in front of her snow-bound house. But when McKenna took her guests on a quick sight-seeing tour, including a visit to her alma mater, the all-women's college, Vassar, at nearby Poughkeepsie, Caitlin feigned disgust at the students in their regulation blue jeans. 'Ridiculous!' she commented. 'They look like intellectual witches.'

It soon became clear that, to Caitlin, every woman in America fitted this description. Noticing her husband talking animatedly to an attractive young women at a post-performance reception, she turned to Brinnin and – one instance among many – asked, 'Who is that bitch with him now?' When Brinnin began to explain, she interrupted, 'Does Dylan sleep with her?' Often she realised she was being foolish; she said she could put on a 'first class Queen Mary act' if required. But her competitive nature could not stand the sight of Dylan at the centre of a circle of eager, mainly female listeners. She let her animosity extend to the country and its people. Asked in a kindly, perhaps slightly condescending manner, what she thought of America, she replied aggressively, 'I can't get out of the bloody country soon enough.' Once, when Dylan was girding himself before a reading, she announced, as if to encourage him, 'Just remember, they're all dirt.'

As their New York base the Thomases chose a one-bedroom apartment with integral kitchenette at the Chelsea Hotel, a shabby genteel establishment catering for artists and writers on West 23rd Street. Greenwich Village was perhaps further away than they might have liked. But it was where they liked to meet friends in bars such as the San Remo and the White Horse, slightly west on 10th Street and Hudson. Dylan gravitated towards the latter, which was run by an elderly Bavarian couple. Frequented by Hudson river longshoremen, its atmosphere was similar to a British pub, more Swansea, with its port connections, than London. It offered cheap German food such as schnitzels and bratwursts, and it was round the corner from Ruthven Todd and his quietly spoken new wife Jody, a painter from Oklahoma. Len and Ann Lye were also close, as were some new friends, the sculptor David Slivka and his wife Rose, who wrote on art, antiques and interiors. Although further afield, the Frankenbergs and Williamses could join them when required.

In the mornings Dylan would slope off to the White Horse, leaving Caitlin to work on a journal which she illustrated with her own brand of wild caricature. (Unnervingly, in her more uncommunicative moods, she would take out her notebook and begin sketching everyone around her.) She then liked to go shopping at Macy's or some other department store. Brinnin had provided Dylan with money in advance of his earnings, though this cache soon ran low, and having to ask her husband for dollar handouts only increased Caitlin's resentment. On more than one occasion, when she felt she needed medication, Dylan arranged for her to see Pearl's physician Dr Anne Baumann who more than a year later was forced to threaten legal proceedings in an effort of obtain full payment. In Caitlin's angry depressed state, shopping became an obsession: like a child in a sweet-shop, she found herself wanting to snatch what she saw in front of her and make for the exit. The abundance and variety of consumer goods was almost unbearably enticing for her.

Later, she would join Dylan but, whereas he tended to stick to beer, she had discovered cocktails and rye whisky on the rocks – a potent combination, given New York's liberal licensing hours. (It was impossible, she told Helen McAlpine, for 'a highly trained Britisher' to leave before closing time, even if that was often three o'clock in the morning.) His friends got used to the couple's squabbles, often arising out of her sexual taunts, as when, once at the Todds, she dismissed him as 'just an old fag', and he replied, 'If only I were.' Among his circle, she took to

Oscar Williams, who not only had expressed interest in her writing but also seemed to understand how important it was to her as an impecunious mother in Laugharne that he sold Dylan's work for quick, ready cash. However her special friend was Rose Slivka, who had the knack of keeping her occupied and relatively calm while Dylan was reading and being feted by his mainly female fans (or 'ardents', as he called them). When Dylan appeared at the Museum of Modern Art, for example, Caitlin and Rose went to the theatre to see the dancer, Martha Graham.

At the time Brinnin was promoting an American tour by three other British poets – W. S. Graham, David Gascoyne and Kathleen Raine – which may explain why Dylan's early timetable was so leisurely. The Poetry Center director was also preparing for a talk by Truman Capote in mid-February. Or he may simply have decided, for the sake of Dylan's well-being, not to burden him with too many readings: the first at Columbia University was a full ten days after his arrival. It was followed in quick succession by two appearances at the YM-YWHA where the applause exceeded anything on his first trip. Otherwise for the next month his only engagements outside Manhattan were brief trips to Washington D.C., Burlington, Vermont, and Montreal, Quebec.

As a result Dylan had plenty of time to attend to minor business matters. One was the issue of his representation in the United States. Ann Watkins no longer wanted to handle Higham's British authors who were being taken on by the William Morris agency. However there were problems because, following an earlier row, James Laughlin refused to deal with Helen Strauss, the responsible executive at William Morris. A compromise was arrived at whereby Higham would deal directly with New Directions over existing authors such as Dylan. But Strauss wanted to earn her keep, selling Dylan's poems to magazines – an area Dylan had entrusted on a bilateral basis to the commercial Oscar Williams. So, with Williams in tow, he visited Strauss and an unsatisfactory modus vivendi was reached.

Dylan was able to spend longer than expected messing around with artist friends in the Village. There was an idea he might make a film with Len Lye, who ran several of his own coloured abstract movies for him, in the hope that one might provide the right backdrop for a poem. When nothing seemed right, Dylan offered to write something about a bicycle, Lye remembered.

Suggestions of a film cropped up again when, in anticipation of New Directions' publication of In Country Sleep and Other Poems at the end of February, Time magazine despatched Irving Berlin's daughter, Mary Ellin Barrett, from its research department to interview Dylan with a view to a profile. Finding him hungover at the Chelsea, she took him first to a bar for a restorative drink and then to a nearby steakhouse where he toyed with a plate of oysters while a watchful Caitlin urged him to eat something more substantial. He told Barrett about two projects: one was the completion of his novel *Adventures in the Skin Trade*, the other a film based on the *Odyssey*. Caitlin was at pains to point out that, though the book existed, the film did not. She was being protective of her husband because, only in January, he had discussed such an idea with the film director Michael Powell. Dylan had advised him to talk to Louis MacNeice who had a better classical education, but relented when Powell countered that he was a much better poet than MacNeice.

Within weeks Powell had visited Igor Stravinsky in Hollywood where, in the composer's words, he proposed 'to make a short film, a kind of masque, of a scene from the *Odyssey*; it would require two or three arias as well as pieces of pure instrumental music and recitations of pure poetry. Powell said that Thomas had agreed to write the verse; he asked me to compose the music.' Stravinsky, who had been alerted to Dylan by Auden, offered to write a twelve-minute score for $12,000. Finance proved difficult to raise and the project did not progress, though Stravinsky retained the idea of working with the Welsh poet. At this stage, however, delicate negotiations were still under way, and Caitlin was determined that there should be no media leakage about a project which was not only dear to Dylan but which promised to steer his career in a new and potentially lucrative direction. As a result Barrett's interview meandered in different directions without getting anywhere. *Time* did not run it as it was, though the poet's evasiveness did interest its editors enough to commission a more substantial profile, with unexpected consequences.

After an appearance at the Poetry Center, Dylan was approached by two young women, Barbara Cohen and Marianne Roney, who wanted to record him reading his poetry. They were unable to beat a path through his throng of admirers on that occasion but, encouraged by Brinnin, they telephoned Dylan regularly at the Chelsea. Eventually Cohen managed to speak to him at five o'clock one morning after he had stumbled back from a party. They agreed to meet at the Little Shrimp, the restaurant attached to the hotel. Caitlin again looked on suspiciously as the two women, both twenty-two years old and recently out of college, made their pitch. At the time they had not even set up their company, Caedmon Records, intending to distribute their records through Cohen's employer, the publisher Liveright. But their enthusiasm, coupled with the offer of a $500 advance against the first 1,000 albums, with a 10 per cent royalty thereafter, helped sway Dylan.

He missed his first scheduled recording session, but turned up at the Steinway Hall on 57th Street a week later, on the afternoon of Friday 22 February. He did not know that Laurence Olivier had been there earlier in the day recording a tribute to King George VI who had died a couple of weeks beforehand. Dylan had a sheaf of poems he intended reading, but the sound engineer Peter Bartók (son of the Hungarian composer Béla Bartók) said that these would only fill one side of a long-playing record. Without much ado, Dylan recalled he had recently written 'A Child's Christmas in Wales' for *Harper's Bazaar*. After some scurrying around, a copy of the magazine was obtained, and Dylan gave a lively rendition of his story. It was an astute move because, after the record was pressed by RCA and released on the Caedmon label on 2 April, it sold quietly. As Dylan's name became more widely known, however, this sentimental story, in particular, captured the imagination of America.

On the evening of the recording, the avant-garde film-maker Maya Deren threw a party for Dylan. Recently returned from Haiti, she was enthusiastic about its Voodoo religion, which struck her as both ancient and modern. The young Anatole Broyard, later a *New York Times* book critic, observed the extraordinary scene when Deren played tapes of rhythmic Haitian music. As the drumming reached a crescendo, two people remained dancing – one the squat Deren, the quintessential Manhattan artist with her minimal movement and understated appearance; the other Caitlin, bumping and grinding for Britain with her skirt lifted above her head to reveal legs, thighs and cotton knickers. Before long it was clear the two women were in fierce competition. When Deren tried to shoo her rival off the floor, Caitlin shot out a straight right that left a solicitous guest reeling. Then, spying the collection of small Haitian gods Deren had brought back, she began hurling them against the wall. Only Deren's stricken cries woke a sleeping Dylan who grabbed hold of his wife and, as if suddenly magically empowered, swung her in one remarkable, deft movement through an open door onto a bed in the next room. Since Dylan was in no state to do anything else, Broyard was deputed to watch over her and hold her down if necessary. She threw her arms around his neck and demanded, 'For God's sake, man, love me, love me.' Although he politely declined her invitation, he was one of the few people considered sober enough to take her home. In the car on the way to the Chelsea, she snuggled up to him. When he took her to her room, she asked him in for a drink. 'Another time' he said, preparing to dash. (She was trying to get her own back on Dylan by conducting her own affairs, but, in the circumstances, this was difficult. So, according to her friend Rose Slivka,

Caitlin sometimes went to the water-front when she would pick up a sailor or longshoreman.)

Soon the legend of the battling Thomases had reached the other side of the Atlantic, where the gossipy Edith Sitwell told a friend about their attendance at a party given by Mrs Murray Crane, the rich widow of a former US senator. A long-time patron of artistic causes, she had helped found the Museum of Modern Art, where she sat on the committee which arranged poetry readings. Her soirées were formal affairs where, as even Sitwell archly put it, the watchwords were 'Decorum, Bonne Tenue, and the milder and more restrained forms of Evening Dress'. Undaunted, Dylan flew at Caitlin and, according to Sitwell's informant, 'kicked, punched and bloodily beat' her. After being asked to leave, Dylan reappeared and asked for the money for a taxi.

On the Saturday night after Maya Deren's party, actress Judith Malina observed Dylan banging forlornly on the locked door of the San Remo after closing time. The following evening she saw him again, but this time in full verbal flight on stage at the Cherry Lane Theatre on 8th Street, where she and her husband Julian Beck had appeared with their Living Theater. Oscar Williams had arranged a special performance for the Village artistic community. Tickets were $1 a head, and Dylan had promised to read only his own poems. However the show was nearly cancelled when he arrived claiming to have lost his copy of his poems. Luckily Malina had one, which was duly returned with ten little bookmarks, each with the name of a poem in his meticulous hand. She was one of the few New Yorkers to recognise that Dylan's poetry had some intellectual content. As a result of a fever she heard his 'priestly incantation through a veil of discomfort. Till I crossed into the depth of Thomas' thought beyond the cavernous grandeur of his language.'

Ten days later Dylan and Caitlin travelled north for engagements in the Boston area. They had been offered the use of Brinnin's apartment on the campus of Massachusetts Institute of Technology where their host's mother Frances was also staying. While Dylan gave his talks, Caitlin found her latest ally in the unlikely figure of Mrs Brinnin, a bland woman who cooked excellent meals and never disagreed with anything. At the weekend Brinnin took the Thomases to Salem for a lobster dinner which rivalled the one in Wales the previous year in its awfulness. By the end of the evening the whole outing had taken on a similar doomed air, after Dylan insisted on visiting a strip-tease show in Boston, and Caitlin sank menacingly into one of her silent moods.

Once Dylan returned to find his wife contentedly playing with Frances's make-up. When Brinnin's mother apologised that this was her fault, Caitlin retorted, 'If you want to know God's truth, Dylan thinks

all women should simply wash their faces in cold water, like nuns.'
'Why not?' asked Dylan. 'That's what men do.' 'I've been looking for
just this colour for years,' said Caitlin, ignoring him. 'What's the name
of it, Frances?' 'Slut pink,' Dylan intervened.

Next day the Harvard literary magazine, the *Advocate*, threw a party for
the Thomases. With everything apparently in order, Brinnin was about
to ask Caitlin if she was enjoying herself when, recalling her anguished
plea to Broyard, she announced imperiously, 'Is there no man in America
worthy of me?' Her behaviour became so unpleasant that, when Dylan
was later asked to join a group of students and she wondered if she was
invited too, he replied brazenly, 'Only if you stop being so awful.' She
flounced off, saying she was returning home with Brinnin who, when
he called at his apartment next morning, found a note on the Thomases'
bedroom door which read, 'Stay out, you scum.' Wondering for a
moment how, once again, he might have offended her, Brinnin discovered Caitlin's venom was directed at her husband whose entry had
been barred when he returned in the early hours.

During this second tour Dylan had been trying to extend his repertoire
of readings to include not just modern British poets but also older ones
such as Webster, Donne and Beddoes. That evening he was due to take
this concept further by performing excerpts from Shakespeare and
Marlowe. When he announced he was going to do *Hamlet*, Caitlin
interjected scornfully, 'You – read *Hamlet*. You can't read *Hamlet*.' Throwing
a book at her, Dylan declared, 'I am going to read *Hamlet* as *Hamlet* has
never been read before.' But his wife had a point. She realised he was
moving steadily away from poetry to performance. She could see how
attractive this was for him – a natural progression from his youthful
thespian escapades. But she believed it brought out his worst exhibitionist
traits, encouraging vulgar adulation and, of course, leaving her out of
the limelight. She also realised it took him away from the boring business
of sitting down and writing verse.

Since Brinnin was himself in the middle of a relationship crisis
suffering from migraines whenever he had to deal with the Thomases,
he must have been relieved on 17 March to pack them off, with railway
tickets and a further $400 spending money, on the first stage of their
journey across America to the west coast. Their first stop was at
Pennsylvania State University, where they were met off the train by a
party which included Dylan's poet friend David Wagoner. This time
Dylan was sulking and Caitlin in an emollient mood. She tried to cheer
him up by interesting him in a copy of *Life* magazine which he violently
shoved aside. According to Wagoner, Dylan drank his supper and seemed
incapable of doing anything further. But, as usual, his reading was

perfect, and when he returned to where he was staying – the bachelor
house of Phil Shelley, head of the German department – Caitlin, who
had not accompanied him, was asleep. However she had washed all the
dishes, tidied up and dusted the living room, and changed the sheets
on another bed.

From there the Thomases proceeded, via Chicago, to Flagstaff, Arizona.
However by the time they reached Chicago they were tired of trains
and wanted to spend a night in a bed. So they checked into an expensive
hotel and then, finding their onward Pullman reservation out of date,
were forced to buy a new one. As a result they arrived in Flagstaff with
less than one dollar. Their hosts were Max Ernst and his artist wife
Dorothea Tanning. Since Dylan had not met Ernst either at the 1936
surrealist exhibition in London or through the artist's brief marriage to
Peggy Guggenheim, his invitation almost certainly came through Oscar
Williams and Gene Derwood who were friends of Tanning. Dylan and
Ernst enjoyed each other's company, drinking in bars in Cottonwood
and Sedona, the nearest towns to the artist couple's house. Enjoying his
brief respite from the lecture treadmill, Dylan sent a postcard to Ebie
Williams in Laugharne, announcing that he was in Poker Flat saloon in
Sedona surrounded by genuine cowboys in ten-gallon stetsons and being
treated to rye whisky by a sheriff with two pearl-handled revolvers in
his belt. To Daniel Jones he and Caitlin sent a card with a more sardonic
message: 'We were killed in action, Manhattan Island, Spring, 1952, in
a gallant battle against American hospitality. An American called Double
Rye shot Caitlin to death. I was scalped by a Bourbon.'

The Thomases were prevented from any great excesses by lack of
funds. They wired Brinnin to send $100 immediately, but he was out
of town and did not get the telegram for four days. In addition they
were concerned that carefully engineered financial arrangements in
England had broken down and Magdalen College School in Oxford was
threatening to expel thirteen-year-old Llewelyn unless his fees were paid.
At one stage on the east coast, Dylan had found a rich female well-
wisher who was prepared to give him $1,000 towards the cost of his
son's schooling. But Caitlin, suspecting the woman's motives, had been
rude to her and the offer was withdrawn.

She found these financial pressures more worrying than Dylan. In
Arizona, her silence became a disappearing act. Her hostess noted how,
whenever they were about to go on an expedition, Caitlin was nowhere
to be found, and Dylan, like a fat Pan, would wander around calling for
her. Tanning attributed this behaviour to a dislike of her small pampered
dogs. 'Ugh.' Caitlin declared. 'In England they make bloody little gods
out of them.' (The mangy mongrel Mably clearly did not come in that

category. Tanning had a theory that Caitlin's maternal instinct made her more partial to children than animals.) The first time the Thomases prepared to continue on their journey, they found they did not have enough money and had to turn back. Tanning gave them a couple of prints and Ernst inscribed his book, *Misfortunes of the Immortals*: 'To Dylan and Caitlin. (They hastened back at the first sign) Hélas. Très cordialement Max Ernst.'

Dylan's first stop in San Francisco was the telegraph office where he needed to do some brisk financial juggling to ensure that Llewelyn did not lose his school place. He was able to wire $300 (or so he said) to Oxford, with the help of further sums from Brinnin and William Morris which sent him his Caedmon fee ($500, minus 10 per cent for the agency). David Higham held out the hope that he might be able to obtain a further £100 from Dent if Dylan immediately wrote a promised Prologue to his *Collected Poems* that his British publisher intended bringing out later in the year. However Dylan found it impossible to write on the road. He had made no progress with the *American Journal* he contracted to write for Allen Wingate (whose advance was even now paying Dolly Long £3 a week to look after Colm). And three scripts entitled 'The Small Geography of a Youngish Writer' which he had promised to write for the BBC on board the *Queen Mary* had fallen by the wayside.

The Thomases stayed with Ruth Witt-Diamant, an arrangement that worked well. Dylan may have complained that the fridge in their hostess's house was full of fruit juices rather than beers, while Caitlin was suspicious of the homosexuals who congregated round her husband, showing no interest in her. But the matronly Witt-Diamant had taken the trouble to send children's clothes to her in Wales, and Caitlin was always grateful to people who showed an interest in her and her children. Over the Easter weekend all three were invited to stay with Mary Short, a member of the rich Carmel set who had met Dylan on his previous trip. The outing was similar to Dylan's two years earlier, but for Caitlin's unpredictable presence. Nearing their hostess's house for dinner, she insisted on stopping and eating something because, she said, she would not know anyone there. In a restaurant in Monterey she downed a plate of spaghetti and a bottle of wine, ensuring that the party arrived late. Robinson Jeffers was again present, and Dylan was expected to sing for his supper. After they had eaten, Caitlin announced, 'And now we'll have some fucking poetry.' When he responded with an insult about her 'pea-sized brain', she stormed out of the room. He threw something at her, and followed, never to return. The next day the couple emerged from their room as if nothing had happened. They were charming and Dylan entertained his fellow guests over a lunch-time picnic. On the way back they again stopped at the hot springs at Big Sur and briefly visited Henry Miller. Caitlin later insisted on buying some artichokes, which Miller had been eating and should, she felt, have offered her.

As Brinnin soon learnt on the poets' grapevine, there were other more alarming stories. When Dylan called on Kenneth Patchen, with whom he had corresponded at the start of the Second World War, he turned up drunk and began to cry, partly from the effects of liquor and partly he was upset at his inability to write. They were joined by Caitlin who, according to Patchen's wife, Miriam, insisted that 'I stop spoiling him, that she'd had all this horrible life with him ... and nothing would help, and so on and so forth.'

Returning east, Dylan and Caitlin stopped again in Chicago, from where he made a small tour of the mid-west. The highlight of this part of the trip was a reading sponsored by Poetry, the country's leading 'magazine of verse', which had been started by Harriet Monroe in 1912. The editor Karl Shapiro found himself treading a fine line between encouraging a poet whom the magazine was keen to publish, and feeling aggrieved at Dylan's minor misdemeanours, such as taking his two volumes of D. H. Lawrence's Collected Poems, as well as a copy of a rhyming dictionary that he promised to review but never did. Dylan stayed with a local grandee, Ellen Borden Stevenson, former wife of the politician Adlai Stevenson. She invited one of Dylan's favourite American authors, Nelson Algren, to join them. Algren, who had won the first National Book Award a couple of years earlier for his novel The Man with the Golden Arm, found both the Thomases amusing at first. However when Caitlin started drinking, he realised she had a big problem and could feel only pity for her. As for Dylan, Algren claimed to be 'neither poet nor lush enough to appreciate him fully. You have to feel a certain desperation about everything either to write like that or to drink like that.' He commended his hostess for her 'tolerance of our friend, when he put on his small-boy-got-to-have-his-way-or-he'll-bust-act'.

Dylan was supposed to travel south from Chicago for an engagement in New Orleans on 28 April. However, although this was one date he had particularly urged Brinnin to book, he was exhausted and could not face it. Worse, he told Brinnin that he would contact the organiser at Tulane University, but failed to do so. This story soon did the rounds of the college lecture circuit and, although Brinnin pleaded that this was the only appearance Dylan missed throughout his tours of America, he found subsequent bookings significantly harder to obtain.

On arriving back in New York, the Thomases asked the Slivkas to take them to a lesbian club. A visit to one in Chicago had fallen through.

Typical of their lack of co-ordination, Caitlin approached Rose and said, 'The horny old bugger still wants to go', while Dylan made a similar pitch to Dave, explaining his wife's disappointment at missing out in the windy city. Slivka asked around and found a suitable place in MacDougal Street. To his embarrassment, he found himself haggling with someone over whether she and a friend would 'perform'. Dylan's approach was to 'buy the bar', but Dave told him to put his money away. Eventually Dave left him and Caitlin at the club.

Later that evening, it seems, Dylan and an unidentified male companion moved on to the San Remo shortly before closing time. Already there was the poet Allen Ginsberg who, as a resident of the East Village, did not know Dylan. In his *Journals*, Ginsberg left an unappealing picture of Dylan making the most of his fame. After being introduced, Dylan told Ginsberg how he had just been in a bar where a girl had asked him if he would like to watch her and another girl 'do a trick'. Dylan had declined because he did not have the necessary $50. However, determined to conclude his evening with some lesbian entertainment, he asked Ginsberg if he knew any amateurs who might oblige. Ginsberg said he could only supply one girl, but invited Dylan to join him in his attic. When Dylan spent some time chatting with a girl at the bar, Ginsberg heard some 'hipsters' wondering why 'weak-chinned' men like Dylan enjoyed sexual success. When the two poets left, Dylan at first seemed enthusiastic to join Ginsberg, then said 'I don't know what to do', and finally succumbed to his companion saying he was tired and reminding him that Caitlin was waiting. Having playfully stuck his tongue out at Dylan, Ginsberg was left feeling sorry that he had not made more of the encounter.

Next day, Dylan met Slivka at the mid-town Gotham Book Mart, where he was signing his books and copies of his newly released Caedmon record. When his sculptor friend asked about the previous evening, Dylan said, misleadingly, 'Oh it was quite an event ... after you left'.

Dylan's words did describe aspects of the intervening period, however. That morning the Thomases received a dramatic telegram from Caitlin's mother, which read: 'Fees not arrived therefore Llewelyn dismissed from school Please reply Macnamara'. Since Caitlin (like Brinnin) had been assured by Dylan that this matter had been dealt with, she was furious. She announced she was leaving him and tried, unsuccessfully, to book an immediate return passage. Dylan was mortified and wanted to cancel his signing session at the Gotham Book Mart. Brinnin counselled against precipitate action, and Dylan relented. After a short sleep, he composed himself and looked surprisingly alert as, with Brinnin at his side, he sipped beer and appended his autograph to customers' May Day purchases. However, the store's formidable owner, Frances Steloff, could sense something was wrong: 'He was so quiet and restrained, it seemed to me that he was sad and would have preferred to be left alone.'

After nearly four months in America, Dylan's last engagement was back at the Poetry Center on 15 May, the day before he sailed for home on the *New Amsterdam*. He spent part of that morning visiting Random House which had expressed an interest in publishing him once Laughlin's option had expired after another book.

Before going up to the YH-YWHA, Brinnin called in at the Chelsea, hoping once more to gain his charge's approval for his meticulous accounting. But Dylan could not care less, while Caitlin looked pale and helpless, surrounded by mountains of luggage. She did not attend the reading, which was competent rather than special, except for the fact that Pearl made her way backstage and asked to see Dylan. Her brief marriage had broken up and she was back in New York. Brinnin put them both in the Green Room for twenty minutes (which would have been impossible if Caitlin had been there). Although he had no idea what happened, he got the impression that the ardour in the couple's relationship had passed.

That night, while Dylan slept, Caitlin flicked through the case of papers he had carried with him throughout his tour. She claimed that, along with unpaid bills, she found a number of love letters from different women. The fact that Dylan had put them in his case unopened suggests that they were not important to him. But Caitlin was aghast at her discovery and spent the whole night reading through them. Dylan's last few hours in New York cannot have been much fun.

Since Dylan had been swallowed up by well-wishers the previous evening, Brinnin had been unable to bid the Thomases goodbye. So he cabled them on board ship, and Caitlin replied, half thanking him and half attacking him for the way he had organised the trip. While railing against the awfulness of the liner's food and the fatness of her fellow passengers, she begged him never to encourage Dylan to visit North America again. Adamant that the continent had been an ordeal for her and the ruin of her husband, she suggested presciently that any further visit might be fatal for him.

Despite its enjoyable moments, Dylan's second trip to America had solved nothing, so far as his life or work were concerned. Rather, it had only emphasised the almost unbridgeable gap that had opened up between him and his wife. In theory, travelling together might have helped heal their wounds. Was not one of Caitlin's main grouses her sense of frustration at being left at home in Laugharne, tending their children? However her presence at Dylan's side had only intensified her jealousy and anger. She had hated seeing her husband fawned over – and, even more, seeing the way he enjoyed it. She was fearful he was prostituting his writing talents for his love of performing, and its immediate returns in terms of praise. Her fury was all the greater for being irrational. And this made his efforts to win her round all the more difficult. The impasse in their relationship was to weigh on him and add to his depression.

Waiting for him on his return was a letter from David Higham informing him that Dent was 'howling' for the corrected proofs and the Prologue to his Collected Poems. In an effort to capitalise on Dylan's growing fame, as well as to generate much-needed income for him, his agent had worked hard on Dent to publish this volume later in the year, together with a book version of his Doctor and the Devils script, and to follow these in 1953 with a new edition of his short stories.

Dylan promised, as usual, to attend to these matters. But his own priority was once more re-ordering his domestic affairs. Since he had been unable to work in Delancey Street, it seemed logical for him and Caitlin to return to Laugharne, where Colm was already living with Dolly in the Orchard Park council estate on the hill towards Pendine. The Boat House was still empty, though Maggs, who seemed on the point of a reconciliation with her husband, was making alarming noises about wanting to sell the place, or at least charge rent for it.

In his hut overlooking the estuary, Dylan expressed his relief at being back on home ground by taking out a sheet of paper and writing: 'Letter on Returning to Wales from the United States of America 1952' (it was addressed to Witt-Diamant or perhaps to Brinnin). Underneath he continued:

> At home, sweet Christ, at last,
> Wet Wales and the night jars
> My liver at half mast
> For the death of the high lights,
> This red impromptu ink
> With poppycock and love
> Across the fucking drink
> With a ballpoint I shove

It was atrocious, drunken verse but, as Dylan began to play with words and phrases, he saw how he might develop his Prologue into a poem based on the idea of gathering the local fauna and flora into an ark (or, conversely, book of poems). He put this matter aside to allow him and Caitlin to make their first triumphal post-America visit to London. Caitlin was dressed to impress in Macy's finest: she 'caught our eyes first', noted Helen McAlpine who was there with the 'two Margarets' to greet her off the train, 'and what a catch! Pale grey suit, crrr-isp white shirt, high heeled sandals, sheerest nylons, tonkety-tonk dangelers in her ears surrounded by a piled heap of disciplined curls. What ho little lady! Dylan had on his best rather reserved look. A carefully graded greeting to each of us in turn. A special wink for me though! So happy we all are to see them again ... London has felt so empty since their going.'

Helen McAlpine did not specify the 'two Margarets'. One was obviously Margaret Taylor and the other almost certainly Marged Howard-Stepney, a wealthy Welsh woman who had over the previous year emerged as a new patroness. A cousin of Frances Hughes, she owned a 10,000-acre coal-bearing estate near Llanelli. Her grandfather, Sir Arthur Cowell-Stepney, a mentally deranged one-time Liberal MP, had deserted his wife, renounced his baronetcy and gone to live in the United States where he had a fatal heart attack on an expedition to collect beetles in the Arizona desert. His daughter had died earlier in 1952, leaving her only daughter Marged with a vast income, a drink problem and a desire to help lost souls such as Dylan. Normally Maggs would never have allowed a rival onto her patch but, living apart from her husband, even she had been feeling the pinch. As the price of a reconciliation, or at least his continued financial support, she had promised again to scale down her interest in the Thomases. Marged Howard-Stepney, or Dylan's 'new County wet nurse', as Caitlin called her, had offered to step into the breach, perhaps by paying the rent for the Boat House, perhaps by buying it outright.

As well as visiting Lord's while in London, Dylan also took the opportunity of calling on E. F. Bozman, the editorial director at Dent who further impressed on him the urgency of the Prologue to his Collected Poems. Dylan also saw Donald Taylor about complications over The Doctor and the Devils. Dent wanted to publish the script under Dylan's name alone, but Taylor was still angling for a joint credit which pushed back publication into the following year.

Although this London meeting was in mid-June, Bozman had to wait three more months before seeing any sign of the Prologue. Over the summer Dylan ditched any idea of completing this work in prose. But as the 166 worksheets of the poetry version in the Houghton Library at Harvard University indicate, progress was painfully slow. Dylan was beset by illness (pleurisy, he claimed) and by worse than usual financial complications, including the threat of an imminent prosecution for failing to pay his National Insurance. As a result he wrote a grovelling verse letter, couched in a vaguely romantic vein, asking for Marged Howard-Stepney's help. Caitlin was livid when she found a draft which started, 'My dear Marged, You told me, once, upon a time, to call on you when I was beaten down, and you would try to pick me up.' Dylan felt forced to write his wife an appeasing letter, apologising for his 'heart-throb lies' to Marged. It is difficult to see what Caitlin objected to so strongly. Dylan's tone to Marged was abasing, but Caitlin had seen that before and, although she may not have liked it, she had condoned it in the hope of financial reward. Sexual jealousy was a factor: Marged was blonde and better looking than Maggs, though the worse for drink. She had been to bed with John Davenport, and Caitlin was convinced she wanted to add Dylan to her conquests. At root, however, Caitlin disliked Marged for seeking to sideline her. Feeling left out of the conversation once at Marged's house, Caitlin reached for a torch on the mantelpiece and crashed it down on Dylan who temporarily passed out. 'My God!' screamed a distraught Marged. 'You may have killed a genius.' But Caitlin was beyond caring, the incident only emphasising the sad depths the Thomases' marriage had reached.

Otherwise Caitlin set herself resignedly to living in Laugharne. The place had its own manageable routine. She no longer thought of doing anything with her journal about America. Despite Helen McAlpine's offers to type it up for her, she found it too painful, personal and best forgotten. But she was determined to resist Dylan's lame suggestions that she join the Women's Institute or take up gardening. She still had ten years' active life in her, she liked to say. And to make her point, she indulged the taste for casual sexual relationships that had been a feature of her stay abroad.

If financial and matrimonial difficulties weighed heavily on Dylan, so did vexing personal issues. His recent trip had been physically exhausting (doubtless contributing to his illness on his return). It had also brought into sharp focus what he should be doing with his talents. He realised – as if Caitlin did not frequently tell him – that he was becoming more of a performer than poet. He told Charles Fry, who had been awaiting a manuscript about his travels, that as he made his way across the United States speaking to often disinterested audiences, 'I began to feel nervous about the job in front of me, the job of writing, making things in words, by myself, again. The more I used words, the more frightened I became of using them in my own work once more. Endless booming of poems did not sour or stale words for me, but made me more conscious of my obsessive interest in them and my horror that I would never again be innocent enough to touch and use them. I came home fearful and jangled.' There was a hint of this in a repeat interview he had given Harvey Breit for the *New York Times* where he had remarked on the way certain words had lost either 'their meaning or their goodness. The word "honor" for instance. A world fit for heroes. A world fit for Neros is more like it.' When asked why this had happened, he answered elliptically, 'The wrong people crowed about them.' It was a statement of disillusion about popular culture, and a call to himself to get back to the drawing board.

The root of the problem, Brinnin understood, was the poet's 'inner, barely spoken fear that he had already written all the poems he was going to write'. Loath to make matters worse by urging Dylan away from his work, Brinnin made little effort to contact him when in Europe with Howard Moss of *The New Yorker* during the summer. But, as he admitted in *Dylan Thomas in America*, Brinnin had his own anxieties and ambivalences. His reason told him that Dylan had had enough of America. Dylan himself made this clear in the same interview with Breit when he said that he did not expect to be back for a while: 'I will have had the universities and they will have had me.' But Brinnin knew that if he met Dylan, the subject would come up, and he would be hard pushed not to suggest a suitable compromise, such as helping him realise the promise of a job offer at a California university, or even, possibly, vacating the post of Director of the Poetry Center for him.

In the meantime America continued to prey on Dylan. His occasional pieces for the BBC seemed to dwell on it. In July he broadcast selections from two of his favourite American poets, Theodore Roethke and Robert Lowell. In New York Oscar Williams had begun selling copies of Dylan's manuscripts to rich female fans as well as to magazine editors. To keep him sweet, Dylan said he also intended recording some of Williams's own poems, along with another pot-pourri of work by more radical American poets, such as Vachel Lindsay and Carl Sandburg. Nothing came of these ideas, though Dylan did finish his much delayed digest of Edgar Lee Masters's *Spoon River Anthology* which he sent to Douglas Cleverdon in August.

His other outstanding work for Cleverdon was *The Town That Was Mad*, or *Llareggub*, as he now referred to it. But although *Botteghe Oscure* had published the half-finished script in April, Dylan still struggled to complete the rest. He tried to get the BBC to put him on a salary for six weeks so that he was not tempted by other offers of work and could complete it. Realising that, from a bureaucratic viewpoint, this was not feasible, Cleverdon lobbied his financial colleagues to pay Dylan five guineas for every thousand words of the script he received. At the time he still hoped for a series, telling Dylan, 'If only we can get Llareggub on the air, we can start the ball rolling and enable you to live on the proceeds of one script while you are writing the next.' Such was his personal commitment that he even proposed recompensing the Corporation out of his own salary if everything fell through.

This scheme received a fillip when, in September, at the end of his European trip, Brinnin managed to get through to the Boat House on the telephone and speak to Caitlin who informed him Dylan was in London. The two men arranged to meet at Old Mother Red Cap in Camden Town, where Dylan was talking reluctantly of having to retreat to in the autumn. They drank bitter and played bar football in a leisurely manner. But despite Brinnin's caveats, Dylan did not delay long before asking about the possibility of another trip to the United States. His main concern was what he might do: he was worried that his readings were getting stale and suggested he might extend his range of dramatic readings. But what then? At this stage Brinnin asked about the progress of Llareggub, adding that this could provide a whole new programme, which he could either read himself or have read by others. Although sceptical of Americans mastering a Welsh accent, Dylan was enthusiastic, and promised to send Brinnin a script by March with a view to a performance some time in May. There was just one problem: what to call it? Brinnin thought Llareggub would not go down well with American audiences. 'What about Under Milk Wood?' suggested Dylan, summoning a phrase that suggested innocence and sensuality. And so, in October, a reading performance of a work of this name was announced in the Poetry Center's bulletin of advance information for the following May.

Shortly before meeting Brinnin in London Dylan had completed another difficult project – his verse Prologue to his Collected Poems. It was a piece of superior craftsmanship rather than poetic genius. In its cheerful evocation of the natural world around Laugharne, it dealt with themes his readers had come to expect. It had extravagant lines such as 'Seaward the salmon, sucked sun slips', and puns, including the use of the words 'undie' (in both a Gothic horror and, subliminally, a clothing sense) and 'agape' (meaning 'wide open' but alluding to the Christian tradition of selfless brotherly love). It made references, depending on one's level of understanding, to America ('the cities of nine/Days' night'), jazz (the dove with her 'blue notes'), nuclear war ('Out of the fountainhead/Of fear, rage red, manalive') and the troubled contemporary world ('at poor peace'). An indication of the pains Dylan had taken – and also of the poem's trickiness – was its reverse rhyming scheme: in two sections of fifty-one lines, the first and last lines rhymed, the second and the next to last, and so on. Dylan told Bozman he could not say why he had 'acrosticked' himself in this way. If he had abandoned his earlier stated aim of throwing light on his methods of work and aims, he did write something which, in technique and in concept (with its central conceit of an ark), worked well as a Prologue. It was Dylan's last completed poem and, unwittingly, reflected as much, from its first line 'This day winding down now' to its final reference to 'God speeded summer's end'. Dylan had few illusions about it himself, telling Charles Fry, 'for a whole year I have been able to write nothing, nothing, nothing at all but one tangled, sentimental poem as preface to a collection of poems written years ago.'

True enough, he still had not finished a version of Llareggub for the long-suffering Princess Caetani, whose further forbearance he had to crave. However publication of Collected Poems, 1934–1952 on 10 November brought an encouraging response. Sophisticated reviewers such as Cyril Connolly in the Sunday Times, Philip Toynbee in the Observer and Stephen Spender in the Spectator competed to incorporate Dylan into the English-speaking canon. Toynbee went so far as to call him 'the greatest living poet'. There was some sniping from the sidelines by critics associated with the Movement, such as John Wain who had no time for his 'disastrously limited subject matter'. But the public was prepared to read what Dylan had to offer, and Dent's first edition of 5,000 copies was soon reprinting.

Bozman had been kept waiting for the Prologue until two months before publication. Unhappy about a brief explanatory note his publisher then added, Dylan sent a replacement which included his much-quoted, if confusing remark that his poems were 'written for the love of Man and in praise of God, and I'd be a damn' fool if they weren't'. As late as 7 October he was cabling Bozman: 'Do really think most vital use new note whatever delay.' Despite these last-minute changes, his publisher was canny enough to encourage him to finish his two other ongoing projects for Dent, The Doctors and the Devils and a volume of stories. The filmscript required no further work (Dylan was not keen on it anyway), but the latter book called for ferreting around to discover what had already been published in Britain and what had not. (Dylan was helped in this by the appearance of a knowledgeable bibliographer, John Alexander Rolph. Certain stories still deemed unacceptable by Dent had appeared in obscure magazines, as well as in Selected Writings, issued by New Directions in the United States in 1946.) Dylan's notes contain lists of possible stories, including some, such as 'Bob's My Uncle', that he had not even written. The gist of these, as suggested by Bozman, was that Dylan should aim to recreate his Welsh childhood in the manner of Portrait of the Artist as a Young Dog. Dylan managed to write one modest story 'The Followers', which summoned up something of the Swansea pub life he was rediscovering with friends such as Dan Jones. One of the characters had the unWelsh name Katinka, which Dylan can only have borrowed from Peter DeVries's American wife. But when Bozman took this a step further and suggested Dylan might consider writing an autobiography, Dylan pointed to *Portrait of the Artist as a Young Dog* and said he had neither the inclination nor the material to write another.

He was not particularly surprised when, on 16 December, his seventy-six-year-old father died. D.J. had been ill in one way or another for most of the preceding two decades. He had fought off cancer, but his final years were marred by deteriorating eyesight. Even if unable to read the notices, he would have been told of the success of Dylan's *Collected Poems* and been satisfied. On the day before he died D.J. got up and went into the kitchen at Pelican where Florence (whom he mistook for his mother) was making onion soup. Later, back in bed, he resigned himself to his fate and declared, 'It's full circle now.' According to Caitlin, Dylan was the only mourner when his father was cremated and buried – not, as might have been expected, in Laugharne, Carmarthen or Swansea, but alongside his brother Arthur in a plot in Pontypridd. Although close to the Crematorium, the Welsh industrial town where he had worked as a young schoolmaster was more important to D.J. than has been recognised. After the ceremony (non-religious in keeping with D.J.'s wishes), Dylan went on a three-day bender. On his return to Laugharne, Florrie said she expected he would do just the same when she died. But drink, as usual, was masking real emotions. As Caitlin realised, Dylan was more affected by his father's death than even she had expected. In a subdued manner, he told her that D.J. had been responsible for all he had ever learnt. His pain came from realising how little he had been able to communicate with a man who had exercised such great influence over his life. But when, to ease his gout, Dylan took to using D.J.'s walking stick, she dismissed it as another of his affectations.

In recent years Dylan had been able to rely on his sister's help at times of family crisis. But Nancy had returned with Gordon Summersby to India, from where news now came that she also was seriously ill, suffering from cancer. As usual with Dylan, publication of a book seemed to make little impact on his bank balance. Beset by a claim from the Inland Revenue for tax on his earnings in the United States in 1950, he pleaded for financial assistance from Stephen Spender, whose generous review of his *Collected Poems* had pleased him above all others. It was an odd move: he might have approached someone more wealthy, particularly as he was lukewarm to Spender as a man, and often disparaging about him professionally. But the review had convinced him that Spender understood what he was trying to do with his verse, and Dylan retained a romantic view of the community of poets.

He sensed a change in Spender's direction too. The pre-war Communist fellow traveller had shaken off Auden's influence and was shortly to become editor of the cultural magazine *Encounter* (though unbeknownst to him it was partially funded by the CIA). Spender was now championing not only Dylan but Edith Sitwell against the Movement, the robust and precise poets who had reacted against the Apocalypse since the war. As a result the old battle-lines in the poetic establishment between the politically engagés and the romantics were being redefined. As recently as 1949 the emotional Roy Campbell had had a famous spat with Spender, whom he regarded as a throw-back to 'Macspaunday' of the 1930s. Campbell had also delighted Edith Sitwell by taking on Geoffrey Grigson for different reasons. Campbell and Sitwell formed a close alliance, promoting aesthetic and religious, rather than social, values in poetry. (He was responsible for her converting to Roman Catholicism in 1955.) This was the school that Dylan naturally inclined towards. He always tried to help Campbell, partly as a friend, and partly, for the same reason he looked to Spender, because he was a fellow poet. He had reviewed Campbell's autobiography for the *Observer* the previous year (a newspaper association that he hoped would lead to further commissions, but he never managed to complete one more.) In November Dylan had agreed to assist Sitwell by sharing the reading with her in a public performance of Humphrey Searle's musical setting of her poem *The Shadow of Cain*. Ironically the poem, which Dylan did not like, was a protest against the dropping of the atomic bomb on Hiroshima. Spender, by then a regular at Sitwell's Sesame Club gatherings, showed his colours by attending the production at the Palace Theatre in London.

In early January 1953 Dylan and Caitlin took a break from family, work and other problems and went to Swansea for a couple of days of carousing with Dan and Irene Jones. As he was often in town to record for the BBC, Dylan had got into the habit of staying with his old friends in Rosehill Terrace, Sketty. When the Jones's young son (called Dylan, after him) was struck with epiphysis, a bone disease which affected his heel, Dylan sent a list of the best 'bone-boys' in London, signing off characteristically, 'The last is best but all are top. Yours, with love, bottom.' Dylan Jones and his young sister Cathrin became used to the detritus in their visitor's room – apple cores, sweet packets and detective novels which the poet bought at his friend Ralph Wishart's bookshop opposite Swansea railway station and exchanged on a three for two basis. Once when playing a cricket 'test' match, the older Dylan broke a window. When he came with Caitlin, the grown-ups would spice up long boozy evenings by acting out impromptu plays of a surrealistic Goon-like nature. One called *Bizimuth* survives in an old wire tape recording. It calls for a cast of five: Arnold, an impotent architect; Patricia, his wife; Derek, 'a queer, Arnold's master'; Phoebe, 'a lesbian, pervertedly in love with Derek (maid), formerly Patricia's mistress'; and Arthur, 'child of all the above, of doubtful parentage, sex and inclinations'. The Warmley spirit still survived after more than two decades. On this occasion, as was their habit, Dylan and Dan went to the Odeon cinema in Sketty to see a film which Dan noted in his diary as *The Silent Man*. This may have been the old silent Western of that name, but it was more likely *The Quiet Man*, John Ford's recent fond evocation of his Irish background.

Either name was eerily appropriate, in the light of what happened on 10 January, the day after the Thomases returned to Laugharne. In the late afternoon, the peace of the town was disturbed by the murder of a seventy-seven-year-old spinster, Elizabeth Thomas. Someone entered her cottage in Clifton Street through a small ground-floor window and bludgeoned her to death. The man arrested for her murder was George Roberts, known as Booda, one of the family of ferrymen who lived next door to the Thomases. Booda, a deaf mute, had been witnessed standing outside the victim's house. Dylan had known the Robertses since before the war when Booda's Uncle Jack rowed him across from below Llanybri on his first visit to Laugharne. As colourful neighbours, they were well known to Dylan's visiting friends such as the McAlpines. Because his disability prevented him from doing much else, Booda, in particular, performed odd jobs for the Thomases, sometimes looking after their children. A well-known photograph shows him carrying Dylan across the estuary at low tide in 1940.

Such was the turbulence within the Boat House, however, that the murder was scarcely mentioned by the Thomases, even in Caitlin's chatty letters to Helen McAlpine. Normally Dylan liked telling people about the wild habits of Laugharne's benighted townspeople. But he was even more silent than his wife. It was as if the incident had taken place on the far side of a psychic boundary he could not cross. In the midst of his own misery, the idea of this strong deaf and dumb man resorting to violence against an innocent victim was too much to handle. Over the next few weeks, the case became a cause célèbre taken up by the national newspapers, as it moved from the local magistrates' court in St Clears to the Glamorgan Assizes in Cardiff. On 24 March the case was thrown out, largely because a judge found it impossible to believe that the police could or should have extracted an eight-page 'confession' from a man who did not even speak deaf and dumb language. But at no time did Dylan stand up and declare that Booda was innocent. He preferred to ignore a matter which took place on his doorstep. Caitlin wrote a strong though ambiguous poem in which she expressed sympathy and solidarity with Booda. However she seemed to imply his guilt, blaming his family for locking him in a loveless prison from which he had been forced to break out.

Dylan coped by immersing himself in a period of frenzied, if not particularly productive, activity. On 13 January he was in London for a further performance of *The Shadow of Cain*, this time broadcast by the BBC from the Albert Hall, with him reading all the verse, as Edith Sitwell was in the United States. Dan Jones heard it in Swansea and thought it 'terrible'. Afterwards Dylan attended a party in Searle's studio in Ordnance Hill where he 'danced wildly and stuffed sausage rolls down the ladies' cleavages'. (Searle lived close to the McAlpines in St John's Wood, which had temporarily taken over from Camden Town as Dylan's centre of operations when in London.)

Next day Dylan returned to Swansea to record three ballads by Vernon Watkins for the BBC. Dan Jones bought 'a lot of drink', including 'Irish' 'whisky' (the two sets of quotation marks in his diary implying that this was a misnomer), and threw a small party for friends, including Watkins, the BBC producer Aneirin Talfan Davies and the jeweller Alban Leyshon. The following morning the funeral of Booda's alleged victim took place in Laugharne. As if determined to ignore it, Dylan hit the Swansea pubs with Dan, visiting the Tenby, Red Cow and King's Head (with a visit to at least one other hostelry and to Ralph's bookshop in between). After a lunch-time pint or two in the Metropole, they went to the cinema. Dan noted the film they saw as *The Osage Trail*, though it was more likely to have been a mediocre 1952 Western called *Fort Osage*. They ended up at the Station Inn before Dylan caught the train home.

On 21 January Dylan was back in London, having drinks with the unlikely combination of Marged Howard-Stepney and his bibliographer John Alexander Rolph. She was on the point of buying the Boat House outright from Maggs Taylor and had apparently offered Dylan further financial help. The very next day she was discovered dead on the carpet of her Hampstead house. She had taken an overdose of sleeping pills but, since there was no obvious indication that she had done this intentionally, the coroner returned a verdict of misadventure. Any hopes Dylan might have had of her leaving him some money were dashed when it was found she had died intestate. Having to deal with a third death in a matter of weeks, Dylan overdid the degree of closeness when he said his 'best friend in the world ... [had] died of drink and drugs'.

But he was upset at the loss of another intimate, in this case the potential benefactor who would have allowed him to maintain a base at the Boat House.

Her loss was all the more difficult and the whole period more bewildering because, since early December, he had known that Caitlin was again pregnant. She told friends (though not, it seems, her husband) that she was not sure who the father was. Even if the unborn baby had definitely been Dylan's, the outcome would have been the same. Caitlin decided to have another abortion and accompanied Dylan on his latest trip to London. They stayed with Cordelia Sewell and Harry Locke who had married and were living in King Street, Hammersmith. Caitlin painted a grim picture of a back-street abortionist poking inside her (with Dylan nowhere to be seen). Her experience coloured her attitude to Dylan winning the Foyle's Poetry Prize for 1953. She felt that he might have spent on her some of the welcome £250 which constituted the award. Instead it went on Llewelyn's fees at Magdalen College School and presumably on her abortion.

Passing back through Swansea in the first week of February, Dylan was intending to work on a four-part series of readings from Welsh poets for the BBC. But his voice had broken down under the strain of the past couple of months and the recording had to be postponed. Dylan and Caitlin, who was still with him, quarrelled 'bitter[ly]'. They retired to a freezing overcast Laugharne – he to bed 'feeling more crooked than ever'; she to vegetate, 'feeling like death'.

In Swansea again the following week to complete his recording, Dylan went with Dan Jones to the Uplands Hotel where, by chance, they met an old school friend Guido Heller, who lived on Gower. Unaware of recent developments, Heller was delighted to find Dylan's humour apparently unchanged. Observing a terrier beside the bar, Dylan remarked, 'I do like a dog, but that dog has got to have a really nice brown arse.' His eyes lit up when Heller mentioned a disused rectory at Rhossili where the Thomases might live. However he became less enthusiastic when Heller reminded him there was no pub in the vicinity.

His brother-in-law Gordon Summersby in Bombay removed some pressure by promising to look after his mother financially. Florrie herself was almost unnaturally ebullient, particularly after Caitlin sent Aeronwy to stay and share her bed. Dylan's immediate problem was his own accommodation. With a further visit to America looming (and Caitlin predictably unhappy about it), even he realised he could not leave his wife and children without a roof over their heads. When Maggs next came to Laugharne, they had a heated row and she beat a tearful retreat. Caitlin painted a dramatic picture of a terrified Ebie Williams taking their patroness to Carmarthen station, as she wailed in the back seat, her blue hair flapping wildly over her face. The upshot was that the Thomases could stay in the rat-infested Boat House, but only if they were prepared to pay £2 a week in rent.

Faced by further pressing bills, Dylan was forced to hand over responsibility for paying them to his agent. Higham was only able to do this by halting all other disbursements to Dylan who became more than ever dependent on unpredictable amounts of cash that Oscar Williams was able to generate from sales of his poetry to magazines or, in manuscript form, to wealthy 'ardents' in the United States. This often led to misunderstandings, as when Williams sought to sell Howard Moss at The New Yorker a copy of Dylan's latest poem, 'Prologue'. He also tried to assist Karl Shapiro at Poetry (Chicago) in putting together a Dylan Thomas issue. But when the magazine needed at least one new poem to make the venture worthwhile, Williams could not supply it. The only possible candidate was 'Prologue' and its sale to periodicals was being handled by Helen Strauss as part of the build-up to the publication of the American edition of his Collected Poems by New Directions in March.

This only emphasised Dylan's medium-term problem that he still had not resolved the issue of his trip to the United States. Caitlin accused him of wanting to go there for 'flattery, idleness and infidelity'. He bridled at this, saying with only the slightest hint of smirk, that he was going for 'appreciation, dramatic work, and friends'. He tried to placate her with promises of taking her abroad to somewhere cheap and sunny on his return. (He mentioned Portugal from where Roy Campbell had extended an invitation to visit.) But Caitlin had heard such undertakings before.

His relationship with Caitlin in tatters, Dylan found a berth during March with the Lockes in Hammersmith, the latest of his homes from home in the capital. There was talk of his paying rent, but this never materialised, probably offset against the help he gave Harry in writing some cabaret sketches. In return Harry would listen to snatches of Under Milk Wood which was due for its first reading in the United States in two months' time. Dylan carried the manuscript in a battered briefcase; sometimes tinkering with it at the local Ravenscourt Arms, sometimes staying up all night to work on it. In the middle of the month he took it with him to Cardiff where he tried out parts on another audience, the members of the University's English Society. However the play's first semi-official reading was marred when he managed to leave it there (inside the briefcase) and had to make strenuous long-distance efforts to retrieve it.

This project delayed Dylan's journal about his earlier American trip for Allen Wingate, which charitably granted him a further extension. Undeterred, David Higham negotiated a contract for him to produce a book on Welsh fairy tales for the Oxford University Press. From across the Atlantic the Grove Press offered Dylan $150 to write an introduction to an edition of the Nigerian author Amos Tutuola's The Palm-Wine Drinkard, a book whose 'young English' he had praised in an Observer review. Dylan promised to complete this on board ship to New York, but disappointingly he did not. Having declared his interest in emerging African writing, he might have taken the opportunity to explore the links between Welsh and Nigerian literary cultures, with their strong oral traditions and their contrasting colonial relationship with the English language.

A year earlier, after his Time interview, he had proudly told friends that the magazine was working on his profile and might contact them for reminiscences. Reporters were duly despatched but, when the article finally appeared on 6 April, the mountains of research had been whittled down and incorporated into a review of Collected Poems. Nevertheless, it spared Dylan nothing, declaring, 'He borrows with no thought of returning what is lent, seldom shows up on time, is a trial to his friends, and a worry to his family.' John Arlott noted how Dylan had earlier taken to buying Time and studying it minutely. When the piece was published, Dylan wryly began to read to his friends, ' "Blubber-lipped, gooseberry-eyed Welsh poet Thomas" '. Then recalling the original reporter, he added, 'Bloody hell, and she said she loved me.'

Within days Dylan had an opportunity to discuss the article with friends when he went to Cardiff to record his first ever television programme, 'Home Town – Swansea', a small-screen variation on the 'Swansea and the Arts' feature he had done for BBC radio in 1949. The idea was to show the town's artistic life through the medium of Janes's paintings. As well as Dylan and Janes, Dan Jones and Vernon Watkins also appeared, with Wynford Vaughan-Thomas as the link-man. Dylan was in Swansea a few days later to record an indulgent programme of Dan Jones's devising about the infelicity of hexameters as a poetical form. As a result he was able to consult his Swansea solicitor and friend, Stuart Thomas, who, after taking counsel's advice, decided to sue Time for defamation. But before a writ could be issued at the end of the month, Dylan had sailed for New York on 16 April. He did not know it at the time but, to cap a dire six months, his sister Nancy died in Bombay on the same day.

TWENTY-ONE

TO BEGIN AT THE BEGINNING

The relationship between life and death had been a favoured poetic theme of Dylan. Sometimes he seemed more aware of the process of the natural world rushing towards its destruction, as in 'The Force that through the green fuse'; at other times, buoyed by the darker imaginings of the metaphysical poets, he focused on the resilient and even regenerative capacity of inert objects, such as the eyes of the corpse in the line in 'Light breaks where no sun shines' – 'The film of spring is hanging from the lids.' After so many personal setbacks over the previous six months, he was determined to introduce new vitality to his still far from completed play for voices *Under Milk Wood*.

After Brinnin met him off the SS *United States* on the morning of 21 April 1953, Dylan checked into the Chelsea Hotel. The two men then set off on a refamiliarisation tour of downtown bars. Around late afternoon they reached the White Horse Tavern, where the owner Ernie Wohlleben sent over a bottle of Scotch as a welcoming present, and Dylan seemed genuinely pleased to be back among familiar faces. By the time they moved uptown, to meet Howard Moss of *The New Yorker* and another colleague at the Algonquin, he was very drunk. They were joined by an unfamiliar figure, Liz Reitell, Brinnin's new assistant at the Poetry Center. Tired of Dylan's promises and evasions about the progress of *Under Milk Wood*, Brinnin had charged her with all aspects of getting the play onto the stage, including arranging a cast.

She was a tall, striking thirty-two-year-old, with a generous rouged mouth and a shock of thick black hair, which fell over dark enquiring eyes in a fashionable fringe. A model of New York chutzpah, she smoked, drank and talked tough. Her background was in the arts: an alumna of the exclusive liberal Bennington College (where she had first met Brinnin while he was on a dance scholarship), she had worked as a costume designer, painter and actress. She had been married twice, the first time, for only one year when she was twenty, to Adolph Green, the writer of musicals, through whom she had become a close friend of Leonard Bernstein. From a close-knit family of German Dunkards, a

Pietist sect like the Mennonites, her father was a professor of economics who had written a popular fishing manual.

When she first saw the man she had to work with, she took an instant dislike to the 'tousled little drunk'. Dylan was more impressed, though her forward manner and svelte good looks initially put him ill at ease. Brinnin had already disturbed him by saying she was furious at the lack of progress on *Under Milk Wood*. 'I could see Dylan shrinking in the face of so much authority', he observed, 'and staring at the briefcase she placed on the floor beside her as though it contained orders for his immediate arrest.' Dylan spilled his martini, and his conversation clammed up. Eventually he announced in his corny way that, as this was his first night back in the country, he wanted to celebrate with something particularly American. After various suggestions such as climbing the Statue of Liberty were rejected, he and Brinnin went to a production of *Guys and Dolls*. But, after three years on Broadway, the staging had become so lacklustre that they left after fifteen minutes and called it a day.

Try as Dylan might, he could not escape the spectre of death. Within forty-eight hours he was back in the White Horse having a lunch-time drink, when Ruthven Todd walked in with the news that Norman Cameron had just died. At Dylan's request, Todd collected three books by Cameron from his house. On his return, Dylan began, slowly and solemnly, to read aloud from them. The only other customers were truckers and longshoremen, who all stopped to listen. Dylan explained that a friend, a poet, had just died. This was his version of a wake.

Brinnin was determined not to involve himself in Dylan's private affairs on this trip. The two men did not meet again until, on 25 April, Dylan flew to Boston for a short reading tour of the north-east. He based himself in his agent's apartment in Memorial Drive, Cambridge (with Brinnin's mother also in residence to cook for him). By chance living next door were the British scientist Jacob Bronowski and his wife Rita. Primarily a scientist, and now a visiting professor at MIT, Bronowski, as a young man, had been one of the experimental poets who came out of Britain's Cambridge University in the late 1920s. As a young man in the circle of Robert Graves in Majorca, he had known George Ellidge, whose ex-wife, Mary, had accompanied Dylan to the Festival of Britain. Through her and her son Mark, who was at Magdalen College School with his son Llewelyn (and with Margaret Taylor's son Sebastian), Dylan had become friendly with the Bronowskis when they lived at Monks Risborough, outside Oxford.

Returning home occasionally, between trips to New York and to his other job, teaching at the University of Connecticut at Storrs, Brinnin was gratified to find his guest hard at work on *Under Milk Wood*. It was not easy for Dylan: he felt pressurised by Liz Reitell's regular telephone calls from New York, where she was already rehearsing a cast and anxious to know when she would receive the next drafts of the script. In an unfamiliar environment, his poet's sense of rhythm was also elusive: as Brinnin remarked, 'It was as if he had the words but could not find the melody.' As a result Dylan was unusually tense, particularly in the build-up to his first solo reading of the play in Harvard's Fogg Museum. He relaxed by going across the hallway to talk about his recently widowed mother with Rita Bronowski, while she was ironing. Reluctantly, Brinnin still felt he had to bolster Dylan's spirits by taking him, for example, to the Old Howard, the revue theatre where Caitlin had balked at the strip-tease the previous year. Despite the yet unfinished text, the reading on 3 May went well, however, and Dylan was pleased that the audience laughed in the right places.

Over the next ten days or so, Dylan criss-crossed the east coast. After first going south to Washington and Lynchburg, Virginia, he returned to New York for a glittering party given for him by Victor Weybright, publisher of the New American Library, who, at Oscar Williams's urging, had published extracts from Dylan's pre-war 'novel', *Adventures in the Skin Trade*, and who was now offering a healthy advance of $2,000 – $500 in cash on signing, followed by $1,500 on the book's completion. Only a few days earlier Dylan had been lost for words when confronted by I. A. Richards, the Harvard (and former Cambridge) academic whom he respected. But his reticence among academics disappeared in the company of professional writers such as Gore Vidal, Michael Arlen and Louis Auchincloss. The only problem was that, in agreeing to go to Weybright's, Dylan failed to attend a reception for him by the New York chapter of PEN – an invitation which Brinnin had accepted on his behalf.

Afterwards Dylan went for a hamburger and on to old haunts at the San Remo and the White Horse. The sense of a massive hangover pervades the depressed letter he sent Caitlin the following day from the Chelsea Hotel where he was staying in the room they had shared the previous year. He recounted his punishing schedule, sent her a cheque for $250 (part of the proceeds of his Weybright coup) and told her about his plans to take her away when he returned, not to Portugal this time, but to Majorca where he had learnt that it was possible to rent a house and, significantly, employ servants for very little money. His mood perked up during the afternoon when he ran through what existed of his *Under Milk Wood* script with the group of actors Liz Reitell had assembled for the premiere the following week. Their professionalism encouraged him to tackle various scenes in different ways. He also made a few linguistic and cultural adaptations for an American audience, such as ensuring that Butcher Beynon went after 'squirrels' rather than 'corgis' with his cleaver. He was in good form, therefore, for his latest poetry reading, a standing-room only occasion, at the YM-YWHA that evening. Among the appreciative audience was Pearl Kazin, now working for The New Yorker.

After a quick dash to Philadelphia for a reading, Dylan returned to New York two days later (a Saturday) for a rehearsal of Under Milk Wood. Afterwards he went to the Algonquin for drinks with Liz Reitell. How he spent the rest of the weekend is not known but, when Brinnin went to Boston station on Monday morning, he found Pearl waiting there also. The plot took a twist when Dylan failed to arrive on his scheduled train. On phoning his apartment, Brinnin found that Dylan had cabled to say he was coming by plane. At the airport Brinnin was taken aback to see Dylan sauntering down the ramp in a pair of dark glasses, which he interpreted as a 'new and ominous sign'. He learnt that Dylan and Pearl had agreed to spend the day together, prior to his next reading at Massachusetts Institute of Technology. At a smallish party afterwards, Brinnin noted that Dylan and Pearl were the subjects of inquisitive gossip as they moved about 'as an intimate twosome'.

When Brinnin called the following morning to drive him to the airport for a flight to North Carolina, Dylan mentioned spending the night with Pearl at the house of a mutual friend, but his only further comment was that he believed she had already returned to New York. The next day Dylan was back in Boston en route for Storrs in Connecticut to give a reading and to address Brinnin's graduate class. His schedule of appearances over the previous few days had been more arduous than anything on his earlier trips. Motoring from Boston, Brinnin claims to have discussed this with Dylan and received some hazy non-committal assent when he said he did not want to be responsible for another tour of this kind.

In Dylan Thomas in America, Brinnin also made play about how, when he and Dylan were at Storrs, Liz Reitell called from New York with frantic enquiries about the Milk Wood script which was due to be performed the following day. She offered to make her way to the campus to help the author with the finishing touches overnight. Dylan convinced her this was unnecessary, but promised to work on it himself. There is no supporting evidence for this: after his talk, Dylan repaired for drinks with the Dean, in whose house he was staying, and off to bed. However next morning, on the train to New York, Dylan did pore over his manuscript, albeit with a bottle of beer in hand. After another rehearsal, he went to Rollie McKenna's apartment close to the Poetry Center for a further session of feverish writing. With less than an hour to go, he still had not finished. With Liz making noises that the performance would have to be cancelled, he was forced to curtail his frantic burst of creativity and devise a makeshift ending.

At 8.40 p.m. the house lights dimmed, and a single spot picked out Dylan on stage, in his role as narrator. Then, as his five fellow actors came into view, his Welsh lilt could be heard: 'To begin at the beginning ...' For a couple of minutes, members of the audience remained silent and still, as they made efforts to picture 'the small town, starless and bible-black'. Then, with the arrival of Captain Cat, they realised they were not going to have to sit through a difficult avant-garde piece: they could sit back and enjoy themselves. They were treated to a life-affirming portrait of a Welsh community which mixed the spirit of Celtic whimsy with the social realism (and some of the technical tricks) of wartime documentary, leavening them with coarser elements from the demotic depths of BBC light entertainment. At the end, after the cast had taken fourteen curtain calls, Dylan stepped back to receive applause alone. He still managed to look faintly sheepish as he repeated, 'Thank you, thank you.'

After this performance, Dylan went to ground in New York for six days. When he met Brinnin again in Massachusetts, he seemed not only more relaxed but much happier. He was already talking about another 'play for voices' which he envisaged as a collaboration between himself and Nancy Wickwire, an American actress in the Under Milk Wood cast who had trained at the Old Vic. It was the love story of two people who were never lovers, telling of a couple in a Welsh industrial town who pass close to one another throughout their lives but never meet.

It soon became clear that there had been a dramatic change in Dylan's relationship with Liz. For three weeks, she had badgered him to finish the play. With the production successfully launched, she was able to turn her nurturing instincts towards him personally. She found a man genuinely amazed that someone had taken his play seriously and had devoted time and energy to helping him achieve what he intended. The last woman to have done that was Pamela Hansford Johnson twenty years earlier. It was not the sort of treatment he was used to from Caitlin.

After a noisy back-stage drinks party at the Poetry Center, he might have paired off with either Pearl Kazin or Jeanne Gordon, who were both present. Instead he departed with Liz. Over the next few days, with no script to burden them, they drifted round the Village, visiting friends, sitting in bars and enjoying each other's company. Dylan was particularly taken by the way Liz made brisk sketches of characters they met and places they visited. Her artistic skills matched his verbal dexterity.

It was a measure of the divide in Dylan's marriage that he did not even bother to tell Caitlin about the play's New York success until at least a week later. He referred to it in only the most perfunctory manner: 'I've finished that infernally eternally unfinished "Play" and have done it in New York with actors.' By then he was back in Cambridge, Massachusetts, staying at Brinnin's on Memorial Drive.

By chance Igor Stravinsky was in Boston, conducting performances of his opera The Rake's Progress, based on Auden's libretto. This inspired Boston University's ambitious opera workshop to think about sponsoring a further collaboration between Stravinsky and a poet. On 20 May Sarah Caldwell, the workshop's director, cabled Dylan, care of Brinnin at the YM-YWHA, asking if he might be interested in such a project. The next day, having picked up a copy of the score of The Rake's Progress from the Bronowskis, Dylan was ensconced in the exiled Russian composer's suite at the Copley Plaza hotel in Boston. His nervousness showed in the number of cigarettes he smoked. But this endeared him to the bed-ridden Stravinsky, who, in many ways, was similar – small in stature, sensitive, childishly playful, and eclectic in his influences. Before long they had agreed to work on an opera about a man and a woman, the only survivors of an atomic catastrophe, rediscovering the physical world around them and having to create a new language and new theories about the origins of the universe. Stravinsky was generous enough to attribute the idea to Dylan and, indeed, the concept sounded similar to the poems Dylan had been trying to write in his 'Country Heaven' sequence. Stravinsky invited his new friend to stay with him and develop it in Los Angeles. 'What a beautiful man,' enthused Dylan. 'Sweet as a bee and small as a grasshopper.'

As Brinnin and anyone else who saw him recognised, Dylan was very excited. While he had reported in a low-key manner to Caitlin about the performance of Under Milk Wood, he was unable to contain his enthusiasm about the Stravinsky project. He wrote to tell her categorically that they were bound for Hollywood in July. They were going to stay for a month with Stravinsky in a 'huge easy house in the hills'. (In fact the composer's house was small and he was contemplating building an extension to accommodate the Thomases.) Dylan told Caitlin about his meeting in Boston: 'we've thought of an opera and it is – for me – so simple that the libretto can be written in the time we're out there.' He promised that he was not making things up: 'it can and will be.' What was more, he had been promised an advance of £500, plus a first-class passage, another £500 when finished, '& then royalties until we die'. After that, they would go, as agreed, on their trip to Majorca.

Dylan may not have been writing poetry, but he was being creative, and that was a good sign. After dinner, washed down with a bottle of vin rosé that Stravinsky had given him, Dylan insisted on going to a south Boston nightclub to listen to the popular singer, Johnnie Ray, who he said was a favourite of Caitlin. Next morning, a Saturday, he sang pieces of opera all the way to the airport to catch his flight to New York. He was still in cheerful mood on Sunday afternoon when, with Liz Reitell in tow, he came to a boozy party prior to another particularly seamless reading at the Poetry Center. Afterwards he went to an Irish bar with the Mississippi-born novelist William Faulkner, but the two writers kept being interrupted and never had a proper conversation. Dylan later sloped off into the night with Liz.

He had been thinking of returning home on 26 May. But that was only two days off, and Dylan was keen to spend some time with his new lover. He informed Caitlin he had been unable to book his intended flight because so many 'rich bitches' were travelling to London for Queen Elizabeth II's Coronation on 2 June. Professing his 'eternal untouched love', he claimed he had rebooked for the day before this event, but in fact he did not fly until the day after.

His last ten days in New York turned out rather differently from expected. On 26 May, he fell down the stairs while at dinner before a performance of Arthur Miller's award-winning play The Crucible, which drew a chilling parallel between the seventeenth-century witch-hunts in Salem, Massachusetts, and the ongoing Congressional investigation into un-American activities. No doubt he had been drinking, because it was not until halfway through the play that he began to feel excruciating pain. When it became obvious he had again broken his arm, Liz took him to her fashionable doctor, Milton Feltenstein, who put the limb in plaster and eased Dylan's discomfort by injecting him with some analgesic or narcotic. He also treated Dylan's gout and gastritis, warning him that he needed to cut down his alcohol intake. But Dylan had gained a taste for what he called Feltenstein's 'winking needle'. Miller was unimpressed, later describing Dylan as methodically making his way out of the world.

Two days later, when Dylan participated in another reading of Under Milk Wood at the Poetry Center, he had his arm in a black sling. When Brinnin took the opportunity to ask Liz if Dylan had told her about his affections, she replied, 'Of course. But what does that mean from a man in such obvious misery?' The accident had clearly punctured his buoyancy, for he felt ill, and afterwards Liz had to hurry him back to the Chelsea. For his remaining few days in the United States, he seemed only to go through the motions, as he carried out necessary duties such as accompanying Liz on a brief trip to Washington to sort out his tax matters. When, on 2 June, his final day in New York, he turned up to record some further poems for Caedmon, he swore so profusely at the microphone that Barbara Cohen cut his expletives from the tape. That night Liz was so worried about Dylan's health that she phoned Brinnin in Boston to say she did not think he could make it. He was watching the Coronation of Queen Elizabeth II at the Bronowskis. He told her to let him go: 'he always gets where he's going.' However the usual round of pre-departure celebrations did not materialise and, the next day, Dylan was spirited to the airport by Liz alone.

There was a familiar scene in London on Dylan's return. Bored with Laugharne, where she had been painting the Boat House, Caitlin took the opportunity to travel to the capital to greet her husband. She also wanted to attend a Coronation party given by Margaret Taylor. When a travel-weary Dylan reached Maggs's house, he found the celebrations still in progress after two days. The sight of his drunken friends depressed him, he was tired, and he wanted to return home immediately.

But Caitlin, as usual, was keen to stay and enjoy some sophisticated company. Since she easily won that round, Dylan did not reach a grey, wet Wales until the following week. By the time his arm had been recast in plaster, it was mid-June before he sat down at his desk. Among the first batch of letters he wrote was one to Liz which started, 'I miss you terribly much,' and continued, 'We were together so much, sick, well, silly, happy, plagued, but with you I was happy all the time.' He asked her to send any business letters to the Boat House, but personal ones to him, care of the Savage Club.

At first sight, his finances seemed reasonably healthy. Higham's system of paying Caitlin's bills directly had worked well. And, from a professional point of view, Dylan had had a successful American trip. He returned with an attractive financial incentive to finish *Adventures in the Skin Trade* for Victor Weybright; he had high expectations of going to California to work on an opera for Stravinsky; and, most promisingly, he had a passable manuscript of *Under Milk Wood* in his bag. Already, in New York, he had been offered $750 for serialisation rights to the finished version of this by Cyrilly Abels, managing editor of *Mademoiselle*, who had attended the premiere. In the expectation that Dent would be unwilling to publish a play with obvious bawdy references, he cheekily offered it to Charles Fry at Allen Wingate, probably as much from a sense of guilt at not having completed his American journal as from anything else. According to the word in publishing circles, Fry offered £1,000 for the manuscript, but his partner Anthony Gibbs said that was more than they could afford.

However David Higham had been alerted by New Directions that

Under Milk Wood was a potentially valuable property. (After attending the New York premiere, James Laughlin sent a memo to his deputy, Bob MacGregor: 'That "play" of Dylan's is pretty good. Have you written to Higham about publishing it? "Under Milk Wood" that is.') Higham communicated this to Dent, which had published *The Doctor and the Devils* during Dylan's absence and had been agreeably surprised by the sales. Martin Dent, the chairman, was not too high-minded to pass on a commercial success. 'As you say, it's a bit broad in places,' he told his editor Bozman, 'but I'm sure it's too good, too authentic Dylan Thomas to let it go.' And he added that 'to turn it down might be to lose the author.'

Within a short time visitors started appearing in Laugharne. Ruth Witt-Diamant, who had been on a sabbatical in Europe, arrived there at the end of June. When she went to Pelican, she was asked by Florrie Thomas: 'Are you church or chapel?' Having been brought up as a Jew, she replied she was not of any organised creed. After travelling around Wales on her own, she met up again with the Thomases at the International Musical Eisteddfod in Llangollen, on the river Dee, near Wrexham, during the second week of July. Dylan was there with journalistic accreditation from the BBC to make a programme about this annual jamboree of music and dance. He did a professional job of contrasting the ordinariness of the Welsh town with the unusual nature of participants from as far away as Java, decked out in full folk regalia. The scribbled notes he made as he sat at the bar in the vast 10,000-seat marquee give a sense of his wry amusement. He jotted down the name of the Breton bagpipe, reminded himself of the 'lovely Czech dancers (specially one)' and remarked on the autograph-hunters: 'Do they swap three Ukrainians for an Indonesian?' Despite the singing and dancing, it was a curious encounter: 'Everyone so odd to the Welsh, and the Welsh certainly not the least odd as they lie, squat, chew, spit etc.' Witt-Diamant remembered the new Queen making an appearance and Dylan being close enough to touch her, but there was no mention of this in the broadcast piece.

Another friend spending the summer in Europe was Ted Roethke. Dylan had not seen him on his recent trip to the United States, though he had often drawn on his poetic contacts who provided a useful counterbalance to Brinnin's. Learning that Roethke and his new wife Beatrice were hoping to go to Ireland, her ancestral home, Dylan suggested that they come to Laugharne, from where he and Caitlin might join them on a jaunt across the Irish Sea. As promised, Dylan recommended Roethke to John Davenport, who was working as a BBC producer, as a good speaker of his own poems on the wireless. When Roethke told a mutual acquaintance in New York about the proposed trip to Ireland, adding that it would 'make literary history', Oscar Williams got to hear of this and wrote asking Dylan if he was the 'literary' or the 'history'. (He also sent news of his sale of Dylan's lacklustre story 'The Followers' to Weybright's New American Library.) Roethke never made the journey to Wales, let alone Ireland, as he became too caught up with Davenport and the metropolitan literary scene. When the Thomases came to London later in July, Caitlin was on top form with her put-downs. 'Where's your Irish accent?' she asked Beatrice Roethke aggressively.

Caitlin may have scuppered the Irish trip for she had ideas of her own. She was determined that her ten-year-old daughter should have the opportunity of following the dancing career that she herself had been denied. Consequently, she had identified the Arts Educational School, a boarding establishment in Tring, Hertfordshire, as a suitable place for Aeronwy to go. The fees were £67 a term, slightly more than Llewelyn's at Magdalen College School. It was typical of the Thomases' extraordinary lifestyle that, despite financial hardships, they could still contemplate sending two children away to school. Caitlin persevered, even gaining David Higham's agreement that he would pay the cost of Aeronwy's school clothes (another £60) directly from Dylan's earnings. Having got her child into school in September, Caitlin intended returning with Colm to Elba where she had contacted Giovanni Chiesa, the innkeeper with whom she had started an affair when on the island six years earlier. He replied enthusiastically, 'Carissima Signora Caterina, Your letter is very agreeable, and I thank you very much for your thoughts and recollection of me.'

With Maggs Taylor again making justifiable noises (through her solicitor) about wanting at least a fair rent from the Thomases' use of the Boat House, Caitlin's unilateral initiatives suggested she had finally had enough of living with Dylan and wanted to make her own way. But she was afraid to take the plunge, which led to a period of dangerous drift in Laugharne. Other factors entered the equation. For example, in June Bill McAlpine was posted to Tokyo by the British Council, which meant Caitlin's best friend Helen would no longer be on hand to make clothes for the children and generally to keep her sane. Soon afterwards, Witt-Diamant's visit reminded the Thomases that they had a place to stay in San Francisco. Ruth particularly took to Aeronwy and offered to look after her for six months.

In the background was the unfinished matter of *Under Milk Wood*. By mid-summer Dylan had at least four clients clamouring for it – Dent, *Mademoiselle*, the BBC and the patient *Botteghe Oscure*. On 23 July Dylan informed Higham he still had twenty pages of the manuscript to complete. Various notes which are not easy to date indicate that he was at least tinkering with the text: for example, introducing, 'A new small character. Mrs Beynon's Billy, who is always faking up signs of antiquity in caves and hills. See p 14. Flints and arrows. Cave paintings. Skulls. At the end he finds a real skull and comes screaming home.' The boy is mentioned but is not developed as a character in the published play.

Around the same time Dylan received further bits of contrasting and confusing information. Boston University told him that it had been unable to raise the money for the proposed opera. Although Stravinsky was still keen to collaborate, funds would have to be found from elsewhere. A putative writers' conference in Pittsburgh might underwrite Dylan's, and perhaps Caitlin's, passages, and they could also stay with Witt-Diamant in San Francisco. This became more feasible when he heard from a specialist New York agent who proposed to arrange him a lecture tour with a guaranteed gross income of over $1,000 a week. On the other hand, if he stayed in Britain, he was hoping, fancifully, that negotiations with Rank would lead to a high-paying contract to write a script of a film of the *Odyssey*.

These possibilities were playing around in Dylan's mind when, in early September, at the end of a summer vacation in Europe, Brinnin again turned up in Laugharne. He had been commissioned by *Mademoiselle* to write a profile of Dylan to accompany its serialisation of an abridged script of *Under Milk Wood*. The magazine had also hired his friend Rollie McKenna to take the accompanying photographs. There was more than a hint of *Mademoiselle* attempting to steam-roll Dylan into producing the script, with Brinnin condoning these tactics in the hope that he might encourage Dylan to appear yet again at the Poetry Center.

On 5 September, Brinnin and McKenna motored to Laugharne, where she shot film of the Thomas family, their neighbours and environs. Caitlin celebrated their arrival by cooking a brace of duck (possibly the gift of a local lover, Howard Dark, who ran a sporting shop in Carmarthen). The meal was a disaster: with her ability to let her actions do her talking, she contrived to serve two bloody, undercooked birds which, with Llewelyn smirking at the far end of the table, had to be abandoned. Together with Dylan and Florrie, the two Americans drove to the Llanstephan side of the estuary to photograph places, such as Fernhill, which had been significant in Dylan's life. The party visited various relations of Florrie's, such as her cousins, the Morrises, at Llwyngwyn Farm. Returning down the road from there, they passed an old man whom Florrie, according to Brinnin's account, introduced as her brother Tom, adding that he had lived alone since losing his wife forty years earlier. Since he was standing outside a house which could only have been Blaencwm, he must have been her brother Bob, and, of course, he had never married.

After speaking with Dylan, Brinnin realised his friend was plagued with indecision about his immediate future. Dylan seemed to want to move from Laugharne: a recent increase in weapons testing at Pendine was making life intolerable and writing impossible, he said, and the way the house shook from time to time confirmed this. Yet Dylan did not want to admit any desire to go to America. He sensed that danger lay that way. He also realised that Caitlin was opposed to his going alone, and any inkling that that was his preference would cause further friction. Some sort of consensus was reached only after Brinnin raised the possibility of further appearances, including productions of *Under Milk Wood*, at the Poetry Center, and said his travel budget might be stretched to include Caitlin. In Brinnin's account, he is careful not to give any impression of forcing Dylan's hand. However the circumstances, with the pending *Mademoiselle* profile, suggest more to the story.

Back at London's Park Lane Hotel a few days later, Brinnin received a call from Dylan saying his film deal with Rank had fallen through and he was definitely coming to New York with Caitlin in mid-October. He would do the *Under Milk Wood* productions, as discussed, undertake a few more appearances, travel to California, and spend time with Stravinsky. Brinnin lost no time in scheduling Dylan's first performance of the play for 24 October. When advised that it would be difficult to book two sea passages at such short notice, Brinnin cabled suggesting Dylan come by plane and Caitlin follow as intended by sea. Dylan replied that he was flying alone, leaving Caitlin's intentions gapingly unclear.

A positive feature of Brinnin's visit to Laugharne was that Dylan had recited some lines from 'Elegy', a short poem, with intriguing changes of rhythm, about his father. Significantly, at this stage in his life, he tried to make his peace with the father he had never been close to. His poem emphasised the kindness beneath D.J.'s proud unyielding exterior but, unlike 'Do not go gentle into that good night', it bid him a peaceful passage to the next life. He hoped to send it to Stephen Spender at *Encounter*. But this proved only one of many projects Dylan could not finish. It lay in several drafts among the clutter on his desk in the shack, which included careful lists of people he had to contact, letters from various clubs which wanted him to talk, computations of amounts of money he owed, and, his latest diversion, details of horses to back and bets to place at the bookmaker's. There was a diet from a Sunday tabloid newspaper, as well as details of medications he might or should be taking (codeine, fenox 'for nose' and 'calomel' [liver]). One feature of his parlous health at this time was a series of short blackouts, possibly linked to a blood clot on his temple. That could have resulted from falling again when drunk. But, along with the wheezing chest, gout, gastritis and general fatigue, it was more likely another symptom of deteriorating general health, which was exacerbated by his refusal to curtail his drinking or smoking.

On the Monday of his last week in Wales, Dylan travelled to Swansea to make another programme for the supportive Aneirin Talfan Davies at the BBC. The subject could not have been closer to home – the town of Laugharne. Taking a different tack from his recent depressed line, Dylan was in benevolent mood about 'this timeless, mild, beguiling island of a town'. He noted appreciatively that, though still regarded as a foreigner, he was 'hardly ever stoned in the streets any more, and can claim to be able to call several of the inhabitants, and a few of the herons, by their Christian names'. When he met Vernon Watkins briefly, he told him about Stravinsky and recited his unfinished Elegy.

As he prepared for his departure over the next few days, he had his hair cut and acquired a new pair of trousers. Caitlin was worried about his blackouts, so when they ran into her doctor, Eric Hughes, on a visit to the cinema in Carmarthen, she asked his opinion. He suggested that they call at his house after the film, but Dylan managed to avoid this ad hoc medical consultation. When finally ready to leave for London with Caitlin at the weekend, it is said that, as if an intimation of his mortality, he turned back three times to kiss his mother goodbye.

The Thomases stayed with the Lockes in Hammersmith. With Caitlin still angry that Dylan was going, they spent a turbulent last few days together. One evening Dylan on his own visited Philip Burton who wanted to hear about the progress of Under Milk Wood, but found his friend more exercised by the new play for voices he had envisaged as a vehicle for himself and Nancy Wickwire. Dylan's idea about two people who grow up in a small Welsh town but never meet had been given a name, Two Streets. He was contemplating having his two characters converge at the end of the play; otherwise their only link was the mid-wife who delivered them both. 'What a rich, Dylanesque character she would have been!' noted Burton.

Since Dylan talked of needing money for his children's education, Burton suggested telephoning his ward, the actor Richard Burton. Still in his twenties, Richard had worked with Dylan on the 1946 BBC production of David Jones's In Parenthesis. He used to tell how Dylan screamed the words 'Mam, Mam' so loud that all the professional actors looked up in amaze-ment. Dylan simply said, 'You try that with a cigarette in your mouth.' Now Richard was prospering on the West End stage and Philip thought he might lend Dylan the required £200. When on the telephone there and then, Richard said he did not have the cash to hand, but might be able to obtain it, Dylan, showing his desperation, offered a sweetener – the rights to *Two Streets*, which he described down the line.

When nothing materialised from that conversation, Dylan talked to Philip Burton about his opera for Stravinsky and read him some passages from *Under Milk Wood*. Burton pointed out, in the light of later claims about Dylan having a death wish, that the opera was about life triumphing over death – a favourite theme of the author. In addition, the whole tenor of Dylan's talk was about developing new strands to his artistic repertoire that would take him through to old age.

Dylan had arranged to deliver the manuscript of *Under Milk Wood* to Douglas Cleverdon on Monday 12 September, but although the BBC producer invited him and his agent David Higham to a celebratory meal at Simpson's in the Strand, Dylan preferred to work on the final paragraphs at the Lockes', and failed to turn up. Eventually on Thursday 15 October, four days before his departure, Dylan delivered a hand-written version to Cleverdon at the BBC. However he said he needed his copy back in two days' time, as this was his only one, and he required it for his readings in New York. Cleverdon immediately put a secretary to typing the text, with a view to duplicating it. He duly returned Dylan's copy, but the following day had a frantic call from the author, saying he had lost it in a pub or a taxi. Cleverdon told him not to worry as he would have another duplicated on Monday, the day of Dylan's departure, and would deliver it to him before he left.

On Monday a party comprising Caitlin, Harry and Cordelia Locke, and Margaret Taylor assembled to toast Dylan's departure over lunch-time drinks. When they reached the air terminal on Cromwell Road in good time for him to catch the 5.45 bus for a 7.30 Pan American flight, the bar was closed. The group took on a dispirited air that descended into angry exchanges between Dylan and Caitlin. The mood lifted when they were joined by Cleverdon, with three immaculately roneo-ed copies of *Under Milk Wood*. Dylan was so grateful that he told the BBC producer to keep the original if it turned up. He mentioned three or four pubs where he might have lost it: without much fuss Cleverdon discovered it in one of them, the Helvetia in Old Compton Street.

In the end Dylan could stand the recriminations no longer. Although the bus did not go for half an hour, Dylan saw it standing empty and asked Locke to accompany him to it. Having climbed to the upper deck, he told his friend to return to the others, adding, 'I want to look out.' Eventually the driver came and the bus prepared to depart. Locke's last sight was of Dylan, as cheekily ambivalent and difficult to read as ever, shaking his head and turning his thumbs down.

TWENTY-TWO

THE GATES OF HELL

Dylan's fourth visit to New York started on the wrong foot. He had been expected six days before 20 October 1953 but, when Liz Reitell went to Idlewild airport to meet his plane on the earlier date, his name was not on the passenger list. It transpired that Brinnin's ticket had not reached Laugharne until after Dylan left home for London. By the time it caught up with him, it was out of date and had to be changed. This messed up his booking at the Chelsea Hotel where he was upset to be told he could not have his usual quarters, fronting on 23rd Street, but had, for the time being at least, to take a small room at the back.

He had wanted a drink as soon as he stepped off the plane, but Liz had pointed out that airport workers were on strike and this would mean crossing a picket line. He reluctantly agreed to forgo his pick-me-up 'but only for you and the Rights of Man'. On the journey into Manhattan he gave her his usual rigmarole about the rigours of his flight. But his main beef was about the 'terrible week' he had just experienced. He said he had missed her terribly and immediately wanted to go to bed with her. When they surfaced, he showed the sort of attentiveness Liz had hoped for. He had no inclination to visit his usual drinking haunts. In fact he did not want to see anyone, but was happy to play the role of sightseer and lover, and to wander round the city with Liz, before taking an early meal at the Jai Wai restaurant where he was content with a simple clam dish. Later he and Liz went to the Poetry Center for a rehearsal of the latest version of Under Milk Wood, the first performance of which was only four days away. He spent some time deciphering and correcting errors in the BBC typist's transcription. After Brinnin called to welcome him, Dylan felt relaxed enough to drop in at the White Horse for a late-night drink. It may have been on this occasion that he met his young poet friend, David Wagoner, greeting him with a toast, 'The Sons of Roethke never eat when they can drink'. (Wagoner had studied under Roethke.) Also present was Oscar Williams about whom Dylan said, when he went to the lavatory, 'I can't fart without having Oscar come running up with a roll of toilet paper.'

When Dylan offered Liz some orange juice in bed next morning, she had a brief sense that the Gods of romance were on her side. In her later notes, she quoted Dylan as saying, 'You're neither my nurse nor my manager; you're my love.' But he was constitutionally unable to maintain this sort of attentiveness to a woman. On his second day in New York, he seemed much more nervous: when he and Liz walked down to her apartment on Charles Street, he saw a billboard advertising the new Tony Curtis film Houdini which somehow disturbed his equilibrium. Only a few weeks earlier he had written to Marguerite Caetani comparing his own condition to that of the great escapologist. When Liz invited him into her place, he declined. Later he said he did not feel well and retired to bed for the afternoon. Liz decided to give him half a gram of phenobarbitone and leave him for the night. The following day, after another rehearsal, Dylan joined her and a friend for a meal at Herdt's where he ate pork chops. (She later described this as his 'last real meal'.) On the Friday she had to work, which seems to have annoyed him. He took it as a licence to get roaringly drunk with a literary critic, Bill Troy, and some representatives of a movie distributor, Cinema 16, which had been trying to contact him since July about participating in a symposium on film and poetry. On Liz's return, she had to dismiss these visitors from Dylan's room. When Troy warned her against romantic involvement because it would lead to hurt, she put him in his place with her comment that she had 'been there and back'.

But by then the alcoholic damage she had been trying to guard against had been inflicted. Dylan was in bad shape when he and Liz went to the 'Y' for another rehearsal. Liz had to take his place in the reading, as he moped and shivered under blankets. He told Herb Hannum, an architect friend of Liz, that he was no longer capable of things he had done as a young man, adding he had 'seen the gates of hell' and was 'frightened'. More positively, he talked of changing his ways, informing Liz specifically that he 'really want[ed] to go on'.

After staying the night with him, Liz slipped out early next morning to go to her apartment for a change of clothes. When she returned, Dylan had left a note, asking her to meet him at the Chelsea Chop House for breakfast. He was talking to Hannum and still looking very sick. With a performance of Under Milk Wood due in the evening, Hannum suggested he should consult Dr Feltenstein. After initial resistance, Dylan soon found himself in the surgery of the physician with the 'winking needle'. Feltenstein gave him a shot of Adrenocorticotrophic hormone (ACTH), a steroid regarded as a pharmaceutical panacea of the moment. Its dual role was to reduce the inflammation of Dylan's gout and provide a stress-relieving adrenaline boost. As a further energiser, Feltenstein also gave Dylan a prescription of Benzedrine, or amphetamine.

As they emerged and walked along Third Avenue, Dylan told Liz about the 'feeling of dread' like a band of pressure inside his head. But soon the medication kicked in, and he perked up physically, even if, at another rehearsal, he alarmed Brinnin with his ashen looks and, in particular, the dullness of his sunken eyes. After this latest run-through, he and Liz went to Rollie McKenna's nearby flat to relax and on to a dark, old-fashioned restaurant, where he was almost his old self. He asked Liz about her life, though when she responded, and started telling him about how bored she was working at the 'Y' and how she wanted to paint, he switched off. Nevertheless she enjoyed herself: 'we were both peaceful with each other.' The production went well and, at a later party at McKenna's, Dylan talked animatedly and appeared not to drink. When a guest asked why, he replied, 'It's just that I have seen the gates of hell, that's all.'

The following day, a Sunday, a matinée of the play was scheduled. Dylan started brightly, as the Chelsea Hotel management had finally managed to change his room. 'Then we'll be all right,' he told Liz, as if where he slept had some magical power. Around noon, they both visited Brinnin in his hotel for a discussion about finance. Brinnin was taken aback by Dylan's distant, grasping attitude, which seemed to take no notice of the close relationship he thought they had developed. He later learnt from McKenna that both Dylan and Liz believed he had been ignoring the Welshman. There was an element of truth: the abstemious Brinnin still felt distaste for some of the places Dylan frequented in the Village, but he trusted his friend was being well looked after by Liz.

The afternoon show of Under Milk Wood was, by all accounts, the best yet. Even Dylan admitted this was the one he had been waiting for. Afterwards he was invited to a party in Sutton Place given by one of his 'ardents'. Dylan was attracted to this women which did not please Liz, though she agreed to accompany him there. With this added sexual tension, Dylan fell apart. He gulped down tumblers of Irish whiskey, before becoming boisterous and disappearing upstairs with his hostess. He broke off from this activity when Brinnin appeared and the two of them, with Liz also, had a tearful reconciliation in which they agreed that though there had been periods of mutual misunderstanding, these were unimportant. The clouds seemed to lift again, as Dylan clasped Brinnin and said, 'John, you know, don't you? This is for ever.' But then, extraordinarily, Dylan turned away and seemed to forget everything he had said. He resumed his dalliance with his hostess, before lapsing into total drunkenness on the floor. When an upset Liz and Brinnin moved to leave on their own, Dylan got up and followed them sheepishly, announcing, 'Here I am.'

On the journey back to the Village by taxi, he asked Liz to accompany him to the White Horse, but she refused. When she stopped the cab at her apartment, Dylan announced in his most stentorian tones, 'I used to have a friend who lived near here.' Liz told him simply, 'You still do.' He carried on to the White Horse where one of the regulars set him up with a girl whom he brought back to the Chelsea for the night.

Next day Liz had had enough and resolved to tell Dylan she was not prepared to carry on with their relationship. An opportunity arose when he called her at the 'Y' in the afternoon and said he wanted to see her 'terribly'. When she joined him at the Algonquin, he had been drinking heavily. He was engaged in a conversation with a Dutchman about war. This was no ordinary exchange of views, however. Dylan started raving about the horrors of combat, falsely implying that he had been involved in active service himself. After a waiter tried to quieten him, Dylan became even more hysterical about blood, mutilation, burning and death. Only when Liz took his hand, did he stop, break down and cry.

In the street outside, he started up again, swearing and making faces at passers-by, and tottering in an unfortunate parody of a drunk. When he noticed that a double bill comprising a Western and a Mickey Spillane thriller was playing at a 42nd Street cinema, he wanted to see it. Emerging much calmer and more sober, he took Liz to Goody's, a Village bar she liked. However when she started speculating if someone was homosexual, saying it was difficult to tell, he became agitated. He said he thought he was going mad and he was concerned that it might be because he was homosexual himself, and always had been. On his way back from a cigarette machine, he noticed a young couple kissing and spat out, 'How filthy'. When she remarked he sounded like a Puritan, he replied, 'I am a Puritan,' as if discovering something about himself for the first time. He later declared that perhaps the 'right doctor' might be able to help him. When Liz told Brinnin about this incident, she said Dylan could not even utter the word 'psychiatrist' and added, 'I couldn't help thinking this nice specialist he had in mind was his own father – the dying man he wanted to confess to and get absolution from.' She described his condition as 'homosexual panic', which, as a woman of the world, she had found in half the men she had known. When Brinnin wondered if Dylan's incessant lunging after women had anything to do with this, she reassured him: 'If it's his performance in bed you're worried about, don't. You have my word for it.'

On 27 October, the following day, Dylan was thirty-nine, and so was his friend Dave Slivka, who had been born in Illinois on exactly the same day. Slivka and his wife Rose held a party in their Washington Street house to celebrate this double anniversary. They prepared an excellent spread, Liz bought a bottle of bourbon, and Jody Todd, from around the corner, made a banner reading 'Dylan and David', with two angels to hold it up. But after half an hour Dylan ground to a halt. He stopped talking, said he was sick, and had to be driven back to the Chelsea, where he threw himself on his bed and made a gloomy speech about being a 'filthy, undignified creature'. When Liz begged him to do something about it, he took offence and shouted at her not to 'go on about it'. He started talking about Caitlin and the guilt he felt towards her. 'She's crying too,' he said, though it was not clear if this was a statement of fact, comfort or condemnation. Liz's efforts to leave only brought the response, 'That won't help my agony.'

Dylan had become an embarrassment. His tough-minded lyricism had helped refresh American poetry, suggesting a way out of its post-war aridity, while his charismatic voice had introduced new audiences to the possibilities of both the written and the spoken word. Yet now he was a snivelling wreck — a not unprecedented fate among poets (Chatterton and Rimbaud were earlier examples), but Dylan's troubles seemed self-inflicted. When Brinnin put in a late telephone call to wish him a happy birthday, he was not certain that Dylan even realised who he was.

As often, when performances were required, Dylan rallied next day when he took part in Cinema 16's discussion at City College on film and poetry with Arthur Miller, Maya Deren and others. He played the ingenue, drawing laughs by deflating the pretensions of his fellow panelists. True to form, he averred that the most 'poetic' films were by Charlie Chaplin and the Marx Brothers. Later, a crowd from the symposium repaired to the White Horse where Liz idly sketched. Dylan took pleasure in her rough drawings and handed them round the room. A sceptical observer of this convivial scene was George Reavey who had been worried about Dylan's pallor on the platform at City College. Like others who knew Dylan, he had heard alarming stories. He did not like Liz and her circle, regarding them as bad influences. So he restricted himself to 'a word or two' with Dylan who readily accepted his invitation to call at his house on West 15th Street, but seemed 'somehow very very sad and sick looking'. When Dylan failed to make contact, Reavey became worried and called his hotel. He later claimed his messages were not delivered, and access was generally barred by Liz. In the light of subsequent developments, such recollections need treating with caution. But they are indicative of the concern, as well as the growing division and competitiveness, among Dylan's New York friends.

The next few days passed in a blur, as Dylan went through the motions at various social engagements. Having promised Liz he would drink nothing but beer, he had lunch with Georgia Williams on 29

October. He spent the afternoon with her in Sutton Place, instead of cutting his *Under Milk Wood* text for *Mademoiselle*, whose managing editor Cyrilly Abels had invited him for dinner that evening. Nevertheless Dylan negotiated this more formal occasion with aplomb, swapping ghost stories with the writer Santha Rama Rau, the sophisticated Wellesley-educated daughter of a former Indian ambassador to the United States.

When Liz saw him the following evening, he was with the enigmatic Herb Hannum, a friend of hers. She had come to pick Dylan up before going to dinner with Ruthven and Jody Todd. A passing 'ardent', who had apparently asked Dylan to marry her, suggested they all join her for a meal in Sutton Place. But Dylan had had enough of her and, to her annoyance, insisted on keeping his prior engagement. Earlier he had been to see Velma Varner, who ran the children's list at Viking. He was clearly pitching something to her, which appeared in a list of projects in a notebook around this time as 'A Children's Book, illustrated by self' – a poignant indication of his future plans. With the help of Oscar Williams, he also managed to secure a further $500 from trusting Victor Weybright against delivery of the completed *Adventures in the Skin Trade*. The money was delivered to the Chelsea Hotel.

In town next day, a Saturday, was a friend of Liz, Rassy Nance, with whom Dylan had stayed on a campus reading tour. Happy to see her again and flush with cash, he arranged to take her and Liz out to an expensive lunch at Luchow's, a well-known German restaurant on 14th Street. He did not eat much, but it was an enjoyable reunion and the three of them agreed to meet again later in the evening, after Dylan had been to dinner with Harvey Breit of the *New York Times*. He did not show up. Instead he joined Dave Slivka and others in the White Horse where his movements were observed, probably not for the first time, by a detective hired by *Time* magazine to accumulate evidence in defence of its pending libel suit. The sleuth noted that Dylan downed glasses of lager, whisky and beer within minutes of arriving at the bar. Later Slivka took him to a restaurant in the hope that some food would counter the effects of the alcohol. Instead Dylan became morose, and started talking about his family. He moved on to the subject of sex, which he described in graphic detail, recalling the loss of his virginity, which he said had taken place in the back of a lorry in Swansea. He was still carousing at 2.30 in the morning, when the *Time* detective observed him 'taking Benzedrine'.

Dylan's friends have denied using drugs, but when Reavey saw him at the White Horse the following afternoon (together with Liz and Hannum, which did not please him), he thought, without prompting, that his friend 'looked a bit drugged'. When Reavey asked about Caitlin, Dylan, not for the first time, answered distractedly 'that he wasn't sure if he still had a wife'. Hannum had a book by Norman Cameron which caused Dylan to voice concern about people dying so young. Reavey could not escape the conclusion that 'he was thinking about himself.'

Earlier, complaining of 'a real horror' of a hangover, Dylan had telephoned Liz with a story about having thrown a girl out of a taxi on his way home the previous night. This was probably an invention to placate Liz after standing her up, because the private eye did not mention the incident – a symptom, perhaps, of Korsakoff's syndrome, a psychosis that afflicts chronic alcoholics, causing them to compensate for sudden memory losses by inventing stories they believe are true.

At an up-town party that Sunday evening, Dylan made a fool of himself by chasing a dancer round the room. According to Brinnin, he was so violent that the young girl suffered concussion. However, David Wagoner, who was present, said this was untrue: the girl, whom he did not know, was injured in a freak accident while demonstrating a dance with him. By midnight, when Dylan moved on for a nightcap at Howard Moss's, he was very drunk. He managed to read some poems, finishing with Auden's 'September 1, 1939'. But his vision was blurred and his coordination poor. After making great play of seeing a non-existent mouse – which, in reality, always terrified him – he went out onto a balcony, stumbled into a rose bush and scratched an eyeball.

He was back at the White Horse the following evening, 'really looking sick and even more depressed', according to Reavey, who could see that the scratched eyeball was real enough and who heard confirmation of the previous night's excesses when Liz arrived and 'said a few things that implied that the party had been rather a wild one and there had been a lot of jumping over a table. Christ, I thought, why are they taking him to parties like that? The man can hardly stand on his feet.'

Dylan managed to rouse himself next day to sign a contract with Felix Gerstman, the lecture tour agent who had approached him some months earlier. After a short nap, he kept an appointment in the late afternoon to have cocktails with Santha Rama Rau and the theatrical producer Cheryl Crawford who was keen to put *Adventures in the Skin Trade* and perhaps *Under Milk Wood* onto the commercial stage. By the evening, he was exhausted and took to his bed where, with Liz at his side, he either slept fitfully or remonstrated tearfully about the misery of his existence and his wish to die. He was still restless, however. At around two o'clock in the morning he got up and said he needed a drink. He promised to be back in half an hour, but was gone for two hours or more. On his return, he is supposed to have burbled, 'I've had eighteen straight whiskies. I think that is the record.' This was impossible, as Ruthven Todd discovered when he checked with the barman and owner of the White Horse. Dylan had taken a taxi to his favourite pub, and stayed there until closing time at four. The consensus was that he cannot have drunk more than six measures of Old Grandad whisky. So far as Liz was concerned, any was too much.

At this stage Dylan had been in New York for a fortnight and, so far as is known, had not been in touch with his family. Back in Britain, Caitlin was still seething towards him. That very day, she had contacted David Higham from the Lockes' house in Hammersmith, thanking him for again sorting out her finances, which had been left in a worse state than usual. She laid into Dylan's irresponsible behaviour and said she intended to have nothing more to do with him, except financially on behalf of her children. Not having heard from Dylan, she had just posted him a vitriolic letter, accusing him of being not only weak, drunken, unfaithful and deceitful, but mean and stingy as well. Threatening to kill herself or go on the streets, she announced she never wanted to go near him again. She told him he could consider himself 'free as shit'. The letter was addressed to him care of John Brinnin in Cambridge, Massachusetts, so he never saw it. However when Edith Sitwell breezed into town a few days later, she was given a version of this story which, in her gossipy way, she quickly passed on to Kenneth Clark's second wife Jane, whom she informed about the 'wretched Caitlin's appalling telegram, received by Dylan a week or ten days before he died. She telegraphed to him, "You have left me no alternative but suicide or the streets. Hate. Caitlin." From that moment he never stopped drinking.' Sitwell's 'telegram' was almost certainly a precis of Caitlin's letter, and the grande dame probably received her information in garbled fashion from her friend John Brinnin. However, it is conceivable that Dylan did receive a cable along these lines. Or, perhaps, he knew intuitively what it might say and felt guilty.

On Wednesday 4 November Dylan had a date to catch a ferry across the Hudson to a well-known clam house in Hoboken, New Jersey. His companions were to be Hannum and Todd who recalled, 'Dylan wanted to visit the men-only bar and crunch clam-shells under his feet on the sawdust-strewn floor.' But when Todd telephoned the Chelsea in the morning, Dylan said he felt awful and, delighting in the Americanism, asked to take a rain-check. Somehow he roused himself to accompany Liz for a couple of beers at the White Horse. But he felt sick and had to go back to the hotel, where Liz insisted on calling Doctor Feltenstein. On the second of three visits that day, the physician gave Dylan another shot of ACTH and counselled an immediate course of medical treatment.

Dylan, the trouper, was only concerned that this would mean his having to miss some up-coming reading engagements. When this time the cortisone failed to do its trick, Dylan collapsed and began to hallucinate. On a third call, Feltenstein prescribed a strong sedative, half a grain of morphine sulphate, which put Dylan to sleep. He also suggested that the increasingly distressed Liz might find someone else to help her share her bedside vigil. Todd and Slivka were out, so she asked an artist friend, Jack Heliker, to join her. Dylan was still alert enough to mumble when he arrived, 'This is one hell of a way to greet a man, isn't it?'

He may have said a few more words: when Liz tried to reassure him that his horrors would abate, he answered, 'Yes, I believe you.' Around midnight, Liz saw his breath tighten and his face turn blue. Again she telephoned Feltenstein but he was not available. The hotel porter called the police who summoned an ambulance. Within minutes Dylan, in a deep coma, had been admitted to the emergency ward of St Vincent's, a private Roman Catholic hospital on 11th Street at Seventh Avenue. The time was 1.58 a.m. on Thursday 5 November.

Half an hour later a tearful Liz roused Brinnin in Massachusetts and told him the news. He caught the first available flight to New York and, by eight, had reached the hospital where Liz had been joined by Ruthven Todd. By then, Dylan's doctors were clear that he was suffering from acute alcohol poisoning. The phrase 'a severe insult to the brain' was bandied about, though its origins are unclear. His coma was a bad sign, but his ability to maintain vital physical functions was more positive. The main worry was his difficulty in breathing, a result of having been given a substantial dose of morphine by Dr Feltenstein. After ascertaining that Dylan's condition was precarious, but not completely hopeless, Liz, Brinnin and Todd began to call those close to him, both in New York and overseas.

At this point the simmering rivalry between Dylan's local friends flared into open hostility. On the one hand was a definite inner circle centred on these three and the Slivkas; on the other, a group, headed by George Reavey and Oscar Williams, who felt excluded. As well as being closer to Caitlin, they considered they had known Dylan longer and were the true guardians of his interests, literary and otherwise.

Their war of words and deeds would have been hilarious, if not for the circumstances. Reavey claimed his first knowledge of Dylan in hospital came from reading the evening newspaper at around 7 p.m. (He later gloated that only one paper had seen fit to mention that Liz had been in Dylan's room at one in the morning, and then it said she had been working with him on a manuscript.) However Todd recalled that Reavey and his wife Irene, as well as Oscar Williams, were at St

Vincent's by the late afternoon. Williams telephoned Ellen Stevenson in Chicago who had been supporting Dylan by buying his manuscripts and who now offered to pick up the bill for the best medical care in Manhattan. But since a treatment regime had already started at the hospital, this generous proposal was turned down, confirming Reavey in his unfounded suspicions that the other group had something to hide, and did not want independent specialists intruding.

Brinnin and Robert MacGregor, New Directions' representative on the scene since Laughlin was out of town, decided not to call Caitlin directly but to allow David Higham to convey the news. She was back in Laugharne where, later that evening, she was sitting in the school hall, listening with an appreciative audience to Dylan's broadcast about the town, when she was passed a telegram which told her simply that Dylan had been 'hospitalised' in New York. She found this odd, not least because this was the first time she had seen this word. But she still felt so angry towards her husband, because of the dire financial situation he had left her in, that she put the matter to one side. On a certain level, she even felt some satisfaction that he was also suffering.

Overnight Daniel Jones contacted Dr Charles MacKelvie, a Swansea doctor who was a friend of the Thomas family. He thought a professional voice would be useful in cabling Dylan's clinical team at St Vincent's with 'possible valuable information about Dylan Thomas'. They put on record that eight weeks earlier he had had a 'haematome' or blood clot on his right temple, followed by a short blackout 'without aura', meaning without any symptoms of epilepsy, hysteria or related phenomena. They also noted his 'alcohol addiction'. However his condition was potentially slightly improved after a tracheotomy allowed him to breathe more easily.

Next morning, Caitlin was shaken out of her matrimonial bitterness by a telephone call from Oscar Williams, who plied her with gloomy prognostications, as well as insinuations that Dylan was being denied proper medical care. When she became hysterical, and demanded that Higham get her to New York as soon as possible, he prevaricated until Daniel Jones and Vernon Watkins agreed to guarantee her passage. For specific help she turned to the much maligned Margaret Taylor who arranged for the American embassy to open specially the following day (a Saturday) to give Caitlin a visa. Maggs also booked a transatlantic air passage with Thomas Cook for Sunday night, though an influential friend managed to bring this forward by twenty-four hours. With no idea how long she would be away, Caitlin, typically, did not stint on luggage. Shortly before her departure, she cabled Oscar Williams, giving him her flight details and asking him to ensure that Bob MacGregor was on hand at the airport with the equivalent of £43 to pay for her excess fare.

The two camps sent competing representatives to meet the flight. On a cold slushy morning, David and Rose Slivka arrived at the airport with Bob MacGregor and a doctor from the hospital. Also waiting were Reavey and Williams, the latter of whom, according to Todd, sidled up to MacGregor and said, 'We must hurry out a book of his papers.' MacGregor did not mention this remark in his account to David Higham, but did say that Rose was Caitlin's 'best feminine friend in New York'. He also poured scorn on 'the absurd lengths to which [Williams] went to be the official sympathiser'. At the airport Reavey claimed to have greeted Caitlin, but Slivka managed to pile her into the station wagon he had borrowed from Rollie McKenna. With a police escort, he then drove at top speed into Manhattan, followed by Reavey and Williams who at one stage managed to overtake.

First stop was the hospital where an addled Caitlin greeted Todd: 'Is the fucking man dead yet?' When she first saw her husband trussed in an oxygen tent, breathing through his throat, she broke down. 'This is not my Dylan,' she cried. 'I don't want to be here.' Reavey made much of the fact that her place at Dylan's side was then taken by Liz.

Caitlin was escorted to the Slivkas' house to compose herself. However Reavey was convinced that she was being drawn into a conspiratorial web. His wife Irene who, Len Lye thought, had been egging him on managed to get through by telephone to Caitlin who, now unwinding and with a drink, wailed, 'Where are you? Where is George? Where is Oscar? Why aren't you over here.' At the Slivkas', Reavey claimed to find Caitlin under the impression that Dylan was dead. When he assured her this was not true, she 'broke down and wept on my shoulder, which was better in the circumstances than just drinking rye and having light conversation with that riff-raff. Then after a time she took a bath – "I want to be like a bride", she said, and prepared to return to the hospital.'

In a stressful situation, both Slivka and Reavey were coping as best they could, but they were working at cross purposes: the one, perhaps adopting the escapist approach of an artist, trying to take Caitlin's mind off the pain of her ordeal; the other hoping that her presence at Dylan's bedside might yet lift him out of his coma. By the time Caitlin returned to the hospital, the balance of the equation had changed because she had been drinking heavily. She had taken pains to look her most striking, in a tight-fitting black wool dress, with her hair loosely tied up. But, ill-advisedly, she carried a bottle of whisky and was out of control. In a fit of anti-clerical rage, she tried to tear down a crucifix and pieces of religious iconography in Dylan's ward. She swore profusely and had to be restrained when she man-handled Brinnin, whom she blamed for enticing Dylan back to the United States. When taken in to see Dylan by the matron, she tried to clamber onto her husband's bed and kiss him. At this stage attendants were called; a staff doctor ordered her to be put in a strait jacket and committed to Bellevue, New York's grim public mental hospital. The Brinnin–Todd party thought this an indignity too far and, calling on Doctor Feltenstein for professional contacts and financial help, arranged for Caitlin to go to the Rivercrest, a private psychiatric clinic on Long Island.

As Liz Reitell resumed her vigil at Dylan's bedside, two of his earlier girlfriends were thinking about him in their different ways. Emily Holmes Coleman had converted to Catholicism and was living back in England. Having read about his coma in the newspapers, she had lain awake on the Saturday night and said a complete rosary for him. At communion on Sunday, the Dies Irae was sung because, significantly for Dylan, it was Remembrance Day. Although aware she had not seen him for years, she was cheered that she had read a recent statement in which he spoke of God. So she prayed, 'God – because he had much sweetness in him and was a poet, a real one, I ask you to save him, now or at his death.'

'What of Pearl?' Helen McAlpine later asked George Reavey from Tokyo. 'Did she appear at all? She was the only important one.' That weekend Pearl was attending a literary conference at Bard College, a liberal arts establishment on the Hudson, ninety miles north of New York. Other participants included Saul Bellow, who taught there, Ralph Ellison and a near hysterical John Berryman, who was heard to declare that, if Dylan passed away, poetry would die with him. On a country walk, he intoned, between long gulps of air: 'I'm breathing for Dylan, if I breathe for him perhaps he will remain alive.' After driving back to New York on Sunday evening with Ellison and Pearl, Berryman insisted that, although it was almost midnight, they should go to St Vincent's to see Dylan. Ellison declined because he felt the others' grief was 'so intensely private'. In recounting her last poignant moments with her former lover, Pearl eschewed all passion. She noted that a nun let them into the ward and, when they stood by the bed, Berryman looked very quiet and very miserable. She made no mention of her own feelings, though they seemed to incorporate both understanding and frustration from her later observation that Dylan had drunk himself to death because he knew he had written his best poetry: anything else would be a poor imitation.

Berryman returned in the morning and, by a strange quirk of fate, was the only person to see Dylan draw his last breath, shortly before

1 p.m. on Monday 9 November. Liz, who had been at his bedside, had taken a short break. Caitlin was still an in-patient at the Rivercrest clinic. When collected by Rose Slivka the next day, she was not aware that her husband had died.

A post-mortem recorded the immediate cause of death as pneumonia – a common outcome with someone in a coma. This was linked to emphysema, which reflected Dylan's history of smoking (and possibly also his taking of morphine). Though his heart was in poor shape (the flabbiness of his heart muscle and the calcification of his arteries would almost certainly have led to his death within ten years, according to Dr Charles MacKelvie), his liver, surprisingly, was healthier than expected, with little obvious sign of cirrhosis. However there had been pressure on his brain from the build-up of cerebro-spinal fluid. This was caused by the 'chronic alcoholic poisoning' of his system, which his leading neurosurgeon Dr William de Gutierrez-Mahoney had no doubt was the cause of Dylan's death.

The obituaries began to appear on 10 November. The New York Times drily summarised his poetic achievement, concluding that he 'was the best of the younger poets who wrote in English, meaning the generation after T. S. Eliot and W. H. Auden.' On the other side of the Atlantic, The Times (of London) adopted an unusually personal tone, suggesting Dylan had 'live(d) Christianity in a public way, leaving a body of work which reflected this – 'a poet narrow and severe with himself and wide and forgiving in his affections'. While acknowledging Dylan's individuality, it positioned him firmly at the centre of English letters: 'No one has ever worn more brilliantly the mask of anarchy to conceal the true face of tradition.'

Although printed anonymously, this notice was written by Vernon Watkins who gave voice to the devastating loss felt not just by Dylan's immediate friends but also by an extraordinary number of people who had come in contact with him, either personally or through his poetry. The literary critic, Alfred Kazin, who knew Dylan through his sister, Pearl, added his bit in his journal: 'Dylan. How much light goes out with the passing of our wizard, our beautiful careless singer. With everything you can say against the automatism, even the lonely self-infatuation of this man, he embodied the deepest cry of poetry, he was our young singer! What lonely pride, I say, what unforgettable bounty of the word.' Even Philip Larkin managed to extricate himself from the baleful influence of Kingsley Amis: 'I can't believe that D. T. is truly dead. It seems absurd. Three people who've altered the face of poetry, and the youngest has to die.' (The others were Auden and Eliot.)

Having been absent during much of Dylan's time in the United States,

James Laughlin sprang into action to organise a support fund for Caitlin and her children. With the help of a committee comprising W. H. Auden, e. e. cummings and other literary luminaries, he raised over $20,000 within two months. In Britain, T. S. Eliot, Louis MacNeice and Goronwy Rees put their names to a similar initiative (Rees even unsuccessfully lobbied Prime Minister Sir Winston Churchill for a civil list pension for Caitlin), while the two leading newspapers in Swansea and Cardiff also raised money from their readers. 'The death of poor old Dylan Thomas was one ghastly mess,' Laughlin told another of his authors, the Roman Catholic poet and priest Thomas Merton. 'Surely there was a miracle that anyone who was so helplessly messed up in his living could have turned out such beautiful poems. That was some kind of Grace all right for there could be no other explanation.'

After returning from the Rivercrest, Caitlin stayed with the Slivkas. As a sculptor, David Slivka thought he might help raise money for the support fund by making Dylan's death mask with a well-known colleague, Ibram Lassaw. Uncertain as to Caitlin's reaction, he arranged for someone from the British embassy to obtain her permission on behalf of 'two anonymous American artists'. He took a cast at the mortuary where Dylan had been laid to rest in a suit and tie that led Ruthven Todd to quip, 'Dylan wouldn't be seen dead in that.' Later a surreal situation developed where Slivka worked on Dylan's cast in his basement studio, while Caitlin received visitors upstairs, unaware what her host was doing.

In the charged atmosphere of the moment, old rivalries soon surfaced. When George Reavey began peppering correspondents in Britain with a defamatory version of the events leading to Dylan's death, Ruthven Todd responded with an alternative account. With Liz Reitell's assistance, Todd tried to salvage from the Chelsea what he could of Dylan's papers, including copies of *Under Milk Wood*. Anything in Dylan's hand was already prized and marketable. Todd told of seeing Oscar Williams remove a Dylan manuscript from a book in his house. By affecting a clinch, he managed to retrieve it from Williams's pocket.

Mutual suspicions were temporarily forgotten when, on Friday 13 November, four hundred people crammed into St Luke's episcopalian church in lower Manhattan to pay their respects at a memorial service. As the Pro Musica Antiqua choir sang motets by the Elizabethan composer Thomas Morley, only a solitary figure at the back bore witness to the troubled background to Dylan's death. This was Liz Reitell, condemned to the unenviable position of the mistress — unable to mourn openly and feeling, as she put it, 'the loneliest person in the world'.

At Dylan's interment in Laugharne eleven days later, Margaret Taylor found herself in a similar situation, though she viewed it more positively. 'I know I must not show my grief,' she wrote to the McAlpines in Tokyo, 'first, because I have no right to any signs of sorrow which must be Caitlin's exclusive right and, two, for Alan's poor sake I must not seem to grieve – the result is therefore satisfactory in that I do think I have been able to help Caitlin by being cheerful and calm.'

On the day of the funeral, Dylan lay in an open coffin in Pelican. When mourners were uncertain how to react to a body trussed in the American sepulchral style satirised by Evelyn Waugh in The Loved One, Florrie put them at their ease and encouraged them to look with the words, 'But he's nice.' In lustrous late autumn weather, the coffin was carried up the main street to St Martin's church by six local bearers. As it entered the lychgate a cock began to crow. Afterwards John Davenport heard what he thought was the perfect epitaph from Ebie Williams: 'He was a very humble man.' By common assent, the proceedings passed as Dylan would have liked, even if his widow did get drunk at the subsequent wake in Brown's and tipped a tray of beer over Fred Janes.

While Caitlin made little attempt to restrain her grief, others kept their wits about them. Having been at her side, physically supporting her, during the service, Dan Jones took the opportunity to talk to David Higham and Stuart Thomas about setting up a trust to care for Dylan's family over the long term. The idea was that Dylan's best friend, literary agent and solicitor would oversee his posthumous affairs, assuming responsibility for, loosely, his texts, copyrights and finances. Interest in Dylan's work was, predictably, great, and important decisions needed taking about literary works, such as Under Milk Wood. The three men felt Caitlin was in no fit state to decide. They had no idea what they were letting themselves in for: legal problems relating to the Trust were to drag on for almost half a century.

Determined to brook no delay, Dan and Stuart Thomas took Caitlin to the Carmarthen district probate office at the end of November to obtain letters of administration confirming her as her husband's sole heir. (Dylan had died intestate, with assets worth £100.) Although, rationally, she understood the sense of this, she was not ready for it on an emotional level. The following day she went to London to stay with the Lockes. After an evening's drinking, she made a botched suicide attempt, throwing herself from a third storey window. A shop front broke her fall and prevented her doing worse than breaking her collar-bone. However she seemed a danger to herself and, only three weeks after leaving the Rivercrest clinic, she agreed to sign into the Holloway Sanitorium, a mental hospital in Virginia Water, Surrey.

Refusing to stay long, she returned to Wales where her spirits were boosted by friends who came to visit – among them, Dan and Irene Jones who spent what Caitlin described as a 'mocking madhouse Christmas' in Laugharne. Dan was appalled at what he found. In her angry, self-lacerating widowhood Caitlin had become more violent and sexually rapacious than ever, and he wondered if she should not be compulsorily committed to an asylum. He compromised by hurriedly having her sign the trust deed. On 28 December Caitlin duly settled her inheritance, including all Dylan's copyrights, in a trust, the income of which was to be divided 50:50 between herself on the one hand and her three children on the other.

He and his co-trustees now had full authority to proceed. At the top of Dan's agenda was the future of Under Milk Wood. The BBC was scheduled to give the play its first broadcast on 25 January 1954. Douglas Cleverdon had secured Richard Burton to take Dylan's part of the First Voice (or narrator). Initially the wary BBC authorities wanted alterations to the text on grounds of decency. They were eventually satisfied with three cosmetic cuts. However Dan refused to allow Cleverdon to include changes that Dylan had made to the text in New York. Although Liz Reitell and Ruthven Todd vouched for these additions, Dan seemed to foresee complications if they were permitted.

On the eve of the transmission, Burton and the cast performed an extract from the play at a gala for the Dylan Thomas memorial fund at the Globe Theatre, London. Louis MacNeice, who helped organise the event, read Canto XVIII from his Autumn Sequel, a tribute to his friends, in which Dylan featured as Gwilym. Although still in America, Edith Sitwell composed a 'personal tribute', while Burton also read Dylan's poems. When asked what Dylan would have thought of the evening, which raised £1,169 5s., Caitlin said, 'He would have liked the cheque.'

The broadcast of the full version of Under Milk Wood the following night was well received, even if listeners in Wales were annoyed that the Third Programme's coverage did not extend to parts of the principality, including Laugharne. When it was suggested that the Welsh Home Service might repeat the play, the local head of programmes refused, saying it was not 'for family or home listening'. The affection with which Dylan portrayed his characters was ignored. As in the days of Caradoc Evans, the chapel influence balked at suggestions of Welsh hypocrisy and saw only malicious satire.

Dan Jones continued preparing the text for publication by Dent in May. He stuck to his conviction that all American additions were of uncertain provenance and therefore superfluous, but undermined his literalist case by changing the town's name from Llareggub to Llaregyb. The book was an immediate success, selling 13,000 copies in Britain in its first month, and over 53,000 in its first year. Its text became the jewel in a clutch of copyrights which by 1956–57 generated an income of £16,043 – not a huge amount, but better than the £500 or so a year that David Higham had forecast in the civil list application to Downing Street. At the same time Caedmon's records were introducing Dylan and his poetry to a new audience, particularly in America. Before long Dylan was being studied in schools and universities. The returns to the estate grew accordingly, plateauing at around £90,000 a year in 1990 – a figure which had hardly changed in 2002.

Nevertheless Caitlin was soon complaining to Higham that (in his words) 'she didn't feel happy about the Trustees and wanted to know whether she could change them!' When told this was impossible, she struck out in different directions. Having avoided Liz Reitell in America, she wrote to her seeking 'the truth'. Despite a conciliatory tone, she could not avoid berating her husband's last lover, asking if Liz and Dylan had felt any guilt about betraying her. She inveighed against the countless women who had thrown themselves at him, adding self-indulgently that she was now quite ready to believe that his love for her had been nothing but a vast incomprehensible sham.

Feeling restricted in a place with so many difficult and unresolved memories, Caitlin planned to take Colm to stay with Ruth Witt-Diamant in San Francisco, but that fell through. She still wanted to go to Elba, where she had hopes of reviving her 1947 holiday romance, but finances prevented it. Angry that she was expected to live on an income of £8 a week from the trustees, she threw herself into a series of indiscriminate sexual flings. By May Dan Jones reported: 'A group of Laugharne men openly share Caitlin, and there are almost nightly orgies at the Boat House about which the police have been informed; at one of these all-night sharing out sessions the deaf-mute Booda was badly beaten up. All this takes place in the presence of whatever children happen to be there.' Jones added that he had heard from Florrie and one of her female friends how Caitlin had made a sexual assault on Llewelyn, though he conceded that this might have been an attempt to shock the two old ladies rather than anything else.

Recognising the attention-seeking aspect of Caitlin's wayward behaviour, the normally garrulous Florrie turned a blind eye. She had decided that this was her best strategy if she were to play a role in bringing up her grandchildren (among whom she was particularly close to Aeronwy). She only vented her feelings to one or two people, such as Fred and Mary Janes, to whom she wrote, '[Caitlin] doesn't seem to think of her kiddies ... What a life she lives. What a shame. It's the children I feel for and I feel mad. She is still Dylan's widow, bless him, he is far better off dead than the husband of such a woman if one can call her that.'

Caitlin was not placated when, over the summer, the trustees bought the lease of the Boat House from Margaret Taylor for a very reasonable £1,300. With a sense of desperation Stuart Thomas agreed to fund her trip to Elba in October. There she quickly tired of the innkeeper Giovanni Chiesa and launched into an affair with an eighteen year old miner. The locals amused themselves by shouting 'prostituta, prostituta' when she passed. On her return to London in April 1955, she claimed she was pregnant and soon had another abortion.

By then she had begun writing a self-indulgent memoir, *Leftover Life to Kill*, which was largely about her reaction to Dylan's death and its aftermath. Well before it was published in May 1957, it was preempted by *Dylan Thomas in America*, Brinnin's revelatory account of his four year long relationship with her husband. Vernon Watkins was so incensed that Dent, Dylan's British publishers, should be responsible for this unflattering portrait that he refused to allow them to put out Dylan's letters to him. (As an unusual compromise, an edition appeared under the joint imprint of Dent and Faber.)

With the benefit of hindsight, others still wanted to make sense of Dylan's death. Alcohol had done the physical damage, of course; but why had he got himself into a state where, as Arthur Miller later remarked, Dylan could, with a week's abstinence, have been 'as healthy as a pig'? Taking his cue perhaps from Liz Reitell, who went to work for him and his wife, Marilyn Monroe, Miller observed in his 1987 autobiography *Timebends* that, having read Dylan's 'confessional' on his father (presumably *do not go gentle into that good night*), he felt that the Welshman had throttled himself for achieving fame while his father had died an unknown, failed man. 'Thomas was making amends by murdering the gift he had stolen from the man he loved.'

Dylan did take D.J.'s death worse than expected. But that was not the reason for his own demise. Others have pointed to his deepening concern that his poetry no longer had the spontaneity and verve of his youth. Again there is some truth in this: a laboured artificiality lies behind the mellifluousness of his 'Prologue', for example. But his last work, *Under Milk Wood*, was well-received even in his own lifetime. He was looking forward to working with Stravinsky and talked enthusiastically about future projects.

A more realistic explanation lies in the dynamics of his doomed relationship with Caitlin. Most of his friends attest to his deep love of his wife whom he tended to idolise. In practical terms, however, their marriage had developed the worst aspects of what modern psychotherapists call co-dependency, with each of them covering for the alcoholic excesses of the other. This behaviour had taken its mental toll, sapping his creative energy. Dylan's visits to the United States had introduced him to new possibilities and new loves that had enabled him to see some way out of his impasse, even if it meant questioning the centrality of Caitlin in his life. Her recognition of this only fuelled her resentment at being left at home with the children, feeling unfulfilled and second-rate. However the strict rules of their partnership ensured that he could never free himself from her. He could not even acknowledge to himself that his love for her was in doubt. He only knew he could do nothing about it. So, as she ranted about his fecklessness and perfidy, he was left feeling angry and impotent.

Ruthven Todd was given the first shot at writing an official biography but, befuddled by drink himself, he found the task beyond him. Determined not to become part of a myth-making machinery about his friend, he had difficulty picking his way through the recollections of people who insisted on writing themselves into Dylan's story and giving it their own interpretations. If a single incident was witnessed by six people, he wrote, six different patterns of behaviour were reported. When he resigned from the job in 1962, the responsibility passed to another of Dylan's old friends, Constantine FitzGibbon, who quickly polished off a life for publication in 1965. This remained the standard biography of Dylan until Paul Ferris's more accomplished work in 1978.

In time Caitlin began to forgive the husband she felt had betrayed and abandoned her. Signs of a healing process were evident in October 1955 when she applied for a licence to re-bury Dylan in the grounds of his beloved Boat House. She was motivated partly by a dislike for St Martin's church, which she felt had neglected his grave for stuffy moralistic reasons. Her petition reached the office of the Secretary of State for Wales who could see no objection. However, having made her point, Caitlin did not pursue her application.

Caitlin continued to move desultorily between Britain and Italy until October 1957, when she met Giuseppe Fazio, a good-looking Sicilian with a talent for languages, who had found a niche in the Italian film business. Eleven years her junior, he had the patience and firmness to deal with her. She went to live with him in Catania where, in March 1963, at the advanced age of forty-nine, she bore him a son, Francesco.

The birth of a child encouraged her to step up her battle with the Trust for more funds. In 1964 she received £5,500 as her half share of the trust's post-tax income, as well as additional personal royalties from the successful Broadway play, Dylan, by Sidney Michaels, which was based partly on her book and partly on Brinnin's. Even so, she wanted more money to fund a expensive lifestyle that ran to an apartment in

Rome. In March 1966, with the help of the trustees, she sued for the return of the original manuscript of *Under Milk Wood*, which Douglas Cleverdon had sold claiming it to be his. It proved an expensive gamble when she lost and was forced to pay costs. Two months later she turned her fire on the trustees, suing them for withholding £9,000 due from the sale of five of Dylan's letters to an American magazine. Wynford Vaughan-Thomas who had taken over as trustee from a disgruntled Dan Jones, remonstrated with Caitlin that over the previous decade she and her family had received 'the best part of a quarter of a million pounds' or 'a yearly income greater than that paid to the Prime Minister'.

Stuart Thomas, the administrator of the trust, might have been more emollient. He did well out of the connection, charging generous expenses to the trust's account. At one time he threatened to make a mockery of the set-up by arranging for his friend Kingsley Amis to become a trustee in place of Vaughan-Thomas who died in 1987. Amis could not abide Dylan either as a man or as a poet, though, occasionally, as when he opposed the 'novelisation' of *Under Milk Wood*, he brought his experience as a writer to the management of Dylan's literary affairs. Stuart Thomas, to give him his due, played a difficult hand with some skill. Despite Caitlin's furies, he performed his duty in keeping the trust not only intact but financially buoyant.

Gradually, around 1970, Caitlin began to conquer her alcoholism and lived the last two decades of her life sober and lucid, if still uncompromising. When, after several efforts, she reworked her memoirs, she pointed unsentimentally to alcohol as the bane of her life. (The book, which was both clear and moving, was published posthumously in 1997 as *Double Drink Story*.) Even as the demons began to disappear, she remained inconsistent to the last, making it known before she died in 1994 that, for all her devotion to her Italian family, she wanted to be buried beside her husband in the same Laugharne churchyard from which she had once wanted him moved.

Her passing did not make life any easier for the trust, for her son Francesco went to court, claiming that, as her heir, he was due her half-share in her husband's estate. Caitlin had discussed this with her other children, but they were understandably unenthusiastic, or they might have allowed the trust to be broken. As it was, the estate withstood Francesco Fazio's repeated legal assaults and his case was dismissed from the High Court in London in July 2002.

Strangely Dylan's mother never benefited from the trust. Although helped by the actor Emlyn Williams who devised a successful one-man show about her son, she lived partially on national assistance until her death in the Boat House in August 1958. Of Dylan's children, Llewelyn went to Harvard and enjoyed a successful career in advertising, before dropping out and seeking anonymity. Keeping matters in the family, he married Rhiannon, Stuart Thomas's step-daughter, but later divorced. He died of cancer in 2000 in the Devon town of Dawlish where he liked to be known as Tom Llewelyn. His and Rhiannon's Australian daughter Jemima was able to inherit his share in Dylan's estate. Colm, like his brother, spent time in Australia, before settling in Italy. Aeronwy trained as a nurse before joining her mother in Italy. After marrying a Welshman, Trefor Ellis in 1973, she moved to New Malden, Surrey, where, as a member of her local church, she enjoys a suburban existence very different from her mother's. With charm and tenacity, she acts as the public face of the Dylan Thomas family.

As for others in the story, Liz Reitell maintained a feisty dignity, even if, latterly, she tended to overemphasise the importance of her relationship with Dylan, calling it the 'greatest love experience' of her life. This was after she had married the architect Herb Hannum, whom she had introduced to Dylan, and worked in New York for Arthur Miller and Marilyn Monroe. Then, abandoning the arts for the environment, her passion for wilderness took her to Montana where she married for a fourth time before dying in February 2001. Adopting a more conventional course, Pearl Kazin married the distinguished Harvard sociologist Daniel Bell in 1960, had a son, and lives in Cambridge, Massachusetts, where she shows little sign of wanting to revisit her affair with Dylan. Her last known publication was an essay on her former Harvard tutor F. O. Mathiessen in *The American Scholar*.

Despite turbulence, Dylan's literary reputation remains intact half a century after his death. Inevitably, the interest shown in his work in the wake of his dramatic demise was followed by a period of reassessment. In England he came under attack from a critical school influenced by the Movement poets and given intellectual fire-power by the Cambridge professor F. R. Leavis. Leading the charge was David Holbrook whose 1962 book *Llareggub Revisited* portrayed Dylan as infantile and his poetry largely meaningless. Meanwhile, at a time of national resurgence in Wales, Dylan, unlike his near name-sake R. S. Thomas, was dismissed for ignoring the true matter of his home country.

That did not prevent him taking his place in Poets' Corner in London's Westminster Abbey in 1982 nor having an expensive part-European Community funded Centre named after him in Swansea in 1995. As the epitome of the romantic poet, he remained popular, even if many of his audience knew little more than *Under Milk Wood* and a dozen of his poems. To the horror of a few die-hard nationalists, he became, with the inexorable logic of the MTV generation, a symbol of modern Welsh culture. When the European Union held a competition for an essay about Wales, Welsh-born Commissioner Neil Kinnock presented the only prize with the requisite community-wide appeal – a first edition of *Under Milk Wood*. Dylan would have loved both the irony and the recognition.

NOTES

For the sake of space, I have used certain abbreviations. These relate to people – as in DT (Dylan Thomas), PHJ (Pamela Hansford Johnson), DJ (Daniel Jones), CT (Caitlin Thomas), KR (Keidrych Rhys), JL (James Laughlin), VW (Vernon Watkins), OW (Oscar Williams), DH (David Higham), MT (Margaret Taylor) JMB (John Malcolm Brinnin)

Or to institutions – SGS (Swansea Grammar School), SWEP (South Wales Evening Post), HoW (Herald of Wales), SWWG (Swansea and West Wales Guardian)

Or to libraries - NLW (National Library of Wales), HRC (Harry Ransom Humanities Research Center at the University of Texas at Austin). Some universities and libraries are noted in an abbreviated form e.g Indiana (University of Indiana at Bloomington) or Berg (the Berg collection at the New York Public Library)

And even to books – MFDT (My Friend Dylan Thomas by Daniel Jones)

CE (Colin Edwards) refers usually to interviews in his papers and tapes in the National Library of Wales

CL refers to the second or new edition of Dylan Thomas The Collected Letters edited by Paul Ferris and published in 2000. A number refers to the relevant page in this edition.

KT refers to the Ph D thesis and related research papers written by Kent Thompson and lodged in the archives of Swansea University Library

The number preceding each reference is the relevant page; subsequent entries on the same page have not been numbered.

CHAPTER I

5 the family raised £350: I am grateful to Kevin Lane, present owner of 5 Cwmdonkin Drive for background information

6 the 'quiet, retiring' George: description by Harry Leyshon CE

7 a Bible and hymn-book for the pulpit: Harry Leyshon CE

10 Gwilym Marles who died three years later: for further information on the Rev William Thomas, see Gwilym Marlais: Dylan Thomas's illustrious forebear by John Edwards New Welsh Review winter 1999–2000

one obituary: The Unitarian Herald December 1879

'I have been pursued' and 'find for me a good brain doctor' : Gwilym Marles to the Rev RJ Jones 7 May 1877 and 12 May 1879 NLW

11 Significantly, on 14 September 1892: see records of Johnstown primary school

and of the National and Practising School, Carmarthen, in Carmarthen county record office.

12 'You will see by the above the hours': for details of pay and hours, see DB/6/48 and DB/6/51 in the papers of the Great Western Railway in Carmarthen county record office

the only extra-curricular activity: details from letter from Thomas Parry, principal of University College, Aberystwyth, to Bill Read 18 December 1963 HRC

According to his future wife Florrie: interview with Ethel Ross Swansea College of Education Arts Festival magazine 1966

13 Eighteen year old Florrie: she was actually in Swansea on day of census

CHAPTER 2

17 box-like room: DT to PHJ c. 3 July 1934 CL 172

18 'A precocious child': DT to PHJ early Nov 1933

'a world within the world of the sea-town': Reminiscences of Childhood BBC Home Service 15 February 1943. Printed The Listener 25 February 1943. Repeated (second version) Welsh Region Children's Hour 21 March 1945

'from the robbers' den': Reminscences of Childhood second version

Addie Drew specifically remembered: CE

19 'He used to climb the reservoir railings: Return Journey BBC Home Service 15 June 1947, with many subsequent repeats

'the majority of literature': DT to Trevor Hughes early January 1933 CL 27

a 'mixture of genuine affection and amused contempt': Haydn Taylor, unpublished memoir

20 Resident in the same establishment: Trevor Hughes, memoir, Buffalo

21 his nickname Le Soldat: mentioned Walford Davies reviewing James A. Davies, A Reference Companion to Dylan Thomas, NWR No 46 1999 pp 70–75

'It'll be just the same':' quoted Fitzgibbon, Dylan Thomas p 41

22 'distant, terrible, sad music of the late piano lessons': Return Journey

'my grave poem': Evelyn Burman Jones in Dylan Thomas Remembered (tape produced by Dylan Thomas Society)

23 'a big voice for a small boy': Gwen James CE

Mervyn's home-life: The Levys came from Liverpool. Louis Levy was one of seven brothers - one of whom, Goodall (known as Goodie) was a jeweller and property developer who also married into the Rubenstein family. Harris Rubenstein, father of Goodie's wife Selina, made his fortune from a chain of wallpaper shops. Dolly Levy was born Zeiler.

24 no interest in the paintings and art books: KT

a competition: although she described it as a short story competition, the item was more likely to have been a poem - either his contribution to Boys Own Paper in February 1927 or the lines attributed to him in a competition in Everyman on 10 October 1929

25 His mother recalled: CE

26 'I did not care what the words said: Poetic Manifesto Texas Quarterly Winter
1961

'the Spinster's Friend': DT to PHJ early November 33 CL 61

From an early age: Addie Drew and Doris Fulleylove CE

I Like/ My Bike: Tom Warner CE

a 'dinner wagon': Fulleylove CE

despatched the wrong material: another version told by Florrie to Colin Edwards
is that she put them on the mantel-piece and accidently burnt them CE

27 My Party and 'As eager captains': HRC

CHAPTER 3

28 'Sleep with your wife, sir?': The Fight, but other sources e.g CE

29 'a hard time school-teaching': Jones MFDT p 11

Florrie noted that her nine year old son: Florrie to Ethel Ross 1 March 1957
Swansea University archives

When, despairing of Dylan's repeated failures: J. Morgan Williams CE

Thirty-third in trigonometry would suggest: Return Journey

One of his physics exercise books: this is in the property of Jeff Towns, to whom
I also owe the perception about the similarities between physics lesson and poem

'The Song of the Mischievous Dog': SGS Magazine December 1925

'His Repetoire': SGS Magazine December 1926

31 'The Watchers': SGS Magazine March 1927

'Missing': SGS Magazine July 1928

Idwal Rees read: Rees recalled (CE) this was a poem about the armistice. His
memory might have been muddled, or he might have remembered
the slightly later poem Armistice SGS Magazine December 1930

His Requiem: Western Mail 14 January 1927

32 'I wrote endless imitations': Fitzgibbon The Life of Dylan Thomas p 48. A slightly
different version is in Poetic Manifesto Texas Quarterly Winter 1961

Dylan's parents were so proud: Florrie Thomas, interview with Ethel Ross Swansea
School of Education etc

33 Jones doubted whether: Jones MFDT

34 'I ran down everything' DT to Percy Smart 7 March 1931 CL

He 'seemed to lack the coarseness': SGS Magazine April 1930

Things We Cannot Credit: SGS Magazine April 1930

'ugly, lovely': Reminiscences of Childhood

One young master: J. Morgan Williams CE

'You don't know how True-Blue': DT to PHJ March 34 CL 125

35 'Don't you go about jeering: DT to PHJ 9 May 1934 CL 154

'The Fight': written in 1939, first published in Life and Letters Today December
1939 and included in his Portrait of the Artist as a Young Dog in 1940.

his first known letter: DT to DJ 30 December 1927 Jeff Towns

36 Dan's previously unknown diary: I grateful for Daniel Jones's daughter Cathy and her husband Rob Roberts for making this available

37 Dan later recalled: Jones MFDT

Vier Lieder: Daniel Jones archive A 41 NLW

meticulous programmes: HRC

'I'm fed up with sculpture' MFDT

'This luxury has its inconveniences: unpublished manuscript, no date, owned by Jeff Towns

38 The Era: Manuscript owned by Jeff Towns

39 she 'whirled away': MFDT

'Tell her you love her, boy': Wynford Vaughan-Thomas, tape Dylan Thomas Society

He said, 'You seem so lovely, Chloe': originally in autograph albumn owned by Dr Bonnie Luscombe, to whom I am grateful for further details of Dylan's visit.

40 Evelyn ('Titch') Philips: see her interview CE

Writing to Geoffrey Grigson: DT to GG spring 1933 CL 33

He later said: DT to HT 16 May 1938 CL 345

CHAPTER 4

42 'ancient peasant Aunt': DT to VW April 1938 (Also creature with a 'cracked sing-song voice': The Peaches, and 'fist of a face': After the Funeral

selling his horse's shoes: CE

43 coming out of a pub and kissing: The Peaches

'in the warm, safe island': The Peaches

44 old family house at 29 Delhi Street: Rate Book St Thomas 1930, West Glamorgan Archives

45 William was drowned: Carmarthen Journal 17 August 1917

Dylan looked up to him: Doris Fulleylove CE

46 At a promotional garden party: details of Nancy's courtship with Haydn Taylor are pieced together from correspondence between Nancy and Haydn Taylor (for which I am grateful to his son Michael Taylor) and from an unpublished memoir by Haydn Taylor (which his daughter Felicity Skelton was kind enough to copy and send me)

'lace curtains and no breakfast': Trick CE

47 Desert Idyll: SGS Magazine December 1929

Modern Poetry: SGS Magazine December 1929

48 He was also thinking about other media: The Films SGS magazine July 1930

'Tendencies of Modern Music': SGS Magazine December 1929

49 he and Dan discussed forming a group of poetry lovers: DJ diary

'Osiris, Come to Iris': for this and other Notebook Poems, refer to Maud (ed.) Dylan Thomas The Notebook Poems 1930–1934

50 'Even that third-former' DT to Percy Smart December 1930 CL 9

noted a transitional period: MFDT p 12

51 Dylan promptly went out and got drunk: DT to Percy Smart 25 June (1931) CL 15

'I have realized how terribly worried Daddy is' Nancy Thomas to Haydn Taylor 24 August 1930

his father had impressed on him: DT to Percy Smart July 1931 CL 18

'a rather short, slightly built, almost girlish figure': Trevor Hughes memoir Buffalo

CHAPTER 5

53 Colleagues recalled: Trevor Ogbourne and WG (Bill) Willis CE

at the annual dinner of the Licensed Victuallers Association: Trick CE

54 'You can do better than that, Thomas.' Mrs Freda Bassett CE

'Some people are too lazy': Old Garbo (also the source, with Return Journey and CE, for further detail)

56 'head in the oven, no nearer heaven': Poem LVII 1930–1932 Notebook NP 105

'I am at the most transitional period': DT to Trevor Hughes February 1932 CL 19

57 'two hours of almost continual chuckling': SWEP 18–20 February 1932

'a remarkable blossoming': Ralph Maud, Notebook Poems p 62

'he stood out should high': HoW 19 September 1936

a six part series on 'The Poets of Swansea': see HoW various dates January to June 1932; also Davies Dylan Thomas's Swansea, Gower and Laugharne

59 'Beer, I may?': recollection by Charles Fisher

Linda Slee: see Tynan Letters (Kenneth Tynan to Elly Horowitz June/July 1948)

60 'I shall never know': interview Jill Davies December 2002

a back-handed farewell notice: SWEP 9 September 1932

62 One of his last pieces: HoW 5 November 1932

'little (Oscar) Wilde words': DT to Percy Smart ?12 December 1932 CL 25

63 'already showing signs of a reporter's decadence': DT to Trevor Hughes early January 1933 CL 28

'to feel November air/ And be no words' prisoner': This is one of a number of poems not in any manuscript notebook which Dylan typed and took up with him to London in August 1933. Professor Ralph Maud has argued plausibly that these 'typescript poems' came from a notebook which covers the seven months bettween July 1932 (the end of one notebook) and January 1933 (the start of the next). When Dylan came to revise this particular poem for his first published book 18 Poems in 1934 he changed the month from November to October - probably to coincide with his birthday. In October 1934 he was twenty. Marking his birthdays in poetry became a tradition. Ten years later, he celebrated his 'thirtieth year to heaven' with his Poem in October (actually written in August 1944).

He observed the obsequies DT to Percy Smart: c12 December 1932 CL 25

64 'No novelists any good except me': DT to Percy Smart ibid.

CHAPTER 6

65 a piece for the Post: SWEP 7 January 1933

66 his 'incurable disease': DT to Trevor Hughes ?early January 1933 CL 28

he claimed that Sir John Squire: DT to Trevor Hughes ibid.

'I continue writing' DT to Trevor Hughes 8 February 1933 CL 32

'She is dead.' DT to Trevor Hughes 8 February 1933 CL 31

Dylan had to counsel his friend: DT to Hughes ?early January 1933 CL 27

67 he pilloried the role: DT to Hughes 8 February 1933 CL 32 For the background see Herald of Wales 24 January and 7 February 1933

68 'Dylan liked a bit of old ham': Eileen Davies CE

When Dylan tried this: Ruby Graham CE

69 'a communist grocer': DT to to PHJ c. 11 November 1933 CL 68

His family, originally from Devon: see Kerith Trick Bert Trick – the original Marx brother New Welsh Review No 54 Autumn 2001 pp 43–51

'that is the only way to get the music': Bert Trick, The Young Dylan, Texas Quarterly Summer 1966

70 'We'd start on modern poetry': Trick CE (unless otherwise indicated Trick's observations come either from this source or from his Texas Quarterly article)

'Dylan had no politics at all': Leslie Mewis to author July 2002

71 Dylan was still a cub reporter: Trick CE

his visitor was seventeen: Country Quest autumn 1960

71–2 Dylan's relationship with Trick: Even with the evidence of the notebooks, it is difficult to pin-point Trick's precise influence on Dylan's poems. At the start of their friendship in 1932, Dylan read Trick some poems which later appeared in his first book, 18 Poems, published in December 1934. Or so Trick remembered over thirty years later in Texas Quarterly. But his recall of dates needs to be treated with scepticism. According to Professor Ralph Maud's precise tabulation (The Notebook Poems), none of the notebook models for the 18 Poems extends back to 1932. The earliest, which found durable form in 'Before I knocked', is from 6 September 1933. Could Dylan have read to Trick from a missing notebook, possibly the one covering the months July 1932 to February 1933? Although Dylan later reprised a handful of his earlier poems (most obviously, The Hunchback in the Park, published in Deaths and Entrances in 1946, but drawing on a poem originally dated 9 May 1932), the majority of those published in his first two collections – 18 Poems and Twenty-five Poems – can be traced to notebook poems written between February 1933 and April 1934.

'And death shall have no dominion': first published New English Weekly 18 May

1933. Trick's effort was not so ambitious, but beguiling enough to be published in SWWG June 1934

His heaven was a Buddhist-style nirvana: 'Now understand a state of being, heaven' 18 May 1933

73 The young man gave a naughty smile: Trick CE; Trick dated this reading to 1933

74 James A. Davies is correct: Davies A Reference Companion p 169

a friend from his Bristol days: information from Taylor's daughter Felicity Skelton

A Little Theatre performance of Sophocles's Electra: Eileen Davies CE; Dylan's poem Greek Play in a Garden HoW 15 July 1933

76 '(Murry) is interested in the symbols of the world': DT to Hughes May 1933 CL 35

Orage asked him bluntly if he were a virgin: see Heppenstall Four Absentees

The bibulous Malcolm Lowry: see Bowker Pursued by Furies

CHAPTER 7

77 For Victor Neuburg, see Calder Marshall The Magic of my Youth, Goulden Mark my Words, and Neuburg Vickybird

78 nice body but poor brain: DT to PHJ January 1934 CL 116. Over the next year, most of Dylan's comments on himself, his work and Pamela are taken from his correspondence with PHJ. Apart from three letters, this correspondence covered the period September 1933 to October 1934. It is found between pages 38 and 194 of the Collected Letters. A few additional observations come from PHJ's diaries for this period, which are in the Lockwood Memorial Library of the State University of New York at Buffalo.

One admirer: interview Canon Fred Cogman August 2002

81 One of the work-sheets: I am indebted to a conversation with the Dylan Thomas expert Robert Williams for this. See also Dylan Thomas and the Welsh language, the article he penned with Ralph Maud in the New Welsh Review 42 (1998)

84 Born Winifred Simpson: 'Runia Tharp' was born in Madras on 18 April 1879 and died in London on 10 November 1970. She had a daughter by Leslie Bellin-Carter and two sons by Charles Tharp. I am indebted for this and related information to Runia Tharp's daughter-in-law Silvia Tharp and her grand-daughter Ros Tharp

'Trying the Modern Experiment': see Calder-Marshall, The Magic of my Youth

88 an anthology of Recent Poetry: this was edited by Alida Monro, widow of the Imagist founder of the Poetry Bookshop.

Graves, no great enthusiast: see Graves The Crowning Privilege

CHAPTER 8

90 'Have you seen the Gauguins?': see Tedlock (ed.) The Legend and the Poet p 23

91 an anthology of English language poems: DT to Glyn Jones March 1934 CL 121

92 the announcement of Dylan's prize: Sunday Referee 13 May 1934

95 'The Orchards': dated October 1934 in the Red Notebook, published The Criterion, July 1936

96 Dylan weighed in with a letter: DT to SWWG 8 June 1934 CL 168

Mainwaring Hughes retaliated: SWWG 15 June 1934

97 'the obscene hypocrisy': SWWG 6 July 1934 CL 177

Geoffrey Grigson's questionaire: New Verse No 11 October 1934

98 'from pit-boy to poet'!': Hansford Johnson Important to me p 143

his scandalous story 'The Burning Baby': 'The Burning Baby' was written before the end of the year and due in a new quarterly 'Art' in January 1935, though not actually published until May 1936 in Contemporary Poetry and Prose. (This was a couple of months before The Orchards was published in The Criterion.) For background on Jones and Dylan's meeting with Caradoc Evans see The Dragon Has Two Tongues Glyn Jones

100 Dylan was influenced: Glyn Jones CE

In May he had told: DT to Hamish Miles (an editor at Cape) ?May 1934 CL 161

He argued in Adelphi: Adelphi Vol 8 No 6 September 1934

'Oh, he's nobody': Glyn Jones archive Trinity College Carmarthen. A.P. Herbert was a friend of Desmond Hawkins. See end of chapter

101 Bert Trick claimed: CE

'And as for the Workers!': DT to Glyn Jones, mid April 1934 CL 141–2

103 'a little too close': DT to Glyn Jones December 1934 CL 206

several Blue Moon writers: Woodcock Letter to the Past

104 Runia Tharp told a Gothic tale: see Grindea Adam International

105 'a curious mixture of slut and whore': MacNiven and Moore (eds.) Literary Lifelines

106 he also claimed to have met: DT to Trick December 1934 CL 204

CHAPTER 9

108 Connolly was 'completely ensared': from a file read by Jeremy Lewis in the Connolly archive in the University of Tulsa. He kindly supplied me with his excellent notes.

several 'ladies representing fashion rather than literature': Connolly Journal and Notebook

109 'Did you say swishing?': for a slightly different perspective on this gathering, see Powell Faces in My Times

Waugh was not aware of any rudeness: EW to Constantine Fitzgibbon 24 December 1964 Waugh The Letters

His own youthful behaviour: according to his friend Noel Annan in Our Age, Waugh said that Dylan reflected what he would have been if he had not found Catholicism. Waugh in his letter to Fitzgibbon said that Robert Byron noted the resemblance between him (Waugh) and Dylan pelting pebbles at bottles: Lewis Cyril Connolly A Life. Lewis tells me that this was a recollection by Gascoyne in an interview with him. No date was given for the trip to Selsey. It sounds like another elaboration on Thomas mythology. In his Recollections of Dylan Thomas London Magazine Vol 4 no 9 1975 Geoffrey Grigson wrote about a similar exercise during his trip with Dylan to Ireland. He and Dylan drew the faces of literary figures on white pebbles and cracked them against the rocks. However his story had an elaboration – that the faces included his bête noir Edith Sitwell. See GG to Constantine Fitzgibbon 4 Oct 1965 Berg.

J.D. Williams using his regular diary column: SWWP 1 January 1935

His ripsoste in an interview: Sunday Referee 30 December 1934

Bert Trick downplayed: SWWG 11 January 1935. Further engagements in this debate came two weeks later (Jennings), 1 February (Hughes) and 8 February (Trick again).

110 Spencer Vaughan Thomas: the Vaughan Thomases were sons of David Vaughan Thomas, a leading Welsh composer. The first review had been in the Morning Post, via if not in the hand of Grigson, on 1 January 1935.

'If there was one empty, dirty milk bottle': Florrie to Ethel Ross Swansea College of Education Arts Festival magazine 1966

111 'what they priggishly call "the class struggle"': DT to Bert Trick ?mid-February 1935 CL 212

reviews of 18 Poems: Adelphi February 1935, Time and Tide 9 February 1935

a basement bar in the King's Road: Heppenstall CE

112 drinking club: Ruthven Todd refers to an unlikely club called Mummy's, where they would compete for favour of girl they called 'Fluffie'; see Todd Dylan Thomas unpublished memoir National Library of Scotland. Dylan referred to Fluffy, 'the chorus-girl with glasses' in a letter to Desmond Hawkins 16 September 1935 CL 227

'Poetry, Jacobean and Metaphysical': DT to Desmond Hawkins 15 May 1935 CL 216

'He had a fund of stories': Hawkins When I was p 118

Alban Berg's then little-known opera Wozzeck: Rayner Heppenstall CE

'Words to him were like flags': Hawkins When I was p 119

earn extra money: Grigson estimated that Dylan made £5 per week this way. See his letter to Bill Read 10 Jan 1964 Berg

modernism's 'Inner Command': Grigson Recollections pp 81–8

113 Norman Cameron's poetry: see Jonathan Barker's introduction to Norman Cameron's Collected Poems Anvil Press Poetry 1990; also Hope Norman Cameron

'Dylan suddenly appeared chez Norman: Hope Norman Cameron

Janes recalled him: unpublished memoir, courtesy Hilly Janes

'I lend once': Taylor A Personal History (for which I rely for much of the other detail about this visit)

115 got drunk, picked up a girl: DT to DJ 14 August 1935 CL 223

116 'wild, unlettered and unfrenchlettered country': DT to BT summer 1935 CL 218–9

'we had a blistery scene': Grigson to Bill Read 10 January 64 Berg 'the blindest blind': DT to Desmond Hawkins 16 September 35 CL 227

'Everywhere I find myself': DT to Trick summer 1935 1935 CL 218

118 WARMDANDYLANLEY-MAN: DT to Dan Jones 14 August 1935 CL 224

'nothing but a protracted dirge': DJ to Thornley Jones 16 November 35 Roberts

119 'the writings of a boily boy': Marjorie Adix in Tedlock (ed.) Dylan Thomas The Legend and the Poet

reminded commentators of James Joyce's Ulysses: see Tindall A Reader's Guide p 142 et al

120 a conscious attempt to 'get away': DT to Glyn Jones December 1936 CL 272

'As Kellner was to the Kit-Kat Club': DJ to Thornley Jones 16 November 35 Roberts

'Dylan is still here': Tom Warner to Dan Jones dated Wednesday posted 16 October 1935 Roberts

122 practice of sponging off Cameron: see Todd archives National Library of Scotland

'When he disappeared': Grigson Recollections

123 'it'll be Rat Week always': DT to OB nd CL 236. Blakeston and Chapman's claims to have had affairs with Dylan were reported in Gay News October 1977

evasive action: see Ruthven Todd's annotation to his personal copy of Fitzgibbon (ed.) Dylan Thomas Selected Letters, property of Jeff Towns

124 'ought to be dashed off to a psycho-analyst': Edith Sitwell to John Sparrow May 1934 quoted Pearson Facades p 307

'I want to ask him some questions: ES to Robert Herring 27 January 1936 quoted Pearson Facades p 308

'She isn't very frightening, is she?': DT to Robert Herring 30 January 1936 CL 240

he 'stands a chance of becoming a great poet': ES to Christabel, Lady Aberconway. Sitwell Selected Letters Lehmann and Parker (eds.) p 54

'charming, a great man': DT to VW 20 April 1936 CL 249

best summaries of his literary beliefs: SWGG 17 January 1936

125 'so tired of sleeping with women I don't even like': Heppenstall Four Absentees p 96

next door to Virginia Woolf's brother: the Stephens' daughter Judith married Wyn Henderson's artist son Nigel

126 a powerful homosexual love story: see Read The Days of Dylan Thomas p 82

CHAPTER 10

128 Caitlin 'unfairly romped' Devas Two Flamboyant Fathers p 78 This book has been useful in sketching out the Macnamara family background.

129 Dillon School of Dancing: Vivien John, unpublished memoir (courtesy Julius White)

Rupert Shephard painted her several times: Shephard diary (courtesy Ben Shephard)

130 Caitlin has put it specifically at 12 April: see Caitlin: Life with Dylan Thomas and Double Drink Story

'Life No 13': DT to VW 20 April 1936 CL 249

131 'from the constipation of logic': Penrose Scrap Book

'came in and tied a mouse to an exhibit': Gascoyne to author September 2001. The cup of boiled string story appears in different places, including Hope Norman Cameron.

132 Fred Janes was back in Swansea: see Hilly Janes Biographical Notes in Alfred Janes 1911–1999 catalogue of retrospective exhibition at Glynn Vivian Art Gallery

en route to Fishguard: see Augustus John to Dorelia McNeil 20 July 1936 NLW

133 Frances Hughes saw things differently: CE

his passengers 'osculating assiduously': Augustus John to Dorelia 20 July 1936 NLW

'possessing it in great milky wads': DT to DH 21 August 1936 CL 265

135 Empson noted revealingly: London Letter Poetry (Chicago) January 1937

136 'I would do, or attempt, anything for you,': Richard Jennings to Edith Sitwell 30 November 1936 Berg

'Have you seen young Dylan Thomas' Twenty Five Poems?': Edith Sitwell to Kenneth Clark 10 January 1937 Berg

'a Young Poet untainted with Eliot': Grigson to Bill Read 10 January 1964 Berg

the fresh-faced full-lipped Coleman: her description of her life and her affair with Dylan are taken from her diaries University of Delaware

138 a passionate affair: DT to Emily Holes Coleman 28 & 29 January 1937 CL 274

'Your new love affair must be "hurried"': Djuna Barnes to Emily Holmes Coleman 10 January 1937 Delaware

139 'brilliant, bitter, and sometimes bawdy invective': minutes of Nashe Society, St John's College Cambridge

141 'It is only among poor failures': DT to Emily Holmes Coleman 29 March 137 Delaware CL 283

'All my friends are failures': DT to George Barker 4 April (1937) CL 284

142 'Gods knows where': telegram DT to Emily Holmes Coleman 6 April 1937 CL 285

'I was not the only one abroad': fragment in Veronica Sibthorp papers NLW

David Gascoyne ran into Dylan: Gascoyne Journal 1936–37 pp 86–7

143 'A nice mess-up all round.': memo BBC Written Archives

'absolutely a physical removal': DT to CT early May 1937 CL 285

144 The last time I slept with the Queen: verse recalled by Todd in his unpublished memoir

Veronica kept an album: descriptions of various drawings and verses over the next two pages come from this album in the National Library of Wales. The Library dates the material to 1936 and 1937, but there is reason to believe later items – up to 1939 - are included.

146 Elizabeth Fusco: her memoir is in CE under the name Elizabeth Milton

147 a close conspiracy: DT to Caitlin Macnamara November or December 1936 CL 271

148 'I spent some time combing': Augustus John to Caitlin Macnamara Thursday Sibthorp papers NLW

'the young irresponsibles': D.J. Thomas to Haydn Taylor, quoted note CL p 287

'with no money': DT to VW 15 July 1937 CL 294

CHAPTER 11

149 The Weekend Book: owned by Jeff Towns

150 they ate in the morning: DT to PHJ 6 August 37 CL 295

'Somebody's boring me': Heppenstall Four Absentees p 139

151 Rhys likened Dylan to Dafydd ap Gwilym: KR to Gwyn Jones 14 March 1937 NLW

'I've told him how absurd': Glyn Jones to KR 18 March 1937 NLW

152 'very experimental and not left' KR to GJ 1 March 1937 NLW

varied pool of talent: see KR to GJ 14 March 1937 NLW

'they all try and write like Dylan': KR to GJ n.d. NLW

'Confident, ear-catching and barely comprehensible': Mathias A Ride Through the Wood p 299

153 a reverse Pilgrim's Progress: DT to Bert Trick summer 1935 CL 220

'a marvellous blend of Dali and St John the Divine': KR to Glyn Jones 27 July 1937 NLW.

'The main obstacle to (Dylan's) fulfilment': Nigel Heseltine to KR 23 March 1937 NLW

found him unchanged: KR to Glyn Jones 6 September 1937 NLW

'The only thing a young Welsh writer should do' KR to Glyn Jones 6 Sept 1937 NLW

A young fellow of Swansea called Tummas: Nigel Heseltine to KR 12 September 1937 NLW

154 Dylan amused the refugee children: Kerith Trick Bert Trick – the original Marx brother New Welsh Review autumn 2001 p 50

'When she smokes a cigarette': VW to Francis Dufau-Labeyrie 30 August 1937 private collection

'Mr Thomas owned a lot of books': Devas Two Flamboyant Fathers

156 'I make one image': DT to Henry Treece 23 March 1938 CL 327

157 'He should do some real work': KR to Glyn Jones 11 December 1937 NLW

158 three poems by Antonia White: see Dunn Antonia White p 235

The cheque was cashed on 25 January: Dylan told Charles D. Abbott of Buffalo University that he would be in London from 24 January. Letter DT to C.D. Abbott 17 January 1938 Buffalo

159 some of the most exciting modern writers: DT to George Reavey March 1938 CL 321

'I have been watching (Dylan's) work': JL to Beatrix Baird 11 February 38 Houghton

a significant unpublished statement: DT to Bob Rees n.d. early 1938 copy West Glamorgan Archives

160 Nicolette told a story: Devas Two Flamboyant Fathers p 193

'We are stages beyond poverty'. DT to Lawrence Durrell early January 1938 CL 309

'Swansea is still the best place': DT to Charles Fisher 11 February 1938 CL 317

'I'm leaving here next week': DT to KR 10 March 1938 CL 320

a rash promise to give Laughlin the American rights: DT to JL 28 March 1938 CL 332/3

161 a mistake: DT to Wyn Henderson 13 July 1938 CL 361;

'a good place': DT to James Laughlin 7 May 1938 CL 340

162 a Victoria Cross: interview with Douglas Williams

'jive-man' Richard Hughes: DT to Henry Treece 1 June 1938 CL 349

163 hoping to write many more stories: DT to Desmond Hawkins 16 March 1938 CL 323

'very Lawrence in style': KR to Glyn Jones 4 November 1937 NLW

'exotic rhapsodies': KR to Glyn Jones 13 March 1938 NLW

'not up to standard': Nigel Heseltine to KR 26 February 1938 NLW

the 'first truly Welsh Anglo-Welsh product': Nigel Heseltine to KR 24 December 1937 NLW

164 'this racial talk': DT to Henry Treece 1 June 1938 CL 349

a mass-poem: DT to Meurig Walters 28 March 1938 CL 333

he offered one of his 'new', realistic tales: DT to George Reavey 16 June 1938 CL 351

165 'How much younger': JL to DT 11 May 1938 Houghton

he did not need an agent: DT to JL 17 May 1938 CL 345

Laughlin did nothing to disabuse him: JL to DT 11 May 1938 Houghton

Dylan claimed ignorance: DT to JL 28 June 1938 CL 356

the agent had only acted for him: DT to JL 27 July 1938 CL 364

'I don't require any more the services of an agent': DT to JL 17 May 1938 CL 346

'queries galore': Beatrix Baird to JL 29 June 1938 Houghton

his 1938 anthology New Directions in Poetry and Prose: The poems printed were How shall my animal, In memory of Ann Jones and I make this a warring absence, though the stories were held back for contractual reasons. Dylan was described as the name on 'the tongue of every young poetry reader in England. His poetry is verbal sculpture – almost fiercely strong.'

'The propaganda is underway': JL to DT 10 July 1938 Houghton

166 'virtually stole' JL to Baird 1 August 1938 Houghton

the 'stage house': Grindea Adam International p 9

'(The Thomases) live in frightful squalor': AJ to Dorelia McNeil August/September 1938 NLW

'neuter': DT to Henry Treece 1 September 1938 CL 373

Charles Fisher: see note in Charles Fisher's personal diary. May 17 1938 'Drove to Laugharne to see Dylan and show him the first chapter of our novel which is apparently all right.' Mr Fisher tells me that Dylan said 'something like "A good start. Fine." We then went over to Browns (where else?)' E-mail 24 January 2003

Fisher happened to be there: CF's diary 9 August 1938. Mr Fisher added, 'I recall this latter part of the evening well. Augustus and I were deeply engaged in talk, but Dylan was saying nothing, not like him at all.' Eventually Dylan said in staccato phrases, 'I'm sorry. I want to say things. It's just ... that I am unable to speak.'

'a terrible war month': DT to VW 14 October 1938 CL 376

'a disappointing school-society' (and further comments): DT to Henry Treece 23 March 1938 CL 327, 16 May 1938 CL 343 and 6 or 7 July 1938 CL 358

168 'What a mincing lot we were!': DT to John Davenport 4 November 1938 CL 386

169 'too often like a man shouting under the sea': DT to T Rowland Hughes 3 November 1938 CL 385.

' Must you be a Georgian writer': DT to John Davenport 14 October 1938 CL 377

'I will not spend a lot of time and money': JL to Miss Johnson at Ann Watkins 17 January 1939 Houghton

'a cliché-ridden humbug': DT to Henry Treece February 1938 CL 316

170 'It really is an insane city': DT to VW 20 December 1938 CL 392

'sit and hate my mother in law': DT to Charles Fisher January 1939 CL 403

171 'I've got the willies of London': DT to Lawrence Durrell 28 December 1938 CL 395

London remained a 'nightmare': DT to VW ?8 January 1939 CL 402

'She's the only woman I've ever loved.': Durrell The Shades of Dylan Thomas Encounter Vol 9 December 1957 pp 56–59

172 'soft, white, silly ravens': DT to VW 20 December 1938 CL 393

CHAPTER 12

173 a 'small, square giant': DT to Desmond Hawkins 12 March 1939 CL 416

174 'very paltry': DT to John Prichard June 1939 CL 433

175 'sort of provincial autobiography': DT to David Higham 11 May 1939 CL 426

his 'earlier world': DT to Richard Church 1 May 1936 CL 254

'As I can't make money by what I write': DT to John Davenport 11 May 1939 CL 428

'Why not an article on Firbank, too?': DT to KR 7 January 1939 CL 400–1

176 'We must have this man's script.': BBC Written archives

'It is mainly a poetry of the elemental physical experience': Seven Autumn 1939

'a little Danzig': DT to VW 25 August 1939 CL 453

177 'If I could pray': DT to D.J. Thomas 29 August 1939 CL 455

two military policemen: see Letters to Vernon Watkins p 71

Lynette Roberts: Earlier Roberts had stayed at Sea View where she recalled Dylan telling her that, as she was there, he could her her any time he felt like it. She reported that 'fortunately' nothing happened. See Lynette Roberts, Parts of an autobiography Poetry Wales 19,2 (1993)

178 'Ca-at. Can I have a plum?' Watkins Portrait of a Friend p.64

Dinner with Mrs David at Minerva: recalled by Ann Starke November 2001

179 a Christmas entertainment: Frances Hughes CE. See also Graves Richard Hughes p 283

'flippant' mock-Joycean title: DT to VW 30 January 1940 CL 497

'all I want is time to write poems': DT to John Davenport 14 September 1939 CL 464

180 'one Daddy to another': DT to Bert Trick 29 September 39 CL 471

'prepared to die for something': Trick CE

declare himself a neutral state: DT to Desmond Hawkins 3 September 1939 Cl 461

'Is it any worse to receive a good salary': DT to Rayner Heppenstall 2 November 1939 CL 480

'I want a war-escaper': DT to VW 13 December 1939 CL 494

182 'a proper city book': DT to JL 15 April 40 CL 511

'my great horror's killing': DT to Sir Kenneth Clark 1 April 1940 CL 508

Rupert Shephard and Lorna Wilmot's visit to Laugharne: see Shephard's diary (source of the clerihew) and Wilmot to Eleanor Scott draft 20 May 1940

183 a total of £126.12s.od: Spender to Francis Brett Young 3 June 1940 University of Birmingham

H.G. Wells meanly declined: H.G. Wells to Stephen Spender 20 May 1940 Houghton

186 'Dylan-shooting begins.': Hansford Johnson Important to me p.146

Another fearful fantasy: DT to VW early September 1940 CL 524

187 'when I tell you I clung to them,': Antonia White to Emily Holmes Coleman 6 November 1940 quoted Dunn p 250

a putative opening: DT to VW 8 August 1940 CL 522

Florrie had optimistically told: Nancy (Thomas) to Haydn Taylor n.d. Taylor papers

188 'Is this Mr Pulham's residence?': see Fitzgibbon With Love

his 'poem about invasion': DT to VW September 1940 CL 526

189 John Royston Morley: he had edited the short-lived magazine Janus which published The Horse's Ha in 1936

'He came in to see me today': BBC Written Archives

five different announcers: DT to John Davenport 8 January 41 CL 533

'so much a visual poem': VW Notes on Dylan Thomas unpublished

'a mixture of Oliver Twist': DT to VW 22 May and 28 May 1941 CL 546/548 also DT to John Lehmann early October 1941 CL 556

190 'When I want advice from Alec Waugh': DT to John Davenport 27 Jan 41 CL 538

a letter of grovelling apology to de la Mare: DT to de la Mare 23 April 1941 Bodleian

'She bites the hand that makes her sick': Evelyn Milton née Phillips CE

191 'There had been a pub on the corner': Trick CE

'I'm not, by the way, thinking of film-work': DT to Kenneth Clark 23 March 1941 Tate Gallery

'I'd rather be a poet anyday': DT to Clement Davenport 2 April 1941 CL 540

Individual Happiness Now (IHN): see Horrocks Len Lye

CHAPTER 13

193 the Gargoyle Club: See Luke David Tennant. For additional material about war-time London, see Sinclair War Like a Wasp, Hewison Under Siege, Stanford Inside the Forties

195 claimed to have been offered work on several scripts: DT to VW 28 August 1941 CL 555

Strand's 'ringing, clinging' offices: DT to Ruth Wynn Owen ?May 1942 CL 560

196 thinking darkly about those who could afford to go to restaurants: DT to VW 28 August 1941 CL 555

197 'Hell of a fine man': Larkin to J.B. Sutton 20 November 1941 (Larkin Letters). For another description, see Hindsights by John Heath-Stubbs, one of the contributors to Eight Oxford Poets. Larkin was to change his attitude after the war.

a party in Christ Church: see Hamburger A Mug's Game

accompanied by his undergraduate friend John Mortimer: see Mortimer Clinging to the Wreckage p 81 ff

198 Dinner with Maclean: Fitzgibbon With Love

'Dylan looked only a little embarrassed': interview with author November 2002; see also Mackworth The Ends of the World

199 As she explained to her sister Brigit: Caitlin p. 91

a recce for a film in Scotland: This was possibly Children's Story, a Strand production for Films of Scotland which appeared in January 1943, or part of an ongoing project to portray different regions in Strand's 'Pattern of Britain' series of films.

200 as he had told another Scots poet Hamish Henderson: see That Dolphin

Torn, That Gong-Tormented Face Dylan in Bloomsbury by Hamish Henderson Cencrastus no. 47 spring 1994

Dylan encouraged Graham to pursue his ambition: W.S. Graham to William Montgomerie 5 July 1942

Even Hugh MacDiarmid: see Hugh MacDiarmid to Valda Grieve 7 July 1942 (MacDiarmid New Selected Letters)

201 'the country's the one place': DT to T.W. Earp 30 August 1942 CL 565

Remembering that Dan Jones; Dan had by now been married, fathered two children and divorced.

202 the tallest man in uniform: Watkins Portrait of a Friend

203 'Once on the dancing floor': Sachaverell Sitwell to Edith Sitwell 25 October 1942 quoted Skipwith (ed.) The Sitwells

Dick Wyndham's fun-loving 21 year old daughter Joan: for this story and accompanying quotes, see Wyndham Love is Blue

'an Oscar Wilde with less talent but no homosexuality': quoted Bakewell Fitzrovia

205 rival condottieri: see Davin Closing Times

fascination with hermaphroditism: see Devas Two Flamboyant Fathers

Dylan and Maclaren-Ross: see Willetts Fear and Loathing in Fitzrovia

206 wondered if Dylan was the right person: Dylan Thomas The Filmscripts p 27

207 'the words were written to be spoken & heard': DT to Donald Taylor ?October 1944 CL 587–8

208 'hack work': Elizabeth Fusco CE

CHAPTER 14

209 'horse-faced and Byronic': Stanford Inside the Forties p 133. For Minton and associates also see Spalding John Minton

210 Gerald Kersh recalled: GK to Constantine Fitzgibbon 1 April 1965 courtesy Paul Duncan

According to his brother Philip: Philip Lindsay made several observations on Dylan's life around this time. I am grateful to Helen Cole of the State University Library in Queensland not only for bringing these citations to my attention but also for arranging them to be copied.

'skipping' down Tottenham Court Road: Fusco CE (and for further observations over the next page)

'one Hogarthian night': John Banting unpublished memoir Tate Gallery archive

been to a psychiatric unit: Lindsay Meetings with Poets p 21 see also CL 601–2

211 rubber fetishism: Lindsay Meetings with Poets p 23

She admits she succumbed: Interview Ann Meo September 2002

'robs his £3-in-Post-Office mistresses': John Gawsworth's diary in Verse Notebook VIII 5–18 December 1940, quoted Sinclair War Like a Wasp

212 Theodora Rosling's betrothal: see Fitzgibbon With Love

Vernon Watkins was married: see Watkins Portrait of a Friend

213 the poem Du Nachbar Gott: see Watkins Portrait of a Friend p 119.

214 'shack at the edge of the cliff': DT to OW 28 March 1945 CL 613

Tom Herbert, an ambitious Welsh-speaking vet: I am grateful to Herbert's widow, now Mrs Jacqui Lyne, for the opportunity to examine his interesting papers.

one of two people who taught him all he knew: see Hastings Evelyn Waugh

'Caitlin wasn't exactly polite': AJ to Mary Keene 5 March 1945 courtesy Alice Kadel

216 'seminal in the evolution': Ackerman (ed.) The Filmscripts p 230

a film life of Charles Dickens: see Fitzgibbon With Love p 166

'Only once did I catch Dylan reading a good book': quoted Lindsay Meetings with Poets p 23

Barnes was unimpressed: Barnes to AT Davies 6 January 1945 BBC Written Archives

217 captions to another Bill Brandt photo-essay: printed in Ackerman Dylan Thomas Companion

'Fitzroy Street could be paved with tits': Banting Memoir Tate Gallery Archive

219 'very dignified, articulate, and charming': AJ to Mary Keene nd Alice Kadel

'Dylan has a split personality': AJ to Mary Keene 5 March (1945) Alice Kadel

'Dylan is an extraordinarily abnormal person': Mary Keene to Henry Yorke nd Sebastian Yorke

Dylan's 'class consciousness': Augustus John to Mary Keene 5 March (1945) Alice Kadel

'I'm delighted that Thomas' cloven hoof': Henry Yorke to Mary Keene 26 February 1945 Sebastian Yorke

the Commercial pub: Now The Seahorse, the former Commercial was earlier known as the Sailors Home Arms, leaving some enthusiasts to suggest that this was the model for the Sailors Arms in Under Milk Wood.

220 an affair with Dylan: Vera Killick never really denied this, telling her family shortly before her death that she retained one great secret. But if she did have an affair with Dylan, it is more likely to have been in Swansea or in London before her marriage.

'as if one were visited by the Gestapo': Mary Keene to Henry Yorke nd Alice Kadel

221 'I'm sorry Dylan was no good': Henry Yorke to Mary Keene 24 June 1945 Sebastian Yorke

'The ordinary moments of walking up village streets': DT to VW 26 February 1945 CL 607/8

'frightened as though I had used the Sten gun myself.' DT to VW 28 March 1945 CL 610

'awfully ill': DT to VW 28 March 1945 CL 610

chipping away ... like an old carpenter: see Watkins Portrait of a Friend p 120

'Less passes Uncle Head's blue-haired pencil': DT to VW 19 April 1945 CL 615

222 a modern existentialist perspective; see Maud Where have the old words got me? p 261

'Crowds queued for hours': Ziegler London at War p. 309

'a little Nagasaki': DT to OW 5 December 1945 CL 639

223 'My dear my dear my dear Caitlin': DT to CT 24 June 1945 CL 619

224 'filmscripts on Rehabilitation': DT to OW 28 March 1945 CL 612

a row with Taylor: See DT to Donald Taylor 8 February 1945 CL 601/2

the eccentricities of rural Wales: DT to OW 30 July 1945 CL 621/2

the Orwellian Ministry of Information: see DT to OW 28 March 1945 CL 613

225 'It is an *essential* part of the feeling': DT to A.J. Hoppé 18 September 1945 CL 633

'for evenings and tears': DT to David Tennant 28 August 1945 CL 629

'joyful': DT to Edith Sitwell 31 March 1946 CL 652

the epitome of the modern Welsh poem in English: see Davies A Reference Companion pp 196–204 ff.

'as if they were packets of cocaine': quoted Fitzgibbon Dylan Thomas p 279

signposted the contents of the book: cf Kipling's Actions and Reactions, Debits and Credits, and Limits and Renewals

226 'because that it all I ever write about': Watkins Portrait of a Friend p 88

CHAPTER 15

227 'a sort of middle-class Lady Ottoline Morrell': Sisman AJP Taylor

'Anybody will do': interview with Lady Spender 27 February 2002. This trip to Oxford may have been the occasion when the Thomases were invited to lunch with the historian A.L. Rowse, who, unable to entertain at All Souls, took them to the Mitre hotel. Caitlin antagonised the sensitive Rowse from the start by announcing as soon as she and her husband arrived, 'We will have white wine'. Rowse felt this was not correct form at a time of austerity. The story is mentioned in A Man of Contradictions, Richard Ollard's biography of A.L. Rowse, though there is no other reference to it.

four days in St Stephens Hospital, London: For hospital stay, see also CL 650

228 renditions of three poems: Dylan claimed he was not allowed to read from Hardy. For description, see Louis Macneice in Ingot December 1954

According to Edith Sitwell: see ES letters to David Horner 18 May and 28? May 1946 and to Denys Kilham Roberts 22 May 1946. Sitwell Selected Letters (Virago)

229 'There is a tremendous risk': Memo 21 November 1945 BBC Written Archives

'a most sensitive and succesful piece of radio': Laurence Gilliam to DT 18 July 1946 BBC Written Archives

230 A Nest of Singing Birds: Picture Post 10 August 1946

'feet apart and head thrown back': quoted Carpenter The Envy of the World p 40

'a trifle too explosive': Arlott Basingstoke Boy p 116

'became almost Superman': quoted Tedlock (ed.) Dylan Thomas The Legend and the Poet pp 41–45

Ruthven Todd lived down the hill at Tilty Mill: see Todd archive National Library of Scotland.

'caused havoc': Spalding John Minton

proved excellent nannies: see Fraser The Chameleon Poet p 299

231 For a short while they were tenants: For details see her autobiography A Goldfish Bowl p 153 ff – though the chronology is difficult to follow.

a statutory 'alcoholically-polite' pass: Lutyens A Goldfish Bowl

an enthusiastic review of Deaths and Entrances: Our Times April 1946

'I'm sorry to smell so awful, Edith': story by Wynford Vaughan Thomas noted Maud (ed.) Dylan Thomas – The Broadcasts p 103

232 One of his drinking partners: interview John Veale December 2002

dinner at Magdalen's High Table: see Taylor A Personal History p 185

She took him to literary societies: Martin Starkie, an undergraduate at the time, recalls Dylan and Margaret Taylor attending a meeting of the university Poetry Society which he ran. Afterwards she was annoyed because Starkie had not ordered a taxi for herself and Dylan. Personal communication June 2003

233 a gathering for Lord David Cecil and Hugh Trevor-Roper: Lord Dacre AJP Taylor and me Sunday Telegraph 16 Sept 1990, quoted Sisman, AJP Taylor

'I disliked Dylan Thomas intensely': Taylor A Personal History p 130

a small diary: this is at the Harry Ransom Center at Austin

234 'We ate ourselves daft': DT to VW 26 August 1946 CL 670

235 'in this tremendous quietness': DT to Donald Taylor 26 August 1946 CL 671

Dylan promised not to enter discussions: DT to JL 1 November 1946 Houghton

'a delightful fellow': Conrad Aiken to Malcom Cowley 27 May 1946 Aiken Selected Letters

236 'yours without any condition': DT to JL 24 November 1946 CL 677

'aghast': ES to John Lehmann 11 December 1946 Sitwell Selected Letters Lehmann and Parker (eds.)

some unwritten stories, which he listed: see list at HRC

'He took his radio acting very seriously': MacNeice Ingot December 1954 pp 28–30

237 Michael Redgrave had expressed an interest: Dylan had indeed met Redgrave. The literary agent Peter Janson-Smith recalls being introduced to him and Dylan at the Café Royal, when down to London from Oxford during the war. As for the script, Dylan later changed the name the anatomist's name to Dr Thomas Rock which he felt was more in keeping with a distinguished scientist. See DT to E.F. Bozman 29 December 1952 CL 957

Dylan became excited: see DT to Graham Greene 11 January 1947 CL 683

'It was all Christmases and birthdays': DT to Osbert Sitwell 23 November 1946 Renishaw Papers 532/6 courtesy Sir Rereseby Sitwell

Dylan was worried about Llewelyn: DT to D.J. and Florence Thomas 12 January 1947 CL 685

238 Ayrton had a flat: see Hopkins, Michael Ayrton

He looked forward to taking off six months: DT to D.J. and Florence Thomas 12 January 1947 CL 686

They took a boat as far as Gravesend: interview Joseph Rykwert, friend of Ayrton December 2002. One version has John Arlott on this trip. This would make sense. He worked with Ayrton on the ENSA Brains Trust. When he first worked full-time job at the BBC after the war, he stayed at Ayrton's flat. Maud's The Broadcasts (p 292) says they went to Gravesend to research a script on Hogarth for the General Overseas Service. When Dylan was recuperating after his immersion in the river, Ayrton took the opportunity to make some well-known sketches of his friend. Colin Edwards had a story that Dylan was arrested for being drunk and disorderly (see his papers in the NLW).

239 'warm-hearted and dull': DT to T.W. Earp 1 March 1947 CL 691

An uncollected poem: the manuscript is in the HRC

240 he collected anecdotes: see notebook in HRC

background research for another talk: possibly, some notes for Dylan's radio talk 'Oxford-Princeton' recorded on 29 December 1946 in an exchange with the New York station WOR.

he might have enjoyed being an undergraduate: Martin Starkie, President of the Oxford University Poetry Club once asked Dylan if he regretted not having been at university. Dylan answered enigmatically, 'If some ways yes, but in most ways no.' Interview June 2003

241 'a clean pink ship in the sea': DT to Edith Sitwell 11 April 1947 CL 696

242 'like a fiend, a good fiend': DT to Edith Sitwell ibid.

When Montale arrived to collect the Spenders: interview Lady Spender March 2002

243 he hoped to finish a radio play DT to DH 24 May 1947 CL 705

possibly Under Milk Wood: Curiously UMW had an Italian antecedent in Fontanamara, Ignazio Silone's 1934 novel about the ravages of fascism on an Italian village, which Dylan had once recommended to Bert Trick.

'I have to stand on my head': DT to John Davenport 29 May 1947 CL 706

'rarefied and damp': DT to Margaret Taylor 20 May 1947 CL 703

244 a rambling, maudlin letter from the Giubbe Rossa: DT to CT May, June or July 1947 CL 707

Dylan pronounced it 'very good': DT to D.J. and Florence Thomas 5 June 1947 CL 713

but not as good as Patrick Hamilton: DT to Donald Taylor 7 June 1947 CL 714

'I am domestic as a slipper': DT to MT 12 April 1947 CL 697

a way of getting Dylan off his back: see Taylor A Personal History

245 'like a live animal': DT to DJ and Florence Thomas 30 June 1947 CL 721

still politely seeking repayment: see Jacopo Treves to DT 10 March 1950 Indiana. DT had been contacted by Arnold A. Bianchi, a friend of Treves in London, in February 1950 NLW. Italian sources also say Dylan was lent 46,000 lire by painter Ottone Rosai.

'Communism in Italy is natural': DT to Bill and Helen McAlpine 1 August 1947

246 a late interview: with Mary Ellin Barrett The Reporter

This last image, implying man's baleful harnessing of the sun's energies: The general tenor of this argument comes from John Goodby's essay The Later Poems and Under Milk Wood from Dylan Thomas in the New Casebooks series edited by him and Chris Wigginton.

CHAPTER 16

248 an unpublished memoir: Cordelia Sewell unpublished ms HRC. I draw on this, with the permission of her daughter Nicola Schaefer, whose own recollections were very helpful

249 Starkie, a Rimbaud expert: see Enid Starkie CE

Early in their friendship: see Davin Closing Times (and for subsequent references to Davin)

250 Dylan's total tax liability: DH to DT 13 May 1948 HRC. For this and other monetary comparisons I have relied on the excellent Economic History Resources site: //www.eh.net/hmit/ppowerbp/

'She's desperate for me': King Yesterday Came Suddenly

'maudlin Magdalen Maggie': DT to CT 2 December 1946 CL 678

251 Brenan had last met Caitlin in Churriana: see Gathorne-Hardy The Interior Castle. Frances Partridge received a version of the dustbin story which ended with Dylan exclaiming 'Forty Thieves!' She heard from Brenan that Dylan – perennially drunk with 'his large baby's head wobbling on its stalk', but 'brilliant, amusing, imaginative and poetical' was threatening to move to Aldbourne. See Partridge Diaries 11 March 1948

252 arranged to meet Bob Pocock: see Bob Pocock to Dan and Irene Jones 5 May 1948 private collection

The McAlpines turned up: Bob Pocock to Dan and Irene Jones n.d summer 1948 private collection

253 the singer Lena Horne: se Buckley The Hornes An American Family

Helen singing Irish ballads to a group of West Indians: DT to John Davenport 12 April 1951 CL 884

'to cook and char': DT to Hermann Peschmann 23 June 1948 CL 753

254 'SHE will go then': DT to CT ?July 1948 CL 756

the Poetry Society in Richmond: description in Stanford Inside the 'Forties p 135

'swamped Milton': The Listener 30 October 1947

256 A Nightingale is Singing: Richard Hughes subsequently worked on the script of A Run for Your Money with Leslie Norman and Charles Frend, the director. The

film, which starred Alec Guinness, High Griffith and Joyce Grenfell, was released in November 1949. See Graves Richard Hughes p 328 ff

'Sydney's carte blanche': DT to Ralph Keene 27 July 1948 CL 758

257 Dylan's day out with MacNeice: see MacNeice's account in Ingot December 1954. Also the letter from MacNeice to his wife 21 July 1948 quoted Stallworthy Louis MacNeice p 369

258 the National Liberal (Club): Dylan was elected to the National Liberal Club in January 1947 and resigned in February 1949. On 10 March 1949 he joined the Savage Club, where his proposer was John Davenport, seconded by Norman Cameron and Parry Jones, principal tenor at Covent Garden. See details at HRC

he bumped into Kenneth Tynan: see Tynan The Life of Kenneth Tynan p 76

'staggering along loaded down with string bags': Alan Brien Sunday Times 25 March 1973

259 Dylan and the Misletoe Bough: story recalled in Paul Redgrave's unpublished ms Bicycle Ride. This encounter took place in late March or early April 1948

260 recalled seeing Dylan with Margaret Taylor: Hamburger A Mug's Game

'Our taste ran to austerity': Brien Sunday Times ibid.

'that crazy Welch fellow Thomas' Kingsley Amis to Philip Larkin 24 March 1947 Amis Letters

'I think a man ought to use good words': Philip Larkin to Kingsley Amis 11 January 1947 Larkin Selected Letters

'Get me some more bloody crème de menthe': letter from Tynan to his old school friend Julian Holland c. Michaelmas 1947 quoted Tynan The Life of Kenneth Tynan

261 Rio Marina reminded him of Wales: see Under Milk Wood's birth-in-exile by David N Thomas New Welsh Review Spring 2001

'A radio play I am writing has Laugharne': DT to John Ormond 6 March 1948 CL 744

'tired of living among strangers': Living in Wales for BBC Scotland recorded 16 June 1949

'I am a Welshman': talk at Scottish PEN Centre at Scotia Hotel, Edinburgh, 4 September 1948

262 'Here I am too near London': DT to Frances Hughes 10 October 1948 CL 766

Dylan replied he would love nothing better: DT to John Banting 17 November 1948 Tate Gallery Archives

263 'Nothing happens to me': DT to VW 23 November 1948 CL 772

Dylan, the supposed film mogul: see DT to John Davenport 17 November 1948 CL 771

264 'In the Spring, we go to Wales': DT to Hector MacIver 17 February 1949 CL 780

'I wake up in the night': see Mosley (ed.) The Letters of Nancy Mitford and Evelyn Waugh

265 'If all the party members were like you': Lindsay Meetings with Poets p 29

which had first published Dylan's poem Ceremony After a Fire-Raid: in an issue dedicated to Lorca, put together by Paul Potts. Dylan was not sure, however, what he felt about lines from Lorca being printed above his poem.

a small private party to meet Holan: for this and other detail, see interviews with Viola Zinkova, Dr Josef Nezvadba and Aloys Skoumal CE; see also Lindsay Meetings with Poets

CHAPTER 17

268 'Now, don't think I'm interfering, dear': quoted DT to Bill & Helen McAlpine 12 November 1949 CL 809

'water and tree room on the cliff': DT to MT 11 May 1949 CL 789

269 'Here I am happy and writing': ibid.

starting a notebook for him: this is in the HRC

a remarkably clear-headed and business-like response: DT to JMB 28 May 1949 CL 790–1

270 'We escaped London and ran smack': Bill & Helen McAlpine to George Reavey end of May 1949 HRC

'about to be X-rayed': DT to Wilfred Grantham 15 July 1949 CL 796

'He looked pretty lively': BBC Written Archives

a former army friend, Desmond Morris: Morris was amazed at his facility with words. see Morris Animal Days p 26–29 interview Desmond Morris July 2002.

271 a talk on Edward Thomas: Dylan included Thomas's poem The Child on the Cliffs, which may refer to Laugharne, in his talk, but he did not mention that Edward Thomas had spent a few weeks there in 1911, portraying it as Abercorran in his novel, The Happy-Go-Lucky Morgans.

Pocock sent an ambiguous note: Bob Pocock to Dan & Irene Jones 12 August 1949 private collection

a minor breakdown: DT to John Davenport 30 July 1949 CL 797

273 'Dylan is very emotional': quoted in Davin Closing Times p 136

274 the I-n-s-u-l-t-s column of Strand magazine: Strand March 1947

living in a slave state: DT to John Davenport December? 1949 CL 821

'I got caught up with rewording': DT to John Davenport December? 1949 CL 821

When Julius and Ethel Rozenberg were executed: DT to OW 22 June 1953 CL 1005

she had seen advertisements for Dylan's forthcoming visit: Elizabeth Bishop to JMB 14 October 1949 Delaware

'If Auden dominated the recent past': Rexroth (ed.) The New British Poets

'because I have gotten the impression' JL to DT 6 December 1949 Houghton

'Have you heard': DT to JL 13 October 1949 CL 803

a New York apartment: belonging to his friend Jean Lawson

276 'I don't want to turn your American visit': JMB to DT 28 November 1949 Delaware; also 22 October 1949

he found Caitlin by turns indifferent: see account in Glyn Jones Notes on Anglo-Welsh Writers NLW

'a kind of colloquial Lycidas': DT to John Davenport December 1949 CL 822

Curnow's meetings with Dylan: see About Dylan Thomas in Curnow Look Back Harder pp 319–325

277 'It would be difficult': DT to MT 28 November 1949 CL 818

'For he hasn't a first class brain': Dan Davin to his wife New Year of 1950 quoted Ovenden A Fighting Withdrawal

'She tended, when in the pub': Davin Closing Times p 139

'it is only frightening when I am whirlingly perplexed': DT to Marguerite Caetani 12 January 1950 CL 826

278 'Thomas's silence is a worry': JMB to Bill Read 30 January 1950 Delaware

How to be a Poet: With illustrations by Ronald Searle, this was published in Circus in two parts in April and May 1950, while Dylan was in America.

279 'I won't have you tied up': quoted Gill Peggy Guggenheim

CHAPTER 18

In writing about Dylan's visits to America, I acknowledge my debt to the work of John Malcolm Brinnin – particularly his book Dylan Thomas in America and his unpublished memoir, letters and invaluable diary which are in the Special Collections department of the Library of the University of Delaware.

282 'it is all an enormous façade': DT to DJ and Florence Thomas 26 February 1950 CL 835

enjoyed American food: DT to DJ and FT ibid

283 Breit's interview: see Breit The Writer Observed

285 'He was most objectionable': see Porter's interview in (Baltimore) Sun Magazine 26 October 1969. Another literary take on the event was Karl Shapiro's poem 'Emily Dickinson and Katherine Anne Porter'

286 'second-rate Charles Laughton': see Breit op cit

'this weekend must be given over to Dylan': JMB to Bill Read Monday (1950) Delaware

287 his novel, Reuben Reuben: In this respect DeVries anticipated not only Kingsley Amis, who satirised Dylan as Gareth Probert in his book That Uncertain Feeling (1955), but also Amis's son Martin who famously suffered McGland's 'agonies of hell' over his bad teeth – though Amis fils did not commit suicide when he had to have them all out

'You'll be able to recognise him easily': JMB to Bill Read Monday (1950) Delaware

'for his own endurance': F.O. Mathiessen to JMB 5 March 1950 Delaware

'a very sick man: Reuben A Brown to JMB 17 March 1950 Delaware

'in a heavy hung-overish desuetude': JMB to Bill Read Monday (1950) Delaware

dinner with Morgan: interview with Frederick Morgan May 2003

289 Elizabeth Bishop and Dylan: see Elizabeth Bishop to Robert Lowell One Art p 202, also Bishop to Pearl Kazin 16 November 1953? One Art p 276

'this vast, mad horror': DT to CT c 11 March 1950 CL 836

'all snivelling and grovelling': Philip Larkin to Kingsley Amis 21 November 1985 Selected Letters

a fleeting visit to Cornell: see David Daiches in Tedlock (ed.) Dylan Thomas The Legend and the Poet

291 'I'm hardly living': DT to CT 15 March 1950 CL 839

'bad actors out of an American co-ed film': DT to CT ibid.

Earlier, at Mount Holyoke: quoted About Dylan Thomas in Curnow Look Back Harder

Dylan in Iowa: see West San Francisco Fault October 1972

292 the only English poet she knew: Another candidate was Professor Brewster Ghiselin, of the University of Utah, a friend of both Brinnin and Ray J. West Jr., who met Dylan briefly when his plane touched down in Salt Lake City. Dylan repaid his courtesy by reading at the University of Utah on his second United States trip 18 April 1952

found it was a boy in drag: Isherwood Diaries 8 December 1953 p 460

293 'Dylan Thomas is here': Kenneth Rexroth to JL 29 March 1950 Selected Letters 137–8; see also California Living Magazine 25 November 1979

Witt-Diamant had a lunch appointment: for a description of this trip, see Witt-Diamant CE

Gavin Arthur: Back in 1928 Arthur had acted in Borderline, an avant-garde film made by Kenneth MacPherson, husband of Winifred Ellerman, known as 'Bryher', the rich patron of literature who had financed the magazine Life and Letters (whose editor Robert Herring was in the cast), as well as the scholarship which sent Dylan to Italy. The star of the film, which explored attitudes to race and colour, was Paul Robeson, in one of his most challenging but little-known roles. Bryher appeared in it, along with her companion the Imagist poet Hilda Doolittle (h.d.)

295 'a quite handsome hellhole': DT to CT 7 April 1950 CL 842–3

another old literary friend, John Berryman: the meeting was recalled by Berryman in 1958, see Mariani Dream Song

'They had conjured up this dangerous little creature': Isherwood Diaries 8 December 1953. Isherwood also recorded some of the additional detail about Dylan's stay in Los Angeles

296 She gave a more decorous version of the story: Winters Best of Times, Worst of Times

297 'My God what a swathe': Ruth Witt Diamant to DT Sunday night probably 23 April 1950 Lilly Library

Dylan at the University of Indiana in Bloomington: I am grateful for David Wagoner's account

298 'wheelbarrowed on to the Queen Elizabeth'. DT to John F Nims and Mrs Nims 17 July 1950 CL 854

party at the Williamses: see acount in Gruen The Party's Over Now pp 29–30

299 Theodore Roethke came: see Roethke Memories and Appreciations Encounter January 1954

Stanley Moss: for his recollections, I am grateful for conversations in April 2003 and at other times

Eugene Walter: see his description in programme accompanying a special presentation of Under Milk Wood by the Joe Jefferson Players' Readers' Theater Mobile Alabama 27 May 1989

300 a piece of information formally: Mike Watkins to David Higham 24 May 1950 HRC The piece for which Harpers Bazaar paid $300 was almost certainly A Child's Memories of Christmas in Wales, an amalgamation of two earlier pieces, usually known as A Child's Christmas in Wales. The magazine printed this in December 1950. Ann Watkins did not take commission. This was not the only personal deal Dylan made, albeit unwittingly, during his trip. Part of Watkins's 24 May letter to Higham – the record of his single meeting with Dylan, starting 'Caught at last!' – told how the poet had got himself into 'some sort of a scrape' by recording, through the auspices of Oscar Williams, seven poems for the Esoteric Record Company. There were legal problems and Watkins intended to keep out. The letter also noted how Dylan's work for Pleasure Dome, the record which accompanied Lloyd Frankenberg's book, had gone without payment. The agency had copies of the discs and were chasing the matter up with the manufactuer, Columbia Records. As well as making personal deals with Kazin, Dylan had sold Over Sir John's Hill – originally in Botteghe Oscure – for cash to Frederick Morgan at Hudson Review. He had taken $50 out of a net sum of $750.87, which was owing to him as royalties from New Directions

a farewell party for Dylan: Dawn Powell to Edmund Wilson 5 June 1950 Powell Selected Letters

'He cranks up that big voice': JL to Kenneth Rexroth 28 April 1950 Selected Letters

CHAPTER 19

302 'kind Friends who helped (Dylan) pack': Conrad Aiken to Edward Burra 29 August 1950 Aiken Selected Letters

'As an author who almost never writes': JL to DT 14 June 1950 Houghton

305 'my reactionary red-nosed club': DT to Pearl Kazin 22 June 1950 owned by Jeff Towns

'If the dark leagues say No': DT to Pearl Kazin 7 August 1950 owned by Jeff Towns. It would appear that this letter was written from Laugharne, using the Savage Club address. He then wrote to Pearl again on 13 August – this time a much lengthier five page letter on headed Savage Club notepaper – written, presumably when he was down in London avoiding Maggs Taylor and seeing Grisewood at the BBC.

307 In a letter to Bill Read: JMB to Bill Read 5 September 1950 Delaware

'arty in clothes and manner' Heppenstall Four Absentees p 180

The wise old bird Wyn Henderson: Henderson to Bill Read 28 February 1964 HRC

308 'All was LIES': DT to Helen McAlpine 14 September 1950 CL 856/7

'I'm in darkness': DT to CT early January 1951 CL 872

This latter project: In his book The Growth of Milk Wood, Cleverdon refers to it as The Village of the Mad. Dylan apparently called it Madtown.

310 'I suppose you've come to throw us out': interview Alice Kadel March 2002

'cheerful animal noise': The Listener 21 December 1950

312 Dylan spent his first few days in Tehran: I am grateful for the use of Bunny Keene's diaries, which were lent to me by his son Richard Brooks-Keene

'depressing and half-made': DT to CT early January 1951 CL 872

'running down the Persian wops': DT to CT January 1951 CL 873

he visited a hospital: DT to CT 16 January 1951 CL 875

'any dusty sunfried place': DT to CT 16 Janaury 1950 CL 876

'Your letter ... made me want to die': DT to CT January/February? 1951 CL 877–8

313 a rather more jaundiced impression: DT to PK January 1951 CL 876/7

'shivering with delight': Mrs Suratgar CE

She admitted a romantic fling: see Ferris Caitlin p 117–8

'Dylan is here': Bill & Helen McAlpine to Mr and Mrs George Reavey 17 March (1951) HRC

314 reluctant to let him start: Douglas Cleverdon to Maurice Brown 13 February 1951 BBC Written Archives

Betjeman did his best: John Betjeman to George Barnes 11 May 1951 Betjeman Letters Vol 1 p 533

prevailed on an Oxford friend, Mary Ellidge: I am grateful to Mary Ellidge's daughter, Julia Davies, for letting me read her mother's unpublished memoir, which includes an account of this visit to the Festival of Britain

315 'conversation consisted of one or two written-out solos': Kingsley Amis to Philip Larkin 29 April 1951 Amis Letters

Amis expanded on: Spectator 29 November 1957

'my horribly cosy little nest': DT to John Davenport autumn 1950 CL 859

In this pretty as a stricture town: DT to Lloyd Frankenberg and Loren McIver 1950–51? CL 909–913

'I'm sick of Laugharne': DT to JMB 12 April 1951 CL 888

'The only person I can't show the enclosed poem': DT to Marguerite Caetani 28 May 1951 CL 891/2

In a talk a couple of years later: this was at the University of Utah in April 1952, and was written up in an account by Marjorie Adix, Tedlock, p 66. See also Maud Where Have the Old Words Got Me? pp 76–80 'which does not say a great deal': DT to Marguerite Caetani 18 July 1951 CL 893

317 Dylan proposed translating: Wall Headlong into Change p 182; further information from interview with Barbara Wall September 2002

'I hope you will beat him sternly': JL to JB 21 August 1951 Delaware

321 'I hate to leave this sea': DT to Ruth Witt-Diamant 10 October 1951 CL 903

if Dylan had a 'London dump': Margaret Taylor to Stuart Thomas 1 December 1953 Thomas Trustees

the corpse had an enormous erection: see Arlott John Arlott

'You are too good': OW to Edward Weeks 25 June 1951 Indiana

'a beauty': OW to Edward Weeks 29 October 1951 Indiana

'I have never had much success': OW to Miss Phoebe Lou Adams 7 November 1951 Indiana

322 sold a story, The Jester, to Botteghe Oscure: it appeared in the April 1952 issue of the magazine – the same one as Dylan's Llareggub

CHAPTER 20

325 he might make a film with Len Lye: See Horrocks Len Lye p 249

326 discussed such an idea with the film director Michael Powell: See Powell Million-Dollar Movie p. 162 Dylan met Powell at the York Minster pub in London on 2 January 1952

Stravinsky: see Stravinsky and Craft Conversations with Igor Stravinsky

Time did not run it: Barrett wrote her own account of the meeting for The Reporter 27 April 1954. Time included some material in a review of Dylan's Collected Poems on 6 April 1953.

Caedmon: I am grateful for conversations with Barbara Holdridge (née Cohen)

327 according to her friend Rose Slivka: in conversation with author April 2003

328 Edith Sitwell told a friend: Edith Sitwell to Jack Lindsay ?March 1952 Selected Letters (Virago) p 345

actress Judith Malina observed Dylan: Malina Diaries

329 According to Wagoner: Personal communication from David Wagoner

330 Dylan sent a postcard to Ebie Williams: DT to Ebie Williams 28 March 1952 noted CE

Tanning attributed this behaviour: see Tanning Between Lives

Ernst inscribed his book, Misfortunes of the Immortals: in the possession of Jeff Towns. The book was written by Ernst with Paul Eluard

331 Over the Easter weekend: Witt-Diamant CE

according to Patchen's wife, Miriam: Smith Kenneth Patchen. Thanks to Jonathan Clark

Algren claimed to be 'neither poet nor lush enough': Nelson Algren to Ellen Borden Stevenson 3 May 1952 HRC

333 Ginsberg left an unappealing picture: Ginsberg Journals. I am, I admit, making

an assumption that Dylan's meeting with Ginsberg happened the same night as the visit to the Lesbian bar. However it is difficult to work out how it could have occurred at any other time. Ginsberg simply dates it 'late April 1952'

a dramatic telegram from Caitlin's mother: Yvonne MacNamara to CT Telegram ?April 1952 Delaware

334 could sense something was wrong: Journal of Modern Literature Special Gotham Book Mart Issue vol 4 no 4 April 1975 p 866

336 Caitlin was dressed to impress: see account Helen McAlpine to George Reavey and wife 17 June 1952 HRC

337 'My dear Marged, You told me, once, upon a time': DT to Marged Howard Stepney ?1952 draft CL 932–3

an appeasing letter: see DT to CT ?1952 CL 933–4

'I began to feel nervous': DT to Charles Fry 16 February 1953 CL 969–70

338 a repeat interview: NYT 17 February 1952

'If only we can get Llareggub on the air': Douglas Cleverdon to DT 26 August 1952 BBC Written Archives

339 why he had 'acrosticked' himself: DT to E.F. Bozman 10 September 1952 CL 935

340 'for a whole year I have been able to write nothing': DT to Charles Fry 16 February 1953 CL 969

his 'distastrously limited subject matter': Mandrake Summer-Autumn 1953

'Do really think most vital': telegram DT to E.F. Bozman 7 October 1952 CL 937

On his return to Laugharne: see Quadrille with Raven chapter 11 by Humphrey Searle, published on the Internet

generous review: Spender called Dylan 'a romantic revolting against a thin contemporary classical tendency......In (his) poetry the reader feels very close to what Keats yearned for – a 'life of sensations' without opinions and thoughts.' Spectator 5 December 1952

342 Dylan's visit to Dan and Irene Jones: information on this and later visits from Dan Jones's diary

343 the peace of the town was disturbed: There is interesting material on this in Thomas Dylan Thomas: A Farm, Two Mansions and a Bungalow

344 his 'best friend in the world: DT to Charles Fry 16 February 1953 CL 969

345 Foyles Poetry Prize for 1953: The recipient the previous year had been Roy Campbell, who had been startled to receive his award from his old sparring partner turned cultural ally Stephen Spender.

quarrelled 'bitter(ly)': Dan Jones diary 5 February 1953

'feeling more crooked than ever'; DT to DH 6 February 1953 CL 963

old school friend Guido Heller: CE

346 'Prologue': it was published in the Atlantic in January 1953

'appreciation, dramatic work, and friends': DT to JMB 18 March 1953 CL 979

347 an Observer review: Observer 6 July 1952

Having declared his interest: See Beyond National Literature? Dylan Thomas and Amos Tutuola in 'Igbo masquerade' New Welsh Review No 60 summer 2003

When the piece was published: Arlott John Arlott Andre Deutsch 1994. The actual words in the review in Time Atlantic 6 April 1953 were 'Dylan Marlais Thomas, 38, is a chubby, bulb-nosed Welshman with green eyes, a generally untidy air, and the finest lyrical talent of any poet under 40.'

an indulgent programme of Dan Jones's devising: Barbarous Hexameters Recorded 13 April 1953

CHAPTER 21

350 extracts from Dylan's pre-war 'novel': these appeared in Weybright's offprint New World Writing in November 1952 and May 1953

353 'I've finished that infernally eternally unfinished "play"': DT to CT c. 23 May 1953 CL 993

Dylan told Caitlin about his meeting in Boston: ibid.

354 Professing his 'eternal untouched love': ibid.

355 'I miss you terribly much': DT to Liz Reitell 16 June 1953 CL 994

Fry offered £1000 for the manuscript: see Gibbs In My Time

356 'That 'play' of Dylan's': memo n.d. New Directions archives Houghton

'a bit broad in places': Martin Dent to E.F. Bozman 10 July 1953 quoted note to CL 1007

Witt-Diamant remembered the new Queen: CE

Learning that Roethke and his new wife, Beatrice: see Seager The Glass House

357 the 'literary' or the 'history': OW to DT 31 July 1953 Thomas Trustees

'Carissima Signora Caterina': Giovanni Chiesa to CT 27 July 1953 Thomas Trustees

361 Locke's last sight: CE

CHAPTER 22

In writing about Dylan's final trip to America, I acknowledge my use of Liz Reitell's diary and other papers which were kindly given to me by her cousin Lois Gridley

366 A sceptical observer of this convivial scene: George Reavey to Helen and Bill McAlpine 21 November 1953 HRC

367 Reavey saw him at the White Horse: ibid.

368 'really looking sick': ibid

a version of this story: Edith Sitwell to Jane Clark 17 November 1953 Berg

perhaps, he knew intuitively: Caitlin had sent Higham unpaid bills amounting to £131.12s 2½d, mentioned additional sums of £46.10, and referred to further unspecified debts. DH internal memo

'Dylan wanted to visit the men-only bar': Todd memoir

372 'We must hurry out a book of his papers': Ruthven Todd to Louis MacNeice 23 November 1953 Thomas Trustees

'to be the official sympathiser': Bob McGregor to DH 12 November 1953 Houghton

373 So she prayed: Emily Holmes Coleman diary 8 November 1953 Delaware

'What of Pearl?': Helen McApline to George Reavey 14 December 1953 HRC

a literary conference at Bard College: see Mariani Dream Song

her later observation: Plimpton Truman Capote p 404

374 'chronic alcoholic poisoning': see Dr William de Gutierrez-Mahoney to Dan Jones 10 January 1954 Rob and Cathy Roberts

Pearl Kazin's brother Alfred spoke for all: Alfred Kazin journal 10 November 1953 Berg

Philip Larkin managed to extricate himself: Larkin to Patsy Strang 11 November 1953 Larkin Letters

375 one ghastly mess: JL to Thomas Merton

376 'I know I must not show my grief': Margaret Taylor to Bill and Helen McAlpine HRC

'But he's nice': see My Friend Dylan Thomas

378 'A group of Laugharne men openly share Caitlin': DJ to Stuart Thomas 18 May 1954 HRC

She only vented her feelings: Florrie Thomas to Fred and Mary Janes 7 June 1955 Hilly Janes

379 with a week's abstinence: Miller Timebends

381 'the best part of a quarter of a million pounds': Wynford Vaughan Thomas to CT draft n.d. NLW

BIBLIOGRAPHY

DYLAN THOMAS'S OWN WORKS, WITH DATE OF FIRST PUBLICATION

18 Poems *Sunday Referee* and Parton Bookshop 1934
Twenty-five Poems Dent 1936
The Map of Love Dent 1939
The World I Breathe New Directions Norfolk, Ct 1939
Portrait of the Artist as a Young Dog Dent 1940
New Poems New Directions Norfolk Ct 1943
Deaths and Entrances Dent 1946
Selected Writings New Directions New York 1946
Collected Poems 1934–1952 Dent 1952
In Country Sleep and Other Poems New Directions New York 1952
The Doctor and the Devils Dent 1953
The Collected Poems of Dylan Thomas New Directions New York 1953
Quite Early One Morning Dent 1954
Under Milk Wood Dent 1954
A Prospect of the Sea ed. Daniel Jones Dent 1955
Adventures in the Skin Trade and Other Stories Putnam 1955
Letters to Vernon Watkins Vernon Watkins (ed.) Dent and Faber & Faber 1957
The Beach of Falesá Cape 1964
Twenty Years A-Growing Dent 1964
Rebecca's Daughters Triton 1965
Me and My Bike Triton 1965
Selected Letters Constantine Fitzgibbon (ed.) Dent 1966
The Doctor and the Devils, and Other Scripts New Directions New York 1966
Poet in the Making: The Notebooks of Dylan Thomas Ralph Maud (ed.) Dent 1968
Early Prose Writings Walford Davies (ed.) Dent 1971
The Poems Daniel Jones (ed.) Dent 1971
Selected Poems Walford Davies (ed.) Dent 1974
The Death of the King's Canary (with John Davenport) Penguin 1978
Collected Stories Dent 1983
The Collected Letters Paul Ferris (ed.) Dent 1985 new edition 2000
Collected Poems 1934–1953 Walford Davies and Ralph Maud (eds.) Dent 1988
The Notebook Poems 1930–1934 Ralph Maud (ed.) Dent 1989
The Broadcasts Ralph Maud (ed.) Dent 1991
Letter to Loren Jeff Towns (ed.) Salubrious Press Swansea 1993

The Filmscripts John Ackerman (ed.) Dent 1995
Under Milk Wood Walford Davies and Ralph Maud (eds.) 'The Definitive Edition'
Dent 1995

BOOKS CONSULTED

John Ackerman Welsh Dylan Granada 1980
A Dylan Thomas Companion Macmillan 1991
Peter Ackroyd T.S. Eliot Hamish Hamilton 1984
Conrad Aiken Selected Letters Joseph Killorin (ed.) Yale University Press 1978
Kingsley Amis Letters Zachary Leader (ed.) HarperCollins 2000
Memoirs Hutchinson 1991
Noel Annan Our Age Weidenfeld & Nicolson 1990
John Arlott Basingstoke Boy Collins Willow 1990
Tim Arlott John Arlott Andre Deutsch 1994
Michael Bakewell Fitzrovia: London's Bohemia National Portrait Gallery 1999
John Bayley The Romantic Survival Constable 1957
John Betjeman Letters Volume 1 Candida Lycett Green (ed.) Methuen 1994
Elizabeth Bishop One Art Letters Robert Giroux (ed.) Farrar, Straus and Giroux
1994
Phyllis Bowen The Baker's Daughter Merton Priory Press 1992
Gordon Bowker Pursued by Furies A Life of Malcolm Lowry HarperCollins 1993
Harvey Breit The Writer Observed Alvin Redman 1957
John Malcolm Brinnin Dylan Thomas in America Dent 1956
Anatole Broyard Kafka was the Rage Vintage 1997
Gail Lumet Buckley The Hornes An American Family Alfred Knopf 1986
Norman Cameron Collected Poems and Selected Translations Warren Hope and
Jonathan Barker (eds.) Anvil Press 1990
Humphrey Carpenter The Envy of the World Weidenfeld & Nicolson 1996
Douglas Cleverdon The Growth of Milk Wood Dent 1969
Emily Holmes Coleman The Shutter of Snow Virago 1981
Cyril Connolly Journal and Notebook David Pryce-Jones (ed.) Collins 1983
Tony Conran Frontiers in Anglo-Welsh Poetry UWP 1997
Andy Croft Letter to Randolph Swingler Shoestring Press 1999
Allen Curnow Look Back Harder Auckland University Press 1998
James A Davies A Reference Companion to Dylan Thomas Greenwood Press 1998
Dylan Thomas's Places Christopher Davies Swansea 1987
Dylan Thomas's Swansea, Gower and Laugharne UWP 2000
Rhys Davies Print of a Hare's Foot Heinemann 1969
Walford Davies Dylan Thomas: New Critical Essays Dent 1972
Dylan Thomas Open University Press, Milton Keynes 1986
Dan Davin Closing Times OUP 1975
Sean Day-Lewis C. Day-Lewis: An English Literary Life Weidenfeld 1980
Nicolette Devas Two Flamboyant Fathers Hamish Hamilton 1985
Jane Dunn Antonia White Cape 1998
Aeronwy Thomas Ellis Later than Laugharne Celtion Publications 1976
William Empson Argufying Chatto & Windus 1987

Paul Ferris Caitlin Hutchinson 1993
          Dylan Thomas The Biography Hodder & Stoughton 1977 new edition
          Dent 1999
Constantine Fitzgibbon The Life of Dylan Thomas Dent 1965
Theodora Fitzgibbon With Love Century Hutchinson 1982
Stephen Fothergill The Last Lamplighter London Magazine Editions 2000
Lloyd Frankenberg The Pleasure Dome Houghton Mifflin 1949
G.S. Fraser A Stanger and Afraid Carcanet Press 1983
Robert Fraser The Chameleon Poet A Life of George Barker Jonathan Cape 2001
Jonathan Fryer Dylan The Nine Lives of Dylan Thomas Kyle Cathie 1993
Jean Overton Fuller The Magical World of Victor Neuburg W.H. Allen 1965
David Gascoyne Journal 1936–1937 Enitharmon 1998
          Selected Prose 1934–1996 Enitharmon 1998
Jonathan Gathorne-Hardy The Interior Castle: A Life of Gerald Brenan Sinclair-
          Stevenson 1992
Anthony Gibbs In My Time Peter Davies 1969
Anton Gill Peggy Guggenheim HarpersCollins 2001
Allen Ginsberg Journals Early Fifties, Early Sixties Grove Press 1977
Rob Gittins The Last Days of Dylan Thomas Macdonald 1986
John Goodby and Chris Wigginton Dylan Thomas New Casebooks Palgrave 2001
Mark Goulden Mark my Words W.H. Allen 1978
W.S. Graham The Night Fisherman Selected Letters of W.S. Graham Michael and
          Margaret Snow (eds.) Carcanet 1999
Richard Perceval Graves Richard Hughes Andre Deutsch 1994
Robert Graves The Crowning Privilege Cassell 1955
Geoffrey Grigson Recollections Chatto & Windus The Hogarth Press 1984
          The Private Art A Poetry Notebook Allison & Busby 1982
Miron Grindea (ed.) Dylan Thomas Memorial Number Adam International Review
          1953
John Gruen The Party's Over Now: Reminiscences of the Fifties Viking 1972
John Haffenden The Life of John Berryman Routledge & Kegan Paul 1982
Michael Hamburger A Mug's Game
Pamela Hansford Johnson Important to Me Macmillan 1974
Merion and Susie Harries A Pilgrim Soul Faber 1989
Selina Hastings Evelyn Waugh Sinclair-Stevenson 1995
Desmond Hawkins When I Was Macmillan 1989
Seamus Heaney The Redress of Poetry Faber 1995
John Heath-Stubbs Hindsights Hodder & Stoughton 1993
Rayner Heppenstall Four Absentees Barrie & Rockcliff 1960
Robert Hewison Under Siege: Literary Life in London 1939–1945 Weidenfeld &
          Nicolson 1977
David Higham Literary Gent Jonathan Cape 1978
Paul Hogarth Drawing from Life David & Charles 1997
David Holbrook Llareggub Revisited Bowes & Bowes 1962
Michael Holroyd Augustus John The New Biography Chatto & Windus 1996
Warren Hope Norman Cameron Greenwich Exchange 2001?
Justine Hopkins Michael Ayrton Andre Deutsch 1994
Roger Horrocks Len Lye Auckland University Press 2001

Margherita Howard de Walden Pages from My Life Sidgwick & Jackson 1965

Christopher Isherwood Diaries Vol 1 1939–1960 Katherine Bucknell (ed.) Methuen 1996

Daniel Jones My Friend Dylan Thomas Dent 1977

Evan John Jones and Robert Cochrane The Roebuck in the Thicket Capall Bann 2001

Glyn Jones The Dragon Has Two Tongues Dent 1968 revised edition University of Wales Press 2001

P.J. Kavanagh People and Places A Selection 1975–1987 Carcanet 1988

Mary Keene Mrs Donald Chatto & Windus The Hogarth Press 1983

Francis King Yesterday Came Suddenly Constable 1993

Philip Larkin Selected Letters Anthony Thwaite (ed.) Faber and Faber 1992

Hilary Laurie Dylan Thomas's Wales Weidenfeld & Nicolson 1999

Doris Lessing Walking in the Shade HarperCollins 1997

Mervyn Levy Reflections in a Broken Mirror Patten 1982

Jeremy Lewis Cyril Connolly Jonathan Cape 1997

Jack Lindsay Meetings with Poets Muller 1968

Michael Luke David Tennant and the Gargoyle Years Weidenfeld & Nicolson 1991

Elisabeth Lutyens A Goldfish Bowl Cassell 1972

Hugh MacDiarmid New Selected Letters Duncan Grieve, Owen Dudley Evans and Alan Riach (eds.) Carcanet 2001

Rollie McKenna Portrait of Dylan Dent 1982

Cecily Mackworth The Ends of the World Carcanet 1987

Julian Maclaren-Ross Memories of the Forties Alan Ross 1965

Louis MacNeice Selected Literary Criticism Alan Heuser (ed.) Clarendon Press 1987

Ian MacNiven and Harry Moore (eds.) Literary Lifelines Faber 1981

Judith Malina The Diaries of Judith Malina Grove Press 1984

Paul Mariani Dream Song The Life of John Berryman William Morrow 1990

Arthur Calder Marshall The Magic of my Youth Rupert Hart-Davis 1951

Roland Mathias A Ride through the Wood Poetry Wales 1985

Ralph Maud Dylan Thomas in Print Dent 1970

Where Have All the Old Words Got Me? University of Wales Press 2003

Arthur Miller Timebends Methuen 1987

Kenneth O. Morgan Rebirth of a Nation Clarendon Press 1981

Desmond Morris Animal Days Cape 1979

John Mortimer Clinging to the Wreckage Weidenfeld & Nicolson 1992

Charlotte Mosley (ed.) The Letters of Nancy Mitford and Evelyn Waugh Hodder & Stoughton 1996

James Nashold and George Tremlett The Death of Dylan Thomas Mainstream Edinburgh 1997

Victor F. Neuburg Jr Vickybird A Memoir The Polytechnic of North London 1983

Keith Ovenden A Fighting Withdrawal OUP 1996

Peter Parker (ed.) The Readers Companion to Twentieth Century Writers Fourth Estate 1995

Frances Partridge Diaries 1939–1972 Weidenfeld & Nicolson 2000

Sebastian Peake A Child of Bliss Lennard Publishing 1989
Joseph Pearce Bloomsbury and Beyond HarperCollins 2001
Hesketh Pearson Pearson and Hugh Kingsmill The Blessed Plot Methuen 1942
John Pearson Facades Macmillan 1978
Roland Penrose Scrap Book Thames and Hudson 1986
George Plimpton Truman Capote Doubleday 1998
Anthony Powell Faces in My Time Heinemann 1980
Dawn Powell The Diaries Tim Page (ed.) Steerforth Press 1995
   Selected Letters Tim Page (ed.) Henry Holt 2000
Michael Powell Million-Dollar Movie Heinemann 1992
Bill Read The Days of Dylan Thomas Weidenfeld & Nicolson 1965
Eiluned Rees Carmarthenshire Memoires of the Twentieth Century Carmarthenshire Antiquarian Society 2002
Kenneth Rexroth The New British Poets New Directions 1949
Kenneth Rexroth and James Laughlin Selected Letters (ed. Lee Bartlett) W.W. Norton 1991
John Alexander Rolph Dylan Thomas A Bibliography Dent 1956
Allan Seager The Glass House The Life of Theodore Roethke McGraw-Hill 1968
Andrew Sinclair Dylan Thomas: Poet of his People Michael Joseph 1975
War Like a Wasp Hamish Hamilton 1989
Adam Sisman A.J.P. Taylor Sinclair-Stevenson 1994
Edith Sitwell Selected Letters John Lehmann and Derek Parker (eds.) Macmillan 1970
   Selected Letters Richard Greene (ed.) Virago 1998
Joanna Skipwith (ed.) The Sitwells and the Arts of the 1920s and 1930s National Portrait Gallery 1994
Larry Smith Kenneth Patchen: Rebel Poet in America Bottom Dog Press 2000
Timothy d'Arch Smith R.A. Caton and the Fortune Press Bertram Rota 1983
Frances Spalding Dance Till he Stars Come Down A Biography of John Minton Hodder & Stoughton 1991
Jon Stallworthy Louis MacNeice OUP 1995
Derek Stanford Inside the Forties: Literary Memoir 1937–1957 Sidgwick and Jackson 1977
Igor Stravinsky and Robert Craft Conversations with Stravinsky Faber 1959
Alvin Sullivan (ed.) British Literary Magazines The Modern Age 1914–84 Greenwood Press 1986
Randolph Swingler Selected Poems Andy Croft (ed.) Trent Editions 2000
Dorothea Tanning Between Lives W.W.Norton 2001
A.J.P. Taylor A Personal History Hamish Hamilton 1983
E.W. Tedlock (ed.) Dylan Thomas: The Legend and the Poet Heinemann 1960
David N Thomas A Farm Two Mansions and a Bungalow Seren 2000
   The Dylan Thomas Trail Y Lolfa 2002
Caitlin Thomas Leftover Life to Kill
   Double Drink Story Virago 1998
   (with George Tremlett) Caitlin Life with Dylan Thomas Secker and Warburg 1986
William York Tindall A Reader;s Guide to Dylan Thomas The Noonday Press 1967

Ruthven Todd Fitzrovia and The Road to the York Minster Michael Parkin Fine Art 1973

Dylan Thomas: A Personal Account unpublished memoir National Library of Scotland

Jeff Towns Dylan Thomas: World and Image Swansea 1995

Henry Treece Dylan Thomas 'Dog Among the Faires' Ernest Benn 1956

Jeremy Treglown Romancing The Life and Work of Henry Green Faber 2000

George Tremlett Dylan Thomas In the Mercy of his Means Constable 1991

Julian Trevelyan Indigo Days MacGibbon & Kee 1957

Kathleen Tynan The Life of Kenneth Tynan Weidenfeld & Nicolson 1987

Kenneth Tynan Letters Kathleen Tynan (ed.) Weidenfeld & Nicolson 1994

Wynford Vaughan-Thomas Madly in All Directions Longmans Green 1967

Bernard Wall Headlong into Change Harvill 1969

Gwen Watkins Portrait of a Friend Gomer 1983

Evelyn Waugh The Letters of Evelyn Waugh ed. Mark Amory Weidenfeld & Nicolson 1980

Anna Wickham The Writings of Anna Wickham ed. R.D. Smith Virago 1984

Paul Willetts Fear and Loathing in Fitzrovia Dewi Lewis 2003

Jane Williams (ed.) Tambimutti Bridge Between Two Worlds Peter Owen 1989

Glanmor Williams (ed.) Swansea an Illustrated History Christopher Davies 1990

Shelley Winters Best of Times Worst of Times

Justin Wintle Furious Interiors HarperCollins 1996

George Woodcock Letter to the Past Fitzhenry and Whiteside 1982

Joan Wyndham Love is Blue William Heinemann 1986

Philip Ziegler London at War Sinclair-Stevenson 1995

Osbert Sitwell Chatto & Windus 1998

INDEX